# DESIGN OF AGRICULTURAL TRACTOR

## (*Principles and Problems*)

# DESIGN OF AGRICULTURAL TRACTOR

## (*Principles and Problems*)

**D. N. Sharma, M.Sc (Canada)**
Retd., Professor & Ex-Estate Officer-cum- Superintending Engineer,
Department of Farm Power & Machinery
College of Agricultural Engineering & Technology
Chaudary Charan Singh Haryana Agricultural University
Hisar-125004 (Haryana)
E-mail: dnsharma@hau.ernet.in
and
**S. Mukesh, M.Tech**
Assistant Agricultural Engineer
Department of Farm Power & Machinery
College of Agricultural Engineering & Technology
Chaudary Charan Singh Haryana Agricultural University
Hisar-125004 (Haryana)
E-mail: mukeshjainhisar@rediffmail.com

**Fourth Revised and Enlarged Edition**

**2023**

**JAIN BROTHERS** (NEW DELHI)
16/873, East Park Road, Near Dr. N.C. Joshi Hospital,
Karol Bagh, New Delhi-110005
Phones: 011-23618426, 011-45097398
E-mail : jain_bros@hotmail.com
www. thejainbrothers.com

***Published by:***

**Shri Sunil Kumar Jain**
*for*
**Jain Brothers (New Delhi)**
16/873, East Park Road, Karol Bagh,
New Delhi-110 005
Phones : 011-23618426, 45097398

***Branch Office at :***

1. **M/s SUNIL BOOK SERVICE**
   Fatima Nagar, Opp. Andhra Bank,
   KAZIPET-506004 (A.P.)
   Ph. : 0870-2459617, Mob. : 9390115435
   E-mail : kpkulshrestha@yahoo.com
2. **M/s JAIN BROTHERS**
   Vidya Vihar, Pilani (Rajasthan)
   Phone : 01596-242144



First Edition : 2010
Second Edition : 2012
Third Edition : 2015
Reprinted : 2018
**Fourth Edition : 2023**

***Price*: ₹ 350.00**

ISBN: 978-81-8360-173-3

***Laser Typesetting by:***

**Niyati *Graphics***
754/23, Khajoor Road,
Karol Bagh, New Delhi-110005

***Printed by :***
**BALAJI OFFSET PRINTERS,** New Delhi-110035

# Preface to the Fourth Edition

The encouraging success of the Third edition of the book **"Design of Agricultural Tractor" Principles and Problems"** from students & teacher communally has prompted us to revise and update the text. Objective Questions for every chapter is added in the book. Large number of new drawings and required updation of text is done to make it more useful to students, fieldworker's design engineers and others engaged in design of tractors & agriculture machinery.

Suggestions for further improvement are welcome.

**D. N. Sharma**
**S. Mukesh**

**Date: 20/05/2023**

# Preface to the Second Edition

The encouraging success of the first edition of the book **"Design of Agricultural Tractor–Principles and Problems"** from the user community has prompted the authors to make it more useful to the students, field workers, design engineers and others engaged in the design of tractors and agricultural machinery by presenting this second revised and enlarged edition of the text. One new chapter on design of mechanical and power steering of tractor has been added in the book. Various suggestions received from readers have been considered and relevant additions have been incorporated especially heat balance of engine, solved examples on engine design, constructional details of components of engine, design of flywheel, solved problems on engine governing system, design of forced circulation type of cooling system and weight transfer in two-wheel tractor (Power Tiller) etc. Most of the chapters have been reinforced with additional material wherever it was felt necessary.

Suggestions for the improvement of the book will be highly appreciated.

**D. N. Sharma**
**S. Mukesh**

**January, 2012**

e-mail: dn60sharma@gmail.com, dnsharma@hau.ernet.in
mukeshjainhisar@rediffmail.com

# Preface to the First Edition

Tractor is the basic unit of power at the farm and its population in a region is a good indicator of level of farm power of that area. The tractor is considered the hub of agricultural mechanization as it can be used to operate most of agricultural implements. Farm mechanization is closely related with the **"Tractorization".** Today tractor has become the most important prime-mover for completion of agricultural operations timely and to alleviate the drudgery associated with various farm operations and making the farm practices as pleasant job especially for the younger generation to adopt farming as profession. Use of tractors ensures better quality of work of farm operations, timely completion of farm activities, better management and supervision. In the peak season of agricultural operations, the tractor is used day and night. With the recent technological developments in tractors and due to increase in competition, the manufacturers are introducing many technical features in tractors.

Agricultural Mechanization is a complex subject and involves several components such as design, development, testing, manufacturing, operation, repair and maintenance of tractors and allied farm machinery. Farm mechanization is a dynamic process as the need and type of machines and its power source required continue to undergo a change with the development of agriculture in terms of new crop variety, cropping pattern, inputs used, availability of farm power, shift in power source, increase in the income of the farmers as well as general development of an area. This requires a continuous use of mechanical power on the farm.

We take immense pleasure in presenting you the first edition of book entitled, **"Design of Agricultural Tractor (Principles and Problems)**". In teaching the farm power and machinery aspects over a number of years, the authors have felt a great need for the book on agricultural tractor design written in simple terms so that subject matter can be introduced to the students on modern tractors. The authors have tried to cover the gap in the field of design of farm tractors. The book represents an attempt to deal with special subject on tractor design in a comprehensive way for the students of B.Tech (Agril. Engg) and Post Graduation programmes of different colleges and universities and persons appearing in various competitive examinations related to entrance tests for higher studies or related to different services such as National Eligibility Test (NET), Graduate Aptitude Test in Engineering (GATE), Agricultural Research Services (ARS) and Indian Engineering Services (IES) etc. This publication will not only serve the purpose of text book, it will also spell out the engineering principles that design engineers, manufacturers, construction personnel and technician should consider in the design of modern tractors.

This is the first book of its kind to address systematically the design problems involved in agricultural tractors. It offers comprehensive coverage of design principles. illustrated by more drawings and photographs depicting working components and operational features of engine and systems of tractors and written after more than 35 years of research and teaching experience in the field. This book describes fundamental principles and procedures in design of engine components and different systems of tractor.

The contents of this book are divided in 12 chapters depicting principles of engine components design, constructional material, and importance of air fuel supply system, lubrication, cooling and electrical systems of tractor engine and its governing. Traction theory, mechanics of tractor chassis and its stability, power transmission and hydraulic systems and their design principles have also been included in this book. In addition, human engineering aspects in the design of tractor have been dealt in detail. Apart from basic theory and design principles a number of solved examples have been included to solve the design problems.

During the preparation of the manuscript of this book, the authors have invited suggestions from different sources and have incorporated in it. Authors express their deep sense of appreciation and gratitude to the faculty, colleagues and students of the College of Agricultural Engineering and Technology, CCS Haryana Agricultural University, Hisar for their constructive suggestions. The authors shall be most grateful to their fellow teachers of Agricultural Engineering for their frank criticisms and suggestions for further improvements.

Authors are also thankful to the Publisher M/s. Jain Brothers (New Delhi) for their keen interest in publication of this book. Authors are also thankful to their family members for their patience and continued encouragement in preparation of manuscript of this book.

**D. N. Sharma**

**S. Mukesh**

# CONTENTS


**CHAPTER 1: ENGINE WORKING PRINCIPLES AND DESIGN ........................................ 1–94**

**1.1.** Engines and their Classifications / *1*
**1.2.** Engine Terminology / *21*
**1.3.** Design of 35 hp Tractor Engine / *37*

**CHAPTER 2: CONSTRUCTION MATERIALS FOR TRACTOR COMPONENTS ............ 95–103**

**2.1.** Constructional Details of Different Components of Tractor / *95*

**CHAPTER 3: AIR FUEL SUPPLY SYSTEM OF TRACTOR ........................................ 104–134**

**3.1.** Air Cleaners / *104*
**3.2.** Quantity of Air Intake by the Engine / *106*
**3.3.** Combustion of Diesel Fuel / *107*
**3.4.** Principle Requirements of Fuel Supply System / *110*
**3.5.** Types of Fuel Injection Pumps / *111*
**3.6.** Design of Fuel Injection Pump for Diesel Engine / *114*
**3.7.** Efficiency of FI Pump (η) / *119*
**3.8.** Essential Requirements of Diesel Fuel Injection / *121*
**3.9.** Types of Injectors / *121*
**3.10.** Types of Nozzles / *125*
**3.11.** Atomization of Fuel / *126*
**3.12.** Energy of Diesel Fuel Atomization / *127*
**3.13.** Fuel Injection Time ($t_i$) / *127*
**3.14.** Injection Delay / *127*
**3.15.** Combustion Chambers / *129*
**3.16.** Ignition Lag / *131*

**CHAPTER 4: GOVERNING SYSTEM OF TRACTOR ENGINE ................................... 135–145**

**4.1.** Types of Governors / *135*
**4.2.** Governor Regulation / *139*
**4.3.** Governor Performance Characteristics / *142*

**CHAPTER 5: LUBRICATING SYSTEM OF TRACTOR** ............ **146–155**

5.1. Types of Lubricating Systems / *147*
5.2. Oil Filters / *148*
5.3. Oil Pump / *149*
5.4. Properties of Lubricating Oil / *152*
5.5. Relationship Between Kinematic Viscosity and Absolute Viscosity / *154*

**CHAPTER 6: COOLING SYSTEM OF TRACTOR** ............ **156–170**

6.1. Air Cooling System / *156*
6.2. Water Cooling System / *157*
6.3. Radiator / *160*
6.4. Performance of Fan of Cooling System / *163*
6.5. Water Pump / *165*
6.6. Thermostat Valve / *169*

**CHAPTER 7: ELECTRICAL SYSTEM** ............ **171–177**

7.1. Battery / *172*
7.2. Generator/Dynamo/Alternator / *175*
7.3. Cutout Relay or Current-Voltage Regulator / *176*
7.4. Self Starter / *176*
7.5. Electrical Wiring / *177*
7.6. Electric Units/Solenoid Switch / *177*

**CHAPTER 8: POWER TRANSMISSION SYSTEM OF TRACTOR** ............ **178–205**

8.1. Tractor Transmission Performance / *179*
8.2. Design of Clutch for a Tractor / *180*
8.3. Gear Drive Design / *185*
8.4. Tractor Transmission Types / *189*
8.5. Design Procedure for Gearbox of a Tractor / *192*
8.6. Differential / *194*
8.7. Final Drive / *198*
8.8. P. T. O. Shaft / *199*
8.9. Belt Pulley / *199*

**CHAPTER 9: HYDRAULIC SYSTEM OF A TRACTOR** ............ **206–229**

9.1. Fundamentals of Fluid Power Transmission / *206*
9.2. Hydraulic System of Tractor / *210*
9.3. Hydraulic Pump Performance / *211*

**9.4.** Solved Problems on Pumps for Hydraulic System / ***213***
**9.5.** Design of Hydraulic Cylinders / ***217***
**9.6.** Hydraulic Control in Tractor / ***221***
**9.7.** Hitch System for Farm Machinery / ***224***

**CHAPTER 10: MECHANICAL AND POWER STEERING OF TRACTOR .................. 230–246**

**10.1.** Mechanical Steering System of Tractor / ***230***
**10.2.** Power Steering of Tractor / ***232***
**10.3.** Steering Geometry / ***245***

**CHAPTER 11: TRACTION ........................................................................ 247–262**

**11.1.** Traction / ***247***
**11.2.** Traction Theory / ***250***
**11.3.** Tractor Tyres / ***259***

**CHAPTER 12: MECHANICS OF TRACTOR CHASSIS AND STABILITY .................. 263–279**

**12.1.** Static Equilibrium of Tractor / ***263***
**12.2.** Weight Transfer Phenomenon / ***264***
**12.3.** Maximum Permissible Drawbar Pull (*P*) / ***265***
**12.4.** Longitudinal Stability of Tractor at no Load / ***268***
**12.5.** Lateral Stability of Tractor / ***270***
**12.6.** Weight Transference in Walking Type 2-Wheel Tractor (Power tiller) / ***273***
**12.7.** Centre Gravity of Tractor / ***275***

**CHAPTER 13: HUMAN ENGINEERING IN TRACTOR DESIGN ............................ 280–313**

**13.1.** The Operator-Machine Interface / ***281***
**13.2.** The Operator Exposure to Environmental Factors / ***281***
**13.3.** Thermal Comfort for Tractor Operator / ***282***
**13.4.** Spatial, Visual and Control Requirement of the Operator / ***285***
**13.5.** Operator Exposure to Noise / ***295***
**13.6.** Vibrations in Tractor / ***305***

**APPENDIX ........................................................................ 315–359**

**Annexure-I ........................................................................ 315–316**
**Annexure-II ........................................................................ 317**
**Annexure-III ........................................................................ 318–359**

**OBJECTIVE TYPE QUESTIONS WITH ANSWERS ........................................ 361–376**

**INDEX ........................................................................ 377–384**

CHAPTER 1

# Engine Working Principles and Design

## INTRODUCTION

An engine is a machine designed to convert some kind of energy into another kind of energy to be used for doing mechanical work. A heat engine is a machine which converts heat energy into mechanical energy. Heat is generated by the combustion of fuel such as coal, diesel, petrol, compressed natural gas (CNG), liquefied petroleum gas (LPG), biogas, producer gas etc. This heat is supplied to a working substance at high temperature. By the expansion of this substance in suitable machines, heat energy is converted into mechanical energy, which is used for doing some work. The energy flow of internal combustion engine is given in Fig. 1.1.

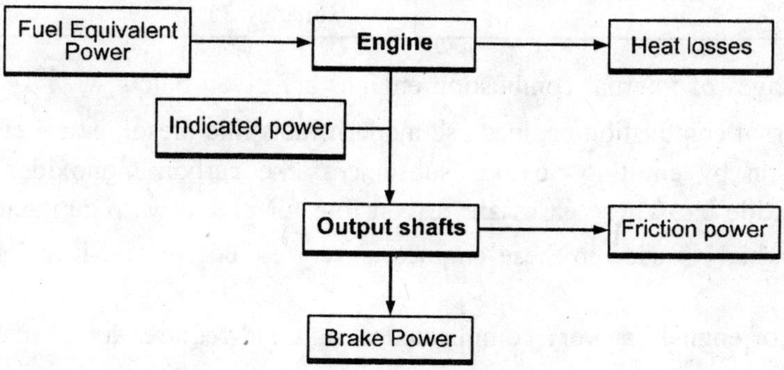


**Figure 1.1. IC engine energy flow**

## 1.1 ENGINES AND THEIR CLASSIFICATIONS

Heat engines can further be divided into two types:

1. External combustion engines.
2. Internal combustion engines.

### External Combustion Engines

When the combustion of fuel takes place outside the cylinder, then it is called as external combustion engine. For example, in the steam engines, coal fuel is burnt in the furnace and the heat is used to boil water in the boiler to generate steam. Then the steam is supplied to the cylinder where it pushes the piston to do some useful work. The used steam is then sent to a condenser, where it is cooled off and the water thus formed is recycled again to the boiler by using a pump.

Now-a-days, this type of engine has become obsolete and internal combustion engines are used widely.

## Internal Combustion Engines

When the combustion of fuel takes place inside the engine cylinder itself, then it is called as internal combustion engine. It uses the expansive forces of the burnt out gases to push the piston downward. The motion of the piston rotates a crankshaft with the help of a connecting rod. For example, the engines used in modern vehicles like scooter, motor cycle, car, bus, truck, tractor etc. are all internal combustion engines.

The difference between the external combustion and internal combustion engines are given below:

| External combustion engines | Internal combustion engines |
|---|---|
| 1. This type of engines are very huge in size and are also heavier. | 1. This type of engines are smaller in size and compact in nature. |
| 2. It cannot be started at once as it takes time to generate steam by boiling the water. | 2. It can be started at once. |
| 3. It is not safe to use, as there is fear of blasting of boiler. | 3. It is comparatively very safe. |
| 4. Thermal efficiency is very low which is approximately 20%. | 4. Thermal efficiency is high which is approximately 35%. |

The disadvantages of internal combustion engines are given below:

1. Since internal combustion engines use modern fuels like diesel, petrol etc, it causes heavy air pollution by emitting noxious substances like carbon monoxide, sulphur dioxide, nitrogen oxide etc. These gases are responsible for global warming, acid rain etc.
2. The fuel which is used in these engines is very expensive and is going to deplete very soon.
3. This type of engine has very complicated design and requires lot of maintenance.

## Classifications of Internal Combustion Engines

Internal combustion engines are classified as given below:

1. **Type of piston movement** According to the movement of piston, it can be classified as:

   ***Reciprocating.*** When the piston moves up and down or from left to right, they are called as reciprocating engines.

   ***Wankel rotary.*** The Wankel engine is a type of internal combustion engine which uses a rotary design to convert pressure into a rotating motion instead of using reciprocating pistons.

2. **Type of mobility** The engines are classified as stationary or mobile as per their mobility.

   ***Stationary.*** Stationary engines are designed without transmission system. These types of engines are generally used in the situations where it is not required to move the engine.

For example, the engines used to pump water, to generate electricity etc.

*Mobile.* Mobile engines are designed with transmission system as used in automobiles and tractors.

3. **Number of cylinders** The engines can be classified as per the number of cylinder it contains as:

   *Single cylinder.* This engine has only one cylinder. For *e.g.* scooter, motor cycle, Eicher Good Earth tractor etc. A single cylinder engine requires a large flywheel (for having more momentum) to move the piston up and down during idle strokes and to overcome the friction between moving parts.

   *Multiple cylinders.* These types of engines have more than one cylinder. A multi cylinder is a combination of several single cylinders which have a common crankshaft, camshaft etc. For *e.g.*, tractor like Eicher 364NC has two cylinders, tractors like HMT 3511, Mahindra B-275, Massey Ferguson 1035DI and Maruti 800 car have three cylinders, tractors like New Holland 5630, HMT 5711 have four cylinders and trucks like Ashok Leyland has six cylinders and more. Tractors are generally provided with multi cylinder engines as they provide more frequent power impulses per revolution of the crankshaft.

4. **Position of engine** The engines can be classified as horizontal engine or vertical engines as per the position or placement of engine is concerned. Generally, the engines used now-a-days are vertical engines.

5. **Engine speed** The engines can be classified according to the speed of engine as under.

   *Slow speed.* Below 350 rpm.

   *Medium speed.* 350 to 1000 rpm. Low and medium speed engines are usually used for stationary work.

   *High speed.* If the engine's rpm is above 1000, then it is called as high speed engine. Tractors and the automobiles are mostly equipped with high speed engines.

6. **Type of thermodynamic cycle** The engines can be classified as given below as per the thermodynamic cycle used for their design.

   *Spark ignition* **(SI).** This type of engine is designed on the basis of Otto cycle. It is also known as Carburetor type or petrol or gasoline engine. In this engine, the fuel is atomized, vaporized and mixed with air in correct proportion before inducting into the cylinder through intake manifold. The ignition of air-fuel mixture in the engine is done with the help of a spark plug which gives an electric spark. These types of engines are generally lighter in design and are used predominantly in automobiles requiring high speeds. But these engines are not good for pulling purpose or for the work which needs high torque.

   *Compression ignition* **(CI).** This type of engine is designed on the basis of Diesel cycle. In this engine, only the diesel fuel is injected at high pressure directly into the combustion chamber above the piston which has highly compressed air. The compression of air inside the cylinder causes rise in temperature and pressure of the air. When the fuel is injected into the combustion chamber, ignition of fuel takes place due to hot compressed air. This type of engine thus does not require any spark plug to ignite the fuel.

7. **Type of stroke** The engines can be classified based on the number of strokes needed to complete one cycle as follows:

   ***Two stroke.*** If the process of suction, compression, power and exhaust are completed within two strokes of piston, then it is called as two stroke engine.

   ***Four stroke.*** If the process of suction, compression, power and exhaust are completed in four strokes of piston, then it is called as four stroke engine.

The classification of the heat engines is given in Fig. 1.2.

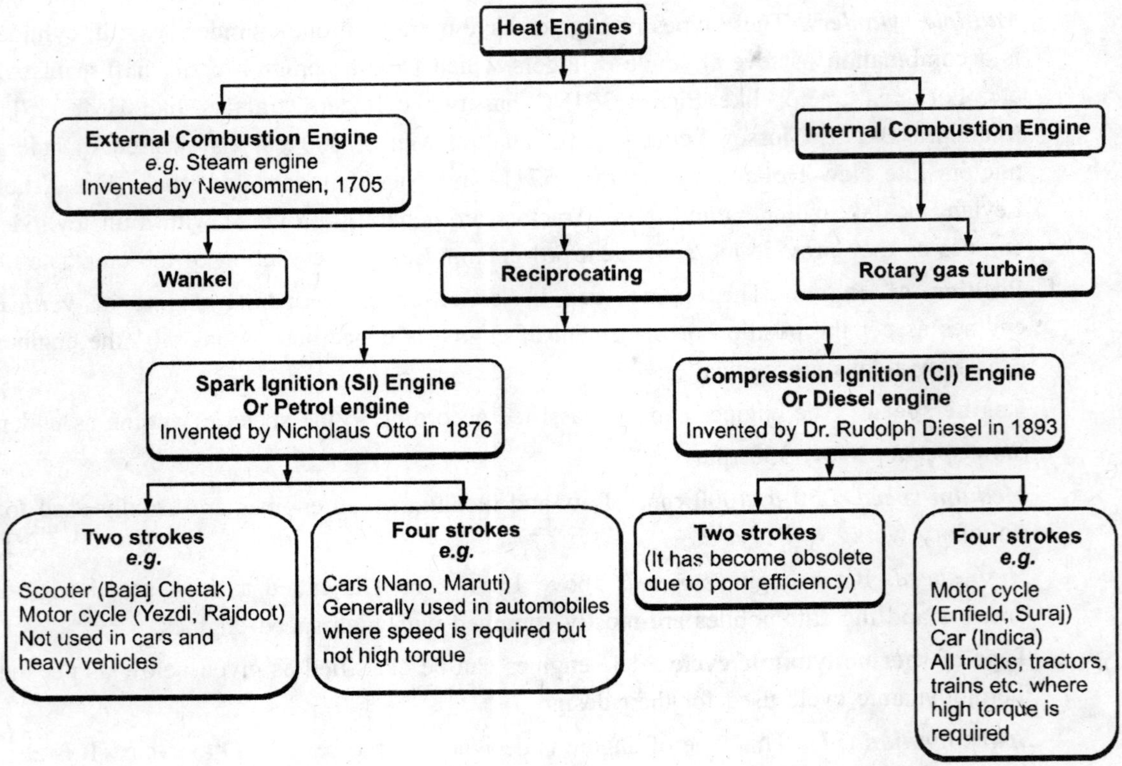


**Figure 1.2. Classification of heat engines**

## Thermodynamic Cycle

A cycle is a series of events that repeat themselves in a regular sequence. There are several types of cylces but the thermodynamic cycles namely Otto cycle and Diesel cycle which are widely used in the internal combustion engines are discussed below:

**Otto cycle.** Engines based upon this cycle are called as Otto engines or spark ignition (SI) engines. The Otto engine was conceived by Beau de Rochas in 1862. But practical form was given by Nicholaus Otto in the year 1876.

The pressure-volume diagram of the Otto cycle is given in Fig. 1.3. In this cycle the heat is taken in at constant volume and rejected at another constant volume of the cylinder. That-is-why, this cycle is also called as constant volume cycle. The sequence of different events like suction, compression, power and exhaust of the Otto cycle are given below:

(*a*) The line *MN* represents atmospheric pressure level and *AB* represents the admission of air slightly below atmospheric pressure [**Suction process**].

(*b*) *BGC* represents the compression of charge (mixture of air and fuel) in the cylinder under adiabatic condition. This operation raises the temperature and pressure of the air [**Compression process**]. Adiabatic refers to that condition where there is no loss or gain of heat from or to the cylinder walls.

(*c*) Ignition starts at the point *C* and the line *CD* represents the pressure rise in the cylinder at constant volume $V_2$.

(*d*) *DE* represents the adiabatic expansion of the gases due to combustion of fuel [**Power process**]. During this process, the temperature and pressure of air falls.

(*e*) Exhaust takes place at the point *E* and the pressure reduces nearly to atmospheric pressure during the exhaust stroke *FA* [**Exhaust process**].

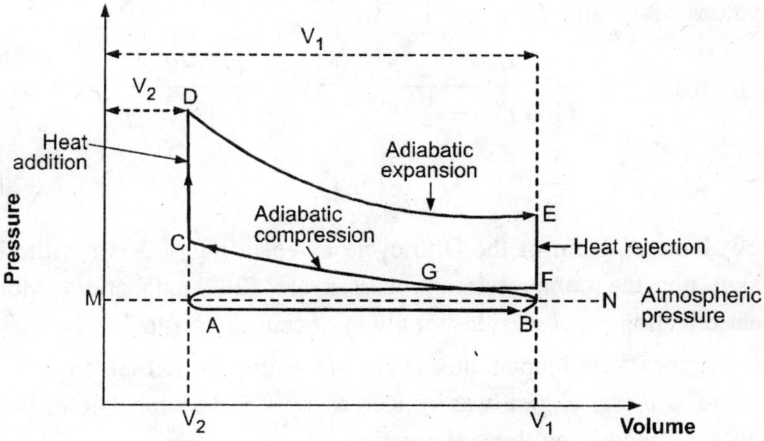


**Figure 1.3. Constant volume cycle**

In the above cycle, heat addition takes place at *CD* and the heat rejection takes place at *EB*. Therefore,

$$\text{Heat added} = Q_1 = C_v\,(T_D - T_C)$$

$$\text{Heat rejected} = Q_2 = C_v\,(T_E - T_B)$$

The theoretical thermal efficiency of the Otto engine is given by

$$\eta_{Otto} = \frac{Q_1 - Q_2}{Q_1} = 1 - \frac{T_E - T_B}{T_D - T_C} \qquad ...(1.1)$$

We know that compression ratio (*r*) is given by

$$r = \frac{\text{total cylinder volume}}{\text{clearance volume}} = \frac{V_B}{V_C}$$

and the air constant (*k*) is given by

$$k = \frac{C_P}{C_v} = \frac{\text{Specific heat at constant pressure}}{\text{Specific heat at constant volume}}$$

For adiabatic process *BC*,

$$\frac{T_C}{T_B} = \left(\frac{V_B}{V_C}\right)^{k-1}$$

$$\therefore \quad T_C = T_B\,(r)^{k-1} \qquad \left[\because\ r = \frac{V_B}{V_C}\right]$$

For adiabatic process *DE*,

$$\frac{T_D}{T_E} = \left(\frac{V_E}{V_D}\right)^{k-1} = \left(\frac{V_B}{V_C}\right)^{k-1} \qquad [\because V_E = V_B \text{ and } V_D = V_C]$$

$$\therefore \quad T_D = T_E\,(r)^{k-1} \qquad \left[\because r = \frac{V_B}{V_C}\right]$$

Putting the values of $T_C$ and $T_D$ in eq. 1.1, we get

$$\eta_{Otto} = 1 - \frac{T_E - T_B}{T_E\,(r)^{k-1} - T_B\,(r)^{k-1}} = 1 - \frac{[T_E - T_B]}{r^{k-1}[T_E - T_B]}$$

$$\eta_{Otto} = 1 - \frac{1}{r^{k-1}} \qquad \ldots(1.2)$$

The pressure-volume diagram of the Otto cycle given in Fig. 1.3 is not the ideal diagram as neither the expansion nor the compression processes are fully adiabatic. Moreover, the heat addition and the heat rejection processes do not always occur at constant volume.

**Diesel cycle.** Engines based upon this cycle are called as Diesel engines or compression ignition (CI) engines. The diesel engine was conceived by Dr. Rudolph Diesel in 1893 to attain a high thermal efficiency by increasing the compression ratio.

The pressure-volume diagram of the Diesel cycle is given in Fig. 1.4. In this cycle the heat is taken in at constant pressure and rejected at another constant volume of the cylinder. That-is-why, this cycle is also called as constant pressure cycle. The sequence of different events like suction, compression, power and exhaust of the Diesel cycle is given below:

(*a*) The line *MN* represents atmospheric pressure level and *AB* represents the admission of air slightly below atmospheric pressure [**Suction process**].

(*b*) BGC represents the compression of air in the cylinder under adiabatic condition. This operation raises the temperature and pressure of the air [**Compression process**].

(*c*) The injection of fuel starts at *C* and stops at *D*. Combustion takes place during this interval at constant pressure. The ratio of the volume at *D* and *C* *i.e.* $V_D/V_C$ is known as cut-off ratio.

(*d*) *DE* represents the adiabatic expansion of the gases due to combustion of fuel [**Power process**]. During this process, the temperature and pressure of air falls.

(*e*) Exhaust takes place at the point $E$ and the pressure reduces nearly to atmospheric pressure during the exhaust stroke $FA$ [***Exhaust process***].

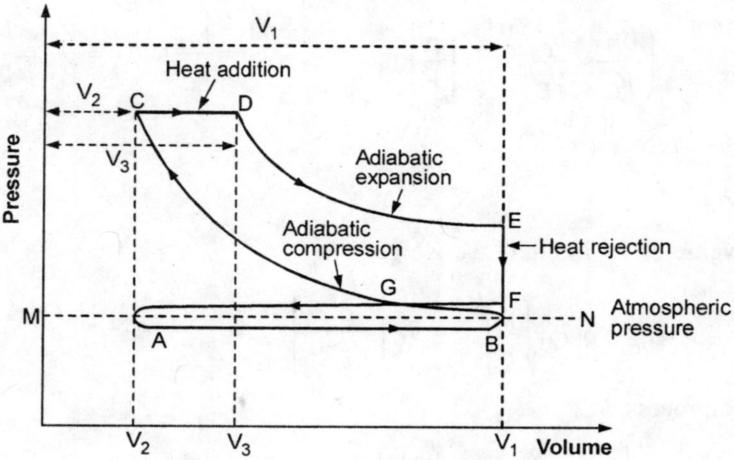


**Figure 1.4. Constant pressure cycle**

In the above cycle, heat addition takes place at $CD$ and the heat rejection takes place at $EB$. Therefore,

$$\text{Heat added} = Q_1 = C_p\,(T_D - T_C)$$

$$\text{Heat rejected} = Q_2 = C_v\,(T_E - T_B)$$

The theoretical thermal efficiency of the Diesel engine is given by

$$\eta_{\text{Diesel}} = \frac{Q_1 - Q_2}{Q_1} = \frac{C_p\,(T_D - T_C) - C_v\,(T_E - T_B)}{C_p\,(T_D - T_C)} \qquad \text{...(1.3)}$$

Since $\dfrac{C_p}{C_v} = k$

The eq. (1.3), becomes

$$\eta_{\text{Diesel}} = 1 - \frac{1}{k}\left[\frac{T_E - T_B}{T_D - T_C}\right] \qquad \text{...(1.4)}$$

The fuel cut-off ratio (ρ) is given by

$$\rho = \frac{\text{Volume at } D}{\text{Volume at } C} = \frac{V_D}{V_C}$$

and, the compression ratio ($r$) is given by

$$r = \frac{\text{total cylinder volume}}{\text{clearance volume}} = \frac{V_B}{V_C}$$

For the process $CD$,

$$\frac{T_D}{T_C} = \frac{V_D}{V_C}$$

$\therefore \quad T_D = \rho\, T_c$

For adiabatic process *DE*,

$$\frac{T_E}{T_D} = \left(\frac{V_D}{V_E}\right)^{k-1} = \left(\frac{V_D}{V_C} \times \frac{V_C}{V_E}\right)^{k-1} = \left[\frac{\rho}{r}\right]^{k-1} \qquad \left[\because \rho = \frac{V_D}{V_C} \text{ and } r = \frac{V_B}{V_C} = \frac{V_E}{V_C}\right]$$

$$T_E = T_D\left[\frac{\rho}{r}\right]^{k-1} \qquad ...(1.5)$$

Putting the value of $T_D$ in eq. (1.5), we get

$$T_E = \rho\, T_C\left[\frac{\rho}{r}\right]^{k-1} = T_C\left[\frac{\rho^k}{r^{(k-1)}}\right]$$

For adiabatic process *BC*,

$$\frac{T_B}{T_C} = \left(\frac{V_C}{V_B}\right)^{k-1} = \left(\frac{1}{r}\right)^{k-1} \qquad \left[\because r = \frac{V_B}{V_C}\right]$$

$$\therefore \quad T_B = T_C\left(\frac{1}{r}\right)^{k-1}$$

Putting the values of, $T_E$, $T_B$ and $T_D$ in the eq. 1.4, we get

$$\eta_{\text{Diesel}} = 1 - \frac{1}{k}\,\frac{\left[T_C\left[\frac{\rho^k}{r^{(k-1)}}\right] - T_C\left[\frac{1}{r}\right]^{k-1}\right]}{\rho T_C - T_C} \qquad ...(1.6)$$

$$\eta_{\text{Diesel}} = 1 - \frac{1}{k}\,\frac{\left[T_C\,\frac{1}{r^{k-1}}\left[\rho^k - 1\right]\right]}{T_C\,(\rho - 1)}$$

$$\eta_{\text{Diesel}} = 1 - \frac{1}{k} \times \frac{1}{r^{k-1}} \times \frac{\rho^k - 1}{(\rho - 1)}$$

Rearranging the above eq., we get,

$$\eta_{\text{Diesel}} = 1 - \left(\frac{1}{r}\right)^{(k-1)}\left[\frac{\rho^{k-1}}{k(\rho - 1)}\right] \qquad ...(1.7)$$

The pressure volume diagram of the Diesel cycle in Fig. 1.4 is not the ideal diagram as neither the expansion nor the compression processes are fully adiabatic, Moreover, the heat addition and the heat rejection processes do not always occur at constant pressure and constant volume respectively.

## Comparison between Otto (SI) and diesel (CI) cycle engines

| Otto cycle engine | Diesel cycle engine |
|---|---|
| 1. It operates on Otto cycle which is also called as constant volume cycle. | It operates on Diesel cycle which is also called as constant pressure cycle. |
| 2. It is also called as spark ignition (SI) engine as spark is used to ignite the air-fuel mixture. | It is also called as compression ignition (CI) engine as the auto-ignition of fuel takes place by the increased temperature due to higher compression of air inside the cylinder. |
| 3. The fuel like petrol having high volatility is used. | It uses diesel fuel. |
| 4. During suction stroke, a mixture of air and fuel in the ratio of 15 : 1 is inducted into the cylinder. | Only air is inducted into the cylinder during suction stroke. |
| 5. Carburetor is used to mix air and fuel which is called as charge before inducting into the cylinder. | Fuel and air are not mixed before inducting into the cylinder. Thus, carburetor is not used. |
| 6. Spark plug is used to generate electric spark which ignites the charge inducted into the cylinder. | Spark plug is not used here. But the ignition of fuel takes place by injecting highly pressurized fuel into the combustion chamber having super heated air due to high compression ratio. |
| 7. The operation of spark plug needs battery or magneto-induction system. | As such battery or magneto-induction system is not required. But now-a-days batteries are provided for easy starting of engine. |
| 8. Fuel injection pump and injectors are not used. | Fuel injection pump is used to pressurize the fuel and injectors are used to atomize the fuel into the combustion chamber. |
| 9. Distributor is used to maintain the timing of sparking in multi cylinder engines. | The timing of fuel injection in different cylinders of a multi cylinder engine is maintained by the fuel injection pump itself. |
| 10. To vary the load and the speed, the quantity of charge is varied. | To vary the load and the speed, the quantity of fuel is varied. |
| 11. Compression ratio of the engine ranges from 4:1 to 8 : 1. Compression pressure inside the cylinder varies from 8 to 10 kg/cm$^2$ and the temperature is about 260 °C | Compression ratio of the engine ranges from 14 : 1 to 22 : 1. Compression pressure varies from 30 to 45 kg/cm$^2$ and the temperature ranges from 650°C to 800°C |
| 12. Since the compression ratio is less, the construction of engine is light and less expensive. | Since the compression ratio is high, the construction of engine needs to be heavy to sustain high pressure and that is why these engines are more expensive. |
| 13. Engine weight per horse power is low. | Engine weight per horse power is high. |
| 14. Operating cost is high due to expensive fuel. | Operating cost is low due to less expensive diesel fuel. |
| 15. Maintenance cost is less due to fewer parts. | Maintenance cost is high due to more parts. |

*Continue......*

*(Continued...)*

| Otto cycle engine | Diesel cycle engine |
|---|---|
| **16.** Due to lower compression ratio, compression pressure attained is low, thus resulting in low combustion pressure. Consequently, the torque obtained is weak. | As the compression ratio is high, compression pressure attained is very high, thus resulting in very high combustion pressure. This is responsible for development of higher torque in diesel engines. |
| **17.** These engines can be used only where high speed and low torque is needed like scooter, motorcycle, cars etc. | These engines are used where high torque is needed like tractor, trucks, trains etc. |
| **18.** Specific fuel consumption is around 290 g per BHP per hour. | Specific fuel consumption is around 200 g per BHP per hour. |
| **19.** Thermal efficiency ranges from 25 to 32%. | Thermal efficiency ranges from 32 to 38%. |
| **20.** Exhaust temperature is low. | Exhaust temperature is high. |
| **21.** Fuel timing is not advanced. | Fuel timing is advanced and it is around 25° before top dead centre (BTDC).The advancement in the timing of fuel is done to accommodate the delay period in the ignition of fuel due to its less volatility. |

## Working Principle of Internal Combustion Engine

The basic component of an internal combustion engine is cylinder. In the cylinder, a close fitting piston moves up and down. The space above the piston inside the cylinder is called combustion chamber where fuel is admitted for explosion. The heat released during the explosion is used to push the piston downward. The piston is connected to a crankshaft with the help of a connecting rod. The reciprocating motion of the piston is converted to rotary motion by the crankshaft. At the end of crankshaft, a flywheel is used for maintaining the momentum of the crankshaft so that the piston moves up and down during dead events like suction, compression and exhaust. The external and internal components of an internal combustion engine are given in Fig. 1.5 (*a*) and Fig. 1.5 (*b*) respectively.

The basic events taking place in the engine are suction, compression, power and exhaust. The process of admission of air and fuel inside the cylinder depends on the type of engine whether it is a spark ignition (SI) engine (petrol engine) or compression ignition (CI) engine (diesel engine). The working of these engines is discussed below.

## Spark Ignition (SI) or Petrol Engine

In this engine, during the process of suction, a mixture of air and fuel called as charge is admitted inside the cylinder. The mixing of air and fuel (generally petrol) is done by carburetor. The ignition of the fuel is done by introducing an electric spark at appropriate time after compressing the charge. That-is-why, this engine is called as spark ignition engine. The electric spark is generated by a spark plug connected to a high induction ignition coil. In case of multi cylinder engine, the timing of sparking in individual cylinder is decided by the distributor.

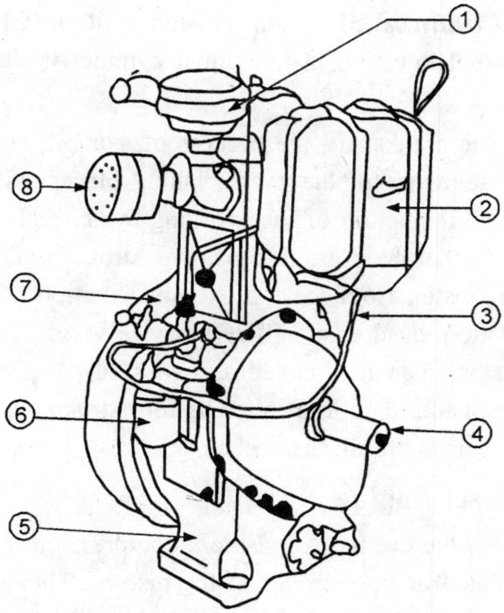


| |
|---|
| 1. Air cleaner |
| 2. Diesel tank |
| 3. Diesel pipe |
| 4. Crank shaft |
| 5. Crank case |
| 6. Diesel filter |
| 7. Fly wheel |
| 8. Exhaust pipe |

Figure 1.5 (*a*). External components of an internal combustion engine

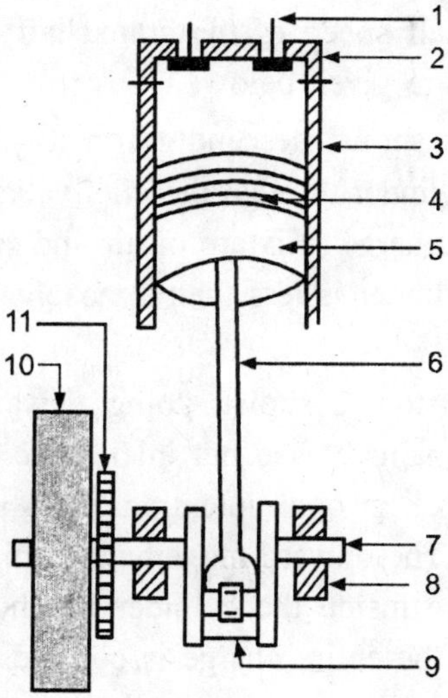


| |
|---|
| 1. Valve |
| 2. Cylinder head |
| 3. Cylinder liner |
| 4. Piston groove |
| 5. Piston |
| 6. Connecting rod |
| 7. Crank shaft |
| 8. Main bearing |
| 9. Big end |
| 10. Fly wheel |
| 11. Timing gear |

Figure 1.5 (*b*). Internal components of an internal combustion engine

## Compression Ignition (CI) or Diesel Engine

During the process of suction, only air is inducted inside the cylinder. Then the air is highly compressed in order to raise the temperature and pressure. The injection of fuel at the end of compression event is done with the help of fuel injection pump and injector. The fuel injection pump is used to highly pressurize the fuel. The pressurized fuel is atomized in the combustion chamber with the injectors. The self-ignition of the fuel takes place, as higher temperature prevails inside the cylinder due to higher compression ratio of the air. As the ignition takes place due to higher compression ratio, this engine is rightly called as compression ignition (CI) engine. In case of multi cylinder engine, the timing of fuel injection in individual cylinder is decided by the fuel injection pump.

To obtain continuous rotation of the crankshaft, the process of suction, compression, power and exhaust have to be repeated. The sequence of the events taking place inside the cylinder is called as working cycle. Based upon the completion of this working cycle, both the spark ignition and compression ignition engines can further be classified as two stroke and four stroke cycle engines. One stroke is the movement of piston from the top extreme position *i.e.* top dead centre (TDC) to bottom extreme position *i.e.* bottom dead centre (BDC) or vice versa. If the working cycle is completed in only two strokes of piston, then it is called as two stroke engine. If the working cycle is completed in four strokes of the piston, then it is called as four stroke engine. The detailed working of two stroke and four stroke engines are discussed below:

## Working of Four Stroke Cycle Diesel Engine

In a four stroke cycle diesel engine, the events like suction, compression, power and exhaust taking place inside the engine are completed in four strokes of the piston. This engine is provided with separate inlet and exhaust valves for inducting fresh air and expelling the burnt out gases. The valves are operated by valve lifting mechanism placed on the cams of camshaft which takes drive from the crankshaft. The camshaft rotates at half speed of the crankshaft. The detailed process happening during the four strokes of the piston are given below:

**Suction stroke:** In Fig. 1.6, the piston is shown descending on its suction stroke. During this stroke, only pure air is inducted inside the cylinder through the inlet valve, whereas, the exhaust valve remains closed. In case of petrol engine, charge (mixture of air and fuel) enters the cylinder during suction stroke. The pressure inside the cylinder is less than atmospheric pressure during this stroke.

**Compression stroke:** In Fig. 1.6, the piston is shown going upward on its compression stroke. During this stroke, the exhaust valve remains closed but inlet valve closes only after 30 to 40° of piston travel from BDC. The inlet valve is kept open intentionally to increase the volumetric efficiency (to induct more air inside the engine). The upward movement of piston does not flush the air through the open inlet valve, as the pressure inside the cylinder has not reached at par with atmospheric pressure. In case of petrol engine, the entire charge is compressed to a small volume called clearance volume which exists above the piston in the cylinder. The compression ratio usually varies from 14 : 1 to 22 : 1 in diesel engines and for petrol engines it is varies form 4 : 1 to 8 : 1. The pressure at the end of compression stroke ranges from 30 to 45 kg/cm$^2$ and the temperature rises to about 800°C. Before the completion of compression stroke, usually before 20° to 30° before top dead centre (BTDC), fuel is injected at high pressure around 200 kg/cm$^2$ inside the cylinder. Advancement in the fuel injection is done as the diesel fuel takes some time (delay period) to ignite. Moreover, the explosion of fuel is realized when the piston is at the top and the piston is pushed downward with full force. In case of petrol engine, spark is introduced at the completion of compression stroke. But the spark timing is not advanced as in diesel engine as petrol burns instantaneously.

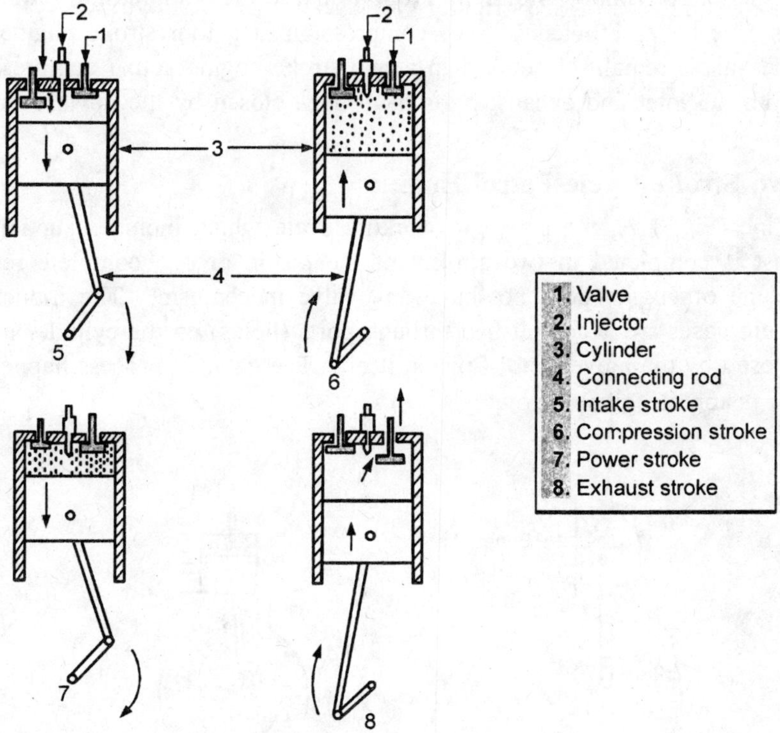


**Figure 1.6. Working principle of four stroke diesel engine**

**Power stroke:** In this stroke, high pressure developed due to combustion of fuel pushes the piston downward (Fig. 1.6). The connecting rod which connects piston and crankshaft transmits the power to crankshaft for useful work. Inlet valve remains closed during this stroke but the exhaust valve is opened 30 to 40° before the piston reaches BDC in order to ensure that proper flushing of burnt out gases is accomplished. The temperature reached during the power stroke is in the range of 1600 to 2000°C. That-is-why, effective cooling mechanism is provided to dissipate the heat energy produced inside the cylinder.

**Exhaust stroke:** The inlet valve remains closed during this stroke and the exhaust valve remains opened. Burnt out gases are expelled through the exhaust valve and the cylinder becomes ready to receive the fresh charge. The process of removal of burnt out gases is called scavenging. The pressure of exhaust gases remains around 3.5 to 5 kg/cm$^2$ which needs a silencer to calm the noise of outgoing gases. The temperature of exhaust gases remains around 650°C.

The thermal efficiency of four stroke engines is better as compared to two stroke engines due to the following reasons:

1. Proper scavenging (removal of burnt out gases), as enough time is available for the exhaust valve to open.
2. Increased volumetric efficiency as more time is available for the inlet valve to open, thus inducting more fresh air.
3. No fuel is wasted through exhaust valve.

4. As the thermal efficiency is directly proportional to the compression ratio, the four stroke engines give better efficiency. The compression in a four stroke engine is effective as both the valves remain closed but in a two stroke engine actual compression starts only after both the inlet and exhaust ports have been closed by the upward movement of the piston.

## Working of Two Stroke Cycle Petrol Engine

In this engine (Fig. 1.7), the complete working cycle which includes suction, compression, power and exhaust is completed in two strokes of the piston or one complete revolution of the crankshaft. This type of engine does not have any valve mechanism. The induction of air and removal of burnt out gases are accomplished through ports (holes) on the cylinder itself. The ports are opened and closed by the movement of piston itself. The detailed process happening during the two strokes of the piston are given below:

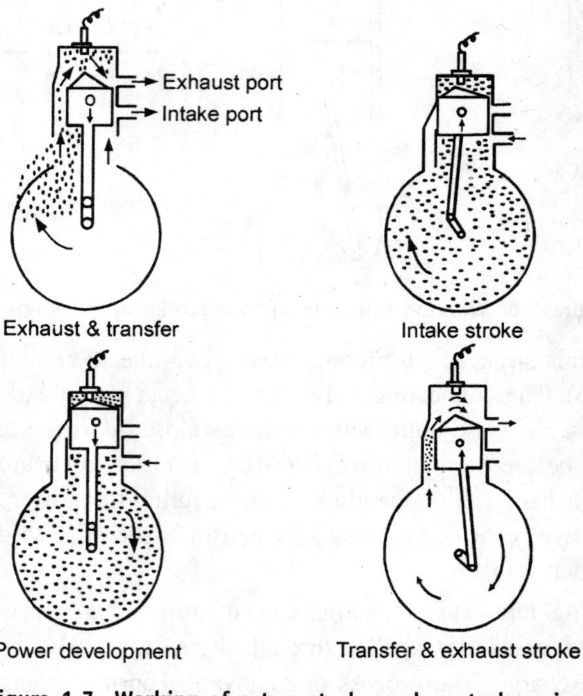


**Figure 1.7. Working of a two stroke cycle petrol engine**

**First stroke:** When the piston is at the bottom dead centre (BDC), the suction port is covered (closed) by the piston and the other two ports *i.e.* exhaust and transfer ports are open (Fig. 1.7). Normally, the exhaust and transfer ports are opposite to each other. Through the transfer port, fresh charge (mixture of air and fuel) is inducted above the piston. Some of the charge directly goes outside the engine through the exhaust port. As the piston moves up, the exhaust and transfer ports are covered by the piston but the suction port is uncovered (opened). Through the suction port, fresh charge from the carburetor enters the crankcase. The upward movement of piston compresses the charge The compression pressure, thus achieved is usually very low, and a spark plug gives an electric spark which causes combustion of fuel.

**Second stroke:** The explosion in the cylinder causes the piston to move downward. The downward movement of the piston closes the suction port and pre-compresses the charge that has been trapped inside the air tight crankcase. This pre-compression of charge is just sufficient to enable the air to flow into the cylinder through the transfer port when the piston reaches near the bottom of its stroke. Further downward movement of the piston uncovers first the exhaust port and then the transfer port. The burnt out gases are expelled through the exhaust port. Moreover, the pre-compressed charge existing in the crankcase is transferred into the cylinder through the transfer port.

## Comparison Between Two Stroke and Four Stroke Engines

| Two stroke engine | Four stroke engine |
|---|---|
| **1.** The process of suction, compression, power and exhaust is completed within two strokes of piston. | The process of suction, compression, power and exhaust is completed in four strokes of piston. |
| **2.** It takes only one crankshaft rotation to complete one cycle. Thus, power is obtained in each crankshaft rotation resulting in smooth operation. Therefore, this engine requires lighter flywheel. | It takes two crankshaft rotations to complete one cycle. In this engine, power is obtained in every two rotations of crankshaft resulting in non-smooth operation. Thus, this engine requires heavier flywheel. |
| **3.** This engine gives less vibration. | It has more vibration. |
| **4.** Theoretically, for the same size of engine, a two stroke engine gives twice the power of four stroke engine. But practically, only 50 to 60% extra power is developed due to poor scavenging (unable to flush out the burnt out gases due to lesser time of opening of ports). | Theoretically, for the same size of engine, a four stroke engine gives half the power of two stroke engine. But practically, four stroke engines are more fuel efficient as more time is available for the intake and exhaust valves to open. Thus, resulting in better volumetric efficiency and proper scavenging of burnt out gases. |
| **5.** In this engine, some of the fuel directly goes outside the engine through the exhaust port without burning. That is why, the thermal efficiency is low. | In this engine fuel is not wasted through exhaust valve. Therefore, the thermal efficiency is more. |
| **6.** In this engine, the intake and exhaust ports remain open during the upward movement of the piston. Thus, actual compression starts only after the piston has passed the ports and thereby resulting in poor compression. | Good compression is achieved. |
| **7.** Compression ratio is directly proportional to the thermal efficiency and thus the poor compression gives poor thermal efficiency | Good compression gives better thermal efficiency. |
| **8.** Ports (holes) are used for inducting air and exhaust purpose which are opened and closed by the movement of piston itself. | Valves are used for intake and exhaust which are operated by valve lifting mechanism operated through camshaft. |

*Continue...*

***(Continued...)***

| | Two stroke engine | Four stroke engine |
|---|---|---|
| 9. | Three ports are used. One for intake, one for exhaust and third one is transfer port connecting the crankcase and the upper portion of cylinder. | Generally two valves are used. One valve for intake and other for exhaust. Now-a-days multiple valves are also being used for getting better volumetric efficiency. |
| 10. | Crankcase is air tight as the air (in case of petrol engine, the charge) enters the crankcase when the piston moves from BDC to TDC. | Crank case is not air tight as the air does not enter the crankcase. |
| 11. | As this engine does not have cam shaft, tappet mechanism etc. the design is easy and the maintenance is very less. | Design is complicated and the maintenance is more due to more parts. |
| 12. | Engine can be operated in clockwise and counter clockwise direction. | Engine can be operated in only one direction. |
| 13. | Weight per horse power is less | Weight per horse power is more due to more parts. |
| 14. | Mechanical efficiency is higher due to the absence of cam shaft, valve lifting mechanism, etc. | Mechanical efficiency is less due to the presence of cam shaft, valve lifting mechanism, etc. |
| 15. | For the same power, this engine is small and compact in size. | It is bigger in size and requires more space. |
| 16. | In this engine, lubrication oil is generally mixed with the fuel which is not more effective resulting in more wear and tear of parts. | Separate lubrication mechanism is provided which gives efficient lubrication and thus wear and tear of parts is reduced. |

**Valve timing diagram:** Valve timing diagram shows the timing (in degrees of crankshaft rotation) of opening and closing of inlet and exhaust valves during one working cycle of an engine. The valve timing diagram of a four stroke diesel engine is given in Fig. 1.8 and the explanation of the same is given below:

**Inlet valve:** The inlet valve is supposed to open when the piston is at TDC and should close when the piston reaches BDC of suction stroke. This will create suction of fresh air due to vacuum created inside the cylinder. But practically, the inlet valve is opened even before the exhaust stroke is completed *i.e.* 10 to 12° before TDC so that it is opened fully as the piston reaches TDC as the valve takes some time for opening. The inlet valve remains open during the entire suction stroke *i.e.* for 180°. Further, during the compression stroke also, the inlet valve is kept open intentionally for about 30 to 35° to increase the volumetric efficiency (to induct more air inside the engine). The upward movement of piston does not flush the air through the open inlet valve, as the pressure inside the cylinder has not reached at par with atmospheric pressure. Thus, theoretically the inlet valve opens for 180° but practically it opens for 220 to 227°. This increase in the timing of opening of inlet valve is one of the reasons for higher thermal efficiency in a four stroke engine as more air is available for better combustion.

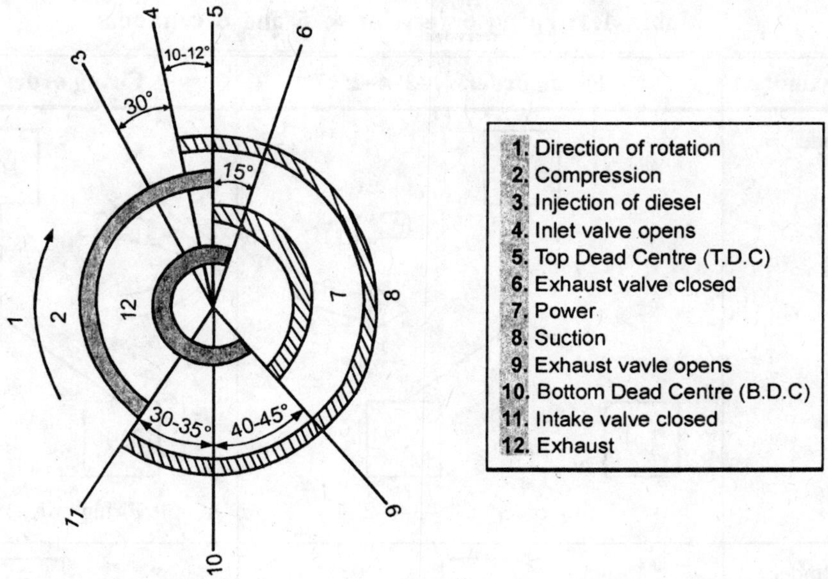


**Figure 1.8. Valve timing diagram of a four stroke diesel engine**

**Exhaust valve:** The exhaust valve is supposed to open when the piston is at TDC and should close when the piston reaches BDC of exhaust stroke. This will expel the burnt out gases formed during the combustion of fuel. But practically, the exhaust valve is opened even before the power stroke is completed *i.e.* 40 to 45° before BDC. The exhaust valve remains open during the entire exhaust stroke *i.e.* for 180°. Further, during the suction stroke also the exhaust valve is kept open for about 15°. Thus, theoretically the exhaust valve opens for 180° but practically it opens for 235 to 240°. This increase in the timing of opening of exhaust valve is one of the reasons for higher thermal efficiency in a four stroke engine as more burnt out gases are flushed out, paving the way for induction of more fresh air.

**Firing order:** The order in which the power stroke in each cylinder of an engine occurs is called firing order. If there are four cylinders, it is not the practice to fire all the cylinders instantaneously or to fire in the sequence 1–2–3–4, as instantaneous firing will need a larger crankshaft and fly wheel to absorb the power. Firing in a sequence like 1–2–3–4 will tend to overload one side of the crankshaft. To overcome this heavy crankshaft has to be provided. Therefore, it a common practice, to follow some firing orders so that loading on the crankshaft is dynamically balanced. The arrangement of crankpin on the crankshaft and the design of the camshaft determine the firing order of the engine. The firing order of 2 and 3 cylinders are generally kept as 1–2 and 1–2–3 respectively as the length of crankshafts is less. The firing orders for 4, 6 and 8 cylinders are given in Table 1.1.

## Rules for Finding Firing Order

**Clockwise direction:**

1. Write the cylinder numbers (half the number of cylinders) in clockwise direction and complete the other remaining number of cylinders in counter-clockwise direction as given in table 1.1.

**Table 1.1: Firing orders for 4, 6 and 8 cylinders**

| For four cylinder | Firing order : 1–3–4–2 | Firing order : 1–2–4–3 |
|---|---|---|
| For six cylinder | 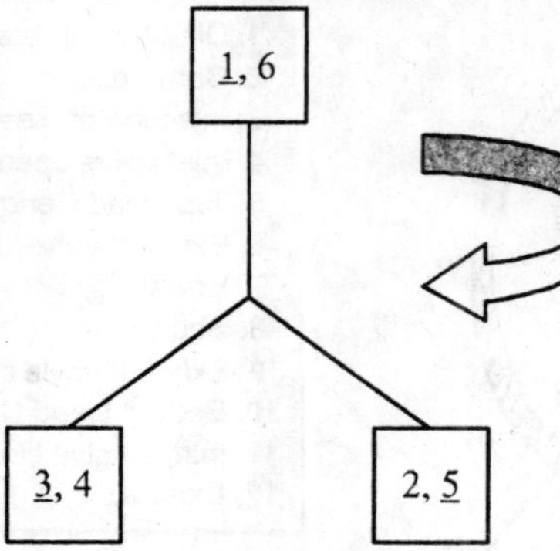  Firing order : 1–5–3–6–2–4 | 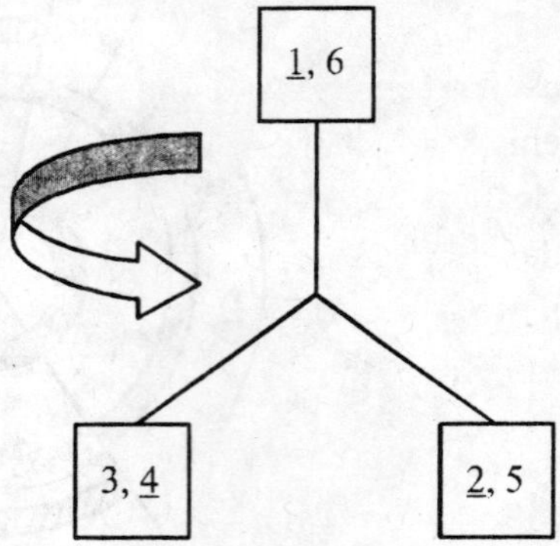  Firing order : 1–4–2–6–3–5 |
| For eight cylinder | 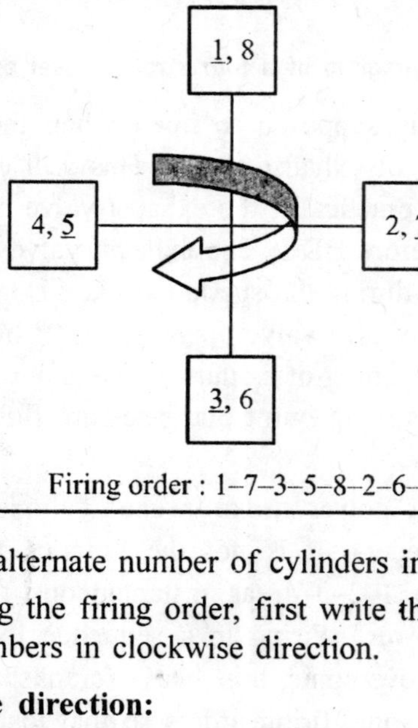  Firing order : 1–7–3–5–8–2–6–4 | 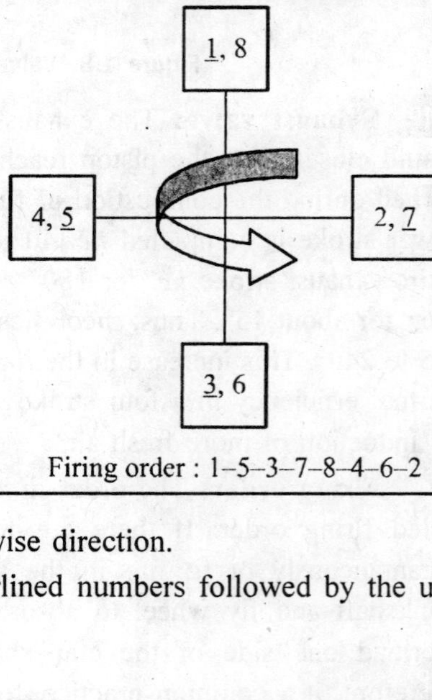  Firing order : 1–5–3–7–8–4–6–2 |

2. Underline the alternate number of cylinders in clockwise direction.
3. For determining the firing order, first write the underlined numbers followed by the un-underlined numbers in clockwise direction.

**Counter-clockwise direction:**

1. Write the cylinder numbers (half the number of cylinders) in clockwise direction and complete the other remaining number of cylinders in counter-clockwise direction as given above.
2. Underline the alternate number of cylinders in counter-clockwise direction.
3. For determining the firing order, first write the underlined numbers followed by the un-underlined numbers in counter-clockwise direction.

**Firing interval:** It is the interval in degrees of crank rotation between successive power strokes in different cylinders. It is given by:

$$\text{Firing interval} = \frac{720°}{\text{No. of cylinders}} \quad \text{[for four stroke cycle engine]}$$

$$\text{Firing interval} = \frac{360^\circ}{\text{No. of cylinders}} \qquad \text{[for two stroke cycle engine]}$$

**Power chart:** It is a sheet showing different processes like suction, compression, power and exhaust happening inside the different cylinders of an engine. This chart gives an idea about what is happening in which cylinder. The knowledge of this chart helps to easily set the tappet clearance (the clearance between the rocker arm and the valve). This clearance is adjusted when a particular cylinder is at compression stroke, as at this stroke both the valves remain closed.

Rules for making a power chart:

1. First determine the firing order of the engine.
2. Determine the firing interval.
3. Determine the crank shaft rotation for one stroke *i.e.* 180° for four stroke engines.
4. Since the firing interval as well as different strokes has to be represented, find the Greatest Common Divisor (GCD) between the firing interval and one stroke.
5. Choose the scale of the crankshaft rotation as per the GCD.

**EXAMPLE 1.1** *Make a power chart for a six cylinder four stroke cycle engine.*

**SOLUTION:**

1. Let the firing order of the six cylinder be 1–5–3–6–2–4
2. Now, Firing interval $= \frac{720^\circ}{6} = 120^\circ$ [∵ it is a four stroke engine]
3. Also we know that one stroke = 180° [∵ it is a four stroke engine]
4. The GCD of firing interval *i.e.* 120° and the stroke *i.e.* 180° is 60°.
5. Therefore, the scale of crankshaft rotation is chosen as 0–60°, 60° –120° and so on.

Now the power chart is constructed as given in Table 1.3.

**EXAMPLE 1.2** *Make a power chart for a three cylinder four stroke cycle engine.*

**SOLUTION:**

1. Let the firing order of the three cylinder engine be 1–2–3
2. Now, Firing interval $= \frac{720^\circ}{3} = 240^\circ$ [∵ it is a four stroke engine]
3. Also we know that one stroke = 180° [∵ it is a four stroke engine ]
4. The GCD of firing interval *i.e.* 240° and the stroke *i.e.* 180° is 60°.
5. Therefore, the scale of crankshaft rotation is chosen as 0–60°, 60°–120° and so on.

Now the power chart is constructed as given in Table 1.4

**TABLE 1.3: Power chart for a six cylinder four stroke cycle engine**

| Crankshaft rotation (in degrees) | The number of cylinder as per firing order | | | | | |
|---|---|---|---|---|---|---|
| | 1 | 5 | 3 | 6 | 2 | 4 |
| 0–60 | Suction | Exhaust | **Power** | **Power** | Compression | Suction |
| 60–120 | Suction | Exhaust | Exhaust | Power | Compression | Compression |
| 120–180 | Suction | Suction | Exhaust | **Power** | **Power** | Compression |
| 180–240 | Compression | Suction | Exhaust | Exhaust | Power | Compression |
| 240–300 | Compression | Suction | Suction | Exhaust | **Power** | **Power** |
| 300–360 | Compression | Compression | Suction | Exhaust | Exhaust | Power |
| 360–420 | **Power** | Compression | Suction | Suction | Exhaust | **Power** |
| 420–480 | Power | Compression | Compression | Suction | Exhaust | Exhaust |
| 480–540 | **Power** | **Power** | Compression | Suction | Suction | Exhaust |
| 540–600 | Exhaust | Power | Compression | Compression | Suction | Exhaust |
| 600–660 | Exhaust | **Power** | **Power** | Compression | Suction | Suction |
| 660–720 | Exhaust | Exhaust | Power | Compression | Compression | Suction |

- It is assumed that No.1 cylinder starts with suction stroke *i.e.* at 0°.
- Since the engine is based on four stroke, the total crankshaft degrees is taken as 720° as it takes two revolution to complete one cycle.
- The shaded area represents overlapping of power in two cylinders.
- There is a overlapping of power in cylinder No.1 and 5 from 480° to 540° (for 60°) and after a brief gap of 60°, again there is a overlapping of power in cylinder No.5 and 3 from 600° to 660° (for 60°) and the process goes on.

**TABLE 1.4: Power chart for a three cylinder four stroke cycle engine**

| Crankshaft rotation (in degrees) | The number of cylinder as per firing order | | |
|---|---|---|---|
| | 1 | 2 | 3 |
| 0–60 | Suction | Power | Compression |
| 60–120 | Suction | Exhaust | Compression |
| 120–180 | **Suction** | **Exhaust** | **Power** |
| 180–240 | Compression | Exhaust | Power |
| 240–300 | Compression | Suction | Power |
| 300–360 | **Compression** | **Suction** | **Exhaust** |
| 360–420 | Power | Suction | Exhaust |
| 420–480 | Power | Compression | Exhaust |
| 480–540 | Power | Compression | Suction |
| 540–600 | **Exhaust** | **Compression** | **Suction** |
| 600–660 | Exhaust | Power | Suction |
| 660–720 | Exhaust | Power | Compression |

- It is assumed that No.1 cylinder starts with suction stroke *i.e.* at 0°.
- The shaded area represents a gap period of power
- There is a gap period of power from 60° to 120° (for 60°), from 300° to 360° (for 60°) and from 540° to 600° (for 60°). Thus, a total gap period of 180° has been distributed equally in three parts for dynamic balancing of the crankshaft.

## 1.2 ENGINE TERMINOLOGY

Various terminology related with internal combustion engine is given in Fig. 1.9.

**Bore** Bore is the diameter of the engine cylinder.

**Top dead centre (TDC) and Bottom dead centre (BDC)** The piston while reciprocating in the cylinder occupies two extreme positions. The upper most position of the piston is called top dead centre (TDC) and the bottom most position is called bottom dead centre (BDC).

**Stroke** The linear distance traveled by the piston from Top Dead Centre (TDC) to Bottom Dead Centre (BDC) is called stroke.

**Stroke-bore ratio** The ratio of stroke (L) and diameter of bore (D) of the cylinder is called stroke-bore ratio (L/D). Generally, this ratio varies between 1 and 1.45 and for tractor engines, this ratio is about 1.25. In square engines, the stroke to bore ratio is one.

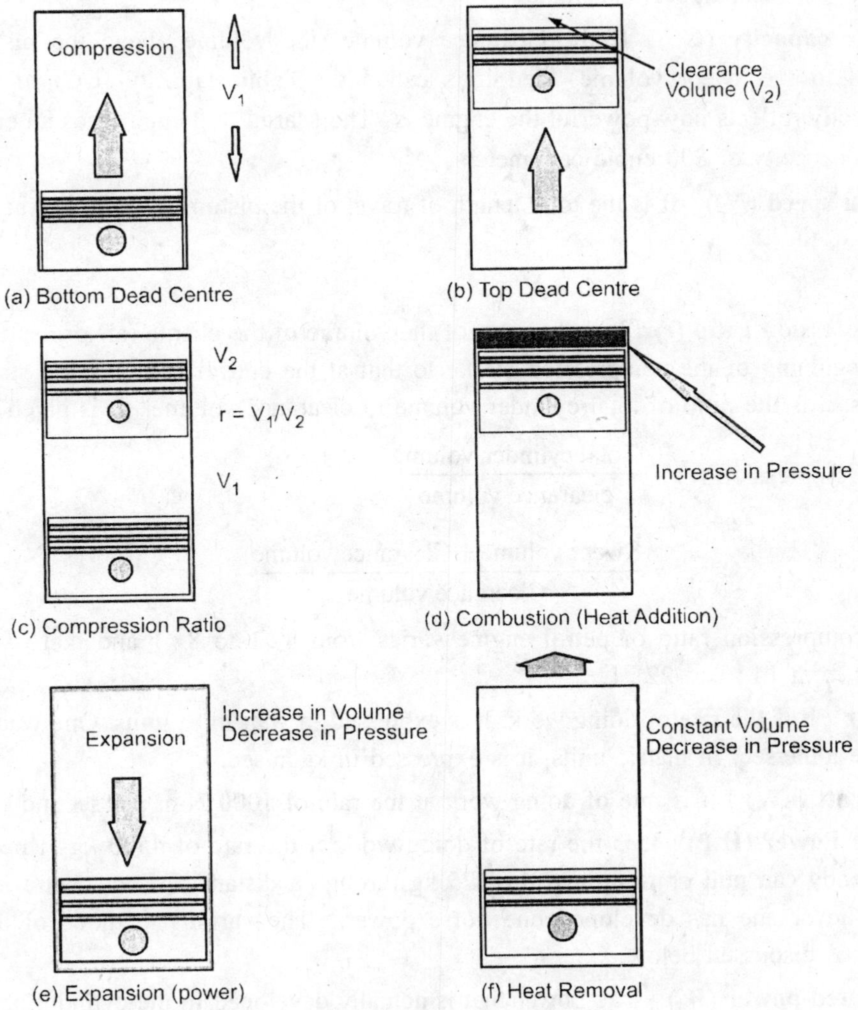


Figure 1.9. IC Engine Terminology

**Swept Volume** It is the volume that the piston displaces during its movement from BDC to TDC. If '*D*' is the bore and '*L*' is the stroke length, then the swept volume is given by $(\pi/4) D^2L$. It is also termed as piston displacement.

**Displacement volume of engine** It is the total swept volume of all the pistons during power stroke occurring in a period of one minute. It is given by

$$\text{Displacement volume} = ALn \times \frac{N}{2} \quad \text{[For four stroke engine]} \quad ...(1.8)$$

$$\text{Displacement volume} = ALn \times N \quad \text{[For two stroke engine]} \quad ...(1.9)$$

Where, $L$ = length of stroke (cm)

$A$ = cross-sectional area of piston ($cm^2$)

$N$ = engine revolution per minute

$n$ = number of cylinder

**Cubic capacity (*CC*)** If the clearance volume (the volume above the piston's TDC) is added to the swept volume, then it is called the cubic capacity (*CC*) of the engine. It indirectly reflects how powerful the engine is? The Maruti 800 engine has an engine having a cubic capacity of 800 cubic centimeters.

**Piston speed ($N_s$)** It is the total length of travel of the piston in a cylinder in one minute. It is given by

$$N_s = 2 \times L \times N \quad ...(1.10)$$

**Compression ratio (*r*)** It is the ratio of the volume of the charge (air or air/fuel mixture) at the beginning of the compression stroke to that at the end of compression stroke. In other words, it is the ratio of total cylinder volume to clearance volume. It is given by

$$\text{Compression } (r) = \frac{\text{Total cylinder volume}}{\text{clearance volume}} \quad ...(1.11)$$

$$= \frac{\text{Swept volume} + \text{Clearance volume}}{\text{Clearance volume}}$$

The compression ratio of petrol engine varies from 4 : 1 to 8 : 1 and that of diesel engine varies from 14 : 1 to 22 : 1.

**Power** It is the rate of doing work. It is expressed in watt in SI units. One watt is equivalent to one joule/sec. In metric units, it is expressed in kg.m/sec.

**Kilowatt (kW)** It is rate of doing work at the rate of 1000 N-m per second.

**Horse Power (H.P)** It is the rate of doing work at the rate of 4500 kg-m per minute or if somebody can pull or push a load of 75 kg through a distance of one metre in one second, then, he or she has developed one horse power. The various methods of defining horse power is discussed below:

**Indicated power ($W_i$)** The power that is actually developed in the cylinder and received by the piston is called indicated power ($W_i$) and it is given by

**In SI Units:**

$$W_i = \frac{PLAn}{60 \times 10^3 \times 10^3} \times \frac{N}{2} \quad \text{[for four stroke engine]} \qquad ...(1.12)$$

and

$$W_i = \frac{PLAn}{60 \times 10^3 \times 10^3} \times N \quad \text{[for two stroke engine]} \qquad ...(1.13)$$

Where $W_i$ = indicated power(kW)

$P$ = indicated mean effective pressure (kPa)

$L$ = length of stroke (cm)

$A$ = cross sectional area of piston ($cm^2$)

$n$ = number of cylinders

$N$ = engine revolutions per minute

**In MKS Units** In MKS units it is known as Indicated Horse Power (IHP) and is given by

$$IHP = \frac{PLAn}{4500} \times \frac{N}{2} \quad \text{[For four stroke engine]} \qquad ...(1.14)$$

$$IHP = \frac{PLAn}{4500} \times N \quad \text{[For two stroke engine]} \qquad ...(1.15)$$

Where, $P$ = indicated mean effective pressure ($kg/cm^2$)

$L$ = length of stroke (m)

$A$ = cross-sectional area of piston ($cm^2$)

$N$ = engine revolution per minute

$n$ = number of cylinders

**Brake power ($W_b$)** It is the power available at the end of crankshaft and is measured by a suitable dynamometer. The brake power is given by following equation:

$$W_b = \frac{2\pi NT}{60 \times 10^3} \qquad ...(1.16)$$

Where, $W_b$ = *brake power, kW*

$N$ = engine revolution per minute

$T$ = engine torque at flywheel, N-m

**Frictional power ($W_f$)** It is the power required to run the engine at a given speed without producing any useful work. This power is used for pumping fuel and to overcome friction. Frictional power ($W_f$) is given by

$$W_f = W_i - W_b$$

and in MKS Units, it is given by

$$FHP = IHP - BHP$$

**Power take off horse power (PTOHP)** It is the power delivered by the tractor through its power take off (PTO) shaft.

**Belt horse power** It is the power measured at the end of a suitable belt, receiving drive from the PTO shaft of the tractor. In general the belt and PTO horsepower of a tractor are approximately the same.

**Drawbar power ($W_{db}$)** It is the power in kilowatt which is available for pulling the loads. It is the power of tractor at the end of the drawbar (the bar which is used between the two lower hydraulic links).In MKS units it is known as drawbar horse power (DBHP).

**SAE power** It is also called as taxable power which is used by Society of Automotive Engineers (SAE) to compare engines on a uniform basis, for tax purposes. It is calculated by

$$\text{SAE HP} = \frac{D^2\, n}{2.5} \qquad \text{...(1.17)}$$

where, $D$ = diameter of cylinder in inches

$n$ = number of cylinders

**Tractive efficiency** It the ratio of output power to input power usually expressed in percent.

**Effect of Environment on Horse power** As per IS: 1601–1960, the observed horse power has to be corrected, as the HP is affected by barometric pressure and atmospheric pressure. The standard operating conditions are:

1. Mean barometric pressure of 736 mm of mercury corresponding to an altitude of 300 m above mean sea level.
2. Water vapour pressure of 27.4 mm of mercury corresponding to a relative humidity of 65 percent at 35°C.
3. Intake air temperature of 35°C.

For decrease in the atmospheric pressure, a deduction from the rated output of the engine shall be made at the rate of 1.4 percent per 100 m of altitude above 300 m. This de-rating is valid up to an altitude of 2500 m. For any increase in the intake air temperature above 35°C, a further deduction shall be made at the rate of 0.25 percent per °C.

**Mean effective pressure** It is the pressure that actually forces the piston downward during the power stroke. It is defined as the average pressure during the power stroke, minus the average pressure during the other three strokes. Mean effective pressure (MEP) is shown in Fig. 1.10.

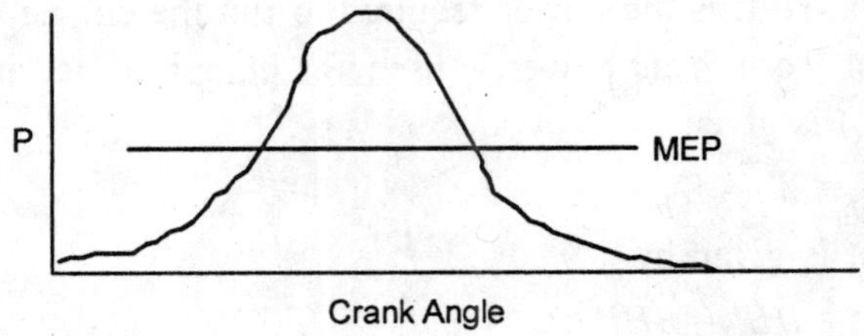


**Figure. 1.10. Mean Effective Pressure (MEP)**

The brake mean effective pressure ($P_b$ in kPa) is given by

**In SI Units:**

$$P_{b.m.e.p.} = \frac{W_b \times 60 \times 10^3 \times 10^3}{LAn \times N/2} \quad \text{[For four stroke engine]} \quad ...(1.18)$$

and

$$P_{b.m.e.p.} = \frac{W_b \times 60 \times 10^3 \times 10^3}{LAn \times N} \quad \text{[For two stroke engine]} \quad ...(1.19)$$

Where $P_{bmep}$ = brake mean effective pressure (kPa)

$W_b$ = brake power, kW

$L$ = length of stroke (cm)

$A$ = cross sectional area of piston ($cm^2$)

$n$ = number of cylinders

$N$ = engine rpm

**In MKS Units:**

$$P_b = \frac{BHP \times 4500}{LAn \times \frac{N}{2}} \quad \text{[For four stroke engine]} \quad ...(1.20)$$

$$P_b = \frac{BHP \times 4500}{LAn \times N} \quad \text{[For two stroke engine]} \quad ...(1.21)$$

Where, BHP = brake horse power

$P_b$ = brake mean effective pressure ($kg/cm^2$)

$L$ = length of stroke (m)

$A$ = cross-sectional area of piston ($cm^2$)

$N$ = engine revolution per minute

$n$ = number of cylinders

**Relationship between different horse powers** As per American Society of Agricultural Engineers Standard, ASAE D497.4 JAN 98, the relationship between different horse powers is given in Fig. 1.11.

**Volumetric efficiency** Practically, the weight of air entering the cylinder due to the vacuum created by the downward motion of the piston is always less than the actual weight of air that should be inducted by filling the piston displacement volume with air at atmospheric pressure and temperature. Thus, the volumetric efficiency is given by

$$\text{Volumetric efficiency} = \frac{\text{Actual volume of air inducted}}{\text{Swept volume}} \quad ...(1.22)$$

In order to increase the volumetric efficiency, superchargers are used in the air intake system which forcibly inducts more air into the cylinder.

**Torque (*T*)** The force applied at any point to cause a turning effect is called torque. The torque ($T$) is the product of force ($F$) and distance ($r$) of force from the centre of shaft. The unit of torque is N-m or kg-m. In the engine, the amount of torque depends upon the pressure exerted by the piston and the length of the crank arm.

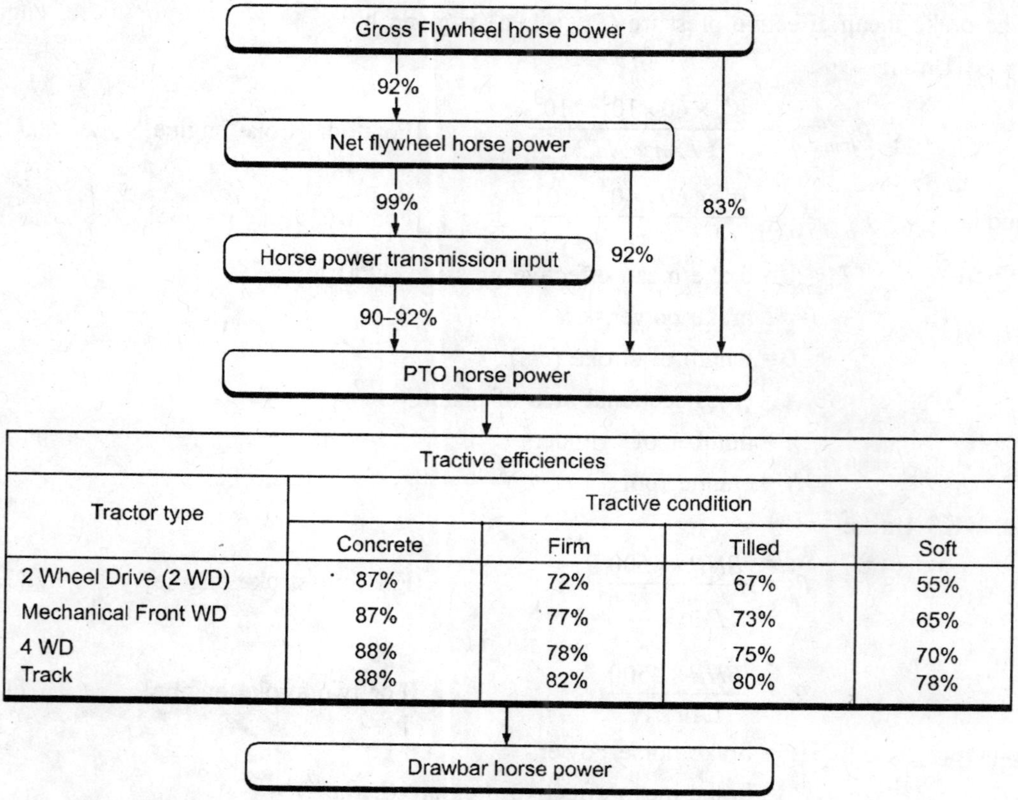


**Figure 1.11. Relationship between various horse powers**

**Specific fuel consumption (SFC):** It is the fuel consumed in grams per hour to produce one kW or one HP. The typical PTO SFC values of tractors are given in Table 1.5.

**TABLE 1.5: Typical PTO SFC values of tractors**

| **Power category (HP/kW)** | **PTO SFC (g/PTOHP/hr)** | **PTO SFC (g/PTO kW/hr)** |
|---|---|---|
| Upto 25 PTO hp (18.65kW) | 205 | 275 |
| Above 25 and upto 35 PTO hp (18.65–26.11 kW) | 200 | 268 |
| Above 35 and upto 55 PTO hp (26.11–41.03 kW) | 195 | 262 |
| Above 55 PTO hp ( Above 41.03 kW) | 185 | 248 |

**Thermal efficiency:** It is the ratio of the output horse power of an engine to the fuel horse power. The brake thermal efficiency is given by

$$\text{Brake thermal efficiency} = \frac{641 \times 10^3}{\text{fuel consumed in g per bhp- hr} \times \text{kilocalories per kg}} \quad ...(1.23)$$

{The above formula is derived from the fact that one hp = 746W = 746 J/s = 178.2 cal/s = 641000 cal/hr}

The thermal efficiency varies from 0.25 to 0.32 in petrol engines and for diesel engines it varies from 0.32 to 0.38.

**Mechanical efficiency:** It is the ratio of the brake power ($W_b$) to indicated power ($W_i$) and is given by

$$\text{Mechanical efficiency} = \frac{W_b}{W_i} \times 100 \qquad ...(1.24)$$

And in MKS units it is given by

$$\text{Mechanical efficiency} = \frac{BHP}{IHP} \times 100 \qquad ...(1.25)$$

**Heat balance equation of an I.C engine:** The analysis of energy balance of an I.C engine generally helps in assessing the total amount of fuel energy converted into useful work and energy lost/ wasted through different systems/channels which can be minimized to improve thermal efficiency of engine.

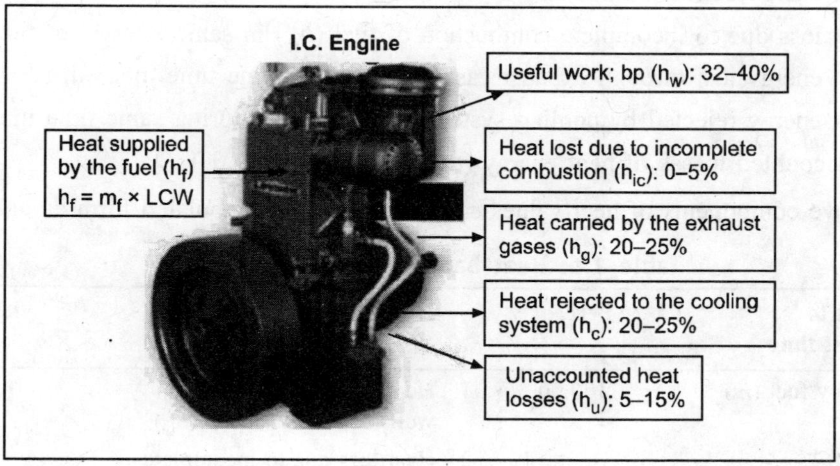


**Figure 1.12. Energy balance of an I.C. engine**

The energy balance equation of an I.C engine is given by

**Energy supplied by fuel** = Energy converted into useful work + Heat lost due to incomplete combustion + Heat energy loss through exhaust gases + Heat rejected by cooling system of engine + Unaccounted energy losses

Or,

$$h_f = h_w + h_{ic} + h_g + h_c + h_u \qquad (1.26)$$

Where

$h_f = m_f \times LCV$, kJ/s or kW

$h_w = bp$, kJ/s or kW

$h_{ic} = m'_f \times LCV$, kJ/s or kW

$h_g = m_g \times C_{pg} \times \delta t$, kJ/s or kW

$h_c = m_w \times C_{pw} \times \delta t$, kJ/s or kW

$h_u$ = unaccounted loss by difference, kJ/s or kW

$m_f$ = mass of fuel, kg
$LCV$ = lower calorific value of fuel, kJ/kg
$bp$ = brake power of engine, kW
$m'_f$ = mass of unburnt fuel, kg
$m_g$ = mass of gas, kg
$C_{pg}$ = specific heat of exhaust gas, kJ/kgK
$m_w$ = mass of water, kg
$C_{pw}$ = specific heat of water, kJ/kgK
$\delta t$ = temperature difference

From above, it is clear that main components of heat balance of an engine are:

*i)* Heat energy input to engine by fuel per unit time ($h_f$) in kJ and taken as 100%
*ii)* Heat energy converted into useful work as brake power per unit time ($h_w$), kJ
*iii)* Heat loss due to incomplete combustion of fuel ($h_{ic}$) in same interval of time, kJ
*iv)* Heat energy lost through exhaust gases ($h_g$) during same time interval, kJ
*v)* Heat energy rejected by cooling system of engine ($h_c$) during same time interval, kJ
*vi)* Unaccounted losses of heat energy (radiation losses etc, $h_u$)

The above components of heat values can be expressed in tabulated form as under:

**Table 1.6: Heat balance of an I.C engine**

| Heat input to engine per unit time | kJ | Percent | Heat expenditure/time | kJ | Per cent |
|---|---|---|---|---|---|
| Heat supplied by fuel ($h_f$) | — | 100.00 | 1. Heat converted to useful work equivalent to bp ($h_w$) | | |
| | | | 2. Heat loss due to incomplete combustion ($h_{ic}$) | | |
| | | | 3. Heat lost in exhaust gases ($h_g$) | | |
| | | | 4. Heat lost to cooling system ($h_c$) | | |
| | | | 5. Unaccounted losses ($h_u$) | | |
| **Total** | — | **100.00** | | | |

**EXAMPLE 1.3** *A 4-stroke cycle diesel engine of 30 kW brake power of a tractor was tested at full load and following results were recorded:*

*i) Indicated power of engine = 37.5 kW*
*ii) Fuel consumption ($m_f$) = 7.5 kg/h*
*iii) Mass of water circulated through cooling system = 7.5 kg/min*
*iv) Inlet and outlet water temperatures = 20°C and 70°C, respectively*
*v) Air to fuel ratio of engine = 25:1*
*vi) Calorific value of fuel (LCV) = 43500 kJ/kg*

*vii) Mean specific heat of exhaust gas= 1.05 kJ/kgK*

*viii) Room temperature = 20°C*

*ix) Temperature of exhaust gas = 430°C*

*Draw an energy balance for test on the basis of kJ and percentages.*

**SOLUTION:**

***i)* Energy input to engine by fuel ($h_f$)**

We know that

$$h_f = m_f \times \text{LCV, kJ/s or kW}$$

$$\therefore \quad h_f = (7.5 \text{ kg/h}/3600 \text{ s/h}) \times 43500 \text{ kJ/kg}$$

$$= 90.625 \text{ kJ/s}$$

***ii)* Heat converted to useful work equivalent to bp ($h_w$)**

We know that

$$h_w = \text{bp, kJ/s or kW}$$

$$h_w = 30 \text{ kW or } 30 \text{ kJ/s}$$

***iii)* Heat loss due to incomplete combustion ($h_{ic}$)**

We know that

$$h_{ic} = m'_f \times \text{LCV, kJ/s or kW}$$

$$m'_f = (5/100) \times 7.5 \text{ kg/h}$$

So,

$$h_{ic} = (5/100) \times (7.5 \text{ kg/h}/3600 \text{ s/h}) \times 43500 \text{ kJ/kg}$$

$$= 4.53 \text{ kJ/s}$$

***iv)* Heat lost in exhaust gases ($h_g$)**

We know that

$$h_g = m_g \times C_{pg} \times \delta t, \text{ kJ/s or kW}$$

$$\therefore \quad h_g = (7.5 \text{ kg} + 25 \times 7.5\text{kg})/3600 \text{ s/h} \times 1.05 \text{ kJ/kgK} \times (430-20)$$

$$h_g = 29.15 \text{ kJ/s}$$

***v)* Heat lost to cooling system ($h_c$)**

We know that;

$$h_c = m_w \times C_{pw} \times \delta t, \text{ kJ/s or kW}$$

$$\therefore \quad h_c = (7.5 \text{ kg/min}/60 \text{ s/min}) \times 4.18 \text{ kJ/kgK} \times (70-20)$$

$$h_c = 26.13 \text{ kJ/s}$$

***vi)* Unaccounted losses ($h_u$)**

We know that

$$h_u = h_f - (h_w + h_{ic} + h_g + h_c)$$

$$\therefore \quad h_u = 90.625 \text{ kJ/s} - (30 \text{ kJ/s} + 4.53 \text{ kJ/s} + 29.15 \text{ kJ/s} + 26.13 \text{ kJ/s})$$

$$h_u = 90.625 \text{ kJ/s} - 89.810 \text{ kJ/s} = 0.815 \text{ kJ/s}$$

Based on the above, the heat balance sheet is drawn as under:

**Heat balance of I.C engine tested**

| Heat input to engine per unit time | kJ/s | Percent | Heat expenditure/time | kJ/s | Per cent |
|---|---|---|---|---|---|
| Heat supplied by fuel ($h_f$) | 90.625 | 100.00 | 1. Heat converted to useful work equivalent to bp ($h_w$) | 30.000 | 33.100 |
| | | | 2. Heat loss due to incomplete combustion ($h_{ic}$) | 4.530 | 4.990 |
| | | | 3. Heat lost in exhaust gases ($h_g$) | 29.150 | 32.170 |
| | | | 4. Heat lost to cooling system ($h_c$) | 26.130 | 28.830 |
| | | | 5. Unaccounted losses ($h_u$) | 0.815 | 0.910 |
| **Total** | **90.625** | **100.00** | **Total** | **90.625** | **100.000** |

**EXAMPLE 1.4** *During testing of a single cylinder, four stroke water cooled diesel engine of a tractor, following data were recorded:*

*Diameter of cylinder = 120 mm*

*Stroke length = 150 mm*

*Mean effective pressure,* $P_m$ *= 7.0 bars*

*Torque = 75 Nm*

*Engine rpm = 2000*

*Fuel consumption = 4.0 kg/hr*

*Calorific value of fuel = 43 MJ/kg*

*Cooling water flow rate = 4.0 kg/min*

*Air used per kg of fuel = 30 kg*

*Rise in cooling water temperature = 40°C*

*Temperature of exhaust gases = 415°C*

*Room temperature = 30°C*

*Mean specific heat of exhaust gases = 1 kJ/kgK*

*Specific heat of water = 4.18 kJ/kgK*

*Determine the following:*

*i) Indicated power of engine*

*ii) Brake power of engine*

*iii) Also draw heat balance sheet of engine for one hour basis in kJ.*

**SOLUTION:**

***i*) Indicated power of engine ($W_i$)**

Now, we know that for a 4-stroke cycle, single cylinder diesel engine

$$W_i = P_m \text{ LAN/2}$$

Where $W_i$ = Indicated power, kW

$P_m$ = Mean effective pressure, kPa

$L$ = Length of stroke, m

$A$ = Area of cross section of engine cylinder, $m^2$

$N$ = Engine revolutions per second

Here, $A = \pi/4 \times (0.12\text{m})^2 = 0.785 \times 10^{-2}\ \text{m}^2$

$L = 0.15\text{m}$

& $N = 2000$ rpm

$P_m = 7.0 \times 10^{-5}$ Pa

Putting values in above equation we get

$$W_i = 7.0 \times 10^{-5}\ \text{Pa} \times 0.15\ \text{m} \times 0.785 \times 10^{-2}\ \text{m}^2 \times (2000/60)/2$$

$$= 19.78\ \text{kW}$$

***ii*) Brake power of engine ($W_b$)**

We know that

$$W_b = 2\pi\text{NT}/1000$$

Where; $W_b$ = Brake power of engine, kW

$N$ = Engine speed, revolutions per second

$T$ = Engine torque, Nm

Putting values in above equation we get

$$W_b = 2\pi\ (2000/60) \times 75\ \text{Nm}/1000$$

$$= 15.70\ \text{kW}$$

***iii*) Heat balance for the engine**

***a*) Energy input to engine by fuel ($h_f$)**

We know that

$$h_f = m_f \times \text{LCV (kJ/s or kW)}$$

$$h_f = (4.0\ \text{kg/h}) \times 43000\ \text{kJ/kg}$$

$$= 172000\ \text{kJ/h}$$

***b*) Heat converted to useful work equivalent to bp ($h_w$)**

We know that

$$h_w = bp\ \text{(kJ/s or kW)} \times 3600\ \text{s/hr}$$

$$h_w = 15.70\ \text{kJ/s} \times 3600\ \text{s/hr} = 56550\ \text{kJ/hr}$$

**c) Heat lost in exhaust gases ($h_g$)**

We know that

$$h_g = m_g \times C_{pg} \times \delta t, \text{ kJ/s or kW}$$
$$h_g = (4.0 \text{ kg} + 30 \times 4.0\text{kg})/\text{h} \times 1.0 \text{ kJ/kgK} \times (415\text{–}30)$$
$$h_g = 47740 \text{ kJ/h}$$

**d) Heat lost to cooling system ($h_c$)**

We know that

$$h_c = m_w \times 60 \text{ min/h } C_{pw} \times \delta t \text{ (kJ/hr)}$$

or,

$$h_c = (4.0 \text{ kg/min} \times 60\text{min/h}) \times 4.18 \text{ kJ/kgK} \times 40°\text{C}$$
$$h_c = 40128 \text{ kJ/h}$$

**e) Unaccounted losses ($h_u$)**

We know that

$$h_u = h_f - (h_w + h_g + h_c)$$

or,

$$h_u = 172000 \text{ kJ/h} - (56550 \text{ kJ/h} + 47740 \text{ kJ/h} + 40128 \text{ kJ/h})$$
$$h_u = 172000 \text{ kJ/h} - 144418 \text{ kJ/h} = 27582 \text{ kJ/h}$$

Based on above the heat balance sheet is drawn as under:

**Heat balance of I.C engine tested**

| Heat input to engine per unit time | kJ/hr | Percent | Heat expenditure/time | kJ/hr | Per cent |
|---|---|---|---|---|---|
| Heat supplied by fuel ($h_f$) | 172000 | 100.00 | 1. Heat converted to useful work equivalent to bp ($h_w$) | 56550 | 32.88 |
| | | | 2. Heat lost in exhaust gases ($h_g$) | 47740 | 27.77 |
| | | | 3. Heat lost to cooling system ($h_c$) | 40128 | 23.33 |
| | | | 4. Unaccounted losses ($h_u$) | 27582 | 16.04 |
| **Total** | **172000** | **100.00** | **Total** | **172000** | **100.00** |

**EXAMPLE 1.5** *During testing of an I.C engine of a tractor under full load conditions, following results were obtained:*

*Indicated power,* $W_i = 37.0$ *kW*
*Brake power,* $W_b = 30.0$ *kW*
*Fuel consumption = 9.0 kg/hr*
*Air used per kg of fuel = 35 kg*
*Temperature of exhaust gases = 450°C*
*Room temperature = 25°C*
*Cooling water flow rate =10 kg/min*
*Inlet temperature of cooling water = 25°C*
*Outlet temperature of cooling water = 75°C*
*Calorific value of fuel = 43 MJ/kg*
*Specific heat of exhaust gases = 1kJ/kgK*
*Specific heat of water = 4.18 kJ/kgK*

*Draw a heat balance sheet per minute basis and also estimate thermal and mechanical efficiencies of the engine.*

**SOLUTION:**

***i)* Heat balance for the engine:**

***a)* Energy input to engine by fuel ($h_f$)**

We know that

$$h_f = m_f \times \text{LCV (kJ/s or kW)}$$
$$h_f = (9.0 \text{ kg/h })/60 \text{ min/h} \times 43000 \text{ kJ/kg}$$
$$= 6450 \text{ kJ/min}$$

***b)* Heat converted to useful work equivalent to bp ($h_w$)**

We know that

$$h_w = \text{bp (kJ/s or kW)} \times 60 \text{ s/min}$$
$$h_w = 30.0 \text{ kJ/s} \times 60\text{s/min} = 1800 \text{ kJ/min}$$

***c)* Heat lost in exhaust gases ($h_g$):**

We know that

$$h_g = m_g \times C_{pg} \times \delta t, \text{ kJ/s or kW}$$
$$h_g = (9.0 \text{ kg} + 35 \times 9.0\text{kg})/\text{hr}/60\text{min/hr} \times 1.0 \text{ kJ/kgK} \times (450\text{–}25)$$
$$h_g = 2295 \text{ kJ/min}$$

***d)* Heat lost to cooling system ($h_c$)**

We know that

$$h_c = m_w \times C_{pw} \times \delta t, \text{ kJ/min}$$

or,
$$h_c = 10.0 \text{ kg/min} \times 4.18 \text{ kJ/kgK} \times (75\text{–}25)$$
$$h_c = 2090 \text{ kJ/min}$$

***e)* Unaccounted losses ($h_u$)**

We know that

$$h_u = h_f - (h_w + h_g + h_c)$$

or,
$$h_u = 6450 \text{ kJ/min} - (1800 \text{ kJ/min} + 2295 \text{ kJ/min} + 2090 \text{ kJ/min})$$
$$h_u = 6450 \text{ kJ/min} - 6185 \text{ kJ/min} = 265 \text{ kJ/min}$$

Based on above the heat balance sheet is drawn as under:

**Heat balance of I.C engine tested**

| **Heat input to engine per unit time** | **kJ/min** | **Percent** | **Heat expenditure/time** | **kJ/min** | **Per cent** |
|---|---|---|---|---|---|
| Heat supplied by fuel ($h_f$) | 6450 | 100.00 | 1. Heat converted to useful work equivalent to bp ($h_w$) | 1800 | 27.91 |
| | | | 2. Heat lost in exhaust gases ($h_g$) | 2295 | 35.58 |
| | | | 3. Heat lost to cooling system ($h_c$) | 2090 | 32.40 |
| | | | 4. Unaccounted losses ($h_u$) | 265 | 4.12 |
| **Total** | **6450** | **100.00** | **Total** | **6450** | **100.00** |

***ii*) Indicated Thermal Efficiency of Engine**

$$\text{Indicated thermal efficiency} = \left[\frac{\text{Indicated power (kW)} \times 60}{\text{Heat supplied (kg/min)}}\right] \times 100$$

Or, Indicated thermal efficiency = $(W_i \times 60 / h_f) \times 100$

Putting values in above equation, we get

Indicated thermal efficiency = (37.0 kW × 60/6450 kJ/min) ×100 = 34.70%

***iii*) Brake Thermal Efficiency of Engine**

$$\text{Brake thermal efficiency} = \left[\frac{\text{Brake power (kW)} \times 60}{\text{Heat supplied (kg/min)}}\right] \times 100$$

Or, Brake thermal efficiency = $(W_b \times 60/h_f) \times 100$

Putting values in above equation, we get:

Brake thermal efficiency = (30.0 kW × 60/6450 kJ/min) × 100 = 27.91%

***iv*) Mechanical Efficiency of Engine ($\eta_m$)**

Mechanical efficiency, $\eta_m$ = (Brake power/Indicated power) × 100

Or, $\eta_m = (W_b/W_i) \times 100$

Putting values in above equation, we get:

$$\eta_m = (30.0 \text{ kW}/37.0 \text{ kW}) \times 100 = 80.43\%$$

**EXAMPLE 1.6** *A four-stroke cycle diesel engine of a tractor is developing a mean effective pressure of 10 bars. It develops a power of 25 kW while running at a speed of 2200 rpm. Take stroke bore ratio as 1.2; calculate the bore and stroke of engine.*

**SOLUTION:**

Diesel engine 4-stroke cycle

Mean effective pressure, $P_m$ = 10 bars

Indicated power developed, $W_i$ = 25 kW

Engine speed = 2200 rpm

Stroke bore ratio, $L/d$ = 1.2

Now, we know that for a 4-stroke cycle engine

$$W_i = P_m \text{ LAN}/2$$

where, $W_i$ = Indicated power, kW

$P_m$ = Mean effective pressure, kPa

$L$ = Length of stroke, m

$A$ = Area of cross section of engine cylinder, m²

$N$ = Engine revolutions per second

Putting values in above equation we get;

$$25 = 10 \times 10^2 \times (1.2\, d) \times \pi/4\, (d)^2 \times (2200/60)/2$$

Or

$$d^3 = 1.446 \times 10^{-3}$$

or $d = 0.1135$ m or 113.5 mm

And $L = 1.2\,d = 1.2 \times 113.5$ mm $= 136.2$ mm

**EXAMPLE 1.7** *A four stroke cycle diesel engine has stroke bore ratio of 1.25. The mean effective pressure recorded was 0.8 MPa. The engine is producing indicated power of 23.5 kW while running at 2000 rpm. Determine the dimensions of engine.*

**SOLUTION:**

4-stroke cycle diesel engine
Mean effective pressure, $P_m = 0.8$ MPa
Stroke bore ratio, $L/d = 1.25$
Indicated power, $W_i = 23.50$ kW
Engine speed = 2000 rpm
Now, we know that for a 4-stroke cycle engine

$$W_i = P_m \, LAN/2$$

Where $W_i$ = Indicated power, kW
$P_m$ = Mean effective pressure, kPa
$L$ = Length of stroke, m
$A$ = Area of cross section of engine cylinder, m²
$N$ = Engine revolutions per second

Putting values in above equation we get

$$23.50 = 0.80 \text{ MPa} \times 10^3 \times 1.25\,d \times \pi/4\,(d)^2 \times (2000/60)/2$$

Or, $d^3 = 1.7945 \times 10^{-3}$

Or, $d = 0.121$ m or 121 mm

And $L = 1.2\,d = 1.25 \times 121$ mm $= 151.25$ mm

**EXAMPLE 1.8** *A four cylinder, 4-stroke cycle diesel engine develops 40 kW power at 35 revolutions/s. The mean effective pressure in each cylinder is 8.5 bars and mechanical efficiency of engine is 80%. Calculate the following:*

*i) Diameter of cylinder*

*ii) Stroke of piston if stroke bore ratio is 1.25:1.*

**SOLUTION:**

Four cylinder, 4-stroke cycle diesel engine
Brake power of engine = 40 kW
Number of cylinders = 4
Mean effective pressure, $P_m = 8.5$ bars
Mechanical efficiency = 80%
Engine speed, $N = 35$ rev/s
We know that

Mechanical efficiency, $\eta_m = W_b/W_i$

Putting values in above equation we get;

$$0.80 = 40 \text{ kW}/W_i$$

Or, $W_i = 40 \text{ kW}/0.80 = 50 \text{ kW}$

Also, for a 4-stroke cycle engine

$$W_i = P_m \text{ LAN}/2 \times n$$

Where $W_i$ = Indicated power, kW

$P_m$ = Mean effective pressure, kPa

$L$ = Length of stroke, m

$A$ = Area of cross section of engine cylinder, m²

$N$ = Engine revolutions per second

$n$ = number of cylinders

Putting values in above equation we get;

$$50 \text{ kW} = 8.5 \times 102 \times 1.25\, d \times \pi/4\, (d)^2 \times \{(2000/60)/2\} \times 4$$

Or, $d^3 = 2.69 \times 10^{-3}$

Or, $d = 0.139$ m or 139 mm say 140 mm

Also, $L = 1.25 \text{ d} = 1.25 \times 140$ mm

$= 17375$ mm say 175 mm

So, the designed dimensions of engine cylinder are 140 × 175 mm

**EXAMPLE 1.9** *A single cylinder four stroke cycle diesel engine of a tractor is having swept volume of 1050 cm³ and is tested at 30 rev/s. A braking torque of 70 Nm and indicator diagram gave a mean effective pressure of 10.5 bars. Calculate the following for the engine:*

*i) Brake power*

*ii) Mechanical efficiency*

**SOLUTION:**

Swept volume of engine = 1050 cm³

Engine speed = 30 rev/s

Brake torque = 70 Nm

Mean effective pressure, $P_m$ = 10.5 bars

***i) Brake power ($W_b$)***

We know that

Brake power of engine, $W_b = T \times \theta/1000$

Where $W_b$ = Brake power of engine, kW

$T$ = Braking torque, Nm

$\theta$ = Angle turned per second = $2\pi\, n$

So, putting values in above equation we get;

$$W_b = 70 \text{ Nm} \times 2\pi \times 30 \text{ rev/s}/1000$$

Or, $W_b = 13.20$ kW

***ii*) Mechanical efficiency ($\eta_m$ )**

We know that for a single cylinder, 4-stroke cycle engine

$$W_i = P_m \text{ LAN/2}$$

Where $W_i$ = Indicated power, kW

$P_m$ = Mean effective pressure, kPa

$L$ = Length of stroke, m

$A$ = Area of cross section of engine cylinder, m²

$N$ = Engine revolutions per second

Putting values in above equation we get

$$W_i = 10.5 \times 10^2 \times 1050 \times 10^{-6} \times 30/2$$

Or, $$W_i = 16.54 \text{ kW}$$

Now, we know that

Mechanical efficiency, $$\eta_m = W_b/W_i$$

Putting values in above equation we get;

$$\eta_m = 13.20 \text{ kW}/16.54 \text{ kW}$$

$$\eta_m = 0.7981 \text{ or } 79.81\%$$

## 1.3 DESIGN OF 35 HP TRACTOR ENGINE

**EXAMPLE 1.10** *Design the engine components of a 35 hp four stroke cycle diesel engine for a tractor.*

**SOLUTION:**

**1. GENERAL**

BHP = 35 hp

Type of engine: Four stroke cycle diesel engine

**Assumptions:**

No. of cylinders = 3

Mechanical efficiency = 75%

Rated engine speed = 2200 rpm

Indicated mean effective pressure (P) = 7 Kg/cm$^2$

Stroke to Bore ratio = 1.25

Now, we know that

$$IHP = \frac{BHP}{\text{Mechanical efficiency}} \quad \text{...(1.27)}$$

Putting the values in eq. 1.27, we get

$$IHP = \frac{35}{0.75} = 46.67.$$

Also, for a four stroke cycle engine

$$IHP = \frac{PLAN}{4500} \times \frac{n}{2} \quad \text{...(1.28)}$$

Where $P$ = indicated mean effective pressure (kg/cm$^2$)

$L$ = length of stroke (m)

$A$ = cross-sectional area of piston (cm$^2$)

$N$ = engine revolution per minute

$n$ = no. of cylinders

Putting the values in the eq.1.28, we get

$$46.67 = \frac{7 \times LA \times 2200 \times 3}{4500 \times 2}$$

$$LA = 9.09 \qquad \text{(Convert } L \text{ in cm as area is in cm}^2\text{)}$$

$$LA = 909$$

$$L \times \frac{\pi}{4} D^2 = 909 \qquad ...(1.29)$$

Moreover, $L/D$ = 1.25 (since stroke to bore ratio = 1.25 (assumed)), the eq. 1.29 becomes,

$$1.25D \times \frac{\pi}{4} D^2 = 909 \quad \text{or} \quad D = 9.7 \text{ cm}$$

Therefore,

Diameter of cylinder = $D$ = 10 cm (say)

Stroke = L = 1.25 × 10cm = 12.5 cm

The dimensions of stroke and bore is given in Fig. 1.13

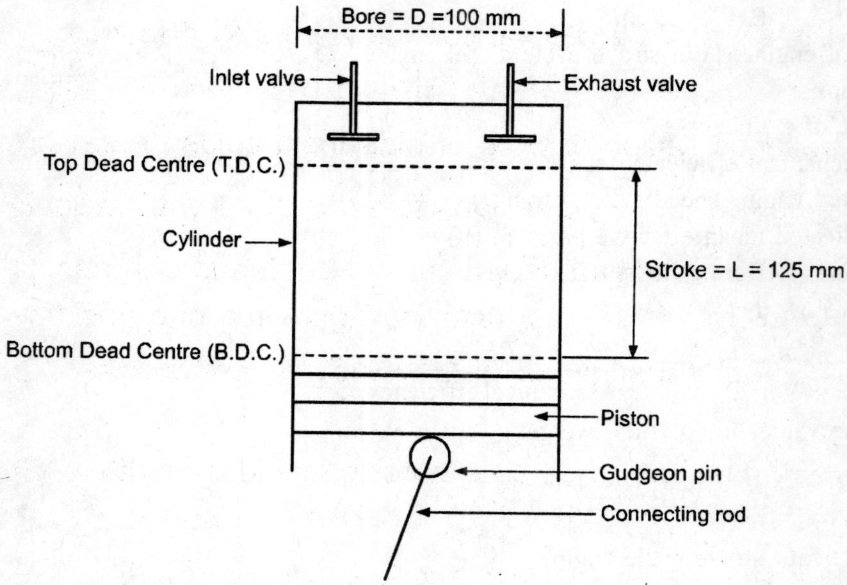


**Figure 1.13. Stroke and bore**

## 2. DESIGN OF CYLINDER

### Cylinder

The primary function of a cylinder is to contain the working fluid i.e. air in case of diesel engine and charge (mixture of air and fuel) in case of petrol engine and the secondary function is to guide the piston. It forms the basic and supporting unit of engine. In case of small engines the cylinder, water jackets and the frame may be cast as one piece. But in larger engines, separate cylinder liners or sleeves are used. The cylinder liners are available in two types: 1. Wet liner and 2. Dry liner. In the wet liner, water in jacket is in direct contact with the outer wall of the liner whereas the dry liner is pressed into the cylinder (Fig. 1.14). The comparison between the dry liner and wet liner is given below:

| Dry liner | Wet liner |
|---|---|
| 1. It is easy to replace a dry liner but the casting is very complicated | It is difficult to replace but the casting is relatively easy. |
| 2. Crankcase or combustion chamber dilution is not possible due to the leakage of water. | Crankcase or combustion chamber dilution is possible due to the leakage of water, if the casting is defective. |
| 3. Decreased heat flow through the composite wall makes lesser heat dissipation. | Heat dissipation is better. |

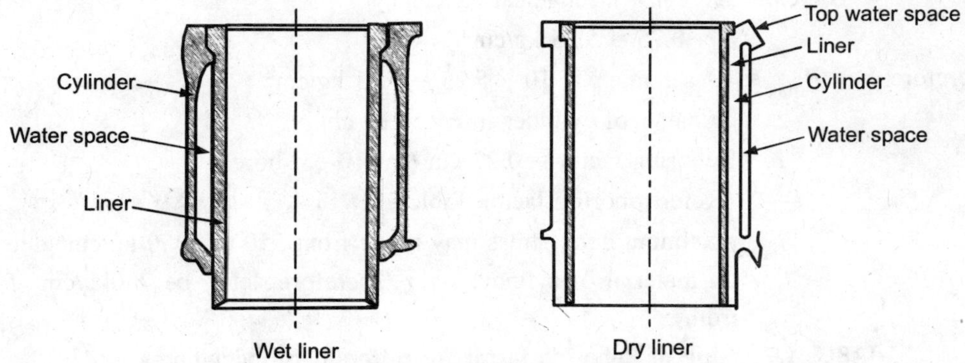


**Figure 1.14. Wet and dry liners**

The cylinder liners are usually made of high grade grey cast iron with homogenous and close grained structure. Some times, to give greater strength, wear and corrosion resistance with less weight, chromium, nickel and molybdenum are added to the cast iron or cast steel. The surface treatments given to make the liner hard and wear resistant are given below:

1. By heating the cast iron liners from inside by passing a high frequency induction current and subsequently water quenching gives a hardness of Rock well C 52 to 55.

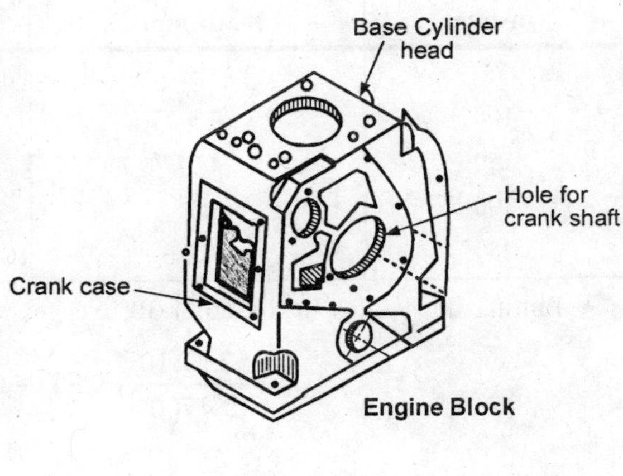

2. In case of cast iron liners with 2% nickel and 0.65% chromium, it is heated to about 840°C, followed by oil quenching and then tempering for about two hours at 180°C. This gives a hardness of Rock well C 50.
3. Chrome plating of cylinder liner gives a very hard and porous surface where a good film of oil can be maintained thus reducing the surface wear appreciably.

Now, let us design the cylinder liner for a 35 BHP engine

**Assumptions:**

Let the cylinder liner be water cooled and made of cast iron.

**(A) Cylinder**

(*a*) ***Thickness of cylinder***: The cylinder liner wall thickness is stressed due to gas pressure and the piston side thrust.

The wall thickness is usually calculated by applying the formula for a thin cylinder. Therefore, thickness of cylinder liner ($t$) in cm is given by

$$t = \frac{P_{max}\ D}{2 f_c} + K \qquad ...(1.30)$$

Where, $P_{max}$ = maximum gas pressure, Kg/cm$^2$

= 9 to 10 times of Brake mean effective pressure (B.m.e.p)

B.me.p = I.m.e.p × mechanical efficiency

= 7 × 0.75 = 5.25 kg/cm$^2$

Therefore, $P_{max}$ = 10 × b.m.e.p = 10 × 5.25 = 52.5 kg/cm$^2$

$D$ = diameter of cylinder in cm = 10 cm

$K$ = Reboring factor = 0.23 cm (for 10 cm bore)

{Refer reboring factor Table 1.7}

$f_c$ = maximum hoop stress may range from 350 to 1050 kg/cm$^2$ depending on material of cylinder liner. Therefore, let $f_c$ be 700kg/cm$^2$ for cast iron

**TABLE 1.7: Value of Reboring factor for different cylinder bores**

| Cylinder bore in mm | Reboring factor K, in mm | Cylinder bore in mm | Reboring factor K, in mm |
|---|---|---|---|
| 75 | 1.5 | 300 | 9.5 |
| 100 | 2.3 | 350 | 10.5 |
| 150 | 4.0 | 400 | 12.5 |
| 200 | 6.0 | 450 | 12.5 |
| 250 | 7.5 | 500 | 12.5 |

Putting the values in the eq. 1.30, we get,

$$t = \frac{52.2 \times 10}{2 \times 700} + 0.23 = 0.60 \text{ cm}$$

But, according to an empirical relation, the thickness of cylinder ($t$) should be

$$t \geq \frac{D}{15} \qquad ...(1.31)$$

[where $D$ = diameter of cylinder in mm]

Putting the values in eq. 1.31, we get

$$t \geq 6.67 \text{ mm}$$

Therefore, let the thickness of cylinder be 7 mm.

(*b*) ***Thickness of jacket wall***: The thickness of jacket wall is given by

$$\text{Thickness of jacket wall (cm)} = 0.032\ D + 1.6 \qquad ...(1.32)$$

[where, $D$ = diameter of cylinder in mm]

Putting the values in eq. 1.32, we get

$$\text{Thickness of jacket wall } (t_j) = 0.032 \times 10 + 0.16$$
$$= 0.48 \text{ cm}$$
$$= 5 \text{ mm (say)}$$

Therefore, let the thickness of jacket wall be 5 mm.

(*c*) ***Thickness of water space***: The water space between the outer cylinder wall and the inner jacket wall is given by

$$\therefore \text{ Water space (cm)} = 0.08\ D + 0.65 \qquad ...(1.33)$$

[where $D$ = diameter of cylinder in cm]

Putting the values in eq. 1.33, we get

$$\text{Water space} = 0.08\ D + 0.65 \text{ cm}$$
$$= 0.08 \times 10 + 0.65 = 1.45 \text{ cm}$$
$$= 15 \text{ mm (say)}$$

Therefore, the water space between the outer cylinder wall and the inner jacket wall is 15 mm.

(*d*) ***Height of cylinder***: The height of cylinder is given by

$$\text{Height of Cylinder} = L + 0.15\ L \qquad ...(1.34)$$

[where, $L$ = Stroke of piston in mm]

Putting the values in eq. 1.34, we get

$$\text{The height of cylinder} = 125 + 0.15 \times 125 = 143.75 \text{ mm}$$
$$= 145 \text{ mm (say)}$$

Therefore, let the height of cylinder be 145 mm.

The dimensions of the cylinder is given in Fig. 1.15.

**(B) Design of flange and studs**

It is assumed that the cylinder is not cast integral with the upper half of the crank case and it is attached to it with the help of flanges, studs and nuts.

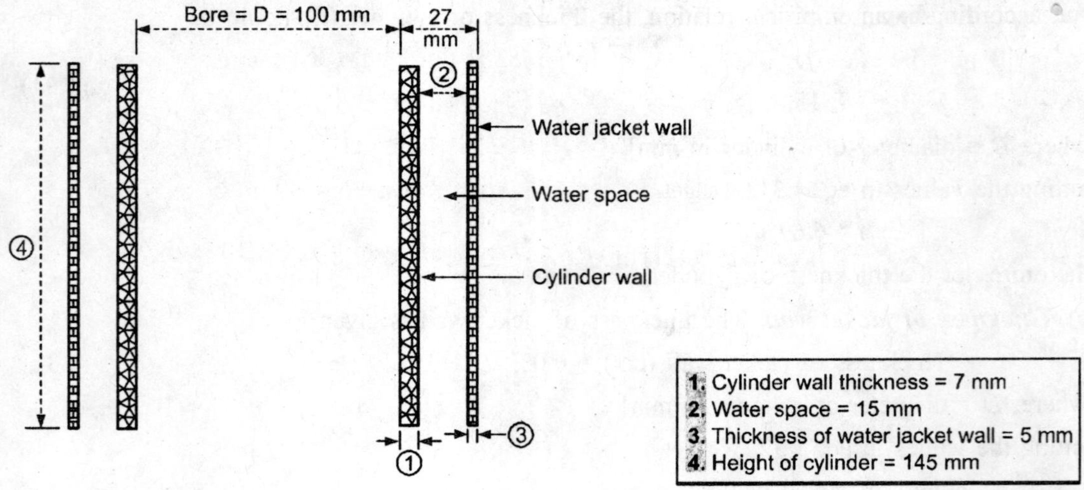


**Figure 1.15. Dimensions of cylinder liner**

(*a*) ***Studs***: Number of studs ($n$) is given by

$$n = \left(\frac{D}{10} + 4\right) \text{ to } \left(\frac{D}{5} + 4\right) \quad \text{...(1.35)}$$

[where, $D$ is the diameter of cylinder in cm]

Putting the values in eq. 1.35, we get

$$n = \left(\frac{10}{10} + 4\right) \text{ to } \left(\frac{10}{5} + 4\right)$$

$$n = 5 \text{ to } 6$$

Therefore, let the number of studs be 6

Core diameter of stud ($d_c$) is given by

$$d_c = D\sqrt{\frac{P_{max}}{nf_t}} \quad \text{...(1.36)}$$

where, $D$ = diameter of cylinder = 10 cm

$P_{max}$ = maximum gas pressure = 52.5 kg/cm$^2$

$n$ = no. of studs = 6

$f_t$ = allowable fibre stress which ranges from 350 to 700 kgf/cm$^2$.

Therefore, let $f_t$ be 450 kgf/cm$^2$.

Putting the values in eq. 1.36, we get

$$d_c = 10\sqrt{\frac{52.5}{6 \times 450}} = 1.39 \text{ cm} = 14 \text{ mm}$$

But core diameter should not be less than 16 mm

Therefore, let the core diameter of stud be 16 mm

Also, the nominal diameter of stud = 16 /0.8 = 20 mm

Pitch of bolts may be taken as $6\sqrt{d}$ to $9\sqrt{d}$ where $d$ is the nominal diameter of stud (its value ranges from 26.8 mm to 40.25 mm)

Therefore, let the pitch of bolts be 35 mm

(*b*) ***Flange***: Flange thickness is made thicker than the wall of the cylinder.

$$\text{Flange thickness } (t_f) \text{ is} = 1.2 \text{ to } 1.4\ t \qquad ...(1.37)$$

where, $t$ is the thickness of cylinder

Putting the values in eq. 1.37, we get

$$t_f = 1.3 \times 7 \text{ mm} = 9.1 \text{ mm}$$

Also, Flange thickness ($t_f$) is = 1.25 to 1.5 $d$ ...(1.38)

where, $d$ is the nominal diameter of stud.

Putting the values in eq. 1.38, we get

$$t_f = 1.4 \times 20 \text{ mm} = 28 \text{ mm}$$

Therefore, let the thickness of flange be 20 mm.

## (C) Design of cylinder head

Generally a separate cylinder cover or head is provided in almost all the engines. A box type section is used, in order to accommodate valves, water passage for cooling and injector in case of diesel engines. The cylinder heads are usually made of close grained cast iron or alloy cast iron containing nickel, chromium and molybdenum. The components of the cylinder head are given in Fig. 1.16.

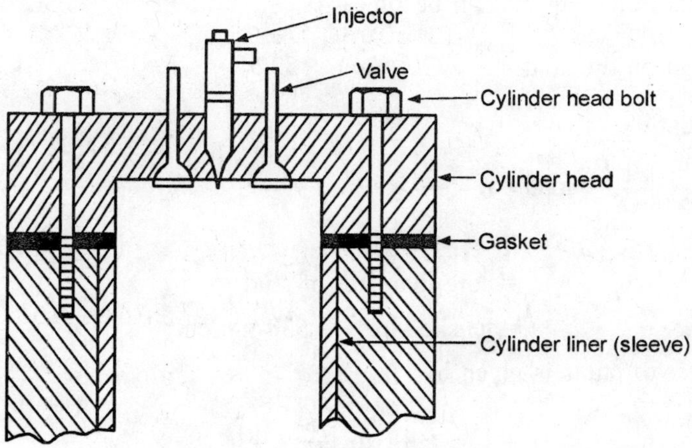


**Figure 1.16. Components of cylinder head**

The thickness of cylinder head is given by

$$t_h = D\sqrt{\frac{CP_{max}}{f_t}} \qquad ...(1.39)$$

where; $t_h$ = thickness of cylinder head in cm

$D$ = diameter of cylinder in cm

$C$ = constant for good cast iron ($C$ = 0.1)

$P_{max}$ = maximum gas pressure = 52.5 Kg/cm$^2$

$f_t$ = allowable stress for material ranges from 350 to 560 kg/cm$^2$.

Putting the values in the above eq. 1.39, it becomes

$$t_h = 10\sqrt{\frac{0.1 \times 52.5}{450}} = 1.08 \text{ cm} = 11 \text{ mm (say)}$$

Therefore, the thickness of cylinder head ($t_h$) be 11 mm

**(D) Studs for cylinder head**

The gas pressure will actually act up to the pitch circle diameter of studs. It is commonly taken that the centre of the stud should be 1.25d to 1.50d from the inner wall of the cylinder where d is the nominal diameter of stud.

The pitch circle diameter ($D_p$) is = $D + 3d$ ...(1.40)

where, $D$ is the diameter of cylinder in cm.

Putting the values in the eq. 1.40, it becomes

$$D_p = 10 + 3d$$

The load on all the studs is given by

$$\text{Load on the stud} = \frac{\pi}{4} \times D_p^2 \times P_{max} \quad ...(1.41)$$

Putting the values in the eq. 1.41, it becomes

$$\text{Load on the stud} = \frac{\pi}{4} \times (10 + 3d)^2 \times 52.5 \quad ...(1.42)$$

But, we know that,

$$\text{load} = n \times \frac{\pi}{4} \times d_c^2 \times f_t \quad ...(1.43)$$

where, $n$ = no of studs

$d_c$ = core diameter of stud

$f_t$ = tensile stress = 630 kgf/cm$^2$

Also, The number of studs is given by

$$n = \left(\frac{D}{10} + 4\right) \text{ to } \left(\frac{D}{5} + 4\right) \quad (1.44)$$

Putting the values in the eq. 1.42, it becomes

$$n = \left(\frac{10}{10} + 4\right) \text{ to } \left(\frac{10}{5} + 4\right)$$

$$n = 5 \text{ to } 6$$

Let core diameter of stud ($d_c$) = 0.8 × nominal diameter of stud ($d$).

Equating and putting the values in eq. 1.42 and 1.43, we get

$$\frac{\pi}{4}(10+3d)^2 \times 52.5 = n \times \frac{\pi}{4} \times (0.8d)^2 \times f_t$$

$$(10 + 3d)^2 \times 52.5 = 6 \times 0.64 \times d^2 \times 630$$

$$(100 + 9d^2 + 30d) \times 52.5 = 2419d^2$$

$$d = 2.09 \text{ cm}$$

Therefore, nominal diameter of stud is 20.9 mm

The pitch circle diameter is given by

Pitch circle diameter ($D_p$) = $D + 3d$ ...(1.45)

Putting the values in the eq. 1.39, it becomes

$$D_p = 10 + 3\ (2.09)$$

$$= 16.3 \text{ cm}$$

Moreover, the pitch of studs is given by

$$\text{Pitch of stud} = \frac{\pi D_p}{n} \quad ...(1.46)$$

Putting the values in the eq. 1.46, it becomes

$$\text{Pitch of studs} = \frac{\pi \times 16.3}{6} = 8.53 \text{ cm}$$

The dimensions of the cylinder head and studs are given in Fig. 1.17

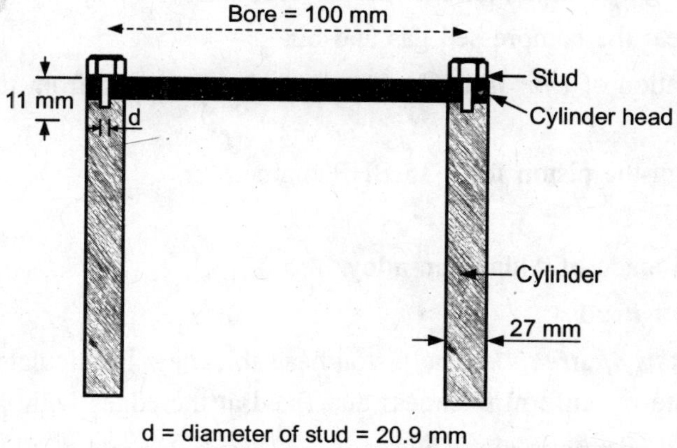


**Figure 1.17. Dimensions of cylinder head and stud**

## 3. DESIGN OF PISTON

Generally trunk type piston which is open at one end is used in internal combustion engines. It is cylindrical in shape which receives the power as a result of the pressure and energy generated by the combustion of fuel. The force of the expanding gases against the closed end of piston forces the piston down in the cylinder. This in turn rotates the crankshaft with the help of connecting rod. Now-a-days, aluminum alloy pistons are widely used due to its lightness and very high thermal conductivity. The parts of the piston are given in Fig. 1.18.

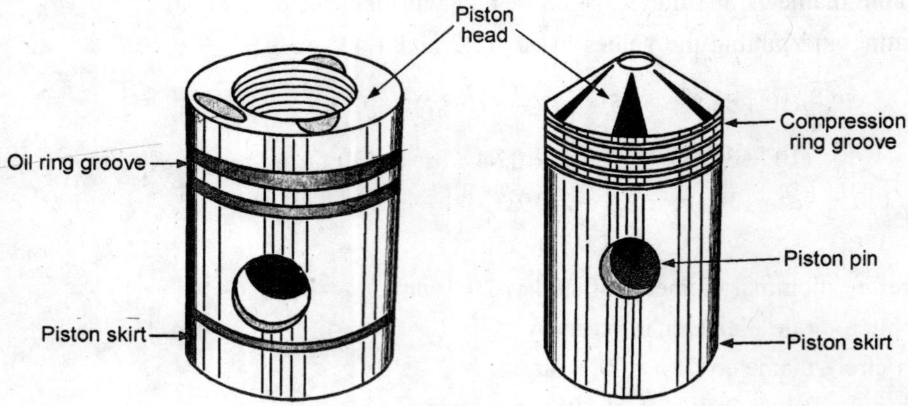


**Figure 1.18. Parts of piston**

The piston consists of the following:

(*a*) Head or crown (top of piston) to carry gas pressure.

(*b*) Skirt (part of piston below piston pin) to act as a bearing for connecting rod side thrust.

(*c*) A piston pin or gudgeon pin to connect it to the connecting rod

(*d*) Piston rings to seal the cylinder so that compressed air is not leaked.

A good piston should have the following characters.

(*a*) Robust construction to withstand high thermal and mechanical stresses.

(*b*) Minimum weight to minimize the inertia forces.

(*c*) Effectively seal the compressed gas and oil.

(*d*) Quick dissipation of heat from the crown to the rings and from the rings to the cylinder walls.

Now, let us design the piston for a 35 BHP engine.

**Assumptions:**

Let the piston be made of Aluminum alloy.

**(A) Thickness of piston head**

***Design on the basis of strength***: The piston head thickness is calculated by assuming that the head is a flat plate of uniform thickness and fixed at the edges with uniform gas loading. The piston head thickness is given by

$$t_p = \sqrt{\frac{3P_{max}\ D^2}{10\ f_t}} = 0.443\ D\sqrt{\frac{P_{max}}{f_t}} \qquad ...(1.47)$$

where, $t_p$ = piston head thickness in cm

$D$ = diameter of cylinder in cm

$P_{max}$ = maximum gas pressure = 52.5 kgf/cm$^2$

$f_t$ = allowable stress in bending, kgf/cm$^2$

For Al alloy $f_t$ may be taken as 600 kgf/cm$^2$

Putting the values in the eq. 1.47, we get,

$$t_p = 0.433 \times 10 \times \sqrt{\frac{52.5}{600}} = 1.28 \text{ cm}$$

Say the thickness of piston head is 13 mm.

An empirical relationship for piston head thickness is given by

$$t_p = 0.03 \text{ D} + 1.5 \text{ cm} \quad \text{... (1.48)}$$

where $D$ is the diameter of cylinder

Putting the values in the eq. 1.48, we get,

$$t_p = 0.03 \times 10 + 1.5$$

$$t_p = 1.8 \text{ cm}$$

$$t_p = 18 \text{ mm}$$

The practical limits for the thickness of piston head for different types of engines are given in the Table 1.8.

**TABLE 1.8: Piston head thickness for different engines**

| Type of engine | Material of piston | Piston head thickness |
|---|---|---|
| Four stroke diesel engine | Aluminum | 0.13 D to 0.16 D |
| | Cast iron | 0.11 D to 0.13 D |
| Four stroke petrol engine | Cast iron | 0.12 D to 0.14 D |

Practically, the thickness of Aluminum alloy piston head is given by

$$t_p = 0.13 \text{ D to } 0.16 \text{ D cm} \quad \text{...(1.49)}$$

where, $D$ is the diameter of cylinder.

Putting the values in the eq. 1.49, we get,

$$t_p = 0.13 \times 10 \text{ to } 0.16 \times 10$$

$$t_p = 1.3 \text{ to } 1.6 \text{ cm}$$

$$t_p = 13 \text{ to } 16 \text{ mm}$$

**Design of piston on the basis of heat dissipation:**

Using the relationship,

$$t_p = \frac{H}{1.456k(T_c - T_e)} \quad \text{...(1.50)}$$

where, $t_p$ = thickness of piston head , cm

$H$ = heat flow through the head in Kcal/hr

$$H = C \times W \times HCV \times BHP$$

where $C$ = 0.05 a constant

$W$ = Specific fuel consumption = 0.2 kg/bhp/hr

HCV = Higher calorific value of fuel = 10500 kcal/kg

BHP per cylinder = 35/3 = 11.67hp

$$\therefore \quad H = 0.05 \times 0.2 \times 10500 \times 11.67$$
$$= 1225.4 \text{ kcal/hr}$$

$k$ = coefficient depends on piston material (for Al alloy = 1.5) and

$T_c - T_e$ = 75°C for Al alloy

Putting the values in eq. 1.50, it becomes,

$$t_p = \frac{1225.4}{12.56 \times 1.5 \times 75°} = 0.86 \text{ cm} = 8.6 \text{ mm}$$

Since the maximum thickness of piston head ($t_p$) comes out to be 18 mm (on the basis of strength) from the above calculations, let the piston head thickness ($t_p$) be 18 mm.

***Radial ribs:*** The radial ribs are provided to make the piston head rigid and to carry the gas and thermal loads. Side thrust from the connecting rod is transmitted to the skirt through the piston pin boss. In order to avoid the distortion of skirt, stiffening ribs are provided at the centre line of the boss and extended around the skirt. In general, four to six ribs are provided. Therefore, let us provide 4 ribs.

The thickness of rib is given by

Thickness of rib = 1/3 to 1/2 $t_p$ ...(1.51)

where $t_p$ is the piston head thickness.

Putting the values in eq. 1.51, we get,

Thickness of rib = 1/3 × 18 to 1/2 × 18 mm = 6 to 9 mm.

∴ Let the thickness of rib be 7.5 mm.

**(B) Piston rings**

Piston rings provide radial pressure so that it maintains seal between the piston and the cylinder bore (Fig. 1.19). Two types of piston rings namely compression rings and oil rings are commonly used. Compression rings are used to effectively seal the compressed gas, transfer the heat from the piston head to the cylinder walls and to absorb some part of the piston shocks due to side thrust. Three to five compression rings are used depending upon the size of the engine. Oil rings are used to scrap the lubrication oil from the liner surface usually splashed by the lubrication system. Engines are provided with one to three oil rings depending upon the size of the engine. The exploded view of piston rings is given in Fig. 1.20.

In our engine, let us provide three compression ring and one oil ring.

Radial thickness of rings

The radial thickness of the rings ($b_r$) is given by

$$b_r = D\sqrt{\frac{3P_w}{f_t}} \quad ...(1.52)$$

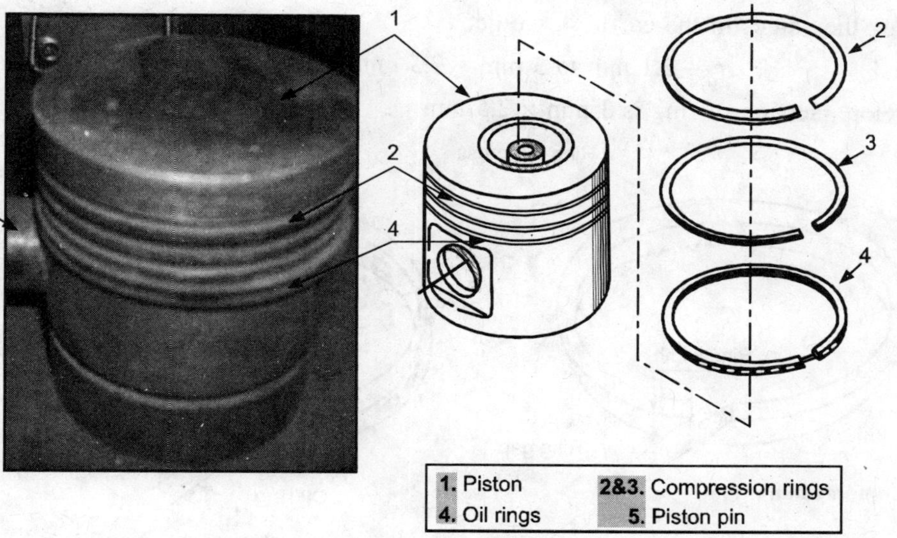


**Figure 1.19. Piston and rings of an IC engine**

where $b_r$ = radial thickness in cm

$D$ = diameter of cylinder in cm

$P_w$ = wall pressure = 0.35 kg/cm$^2$

$f_t$ = permissible stress which ranges from 1000 to 1500 Kg/cm$^2$ for **CI rings.**

Let $f_t$ be 1250 kg/cm$^2$.

Putting the values in the eq. 1.52, we get,

$$b_r = 10\sqrt{\frac{3 \times 0.35}{1250}} = 0.29 \text{ cm} = 3 \text{ mm (say)}$$

Therefore, the radial thickness of the rings is 3 mm.

***Axial thickness of rings***: Empirically, minimum axial width of rings is given by

$$t_a = \frac{D}{10n_r} = \frac{10}{10 \times 4} = 0.25 \text{ cm} = 2.5 \text{ mm} \qquad \text{...(1.53)}$$

where $D$ is the diameter of cylinder, cm

$n_r$ is no of piston rings

Putting the values in the eq. 1.53, we get,

$$t_a = \frac{10}{10 \times 4} = 0.25 \text{ cm} = 2.5 \text{ mm}$$

Therefore, the axial thickness of the rings is 2.5 mm

The axial width ($t_a$) *is also given by*

$$t_a = 0.7 \text{ to } 1 \text{ of } b_r \qquad \text{...(1.54)}$$

where $b_r$= radial thickness of the rings.

Putting the values in the eq. 1.54, we get,

$$t_a = 2.1 \text{ mm to } 3 \text{ mm} = 2.5 \text{ mm (say)}$$

Therefore, section of ring is 3 mm × 2.5 mm

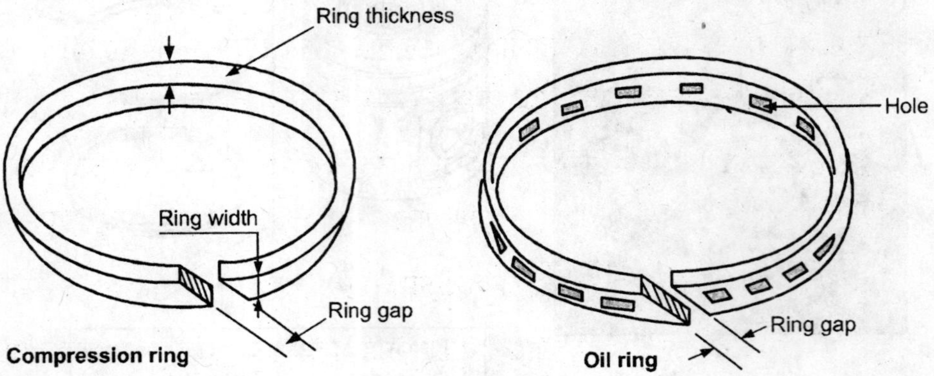


**Figure 1.20. Exploded view of piston rings**

***Other dimensions of ring:*** The width of top land is given by

Width of top land $= 1\ t_p$ to $1.2\ t_p$ ...(1.55)

where, $t_p$ = thickness of piston head, mm.

Putting the values in the eq. 1.55, we get,

$$\text{Width of top land} = 1 \times 18 \text{ to } 1.2 \times 18$$
$$= 18 \text{ mm to } 21.6 \text{ mm}$$
$$= 20 \text{ mm (say)}$$

The width of the top land is made more than the other ring lands to protect the top ring from the high temperature which prevails at the top of the piston.

The width of other ring lands is given by

Width of other ring lands $= 0.75\ t_a$ to $1\ t_a$ ...(1.56)

where $t_a$ = axial thickness of ring.

Putting the values in the eq. 1.56, we get,

$$t_a = 0.75 \times 2.5 \text{ to } 2.5 \text{ mm}$$
$$= 1.9 \text{ to } 2.5 \text{ mm}$$
$$= 2.2 \text{ mm (say)}$$

The gap between the free ring ends is given by

The gap between the free ring ends $(G) = 3.5\ b_r$ to $4\ b_r$ ...(1.57)

Putting the values in the eq. 1.57, we get,

$$G = 3.5 \times 3 \text{ to } 4 \times 3$$
$$= 10.5 \text{ to } 12 \text{ mm}$$
$$= 11 \text{ mm (say)}$$

The gap when the ring is in the cylinder is given by

$$\text{The gap when the ring is in the cylinder} = 0.002D \text{ to } 0.004D \quad ...(1.58)$$

Putting the values in the eq. 1.58, we get,

The gap when the ring is in the cylinder

$$= 0.002 \times 100 \text{ to } 0.004 \times 100$$
$$= 0.2 \text{ to } 0.4 \text{ mm}$$
$$= 0.3 \text{ mm (say)}$$

**(C) Piston barrel**

For better flow of heat, the thickness of the piston barrel should be equal to the head thickness at the top and tapering at the bottom head.

The thickness of barrel at the top ($t_1$) is given by

$$t_1 = b + 0.03\ D + 4.5 = 10.9 \text{ mm} \quad ...(1.59)$$

where, $b = b_r + 0.4$ mm

$b_r$ = radial thickness of the rings = 3

$\therefore$ $b = 3 + 0.4 = 3.4$ mm

Putting the values in the eq. 1.57, we get,

$$t_1 = 3.4 + 0.03 \times 100 + 4.5 = 10.9 \text{ mm}$$

The thickness of barrel at the open end (lower end) ($t_2$) is given by

$$t_2 = 0.25\ t_1 \text{ to } 0.35\ t_1 \text{ mm} \quad ...(1.60)$$

Putting the values in the eq. 1.60, we get,

$$t_2 = 0.25 \times 11 \text{ to } 0.35 \times 11 = 2.75 \text{ to } 3.85 \text{ mm}$$
$$= 3.2 \text{ mm (say)}$$

**(D) Skirt length**

The part of the piston barrel below the ring section up to the open end is known as skirt. It takes the side thrust pressure of the connecting rod. The skirt length can be found by calculating the maximum gas load on the piston. The maximum gas load ($F$) is given by

$$\text{Maxium gas load} = F = \frac{\pi}{4} D^2 \times P_{max} \quad ...(1.61)$$

where $D$ = diameter of cylinder, cm

$P_{max}$ = maximum gas pressure = 52.5 kg/cm$^2$

Putting the values in the eq. 1.61, we get,

$$F = \frac{\pi}{4} \times 10^2 \times 52.5 = 4123.3 \text{ kgf}$$

Now, side thrust in the liner is given by

$$R = (0.03 \text{ to } 0.1)\ F \quad ...(1.62)$$

where, $F$ = maximum gas load, kgf

Let $R = 0.1$ F

$\therefore$ $R = 0.1 \times 4123.3 = 412$ Kgf

Also, $R = l \times D \times P_b$ ...(1.63)

where $R$ = side thrust in the liner, kgf

$l$ = skirt length, cm

$D$ = diameter of cylinder, cm

$P_b$ = bearing pressure = 4.5 kgf/cm$^2$

Putting the values in the eq. 1.63 and rearranging, we get skirt length as

$$l = 412/(10 \times 4.5) = 9.2 \text{ cm}$$

$$= 9.5 \text{ cm (say)}$$

**(E) Piston pin or gudgeon pin or wrist pin**

The piston pin connects the piston and the connecting rod. The gas pressure developed in the cylinder passes through the piston pin to the crankshaft. The piston pins are available in the following three types.

(*a*) ***Full floating***: This pin is free in both piston boss and small end bush of connecting rod. The pin is secured by using circlips against end movements.

(*b*) ***Semi-floating***: This pin is free to move either in piston boss and clamped in the small end of connecting rod or this pin is free to move in small end of connecting rod and clamped to piston boss by means of screw.

(*c*) ***Fixed***: The piston pin is fixed at both the points *i.e.* at piston boss and at the small end of connecting rod.

The piston pin is designed for maximum gas load. The maximum gas load is given by

$$F = l_1 \times d \times P_b \qquad ...(1.64)$$

where $F$ = Maximum gas load = 4123.3 kgf/cm$^2$ (from eq. 1.61)

$l_1$ = length of pin in bearing may be taken as 0.45D i.e. 0.45 × 10 = 4.5 cm

$d$ = diameter of piston pin, cm

$P_b$ = Bearing pressure, kg/cm$^2$. For high quality bronze bushing it may be taken as 250 kgf/cm$^2$

Putting the values in the eq. 1.64 we get,

$$4123.3 = 4.5 \times d \times 250$$

$$d = 3.67 \text{ cm}$$

$$d = 3.7 \text{ cm (say)}$$

Let the material of pin be heat treated alloy steel.

To check the pin in bending, the maximum bending moment (M) on the piston pin is given by

$$M = \frac{F \times D}{8} \text{ kgf – cm} \qquad ...(1.65)$$

where, $F$ = maximum gas load in kgf/cm$^2$

$D$ = diameter of cylinder in cm

Putting the values in the eq. 1.65, we get

$$M = \frac{4123.3 \times 10}{8} = 5154 \text{ kgf} - \text{cm}$$

We also know that

$$M = \frac{\pi}{32} d^3 f_b \qquad \text{...(1.66)}$$

where, $M$ = maximum bending moment, kgf–cm

$d$ = diameter of piston pin, cm

$f_b$ = allowable stress in bending, kg/cm$^2$.

Putting the values in the eq. 1.66 and rearranging, we get

$$f_b = \frac{5154 \times 32}{\pi \times d^3} = \frac{5154 \times 32}{\pi \times 3.7^3} = 1036 \text{ kgf/cm}^2$$

The value of $f_b$ which is well within the safe limits of 1400 kgf/cm$^2$ for the pin of heat treated alloy steel.

To make the pin lighter, it is usually made hollow.

Therefore, let $d_o$ = 3.7 cm and $d_i$ = 2 cm

The maximum bending moment for a hollow pin is given by

$$M = \frac{\pi}{32} \times \frac{d_0^4 - d_i^4}{d_o} \times f_b \qquad \text{...(1.67)}$$

Putting the values in the eq. 1.65 and rearranging, we get

$$5154 \text{ kgf} - \text{cm} = \frac{\pi}{32} \times \frac{3.7^4 - 2^4}{3.7} \times f_b$$

$$\therefore \qquad f_b = 1133 \text{ Kg/cm}^2$$

The value of $f_b$ is well within the safe limits i.e. less than 1400 kg/cm$^2$.

The complete dimensions of the components of piston and cylinder are given the Table 1.9 and Fig. 1.21 and Fig. 1.22. The dimensions of piston pin and rings are given in Fig. 1.23. The arrangement of pistons and valves in a 4-cylinder engine is given in Fig. 1.24.

## 4. DESIGN OF CONNECTING ROD

Connecting rod in an engine connects the piston and crankshaft. The small end of connecting rod connects with piston and the big end of connecting rod connects with the crank pin of crankshaft. It has an eye at the small end usually fitted with bronze bush for the piston pin, a long shank, and a big end opening which is usually split to take the crankpin bearing shells. Connecting rod is primarily used to transmit the push and pull from the piston pin to the crank pin of crankshaft. The components of the connecting rod are given in Fig. 1.25. In some engines, it is also used to transfer lubrication oil from the bottom to the top end *i.e.* from crank pin to the piston pin. Connecting rods are made of mild or medium carbon steel

**TABLE 1.9: Dimension chart of piston and cylinder of engine**

| No. | Particular | Formula | As per formula calculations (using other formulae) | As per earlier calculations | Selected |
|---|---|---|---|---|---|
| 1. | Diameter of cylinder (Bore) | — | — | — | 100 mm |
| 2. | – At crown<br>– At Skirt | 0.944 to 0.996 D<br>0.9993 to 0.9996D | 99.4 to 99.6 mm<br>99.93 to 99.96 | —<br>— | 99.00 mm<br>99.82 mm |
| 3. | Clearance between the piston crown and cylinder | 0.01 D | 1 mm | — | 1 mm |
| 4. | Clearance between the piston skirt and cylinder | 0.0018 D to .0025 D | 0.18 to 0.25 mm | — | 1 mm |
| 5. | Thickness of piston head ($t_p$) for die forged | 0.10 to 0.15 D | 10 to 15 mm | 18 mm | 18 mm |
| 6. | Thickness of piston wall at piston crown | Equal to the thickness piston heat ($t_p$) | 18 mm | 11 mm | 18 mm |
| 7. | Thickness of piston wall at skirt | 0.025 to 0.35 $t_p$ | 4.5 to 6.3 mm | 3.2 mm | 4.5 mm |
| 8. | Height of top land | 0.104 to 0.20 D | 10.4 to 20 mm | 20 mm | 20 mm |
| 9. | Height of other lands | 0.043 to 0.065 D | 4.3 to 6.5 mm | 2.2 mm | 5.5 mm |
| 10. | Side clearance of piston ring<br>– Upper groove<br>– Lower groove | <br>0.15 to 0.20 mm<br>0.08 to 0.12 mm | <br>0.175 mm<br>0.10 mm | <br>— | <br>0.175 mm<br>0.10 mm |
| 11. | Groove axial width<br>– Upper groove<br>– Lower groove | <br>Axial width of ring + side clearance (Upper groove)<br>Axial width of ring + side clearance (lower groove) | <br>2.5 mm + 0.175 mm<br>2.5 mm + 0.10 mm = 2.6 mm | <br>—<br>— | <br>2.68 mm<br>2.6 mm |
| 12. | Difference between the groove depth and radial thickness of the ring (A)<br>– Compression ring<br>– Oil ring | <br>0.77 to 0.95 mm<br>0.92 to 1.1 mm | <br>0.85 mm<br>0.92 mm | <br>—<br>— | <br>0.85 mm<br>0.92 mm |

| | | | | | |
|---|---|---|---|---|---|
| **13.** | Groove radial width<br>– compression ring<br>– oil ring | Ring radial width – ‘A’<br>3 mm – 0.85 mm<br>3 mm – 0.92 mm | <br>2.15 mm<br>2.08 mm | <br>—<br>— | <br>2.15 mm<br>2.08 mm |
| **14.** | Height of skirt | 0.60 to 0.70 D | 60 to 70 mm | 95 mm | 95 mm |
| **15.** | Piston pin diameter<br>– external diameter<br>– Internal diameter | <br>0.30 to 0.38 D<br>— | <br>30 to 38 mm<br>— | <br>37 mm<br>20 mm | <br>37 mm<br>20 mm |
| **16.** | Distances between bosses for full floating pin | 0.30 to 0.40 D | 30 to 40 mm | — | 40 mm |
| **17.** | Ratio of internal diameter to external diameter of piston pin | 0.50 to 0.58 | 20 mm/37mm = 0.54 | — | 0.54 |
| **18.** | Physical length of pin | 0.85 D | 85 mm | — | 85 mm |
| **19.** | Distance between piston lower and pin axis | 0.38 to 0.53 D | 38 to 53 mm | — | 45 mm |
| **20.** | Distance of pin above the centre of skirt | 0.02 to 0.04 D | 2 to 4 mm | — | 2.5 mm |
| **21.** | Height of Piston | Top land + other lands + grooves + skirt length | 20 + 3 × 5.5 + (2.68 + 2.6 + 2.6 + 2.6) + 95<br>= 141.98 mm | 131.6 mm | 142 mm |
| **22.** | Height of cylinder | Stroke + 15 % of clearance | 125 + 0.15 × 125<br>= 143.75 | 125 + 50<br>= 175 mm | 175 mm |

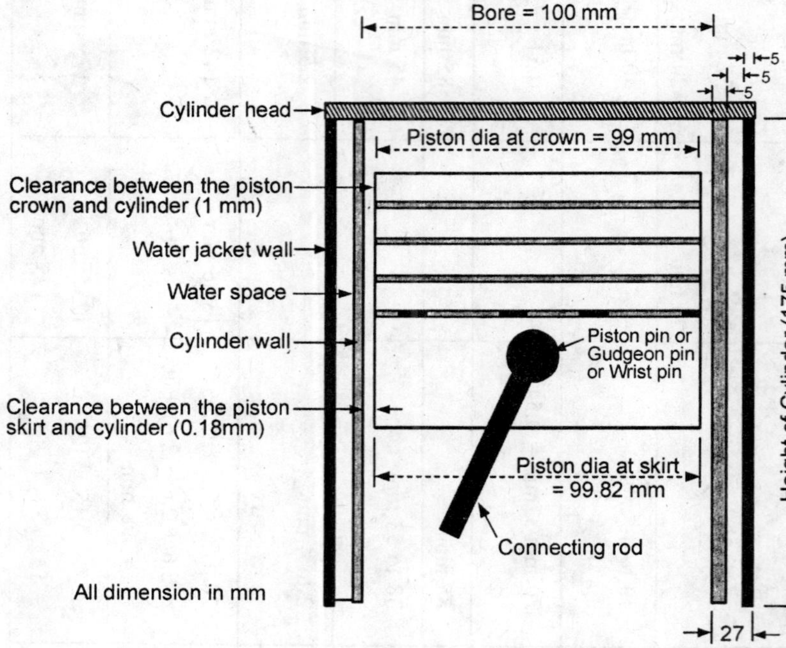


**Figure 1.21. Dimensions of cylinder and piston**

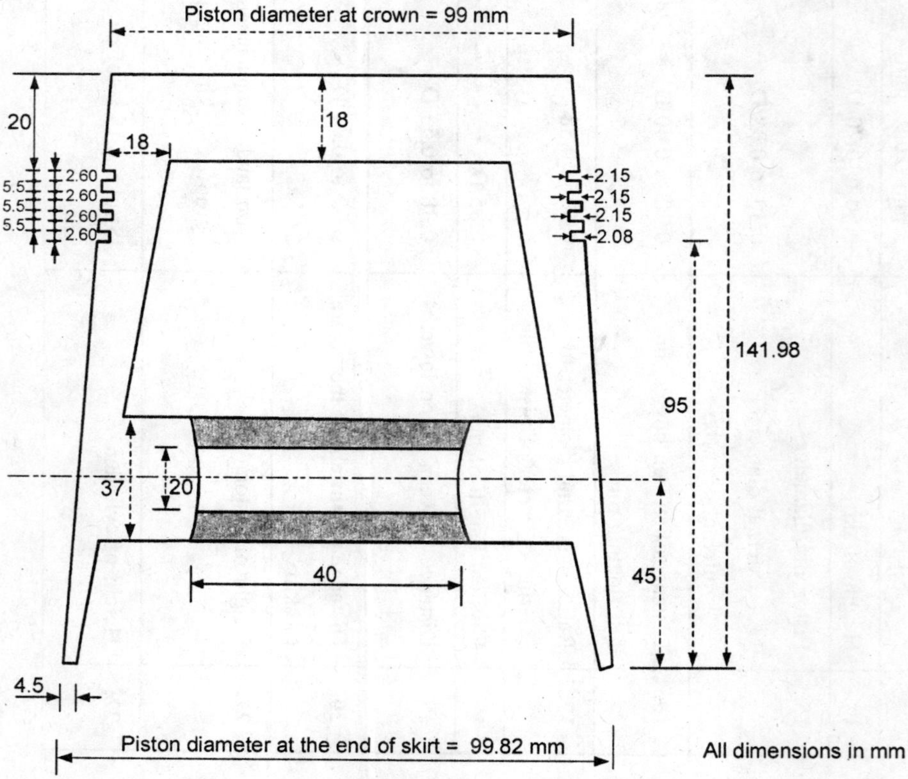


**Figure 1.22. Dimensions of piston**

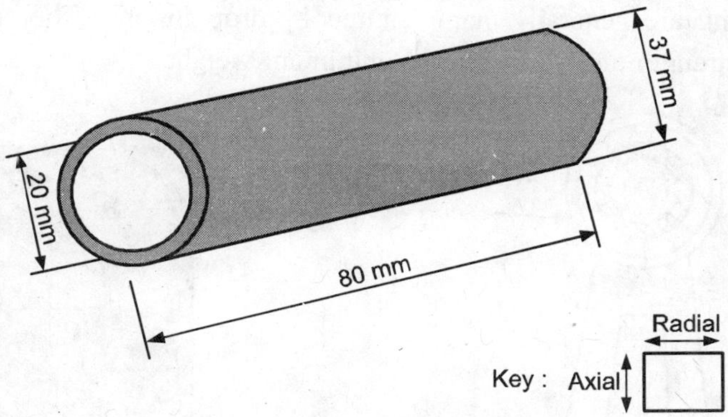


| Type of Ring | Ring section | Groove section |
|---|---|---|
| Top compressing ring | 2.5 (axial) × 3.0 (radial) | 2.15 (radial) × 2.68 (axial) |
| Other compression ring | 3.0 (radial) × 2.5 (axial) | 2.15 (radial) × 2.60 (axial) |
| Oil ring | 3.0 (radial) × 2.5 (axial) | 2.15 (radial) × 2.60 (axial) |

Figure 1.23. Dimensions of piston pin and rings

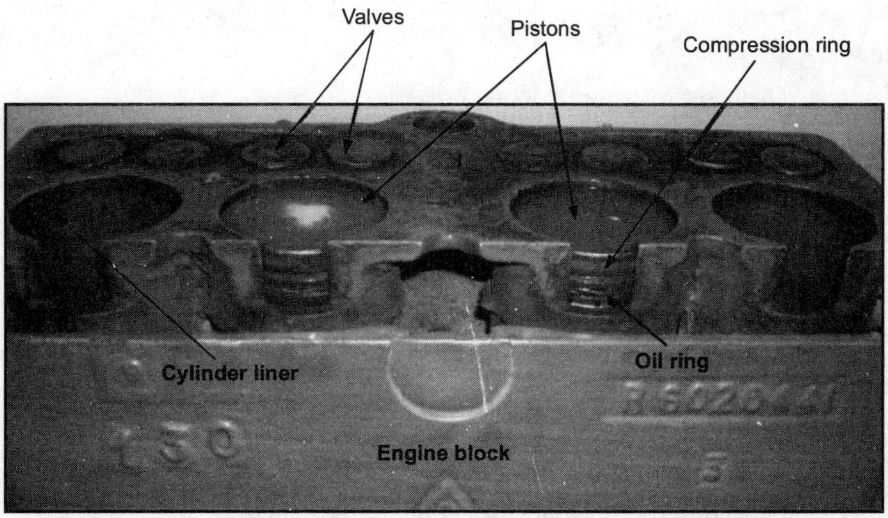


Figure 1.24. Arrangement of pistons and valves in 4-cylinder engine

or alloy steel and are generally manufactured by drop forging. The connecting rod should have adequate strength and stiffness with minimum weight.

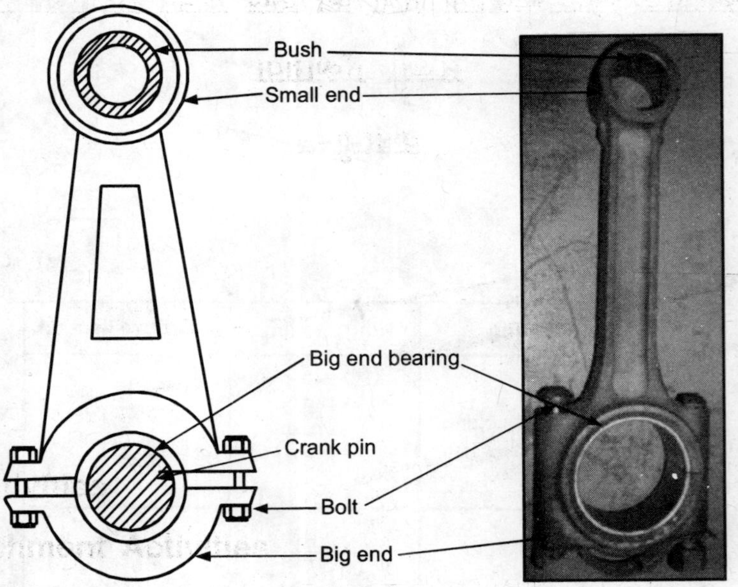


**Figure 1.25. Components of connecting rod**

Now, let us design a connecting rod for a 35BHP diesel engine.

Let the connecting rod be made of drop forging low carbon steel and its length be 300 mm.

Let the weight of reciprocating parts ($W$) = $0.28 \times 10^{-2}$ N/mm$^2$ of piston area.

**(A) Connecting rod section**

The usual shape of connecting rod in high speed engines are I-section or H-section or tubular section.

We know that

$$\text{Diameter of piston} = 99 \text{ mm}$$

$$\text{Stroke length} = 125 \text{ mm}$$

$$\text{Engine speed} = 2200 \text{ rpm}$$

$$\text{Maximum explosion pressure} = 52.5 \text{ kg/cm}^2 = 5.25 \text{ N/mm}^2$$

The maximum value of inertia pressure will be at the beginning of the stroke and will be equal to

$$= \frac{W}{g} r\omega^2 \left(1 + \frac{1}{n}\right) \text{ N/mm}^2 \quad \text{...(1.68)}$$

where, $W$ = weight of reciprocating parts, N/mm$^2$

$r$ = crank radius = stroke length/2 = 125 mm/2 = 62.5 mm

$n$ = $l/r$ = connecting rod length/crank radius = 300 mm/62.5 mm = 4.8

$\omega$ = angular velocity, rad/sec = $(2200 \times 2\ \pi)/60$ = 230.4 rad/sec

Putting the values in eq. 1.66, we get

Maximum Inertia Pressure

$$= \frac{0.28 \times 10^{-2}}{9800} \times 62.5 \times 230.42 \times \left(1 + \frac{1}{48}\right) = 1.4 \text{ N/mm}^2$$

At the beginning of power stroke, the resulting load on piston will be

Load on piston = Explosion load – inertia load

$$= \frac{\pi}{4} D^2 \text{ [Maximum explosion pressure – Maximum inertia pressure]}$$

$$= \frac{\pi}{4} \times 99^2 \, [5.25 - 1.14] \quad \text{Newton}$$

$= 31637$ N

Therefore, Maximum load on piston (P)

= Load on piston × factor of safety. [Let factor of safety be 7]

= 31637 × 7 = 2,21,142 Newton

= 22,114 Kgf

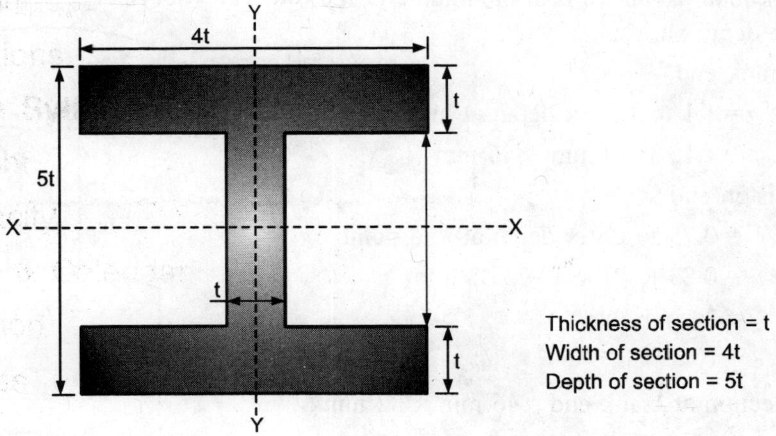


**Figure 1.26. I-Section of connecting rod**

Now, section of the rod can be determined by considering the buckling about axis of *X-X* (Refer Fig. 1.26), by the Rankine formula.

$$\text{Buckling load } (P) \text{ in kg} = \frac{f_{cu} A}{1 + a\left(\frac{l}{k}\right)^2} \qquad ...(1.69)$$

where, $f_{cu}$ = ultimate crushing stress, 3300 kg/cm$^2$ for low carbon steel

$A$ = sectional area *i.e.* 11 $t^2$ (cm$^2$)

$a$ = constant = 1/7500 for mild steel

$l$ = length of connecting rod in cm = 30

$k$ = least radius of gyration about the axis of buckling, cm

$$k^2 = \frac{I}{A} = \frac{\text{2nd moment of Inertia in the plane } x\text{-}x}{\text{Area of section}} = \frac{35t^4}{11t^2}$$

Putting the values in the eq. 1.69, we get

$$22114 = \frac{3300 \times 11t^2}{1 + \frac{1}{7500}\left(\frac{30^2}{3.18t^2}\right)} = \frac{36300t^2}{1 + \frac{900}{23850t^2}}$$

$$36300\, t^4 - 22114\, t^2 - 834 = 0 \qquad \text{...(1.70)}$$

Solving the eq. 1.70, we get

$$t = 8 \text{ mm}$$

Therefore,

Width of flange = 4 × 8 mm = 32 mm

Height of section = 5 × 8 mm = 40 mm

Since the connecting rod is to be manufactured by forging, the sharp corners are rounded off for the easy withdrawal of the section from the dies. The modified section is shown in Fig. 1.27.

The section obtained above is at the middle of the rod. The width is kept constant throughout the length but the depth varies.

Depth at crank end

= 1.1 to 1.25 × depth at mid point

= 1.15 × 40 mm = 46 mm

Depth at piston end

= 0.75 to 0.9 × depth at mid point

= 0.83 × 40 mm = 33.2 mm

= 34 mm (say)

Therefore,

Section at crank end = 46 mm × 32 mm

Section at small end = 34 mm × 32 mm

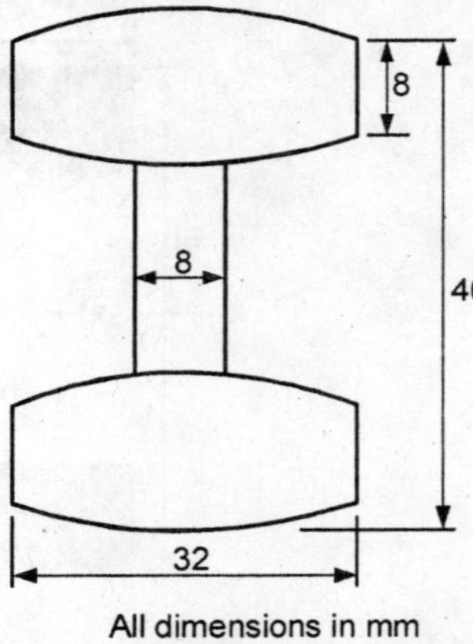


**Figure 1.27. Modified section of connecting rod**

**(B) Dimensions of big end**

The big end bearing carries the maximum gas load. In most cases the big end has removable bearing shells. The shells may be of bronze or steel or brass and a thin lining of cadmium silver or copper lead or lead based babbit of less than 1 mm thickness is usually given on the inner surface of the shells.

The maximum gas load is given by

$$F = l_c \times d_c \times P_b \text{ kg} \qquad \text{...(1.71)}$$

where; $F$ = maximum gas load in kgf = $\pi/4 \times D^2 \times P_{max}$ = $\pi/4 \times 9.9^2 \times 52.5$ = 4041 kgf

$l_c$ = length of crank pin, cm

$d_c$ = diameter of crank pin in cm

$P_b$ = allowable bearing pressure, kgf/cm$^2$ (For pressure lubrication it can be 70 kgf/cm$^2$)

Usually, $l_c/d_c$ ranges between 1.25 to 1.5.

Therefore, let $l_c/d_c$=1.35

Or $l_c = 1.35\ d_c$

Putting the values in the eq. 1.71 and rearranging, we get,

$$4041 = 1.35\ d_c \times d_c \times 70$$

$$d_c^2 = 42.76\ \text{cm}^2$$

$$d_c = 6.5\ \text{cm} = 65\ \text{mm}$$

Therefore $l_c = 1.35 \times 65\ \text{mm} = 88\ \text{mm}$

$= 90$ mm (say)

Therefore,

Diameter of crankpin ($d_c$) = 65 mm

Length of crank pin ($l_c$) = 90 mm

Empirically,

$d_c$ should be = (0.5 to 0.65 ) × cylinder bore

= (0.5 to 0.65) × 100 mm

= 50 to 65 mm

$l_c$ should be = (0.4 to 0.6) × cylinder bore

= (0.4 to 0.6) × 100

= 40 to 60 mm

Thus, diameter of crankpin is safe. But the length of crankpin is on the higher side.

**(C) Design of small end**

The piston pin bearing is usually a high quality bronze bushing or aluminum alloy.

The maximum gas load is given by

$$F = l_p \times d_p \times P_b \text{ kg} \quad \text{...(1.72)}$$

where, $F$ = Maximum gas load in kgf = $\pi/4 \times D^2 \times P_{max} = \pi/4 \times 9.9^2 \times 52.5 = 4041$ kgf

$l_p$ = length of piston pin bearing, cm

$d_p$ = diameter of piston pin = 37 mm (already designed)

$P_b$ = allowable bearing pressure kgf/cm². Usually it ranges from 250 to 315 kgf/cm².

Therefore, let $P_b$ = 300 kgf/cm².

Putting the values in the eq. 1.70, we get

$$4041 = l_p \times 3.7 \times 300$$

$$l_p = 3.6\ \text{cm}$$

Therefore,

Length of small end bearing = 36 mm

Inner diameter of small end bearing = 37 mm

**(D) Bolts for big end cap**

Let the material for connecting rod bolt be nickel alloy steel whose allowable stress ($f_t$) is 1500 kgf/cm$^2$. Now the inertia force,

$$\text{Maximum Inertia Pressure } (F_i) = \frac{W}{g} r\omega^2\left(1+\frac{1}{n}\right) \quad ...(1.73)$$

where, $W$ = weight of reciprocating parts = 2 kgf

$r$ = crank radius = stroke length/2 = 125 mm/2 = 62.5 mm

$n = l/r$ = connecting rod length/crank radius = 300 mm/62.5 mm ≅ 4.8

$\omega$ = angular velocity, rad/sec = (2200 × 2 π)/60 = 230.4 rad/sec

Putting the values in the eq. 1.73, we get

$$\text{Maximum Inertia Pressure } (F_i) = \frac{2}{9.81}\times 0.0625\times 230.4^2\times\left(1+\frac{1}{4.8}\right)$$

$$= 817 \text{ kgf}$$

If two bolts are used, and the core diameter is $d_c$ then, using the relationship we get

$$2\times\frac{\pi}{4}d_c^2\times f_t = 817 \text{ kgf}$$

$$2\times\frac{\pi}{4}d_c^2\times 1500 = 817$$

$$d_c = 0.58 \text{ cm} = 6 \text{ mm}$$

Core diameter of big end cap bolt = 6 mm

$$\text{Outer diameter} = \frac{d_c}{0.8} = \frac{6}{0.8} = 8 \text{ mm}$$

**(E) Connecting rod big end bearing cap**

The maximum bending moment ($M$) in Kgf is given by,

$$M = \frac{F_i\times S}{6} \quad ...(1.74)$$

where, $F_i$ = load on the cap i.e the inertia load = 817 kgf

S = Distance between bolts centre.

= diameter of bearing + twice the thickness of bearing liner + diameter of bolt + some clearance (2 mm)

Thickness of bearing liner = thickness of shell + thickness of bearing metal

But,

Thickness of shell = 0.05 × cylinder bore

= 0.05 × 100 mm = 5 mm

Thickness of bearing metal = 1 mm

Therefore,

Thickness of bearing liner = 6 mm

Thus, $S = 65 \text{ mm} + 2\ (6) \text{ mm} + 8 \text{ mm} + 2 \text{ mm}$

$= 87 \text{ mm}$

Therefore, the bending moment is given by

$$M = \frac{F_i \times S}{6} = \frac{817 \times 8.7}{6} = 1185 \text{ kgf}$$

Now, the bending moment is also given by

$$M = f_b \times Z \qquad \text{...(1.75)}$$

Let $f_b = 1200 \text{ kgf/cm}^2$

And $Z = bc^2/6$

where; $b$ = width of cap = length of crank pin = 9.0 cm

$c$ = thickness of cap, cm

Putting the values in eq. 1.75 and rearranging, we get,

$$1185 = (1200 \times 9.0\ c^2)/6$$

$$c^2 = 0.6583$$

$$c = 0.81 \text{cm}$$

$$c = 9 \text{ mm (say)}$$

Therefore, Thickness of cap = 9 mm

The dimensions of the connecting rod is given in Fig. 1.28

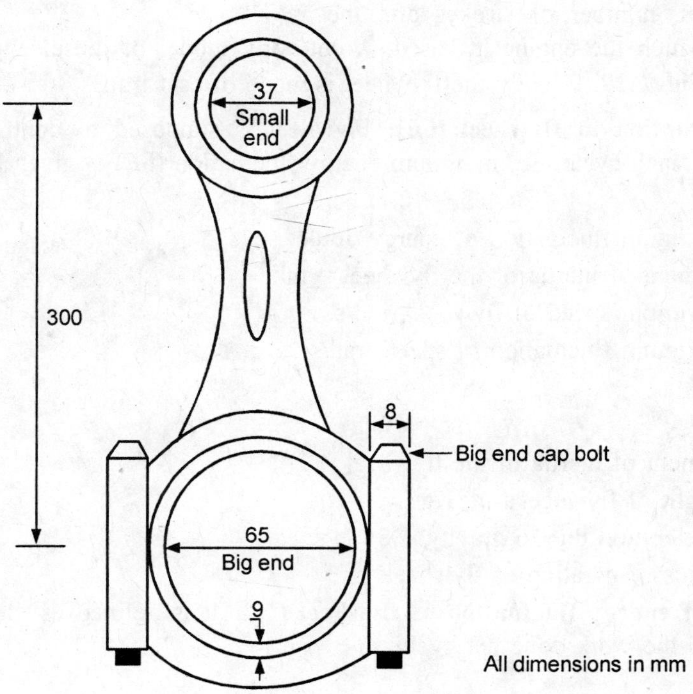


**Figure 1.28. Dimensions of connecting rod**

## 5. DESIGN OF FLY WHEEL

The functions of flywheel are given as follows:

1. It acts as "energy accumulator" *i.e.* it stores energy during power stroke and it acts as energy redistributors during the idle strokes i.e. during suction, compression and exhaust so that a uniform motion is provided by virtue of its inertia.
2. It helps in balancing rotating masses.
3. It also carries ring gear that meshes with the pinion of starting motor.
4. The rear surface of the flywheel is used to serve as one of the pressure surface for the engagement of clutch plate.
5. In small engines, it also serves the purpose of a pulley for transmitting power.
6. The flywheel also carries the identification marks, which helps in adjusting the fuel and valve timing of the engine.

**Figure 1.29. A cut-away model of diesel engine with heavy fly wheel**

The size of the flywheel varies with the number of cylinders, number of strokes and the working cycle on which the engine is based. A cut-away model of diesel engine with heavy fly wheel is shown in Fig. 1.29. Usually the flywheel is made of cast iron.

**Energy fluctuation in flywheel ($\delta E$):** Flywheel is supposed to control the variations in engine speed during each cycle. So, minimum energy fluctuation ($\delta E$) is given by

$$\delta E = \mathrm{I}\ \omega\ \delta\omega \quad ...(1.76)$$

Where $\delta E$ = Maximum fluctuation of energy, Joules

$I$ = Moment of inertia of the flywheel = $mk^2$

$\omega$ = Maximum speed of flywheel, rad/s

$\delta\omega$ = Maximum fluctuation of speed, rad/s

Also,

$$I = (W/g) \times k^2 \quad ....(1.77)$$

Where $I$ = Moment of inertia of the flywheel

$W$ = Weight of flywheel rim, Kg

$g$ = Acceleration due to gravity, 9.81 N/s$^2$

$k$ = Radius of gyration of flywheel, m

**Coefficient of energy fluctuation of flywheel ($C_e$):** It is defined as the ratio of maximum energy fluctuation to the work done per cycle

$$C_e = (E_{max} - E_{min})/(T_m \times \theta) \quad ... (1.78)$$

Or

$$C_e = \delta E/(T_m \times \theta) \quad ... (1.79)$$

Where $E_{max}$ = Maximum energy, J

$E_{min}$ = Minimum energy, J

$\delta E$ = Maximum fluctuation of energy, Joules

$T_m$ = Mean torque, Nm

$\theta$ = Angle of rotation of crank, degrees

**Kinetic energy of flywheel at mean speed ($E_m$)**

$$E_m = ½\, I\, \omega_m^{\,2} \qquad \text{...(1.80)}$$

Where $E_m$ = Kinetic energy of flywheel at mean speed, J

$I$ = Moment of inertia of the flywheel=mk²

$\omega_m$ = Mean speed of flywheel, rad/s

$k^2$ = Radius of gyration of flywheel, m

Also

$$E_m = \delta E/2C_s$$

Where $C_s$ = Coefficient of speed fluctuation

**Coefficient of fluctuation of speed ($C_s$):** Coefficient of fluctuation of speed is defined as the ratio of maximum fluctuation speed to the mean speed.

$$C_s = (\omega_{max} - \omega_{min})/\omega_m = (N_1 - N_2)/N_m \qquad \text{...(1.81)}$$

Where $N_1$ = Maximum speed during cycle, rpm

$N_2$ = Minimum speed during cycle, rpm

$N_m$ = Mean speed during cycle, rpm

**Dimensions of flywheel rim:**

For a flywheel rim of diameter ($d$), mass ($m$) and density ($\rho$), area ($A$) is given by

$$A = m/\pi \times d \times \rho \qquad \text{...(1.82)}$$

Where $A$ = Area of cross section of rim = $b \times t$ (for rectangular section), m²

$b$ = Width of rim, m

$t$ = Thickness of rim, m

$m$ = mass of rim, kg

$\rho$ = Density of material of rim, kg/m³

Figure. 1.30. Dimensions of flywheel of engine

**EXAMPLE 1.10a** *The mean speed of a 30 kW diesel engine of a tractor is 1600 rpm. The speed of engine should not vary by more than 2% of mean speed. The excess energy is 35% of the indicated work per stroke of the engine. Determine the weight of flywheel of the engine if mean radius of gyration of flywheel is 17.5 cm.*

**SOLUTION:**

Engine power, $W = 30$ kW

$C_s = 2\% = 0.02$

Radius of gyration, $k = 17.5$ cm $= 0.175$ m

Engine mean speed, $N_m = 1600$ rpm

Now

Number of working strokes of engine per second $= N_m/60 = 1600/60 = 26.67$ strokes/s

Also

Work done per stroke by the engine

$= W/$ No. of strokes/s $= 30 \times 10^3$ Nm/s/26.67 strokes/s

$= 1.125 \times 10^3$ Nm

Also

We know that maximum excess energy, $\delta E = 35\%$ Indicated work/stroke

$= 0.35 \times 1.125 \times 10^3$ Nm

$= 3.94 \times 10^2$ Nm

Now, we know that;

$$E_m = \delta E/2\,C_s = 3.94 \times 10^2 \text{ Nm} /(2 \times 0.02) = 9.843 \times 10^3 \text{ Nm}$$

Also $$E_m = ½ \times I \times \omega_m^{\ 2} = 1/2 \times m \times k^2 \times \omega_m^{\ 2}$$

Where $E_m$ = Kinetic energy of flywheel at mean speed, J

$I$ = Moment of inertia of the flywheel = $mk^2$

$\omega_m$ = Mean speed of flywheel, rad/s

$k^2$ = Radius of gyration of flywheel, m

Putting values in above equation we get;

$$9.843 \times 10^3 \text{ Nm} = ½ \text{ m} \times (0.175\text{m})^2 \times (2\pi N_m /60)^2$$

Or $$m = 2 \times 9.843 \times 10^3 \text{ Nm}/\{(0.175\text{m})^2 \times (2\pi \times 1600 /60)^2\}$$

$$m = 18.09 \text{ kg say } 20.0 \text{ kg}$$

**Design a flywheel for a 35BHP diesel engine**

We know that

BHP = 35 hp

Speed = 2200 rpm

**Assumptions:**

Let, The maximum variation of energy per revolution = 25% of mean energy

The coefficient of fluctuation of speed = 0.02

The mean velocity of flywheel is limited to 40 m/sec.

95% of the flywheel effect is provided by the rim of the flywheel.

The density of cast iron be 7000 kg/m$^3$

**(A) Flywheel section**

As the engine develops 35 hp at a mean speed of 2200 rpm, the mean energy per revolution is given by

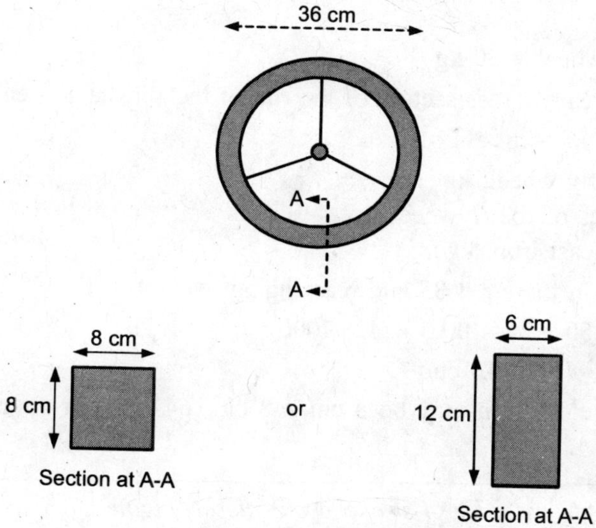


**Figure 1.31. Dimensions of flywheel**

$$\text{Mean energy per revolution } (E) = \frac{35 \times 746 \times 60}{2200} = 712 \text{ Joules}$$

Maximum flutuation of energy/revolution ($\partial E$) = 0.25 × 712 = 178 Joules

$$\text{Maximum speed of flywheel } (\omega) = \frac{2200 \times 2\pi}{60} = 230.38 \text{ rad/sec}$$

Maximum flutuation of speed ($\partial\omega$) = 0.02 × 230.38 = 4.6 rad/sec

Mean radius of the flywheel = 40/230.38 = 0.1736 m = 0.18 m (say)

If $I$ is the moment of inertia of the flywheel, then

$$\partial \text{E} = I\ \omega\ \partial w \qquad \text{...(1.83)}$$

Putting the values in the eq. 1.83 and rearranging, we get

$$178 = I \times 230.38 \times 4.6$$

$$I = 0.168 \text{ Kg-m}^2$$

As 95% of the flywheel effect is provided by the rim of the flywheel, the moment of inertia of the rim of the flywheel will be

$$0.95 \times I = 0.95 \times 0.168 = 0.160 \text{ kg-m}^2$$

If $W$ be the weight of the flywheel rim, then the moment of inertia is given by

$$I = \frac{W}{9.81} \times r^2 \qquad \text{...(1.84)}$$

Putting the values in the eq. 1.84 and rearranging, we get

$$0.16 \text{ kg} - m^2 = \frac{W}{9.81} \times (0.18)^2$$

$$W = 48 \text{ kg} = 50 \text{ kg (say)}$$

Therefore,

The weight of flywheel = 50 kg

If '$A$' m$^2$ be the area of cross section of the rim of the flywheel, then

$$W = 2\pi \times r \times A \times \rho \qquad ...(1.85)$$

where, $W$ = weight of fly wheel, kg

$r$ = mean radius of the flywheel

$\rho$ = density of cast iron, kg/m$^3$

Putting the values in the eq. 1.85 and rearranging, we get

$$50 = 2\pi \times 0.18 \times A \times 7000$$

$$A = 63.16 \text{ cm}^2$$

Therefore, Flywheel section may be 8 cm × 8 cm (64 cm$^2$) or 12 cm × 6 cm (72 cm$^2$) as given in Fig. 1.31.

**EXAMPLE 1.10b** *A single cylinder, 4-stroke cycle diesel engine of a tractor develops 40 kW power at a mean speed of 1800 rpm. The coefficient of fluctuation of energy is 0.35 and fluctuation of engine speed is ± 2.5% of mean speed. If the flywheel diameter is 30 cm and hub of flywheel provides 6% of rotational inertia of flywheel. Determine the mass and dimensions of flywheel rim if density of flywheel material is 7000 kg/m$^3$.*

**SOLUTION:**

Power of engine, $W$ = 40 kW = 40 × 10$^3$ watts or Nm/s

Mean speed of engine, $N_m$ = 1800 rpm or $\omega_m = (2\pi N_m/60)$ =188.5 rad/s

$C_s$ = ± 2.5% = 0.05

$C_e$ = 0.35

Diameter of flywheel = 30 cm = 0.30 m

Density of flywheel material, $\rho$ = 7000 kg/m$^3$

Now

Work done per cycle = 40 × 10$^3$ Nm/s/(1800 rpm/60 s/min)

= 1.33 × 10$^3$ Nm

Now

Maximum fluctuation of energy, $\delta E$ = 0.35 × Work done per cycle

= 0.35 × 1.33 × 10$^3$ Nm

= 4.667 × 10$^2$ Nm

Also, we know that

$$\delta E = \tfrac{1}{2} I \omega_m^2 \times C_s$$

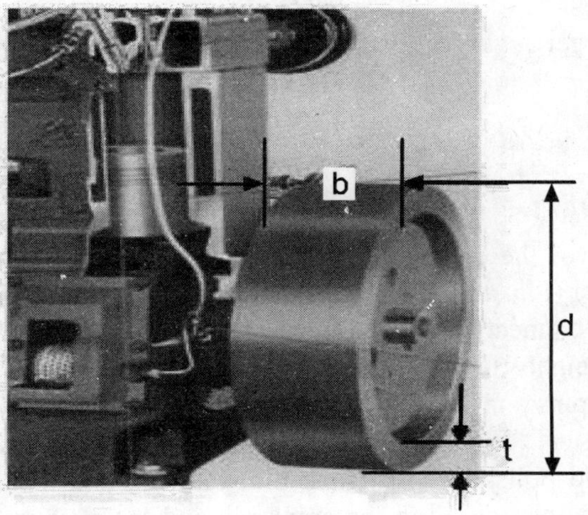


**Figure 1.30: Dimensions of flywheel of engine**

Putting values in above equation we get;

$$4.667 \times 10^2 \text{ Nm} = \tfrac{1}{2} I\,(188.5 \text{ rad/s})^2 \times 0.05$$

Or $$I = (2 \times 4.667 \times 10^2 \text{ Nm})/((188.5 \text{ rad/s})^2 \times 0.05)$$

$$I = 0.525 \text{ kgm}^2$$

Again

$$I_{rim} = 0.94\, I = 0.94 \times 0.525 \text{ kgm}^2$$

$$I_{rim} = mk^2 = 0.4935 \text{ kgm}^2$$

Or $$m = I_{rim}/k^2 = 0.4935 \text{ kgm}^2/(0.15\text{m})^2$$

Or $$m = 21.93 \text{ kg say } 25.0 \text{ kg}$$

Also, we know that;

For a flywheel rim of diameter ($d$), mass ($m$) and density ($\rho$), area ($A$) is given by

$$A = m/\pi d\rho \quad \text{... (1.83)}$$

Where $A$ = Area of cross section of rim = $b \times t$ (for rectangular section), $m^2$

$b$ = Width of rim, m

$t$ = Thickness of rim, m

$m$ = mass of rim, kg

$\rho$ = Density of material of rim, $kg/m^3$

Putting values in above equation, we get

$$A = 25.0 \text{ kg}/\pi\,((0.30 \text{ m}) \times 7000 \text{ kg/m}^3)$$

$$= 3.788 \times 10^{-3} \text{ m}^2$$

Also $$A = b \times t$$

Where, $A$ = Area of cross section of rim, $m^2$

$b$ = width of rim, m

$t$ = Thickness of rim, m

Now, take $$b = 2t$$

Therefore, $$A = 2t \times t = 2t^2$$

Or $t = (A/2)^{0.5}$

Putting values, we get

$$t = (37.88 \times 10^{-4})^{0.5}$$

Or $t = 4.35$ cm say 4.5 cm

And $b = 2t = 2 \times 4.5 \text{ cm} = 9.0 \text{ cm}$

## 6. DESIGN OF CRANKSHAFT

It is the main shaft of the engine which converts the reciprocating motion of the piston into rotary motion or vice-versa (Fig. 1.30). The part that supports the crankshaft in the cylinder block is called main journal. The connecting rod is attached to the crankshaft at crank pin. Crankshaft is provided with counter weights throughout its length for maintaining dynamic balance. The part which connects the crank pins and the shaft is called crank web. Generally the crankshaft is made of drop forged steel or cast steel. The crank pins and main journals are machined to a high precision, case hardened, ground and polished. The crank pin, journals and the main bearings are provided with drilled channels for delivering oil to the crank pin and the main bearings. The crankshaft of a four stroke four cylinder is shown in Fig. 1.32.

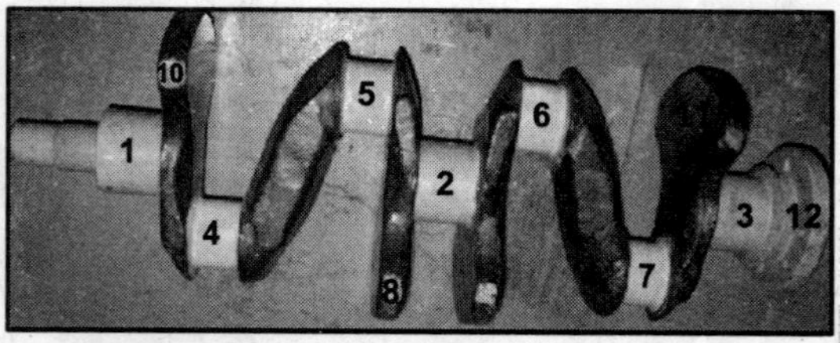


1, 2 & 3. Crank shaft main bearings
4, 5, & 7. Crank pin
8, 9, 10 & 11. Counter weight
12. Flywheel coupling

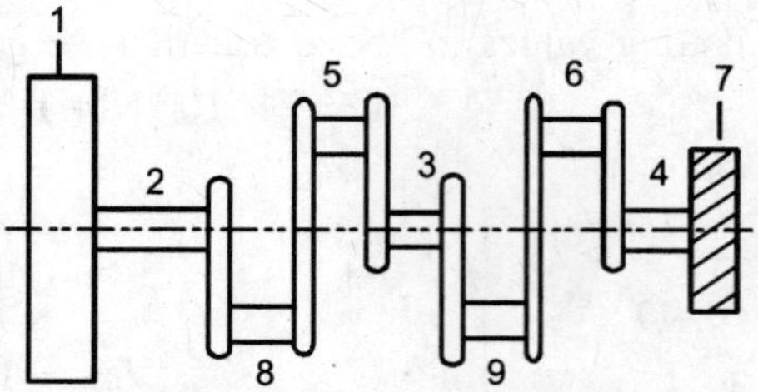


1. Fly wheel
2, 3, 4. Crank shaft main bearing
5, 6, 8, 9. Crank pin
7. Timing gear

**Figure 1.32. Crankshaft of four cylinder four stroke diesel engine**

Let us design a crankshaft for a 35 BHP diesel engine

We know

Bore ($D$) = 100 mm

Stroke ($L$) = 125 mm

Diameter of piston = 99 mm

Engine speed = 2200 rpm

Maximum gas pressure ($P_{max}$) = 52.5 kg/cm$^2$

No. of cylinder = 3

Firing order = 1–2–3

Firing interval = 720°/3 = 240°

Crank throw = 360°/3 = 120°

Length of connecting rod = 300 mm

Diameter of crankpin ($d_c$) = 65 mm

Length of crankpin ($l_c$) = 90 mm

Weight of flywheel (W) = 50 kg

Let us provide centre crank shaft with 4 main bearings and 3 crank pins for accommodating 3 connecting rods. The arrangement of crank pin in a three cylinder engine is shown in Fig. 1.33.

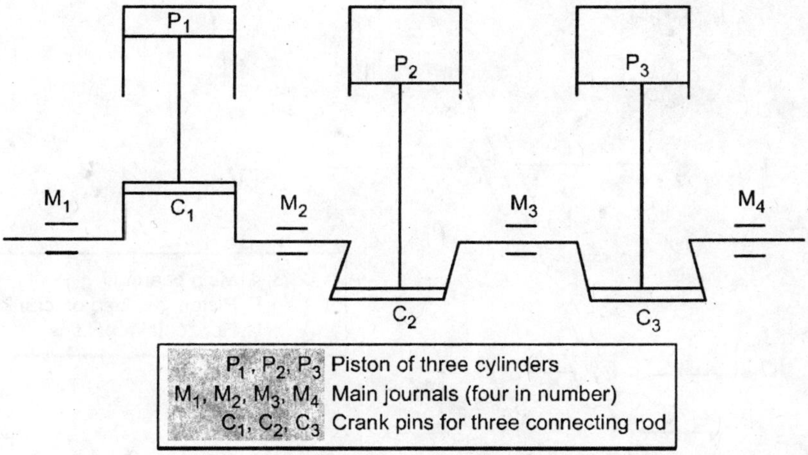


**Figure 1.33. Crank pin arrangement in a three cylinder engine**

In the design of crankshafts,

1. It is assumed that the crankshaft is a simply supported beam at two or three supports.
2. It is designed and checked at least for two crank positions, one when the bending moment is maximum, and the other when the twisting moment is maximum.
3. The additional moment due to the flywheel weight, belt tension and other forces should also be considered.

Now, let us analyze the crank at dead centre when the bending moment is maximum and for the crank at maximum torque position.

## (A) Crank at Dead Centre

Maximum bending moment will act in the crankshaft when the rank is at bottom dead centre or top dead centre. The thrust in the connecting rod will be equal to the piston gas load '*P*'. The forces acting on the crankshaft at dead centre is shown in Fig. 1.34.

The load on the piston is given by,

$$F = \frac{\pi}{4} D^2 P_{max} \text{ kgf} \quad ...(1.86)$$

where, $D$ = diameter of piston, cm

$P_{max}$ = maximum gas pressure, kg/cm$^2$

Putting the values in the eq. 1.86, we get

$$F = \frac{\pi}{4} \times 9.9^2 \times 52.5 = 4041 \text{ kgf}$$

Let us assume that the distance between the main journals ($f$) is

$$f = 2 \times \text{cylinder diameter} = 2 \times 10 \text{ cm} = 20 \text{ cm}$$

Therefore, $a = a = f/2 = 20/2 = 10$ cm (Refer Fig. 1.32)

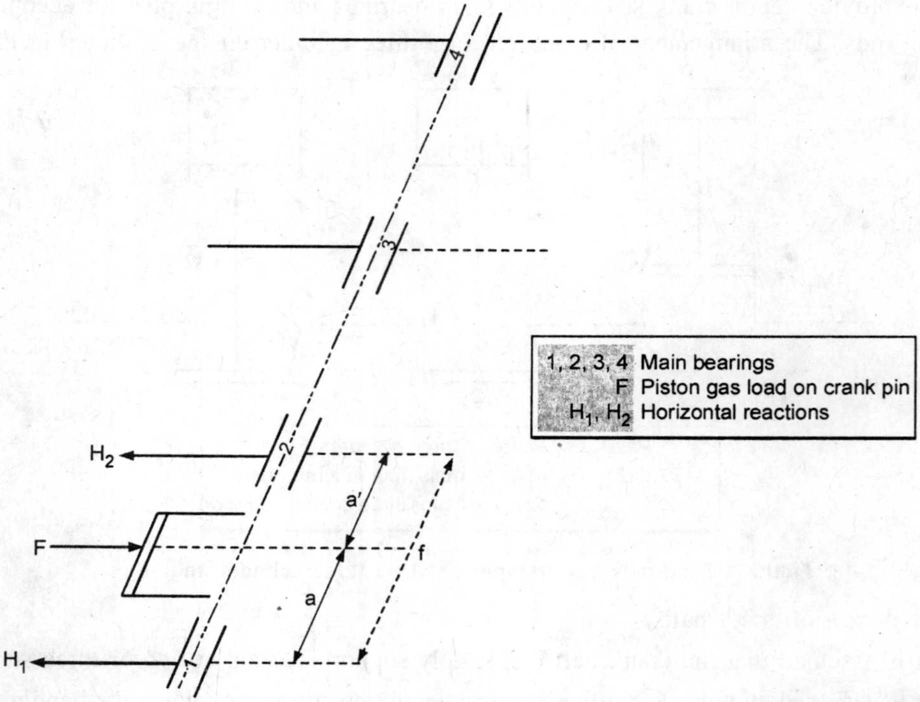


**Figure. 1.34. Crankshaft at dead centre**

Moreover, due to the piston gas load '*P*' on the connecting rod, there will be two horizontal reactions. *i.e.* $H_1$ at bearing No.1 and $H_2$ at bearing No.2 as given in Fig. 1.34.

$$H_1 = H_2 = F/2 = 4041/2 = 2020.5 \text{ kgf}$$

In this position of the crank, the parts like crank pin and crank web will be designed for bending only.

**Crankpin**

The bending moment at the centre of pin is given by

$$M_b = H_1 \times \frac{f}{2} \, kgf \qquad ...(1.87)$$

Putting the values in the eq. 1.87, we get

$$M_b = 2020.5 \times \frac{20}{2} = 20205 \text{ kgf}$$

Also
$$M_b = \frac{\pi}{32} d_c^{\,3} f_b \qquad ...(1.88)$$

where, $f_b$ = allowable stress in bending , kgf/cm$^2$. (Let $f_b$ be 750 kgf/cm$^2$)

$d_c$ = diameter of crankpin, cm

Putting the values in the eq. 1.88 and rearranging, we get

$$20205 = \frac{\pi}{32} d_c^3 \times 750$$

$$d_c = 6.49 \text{ cm}$$

Hence, the earlier design of crank pin (dimension obtained while designing the connecting rod) is safe.

Therefore, let the

Diameter of crankpin be 65 mm

Length of crankpin be 90 mm.

**Main bearings**

Let the lengths of main bearings be equal. The length of main bearing is given by

Length of main bearings = 0.62 to 0.85 × cylinder bore

= 0.85 × 100 mm

= 85 mm

**Left hand crank web**

There will be two stresses on the web, one direct compressive stress and the other bending stress due to the gas load $P$.

Let the thickness of web $(t) = 0.65\, d_c + 6.35$ mm where $d_c$ = diameter of crankpin

or $= 0.65 \times 65 + 6.35 = 48.6$ mm

$t = 50$ mm (say)

Let the width of web $(w) = d_c \times 9/8 + 12.7$ mm where $d_c$ = diameter of crankpin

or $= 65 \times 9/8 + 12.7$ mm

$= 85.8$ mm

$w = 86$ mm (say)

Hence, Thickness of web $(t) = 50$ mm

Width of web $(w) = 86$ mm

Now, bending moment $(M_b)$ for the reaction $H_1$ is given by

$$M_b = H_1 \left( \frac{f}{2} - \frac{l_c}{2} - \frac{t}{2} \right) \quad \text{...(1.89)}$$

where, $f$ = distance between the main journals, cm

$l_c$ = length of crank pin, cm

$t$ = thickness of the web, cm

Putting the values in eq. 1.89, we get

$$M_b = 2020.5 \left( \frac{20}{2} - \frac{9.0}{2} - \frac{5.0}{2} \right)$$

or $M_b = 2020.5\,(10 - 4.5 - 2.5)$

or $M_b = 6062$ kgf – cm

Now, section modulus of arm ($Z$) is given by

$$Z = \frac{wt^2}{6} \qquad \text{...(1.90)}$$

where, $w$ = width of the web, cm; $t$ = thickness of the web, cm.

Putting the values in eq. 1.90, we get

$$Z = \frac{8.6 \times 5^2}{6} = 35.8 \text{ cm}^3$$

Therefore, bending stress ($f_b$) is given by

$$f_b = \frac{M_b}{Z} = \frac{6062}{358} = \text{kgf/cm}^2$$

Direct Compressive stress ($f_d$) is given by

$$f_d = \frac{H_1}{wt} = \frac{2020.5}{8.6 \times 5} = 46.9 \text{ kgf/cm}^2$$

Total stress on the web = bending stress + direct stress

$$= f_b + f_d$$

$$= 169 + 46.9 = 215.9 = 216 \text{ kgf/cm}^2 \text{ (say)}$$

which is well below the limit of 750 kg/cm$^2$. The allowable stress for different materials is given in the Table No. 1.10.

**TABLE 1.10 : Allowable stress for different materials**

| Material | Allowable stress in bending (kg/cm$^2$) | Allowable stress in shear (kg/cm$^2$) |
|---|---|---|
| Carbon steel | 560 to 750 | 310 to 420 |
| Alloy cast iron | 350 to 470 | 350 to 470 |
| Chrome nickel or other alloy steel | 1300 to 1750 | 725 to 970 |

**Right hand crank web**

Since, it has been assumed that the main bearings are of the same length and $H_1 = H_2$, therefore, the analysis of the right hand crank arm will be the same as for left hand crank arm. Therefore, dimensions of left crank arm will be applicable to the right hand crank.

**Shaft under flywheel**

Bending moment due to flywheel weight ($M_f$) is given by

$$M_f = \frac{W \times g}{4} \text{ kg} - \text{cm} \qquad \text{...(1.91)}$$

where, $W$ = weight of flywheel, kg

$g$ = distance between flywheel and centre of main bearing (No.4) adjacent to the fly wheel, cm (Refer Fig. 1.35).

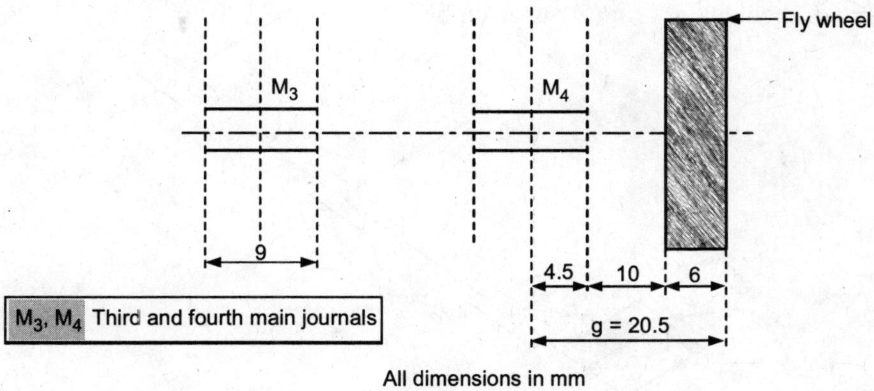


**Figure 1.35. Distance between fly wheel and main bearing**

Putting the values in the eq. 1.91, we get

$$M_f = \frac{50 \times 20.5}{4} = 256.25 \text{ kg} - \text{cm}$$

Also, $$M_f = \frac{\pi}{32} d_w^2 \times f_b \qquad ...(1.92)$$

where, $M_f$ = Bending moment due to flywheel weight, kg–cm

$d_w$ = Diameter of flywheel shaft, cm

$f_b$ = Allowable bending stress for alloy cast iron, kg/cm$^2$ (Let it be 420 kg/cm$^2$)

Putting the values in the eq.1.92, we get

$$256.26 = \frac{\pi}{32} d_w^2 \times 420$$

or $$d_w = 62 \text{ mm}$$

Therefore, diameter of shaft under flywheel = 62 mm

## (B) Crank at angle of maximum torque

The twisting moment on the crankshaft will be maximum when the tangential force is maximum. The angle usually lies between 25 and 35° from the dead centre for petrol engines and between 30 to 40° for diesel engines. At this angle, the gas pressure will not be maximum.

The forces acting on the crankshaft when it is at an angle of maximum torque is given in Fig. 1.36.

**Assumption:**

Let the crank angle be 36° at maximum torque.

Let the gas pressure be 40% of maximum explosion pressure at maximum torque *i.e.*

40% of 52.5 Kgf/cm$^2$ = 21 kgf/cm$^2$.

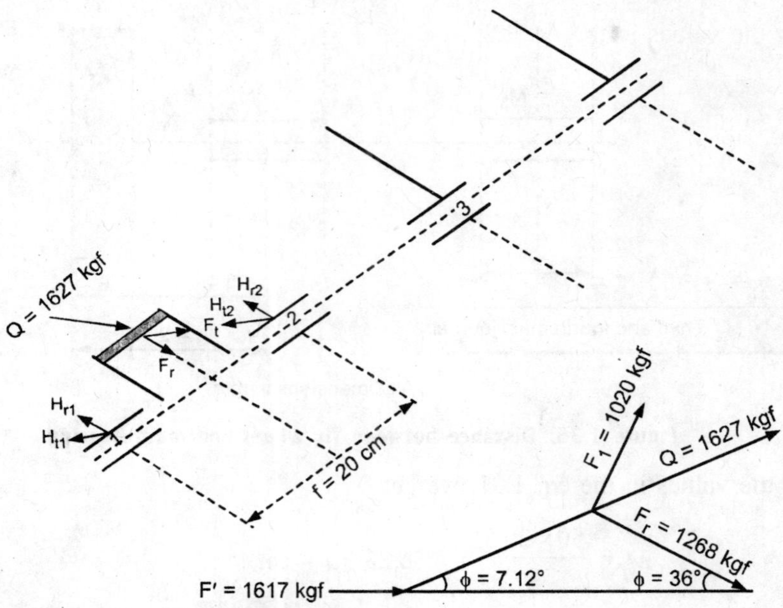


| | |
|---|---|
| 1, 2, 3, 4 | Main bearings |
| Q | Connecting rod thrust on crank pin |
| $H_{r1}$, $H_{r2}$ | Horizontal radial reactions |
| $H_{t1}$, $H_{t2}$ | Horizontal tangential reactions |

**Figure 1.36. Crank at an angle of maximum torque**

Piston gas load ($F'$) is given by

$$F' = \frac{\pi}{4} D^2 P \text{ kgf} \qquad ...(1.93)$$

Putting the values in the eq. 1.93, we get

$$F' = \frac{\pi}{4} \times 9.9^2 \times 21 = 1617 \text{ kgf}$$

If $F'$ is the gas load along the cylinder centre line, then the thrust '$Q$' along the connecting rod is given by

$$Q = \frac{F'}{\cos \phi} \qquad ...(1.94)$$

and

$$\sin \phi = \frac{\sin \theta}{L/R} \qquad ...(1.95)$$

where, $L$ = length of connecting rod

$R$ = crank radius

Given $\theta$ =36°

Therefore,

$$\frac{L}{R} = \frac{\text{Length of connecting rod}}{0.5 \times \text{stroke}} = \frac{300}{0.5 \times 125} = 4.8$$

Putting the values in the eq. 1.86, we get

$$\sin \varphi = \frac{\sin 36°}{4.8}$$

$$\therefore \quad \varphi = 7.12$$

Now, tangential and radial component of '$Q$' are

$$F_t = Q \sin (\theta + \varphi) \text{ and} \quad ...(1.96)$$

$$F_r = Q \cos (\theta + \varphi) \quad ...(1.97)$$

Now, putting the values in the eq. 1.85, we get

$$Q = \frac{F'}{\cos\varphi} = \frac{1617 \text{ kgf}}{\cos 7.12} = 1627 \text{ kgf}$$

Putting the values in the eq. 1.96 and 1.97, we get

$$F_t = 1627\sin (36 + 7.12) = 1020 \text{ kgf}$$

$$F_t = 1627 \cos (36 + 7.12) = 1268 \text{ kgf}$$

Therefore,

$$H_{t1} + H_{t2} = \frac{F_t}{2} = \frac{1020}{2} = 510 \text{ kgf}$$

$$H_{r1} = H_{r2} = \frac{F_r}{2} = \frac{1268}{2} = 634 \text{ kgf}$$

**Crankpin**

Bending moment at the centre of crankpin is given by

$$M_b = H_{r1} \times \frac{f}{2} \text{ kg-cm} \quad ...(1.98)$$

Putting the values in the eq. 1.98, we get

$$M_b = 634 \times \frac{20}{2} = 6340 \text{ kg–cm}$$

Twisting moment is given by

$$M_t = H_{t1} \times R \text{ kg} - \text{cm} \quad ...(1.99)$$

where, $R$ = crank radius = half of the stroke.

Putting the values in the eq. 1.99, we get

$$M_t = 510 \times 6.25 = 3188 \text{ kg-cm}$$

Equivalent twisting moment is given by

$$M_{te} = \sqrt{M_b^2 + M_t^2} \quad ...(1.100)$$

Putting the values in the eq. 1.100, we get

$$M_{te} = \sqrt{6340^2 + 3188^2} = 7096 \text{ kg–cm}$$

Also $$M_{te} = \frac{\pi}{16} d_c^3 f_s \qquad ...(1.101)$$

where, $M_{te}$ = Equivalent twisting moment, kg-cm

$d_c$ = diameter of crankpin, cm

$f_s$ = Allowable shear stress, kg/cm$^2$ (Let it be 350 kg/cm$^2$)

Putting the values in the eq.1.101, we get

$$7096 \text{ kgf–cm} = \frac{\pi}{16} d_c^3 \times 350 \text{ kgf/cm}^2$$

$$\therefore \quad d_c = 4.7 \text{ cm}$$

Diameter of crankpin = 4.7 cm, which is small as compared to the diameter already calculated.

**Shaft under the flywheel**

Total bending moment will be the same as before, *i.e.* $M_b$= 256.25 kgf–cm

Twisting moment is given by

$$M_t = F_t \text{ x } R = 1020 \times 6.25 = 63750 \text{ kgf–cm}$$

Resultant moment ($M_r$) is given by

$$M_r = \sqrt{M_b^2 + M_t^2} = \sqrt{256.25^2 + 63750^2}$$

$$= 63750.5 \text{ kgf – cm}$$

Also, $$M_r = \frac{\pi}{160} d_w^3 fs \qquad ...(1.102)$$

where, $M_r$= resultant moment, kg-cm

$d_w$ = diameter of flywheel shaft, cm

$f_s$ = allowable shear stress, kg/cm$^2$ .

Putting the values in the eq.1.102, we get

$$63750.5 \text{ kgf – cm} = \frac{\pi}{16} \times 6^3 \times f_s \text{ kgf/cm}^2$$

$$f_s = 1503 \text{ kgf/cm}^2$$

$f_s$ = 1503 kgf/cm$^2$ is more than the safe limit of 310 to 420 kgf/cm$^2$ for carbon steel shaft. Therefore, redesigning the diameter of flywheel shaft, we get

$$d_w^3 = \frac{63750.5 \times 16}{\pi \times 420}$$

$$d_w = 90$$

Hence, Diameter of shaft under the flywheel = 90 mm

## Journals

Since the bearing No. 4 is heavily loaded due to the presence of flywheel, our design for the all journals will be based on journal No. 4.

Total reactions at this bearing is given by

$$R_j = \frac{F}{2} + W \text{ kgf}$$

$$R_j = \frac{4041}{2} + 50 = 2071 \text{ kgf}$$

Also $$R_j = l_j \times d_j \times p_b \quad ...(1.103)$$

where, $l_j$ = length of journal = 8.5 cm

$d_j$ = diameter of journal, cm

$p_b$ = bearing pressure which ranges from 50 to 85 kgf/cm$^2$

Putting the values in the eq.1.103, we get

$$\therefore \quad d_j = \frac{R_j}{l_j\, p_b} = \frac{2071}{8.5 \times 50} = 4.9 \text{ cm} = 50 \text{ mm (say)}$$

Hence, Diameter of shaft at journals is 50 mm.

The dimensions of the crankshaft are given in Fig. 1.37.

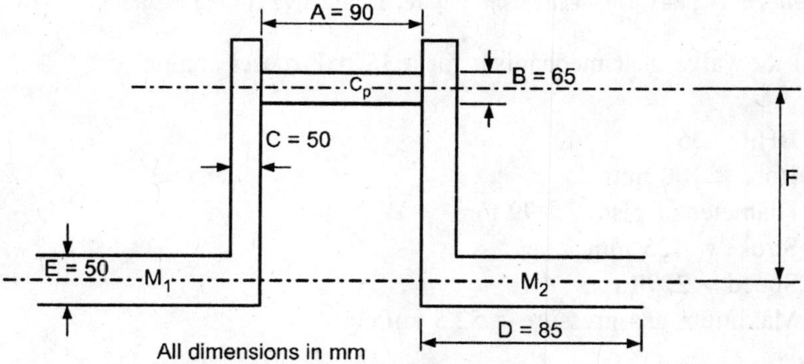


A Length of crank pin
B Diameter of crankpin
C Thickness of crank web
D Length of main bearing
E Diameter of main journal
F Centre to centre distance between main journal and crank pin
$M_1$, $M_2$ Main journals
$C_p$ Crank pin

**Figure 1.37. Dimensions of crankshaft**

## 7. DESIGN OF VALVE GEAR MECHANISM

Valve gear mechanism is a combination of parts which operate or actuate the valves like intake and exhaust at proper time with respect to the position of the piston and crankpin and keep them open during the required time. The valve gear mechanism varies in its construction depending upon the type, speed and size of the engines. A good valve should open and close at definite crank angles with a minimum of noise, wear and corrosion. It should be light in weight to reduce inertia forces. The components of the engine valve mechanism are given in Fig. 1.38.

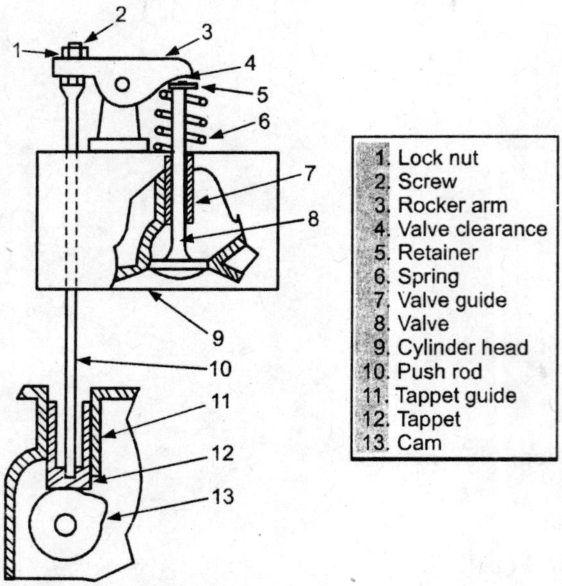


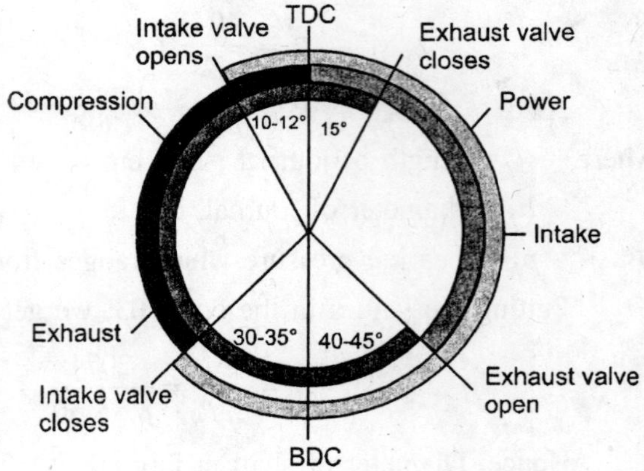


**Figure. 1.38: Components of engine valve mechanism** **Figure. 1.39: Valve timing diagram of 4-stroke cycle engine**

Let us design the valve gear mechanism for a 35BHP diesel engine

We know

BHP = 35

Bore = 100 mm

Diameter of piston = 99 mm

Stroke = 125 mm

Speed = 2200 rpm

Maximum gas pressure = 52.5 kgf/cm$^2$

**Assumptions :**

Let the valves be of poppet or mushroom type as given in Fig. 1.40 and made of carbon steel.

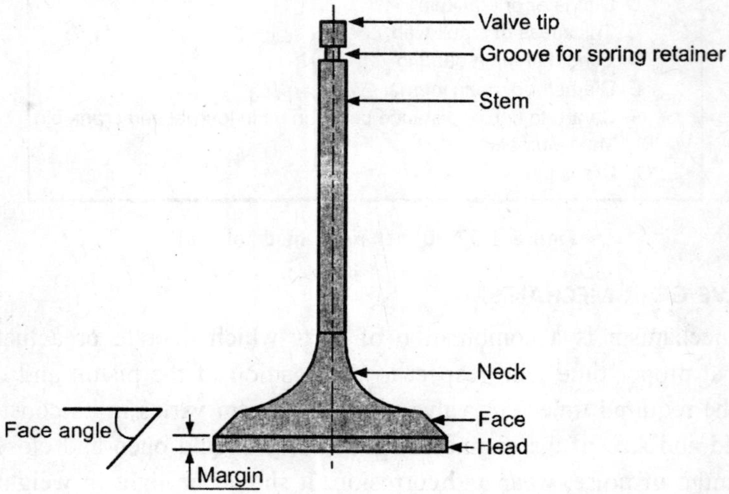


**Figure 1.40. Poppet or mushroom valve**

## (A) Design of valve

The size of the valve ports depends upon the cylinder diameter and the cylinder centre distances. If the cylinder diameter is large, large ports are used. A valve port is shown in Fig. 1.41.

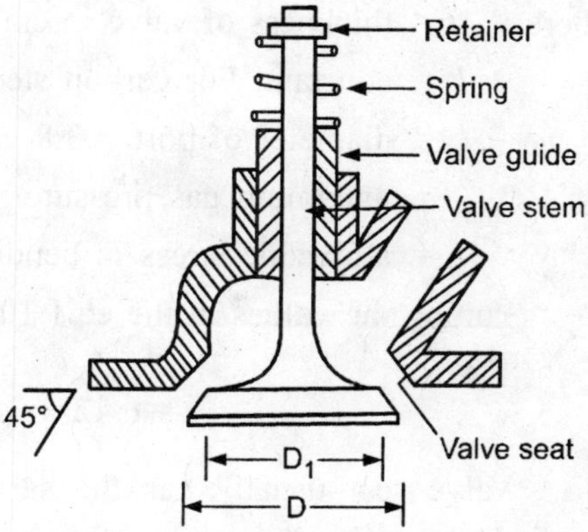


**Figure 1.41. Valve port**

The size of the valve head may be determined from the relationship,

$$a_p \times v_p = a_{po} \times V_{po} \qquad \text{...(1.104)}$$

where; $a_p$ = area of piston, $cm^2$

$= \frac{\pi}{4} \times (9.9)^2 = 77\ cm^2$

$v_p$ = mean piston velocity, m/min

$= 2\ LN = 2 \times 0.125 \times 2200 = 550$ m/min

$a_{po}$ = area of port, $cm^2$

$v_{po}$ = mean velocity of gas through the port m/min.

For automotive engines it ranges from 3000 to 4500 m/min. (Let $V_{po}$ = 3750 m/min.)

Putting the values in the eq.1.104 and rearranging, we get

$$77 \times 550 = \frac{\pi}{4} d_{po}^2 \times 3750 \text{ m/min}$$

$$d_{po} = 3.8 \text{ cm}$$

Hence, Diameter of port ($d_{po}$) = 3.8 cm.

**For Exhaust valve**

For seat angle (α) of 45°, the projected width of the valve seat may be taken empirically as

$= 0.05\ d_{po}$ to $0.07\ d_{po}$

or $= 0.05 \times 3.8$ cm to $0.07 \times 3.8$ cm

or $= 0.19$ to $0.27$ cm $= 0.25$ cm (say)

The diameter of exhaust valve head is given by,

Diameter of valve head = diameter of port + (2 × width of valve seat) ...(1.105)

Putting the values in the eq.1.105, we get

Diameter of exhaust valve head = 3.8 + 2 × 0.25 = 4.3 cm

Thus, the diameter of exhaust valve head is 43 mm.

Now, the lift of the valve is given approximately as,

$$l = \frac{d_{po}}{4\cos\alpha} = \frac{3.8}{4\cos 45°} = 1.25 \text{ cm}$$

The thickness of the valve head is given by,

$$t = k d_p \sqrt{\frac{P_{max}}{f_t}} \qquad \text{...(1.106)}$$

where, $t$ = thickness of valve in cm

$k$ = constant. For carbon steel $k = 0.42$

$d_p$ = diameter of port = 3.8 cm

$P_{max}$ = maximum gas pressure = 52.5 kg/cm$^2$

$f_t$ = allowable stress in bending, kgf/cm$^2$. For carbon steel $f_t$ = 560 kgf/cm$^2$

Putting the values in the eq.1.106, we get

$$t = 0.42 \times 3.8\sqrt{\frac{52.5}{560}} = 0.488 \qquad t = 5 \text{ mm (say)}$$

Valve seat usually has the same angle as the valve seating surface. But, it is generally practiced to make the angle of valve seat as ½ to 1 degree larger than the valve angle. This interference angle results in more effective seat.

$$\text{Valve seat angle } (\alpha') = \alpha + 1°$$
$$= 45° + 1°$$
$$= 46°$$

$$\text{Valve stem diameter} = d_{po}/8 + 6.35 \text{ mm}$$
$$= 38/8 + 6.35 \text{ mm}$$
$$= 11 \text{ mm}$$

The dimensions of exhaust valve are given in Fig. 1.42

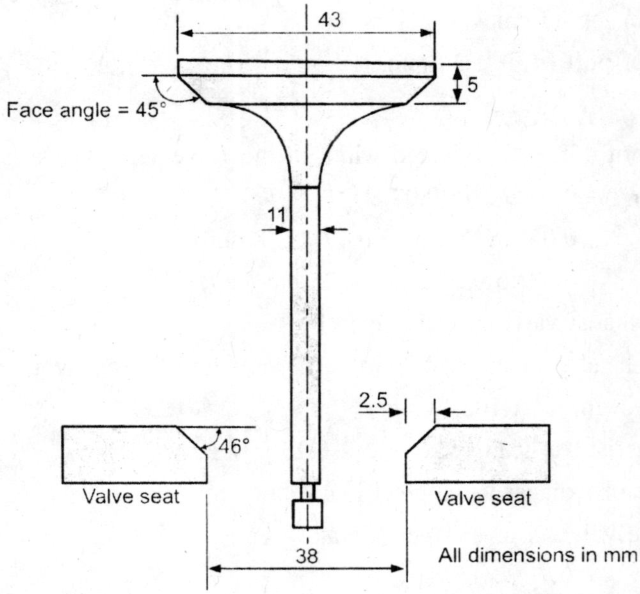


**Figure 1.42. Dimensions of exhaust valve**

## (B) Force analysis at various points of rocker arm assembly

The valve gear arrangement along with the rocker arm assembly is given in Fig. 1.43.

Let the gas pressure in the cylinder when the valve starts to open is 7 kgf/cm$^2$.

Let the pressure on the top side of valve is 1.05 kgf/cm$^2$

Let the exhaust valve opens at 40° B.B.D.C and closes 10° A.T.D.C.

We know that the

Diameter of exhaust port = 38 mm

Diameter of exhaust valve head = 43 mm

The total load at the exhaust valve *i.e.* point *B* is equal to gas load when it opens plus spring load. Now when the valve opens, the cylinder pressure acting on its face *i.e.* on 43 mm diameter is 7 kgf/cm$^2$, while the pressure on its top side *i.e.* on 38 mm diameter is 1.05 kgf/cm$^2$.

Therefore,

$$\text{Net gas load} = \frac{\pi}{4} \times 4.3^2 \times 7 - \frac{\pi}{4} \times 3.8^2 \times 1.05$$

or $$= 101.62 - 11.9.$$

$$= 90 \text{ kgf}$$

Spring load may be taken as 0.5 kgf/cm$^2$ of valve area. Therefore, the spring load is

$$\frac{\pi}{4} \times 4.3^2 \times 0.5 = 8 \text{ kgf}$$

Therefore, total load at point *B* = Net gas load + spring load

Or $$= 90 + 8 = 98 = 100 \text{ kgf (say)}$$

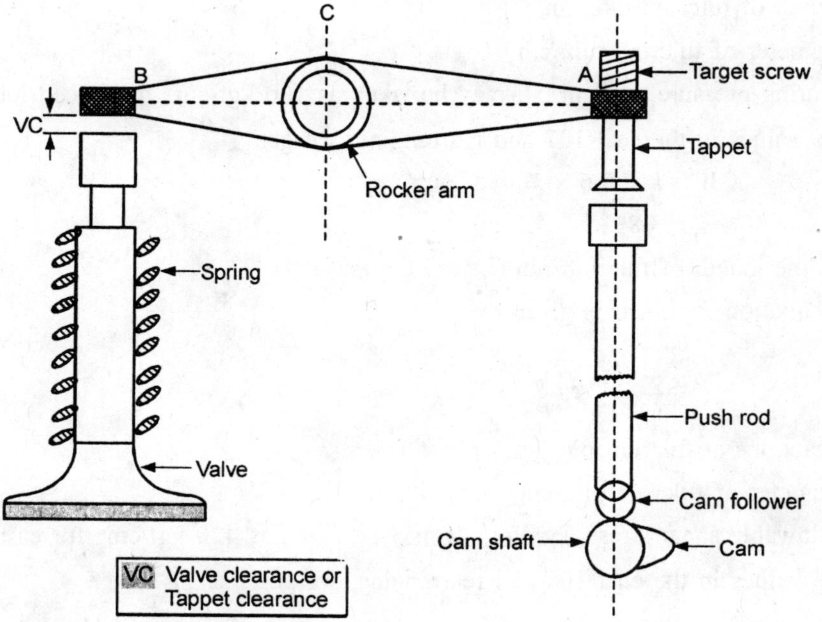


**Figure 1.43. Valve gear arrangement**

The load at point *A* will depend upon the lever ratio *y*/*x* (Refer Fig. 1.44). The lever ratio *y*/*x* often depends upon the availability of space. For moderate and slow speed engines, the lever ratio is always 1. But for high speed engines, it ranges from 1/1.5 to 1/1.6. But generally, it is taken as 1/1.3 to minimize the inertia forces. Moreover, the distance '*x*' should not be less than five times the valve lift.

Thus, $y/x = 1/1.3$

Now, *x* should be at least 5 times of lift of valve.

Thus, $x = 5 \times 1.25 = 6.25$ cm and

$y = 6.25/1.3 = 4.8$ cm

Therefore, load at point

$$A = 100 \times (x/y) = 100 \times (6.25/4.8) = 130 \text{ kgf}$$

Thus,

The load at point $C$ = Load at point $B$ + Load at point $A$

= 100 + 130

= 230 kgf

### (C) Fulcrum pin

Reactions at fulcrum pin $C$ = 230 kgf

The bearing equation is given by

$$P = l_f \times d_f \times P_b \qquad ...(1.107)$$

where, $P$ = Reactions at fulcrum pin, kgf

$l_f$ = length of fulcrum pin, cm

$d_f$ = diameter of fulcrum pin, cm

$p_b$ = bearing pressure, kgf/cm$^2$. It may be taken as 100 kgf/cm$^2$ for forced lubrication.

Putting the values in the eq.1.107 and rearranging, we get

$$230 = l_f \times 0.6 \times 100$$

$$l_f = 3.83$$

Therefore, the length of fulcrum pin ($l_f$) = 4 cm (say).

Also, the equation for shear is given by

$$P = 2 \times \frac{\pi}{4} d_f^2 \times f_s \qquad ...(1.108)$$

where, $P$ = Reactions at fulcrum pin, kgf

$d_f$ = diameter of fulcrum pin, cm

$f_s$ = Allowable shear stress, kgf/cm$^2$. It may be taken as 420 kgf/cm$^2$ for carbon steel

Putting the values in the eq.1.108 and rearranging, we get

$$230 = 2 \times \frac{\pi}{4} d_f^2 \times 420$$

Or $d_f = 0.6$ cm

Therefore, the diameter of fulcrum pin ($d_f$) = 0.6 cm = 6 mm.

But, practically, $l_f/d_f$ varies from 1.25 to 2.

Taking $l_f/d_f$=1.5, the bearing equation becomes,

$$230 = 1.5d_f^2 \times 100$$

$$d_f = 1.24 \text{ cm} = 1.25 \text{ cm (say)}$$

Therefore, $l_f = 1.25 \times 1.5 = 1.875$ cm = 2.0 cm (say)

Hence, Diameter of fulcrum pin = 12.5 mm

Length of fulcrum pin = 20 mm

A bush of 3 mm thick may be provided in the boss.

Therefore, Inside diameter of boss = 1.25 + 2 (0.3) = 1.85 cm = 18.5 mm

## (D) Rocker arm

Now to find the dimension of the rocker arm (Fig. 1.41) adjacent to the boss, the lever arm from point *B i.e. y* is equal to 4.8 cm.

Therefore, the moment is given by

$$M = \text{Force at } B \times \text{lever arm}$$
$$= 100 \times 4.80$$
$$= 480 \text{ kgf-cm}$$

If the material of the rocker arm is carbon steel, $f_b$ = 420 kgf/cm$^2$

Also,

$$M = f_b \times Z \quad \text{...(1.109)}$$

Where $M$ = Bending moment, kgf-cm

$f_b$ = Allowable bending stress, kg/cm$^2$

$Z$ = Sectional modulus

Putting the values in the eq.1.109, we get

$$480 = 420 \times Z$$

$$Z = 1.14 \text{ cm}^3 \quad \text{...(1.110)}$$

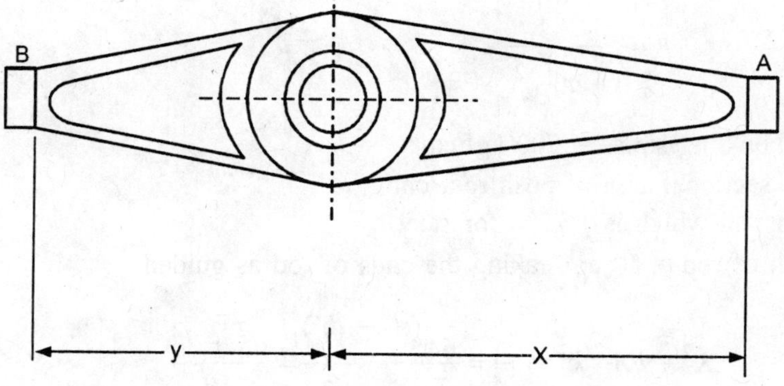


Figure 1.44. Rocker arm

Let the depth of I-section to be used in rocker arm be 2.6 cm. Therefore, the dimensions are given by

$$\text{Depth} = 6t = 2.6 \text{ cm}$$

$$\text{Width} = 2.5\ t$$

*or* $$t = 2.6/6 = 0.433 = 0.45\text{cm (say)}$$

or $$I_{xx} = \frac{\frac{1}{12}(BH^3 - bh^3)}{12}$$

$$I_{xx} = \frac{1}{12}(2.5t\,(6t)^3 - 1.5t(4t)^3)$$

$$I_{xx} = \frac{1}{12}(540t^4 - 96t^4) = \frac{444}{12t^4}$$

$$\therefore \quad Z_{xx} = \frac{I_{xx}}{y} = \frac{444}{12}t^4 \times \frac{1}{3t}\frac{111}{9}t^3 = 12.33t^3 \qquad \text{...(1.111)}$$

Equating eq. 1.110 and 1.111, we get

$$Z = 1.14 = 12.33\ t^3 \qquad \text{...(1.112)}$$

Solving the cubic eq. 1.112, we get

$$t = 0.45 \text{ cm.}$$

Hence,

Depth of I-section of rocker arm = $6t = 6 \times 0.45$ cm = 2.7cm

Width of I-section of rocker arm = $2.5\ t = 2.5 \times 0.45$ cm = 1.125 = 1.2 cm (say)

## (E) Push rod

Push rods are driven by the valve lifter or tappets which gets drive from camshaft. The push rod in turn opens the valves. Push rods are subjected to buckling and it is designed by using Rankine Gordon formula.

The load on the push rod ($P$) = load at point $A$ = 130 kgf

The length of the push rod depends upon the height of engine and other design. Let us assume the length of push rod as 50 cm.

Applying Rankine Gordon formula

$$P = \frac{f_c\,A}{1 + a(\frac{l}{k})^2} \qquad \text{...(1.113)}$$

where, $f_c$ = safe buckling stress = 700 kgf/cm$^2$

$A$ = cross sectional area of push rod, cm$^2$

$a$ = a constant which is 1/7500 for steel

$l$ = length of rod = 50 cm, taking the ends of rod as guided

$$K^2 = I/A = k^2 = \frac{I}{A} = \frac{\frac{\pi}{64}(d_0^4 - d_i^4)}{\frac{\pi}{4}(d_0^2 - d_i^2)} = \frac{d_0^2 + d_i^2}{16}$$

where $d_o$ = outer diameter of push rod

$d_i$ = inner diameter of push rod

Now, $d_o/d_i$ is usually 1/0.6 to 1/0.8

Therefore, let $d_i = 0.6\ d_o$

Thus $A = \frac{\pi}{4}(d_0^2 - 0.36d_0^2) = 0.16\pi d_0^2$ and

$$k^2 = \frac{d_0^2 + 0{,}36d_0^2}{16} = \frac{1.36d_0^2}{16} = 0.085\ d_0^2$$

Putting the values in the eq. 1.113, we get,

$$130 = \frac{700 \times 0.16\pi d_0^2}{1 + \frac{1}{7500} \times \frac{2500}{0.085d_0^2}}$$

or $352\ d_0^4 - 130\ d_0^2 - 510 = 0$ ...(1.114)

Solving the bi-quadratic eq. 1.114, we get,

$d_o$ = 1.18 cm = 1.2 cm (say)

Hence, Outer diameter of push rod ($d_o$) = 12 mm

Inner diameter of push rod ($d_i$) = 0.7 × $d_o$ = 0.7 × 12 = 8.4 mm.

The dimensions of the push rod are given in Fig. 1.45.

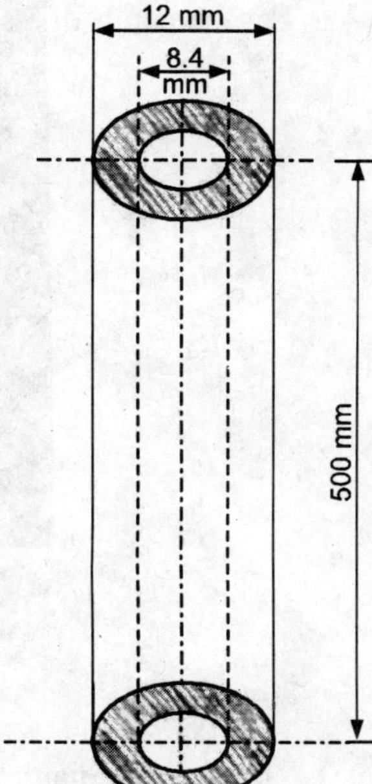


**Figure 1.45: Dimensions of push rod**

## (F) Adjusting screw

This screw remains under compression and the load to be carried by it is 100 kgf. Assuming safe stress of 500 kgf/cm$^2$, diameter of screw is found by using the relationship,

$$100 \text{ kgf/cm}^2 = \frac{\pi}{2} \times d_c^2 \times 50$$

or $d_c = 0.5$ cm

$$\text{Nominal diameter} = \frac{d_c}{0.8} = \frac{0.5}{0.8} = 0.625$$

Suitable dimension for the circular end of the rocker arm to carry this stud will be

Diameter = 2 × 0.625 = 12.5 mm

Depth = 2 × 0.625 = 12.5 mm

## (G) Cam

A cam is an eccentric projection on a revolving disk used for opening and closing of a valve through the other parts. Let the cam be forged as one piece with cam shaft. The timing gear of IC engine is shown in Fig. 1.46.

Cam shaft diameter = 0.16 cylinder bore + 1.27 cm

= 0.16 × 10 cm + 1.27 cm

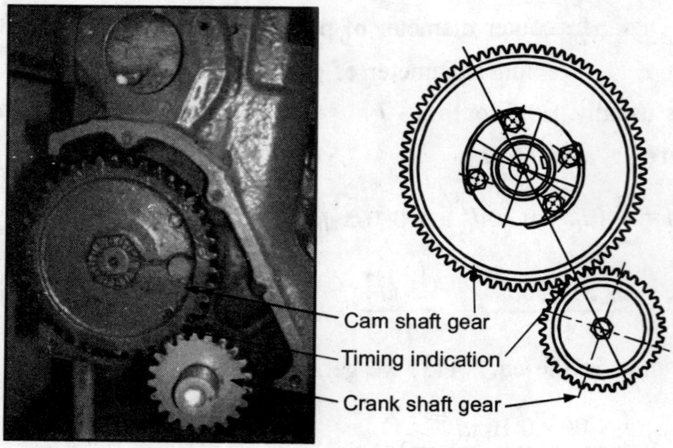


Figure 1.46. Timing gears of IC engine

= 2.87 cm

= 30 mm (say)

Base circle diameter = cam shaft diameter + 0.3 cm

= 3 cm + 0.3 cm

= 33 mm

Cam width = 0.09 × cylinder bore + 6 mm

= 0.09 × 100mm + 6 mm

= 9 + 6 mm

= 15 mm

The dimensions of the cam are given in Fig. 1.47.

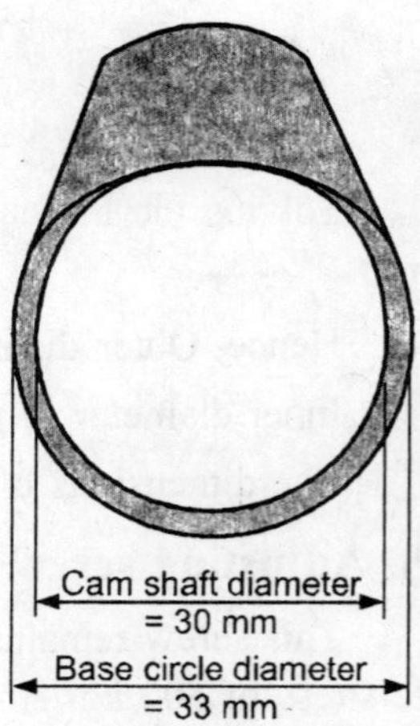


Figure 1. 47. Dimensions of cam

## (H) Intake valve

Higher engine output can be obtained by better cylinder charging and better cooling of the exhaust valves. For this purpose, intake ports are made 20 to 40 % larger than exhaust valves. Let the dimensions of intake valve be 30% more than the exhaust port.

Let the seat angle ($\alpha$)-be 30°

Therefore,

Diameter of intake port ($d_{po}$) = Diameter of exhaust port × 1.3

= 3.8 cm × 1.3 = 5.0 cm = 50 mm

For seat angle ($\alpha$) of 30°, the projected width of the valve seat may be taken empirically as

$= 0.05\ d_{po}$ to $0.07\ d_{po}$

∴ Projected width of valve seat = 0.05 × 5.0 cm to 0.07 × 5.0 cm

= 0.25 cm to 0.35 cm

= 0.30 cm

The diameter of intake valve head is given by

Diameter of valve head = diameter of port + (2 × width of valve seat)

Therefore,

Diameter of intake valve head = $d_{po}$ + 2 × 0.3 cm

= 5.0 + 2 × 0.3 = 5.6 cm = 56 mm

Now, the lift of the valve is given approximately as

$$L = d_{po}/4 \cos\alpha = 5/4 \cos 30° = 1.4 \text{ cm}$$

The thickness of the valve head is given by,

$$t = kd_{po}\sqrt{\frac{P_{max}}{f_1}} \qquad \text{...(1.115)}$$

where, $t$ = thickness of valve in cm

$k$ = constant. For carbon steel $k$ = 0.42

$d_{po}$ = diameter of intake port =5.0 cm

$P_{max}$ = maximum gas pressure = 52.5 kg/cm$^2$

$f_t$ = allowable stress in bending, kgf/cm$^2$. For carbon steel $f_t$ = 560 kgf/cm$^2$

Putting the values in the eq. 1.115, we get

$$t = 0.42 \times 5.0\sqrt{\frac{52.5}{56.0}} = 0.640$$

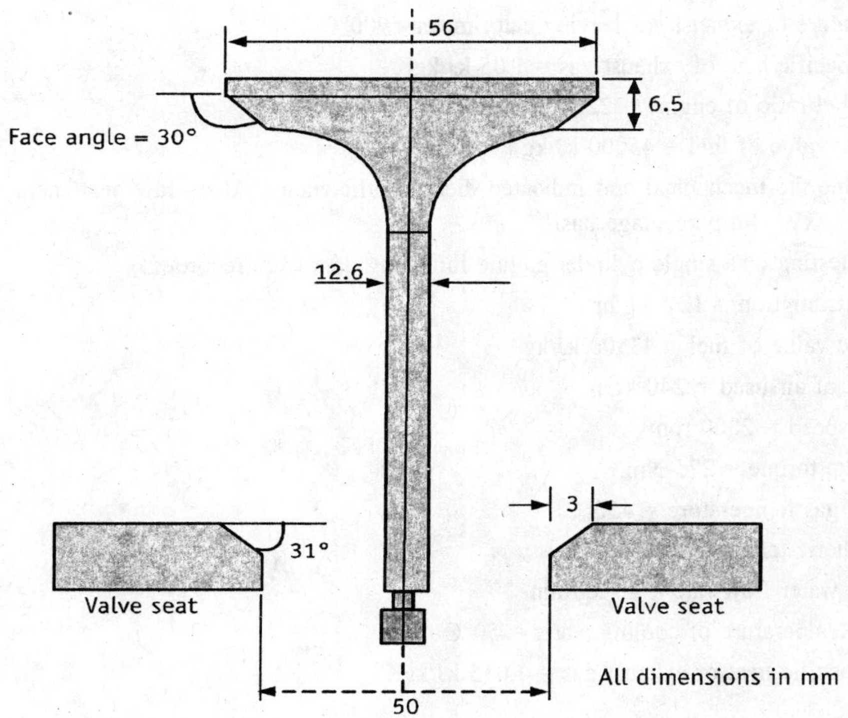


**Figure 1.48. Dimensions of intake valve**

$t = 6.5$ mm (say)

Valve seat angle $(\alpha) = 30° + 1° = 31°$

Valve stem diameter $= d_{po}/8 + 6.35$ mm

$= 50/8 + 6.35$ mm

$= 12.6$ mm

The dimensions of rocker arm, push rod, fulcrum pin, adjusting screw and cam for intake valve can be the same as that designed for exhaust valve, as the load on exhaust valve is higher as compared to intake valve. The dimensions of the intake valve are given in Fig. 1.48.

## EXERCISES

1. At a full load testing of a tractor engine following results were obtained:
   Indicated power of engine = 30 kW
   Brake power of engine = 24 kw
   Fuel consumption of engine = 9.5 kg/h
   Amount of water circulated in radiator = 6.0 kg/min
   Inlet and outlet water temperatures = 20°C and 70°C respectively
   Exhaust gas calorimeter water circulation rate= 10 kg/min
   Inlet and outlet temperatures of water in calorimeter= 20°C & 70°C respectively
   Temperature of exhaust gas leaving calorimeter= 900°C
   Mean specific heat of exhaust gas = 1.05 kJ/kgK
   Air to fuel ratio of engine = 22:1
   Calorific value of fuel = 45000 kJ/kg
   Determine the mechanical and indicated thermal efficiencies. Also draw heat/energy balance for engine on kW and percentage basis.
2. During testing of a single cylinder engine following data were recorded:
   Fuel consumption = 12.5 kg/hr
   Calorific value of fuel = 43500 kJ/kg
   Amount of air used = 240 kg/h
   Engine speed = 2000 rpm
   Net brake torque = 275 Nm
   Exhaust gas temperature = 450°C
   Atmospheric temperature = 25°C
   Cooling water flow rate = 20 kg/min
   Rise in temperature of cooling water = 50°C
   Mean specific heat of exhaust gas = 1.015 kJ/kgK

Calculate the following:

*i*) Brake power

*ii*) Brake thermal efficiency

*iii*) Draw energy balance for the engine on kW basis

Draw a heat account in kJ/minute for a diesel oil engine using 10 kg/h of oil per hour having calorific value of 42500 kJ/kg. The engine develops 40 kW indicated power and 30 kW brake power. Jacket water was circulated at the rate of 9.5 kg/minute with temperature rise of 49°C.

**3.** A 4-stroke cycle diesel engine is developing mean effective pressure of 9.0 bars and developing power at the rate of 20 kW at 2000 rpm. Consider stroke bore ratio as 1.5. Calculate the bore and stroke of the engine.

**4.** A four stroke cycle, single cylinder diesel engine has 100 mm cylinder diameter and 150 mm stroke length. The engine is producing 30 kW indicated power at 2200 rpm. Find the mean effective pressure of the engine.

**5.** A four stroke cycle, 4 cylinder diesel engine has stroke bore ratio of 1.25. The engine is producing indicated power of 40 kW at 2000 rpm. The mean effective pressure recorded with an indicator was 10.0 bars. Find dimensions of engine.

**6.** A 4-stroke cycle, single cylinder diesel engine has a stroke bore ratio of 1.25. The piston displacement is 350 $cm^3$ and its compression ratio is 16:1. Calculate:

*i*) Cylinder diameter and length of stroke

*ii*) Swept volume of the engine

**7.** A 4-stroke cycle, four cylinder diesel engine of a tractor has cylinder diameter 100 mm and stroke length 130 mm. The speed of engine is 1800 rpm. Mean effective pressure of engine is 10 bars and mechanical efficiency is 85%. Calculate following for the engine:

*i*) Indicated power

*ii*) Brake power

**8.** A tractor is fitted with a four cylinder, 4-stroke cycle diesel engine. It is operating at a speed of 2000 rpm. If its cylinder diameter is 110 mm and stroke length is 140 mm, calculate:

*i*) Stroke bore ratio

*ii*) Piston speed

*iii*) Displacement volume

**9.** A 4-stroke cycle diesel engine has displacement volume of 18.75 litres and is working at 2000 rpm. It produces a torque of 1050 Nm. The mean indicated pressure in its cylinder is 9.5 bars. Calculate:

*i*) Indicated power

*ii*) Brake power

*iii*) Frictional power

**10.** A 4-stroke cycle diesel engine of a tractor has following details:

*i*) Number of cylinders = 4

*ii*) Cylinder diameter = 100 mm

*iii*) Stroke length = 150mm

*iv*) Compression ratio = 16:1

Determine the following:

*a*) Piston displacement

*b*) Displacement volume

*c*) Stroke bore ratio

*d*) Piston speed

**11.** A diesel engine of a tractor running at 1800 rpm develops a torque of 150 Nm. Calculate the brake power of the engine.

**12.** A 4-cylinder, 4-stroke cycle diesel engine of a tractor has a bore of 110 mm and stroke of 130 mm. The engine develops 42.5 kW brake power at 2200 rpm and consumes 9.5 l/hr diesel (specific gravity 0.86). If mechanical efficiency of the engine is 84% and calorific value of fuel is 42500 kJ/kg, calculate:

*i*) Indicated power of engine

*ii*) Mean effective pressure of engine

*iii*) Thermal efficiency of engine

**13.** A 4-cylinder, 4-stroke cycle diesel engine of a tractor has a bore of 98 mm and stroke of 120 mm and develops brake power of 37.5 kW at 2200 rpm. Calculate the following for the engine, if the mechanical efficiency is 85%

*i*) Mean effective pressure

*ii*) Brake power per unit of piston displacement

*iii*) Displacement volume.

**14.** Design a cylinder liner, cylinder head and studs for liner and cylinder cover made of cast iron for a vertical 4-stroke diesel engine which has following specifications:

(*i*) BHP : 10, RPM : 1000, I.M.E.P : 3.5 kg/cm$^2$, Mechanical Efficiency : 0.8

(*ii*) Assume any other data required.

**15.** Design aluminium alloy liner, head and piston for a 2-stroke cycle engine, which has the following specifications :

(*i*) BHP : 10, Maximum gas pressure: 80 kg/cm$^2$, B.M.E.P: 7.5 kg/cm$^2$

(*ii*) Speed : 500 rpm. Assume any other data needed

**16.** Design the thickness of a plain cylinder head for 300 mm cylinder. Maximum gas pressure is 32 kg/cm$^2$. Design the studs for cylinder cover.

**17.** Design a cast iron piston for a 4-cylinder tractor engine with following specifications:

(*i*) Cylinder bore: 100 mm, Stroke: 120 mm, Speed: 2200 rpm,

(*ii*) Maximum gas pressure: 50 kg/cm$^2$, B.M.E.P: 6.5 kg/cm$^2$,

(*iii*) Fuel consumption : 0.17 kg/BHP/hr. Assume any data required.

**18.** How many times the BHP of a tractor engine increases or decreases if the piston diameter is increased by 25% while all other parameters remain constant.

**19.** Calculate the average pressure in a 4-stroke cycle tractor engine with following specifications:

(*i*) Engine size : 100 × 120 mm

(*ii*) Engine speed : 2200 rpm

(*iii*) No. of cylinders : 3
(*iv*) BHP of Engine : 45
(*v*) Mechanical efficiency : 80%

**20.** A 2-stroke four cyiinder engine having bore diameter of 250 mm and stroke length 500 mm is working at 150 rpm. The mean effective pressure is 7 kg/cm$^2$. Its mechanical efficiency is 86%. Then calculate the following :

(*i*) IHP (*ii*) BHP and (*iii*) Stroke bore ratio.

**21.** An internal combustion engine is having a clearance volume of 40 cm$^3$. Its stroke length is 120 mm and bore diameter is 100 mm. Calculate the compression ratio of the engine.

**22.** Calculate the diameter of 2-stroke cycle internal combustion engine with following specifications:

(*i*) No. of cylinders : 2
(*ii*) Speed : 2000 rpm
(*iii*) Stroke bore ratio:1.5
(*iv*) Average gas pressure: 7 kg/cm$^2$
(*v*) IHP : 25

**23.** A four stroke cycle engine having stroke length of 100 mm is working on a compression ratio of 15:1. If volume displaced in one time is 1520 cc. Calculate the diameter of the piston.

**24.** Design a connecting rod and crank shaft for a 4-stroke petrol engine having following data :

(*i*) Piston dia : 100 mm
(*ii*) Stroke : 140 mm
(*iii*) Length of connecting rod (centre to centre) : 315 mm
(*iv*) Weight of reciprocating parts : 1.82 kgf
(*v*) Speed : 1500 rpm with possible overload: 2500 rpm
(*vi*) Compression ratio: 4:1
(*vii*) Maximum explosion pressure: 24.5 kg/cm$^2$
(*viii*) At maximum torque *i.e* 36°, the gas pressure: 9.75 kg/cm$^2$
(*ix*) Weight of fly wheel : 5450 kgf
(*x*) Total belt pull: 675 kgf
(*xi*) Assume suitable data required. If the intake valve has face angle of 30° and maximum head dia is 35.3 mm, the cam lift is 7.11 mm and stem diameter is 9.5 mm calculate the valve opening area also.

**25.** Design connecting rod for a 3 cylinder 4-stroke diesel engine of a 30 HP tractor with following specifications:

(*i*) Mechanical efficiency : 80%
(*ii*) Speed 1300 rpm with a possible over speed of 2500 rpm
(*iii*) Length of connecting rod: 300 mm
(*iv*) Weight of reciprocating parts: 2kgf
(*v*) Assume suitable data if required

**26.** Design a plain carbon steel crankshaft for 400 × 600 mm single acting 4-stroke cycle single cylinder engine operating at 200 rpm. The mean effective pressure is 4.5 kg/cm$^2$ and the maximum combustion pressure is 26.25 kg/cm$^2$. At maximum torque when crank is 36°, the gas pressure is 9.75 kg/cm$^2$. The ratio of connecting rod and crank radius is 4.8. The weight of fly wheel is 5450 kgf and is also used as pulley. The total belt pull is 675 kgf. Assume suitable missing data.

27. A 42.5 kW, 4-cylinder diesel engine of a tractor is running at an average speed of 2200 rpm. Design a flywheel for the engine if its speed is to vary upto ± 2.0% of average engine speed. Assume any other data if required.
28. Calculate the BHP developed in a 4 cylinder 15 × 25 cm engine with 2000 rpm and mean effective pressure of 30 kgf/cm$^2$ when operating as a
    (*a*) 2-stroke cycle engine
    (*b*) 4 stroke cycle engine.

CHAPTER 2

# Construction Materials for Tractor Components

## INTRODUCTION

Tractor and farm machine should be made out of correct easily workable, machinable, cheaper and locally available material and also minimum quantity of material should be consumed. The wearing parts of the tractor should be made of wear resistant material. The components of the tractor/machine should be made of corrosion resistant materials or protective coatings or treatments for vulnerable parts should be used. Proper choice of material of construction of tractor and its elements is a very crucial objective for the rational design of a tractor. It should be readily shaped, forged, welded, cast and should be easily machineable. It should be corrosion resistant and above all, the material of construction should be cheap and locally available. The material of construction of engine components and different systems of agricultural tractor is reported in Table 2.1.

## 2.1 CONSTRUCTIONAL DETAILS OF DIFFERENT COMPONENTS OF TRACTOR

**TABLE 2.1: Material of construction of different components of tractor**

| System/Part | Material | Composition/properties | Heat Treatment |
|---|---|---|---|
| **Engine components** | | | |
| Cylinder block | Grey cast iron, iron alloy with nickel or chromium or cast aluminum, or welded steel | | Casting |
| Cylinder liner | Closed grain cast iron or nickel cast iron, or cast steel | Ni = 2%, Cr = 0.65% | Casting, induction hardening, quenching, chrome plating. |
| Cylinder head | Cast iron or grey iron, or aluminum alloy or alloy steel | | Casting |
| Cylinder head gasket | Copper and asbestos or steel and asbestos | | |
| Piston | Aluminum alloy or cast iron or semi steel | | Casting |
| Piston rings | Grey cast iron, or pressed alloy steel, | Some times rings are plated with cadmium, tin or chromium | Casting and plating |

*Continued...*

*(Continued...* **TABLE 2.1)**

| System/Part | Material | Composition/properties | Heat Treatment |
|---|---|---|---|
| Piston pin | Alloy steel, forged steel or aluminum alloy | | Casehardening, forging |
| Connecting rod | Alloy steel or aluminum alloy | | Drop forging |
| Big end bearing | Steel backed copper lead or steel backed cadmium silver or bronze or white metal | | |
| Crank shaft | Heat treated alloy steel | | Casting or forging, Induction hardening |
| Main bearings | White metal, steel backed Babbitt base | | |
| Valves | Special alloy steels or forged steel | With relatively high percentage of chromium, nickel and chromium | Forging |
| Valve seat | Wear resistant alloy steel | | |
| Valve guide | Grey cast iron | | |
| Valve spring | High grade spring steel wire | | |
| Camshaft | Alloy steel or chilled cast iron | | |
| Push rod | Forged steel | | Drop forging, casting |
| Crankcase | Cast iron or welded steel | | Forging |
| Manifolds | Cast iron or cast aluminum | | Casting |
| Studs and bolts | Carbon steel | | Casting |
| Gaskets | Copper and asbestos or cork | C = 0.4%, Cr = 1.0% | Quenching and tempering |
| Fly wheel | Cast iron | | Casting |
| Timing gears | Cast iron or forged steel | | Case carburizing, hardening and tempering |
| **Castings and housings (For tractors less than 60 HP)** | | | |
| 1. Transmission gear housing<br>2. Differential housing<br>3. Engine crank case | Graded cast iron<br>Grade-20<br>Grade-25 | TS, CS and SS of different grades of cast iron are:<br>20 kg/mm$^2$, 72kg/mm$^2$, 23 kg/mm$^2$ | Casting |

*Continued...*

**(Continued... TABLE 2.1)**

| System/Part | Material | Composition/properties | Heat Treatment |
|---|---|---|---|
| 4. Axle housing | Grade-30 | 25 kg/mm$^2$, 85 kg/mm$^2$, 29 kg/mm$^2$<br>30 kg/mm$^2$, 95 kg/mm$^2$, 34.5 kg/mm$^2$<br>For making graded cast iron Ferro-chrome and Ferro-silicon are added to molten metal *e.g.* for 25 grade cast iron: A type carbon flakes with size >4 as per ASTM, Pearlite >90% and maximum 10% Ferrite | |
| **Castings and housings (For tractors of 60 HP and above)** | | | |
| 1. Axle housings<br>2. Axle hubs<br>3. Differential housings | Spheroidal Graphite-iron<br>SG 400/2<br>SG 500/7 | TS, Elongation, Hardness (B) and Matrix are: 40kg/mm$^2$, 12%, 201 Max, Ferrite 50 kg/mm$^2$, 7%, 170–241, Ferrite and Pearlite | Casting |
| **Gears** | | | |
| Crown wheels and Tail pinions | En 353 steel | C = 0.18–0.23%,<br>Cr = 0.4–0.6%,<br>Ni = 0.4–0.7%,<br>Mn = 0.7–0.9%,<br>Mo = 0.15–0.25%,<br>Si = 0.1–0.35% | Case carburizing, hardening and tempering |
| Other transmission gears | SAE-8620 steel | C = 0.17–0.20%,<br>Cr = 0.75–0.25%,<br>Ni = 1.0–1.5%,<br>Mn = 0.5–1.0%,<br>Mo = 0.08–0.15%,<br>Si = 0.1–0.35%, | Case carburizing, hardening and tempering |
| | 20 Mn Cr 1 steel | C = 0.17–0.22%,<br>Cr = 1.0–1.3%,<br>Mn = 1.0–1.45%,<br>Si = 0.1–0.35% | |

*Continued...*

*(Continued...* **TABLE 2.1)**

| System/Part | Material | Composition/properties | Heat Treatment |
|---|---|---|---|
| Shafts with fixed gear trains | C-45 grade plain Carbon steel | C = 0.4–0.5%, Mn = 0.6–0.9, | Toughened, Hardness after toughening = 30–34 Rc, Induction hardening, Hardness after induction hardening 50–54 Rc |
| Shafts on which moving or shifting gears used | SAE 8620 steel or | C = 0.17–0.20%, Cr = 0.75–0.25%, Ni = 1.0–1.5%, Mn = 0.5–1.0%, Mo = 0.08–0.15%, Si = 0.1–0.35% | Case carburization and Case hardening |
| | 20 Mn Cr 1 steel | C = 0.17–0.22%, Cr = 1.0–1.3%, Mn = 1.0–1.45%, Si = 0.1–0.35% | -do- |
| Axle shafts | C-45 grade plain Carbon steel | C = 0.4–0.5%, Mn = 0.6–0.9 | Toughening and case hardening, Hardness after toughening = 30–34 Rc, Hardness after induction hardening 50–54 Rc |
| | 40 Cr 1 steel | C = 0.35–0.45, Cr = 0.9–1.2% Mn = 0.6–0.9% | Toughening and case hardening. Hardness after toughening = 30–34 Rc, Hardness after induction hardening 52–56 Rc |
| **Structural parts of tractor** | | | |
| Structural parts | M.S angles, M.S. plates or structural steel<br>Fe 410 WA steel | C = C = 0.25 + 0.03%, Mn = 1.6%, S = 0.055%, P = 0.055% | Weldable M.S. steel<br>Rolled and weldable quality |

*Continued...*

*(Continued...* **TABLE 2.1)**

| System/Part | Material | Composition/properties | Heat Treatment |
|---|---|---|---|
| | Fe 410 WB steel | C = 0.22 +0.03%, Mn = 1.6%, S = 0.05%, P= 0.04%, Si = 0.04% | Rolled and weldable quality |
| | ST-42 W | C = 0.2 +0.03%, Mn = 1.6%, S = 0.05+ 0.005%, P = 0.055+0.005% | Rolled and weldable quality |
| **Sheet Metal Components** | | | |
| Components not providing aesthetic look | Hot Rolled Sheets | | Derusting and painting |
| Components providing aesthetic look | Cold Rolled Sheets | Controlled carbon 0.13% | Degreasing and Phosphated to get surface suitable for painting |
| **Plastic Parts** | | | |
| Battery tray | Plastic | Excellent corrosion resistance and long life | Forming or moulding |
| Battery Covers | Plastic | -do- | -do- |
| Dash-Boards | Plastic | -do- | -do- |
| **Rubber Parts** | | | |
| Cushioning of sheet metal parts and Grommets in wiring | Butyl Rubber | Weather resistant, oil resistant and does not crack over period of time. It does not give smell | |
| **Miscellaneous parts** | | | |
| Fasteners (Nut/bolts) | Class 8.8 and | For normal applications with C = 0.4% | Quenching and tempering heat treated to get 22–28 Rc |
| Link pins | Class 10.9 | Severe applications with C = 0.4%, Cr = 1.0% | Quenching and tempering heat treated to get 30–36 Rc |
| | Medium carbon steel | C = 0.35–0.6% high resistance to shearing and bending | 26–30 Rc |

**TABLE 2.2: Details of important components/assemblies of agricultural tractor**

| Sr. No. | Name of component | Diagram/photo | Main features |
|---|---|---|---|
| 1. | Engine block | <br>(a) Single cylinder (b) Four cylinders<br>Engine blocks of IC engines | Engine block is an individual or monoblock grey cast iron or aluminium alloy casting construction, which houses the engine cylinders, where combustion of fuel takes place for the development of power. In the block, around the cylinders there are passages for circulation of cooling water. Oil passages are also drilled in the block for carrying the lubricating oil to various engine components for lubrication. At the top of block, cylinder head is attached which houses valves and fuel injectors. On the lower end of the block crankcase is provided which has a no. of bearings to support the crank shaft known as main bearings. |
| 2. | Cylinder head | 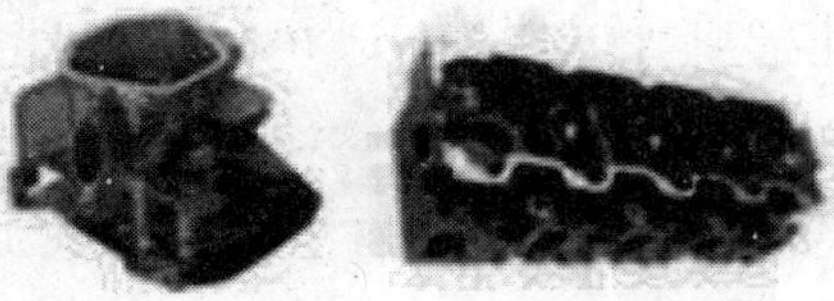<br>(a) Single cylinder (b) Multi cylinders<br>Cylinder heads | Cylinder head is a cast iron or aluminium alloy construction fitted to the engine block at the top with the help of studs. Gasket is provided between the cylinder head and block for leak proof/gas tight joint. It forms a gas tight combustion chamber above each cylinder. Valve openings with complete valve operating mechanism are provided in the cylinder head. It also contains water jackets. Fuel injectors are fitted in the cylinder head for injection of diesel fuel as per firing order of engine. |
| 3. | Cylinder liners | <br>(a) Dry cylinder liners (b) Wet cylinder liners<br>Cylinder liners of IC engines | These are replaceable type special alloy casting barrel having flange at the top fit in the groove and to keep in position. These are further hardened by nitriding or chromium plating to improve resistance to corrosion & wear. Liners are dry type or wet type . Dry liner's outer surface bears against the inside surface of cylinder block casting while, the outer surface of wet liner is in direct contact with cooling water. Water tight leak proof joints between liner & block by using packing rings of synthetic rubber are provided. |
| 4. | Valves | <br>(a) Valves (b) Valves in cylinder head of engine<br>Inlet & exhaust valves of IC engines | Valves allow admission of air or air-fuel mixture in the engine cylinder and force the exhaust gases at correct timings. Generally poppet valve or mushroom valve being simple in construction and better sealing efficiency are used. Inlet valves are made of silico-chrome steel, while, exhaust valves are made from silico-chrome steel with moly-bdenum. The stems are chromium plated to make them wear resistant. Inlet valves are larger than exhaust valves. |

*Continued...*

(*Continued....*TABLE 2.2)

| Sr. No. | Name of component | Diagram/photo | Main features |
|---|---|---|---|
| 5. | Piston |  Pistons of IC engines | Piston is a light weight specially shaped strong & durable cast iron, steel or aluminium alloy with high thermal conductivity construction. Its head or crown should form desired shape of combustion chamber in cylinder with the help of cylinder head. Piston forms a seal in the combustion chamber and transmits the force of explosion due to burning of fuel to the crank shaft. It serves as a guide & bearing for small end of connecting rod. Ring grooves of appropriate size for compression & oil rings are provided on the piston, which seals the compression & lubricate cylinder walls. |
| 6. | Piston rings | 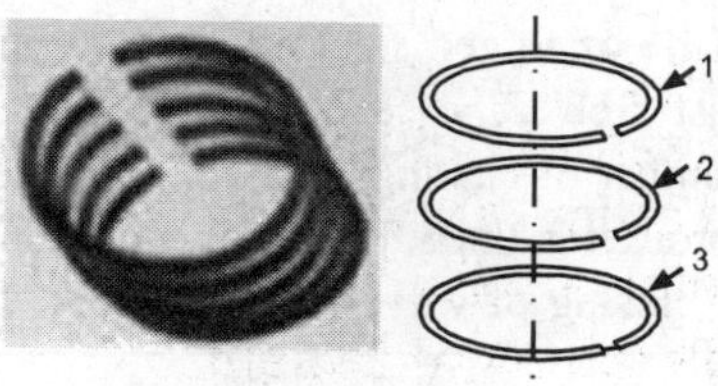  Piston rings | Piston rings are individually cast & properly machined to exert uniform pressure against the cylinder wall. A gap is provided in the rings for easy fitting on the piston and gap is almost closed when piston is in the cylinder. There are two types of rings *i.e.* compression ring & oil ring. Main function of compression ring is to seal high gas pressure in the combustion chamber against leakage and to dissipate heat from piston crown to the cylinder wall & controlling oil. Oil ring maintains a thin oil film on cylinder walls to minimize ring & cylinder wear and help in heat dissipation. These are made from fine grain alloy cast iron having silicon & mangenese, alloy steel, stainless steel. Generally three rings out of which one is oil ring are used. |
| 7. | Piston pin |  Piston pin or gudgeon pin | Piston pin or gudgeon pin connects the piston with small end of connecting rod. It is floating type pin which passes through the bosses of piston and bush of small end. It is generally hollow type pin made of case hardened steel. |
| 8. | Connecting rod |  Connecting rod | It is drop forged 'I' section generally made from steel or duralumin which converts the reciprocating motion of piston into rotary motion of crank shaft. Small end of CR generally has solid eye for holding the piston pin and is connected to the piston. Big end is connected to crank pin and is always split. A hole is drilled between two ends of connecting rod to carry lubricating oil from big end to small end for lubrication of piston pin & piston. |
| 9. | CR bearings | 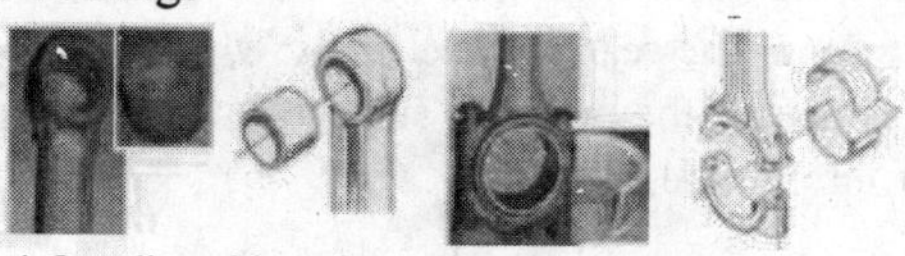 (a) Small end bearing (b) Big end bearing<br>Connecting rod bearings | **Small end bearing**: In the solid eye type small end bush is used for holding piston pin.<br>**Big end bearing:** It is split type made from babbitt metal which fits the crank shaft. Big end of connecting rod is attached to the crank pin through the split bearing. |

*Continued...*

(*Continued....*TABLE 2.2)

| Sr. No. | Name of component | Diagram/photo | Main features |
|---|---|---|---|
| 10. | Crank shaft |  (a) Single cylinder  (b) Four cylinder Crank shafts of IC engines | It is special type of shaft which converts to and for motion of piston into rotary motion. The engine power is received by this shaft through CR for further transmission to clutch, gear box, differential and finally to rear wheels. On front end of this shaft timing gear is fitted, while, on the rear end fly wheel is mounted which balances the engine. Crank shaft is made by casting or drop forging of steel, steel alloys. It is supported in main bearings in lower portion of engine block. |
| 11. | Cam shaft |  (a) For single cylinder 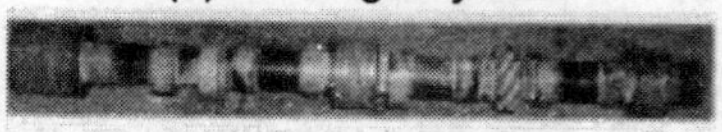 (b) For four cylinders Camshafts of IC engines | It is a shaft which consists of a number of cams at appropriate position as integral part for opening/ closing of valves as per timings of engine. It is made of forged steel alloy or chromium alloy steel, cast iron & case hardened. It is supported in a number of bearings and on its front end timing gear/ sprocket is fitted. Throw of cams controls the opening & closing of valves. |
| 12. | Timing gear |  Timing gears of engine | The drive from crankshaft to cam shaft is either a chain or a gear drive. Gear that drives the cam shaft for operation of valves at correct times. Timing gears are generally made of cast iron, steel, aluminium or laminated fibre. The timing gears of engine must be in the ratio of 2:1. |
| 13. | Injector | 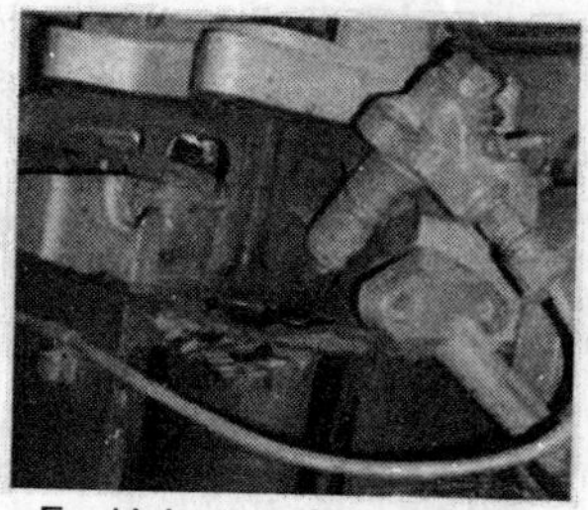 Fuel injector of IC engine | It is a part of fuel injection mechanism which injects metered amount of fuel in fine spray form according to load and speed in IC engine cylinder. Nozzles are made of high quality steel. Generally two types of nozzles namely multi hole nozzle or single hole pintel type of nozzle are used. Multi hole nozzle is mostly used in DI engines, while, single hole pintel nozzle is used in diesel engine with divided combustion chambers. |
| 14. | Fly wheel |  Flywheel of IC engine | It is usually a cast iron wheel that acts as energy accumulator to provide uniform motion to engine by inertia and to balance the rotating masses. It carries a ring gear that meshes with pinion of starting motor. The rear surface of fly wheel is used to serve as one of the pressure surface for the engagement of clutch plate. |

*Continued...*

(*Continued*....TABLE 2.2)

| Sr. No. | Name of component | Diagram/photo | Main features |
|---|---|---|---|
| 15. | Transmission gear box | <br>(a) Sliding type gear box<br>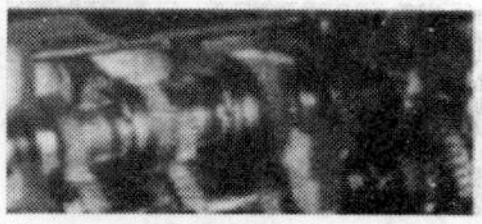<br>(b) Constant mesh gear box<br>Transmission gear box of tractor | Sliding gear box is simplest type of gear transmission where desired speed ratios are obtained with the movement of gear lever. The lever slides the selected gears on to their shafts. It is very efficient *i.e.* highest transmission efficiency.<br>Constant mesh gear box is basic and simple type transmission where all the pairs of helical gears on main and counter shafts are always in mesh and do not move on their shafts. The gears are engaged/ disengaged by splined sleeve couplings with a gear lever. |
| 16. | Transmission gears | 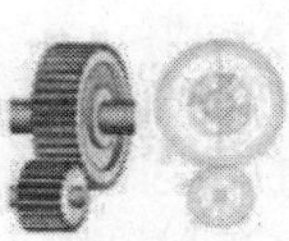<br>(a) Spur gear<br>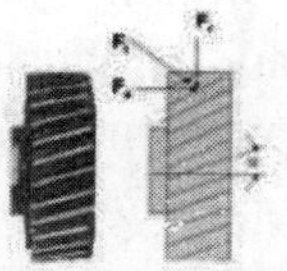<br>(b) Helical gear<br><br>(c) Bevel gear<br>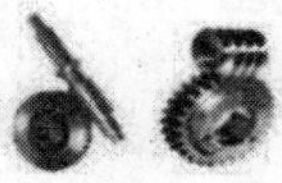<br>(d) Worm gear<br>Different types of gears used in tractor | Gear is toothed wheel which meshes with another part for transmission of power. Spur gears transmit power between parallel shafts at a constant angular velocity ratio, while in spiral gears the teeth are cut in the form of helix on their pitch cylinders. These can be used to transmit power between both parallel and non-parallel shafts. Bevel gears are pair of gears used to connect two shafts whose axes intersect. The teeth may be straight or spiraled with respect to cone element. Worm gears are widely used to transmit power at high velocity ratio between non-intersecting shafts but not necessarily at right angles. |
| 17. | Transmission shafts | <br>Transmission shafts of tractor | Shafts of appropriate diameter of adequate strength & rigidity are used to transmit engine power to various outlets in the tractor under various operations and loading conditions. These are usually circular in cross section and are subjected to torsion, bending and axial loads. Shafts are made of C-45 grade plain carbon steel and steel alloys. |
| 18. | Bearings | 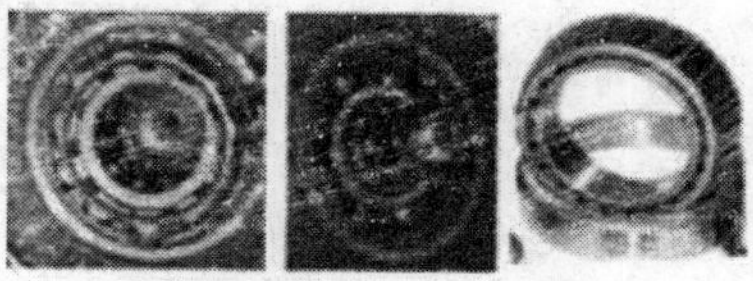<br>Different types of bearings | Bearing is the support or carrier for a rotating shaft which has capability of reducing friction effectively. Journal bearing, ball bearing, roller or taper roller bearings are commonly used. Antifriction & white metals, brass, gun metal and various alloys are used in the bearings. |
| 19. | Fasteners | <br>Fasteners/Nuts & bolts | Fasteners like through bolts, stud bolts, cap screws, machine screws and set screws are used for joining two separate parts of a machine elements & structures. Heads of bolts are hexagonal in shape, while, nuts are commonly square or hexagonal shapes having internal threads. |

CHAPTER 3

# Air Fuel Supply System of Tractor

## INTRODUCTION

In internal combustion diesel engines for development of power, clean air must be compressed in the engine cylinder up to self-ignition temperature of diesel fuel and correct amount of fuel must be injected in the engine cylinder at correct time. Diesel fuel must be injected into cylinder at appropriate rate against the compression pressure of air and it must be mixed with air and vapourized. Clean air as well as clean fuel is necessary for satisfactory working of tractor engine as it has to work under dusty conditions in the field. Function of air fuel supply system is to provide clean air during suction strokes of engine cylinder and to supply/inject fuel to engine cylinder in atomized form at very high pressure according to operating conditions. This system is composed of pre-cleaner, air cleaner, diesel tank, strainer, fuel feed pump, fuel filters (primary and secondary), fuel injection pump, injection nozzle etc. Air-fuel supply system of tractor and its schematic representation is depicted in Fig.3.1.

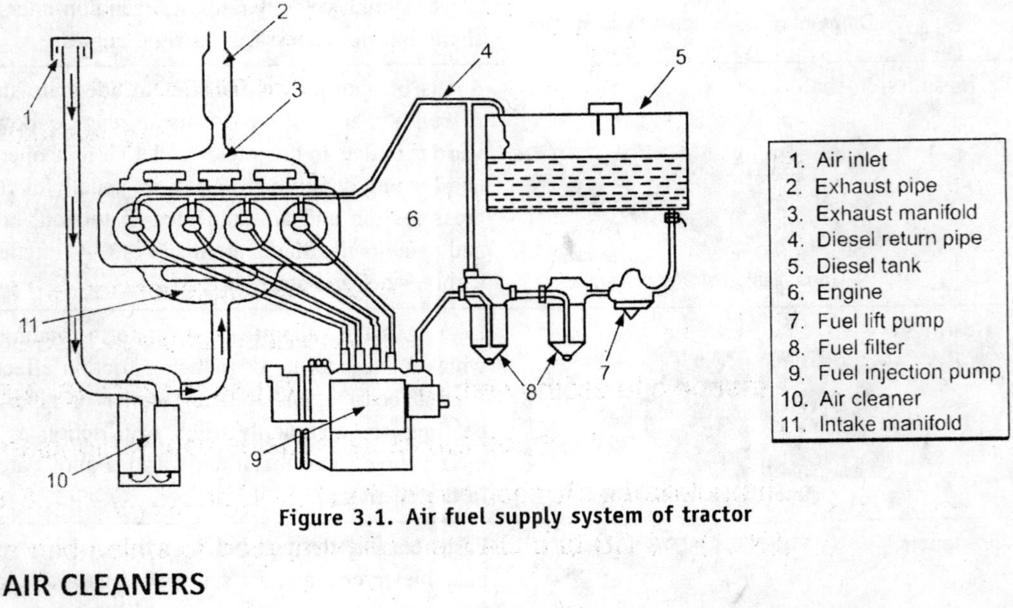


**Figure 3.1. Air fuel supply system of tractor**

## 3.1 AIR CLEANERS

For satisfactory performance and long life of engine, air cleaner is very essential. It must remove all dust effectively from large volume of incoming air required by an engine for combustion of fuel and development of power. In almost all cases, pre-cleaners are used to partially clean the incoming air.

Use of pre-cleaner reduce the dust load on main cleaner and thus improves its efficiency and service life. Generally pre-cleaner removes 90% or more dust from the incoming air in an I. C. engine. Main factor in the design of air cleaner is maximum air flow through it.

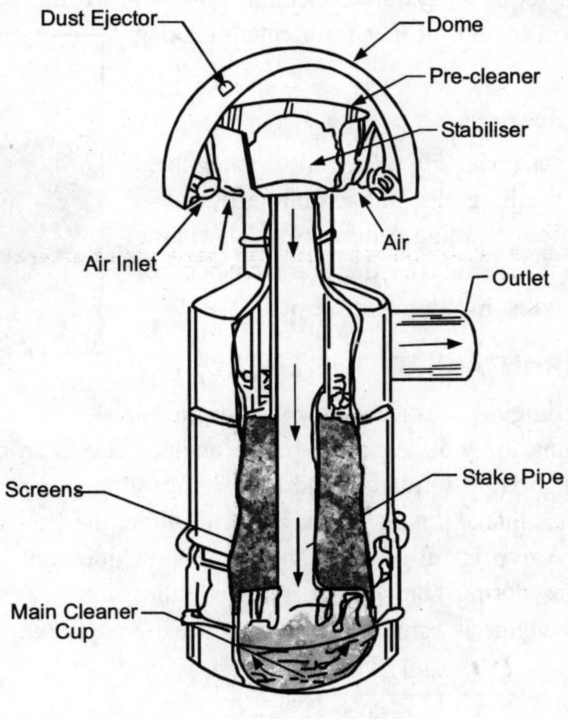


**Figure 3.2. Oil bath air cleaner**

Main features of an ideal air cleaner are:

- Simple in design
- Lower cost
- Higher dust removal efficiency
- Compact in size
- Lower resistance to air flow
- Longer life (durability)
- Should be able to reduce noise of intake air
- Minimum repair and maintenance requirements and
- Should be able to suppress back fire from the engine

There are two types of air cleaners *i.e.* (*i*) Oil bath type and (*ii*) dry type.

## 3.1.1. Oil Bath Type Air Cleaner

Details of oil bath type of air cleaner are furnished in Fig. 3.2. It has got a bowl type container filled with mobile oil (the same oil which is used in lubrication system) and above it, a strainer is placed. The air enters into the air cleaner through pre-cleaner where majority (90%) of dirt/dust is removed. Then the air enters the oil bath/ oil filled in the bowl where dust particles are caught by the oil as it makes a sharp 180° turn. Then the air passes through oil saturated screen which further removes finer dust particles from the air and only clean air enters the engine cylinder. Oil bath type air cleaners require periodical cleaning of oil bowl and screen. Optimum oil level should also be maintained in the air cleaner for greater cleaning efficiency of air cleaner.

### 3.1.2. Dry Type Air Cleaner

In dry type air cleaner (refer Fig 3.3), resin-impregnated paper element is used for cleaning air. This is quite efficient in dust removal. It maintains air cleaning efficiency at all engine speeds. It must be handled carefully as there are chances of cracks or development of holes in the paper element.

**Figure 3.3. Dry type air cleaner**

## 3.2 QUANTITY OF AIR INTAKE BY THE ENGINE

In an internal combustion engine, fresh charge of air is to be introduced for accomplishing the working cycle of the engine. The fresh charge of air should have desired velocity for proper mixture formation and high combustion rate in the combustion chamber. In four stroke engines the air intake duct is so shaped as to direct the flow of fresh air at appropriate speed (50–130 m/s when valve is fully open) and its motion does not stop after admission into cylinder rather it intensifies during compression. The amount of air admission in the combustion chamber of 4-stroke cycle engine is estimated by the following equation.

$$W_a = \frac{C_a \times n \times V_s \times N}{2 \times \rho_a \times 60} \quad ...(3.1)$$

where, $W_a$ = quantity of air entered in the engine, kg/s
$C_a$ = coefficient of air admission in engine cylinder (0.8–0.9 for diesel engines)
$n$ = number of cylinders
$V_s$ = piston displacement (swept volume), $m^3$
$N$ = crankshaft speed, rpm
$\rho_a$ = density of air entering the cylinder, $kg/m^3$

The quantity of air intake by the engine by volume is given by

$$V_a = \frac{C_a \times n \times V_s \times N}{2 \times 60} \quad ...(3.2)$$

where, $V_a$ = volume of air entered in the engine, $m^3/s$.

Or alternatively,

$$V_a = \frac{n \times V_s \times N \times \eta_v}{1.2 \times 10^5} \quad ...(3.3)$$

where, $V_a$ = volume of air entered in the engine, $m^3/s$
$V_s$ = displacement volume, litres
$n$ = number of cylinders
$N$ = crankshaft speed, rpm
$\eta_v$ = volumetric efficiency (generally 85–90% for diesel engines)

**EXAMPLE 3.1** *A 3-cylinder diesel engine of a tractor, having 100 mm cylinder diameter, and 100 mm stroke running at 1600 rpm has air to fuel ratio of 14.5:1. Assuming that coefficient of air admission in the engine is 0.85, calculate the quantity of air and fuel supplied to engine per minute. Assume that density of air at intake is 1.209 kg/m³.*

**SOLUTION:**

$n = 3$

$N = 1600$ rpm

$D = 100$ mm

$L = 100$ mm

$C_a = 0.8$

A/F = 14.5:1

We know that

Swept volume or piston displacement

$$(V_s) = (\pi/4)\, d^2 \times L$$

$$\therefore \quad = (\pi/4) \times 10 \times 10 \times 10$$

$$= 785 \text{ cc or } 7.85 \times 10^{-4} \text{ m}^3$$

Now, using equ. 3.1 and putting the values, we get

$$W_a = \frac{0.85 \times 3 \times 7.85 \times 10^{-4} \times 1600}{2 \times 1.209 \times 60}$$

$$= 0.032 \text{ kg/s or } 1.94 \text{ kg/min}$$

Also, we know that

A/F = 14.5 : 1

$$\therefore \quad W_f = W_a / 14.5 = 1.94/14.5$$

$$= 0.134 \text{ kg per minute.}$$

Thus, the quantity of air and fuel supplied per minute is 1.94 and 0.134 kg respectively.

## 3.3 COMBUSTION OF DIESEL FUEL

### 3.3.1. Air Fuel Ratio Based on Chemical Combustion Equation

Atmospheric air contains 23% oxygen and 77% nitrogen by weight and 21% oxygen and 79% nitrogen by volume. By knowing composition of hydrocarbon fuels and carbon, hydrogen and other constituents present in the air, the amount of air required for complete combustion of fuel can be determined. For example the combustion equation for diesel fuel ($C_{16} H_{34}$) is given below.

$$C_{16}H_{34} + 24.5\ O_2 + 92.12\ N_2 \rightarrow 16\ CO_2 + 17\ H_2O + 92.12\ N_2 \quad ...(3.4)$$

Now, convert eqn. 3.4 chemical combustion equation to mass units by multiplying the number of atoms by their atomic weights.

We get,

$$1\,(226) + 24.5(32) + 92.12(28) \rightarrow 16(44) + 17(18) + 92.12(28) \quad ...(3.5)$$

$$226 + 784 + 2579.36 \rightarrow 704 + 306 + 2579.36 \quad ...(3.6)$$

Dividing the eq. 3.6 by 226, we get

$$1 + 3.47 + 11.413 \rightarrow 3.115 + 1.354 + 11.413 \quad ...(3.7)$$

From combustion eqn. 3.5 of diesel fuel, it is clear that when one mole of fuel is burnt with 24.5 moles of oxygen accompanied with 92.12 moles of nitrogen in the air, 16 moles of carbon dioxide and 17 molecules of water are produced. Chemically air to fuel ratio of diesel fuel is given by

$$A/F = (\text{Weight of } O_2 + \text{Weight of } N_2)/\text{Weight of fuel}$$

$$= (3.47 \text{ kg} + 11.413 \text{ kg})/1 \text{ kg} = 14.46{:}1$$

It is clear from above analysis that about 14.46 kg of air is needed for stoichiometric combustion of 1 kg of diesel (Cetane). It is also clear that one kg of diesel burnt releases about 3.2 kg of $CO_2$ and almost 1.35 kg of water ($H_2O$).Similarly, air to fuel ratio of other fuels can be calculated.

Generalized form of combustion equation for hydrocarbon fuels is given below, which can be used for estimation of air to fuel ratio, less or excess amount of air required for combustion of fuels and quantities of exhaust products of the engine.

$$C_mH_n + (m + n/4)O_2 + 3.76\,(m + n/4)N_2 \rightarrow m\,CO_2 + n/2H_2O + 3.76\,(m + n/4)\,N_2 \quad ...(3.8)$$

But, most fuel combustion system operate with excess air to ensure that virtually whole amount of fuel is burnt completely. So, combustion of any fuel whose constituents are known can be analyzed by assuming complete combustion. But, in actual practice combustion is never quite complete.

Theoretical weight of air required per kg of fuel for complete combustion is given by

$$W_a = 100/23\ [\ (8/3\ C + 8H_2 + S)–O_2] \quad ...(3.9)$$

Theoretical volume of air required for combustion of 1 kg of fuel

$$V_{th} = 100/20.9\ [\ C/12 + H_2/4–O_2/32\ ] \quad ...(3.10)$$

Weight of Carbon produced per kg of exhaust gas is given by

$$W_c = [3/11\ CO_2 + 3/7\ CO)],\ \text{kg} \quad ...(3.11)$$

**EXAMPLE 3.2** *An engine of tractor burns diesel ($C_{16}H_{34}$) with 10% excess air and develops* 30 kW *with 24% thermal efficiency based on higher heating value of fuel. Calculate*

*(i) the fuel feed rate to engine*

*(ii) the air-fuel ratio*

*(iii) the quantity of air flow rate in the engine*

*(iv) Volumetric composition of exhaust dry gases.*

**SOLUTION:**

**(*a*) Fuel feed rate to the engine**

Fuel used = diesel ($H_{16}H_{34}$)

Power developed by the engine: =30 kW

Thermal efficiency of engine = 24%

Now, higher heating value of diesel fuel = 47261 kJ/kg (we know)

Now, amount of fuel used to develop 30 kW at a efficiency of 24%

$$m_f \text{ (kg/s)} = \text{Power (kW)}/(\eta_t \times \text{HHV (kJ/kg)} \qquad \text{(as 1 kJ = 1 kW-s)}$$

$$= 30 \text{ kW}/\ (0.24 \times 47261 \text{ kJ/kg})$$

$$= 0.002645 \text{ kg/s or } 2.645 \text{ g/s}$$

**Ans.**

Therefore, fuel flow rate in the engine is 2.645 g/s.

**(b) Air fuel ratio of engine**

Writing combustion equation for diesel fuel we get,

$$C_{16}H_{34} + 24.5\ O_2 + 92.12\ N_2 \rightarrow 16\ CO_2 + 17\ H_2O + 92.12\ N_2 \qquad \text{...(3.12)}$$

Since, 10% excess air is used in the engine, the combustion equation would be modified as given below.

$$C_{16}H_{34} + 24.5\ O_2 + 2.45\ O_2 + 92.12\ N_2 + 9.212N_2$$

$$\rightarrow 16\ CO_2 + 17\ H_2O + 92.12\ N_2 + 9.212\ N_2 + 2.45\ O_2 \qquad \text{...(3.13)}$$

Eqn. 3.13 is all balanced with excess air.

or, $$C_{16}H_{34} + 26.95\ O_2 + 101.332\ N_2$$

$$\rightarrow 16\ CO_2 + 17\ H_2O + 101.332\ N_2 + 2.45\ O_2 \qquad \text{...(3.14)}$$

Now, combining $O_2$ and $N_2$ which is called as air together, we get

$$C_{16}H_{34} + 128.282 \text{ air} \rightarrow 16\ CO_2 + 17\ H_2O + 101.332\ N_2 + 2.45\ O_2 \qquad \text{...(3.15)}$$

The molecular weight of diesel (Cetane) is 12 × 16 + 1 × 34 = 226.

Now using combustion eqn. 3.15, the air fuel ratio is estimated as under:

$$\text{A/F} = \frac{128.282 \text{ k mol of air} \times 28.967 \text{ kg per k mol of air}}{1 \text{ k mol of cetane} \times 226 \text{ kg per k mol of cetane}}$$

$$\text{A/F} = 16.44\text{kg of air/kg of diesel or } 16.44:1$$

**(c) Quantity of air flow rate in engine**

In order to burn a mole of diesel fuel, volume of dry air required is given by

$$V = \text{mRT/P} \qquad \text{...(3.16)}$$

$$= (128.282 \text{ k mol of air/k mol of cetane}) \times (8.3143 \text{ kN-m/k mol of air}) \times 308°\text{K}/101.3 \text{ kN/m}^2)$$

$$= 3242.9 \text{ m}^3\text{/k mol of air}$$

Now, 226 kg/k mol of cetane fuel may be taken as 226 g/g mol of fuel.

Since, the fuel flow rate in the engine is 2.64 g/s which may be converted in g mol of fuel as under

$$m_f = (2.64\text{g of fuel/s})/(\ 226 \text{ g/g mol fuel}) = 0.00117 \text{ g mol/s}$$

Multiplying fuel flow rate with volume of dry air needed as calculated by eqn. 3.16,

We get, $V_a = (0.00117 \text{ g mol fuel/s}) \times (3242.9 \text{ m}^3\text{/k mol of fuel})/(1000 \text{ g mol/k mol of fuel})$

$= 3.794 \times 10^{-3} \text{ m}^3\text{/s}$ or about 3.8 litres per second.

**(d) Volumetric composition of dry combustion gases**

From combustion eqn. 3.15, it is clear that

| | | |
|---|---|---|
| 16 mols of $CO_2$ | = 16/119.782 | = 13.36% of $CO_2$ |
| 101.332 mols of $N_2$ | = 101.332/119.782 | = 84.597% $N_2$ |
| 2.45 mols of $O_2$ | = 2.45/119.782 | = 2.05% $O_2$ |
| 119.782 mols total | | 100.0% |

## 3.4 PRINCIPLE REQUIREMENTS OF FUEL SUPPLY SYSTEM

The principle requirements of fuel supply system are:

1. To supply the correct fuel charge to each cylinder according to load and speed.
2. To inject fuel at correct time in cylinder.
3. To facilitate efficient fuel utilization by atomizing the charge at the time of injection.
4. It should not be subjected to undue wear or require frequent adjustment and servicing.

The fuel injection system of a diesel engine is given in Fig. 3.4 and the parts of the same is given in Fig. 3.5.

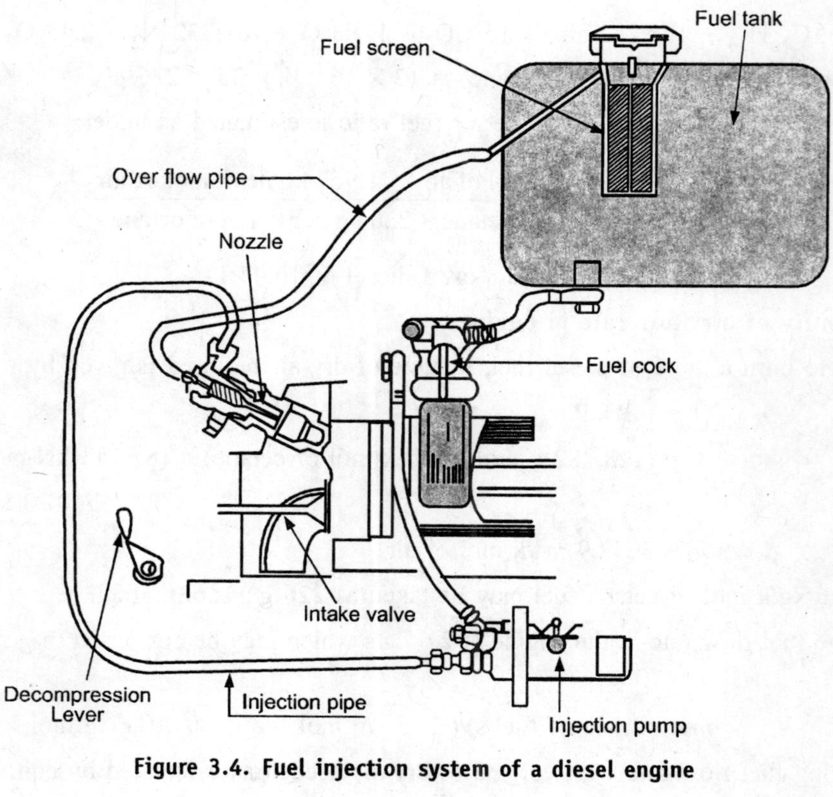


**Figure 3.4. Fuel injection system of a diesel engine**

| | | | |
|---|---|---|---|
| 1. | Fuel cock | 2. | Fuel filter primary |
| 3. | Fuel filter secondary | 4. | Filter air bleed screw |
| 5. | F.I Pump | 6. | Bled tap |
| 7. | High pressure pipes | 8. | Exhaust manifold |
| 9. | Fuel feed pump | 10. | Hand primer |

**Figure 3.5. Parts of fuel injection system of a tractor**

## 3.5 TYPES OF FUEL INJECTION PUMPS

The main function of fuel injection pump is to supply fuel at required pressure in metered quantity according to power and speed and at correct time *i.e.* 27° before compression at TDC, though the exact timing of fuel injection differs from engine to engine. The constructional details of a fuel injection pump is given in Fig. 3.6.

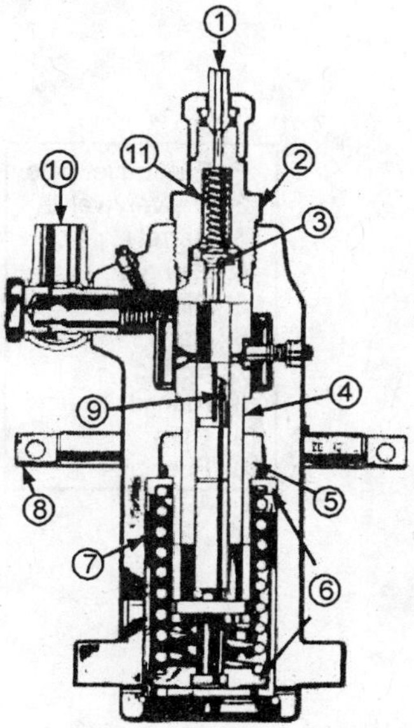


| | |
|---|---|
| 1. | Fuel outlet to nozzle |
| 2. | Delivery valve holder |
| 3. | Delivery valve assembly |
| 4. | Sleeve |
| 5. | Toothed control sleeve |
| 6. | Spring seats |
| 7. | Return spring |
| 8. | Control Rack |
| 9. | Pump element |
| 10. | Fuel Inlet |
| 11. | Delivery valve spring |

**Figure 3.6. Constructional details of fuel injection pump**

Main types of fuel injection pumps are:

1. Individual or in-line injection pump
2. Distributor type fuel injection system

### 3.5.1. Individual or In-Line Injection Pump

It is constant stroke, lapped plunger type pump operated by cam (timed and metered type). Individual or in-line injection pump is given in Fig. 3.7.

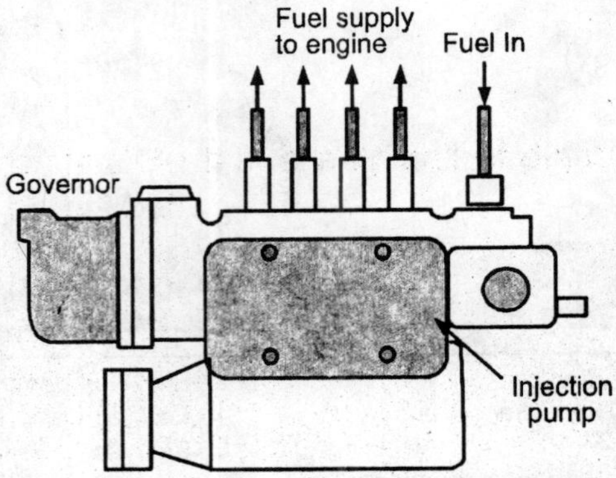


**Figure 3.7. Individual or in-line injection pump**

### Parts of fuel injection pump

(*i*) Driving units *i.e.* Cams

(*ii*) Pump element: This include  plungers and barrels

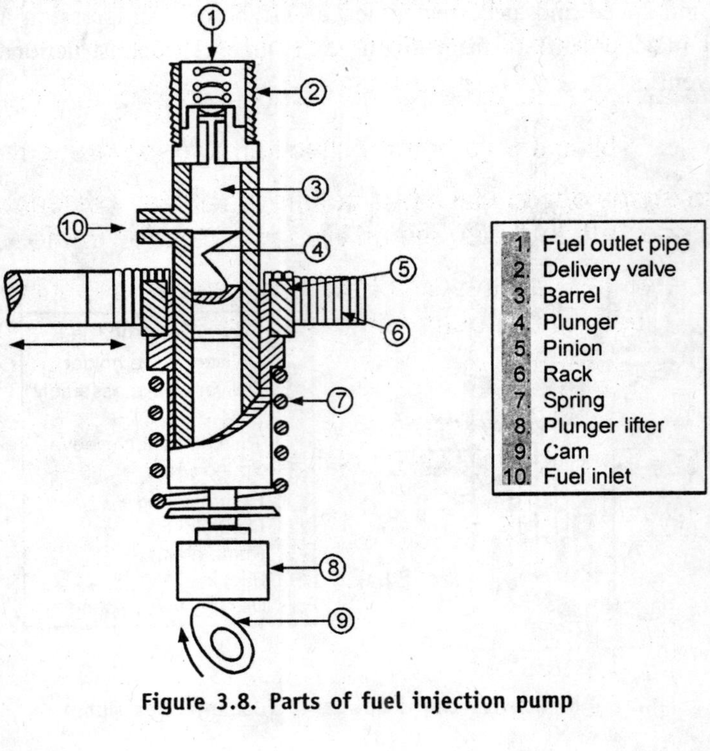


**Figure 3.8. Parts of fuel injection pump**

(*iii*) Delivery Valve (D.V): Delivery valve assembly consists of:

(*a*) Delivery valve seat

(*b*) Delivery valve

(*c*) Delivery valve spring, spacer and holder

(*iv*) Plunger guide

(*v*) Spring and spring seat

(*vi*) Spring lock

The parts of fuel injection pump are given in Fig. 3.8.

Quantity of fuel delivered by each stroke of pump is controlled by rotation of piston by a rack attached directly/indirectly to a governor. The rack pinion assembly is given in Fig. 3.9 and the position of plunger during fuel delivery stroke is given in Fig. 3.10.

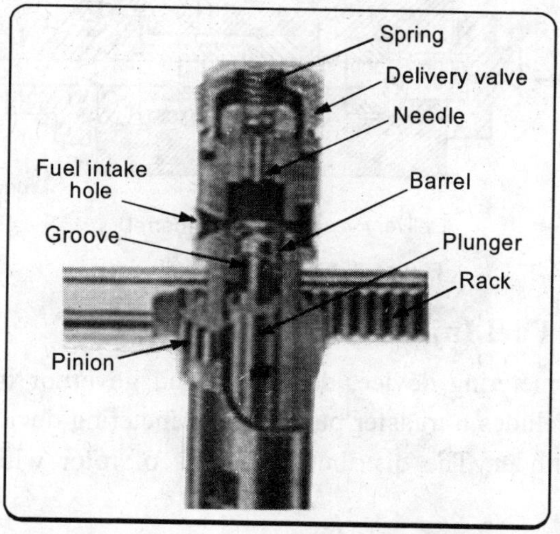


**Figure 3.9. Rack-pinion assembly of fuel injection pump.**

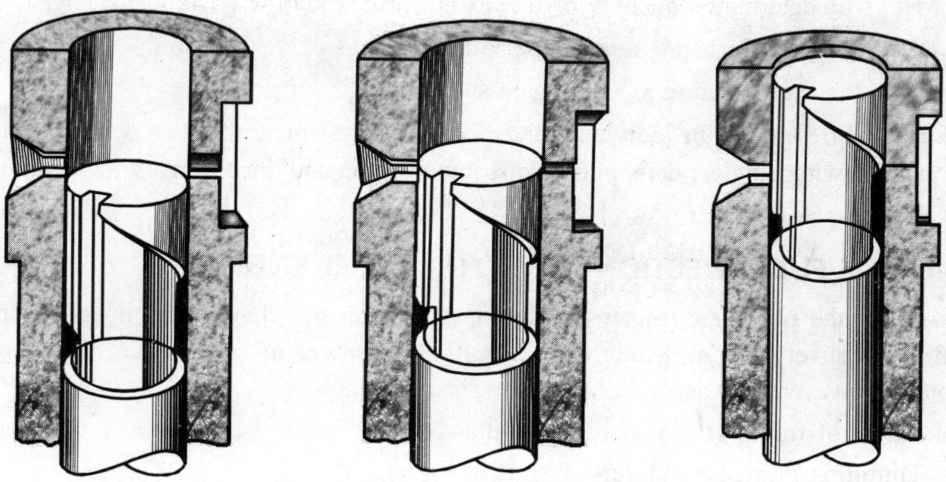

**Figure 3.10. Position of plunger during fuel delivery stroke.**

### Functions of delivery valve

(*i*) It seals the suction chamber and delivery chamber.

(*ii*) It reduces the pressure of delivery nozzle valve of injection into its position after spraying the fuel in combustion chamber.

A relief valve is provided for prevention of damaging the engine parts due to excessive pressure.

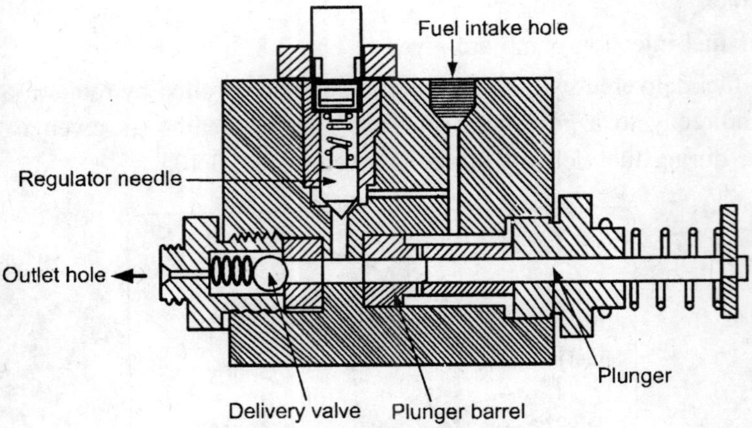


**Figure 3.11. Delivery valve**

## 3.5.2. Distributor Type Fuel Injection System

It consists of pump, metering device, distributor and governor in one unit. The distributor type fuel injection system includes a transfer pump, a fuel metering device, a pressurized distributor and an injector in each cylinder. The distributor consists of rotor with two small radial pistons driven by cam.

### Functions:

1. Meters predetermined quantity of fuel as determined by the governor of engine
2. Delivers fuel at high pressure to nozzle in the range of $1 \times 10^4$ to $2 \times 10^4$ kPa
3. Times the fuel injection as per engine speed.

The main difference with individual and distributor system is that this system replaces the individual pumps with single pump plus a distributor rotor and incorporates a governor in the housing.

## 3.6 DESIGN OF FUEL INJECTION PUMP FOR DIESEL ENGINE

In order to select the plunger diameter and stroke of plunger barrel type fuel injection pump, the quantity of fuel delivery per cycle must be known. The amount of fuel feed per cycle of a fuel injection pump however, will depend on following parameters:

- Extent of filling of space above the plunger with fuel.
- Throttling in intake and cut-off ports of barrel.
- Relieving action of delivery valve.

- Compressibility of fuel.
- Resilience of fuel feed devices.
- Leakage of fuel through clearances in plunger, barrel and nozzle.

This is estimated by following equation.

$$Q_d = \frac{P_b \times SFC \times V_s}{\rho_d} \quad ...(3.17)$$

where, $Q_d$ = Fuel delivery per cycle, $m^3$

$P_b$ = Break mean effective pressure, $N/m^2$

$SFC$ = Specific fuel consumption, kg/(W.Sec)

$V_s$ = Piston displacement (swept volume), $m^3$

$\rho_d$ = Density of diesel, $kg/m^3$

Also, The specific fuel delivery per cycle is determined by following equation

$$q_d = \frac{Q_d}{V_s} \quad ...(3.18)$$

where, $q_d$ = is fuel delivery per cycle/litre of cylinder working volume (usually 50–80 $mm^3$/litre).

**EXAMPLE 3.3** *A tractor has 10 × 10 cm size, 3 cylinder diesel engine running at a speed of 2000 rpm and develops 25 kW power and consumes 7.5 litres/hr diesel at full load. Calculate the fuel delivery rate of fuel injection pump of tractor engine if break mean effective pressure is 0.75 MN/m² and density of diesel fuel is 830 kg/m³.*

**SOLUTION:**

No. of cylinders: 3

Cylinder diameter: 10 cm

Stroke length: 10 cm

Brake Power: 25 kW

Fuel consumption: 7.5 litres/hr

Brake mean effective pressure: 0.75 $MN/m^2$

Density of diesel: 830 $kg/m^3$

Now, Fuel consumption rate = 7.5 litres/hr × 0.8 kg/litre = 6 kg/hr

And,

$$\begin{aligned} SFC &= \text{Fuel consumption rate (kg/hr)/Brake power (kW)} \\ &= 6 \text{ kg/hr}/25 \text{ kW} = 0.240 \text{ kg/kWh} \\ &= 0.240 \text{ kg/kWh} \times 2.78 \times 10^{-7} \text{ kWh/W.s} \\ &= 6.67 \times 10^{-8} \text{ kg/Ws} \end{aligned}$$

Also,

Piston displacement or swept volume

$$\begin{aligned} V_s &= (\pi/4)\, d^2\, L \\ &= (\pi/4) \times (0.10)^2 \times (0.10) \\ &= 7.85 \times 10^{-4} \text{ m}^3 \end{aligned}$$

and $\rho_d = 830 \text{ kg/m}^3$

We know that, $$Q_d = \frac{p_b \times SFC \times V_s}{\rho_d}$$

or $Q_d = 7.5 \times 10^{-5} \text{ N/m}^2 \times 6.67 \times 10^{-8} \text{ kg/W.s} \times 7.85 \times 10^{-4} \text{ m}^3/830 \text{ kg/m}^3$

$Q_d = 0.473 \times 10^{-7} \text{ m}^3/\text{cycle}$

$Q_d = 0.473 \times 10^{-7} \text{ m}^3/\text{cycle} \times 10^6 \text{ cm}^3/\text{m}^3$ (because $1 \text{ m}^3 = 10^6 \text{ cm}^3$)

$Q_d = 0.0473 \text{ cm}^3/\text{cycle}$ or $47.3 \text{ mm}^3/\text{cycle}$

Also, specific fuel delivery rate of FI pump is given by

$q_d = Q_d/V_s = 47.3 \text{ mm}^3/7.85 \times 10^{-4} \text{ m}^3 \times 10^3 \text{ litres/m}^3$

$q_d = 60.25 \text{ mm}^3/\text{litre}$.

Based on fuel delivery per cycle, the diameter and stroke of pump plunger can be selected from Table 3.1.

**TABLE 3.1: Plunger diameter and stroke for different range of fuel delivery**

| Plunger diameter, mm ($d_p$) | Plunger stroke, mm ($S_p$) | Maximum range of fuel delivery/cycle, $\text{mm}^3$ | Number of plunger sections of FI pump |
|---|---|---|---|
| 7,8,8.5,9,10 | 8 | 25–150 | 1,2,3,5,6,8,12 |
| 8,8.5,9,10,11,12 | 10 | 35–250 | 1,2,4,6,8,12 |
| 10,12,13,14,16 | 12 | 120–800 | 4,6,8,12 |

**EXAMPLE 3.4** *A diesel engine of a tractor has brake thermal efficiency of 30%. If calorific value of diesel is 42500 kJ/kg, find out brake specific fuel consumption of the engine.*

**SOLUTION:**

Brake thermal efficiency of engine = 30%

Calorific value of diesel fuel = 42500 kJ/kg

Now,

We know that for a diesel engine

Brake thermal efficiency = $W_b/(m_f \times CV)$

Where; $W_b$ = brake power of engine, kW or kJ/s

$m_f$ = mass of fuel, or brake specific fuel consumption, kg/kWh

$CV$ = calorific value of fuel, kJ/kg

So, putting values in above equation we get:

$0.30 = 1 \text{ kJ/s} \times 36000 \text{ s/hr}/(m_f \times 42500 \text{ kJ/kg})$

Or, $m_f = 1 \text{ kJ/s} \times 36000 \text{ s/hr}/(0.30 \times 42500 \text{ kJ/kg})$

$m_f = 0.282 \text{ kg/kWh}$

Or, $m_f = 282 \text{ g/kWh}$

So, brake specific fuel consumption of tractor engine is 282 g/kWh

**EXAMPLE 3.5** *A diesel engine of a tractor develops 30 kW power. The indicated thermal efficiency of engine is 30% and ite mechanical efficiency is 80%. If specific gravity of diesel fuel is 0.89 and calorific value of fuel is 42500 kJ/kg. Determine the following:*

*i) Fuel consumption of engine*

*ii) Indicated specific fuel consumption*

*iii) Brake specific fuel consumption*

**SOLUTION:**

Thermal efficiency of engine = 30%

Engine brake power = 30 kW

Mechanical efficiency of engine, $\eta_m$ = 80%

***i)* Indicated power ($W_i$)**

We know that

$$\eta_m = W_b/W_i$$

Where $\eta_m$ = mechanical efficiency of engine

$W_b$ = brake power of engine, kW

$W_i$ = indicated power of engine, kW

Putting values in above equation, we get

$$0.80 = 30 \text{ kW}/W_i$$

Or $$W_i = 30 \text{ kW}/0.80 = 37.5 \text{ kW}$$

Also, we know that

Indicated thermal efficiency $= W_i \times 3600/(m_f \times CV)$

Putting values we get

$$0.30 = 37.50 \text{ kW} \times 3600 \text{ s/h}/(m_f \times 42500 \text{ kJ/kg})$$

Or, $$m_f = 37.50 \times 3600/(0.30 \times 42500) = 10.588 \text{ kg/h}$$

Or, Fuel consumption of engine = $m_f$/S.G = 10.588 kg/h/0.89 = 10.90 l/h

***ii)* Indicated specific fuel consumption (*isfc*) of engine**

$$isfc = m_f/W_i = 10.566 \text{ kg/h}/37.5 \text{ kW}$$
$$= 0.28235 \text{ kg/kWh}$$

Or, $$= 282.35 \text{ g/kWh Ans}$$

***iii)* Brake specific fuel consumption (*bsfc*) of engine**

$$bsfc = m_f/W_b = 10.588 \text{ kg/h}/30 \text{ kW}$$
$$= 0.353 \text{ kg/kWh}$$

Or, $$= 353 \text{ g/kWh}$$ **Ans.**

**EXAMPLE 3.6** *A tractor fitted with 90 × 100 mm size 4 cylinder 4-stroke cycle IC diesel engine with compression ratio of 16:1 develops 40 IHP at a operating speed of 2000 rpm. It consumes 8.5 litres/hr diesel at full load. Assume that mechanical efficiency of engine is 85% and density of diesel is 830 kg/m$^3$. Calculate the fuel delivered per cycle by the FI pump of engine. Also select the size of plunger barrel of fuel injection pump of the engine.*

**SOLUTION:**

Type of engine: 4-stroke cycle diesel engine
No. of cylinders: 4
Engine rpm ($N$): 2000
Piston size ($d$): 90 mm
Stroke length ($S$) : 100 mm
IHP: 40 hp
$\eta_m$: 85%
Density of diesel: 830 kg/m$^3$
Now, we know that

$$IHP = \frac{PLAN}{4500} \times \frac{n}{2} \quad \text{...(3.19)}$$

Putting the values in Eq. 3.19, we get

$$40 = \frac{P_{i.m.e.p.} \times 0.10 \times \frac{\pi}{4} \times (9.0)^2 \times 4}{4500} \times \frac{2000}{2}$$

$$P_{i.m.e.p.} = \frac{40 \times 45000}{0.10 \times \frac{\pi}{4} \times (9.0)^2 \times \frac{2000}{2} \times 4}$$

or $\quad = 7.07 \text{ kg/cm}^2$

Now, $\quad \eta_m = 85\%$

Therefore, $\quad \text{BHP} = \text{IHP} \times \eta_m$

$= 40 \times 0.85 = 36$ hp or 26.9 kW

Also $\quad P_{b.m.e.p.} = \dfrac{P_{i.m.e.p}}{\eta_m}$

or, $\quad P_{b.m.e.p.} = 7.07 \text{ kg/cm}^2 \times 0.85 = 6.55 \text{ kg/cm}^2$

Now, fuel consumption of engine

= 8.5 litres/hr = 8.5 litres/hr × 0.8 kg/litre

= 6.8 kg/hr

Also, $\quad$ SFC = Fuel consumption (kg/hr)/Brake power (kW)

= 6.8 kg/hr/26.9 kW = 0.253 kg/kWh

$= 0.253 \text{kg/kWh} \times 2.78 \times 10^{-7} \text{ kWh/W.s} = 7.03 \times 10^{-8} \text{ kg/W.s}$

Also, Piston displacement or swept volume

$$V_s = (\pi/4)\, d^2\, L$$

$$= (\pi/4)\,(0.09)^2 \times 0.10 \text{ m}^3$$

$$= 6.36 \times 10^{-4} \text{ m}^3$$

And $\quad \rho_d = 830 \text{ kg/m}^3$

Now, we know that, quantity of diesel delivered per cycle by the fuel injection pump is given by

$$Q_d = \frac{p_b \times SFC \times V_s}{\rho_d}$$

Or $$Q_d = \frac{6.55 \times 10^{-5}\ (\text{N/m}^2) \times 7.03 \times 10^{-8}\ (\text{kg/W.s}) \times 6.36 \times 10^{-4}\ (\text{m}^3)}{830\ \text{kg/m}^3}$$

$$Q_d = 0.353 \times 10^{-7}\ \text{m}^3/\text{cycle}$$

$$Q_d = 0.353 \times 10^{-7}\ \text{m}^3/\text{cycle} \times 10^6\ \text{cm}^3/\text{m}^3 \qquad (\text{because } 1\ \text{m}^3 = 10^6\ \text{cm}^3)$$

$$Q_d = 0.0353\ \text{cm}^3/\text{cycle or } 35.3\ \text{mm}^3/\text{cycle}$$

Also, specific fuel delivery rate of FI pump is given by

$$q_d = Q_d/V_s = 35.3\ \text{mm}^3/6.36 \times 10^{-4}\ \text{m}^3 \times 10^3\ \text{litres/m}^3$$

$$q_d = 55.5\ \text{mm}^3/\text{litre}$$ **Ans.**

Now based on 55.5 mm$^3$/litre, from Table 3.1, we can select the dimensions of FI pump plunger as under:

$$d_p = 8\ \text{mm and } S_p = 8\ \text{mm}$$

or, $$d_p = 8\ \text{mm and } S_p = 10\ \text{mm}$$

## 3.7 EFFICIENCY OF FI PUMP (η)

The efficiency of fuel injection pump is given by

$$\eta = \frac{Q_d}{Q_{th}} \qquad \text{...(3.20)}$$

where, $Q_d$ = fuel delivery per cycle by the pump

$Q_{th}$ = theoretical pump delivery per cycle

$Q_{th} = A_p \times S$ ...(3.21)

$A_p$ = cross sectional area of plunger = $(\pi/4)\ d_p^2$

$d_p$ = plunger diameter

$S$ = active stroke of plunger in barrel

Rearranging eqn. 3.20 and 3.21, we get

$$Q_d = A_p \times S \times \eta \qquad \text{...(3.22)}$$

where, $\eta$ = efficiency of pump which is generally 0.75–0.90.

**EXAMPLE 3.7** *A three cylinder, 4-stroke cycle diesel engine developing 30 kW brake power at 2400 rpm . The specific fuel consumption of engine is 0.20 kg/kwh. Assume that the fuel injection pump of this engine has full stroke displacement of 4 times the rated engine fuel consumption and if the injector pump plunger has stroke length twice its diameter. Assuming that density of diesel is 830 kg/m$^3$, then calculate the following:*

*(i) Total fuel delivery rate (cm$^3$/s) of pump to the engine*

*(ii) Pump plunger diameter*

*(iii) Plunger stroke length*

**SOLUTION:**

Type of engine = 4-stroke cycle diesel engine

No. of cylinders = 3

Brake power of engine = 30 kW

Rated speed of engine = 2400 rpm

Specific fuel consumption = 0.20 kg/kWh

Plunger full stroke displacement = 4 times rated engine fuel consumption

Plunger stroke length = twice plunger diameter

***(i)* Total fuel delivery rate (cm³/s) of pump to the engine**

According to problem, total fuel supplied to the engine per second is given by

$$Q = \frac{SFC \times \text{Brake power of engine (kW)}}{60 \times 60 \times \rho_d}, \frac{\text{m}^3}{\text{s}} \tag{3.23}$$

Putting values in eqn. 3.23, we get

$$Q = 0.20 \text{ kg/kWh} \times 30 \text{ kW/ } (60 \times 60 \times 830 \text{ kg/m}^3)$$
$$= 2.01 \times 10^{-6} \text{ m}^3\text{/s or } 2.01 \text{ cm}^3\text{/s (as } 1\text{m}^3 = 10^6 \text{ cm}^3)$$

***(ii)* Pump plunger diameter**

Fuel stroke displacement = 4 × rated engine fuel consumption

Also fuel consumption/second = 2.01 cm³/sec

$$= 0.201 \times 10^{-5} \text{ m}^3\text{/sec}$$

Therefore,

$$\text{Fuel stroke displacement} = 4 \times 0.201 \times 10^{-5} = 0.804 \times 10^{-5} \text{ m}^3\text{/sec}$$

Hence, Fuel supplied per cylinder = Fuel stroke displacement/No. of cylinders

$$= 0.804 \times 10^{-5}/3, \text{ m}^3\text{/sec} = 0.268 \times 10^{-5} \text{ m}^3\text{/sec}$$

Let, $L$ is the stroke length and $d$ is the bore of plunger,

Then, $\text{fuel supplied/stroke} = \pi/4\ d^2 \times L$ (cu. cm) ...(3.24)

$\text{fuel supplied/sec} = (\pi/4)\ d^2 \times L \times (1/60) \times N$ ...(3.25)

where, $n$ = rpm of cam shaft and for 4-stroke engine

$= N/2 = 2400/2 = 1200$ rpm

Therefore, $\text{fuel supplied/sec} = (\pi/4)\ d^2 \times 2d \times (1/60) \times 1200$

$= 31.47\ d^3$ c.c/s

$= 31.47\ d^3 \times 10^{-6}$ m³/s ($L = 2d$ given)

or, $31.47\ d^3 \times 10^{-6} \text{ m}^3\text{/s} = 0.268 \times 10^{-5} \text{ m}^3\text{/sec}$

or, $d^3 = 0.268 \times 10/31.47 = 0.085$

or, $d = 0.445$ cm = 4.45 mm say 5.0 mm **Ans.**

***(iii)* Stroke length of plunger**

Stroke length of plunger ($L$) is given by

$L = 2d = 2 \times 4.45$ mm = 8.90 mm say 9.0 mm **Ans.**

## 3.8 ESSENTIAL REQUIREMENTS OF DIESEL FUEL INJECTION

1. At the beginning of fuel injection, the rate of fuel feed rate in the cylinder should not be too high. This will result in less fuel accumulation in the combustion chamber during ignition lag and pressure increase will also be less intensive during combustion process. On the other hand too low fuel delivery rate will result in poor atomization of fuel which will increase the ignition lag.
2. For proper utilization of air in diesel after combustion begins, the majority of fuel should be supplied at an increasing rate so that drops of diesel reach the remotest point in the combustion chamber. The rate of fuel delivery should increase gradually, and comparatively small quantity of fuel should be supplied at a decreasing rate.
3. Dribbling of fuel from the nozzle is not desirable. Therefore, fuel injection should end abruptly.
4. Fuel injection at full delivery rate should last up to a crank rotation angle of 35–40°.
5. After termination of main fuel delivery, there should not be any additional injection of fuel.

## 3.9 TYPES OF INJECTORS

Fuel in diesel engines is injected in compressed air having a pressure of 3–4 MN/m$^2$ and temperature of 450–550°C. Delivery of fuel from the fuel injection pump begins before TDC and terminates either before or after TDC. Maximum rate of pressure increase is 1 MN/m$^2$.deg. Most appropriate angle at which fuel injection begins is 20° before TDC. The location of an injector is given in Fig. 3.12 and its components are given in Fig. 3.13.

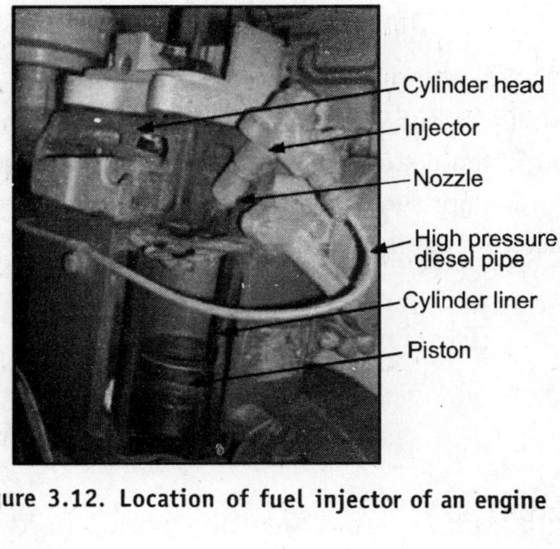


Figure 3.12. Location of fuel injector of an engine

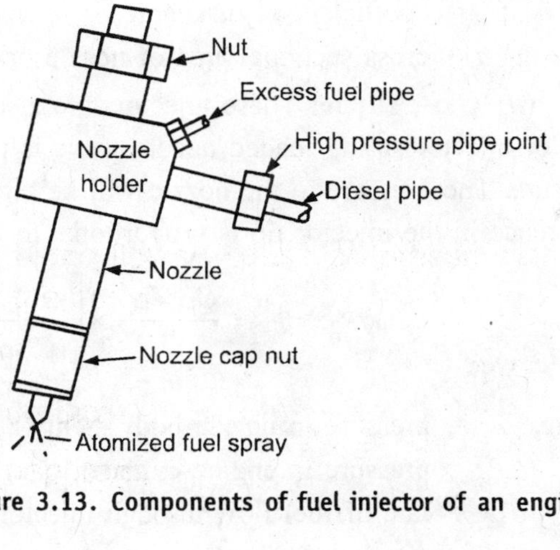


Figure 3.13. Components of fuel injector of an engine

There are two types of fuel injectors:

*(i)* **Open type:** Open type injectors are not provided with fuel shut-off device between the delivery pipe and orifice of spray nozzle. The injection pressure in this type of injector changes sharply and nozzles used are without shut-off device as a result of which fuel may leak from the orifice at the end of fuel injection. Generally nozzle orifice gets clogged and makes the engine smoke.

*(ii)* **Closed type:** In closed injectors, the pressure difference between nozzle body and nozzle tip at lower fuel flow rate is considerable which is used to increase the velocity of fuel stream and overcome the resistance in delivery valve. In this type of injector the pressure at which the needle valv,e begins to rise is about 20–25 $MN/m^2$ and maximum atomization pressure should be 40–60 $MN/m^2$. This ensures adequate atomization of diesel fuel even at lower engine speed and fuel delivery per cycle.

### 3.9.1. Design of Injectors

Increase in engine speed and diesel fuel delivery per cycle will increase injection pressure and consequently, the velocity of diesel fuel outflow from the nozzle orifice increases, which will result in finer atomization of diesel fuel.

*(i)* **Open type:** Open type injectors are not provided with fuel shut-off device between the delivery pipe and orifice of spray nozzle. The pressure difference in the injector is proportional to the square of fuel flow rate through the nozzle as given by following equation.

$$P_n - P_c = \frac{Q_i^2 \times \rho_d}{2\,(C_d a)^2}, \text{ N/m}^2 \qquad \text{...(3.26)}$$

where, $P_n$ = pressure in nozzle body, $N/m^2$
$P_c$ = pressure in engine cylinder, $N/m^2$
$Q_i$ = rate of fuel flow through injector per second
$\rho_d$ = density of diesel, $kg/m^3$
$C_d$ = coefficient of discharge
$a$ = cross sectional area of nozzle orifice, $m^2$

*(ii)* **Closed type:** These injectors are also known as hydraulically controlled injectors. In this type of injector spring loaded needle valve is provided in the nozzle. This valve is opened by fuel pressure. The pressure in the nozzle will be higher than the pressure in the nozzle tip. The pressure difference in the injector tip is proportional to the square of fuel flow rate through the nozzle.

$$P_n - P_c = \frac{Q_i^2 \times \rho_d}{2} \times \left[\frac{1}{(C_d a)^2} + \frac{1}{(C_{d1} a_1)^2}\right], \text{ N/m}^2 \qquad \text{...(3.27)}$$

where, $P_n$ = pressure in nozzle body, $N/m^2$
$P_c$ = pressure in engine cylinder, $N/m^2$
$Q_i$ = rate of fuel flow through injector per second
$r_d$ = density of diesel, $kg/m^3$
$C_d$ = coefficient of discharge

$a$ = cross sectional area of nozzle orifice, $m^2$

$C_{d1}$ = coefficient of discharge of passage between the needle cone and seat

$a_1$ = cross sectional area of passage between the needle cone and seat, $m^2 \cong C_{d1}\ \pi d_c \times \sin\phi$

$d_c$ = mean diameter of cone seating surface of needle, m

$x$ = needle valve lift, m

$\phi$ = half apex angle of shut-off needle cone, degrees

**EXAMPLE 3.8** *A tractor is provided with a 4-stroke cycle diesel engine with following specifications:*

(i) *Brake mean effective pressure: 0.70 MN/m²*
(ii) *Brake power: 30 kW*
(iii) *Engine rpm: 2200*
(iv) *No. of cylinders: 3*
(v) *Piston displacement: 785 cc*
(vi) *Pressure in combustion chamber at the time of fuel injection: 3 MN/m²*
(vii) *Fuel injection pressure in the injector nozzle: 20 MN/m²*
(viii) *Consumes 32 litres of diesel in 4 hours at full load and rated engine speed.*
(ix) *Density of diesel: 830 kg/m³*

*Calculate the following:*

(i) *Effective specific fuel consumption*
(ii) *Fuel delivery rate by FI pump*
(iii) *Length of stroke and diameter of plunger of FI pump*
(iv) *Design open type fuel injector*

**SOLUTION:**

Brake mean effective pressure = 0.70 MN/m²
Brake power = 30 kW
Engine rpm = 2200
No. of cylinders = 3
Piston displacement = 785 cc
Pressure in combustion chamber at the time of fuel injection = 3 MN/m²
Fuel injection pressure in the injector nozzle = 40 MN/m²
Consumes 32 litres of diesel in 4 hours at full load and rated engine speed.
Density of diesel: 830 kg/m³

**(i) Specific fuel consumption (SFC)**

We know that,

Fuel consumption rate = Total fuel consumed (l)/Time (hr)

= 32 litres/4 hr = 8 l/hr

or, = 8 l/hr × 0.8 kg/l = 6.4 kg/hr

Now, SFC = Fuel consumption rate (kg/hr)/ Brake power (kW)

$= 6.4$ kg/hr/30 kW $= 0.213$ kg/kWh

$= 0.213$ kg/kWh $\times 2.78 \times 10^{-7}$ kWh/W.s

$= 5.93 \times 10^{-8}$ kg/W.s

***(ii)* Fuel delivery rate by FI pump**

Now, $V_s = 785$ cc or $7.85 \times 10^{-4}$ m$^3$

$P_b = 0.7$ MN/m$^2$ or $7.0 \times 10^5$ N/m$^2$

Now, we know that, quantity of diesel delivered per cycle by the fuel injection pump is given by

$$Q_d = p_b \times \text{SFC} \times V_s/\rho_d$$

or $Q_d = 7.0 \times 10^{-5}$ N/m$^2 \times 5.93 \times 10^{-8}$ kg/W.s $\times 7.85 \times 10^{-4}$ m$^3$/830 kg/m$^3$

$Q_d = 0.393 \times 10^{-7}$ m$^3$/cycle

$Q_d = 0.393 \times 10^{-7}$ m$^3$/cycle $\times 10^6$ cm$^3$/m$^3$ (because 1 m$^3$ = $10^6$ cm$^3$)

$Q_d = 0.0393$ cm$^3$/cycle or 39.3 mm$^3$/cycle

Also, specific fuel delivery rate of FI pump is given by

$q_d = Q_d/V_s = 39.3$ mm$^3$/$7.85 \times 10^{-4}$ m$^3 \times 10^3$ litres/m$^3$

$q_d = 50.06$ mm$^3$/litre **Ans.**

***(iii)* Size of plunger barrel of FI pump**

From above,

$Q_d = 0.0393$ cm$^3$/cycle or 39.3 mm$^3$/cycle and

$q_d = 50.06$ mm$^3$/litre

Now, based on above fuel delivery rate, the size of plunger and its stroke is selected from the Table 3.1.

$d_p =$ 8 mm and $S_p$ = 8 mm

or, $d_p =$ 8 mm and $S_p$ = 10 mm

***(iv)* Design of open injector**

$P_n = 20$ MN/m$^2$

$P_c = 3$ Mn/m$^2$

And, $P_n - P_c = 20$ MN/m$^2$–3 MN/m$^2$

$= 17$ MN/m$^2$

Also, we know that for a 4-stroke cycle engine with 2200 rpm no. of fuel injections in one minute = RPM/2 = 2200/2 =1100

or, No. of fuel injections cycles/s = 1100/60 s = 110/6

Now, $Q_i = Q_d \times$ No. of fuel injections cycles /s

$Q_i = 39.3$ mm$^3$/cycle $\times$ 110/g cycles/s

$Q_i =$ 720.5 mm$^3$/s or $7.205 \times 10^{-7}$ m$^3$/s

Now for open injectors, the pressure difference in the injector is proportional to the square of fuel flow rate through the nozzle as given by following equation:

$$P_n - P_c = \frac{Q_i^2 \times \rho_d}{2(C_d a)^2}, \frac{N}{m^2} \qquad ...(3.28)$$

Putting values in eqn. 3.28, we get

$$17 \text{ MN/m}^2 = (7.205 \times 10^{-7})^2 \times 830 \text{ kg/m}^3/2\ (0.9 \times a)^2$$

or, $$2\ (0.9 \times a)^2 = (7.205 \times 10^{-7})^2 \times 830 \text{ kg/m}^3/17 \text{ MN/m}^2$$

or, $$2 \times 0.81\ a^2 = 51.84 \times 10^{-14} \times 830/17 \times 10^6$$

or $$1.62\ a^2 = 25.31 \times 10–18$$

$$a^2 = 25.31 \times 10^{-18}/1.62 = 15.62 \times 10^{-18}$$

$$a = 3.95 \times 10^{-9} \text{ m}^2$$

or $$a = 3.95 \times 10^{-3} \text{ mm}^2 \quad (\text{As } 1 \text{ m}^2 = 10^6 \text{ mm}^2)$$ **Ans.**

## 3.10 TYPES OF NOZZLES

The nozzles are made of high quality steel and the selection of type of nozzle used is based on following parameters.

- Shape of combustion chamber
- Design of fuel feed devices
- Operating conditions of diesel engine.

Generally two types of nozzles are used in injectors of injectors.

**(*i*) Multi-hole nozzle :** This is used in direct injection (DI) engines. The direct injection system in comparison with pre-chamber or swirl chamber systems, gives a saving of 10–15% on the basis of average fuel consumption. With the direct injection system, the motion of the air-fuel

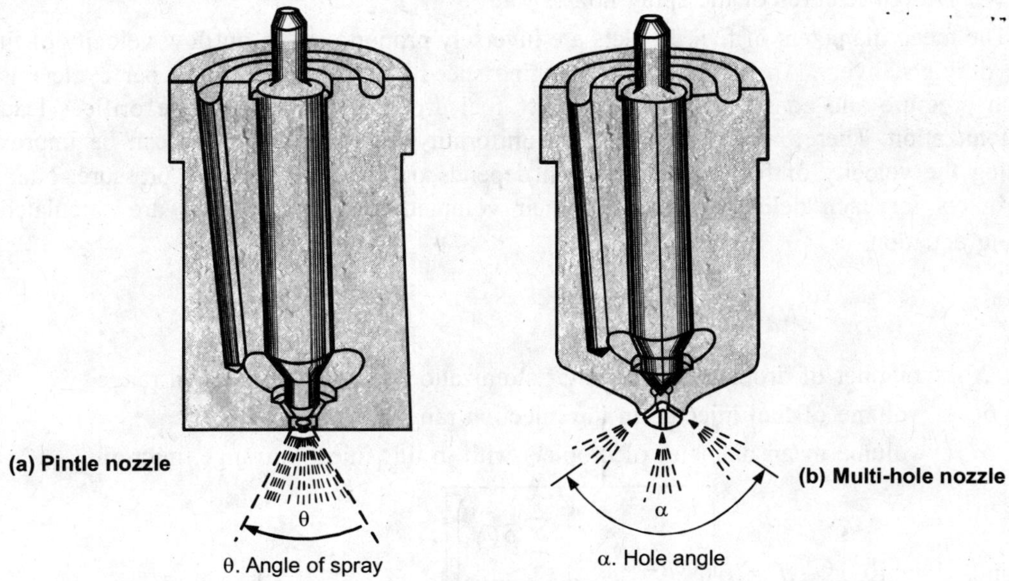


**Figure 3.14. Different types of nozzles**

mixture is less intense than with other combustion systems, and thus, entails less heat transfer to the walls of the combustion chamber. This type of nozzle is provided with a spring loaded needle valve with shut-off cone and body with 2–4 spraying orifices with diameters ranging from 0.15 to 0.45 mm and valve opening pressures of 20 MPa or above. Needle valve opening pressure is adjusted with the help of an adjusting screw. Needle valve lift is also adjustable. In multi-hole nozzles maintenance of correct orifice size and valve opening pressure is very vital and important for proper atomization of fuel in the combustion chamber. Different types of nozzle is given in Fig. 3.14.

***(ii)* Single hole pintel type nozzle :** This is used in non DI engines. Pintle has the form of two truncated cones with smaller base together and has several throttling sections. This type of nozzle is used in diesel engines with divided combustion chambers. Usually the pintle diameter is about 2 mm and needle valve diameter is 6 mm and maximum spray cone angle of 25° during injection. This nozzle ensures fine atomization of the fuel with considerable variation in engine speed. This type of nozzle does not jam, rises sharply and lowers quite accurately on to its seat.

The required injection pressure in the engine can be maintained by adjusting the spring tension of returning spring of the nozzle. Spring loaded delivery valve is incorporated in the nozzle to prevent dribbling of excess fuel into the cylinder after the injection stroke of piston has been completed.

## 3.11 ATOMIZATION OF FUEL

The atomization of liquid fuel being injected in the combustion chamber of a diesel engine is very vital and its fineness and uniformity depend on following parameters:

- Velocity of fuel droplets.
- Physical properties of fuel.
- Physical properties of compressed air in the engine cylinder.
- Design features of the spray nozzle.

The mean diameters of fuel droplets are inversely proportional to outflow velocity of fuel and change during delivery. An increase in the engine speed and delivery of fuel per cycle raises the injection pressure and consequently the velocity fuel droplets from the nozzle orifices leading to finer atomization. Therefore, the fineness and uniformity of fuel atomization can be improved by increasing the velocity of fuel particles which depends on the fuel injection pressure. Number of fuel droplets for each delivery range and their volumetric mean diameters are calculated from following equation.

$$N_d = \frac{6 \times 10^9 \times \delta Q}{\pi d_v^3} \qquad ...(3.29)$$

where, $N_d$ = number of droplets formed after atomization in a given injection range

$\delta Q$ = volume of fuel injected in the injection range, $mm^3$

$d_v$ = volume mean diameter of droplets with in this injection range, micron

and,

$$d_v = \sqrt[3]{\left[\left(\frac{6 \times 10^9}{\pi}\right) \times \left(\frac{\sum_{i=1}^{n} \delta Q_i}{N_d}\right)\right]} \qquad ...(3.30)$$

Atomization is considerably affected by the physical properties of fuel. A fuel with lower viscosity and forces of surface tension is atomized finer.

## 3.12 ENERGY OF DIESEL FUEL ATOMIZATION

The energy of atomization of fuel in the combustion chamber of an engine is the kinetic energy of diesel fuel jet coming out of spray orifices of the nozzle and it is given by following equation.

$$E_d = \frac{V_d^2}{2} = \frac{C_v\,\delta P}{\rho_d}, \frac{J}{kg} \qquad ...(3.31)$$

where, $E_d$ = specific energy of atomization of diesel fuel, J/kg
$V_d$ = velocity of diesel outflow, m/s
$C_v$ = velocity coefficient, generally 0.7
$\rho_d$ = density of diesel fuel, kg/m$^3$ (830 kg/m$^3$)

The specific energy of atomization of diesel is given in Table 3.2

**TABLE 3.2: Specific energy of atomization of diesel**

| Mechanical atomization at $\delta P$ (MN/m$^3$) | Diesel fuel parameters | |
|---|---|---|
| | Outflow velocity (m/s) | Specific kinetic energy of atomization (J/g) |
| 10 | 108 | 5.9 |
| 25 | 170 | 14.8 |
| 45 | 229 | 26.5 |

Energy of air-fuel mixture formation in mechanical atomization is given by

$$E_{mix} = E_d + E_a \qquad ...(3.32)$$

where, $E_a$ = specific energy of air stream used for mixture formation in the combustion chamber of engine

From eq. 3.31, it is clear that during mechanical atomization of diesel fuel, the mixture formation can also be improved by using the kinetic energy of compressed air in the combustion chamber of engine.

## 3.13 FUEL INJECTION TIME ($t_i$)

The fuel injection time of a diesel engine is calculated as given below.

$$t_i = \frac{\theta}{360} \times \frac{1}{N} \times 60 \qquad ...(3.33)$$

where, $t_i$ = fuel injection time, minutes
$\theta$ = crank rotation angle, degrees
$N$ = engine rpm

## 3.14 INJECTION DELAY

More injection lag period will not only increase the amount of fuel injected up to ignition but, also improve homogeneity of air-fuel mixture for self ignition.

Percent of fuel injection during delay

= (Delay in time of injection/Time of injection) × 100

= (Delay degrees/injection degrees) × 100

Optimum angle of injection advance depends on engine design, its compression ratio, the pressure and temperature of air at inlet, design of injectors and crankshaft speed.

**EXAMPLE 3.9** *In an IC engine running at 2200 rpm, the fuel injection pump delivers fuel for an interval of 20° crank rotations. The engine has an ignition delay of 0.0011 seconds. The period of rapid fuel combustion is 5° of crank rotation. Calculate:*

*(i) Injection lag in terms of crank shaft rotation*

*(ii) Percentage of fuel injected during injection delay*

*(iii) Percentage of fuel injected during injection delay and rapid combustion.*

**SOLUTION:**

Engine speed: 2200 rpm

Fuel injection interval: 20° crank rotation

Injection delay time $t_d$: 0.0011 seconds

Time period of rapid combustion: 5° of crank rotation

(*i*) Injection lag in terms of crank shaft rotation

Now using the relationship,

$$t_i = \frac{\theta}{360} \times \frac{1}{N} \times 60 \quad \text{...(3.34)}$$

where, $t_i$ = fuel injection time, seconds

$\theta$ = crank rotation angle, degrees

$N$ = engine rpm

From eqn. 3.34, time required by the crank shaft to rotate one degree is given by

= (1/360) × 60/2200 seconds

Therefore, crank rotation during the period of injection delay

= (2200 × 360/60) × 0.0011 seconds

= 14.52 degrees.

(*ii*) Percentage of fuel injected during injection delay

Now, putting values in eqn. 3.34, time of injection is given by

$t_i$ = (20/360) × (60/2200) seconds

= 1/660 seconds

Percent of fuel injection during delay

= (Delay in time of injection/Time of injection) × 100

= (Delay degrees/injection degrees) × 100

Therefore, percentage of fuel injected during delay = $(t_d/t_i) \times 100$

$= 0.0011/(1/660) \times 100$

$= 72.6\%$

(*iii*) Percentage of fuel injected during injection delay and rapid combustion

Percent of fuel injection during delay and rapid combustion

$$= \left[\frac{\text{Delay in time of injection}}{\text{Time of injection}}\right] + \left[\frac{\text{Degrees of rapid combustion}}{\text{degrees injection}}\right] \times 100 \quad ...(3.35)$$

Putting values in eqn. 3.35, we get

Percent of fuel injection during delay and rapid combustion

$= [0.0011/(1/660) + 5/20)] \times 100$

$= 0.976 \times 100 = 97.6\%$

## 3.15 COMBUSTION CHAMBERS

Combustion chambers can be classified as open combustion chamber and divided combustion chamber. Different types of combustion chambers are given in Fig. 3.15.

(*i*) **Open combustion chambers:** These have the advantage of good mixture formation and lower heat losses through the chamber surface. Good mixture formation is due to high injection pressures and optimum diameter and number of orifices in the spray nozzle with energy of tangential swirl. However, centane number of diesel fuel for such chambers should be within 50–60. Due to direct injection in open combustion chamber, fuel is finely atomized and has 8–10% fuel economy over indirect ignition.

Main disadvantages of this type of combustion chamber are

- High rate of pressure increase during combustion (0.6–1.2 $MN/m^2$.deg) and
- In closed type of injectors the needle valve begins to rise at a pressure of 20–25 $MN/m^2$ and maximum atomization pressure should be 40–60 $MN/m^2$ so, it requires quite high injection pressure for mixture formation.

(*ii*) **Semi-divided combustion chamber:** This type of combustion chamber in piston is modification of open type combustion chamber which ensures development of high power and fuel economy. This has all advantages of open combustion chambers. An intensive swirl motion is created by the air and this additional turbulence in air stream will result in reduced injection

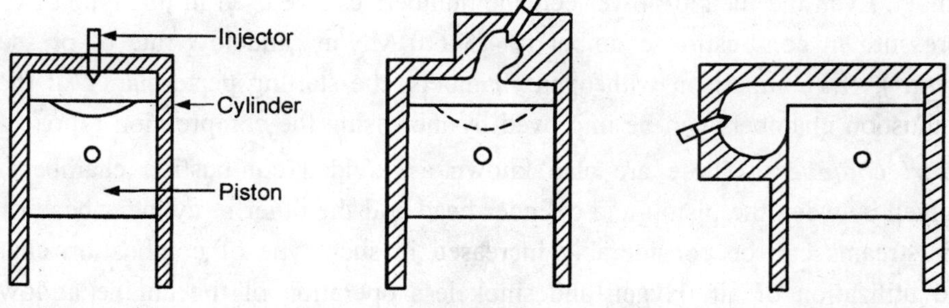


**Figure 3.15. Different types of combustion chambers**

pressure as the needle will begin to rise at a pressure of 15–17.5 MN/m$^2$. Number of spray orifices in the nozzle will also be reduced *i.e.* it may range from two to five. Main draw back of this type of combustion chamber is that the piston head thickness should be more which will result in increased piston mass and inertia loads.

All the direct ignition engines are classified according to their swirl ratio (SR) which is given by

$$SR = N_s / N_e \quad \text{...(3.36)}$$

where, $SR$ : swirl ratio

$N_s$ : swirl speed, rpm

$N_e$ : engine speed, rpm

**EXAMPLE 3.10** *The DI engine of a tractor is operating at a speed of 2200 rpm which is fitted with injector having holes and has injection delay of 16°. Calculate the swirl ratio of engine needed to fan one spray plume half way to the next plume during ignition delay.*

**SOLUTION:**

Since the nozzle of engine is provided with 4-holes, therefore, spray plumes of nozzle are 360°/4 = 90° apart. Theoretically, the air swirl must move 90°/2 = 45° during the delay period.

Now, time available for the air to move during delay period is

$$t = \text{delay (degrees)}/360° \times N_e, \text{ min}$$

$$t = 16°/(360° \times 2200 \text{ rpm}) = 2.02 \times 10^{-5} \text{ min}$$

Now, swirl speed (Ns) of air is given by

$$Ns = 45°/(360° \times t) = 45°/360° \times 2.02 \times 10^{-5}) = 6188 \text{ rpm}$$

$$SR = N_s/N_e = 6188 \text{ rpm}/2200 \text{ rpm} = 2.81$$ **Ans.**

***(a) Pre-combustion chamber***: It is a chamber provided in the cylinder head of an engine which has 20–30% of total clearance volume. During compression, the air flows in pre-combustion chamber at very high velocity ranging from 230–320 m/s and creates mild turbulence. The temperature of pre-combustion chamber ranges between 600–750°C and as the fuel is injected into it, the same is ignited and comes out into main chamber through a small orifice which generates intensive swirling (turbulence). This helps in proper mixing and atomization of unburnt fuel with air in main chamber. Even the fuels of lower centane numbers can be used in this type of chamber. The maximum pressure in combustion chamber is 4.5–6.0 MN/m$^2$ and low rate of pressure increase (0.3–0.5 MN/m$^2$). In comparison with open chambers, the starting performance of diesel engines with pre-combustion chambers can be improved by increasing the compression ratio.

***(b) Swirl chambers***: These are also known as divided combustion chambers where one chamber is given between the piston and cylinder head and the other in cylinder head or block. The energy of air streams can be considerably increased in such type of combustion chambers. This ensures good utilization of air oxygen and smokeless operation of the engine at low excess air coefficients. The intensive motion of air in swirl chamber makes it possible to use closed type of injector with single large diameter orifice. The injector needle will start to rise at a pressure of

12.5–15.00 MN/m$^2$. The maximum velocity of air flow in the swirl chamber should be around 100–200 m/s.

**Advantages of swirl chambers:**

Main advantages of swirl chambers are:

(*i*) As compared to open combustion chambers, maximum pressure and rate of pressure increase in combustion chamber are lower.

(*ii*) The fuel injection pressure is low as a result of which the fuel feed devices would function satisfactorily.

(*iii*) Fuels of different fractional compositions can be used without affecting engine performance.

(*iv*) Proper utilization of air oxygen by the engine would ensure smokeless performance of engine.

(*v*) It makes possible to operate engine at high speeds, with smokeless exhaust and low noise.

**Disadvantages of swirl chambers:**

(*i*) Specific fuel consumption of engine is higher due to higher thermal losses.

(*ii*) Starting of cold engine is poor.

## 3.16 IGNITION LAG

In diesel engines the process of fuel combustion in combustion chambers is considerably affected by its mixing with compressed air and the duration of ignition lag. Ignition lag is the minimum possible time interval from the moment the fuel is injected to the moment it is ignited. The duration of ignition lag is influenced by following parameters:

(*i*) Temperature and pressure of compressed air at the time of fuel injection

(*ii*) The chemical properties of fuel *i.e.* cetane number. Cetane rating is important in diesel engines and it is a measure of how well a fuel ignites spontaneously. Higher the cetane number of fuel, the shorter the ignition lag and smoother engine operation. Diesel ($C_{16}H_{34}$) is the most easily self ignited cetane (cetane number 60) and a-methylanenaphthalene $C_{10}H_7CH_3$ is difficult to ignite (whose cetane number is 0).

(*iii*) Degree of fuel atomization

(*iv*) Extent of swirling motion of air and fuel charge

(*v*) Extent of heat transfer from the hot gases to the walls of combustion chamber.

## EXERCISES

1. Calculate the fluid and air consumption per kWh of a CI engine which uses diesel fuel of specific gravity 0.75, calorific value of 45000 kJ/kg and has a brake thermal efficiency of 30%. The air fuel ratio for the engine may be taken as 20.
2. A diesel engine is having air fuel ratio of 24:1, calorific value of fuel 42500 kJ/kg and brake thermal efficiency of 35%. Find out the following for the engine

   *i*) Brake output   *ii*) Specific fuel consumption

3. The injection pump of an I.C engine running at 1800 rpm delivers fuel once for an interval of 20° of crank shaft rotation. The engine has an ignition delay of 0.0015 seconds. Determine

   *i)* The time lag in terms in degrees of crank shaft rotation between injection and starting of combustion.

   *ii)* The percentage of fuel injected during the period of ignition delay

   *iii)* Percentage of fuel supplied during injection delay and rapid combustion if rapid combustion takes place 5° of crank rotation.

4. Design a cylinder for 30 kW diesel engine running at 1800 rpm and using high speed diesel fuel with calorific value of 45000 kJ/kg. The fuel contains 85% Carbon & 14% hydrogen. For complete combustion 30% extra air is required. Take the mechanical efficiency as 80%, thermal efficiency as 35% and overload as 110%. Assume any other data if required.

5. Find out the orifice size of a single jet nozzle in an injector of diesel engine to deliver $1.00 \times 10^{-4}$ kg of fuel during 25° period of crank rotation of an engine running at 2000 rpm. Assume injection pressure as 150 kg/cm$^2$, pressure at the end of compression as 40 kg/cm$^2$ and specific weight of fuel as 0.78. Take coefficient of discharge of nozzle as 0.92.

6. Determine the volume of fuel per cylinder per cycle in a 4 cylinder, four stroke cycle diesel engine developing 40 kW brake power at 1800 rpm. 32° API oil of specific gravity 0.88 is used as fuel at the rate of 0.292 kg/kWh. The injection pressure is 140 kg/cm$^2$. Determine the diameter of fuel orifice for single & five hole nozzles for this engine, if injection duration is 28° of crank travel. Take coefficient of discharge of injection orifice as 0.60 for both the cases. Also find the power loss in injecting the fuel.

7. A 4-stroke cycle, 4 cylinder diesel engine developing 40 kW brake power at 1800 rpm. 320 API oil of specific gravity 0.88 is used as fuel at the rate of 0.292 kg/kWh. The injection pressure is 140 kg/cm$^2$. If the fuel injection pump has full stroke displacement of 3 times the rated engine fuel consumption and if the injection pump plunger has stroke 1.75 times its diameter, what are the pump plunger bore and stroke dimensions.

8. A 20 kW 4-stroke cycle single cylinder diesel engine running at 1800 rpm on oil having composition by mass C85; H 15% and calorific value 42500 kJ/kg. The diesel oil is burnt with 20% excess air. The volumetric efficiency of engine at 1.015 bars atmospheric pressure and 10°C is 0.80. Mechanical efficiency and thermal efficiencies were 0.85 and 0.32 respectively. Determine the stroke volume of the engine.

9. A four stroke cycle diesel engine of a tractor running at 1800 rpm consumes 4.5 kg of fuel in one hour and develops a torque of 150 Nm. Calculate the brake specific fuel consumption of engine.

10. Calculate thermal efficiency of a tractor engine developing 40 kW power while consuming diesel at the rate of 10.5 litres/h. Take density of diesel as 0.85 and calorific value of fuel is 43000 kJ/kg.

11. A diesel fuel ($C_{16}H_{34}$) is used in I.C engine of a tractor and air supply is 10% excess than theoretically required for complete combustion of fuel. Assuming that no free carbon is left in the exhaust and all the hydrogen is burnt, calculate the following:

    *i)* Analyze the dry exhaust gases by volume

    *ii)* Quantity of water produced per kg of fuel burnt.

12. A 4-cylinder, 4-stroke cycle diesel engine is operating at 1800 rpm and consumes 9.5 kg of diesel (0.86 specific gravity) per hour. Calculate the volume of fuel of individual injectors of the engine.
13. The specific fuel consumption of a 30 kW diesel engine of a tractor is 272 g/kWh. Take calorific value of diesel fuel as 42000 kJ/kg. Calculate the thermal efficiency of the tractor engine.
14. Determine the quantity of air required for a 4-stroke cycle, 4-cylinder engine having a total displacement volume of 3550 CC. Assume volumetric efficiency of engine as 82%.
15. A 25 kW tractor engine is burning diesel ($C_{16}$ $H_{34}$) at an efficiency of 25% while ploughing a field. Calculate the amount of $CO_2$ released in kg/hr assuming that heating value of diesel used is 45 MJ.
16. When one kg of diesel is burnt completely by a tractor engine using 15% more air than required, Calculate the amount of air used and Kg of $CO_2$, $O_2$, $H_2O$ and $N_2$ in products of combustion. Also determine the percent of dry gases present in the exhaust of tractor engine.
17. Calculate the air/fuel ratio and volume percentage of each constituents of dry exhaust gases for the combustion of following fuels:
    (*a*) Cetane, $C_{16}H_{34}$ with, 20% excess air
    (*b*) Octane, $C_8H_{18}$, with 90% of theoretical air
18. A tractor engine is consuming 4.5 kg of diesel, $C_{16}H_{34}$ fuel/hr with 10% excess air and is developing 30 kW power for field operation. Calculate the following:
    (*a*) the fuel feed rate to engine
    (*b*) the air-fuel ratio
    (*c*) the quantity of air flow rate in the engine
    (*d*) Volumetric composition of exhaust dry gases.
19. In a tractor having DI engine, an injector have six holes. The engine operating speed is 2000 rpm and has ignition delay of 18°. Then calculate the swirl ratio of the engine if one plume is half way that of next plume when ignition delay is to be provided.
20. The exhaust gas of IC diesel engine has the following volumetric analysis on a dry basis 9.98% $CO_2$, 2% CO; 4.69% $O_2$ and 83.33% $N_2$. Determine the actual air-fuel ratio on mass basis and also calculate the excess air used for combustion of diesel fuel.
21. When hydrocarbon fuel cetane ($C_{16}H_{34}$) is used in a diesel engine, the air supply is 10% greater than theoretically required for complete combustion. Assume that all the hydrogen was burnt and no free carbon was left in the exhaust. Calculate the volume percentage of constituents of exhaust gases on dry basis. Also determine the quantity of water produced per kg of fuel burnt in the engine.
22. A 40 kW tractor engine is consuming 35 litres diesel in 3.5 hours of field operation. The calorific value of diesel fuel is 42.5 MJ/kg. Calculate thermal efficiency and specific fuel consumption of engine.
23. A four cylinder 4-stroke cycle engine has cylinder diameter of 100 mm and stroke length of 120 mm. It is operating at a speed of 2400 RPM and develops 40 hp. Calculate brake mean effective pressure of engine if mechanical efficiency of engine is 80%. Also design a closed type fuel injector if it consumes 10 litres of diesel per hour at maximum load. Assume that density of diesel fuel is 830 kg/m$^3$.

**24.** A 4-stroke cycle diesel engine has following specifications:

(*a*) Rated power at 2400 rpm = 40 kW

(*b*) No. of cylinders = 4

(*c*) Compression ratio = 16.5 : 1

(*d*) Excess air required for complete combustion = 20%

(*e*) Diesel fuel used has LHV = 42 MJ/kg

(*f*) Determine the following:

(*i*) Amount of air theoretically required for the combustion of one kg fuel

(*ii*) Total amount of combustion products.

(*ii*) Fuel delivery rate

**25.** A 26 kW brake power tractor is operated at 2000 rpm and consumes diesel fuel at the rate of 8.5 litres/h. If compression ratio of engine is 16.5 : 1 and displacement volume is 4250 × $10^{-3}$ L, calculate the fuel delivery rate of FI pump.

**26.** A 3-cylinder, 4-stroke cycle engine having displacement volume of 3.050L while running at a speed of 2400 rpm consumes 9.5 kg/h diesel and 180 kg/h of air and produces 40.5 kW brake power under 100 kPa pressure and ambient air temperature of 300°K. Calculate the following:

(*a*) Theoretical air consumption by the engine

(*b*) Air to fuel ratio.

(*c*) Volumetric efficiency of engine

**27.** A 4-cylinder, 4-stroke cycle diesel engine of a tractor has displacement volume of 2.750L. The compression ratio of engine is 16.5 : 1. While running at a speed of 2400 rpm develops 35 kW brake power and consumes diesel at the rate of 8.5 litres/h. Assume that for mixing of diesel and air 18° crankshaft rotations is available and density of diesel fuel is 830 kg/m$^3$. Calculate the following:

(*a*) Average volume of fuel injected to each cylinder

(*b*) Time of air and fuel mixing

(*c*) Fuel delivery rate of FI pump

(*d*) Select the size and stroke of plunger in barrel of FI pump

(*e*) Size of open type injector for the engine.

**28.** Determine the weight and volume of fuel per cylinder per cycle delivered in 4 cylinders, 4-stroke cycle engine developing 40 kW brake power at 2000 rpm. The specific fuel consumption of engine may be taken as 0.250 kg/kWh. Fuel injection pressure is 14 MN/m$^2$. Also determine the orifice size of 4-hole nozzle for the engine if injection duration is 28° crank travel. Coefficient of discharge of orifice may be taken as 0.65 and specific weight of diesel as 0.830 kg/cc. Assume any other data required.

**29.** In a diesel engine running at 2000 rpm an injector is delivering 1.25 × $10^{-4}$ kg of fuel during 20° crank travel. Assume that pressure at the end of compression stroke is 3.5 MN/m$^2$ and injection pressure of 14.5 MN/m$^2$. Coefficient of discharge of nozzle orifice may be taken as 0.9 and density of diesel fuel as 830 kg/m$^3$.

# CHAPTER 4

# Governing System of Tractor Engine

## INTRODUCTION

Tractor engines usually run under varying loads. The variation of load on the engine tends to vary the engine speeds. So, there will be fluctuations in engine speeds under varying loads if no speed control device is used in the engine. It is essential that the engine of tractor runs at constant speed irrespective of loads. Governing system in tractor engine is provided to regulate and maintain a constant speed under fluctuating loads. It ensures that the engine does not pick up speed at no load and the speed should not fall as the load is increased. In order to regulate engine speeds automatically at varying loads and protect the engine components from high speeds a governor is provided. A governor is a mechanical device which automatically regulates the supply of fuel to the engine according to load so that the engine speed may not go down or vice-versa. The governor automatically maintains all speeds (idling as well as maximum speed) nearly constant once the driver has selected the required engine speed with the accelerator through linkages system. In general, centrifugal type governor having horizontal or vertical axis of rotation are used in the engines of tractors.

## 4.1 TYPES OF GOVERNORS

Governors are of following four types.

(*i*) Mechanical or centrifugal governors

  (*a*) Constant speed governor

  (*b*) Variable speed governor

(*ii*) Pneumatic type governor

(*iii*) Hydraulic type governor

(*iv*) Combined mechanical and pneumatic type governor.

### 4.1.1. Mechanical Type Centrifugal Governor

Mechanical type centrifugal governor is provided in all tractor engines. It works on the principle of centrifugal force and consists of weights, sliding collar, rod connecting the collar, throttle and lever for speed adjustment. The weights are hinged to the cam shaft of fuel injection pump with the help of springs. The distance between weights of governor is directly proportional to centrifugal force and inversely proportion to the spring tension. The collar moves along the axis of shaft according to speeds of rotation of weights. As the speed of rotation of engine changes, the centrifugal weights fly out due to change in centrifugal force. The weights assumes a new position in response to engine speed change and move the collar on the shaft which in turn change the position of control device that will vary the supply of fuel from fuel injection pump to the engine. Reduced fuel supply will result in restoring the normal speed of the engine.

On the other hand if load on the engine is suddenly increased, the speed will decrease and the weights will come closer due to spring tension as the centrifugal force will become lesser than the spring force. This will change (increase) the fuel supply from fuel injection pump to the engine and will result in increase in engine speed to normal value despite heavy loads. Thus, in this way the engine speed regulation at varying loads is controlled by the centrifugal action on the weights of the governor. The accelerator pedal of tractor engine is linked with the governor in such a way that a complete control on engine speed to suit the forward speed and load conditions is maintained. The tractor engines are generally fitted with variable speed governor which regulates engine speed with varying load at any preset value within the speed range. The components of a spring loaded centrifugal type speed governing system is given in Fig. 4.1

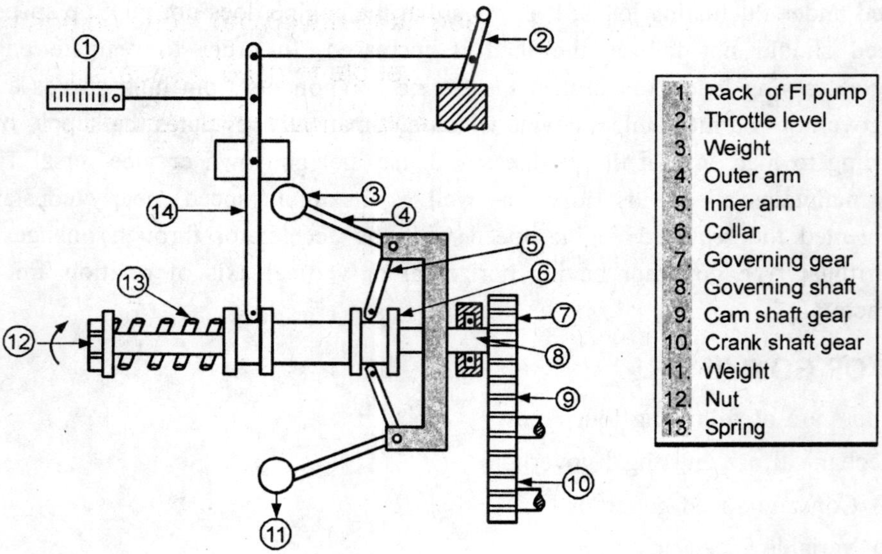


**Figure 4.1. Components of centrifugal speed governor**

In this type of governor, centrifugal force $F_c$ acts on a ball having mass, $m$ rotating about center line at a radius '$r$' with angular velocity '$\omega$'. Then the centrifugal force acting on the ball of governor is given by

$$F_c = mr\omega^2 = mr\left[\frac{2\pi N}{60}\right]^2 \qquad ...(4.1)$$

where, $F_c$ = centrifugal force in kg,

$m$ = mass of ball

$w$ = angular velocity of ball, rad/s

$N$ = speed of drive shaft, rpm.

### 4.1.2. Pneumatic Type Governor

Pneumatic governor operate by the vacuum created by air flow in the inlet manifold of the engine and consists of venturi air flow control unit and diaphragm unit. As the speed of engine increases or decreases, the vacuum in the venturi changes and accordingly the diaphragm is pulled out or pushed in and engine speed is kept under control. Pneumatic governor covers the complete range of engine speeds (idling to maximum).

### 4.1.3. Hydraulic Governor

In hydraulic governor an oil pump takes oil from the oil reservoir and pumps through release valve under pressure. From the release valve oil under pressure enters the cylinder and pushes plunger outwards. The plunger is connected to speed control lever which is connected to fuel control rack. When the plunger moves out it moves control rod to full fuel position against the tension of spring. Other end of plunger has a helix cut in it and plunger also rotates sideways. The helix in the plunger is so arranged that at certain position it connects the hydraulic oil to port. The plunger can be positioned at appropriate place according to throttle opening and according to speed variations of the engine. It is an all speed governor and control speed to suit road and load conditions on the engine.

### 4.1.4. Combined Pneumatic and Mechanical Type Governor

In this type of governor, features of both pneumatic and mechanical governors are combined together for obtaining advantages of both. It is also all speed governor but not used commonly on tractor engines.

**EXAMPLE 4.1** *A centrifugal type of governor mounted on the camshaft of an engine running at speed of 1800 rpm has following specifications as given in Fig. 4.2.*

*Effective lever arm*

$a = 3$ cm

$b = 3.5$ cm

$L = 6$ cm

*Angle of arm with axis of rotation when weights are in closed position,* $\theta = 0°$

*Angle of arms axis of rotation when weights are in open position,* $\theta = 30°$

*Spring tension on the sleeve = 6 kg/cm*

*Find out the weights 'W' attached to the end of arms of the governor.*

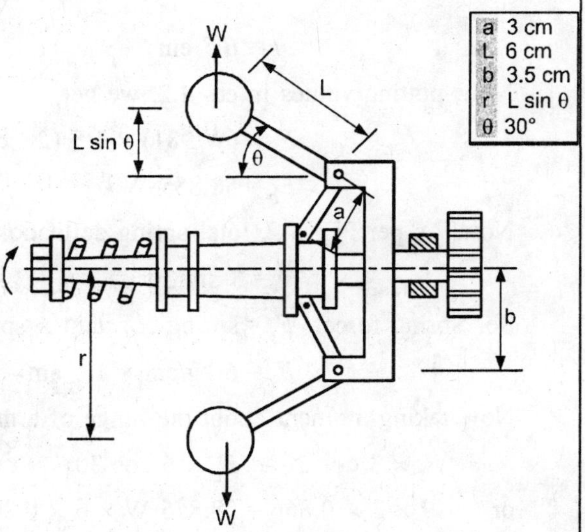


**Figure 4.2. Details of centrifugal governor**

**SOLUTION:**

Refer to the details given in Fig. 4.2 of centrifugal governor. Assume that there are negligible weights of arms of governor and the fly weights are spherical in shape.

Now, we know that centrifugal force in the rotating mass of governor is given by

$$F_c = mr\,\omega^2 = mr\left[\frac{2\pi N}{60}\right]^2$$

or

$$F_c = \left[\frac{W}{g}\right] \times r \times \left[\frac{2\pi N}{60}\right]^2 \qquad ...(4.2)$$

where, $F_c$ = centrifugal force, kg

$m$ = mass of ball

$W$ = weight of rotating mass, kg

$\omega$ = angular velocity of ball, rad/s

$N$ = speed of drive shaft, rpm

At steady state, the above centrifugal force would be balanced by the spring tension of the governor. Since governor is mounted on the cam shaft of the engine and the engine speed is 1800 rpm. Therefore, the speed of governor would be 900 rpm. At 900 rpm of governor the weights make an angle 30° with the axis of rotation (given).

So, as per Fig. 4.2, the effective radius of rotation '$r$' is given by

$$r = b + L \sin \theta = 3.5 + 6 \times \text{Sin } 30°$$

$$= 3.5 + 6 \times \frac{1}{2}$$

$$r = 6.5 \text{ cm}$$

Now, putting values in eq. 4.2, we get

$$F_c = (\text{W}/981) \times 6.5\ (2\pi\ x\ 900/60)^2$$

$$F_c = 58.855 \text{ W kg}$$

Now, As per Fig. 4.2, total spring deflection by the centrifugal force is

$$= 3 \sin 30° = 3 \times 1/2 = 1.5 \text{ cm}$$

So, Spring force, $F_s$ = spring constant × spring deflection

$$F_s = 6 \text{ kg/cm} \times 1.5 \text{ cm} = 9 \text{ kg}$$

Now taking moment about the hinge of arm we get,

$$F_s \times 3 \cos 30° = F_c \times 6 \cos 30°$$

or, $9 \times 3 \times 0.866 = 58.855 \text{ W} \times 6 \times 0.866$

or, $W = (9 \times 3 \times 0.866)/(58.855 \times 6 \times 0.866)$

$$= 0.0765 \text{ kg or } 76.5 \text{ gms.}$$

## 4.2 GOVERNOR REGULATION

It is also known as speed drop of governor with increase in load on engine. Regulation is defined as the ratio of difference between no load and full load speeds to mean equilibrium speed.

$$R_g = \left[\frac{N_n - N_l}{N_m}\right] \times 100 \quad ...(4.3)$$

And
$$N_m = \left[\frac{N_n + N_l}{2}\right] \quad ...(4.4)$$

where, $R_g$ = governor regulation, %

$N_n$ = engine speed at no load, rpm

$N_l$ = engine speed at full load, rpm

$N_m$ = mean equilibrium speed of governor (also known as speed at mean position of ball masses), rpm

Also,
$$R_g = \left[\frac{\omega_n - \omega_1}{2}\right] \quad ...(4.5)$$

And
$$\omega_n = \left[\frac{\omega_n + \omega_l}{2}\right] \quad ...(4.6)$$

where, $\omega_n$ = engine speed at no load, rad/s.

$\omega_l$ = engine speed at no load, rad/s.

$\omega_m$= mean equilibrium speed of governor, rad/s.

The speed drop or governor regulation helps in overshooting or hunting of governor during fuel quantity is corrected when engine loads change.

### 4.2.1. Range of Governor Equilibrium Speed

It is the difference between the maximum and minimum equilibrium speeds, where maximum equilibrium speed is the speed at maximum radius of rotation of the balls and minimum equilibrium speed is the speed at minimum radius of rotation of balls of governor.

### 4.2.2. Sleeve Lift

The distance travelled by the sleeve due to change in equilibrium speed of governor is called as the lift of sleeve.

**EXAMPLE 4.2**

*A watt governor fitted in a low speed diesel engine is rotating at a speed of 150 rpm. If the engine speed is increased to 250 rpm, what would be the change in vertical height of the governor?*

**SOLUTION:**

Initial speed of governor, $N_i$ = 150 rpm

Final speed of governor, $N_f$= 250 rpm

Now, We know that for a watt governor

$$h = 895000/N^2$$

Where $h$ = height of governor, mm

$N$ = speed of governor, rpm

Now,

Initially, $h_i = 895000/N_i^2 = 895000/(150)^2$

$= 39.77$ mm

And after gaining new speed

$h_f = 895000/N_f^2 = 895000/(250)^2$

$= 14.32$ mm

So,

Change in vertical height of watt governor

$= h_i - h_f = 39.77 \text{ mm} - 14.32 \text{ mm}$

$= 25.45$ mm Ans.

**EXAMPLE 4.3** *In a porter governor mass of each ball is 5 kg and mass of sleeve is 30 kg. The governor has equal arms each of 300 mm long and pivoted on the axis of rotation. The radius of rotation is 200 mm when it begins to lift and 250 mm when the governor is at maximum speed. Determine the minimum speed, maximum speed and speed range of governor.*

**SOLUTION:**

$m = 5$ kg

$M = 30$ kg

Arm length, l = 300 mm both the arms of governor are equal

Radius of rotation when sleeve begins to lift, $r_1 = 200$ mm

Radius of rotation when governor is at maximum speed, $r_2 = 250$ mm

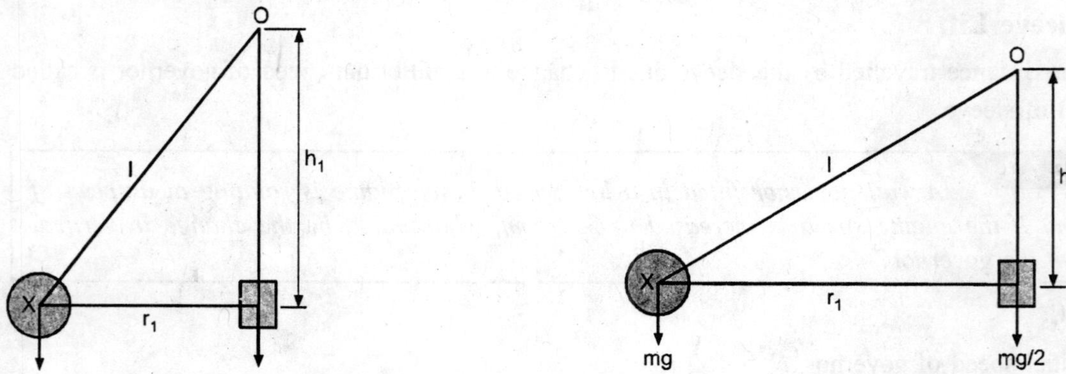


**Figure. (a) Minimum radius of rotation (b) Maximum radius of rotation**

Since, both the arms of governor are equal and height of governor is given by

$$h = \frac{895000}{N^2} \times \left[\frac{m+M}{m}\right]$$

Where $h$ = height of governor, mm

$N$ = speed of governor, rpm

$m$ = mass of each ball, kg

$M$ = mass of sleeve, kg

Now, refer to figure above, when $r_1$ = 200 mm, $h_1$ is given by

$h_1 = (OX^2 - r_1^2)^{0.5} = (300^2 - 200^2)^{0.5}$

$h_1 = 223.61$ mm

And, $N_1^2 = (895000/h_1) \times (m + M)/m$

$= (895000/223.61) \times (5 + 30)/5$

$= 28017.53$

Or, $N_1 = 167.38$ rpm

Again, when $r_2$ = 250 mm

$h_2 = (Ox^2 - r_2^2)^{0.5} = (300^2 - 250^2)^{0.5}$

$h_2 = 165.83$ mm

And, $N_2^2 = (895000/h_2) \times (m + M)/m$

$= (895000/165.83) \times (5 + 30)/5$

$= 37779.65$

Or, $N_2 = 194.37$ rpm

Now, we know that speed range of governor ($N_g$) is given by

$N_g = N_2 - N_1 = 194.37 \text{ rpm} - 167.38 \text{ rpm}$

$N_g = 26.99$ rpm

**EXAMPLE 4.4** *Calculate the governor regulation of a tractor engine where speeds at no load and full load are 1750 and 1650 rpm respectively.*

**SOLUTION :**

Speed at no load, $N_n$ = 1750 rpm

Speed at full load, $N_l$ = 1650 rpm

Now, $N_m = (N_n + N_l)/2 = (1750 + 1650)/2 = 1700$ rpm

Now, we know that,

$$R_g = \left[\frac{N_n - N_l}{N_m}\right] \times 100$$

Putting the values in the above eqn., we get,

$R_g = [(1750 - 1650)/1700] \times 100$

$R_g = (100/1700) \times 100 = 5.882\%$

**EXAMPLE 4.5** *Find out the speed of governor at load having a regulation of 10% and speed at no load is 1800 rpm.*

**SOLUTION:**

$$R_g = 10\%$$
$$N_n = 1800 \text{ rpm}$$

Now, we know that

$$R_g = \left[\frac{N_n - N_l}{N_m}\right] \times 100$$

And

$$N_m = \left[\frac{N_n + N_l}{2}\right]$$

*Putting values in the above equations and rearranging, we get*

$$10 = [2(1800 - N_1)/(1800 + N_1)] \times 100$$

Or, $$1800 + N_1 = 36000 - 20\, N_1$$

Or, $$21\, N_1 = 34200$$

$$N_1 = 1657.15 \text{ rpm}$$

## 4.3. GOVERNOR PERFORMANCE CHARACTERISTICS

Performance of governor of a tractor engine depends on following main parameters:

1. The relationship between the angular velocity of weights and sleeve lift.
2. Resistance of sleeve and fuel control device (regulating gear) affect speed of governor.
3. Characteristics of fuel feed device
4. Relationship between engine torque and fuel supplied by the fuel system.

**Sensitiveness of governor:** It is defined as a percentage of the mean speed of governor and calculated by eqns. 4.3 and 4.4. It is the response of governor to act with certain change in engine speed. If an engine is running with the governor in equilibrium state, engine speed must change to certain rpm before the governor starts to act. This is because of loss of motion in its parts due to friction in joints.

Sensitiveness of governor is also defined as the ratio of mean speed to the speed range of governor over its limit of operation. Mathematically:

Sensitiveness = Mean equilibrium speed/speed range of governor

$$= N_m/(N_n - N_1) \qquad \text{...(4.7)}$$

Where $N_m = (N_n + N_1)/2$

$N_m$ = engine mean speed, rpm

$N_n$ = engine speed at no load, rpm

$N_1$ = engine speed at load, rpm

**Effort of governor:** The effort of a governor is defined as the mean force exerted at the collar sleeve for a given percent change in speed. At steady state of governor there will not be any force at the sleeve. The available work force from the governor is the energy available for moving governor and fuel metering mechanism. It is difference between the force generated by the rotating weights in the open position and the force generated in the closed position, minus force required to overcome spring deflection and friction.

The governor effort may be calculated by following equations:

**For simple watt governor**

$$F_g = N_p \times mg \quad (4.8)$$

Where $F_g$ = governor effort, N
$N_p$ = percent increase in speed
$m$ = mass of each ball
$g$ = acceleration due to gravity, 9.81 N/s$^2$

**For Porter governor**

$$F_g = N_p (M + m)\, g \quad .... (4.9)$$

Where $F_g$ = governor effort, N
$N_p$ = percent increase in speed
$M$ = mass of sleeve
$m$ = mass of each ball
$g$ = acceleration due to gravity, 9.81 N/s2

**For Hartnell governor**

$$F_g = N_p (Mg + S) \quad .... (4.10)$$

Where; $F_g$ = governor effort, N
$N_p$ = percent increase in speed
$M$ = mass of sleeve
$S$ = spring force exerted on the sleeve, N
$g$ = acceleration due to gravity, 9.81 N/s2

Or alternatively,

$$F_g = (S_2 - S_1)/2 \quad ...(4.11)$$

Where $F_g$ = governor effort, N
$S_1$ = spring force exerted on the sleeve at minimum speed, N
$S_2$ = spring force exerted on the sleeve at maximum speed, N

**Power of governor:** It is expressed as product of effort of governor and lift of sleeve as given below.

Power of governor ($W$) = Mean effort of governor ($F_g$) × Lift of sleeve ($L$) ... (4.12)

Or, $$W = F_g \times L \quad ... (4.13)$$

**For Porter governor**

$$W = (F_g/2) \times (2 \times \text{Height of governor}) \quad ... (4.14)$$

**For Hartnell governor**

$$W = F_g \times 2\, N_p \quad .... (4.15)$$

Where $F_g$ = governor effort, N
$N_p$ = percent increase in speed

**EXAMPLE 4.6** *In a porter governor mass of each ball is 5 kg and mass of sleeve is 30 kg. The governor has equal arms each of 300 mm long and pivoted on the axis of rotation. The radius of rotations 200 mm when it begins to lift and height of governor is 223.61 mm and 250 mm when the governor is at maximum speed. With height of governor as 165.83 mm, find out effort and power of governor.*

**SOLUTION:**

$$m = 5 \text{ kg}$$
$$M = 30 \text{ kg}$$

Arm length, l = 300 mm both the arms of governor are equal

Radius of rotation when sleeve begins to lift, $r_1$ = 200 mm

Radius of rotation when governor is at maximum speed, $r_2$ = 250 mm

Height of governor at minimum radius of rotation, $h_1$ = 223.61 mm

Height of governor at maximum radius of rotation, $h_2$ = 165.83 mm

Now, we know that

Sleeve lift, $L = 2\,(h_1 - h_2)$

$$= 2\,(223.61 \text{ mm} - 165.83 \text{ mm})$$
$$= 115.56 \text{ mm}$$

And, also percent increase in speed, $N_p = (N_2 - N_1) / N_2$

$$N_p = (194.37 - 167.38)/194.37$$
$$= 0.1389$$

Now, governor effort ($F_g$) is

$$F_g = N_p \times g\,(m + M)$$
$$= 0.13899.81\,(5 + 30) = 47.69 \text{ N}$$

Also,

Power of governor, $W$ = Effort × Lift

$$W = F_g \times L = 47.69 \text{ N} \times 0.11556 \text{ m}$$
$$= 5.57 \text{ Nm}$$

**Stability of governor:** A governor is stable if it maintains a definite position of equilibrium for each speed within its working limits. The ball masses occupy a definite position for each speed of engine in its working range. The stability and sensitiveness of governor are two different and opposite characteristics.

**Governor haunting:** A large variations in the speed of engine above and below the mean speed continuously due to excessive friction in the joints or lost motion in parts of the governor is known as governor haunting. It may also be due to changing of fuel supply rate in large extent on small change in engine speed. This is due to over compensation of fuel supplies and oversensitivity of the governor. Even a sudden change in fuel supply to the engine by closing the throttle completely will overload the engine and the governor will try to open the throttle creating a situation for governor haunting.

## EXERCISES

1. A watt governor has each arm length 300 mm which are pivoted on the axis of rotation. Determine the following:
   *a)* Governor height
   *b)* Radius of rotation of balls when the governor speed is 250 rpm
2. The particulars of a porter governor whose arms are pivoted on axis of rotation fitted on a diesel engine are as under:
   Mass of each ball = 5 kg
   Length of each arm = 250 mm
   Mass of sleeve = 25 kg
   Minimum radius = 100 mm
   Maximum radius = 150 mm
   Calculate the following:
   *i)* Range of speed
   *ii)* Lift of sleeve
3. A centrifugal type of governor is mounted on the camshaft of a diesel engine running at a speed of 1600 rpm and has following specifications:
   Effective lever arm
   $A = 3$ cm
   $b = 4$ cm
   $L = 7.5$ cm
   Angle of arm with axis of rotation when weights are in closed position, $\theta = 0°$
   Angle of arm with axis of rotation when weights are in open position, $\theta = 45°$
   Spring tension on sleeve = 5 kg/cm
   Find out the weights 'W' attached to the end arms of the governor
4. Calculate the governor regulation of a tractor engine fitted on cam shaft of engine. If engine speeds at no load and full load are 1800 rpm and 1650 rpm respectively.
5. Find out the speed of governor at no load having a regulation of 8% and speed at load is 850 rpm.
6. A porter governor having equal links of 300 mm and pivoted on axis of rotation. Each ball has 5 kg and sleeve has mass of 30 kg. The radiuses of rotation at minimum and maximum speeds are 200 mm and 250 mm respectively. Find out maximum speed, range of speed, governor effort and power of governor.

CHAPTER

5

# Lubricating System of Tractor

## INTRODUCTION

The moving components of IC engine especially crank shaft plain bearings and piston operate at varying temperature, pressure, load and speed. So, their proper and timely lubrication is absolutely essential to reduce friction and ultimately wear and tear in moving parts and increased brake power of the engine. Engine parts which require lubrication are cylinder, piston, piston pin, connecting rod bearing, crank shaft, cam shaft, valve and valve opening mechanism. Lubrication of IC engine is accomplished by circulating a suitable grade of lubrication oil through passages drilled in engine components at appropriate pressure with the help of a gear pump. The lubricating oil is pumped into moving components of engine through oil filter and it flows back downwards into the engine sump provided at the bottom of engine. The cooling of piston by lubricating oil jet is given in Fig. 5.1. Lubricating system in IC engines of tractors is provided to perform following main functions:

1. **Lubrication of moving parts:** To provide thin oil film between moving parts of the engine and separating them completely to reduce friction and their wear and tear.
2. **Cooling of critical components:** The lubricating oil is largely responsible for cooling of piston by direct heat dissipation to cylinder walls and then to cooling system and also cooling of engine bearings.

**Figure 5.1. Cooling of piston by lubricating oil jet**

3. **Cleaning of foreign materials:** The lubricating oil and oil additives clean the various engine parts from the products of wear and tear and also hold the contaminants in suspension form.
4. **Sealing of compression pressure:** Oil film acts as a seal between piston rings and cylinder walls and prevents leakage of gases from combustion chamber.
5. **Engine noise reduction:** The oil film acts as a cushion on moving parts which reduce engine noise.
6. **Frictional power reduction:** To reduce the power required to overcome frictional resistance in moving parts of the engine.
7. **Prevention of corrosion of bearings:** The oil additives in the lubricating oil neutralize the acidic components formed in the oil which may otherwise lead to corrosion and rusting of bearings.

## 5.1 TYPES OF LUBRICATING SYSTEMS

Generally following two types of lubricating systems are used in IC engines.

### 5.1.1. Splash Type

In this type of lubricating system a dipper is provided at the bottom end of connecting rod and lubricating oil is kept in oil pan/sump at the bottom of engine. The dipper provided with connecting rod end scoops the oil during every revolution when it enters the oil pan. The splash is produced due to rotation of crank shaft in the oil pan. The splashed oil mist formed in crank case housing lubricates the main bearing, crank shaft bearing, timing gear, push rod, cylinder liner walls etc. However, the valve mechanism is lubricated with the help of oil cans manually at regular intervals. This type of lubricating system is generally provided in single cylinder engine with closed crank case. Its effectiveness will depend upon size of oil holes, clearance etc. as well as maintenance of proper oil level in oil pan and condition of engine components.

### 5.1.2. Forced Feed Lubricating System

Forced feed lubricating system mainly consists of oil sump, gear pump, oil filter, and drilled oil passages through moving parts and oil pressure gauge as given in Fig. 5.2. In this type of system a gear type pump is provided in engine sump to circulate adequate quantity of lubrication oil to different engine components at a pressure of 0.4 to 0.5 $MN/m^2$ depending upon engine design. The gear pump is driven by cam shaft and it draws oil from the sump through a coarse mesh filter and discharges it into the distribution network *i.e.* drilled passages of crankshaft and cam shaft. The pump forces oil into all the crankshaft and connecting rod bearings and timing gears. Cylinder walls, piston pins and small end bearings of connecting rod are lubricated by the oil coming out from the big end bearing through holes drilled through connecting rod. Surplus oil then flows back to sump. This also washes extraneous impurities *i.e.* wear out products of bearings and clearances between mated parts to the sump by scrapping of oil.

From cam shaft, the oil under pressure goes to the valve mechanism (rocker arm shaft and tappet). Excess oil from the cylinder head is received back to crank case along with the push rod. An oil pressure gauge is fitted with the system to indicate the lubricating oil pressure in the system,

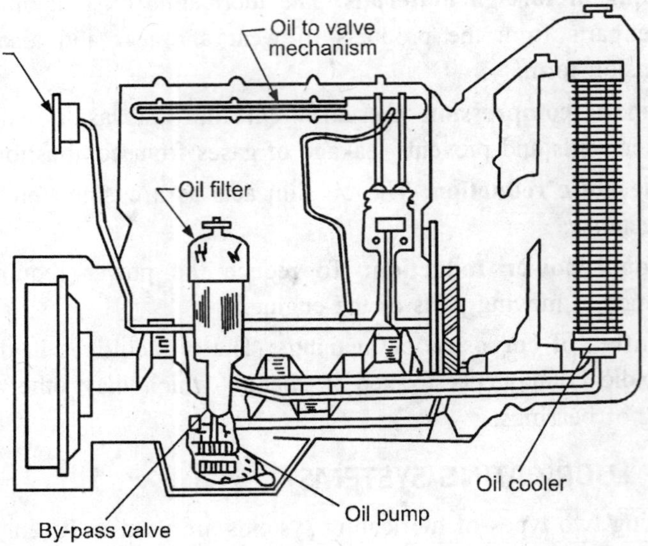


Figure 5.2. Forced feed lubrication system of tractor

The amount of oil in crank case depends on volume of crank case, filters, ducts and consumption of oil during operation. It should be sufficient to enable the oil pump to operate without drawing in air through the oil intake. The specific capacity of diesel engine wet sumps should range between 0.14 to 0.21 litres/kW and for dry sump 0.15 to 0.70 litres/kW. Maintenance of correct level of proper grade of oil in the engine sump as recommended by the manufacturer is very essential.

### 5.1.3. Crank Case Breather

A crank case breather (Fig 5.3) is provided in the engine sump to remove fuel and water dilution of oil due to condensation of water and mixing of diesel as a result of injector dribbling as well as to permit escape of gases to atmosphere which has been blown into the sump by piston. These gases may force the crank case oil to pass the main bearing seals or engine gasket by rupturing them. A small air cleaner is commonly provided in the crank case breather to prevent dirt and dust particles from air entering the crank case breather.

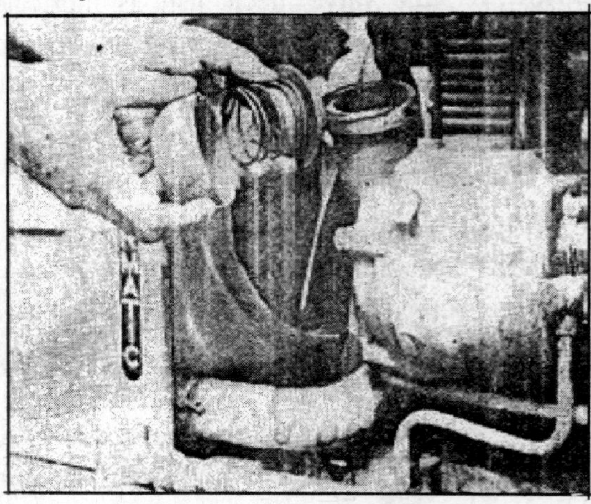

Figure 5.3. Crank case breather

## 5.2. OIL FILTERS

Oil filter keeps the oil free from dirt, dust and any other abrasive type foreign material that collects in the engine sump. Commonly coarse and fine filters are used which trap particles 30–60 and 0.5–1 microns respectively. Wire slit plate and wire gauge filters with 60 micron mesh are used for coarse cleaning. The oil flow rate through oil filters depends on:

- Surface area of filter
- Size of orifice
- Oil pressure on the filter
- Resistance to oil flow
- Viscosity of lubricating oil
- Temperature of lubricating oil

Generally two types of oil filters are used in the lubrication system of tractor:

### 5.2.1. Washable Type Filters

These are also known as metal plate or edge type metal filters. These can be wire gauge type, edge type or centrifugal type filters. These must be cleaned and washed thoroughly after recommended working hours with kerosene oil or diesel.

### 5.2.2. Replaceable Type

The filtering material can be cotton waste, paper or perforated cover type paper. Pleated resin impregnated paper are also used where surface area can be increased by pleating the paper. These are changed after 120 hours of engine operation or with each engine lubrication service. A replaceable type lubrication oil filter is given in Fig. 5.4.

**Figure 5.4. Replaceable type lubrication oil filter**

## 5.3 OIL PUMP

The lubricating oil is circulated in the system with the help of external meshing gear pumps. The pump shaft generally rotates at 4000–5000 rpm and gear ratio between cam shaft and pump is 1.0 : 1.5. The peripheral velocity of the gears should not exceed 10 m/s for satisfactory pump delivery. The required output of a gear type oil pump depends on:

- Quantity of oil fed to crankshaft bearings ( Nearly 60–70% of oil pumped in main line)

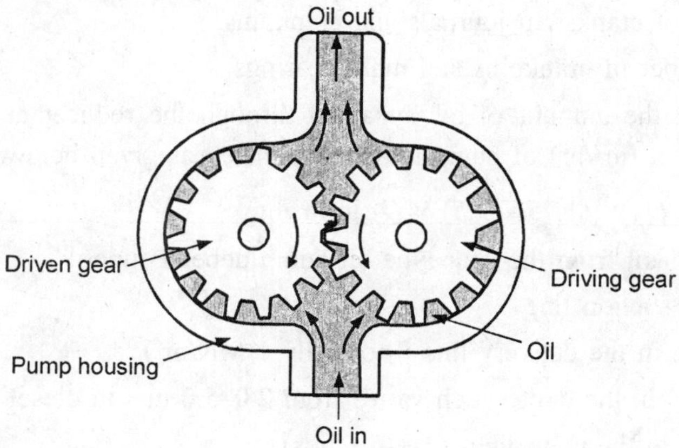


**Figure 5.5. Gear type oil pump**

- Amount of oil delivered to cam shaft and valve mechanism.
- Oil required for cooling of piston crown and lubricate cylinder liner.
- Amount of oil bypassed through pump reducer to fine filter and crank case.
- Additional oil to account for wear and tear in the pump gears with use.

The construction of a gear type oil pump is given in Fig. 5.5.

### 5.3.1. Quantity of Oil Pumped by Gear Pump

For externally meshed gear type pump, the pump discharge is given by

$$Q_{th} = D_p \times N \quad ...(5.1)$$

where, $Q_{th}$ = theoretical flow, l/min

$D_p$ = volume of displacement of pump in one revolution, l/rev

$N$ = pump speed, rpm

$$Q_{act} = D_p \times N \times \eta_v \quad ...(5.2)$$

or,

$$Q_{act} = Q_{th} \times \eta_v \quad ...(5.3)$$

$$Q_{act} = 47 \times \eta_v (d_a^2 - d_d^2) \times b \times N_p \quad ...(5.4)$$

where, $\eta_v$ = volumetric efficiency of pump (0.75–0.85)

$d_a$ = diameter of addendum circle

$d_d$ = diameter of dedundum circle

$b$ = length of teeth (addendum) or height of rotor

$N_p$ = speed of pump driving shaft, rpm at rated engine speed

The volume of oil required in the crankshaft bearings is estimated by following equation.

$$Q_b = C \times N_r \times d_p^2 \times n_p \quad ...(5.5)$$

where, $Q_b$ = amount of oil required in bearings, $m^3/hr$

$C$ = coefficient (generally 0.008–0.012)

$N_r$ = rated speed of crank shaft, rpm

$d_p$ = diameter of crankshaft journals and crankpins, m

$n_p$ = total number of crankpins and main bearings

Now, considering the amount of oil bypassed through the reducer and drain valve in fine filter, the actual oil output ($m^3/hr$) of pump may be estimated as given below.

$$Q_p = (1.75 - 2.5) \times Q_b \text{ in } m^3/hr \quad ...(5.6)$$

Actual delivery of oil from the gear type oil pump depends upon:

- Resistance in suction line
- Back pressure in the delivery line ( normally 1 $MN/m^2$)
- Velocity of oil in the duct which varies from 2.0–5.0 m/s in diesel engines.
- Oil velocities in the main lines (3.8–6.1 m/s)

Also, the specific oil output of pump for different engine is given in Table 5.1.

**TABLE 5.1: Specific oil output of pumps for different engines**

| Sr. No. | Type of engine | $q_p$ ($m^3$/(W–hr)) |
|---|---|---|
| 1. | Diesel engine without oil cooling of piston | $(27–41) \times 10^{-6}$ |
| 2. | Supercharged diesel engine with oil cooling of piston | $(48–68) \times 10^{-6}$ |
| 3. | Petrol engine provided with soft alloy bearings | $(20–27) \times 10^{-6}$ |

## 5.3.2. Pump Torque and Power Requirements

**5.3.2.1. Torque ($T_p$):** The pump torque ($T_p$) is given by

$$T_{th} = \frac{(P \times D)}{2\pi} \times 100 \qquad ...(5.7)$$

where, $T_{th}$ = theoretical input torque, N-m

$P$ = pump outlet pressure minus pump inlet pressure (bar)

The actual torque is given by

$$T_{act} = \frac{(P \times D)}{2\pi} \times 100 \times \eta_t \qquad ...(5.8)$$

where, $\eta_t$ = torque efficiency of pump, %.

**5.3.2.2. Input or shaft power ($W_s$):** The input or shaft power ($W_s$) is given by

$$W_s = T \times N \times 1.05 \times 10^{-4} \text{ in kW} \qquad ...(5.9)$$

where, $T$ = input shaft torque, N-m

$N$ = shaft speed, rpm

**5.3.2.3. Hydraulic/fluid power of pump ($W_f$):** The hydraulic/fluid power of pump ($W_f$) is given by

$$W_f = \frac{Q \times P}{60} \qquad ...(5.10)$$

where, $Q$ = actual pump discharge, l/m

$P$ = pressure across the pump, MPa

And

$$HP_F = \frac{Q \times H}{75} \qquad ...(5.11)$$

where, $Q$ = actual pump discharge, l/s

$H$ = Head, m

**5.3.2.4. Overall efficiency of pump ($\eta_m$):** The overall efficiency of pump ($\eta_m$) is given by

$$\eta_m = \frac{W_f}{W_s} \qquad ...(5.12)$$

This is also equal to the product of torque and volumetric efficiencies, *i.e.*

$$\eta_m = \eta_t \times \eta_v \qquad ...(5.13)$$

**EXAMPLE 5.1** *A gear type pump of lubricating system of an engine operating at a speed of 2200 rpm is developing a pressure of 10 MPa requires input power of 10.7 kW. If its mechanical efficiency is taken as 70%, calculate oil flow rate in the pump in litres/min and its displacement volume per revolution. Also calculate theoretical discharge of pump if its volumetric efficiency is 80%.*

**SOLUTION:**

Shaft power ($W_s$) = 10.70 kW

Pressure developed ($P$) = 10 MPa

Mechanical efficiency of pump ($\eta_m$) = 70%

Pump speed ($N$) = 2200 rpm

We know that

Shaft Power $(W_s) = W_f/\eta_m$

or, $W_f = Ws \times \eta_m$ = 10.7 kW × 70/100

= 7.49 kW

Also, Fluid Power $(W_f) = Q.P/60$

or, $Q = W_f \times 60/P$ = 7.49 kW × 60/10 MPa

= 44.94 Litres/min

Again, $D_p = Q/N = 44.94 \times 10^3/2200$

$= 24.42\ cm^3/rev$

We know that $Q_{th} = Q_a/\eta_v$

or = 44.94 litres/min/0.80 = 56.17 litres/min

## 5.4 PROPERTIES OF LUBRICATING OIL

**Viscosity:** Viscosity (ease with which oil flows) is the most important property of lubricating oil. It is also known as internal resistance of a fluid as one layer is moved in relation to another layer. The lubricating oil must have sufficient viscosity and oiliness to protect the moving parts of engine at necessary speeds, pressures and temperatures. Sir Issac Newton has developed following relationship for viscous force in lubricating oil.

$$F = \mu A \times \left(\frac{z}{v}\right) = \text{constant} \quad \text{...(5.14)}$$

where, $F$ = viscous force in the oil layer, N

μ = absolute viscosity of fluid, mPa.s (centipoises)

$A$ = contact area, $m^2$

$v$ = velocity, m/s

$z$ = distance between two plates or layers, mm

For Newtonian fluids, absolute viscosity is constant as per following expression

$$\mu = (F/A) \times \left(\frac{z}{v}\right) = \frac{\text{Shear stress}}{\text{Shear rate}} = \text{constant} \quad \text{...(5.15)}$$

Based on eqn. 5.14 given by Sir Issac Newton, the viscosity of lubricating oil in piston ring and wall of cylinder, where thick oil film provides hydrodynamic lubrication can be modified to following form.

$$F_t = \mu A \times \left(\frac{v}{t}\right) \quad \text{...(5.16)}$$

where, $F_t$ = tangential shear force in the oil layer, N
$\mu$ = dynamic viscosity of fluid, mPa.s
$A$ = contact area between ring and liner wall, $m^2$
$v$ = ring speed, m/s
$t$ = oil film thickness, mm

According to Poiseville's law of viscosity for laminar fluids, it can be related with fluid flow through capillary tubes as given under:

$$\mu = \frac{\pi p r^4 t}{8VL} \quad \text{...(5.17)}$$

where, $\mu$ = Absolute viscosity of fluid, poises
$P$ = pressure difference, dynes/$cm^2$
$r$ = radius of tube, cm
$t$ = time in seconds
$V$ = volume of liquid, $cm^3$
$L$ = length of tube, cm

**EXAMPLE 5.2** *In a 3 mm diameter and 100 mm long capillary tube viscometer, 200 $cm^3$ of oil having specific gravity of 0.92 passes through the tube in 10 seconds. A head of 8 mm of oil above inlet of viscometer tube maintains a pressure difference through the tube. Calculate the following:*

*(i) Pressure difference across the tube*
*(ii) Dynamic viscosity of the oil*

**SOLUTION:**

Diameter of capillary tube = 3 mm
Length of capillary tube = 100 mm or 10 cm
Head of oil at tube inlet = 8 mm
Specific gravity of oil = 0.92
Volume of oil flow = 200 $cm^3$
Time of oil flow = 10 s

**(*i*) Pressure difference across the tube**

As oil pressure head = 8 mm or 0.8 cm
Now, Specific gravity of oil is 0.92

Therefore pressure head of water column = 0.8 cm × 0.92 = 0.736 cm

Pressure difference across the tube = 0.736 cm of $H_2O$ × 100 Pa/100cm = 0.736 Pa

***(ii)* Dynamic viscosity of oil**

According to Poiseville's law of viscosity

$$\mu = \frac{\pi p r^4 t}{8VL}$$

where, $\mu$ = Absolute viscosity of fluid, poises

$p$ = pressure difference, dynes/cm$^2$

$r$ = radius of tube, cm

$t$ = time in seconds

$V$ = volume of liquid, cm$^3$

$L$ = length of tube, cm

Putting values in the above equation, we get

$$\mu = \frac{\pi \times 7.36 \times (0.15)^4 \times 10}{8 \times 200 \times 10}$$

$$= 7.31 \times 10^{-6} \text{ poises}$$

## 5.5 RELATIONSHIP BETWEEN KINEMATIC VISCOSITY AND ABSOLUTE VISCOSITY

The absolute viscosity of lubricating oil is affected by its density. Therefore, in order to keep viscosity independent of density, its kinematic viscosity is computed by following relationship.

$$\nu = \frac{\mu}{\rho} = \frac{\text{Absolutely viscosity}}{\text{mass density of fluid}} \quad ...(5.18)$$

$\nu$ = kinematic viscosity, centistokes in mm$^2$/s

### 5.5.1. Viscosity Index (VI)

Generally the viscosity of oil is designated by SAE number system. SAE number of oil is a viscosity classification. According to classification drawn by Society of Automotive Engineers in the U.S.A, lubricating oil having higher viscosity has higher SAE number. The viscosity of oil changes with temperature, it declines as temperature of oil increases. It is desirable that engine oil should have minimum change in viscosity over a range of working temperature. The degree with which the viscosity of different oils changes is denoted by viscosity index. Viscosity index refers to the ability of an oil to resist changes in viscosity as the temperature changes. An oil of higher viscosity index can serve as multi-grade oil which can be further improved with the use of additives. Viscosity index (VI) of lubricating oil is calculated from ASTM method D-567 as given under:

$$VI = \left[\frac{L-U}{L-H}\right] \times 100 \quad ...(5.19)$$

where, $L$ = viscosity at 38°C of "L" oil that has arbitrary viscosity index as zero

$H$ = viscosity at 38°C of "H" oil that has arbitrary viscosity index as 100

$U$ = viscosity at 38°C of the oil whose viscosity index is not known.

**EXAMPLE 5.3** *Calculate the viscosity of oil which has following details:*

*Viscosity at 38°C =110 s*

*Viscosity at 99°C = 40 s*

*and L = 136.7 s*

*H = 106.2 s*

**SOLUTION:**

Viscosity of 'L' oil at 38°C = 136.7 s

Viscosity of 'H' oil at 38°C = 106.2 s

Viscosity of oil with unknown index = 110 s

Now, we know that

$$VI = \left[\frac{L-U}{L-H}\right] \times 100$$

Putting values in the above eqn., we get

$$VI = [(136.7 - 110)/(136.7 - 106.2)] \times 100$$

$$VI = (26.7/30.5) \times 100 = 87$$

CHAPTER 6

# Cooling System of Tractor

## INTRODUCTION

Cooling system controls the operating temperature of the engine to protect its components from overheating and seizure. The heat produced by fuel combustion can not be fully converted into useful work. Only 30 to 35% of total heat supplied is converted into useful work. Out of the remaining 65 to 70% heat supplied, some part is dissipated to cooling system, some part is taken away by exhaust gases and some part is lost through radiation. So, quite a large percentage of the heat produced in the engine needs to be removed with the cooling system as engine components like cylinder head, cylinder liner and piston are exposed to temperature as high as 1350–1650°C. Peak combustion temperatures generally exceed the melting point of the engine components. Moreover, such a high engine temperature which may lead to lower volumetric efficiency, pre-ignition, detonation and complete engine failure. Therefore, nearly 33% of heat of combustion of the fuel is removed through cooling system for satisfactory performance of the engine.

Main functions of cooling system are:

- To remove only about 33–35% of heat of fuel combustion of fuel from the engine. Too much removal of heat lowers the thermal efficiency of engine.
- To regulate engine operating temperature *i.e.* to maintain optimum operating temperature of 82–85°C of the engine
- To prevent overheating of the engine
- To protect engine components from thermal stresses and seizure
- To maintain optimum volumetric efficiency and power output of the engine

**Types of cooling systems:** Generally two types of cooling systems are used in tractor engines. They are:

(*i*) Air cooling system and

(*ii*) Liquid or water cooling system

## 6.1 AIR COOLING SYSTEM

In this type of cooling system the engine heat is directly dissipated to atmospheric air. A stream of air is directed over finned surfaces on and around hottest parts of engine like cylinder block and head with the help of a blower. The heat transfer takes place through convection. The contact area of air is increased by providing fins on the engine block and head. The air stream blown continuously comes in contact with the cylinder block and head through fins and the heat is directly removed by the atmospheric air. Effectiveness of air cooling depends on the following parameters.

1. Uniformity of temperature in the cylinder walls and head.
2. Maintenance of temperature of cylinder walls and head.
3. The area of fins on cylinder and head.
4. Designed dimensions of blower fan.
5. Power spent to drive the blower fan.

The unit volume of air at 40°C needed to cool various types of engines and resistance of air flow through the fins area is reported in Table 6.1.

**TABLE 6.1: Volume of air needed to cool various types of engines**

| Sr. No. | Type of engine | Unit volume of air, $v_u$ ($m^3$/(W-hr)) | Resistance to air flow, $P$ ($kN/m^2$) |
|---|---|---|---|
| 1 | Diesel engine with open combustion chamber | 0.05–0.06 | 1–1.8 |
| 2 | Diesel engine with divided combustion chamber | 0.06–0.075 | 1.5–2.4 |
| 3 | Petrol engine | 0.04–0.07 | Up to 1.5 |

### 6.1.1. Volume of Air Required

The total volume of air required for cooling the engine is given by under:

$$V_t = V_u \times W_b \quad \text{...(6.1)}$$

where, $V_t$ = total volume of air needed to cool engine, $m^3$/hr

$V_u$ = unit volume of air needed for cooling, $m^3$/(W-hr)

$W_b$ = brake power of the engine, kW

### 6.1.2. Cooling Fan Efficiency ($\eta_f$)

The efficiency of cooling fan is given by

$$\eta_f = W_d/W_i \quad \text{...(6.2)}$$

where, $W_a$ = air power, kW

$W_i$ = input power to fan, kW

The air power ($W_a$) can be calculated as given by

$$W_a = Q \times p \quad \text{...[6.2 (a)]}$$

where, $Q$ = air flow rate, $m^3$/s

$P$ = total air pressure, $10^3$ Pa

(The resistance of radiator to the flow of air is usually 200–300 $N/m^2$).

## 6.2 WATER COOLING SYSTEM

In water cooling system the heat from the engine is first transferred to the water and then to the air. The cooling water moves through the water jackets provided around the cylinders where heat is transferred from the cylinder walls to the water. The hot water then flows through a radiator where heat is transferred from water to the air passing through the radiator core. Effectiveness of water cooling system depends on the following parameters.

1. Amount of heat rejected through cooling system
2. Rate of water circulation
3. Quantity of heat dissipated by the radiator
4. Higher limit of cooling water temperature
5. Overall dimensions of fan and water pump
6. Power required for operating water pump and fan

Heat dissipated by the engine to cooling water is given by following equation.

$$H_w = W \times C_p \times (T_o - T_i) \quad ...(6.3)$$

where, $H_w$ = heat dissipated to cooling water, kJ/s
$W$ = weight of water circulated per sec, kg/s
$C_p$ = specific heat of water at constant pressure, kJ/kg-°C
$T_o$ = temperature of cooling water at outlet, °C
$T_i$ = temperature of cooling water at inlet, °C

Water cooling systems are broadly classified as given below:

(*i*) Thermo siphon type cooling system:
(*ii*) Forced circulation type cooling system

**EXAMPLE 6.1** *The cooling system of a 40 kW tractor engine maintains a temperature difference of 5.5°C of coolant. Calculate the quantity of water required to maintain above temperature difference. Assume that 0.16 L/s.kW of water is required and the engine rejects 0.58 kW per kW output of engine power.*

**SOLUTION:**

Engine power, $W_e$ = 40 kW

Power rejected by the engine = 0.58 kW/kW output power

Quantity of water required to maintain temperature difference, $Q$ = 0.16 L/s.kW

Now,

We know that quantity of water to be circulated by the cooling system is given by

$$Q_w = W_e \times W_r \times Q$$

Where $Q_w$ = Quantity of water circulated by cooling system, L/s
$W_e$ = Engine power, kW
$W_r$ = Power rejected by the engine, kW/kW power output
$Q$ = Quantity of water required to maintain 5.5°C temperature difference, L/s.kW

Putting values in above equation we get;

$$Q_w = 40 \text{ kW} \times 0.58 \text{ kW/kW} \times 0.16 \text{ L/s.kW}$$

$$Q_w = 3.712 \text{ L/s}$$

## 6.2.1. Thermo Siphon Type Cooling System

In this system of cooling there is no water pump to lift the water from the radiator and put into the water jackets around cylinder block. It is closed type of cooling system where cold water from the lower part of radiator enters the water jackets around the cylinders. Heat of cylinder walls raises the temperature of water in the water jackets. It becomes lighter and rises above and flows into the top of radiator and fresh cold water takes its place. Thus, thermostat is not used. The fan operating at designed speed sucks air through the radiator core and removes heat from the water. The cooled water again moves into lower radiator and re-enter again into the water jackets of engine. In this way cycle continues but the circulation of water is slow. The diagram of thermo-syphon system of cooling is given in Fig. 6.1.

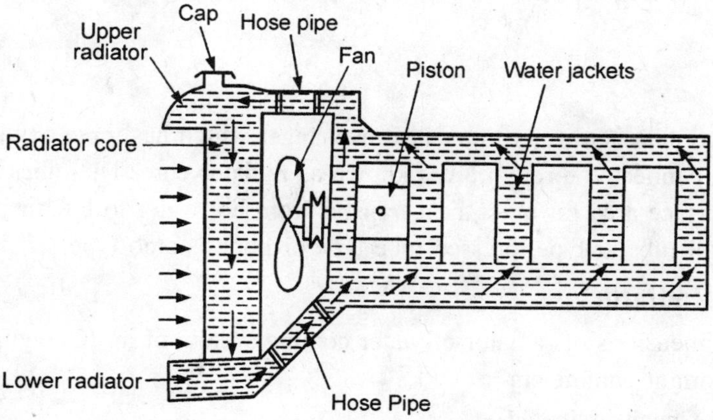


**Figure 6.1. Thermo siphon type cooling system**

### 6.2.2. Forced Circulation Type Cooling System

In this type of cooling system a pump is used to lift the water from the bottom of radiator and force it through the water jackets provided around the cylinders and in the cylinder head. The pump creates more positive circulation of water in the engine. The pump gets drive from the engine crank shaft through V-belt. Centrifugal type of pump takes water from the lower portion of radiator and forces it into engine block. A thermostat valve is also provided to restrict the flow of water through

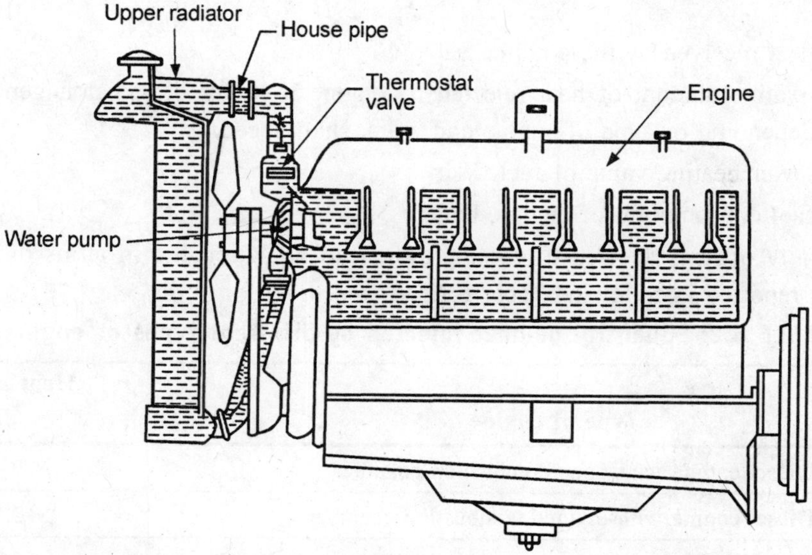


**Figure 6.2. Forced circulation type cooling system of tractor**

the radiator till it gets warmed up after cold start of engine. This valve also helps in maintaining a constant engine operating temperature. Air fan is mounted in front of water pump which sucks air from the radiator core and also blows it across the engine. The operating speed of fan is much higher than the crankshaft speed of engine for higher air flow through the radiator core. Thermo siphon action is also present in this type of cooling system. A forced circulation type of cooling system is most successful and used commonly in tractor engines. Its components are shown in Fig. 6.2.

## 6.3 RADIATOR

Radiator of cooling system is a water-to-air heat exchanger which has three compartments. Top and bottom radiators are connected through tubes known as radiator core. The tubes and fins of radiator core provide high surface area for quick heat transfer from hot water to the air passing between the tubes. Radiator can of tubular type, pressed tube type or honey comb type.

### 6.3.1. Design of Radiator

The overall dimensions of radiator of water cooling system of an IC engine of tractor depend upon following important parameters.

1. Quantity of heat dissipated.
2. Rate of circulation of water through radiator tubes.
3. Velocity of air passing through radiator core.
4. Arrangement of radiator with respect to engine.
5. Design parameters of radiator such as shape, location, number of rows of tubes, number of fins or strips, wall thickness, tubes and fins or strips, material of construction etc.

It is assumed that all the heat rejected by the engine to cooling system is dissipated by the radiator. Amount of heat rejected by the engine to cooling system is given by following equation.

$$H_w = h_r \times LHV \times F_c \qquad ...(6.4)$$

where $H_w$ = heat received by the cooling water, J

$h_r$ = relative amount of heat rejected by engine to water of radiator, generally 24–26% depending on type of engine and crank shaft speed.

$LHV$ = lower heating value of fuel, J/kg

$F_C$ = fuel consumption of engine, kg/hr

The quantity of heat rejected to cooling system of an IC engine in terms of J/(W-hr) for a diesel engine is reported in following Table 6.2.

**TABLE 6.2: Quantity of heat rejected by different types of engines**

| Sr. No. | Type of engine | Heat rejected ($h'_r$), J/(W-hr) |
|---|---|---|
| 1. | Diesel engine with open combustion chamber | 2394–2850 |
| 2. | Diesel engine with divided combustion chamber | 2850–3420 |
| 3. | Petrol engine | 4560–5700 |

So, based on Table 6.2, we can calculate amount of heat rejected to cooling system by using the following relationship.

$$H_w = h'_r \times W_b \qquad \text{...[6.4 (a)]}$$

where, $H_w$ = Total heat rejected to cooling water, J/hr

$h'_r$ = quantity of heat rejected to cooling system by engine, J/(W-hr)

$W_b$ = brake power of engine, W

Now, for the purpose of design of radiator, let us assume that 10% extra heat is rejected to the cooling system by engine. Therefore,

$$H_{rd} = 1.1\ H_w \qquad \text{...(6.5)}$$

Also,

$$H_{rd} = C_h \times A_t \times \Delta T_{w-a} \qquad \text{...(6.6)}$$

or,

$$A_t = H_{rd}/(C_h \times \Delta T_{w-a}) \qquad \text{...(6.7)}$$

where, $A_t$ = total heat dissipation surface of the radiator, $m^2$

$H_{rd}$ = total design heat of radiator, Joules/hr

$C_h$ = heat transfer coefficient, $W/m^2$-deg

$\Delta T_{w-a}$ = mean temperature difference between cooling water and air passing through radiator, °C

$$\Delta T_{w-a} = T_{mw} - T_{ma} \qquad \text{...(6.8)}$$

where, $T_{mw}$ = mean temperature of cooling water in radiator, °C (usually 86–91°C)

$T_{ma}$ = mean temperature of air passing through the radiator, °C

$$T_{ma} = (T_{ao} + T_{ai})/2 \qquad \text{...(6.9)}$$

$$T_{ao} = T_{ai} + \Delta T_a/2 \qquad \text{...(6.10)}$$

where, $T_{ao}$ = temperature of air at outlet of radiator, °C

$T_{ai}$ = temperature of air at radiator inlet, °C

$\Delta T_a$ = amount by which air is heated in radiator, °C (Normally 20–30°C)

Moreover,

$$\Delta T_a = H_{rd}/(3600 \times A_f \times C_a \times V_a \times \rho_a)$$

where, $H_{rd}$ = Total design heat of radiator, Joules/hr

$A_f$ = face area of radiator, $m^2$

$V_a$ = velocity of air, m/s

$\rho_a$ = density of air, $kg/m^3$

$C_a$ = specific heat of air at constant pressure, 1.0 kJ/kg/°C

Now,

Volume of radiator is given by

$$V_r = A_f \times d_r \qquad \text{...(6.12)}$$

where, $V_r$ = volume of radiator, $m^3$

$A_f$ = face area of radiator, $m^2$

$d_r$ = depth of radiator, m (Generally 60–130 mm)

or, $$d_r = A_t/(A_f \times C_{vc})$$ ...(6.13)

where, $C_{vc}$ = coefficient of volumetric compactness, 1/m (usually 600–950 1/m).

By using equ. 6.7 and 6.13 the size of radiator can be calculated.

### 6.3.2. Air Flow Through Radiator

The Quantity of air required for cooling of engine radiator is estimated as given under.

$$M_a = H_{rd}/(A_f \times C_a \times V_a \times \Delta T_a)$$ ...(6.14)

where, $M_a$ = mass of air flow through radiator, $kg/m^3$ (Normally 0.34 $kg/m^3$)

$H_{rd}$ = total design heat of radiator to be removed, kW

$A_f$ = face area of radiator, $m^2$

$V_a$ = velocity of air, m/s (mean velocity of air should be around 7–12 ms)

$C_a$ = specific heat of air at constant pressure, 1.0 kJ/kg/°C

$\Delta T_a$ = amount by which air is heated in radiator, °C (Normally 20–30°C)

**EXAMPLE 6.2** *A 100 × 120 mm four cylinder diesel engine of a tractor running at 2200 rpm develops 45 kW power at rated load. Calculate the quantity of water circulated through the radiator to maintain a temperature difference of coolant by 5.5°C. Also determine the rate of air flow through the radiator for dissipation of engine heat removed by the cooling water. Assume any other data required.*

**SOLUTION:**

100 × 120 mm four cylinder diesel engine

Engine speed = 2200 rpm

Power developed by the engine at rated load, $W_e$ = 45 kW

Coolant temperature difference = 5.5°C

Assume that the power rejected by the engine, $W_r$ = 0.55 kW/kW rated engine power

And, quantity of water required per second to maintain temperature difference,

$$Q = 0.16 \text{ L/s.kW}$$

***i*) Quantity of water circulated ($Q_w$)**

We know that quantity of water to be circulated by the cooling system is given by

$$Q_w = W_e \times W_r \times Q$$

Where $Q_w$ = Quantity of water circulated by cooling system, L/s

$W_e$ = Engine power, kW

$W_r$ = Power rejected by the engine, kW/kW power output

$Q$ = Quantity of water required to maintain 5.5°C temperature difference, L/s.kW

Putting values in above equation we get;

$$Q_w = 45 \text{ kW} \times 0.55 \text{ kW/kW} \times 0.16 \text{ L/s.kW}$$

$$Q_w = 3.96 \text{ L/s.kW}$$

***ii)* Air flow rate ($Q_a$)**

We know that the heat removed by the cooling water is to be dissipated by the air passing through the radiator and is given by following equation

$$H_w = Q_a \times M_a \times C_a \times \delta T$$

Where $H_w$ = Heat removed by the air, kW

$Q_a$ = Air flow rate through radiator, m$^3$/s

$M_a$ = Mass of air, kg/m$^3$ (0.34 kg/m$^3$)

$C_a$ = Specific heat of air, kJ/Kg°C (1.0 kJ/kg°C)

$\delta T$ = Temperature rise of air while passing through radiator, °C

Or, $$Q_a = H_w/(M_a \times C_a \times \delta T)$$

Also, $$H_w = W_e \times W_r$$

Where $H_w$ = Heat removed by the cooling water from engine, kW

$W_e$ = Engine power, kW

$W_r$ = Power rejected by the engine, kW/kW engine power

So,

$$H_w = 40 \text{ kW} \times 0.55 \text{ kW/kW}$$

$$H_w = 24.75 \text{ kW}$$

Assume that rise in temperature of air passing through the radiator ($\delta T$) is 25°C

Putting values in the above equation, we get

$$Q_a = 24.75 \text{ kW}/(0.34 \text{ kg/m}^3 \times 1.0 \text{ kJ/kg°C} \times 25\text{°C}$$

$$Q_a = 2.91 \text{ m}^3\text{/s}$$

## 6.4 PERFORMANCE OF FAN OF COOLING SYSTEM

The output of fan depends on its design and speed and can be determined by following equation.

$$V_f = A_f \times V_a \quad ...(6.15)$$

where $V_f$ = fan output, m$^3$/s

$A_f$ = face area of radiator, m$^2$

$V_a$ = velocity of air, m/s (mean velocity of air should be around 7–12 m/s)

### 6.4.1. Diameter of Fan Blades ($D_b$)

The fan blade diameter is selected based on face area of the radiator as given below.

$$D_b = 2\sqrt{A_f / \pi} \qquad ...(6.16)$$

### 6.4.2. Peripheral Velocity of Fan Blades ($u_f$)

Peripheral velocity of fan blades primarily depends on rpm of fan as given below.

$$u_f = \frac{\pi D_b \times N_f}{60} \qquad ...(6.17)$$

where, $u_f$ = peripheral velocity of fan blade, m/s
$D_b$ = diameter of fan blade, m
$N_f$ = fan rpm

Peripheral velocity of fan blade can also be estimated based on design parameters and resistance of air stream through radiator core.

$$u_f = 0.89 S_f \sqrt{\Delta P} \qquad (6.18)$$

where, $\Delta P$ = resistance of air stream through radiator, $N/m^2$ (usually 600–1000 $N/m^2$)
$S_f$ = shape factor for blades (for flat blades = 2.8–3.5 and for curved blades = 2.2–2.9)

### 6.4.3. Power Requirement of Fan ($W_f$)

The power requirement of fan is given by

$$W_f = \frac{V_f \times \Delta P}{\eta_f} \qquad (6.19)$$

where, $W_f$ = power required to drive the fan, kW
$V_f$ = fan output, $m^3/s$
$\Delta P$ = resistance to air path, $N/m^2$
$\eta_f$ = cooling fan efficiency

### 6.4.4. Cooling Fan Efficiency ($\eta_f$)

The efficiency of cooling fan is given by

$$\eta_f = W_a / W_i \qquad ...(6.20)$$

where, $W_a$ = air power, kW
$W_i$ = input power to fan, kW

Also,

$$W_a = V_f \times \Delta p \qquad ...(6.21)$$

where, $V_f$ = air flow rate, $m^3/s$
$\Delta P$ = total air pressure, $10^3$ Pa (The resistance of radiator to the flow of air is usually 200–300 $N/m^2$)

## 6.5 WATER PUMP

Centrifugal type of water pump as given in Fig.6.3 is mostly used in cooling system of a tractor which forces water into manifolds and distributes uniformly to all cylinders through water jackets in cylinder and cylinder head through thermostat valve. The volume of water circulated by the centrifugal pump is estimated based on quantity of heat received by the cooling system from the engine as given below.

$$V_w = H_{rd}/(C_w \times \Delta T_w \times \rho_w) \quad ...(6.22)$$

where, $V_w$ = volume of water circulated by pump, $m^3/hr$

$H_{rd}$ = total design heat of radiator, Joules/hr

$C_w$ = specific heat of water, 4.19 kJ/(kg-deg)

$\Delta T_w$ = drop in water temperature in the radiator, °C

$\rho_w$ = density of water, $kg/m^3$

Also, Power required to operate the water pump of cooling system is given by

$$W_p = \{(0.5 \text{ to } 1.0)/100\} \times \text{rated engine power (kW)} \quad ...(6.23)$$

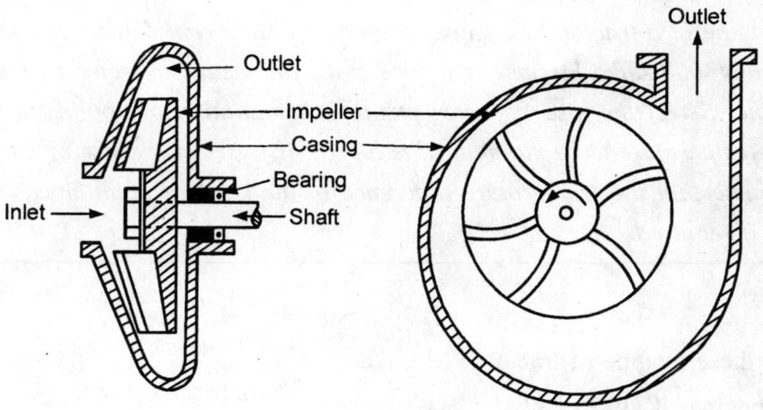


**Figure 6.3. Centrifugal type water pump**

**EXAMPLE 6.3** *A centrifugal type water pump of a cooling s 150 lpm system of a tractor engine, operating at 1000 rpm delivers water at the rate of 150 lpm at a pressure of 0.70 MPa. Calculate the power required to operate the pump. Assume that overall efficiency of pump is 80%.*

**SOLUTION:**

Pump discharge, $Q_p$ = 150 lpm

Pressure developed by the pump, $P$ = 0.70 MPa

Overall efficiency of pump, $\eta_m$ = 80%

Pump speed, $N$ = 1000 rpm

Now.

We know that

$$W_f = Q_p \times P/60$$

Where $W_f$ = Fluid power of pump, kW

$Q_p$ = Pump discharge rate, lpm

$P$ = Pressure developed by the pump, MPa

Putting values in above equation, we get

$$W_f = 150 \text{ lpm} \times 0.70 \text{ MPa}/60$$

$$= 1.75 \text{ kW}$$

Also,

$$W_i = W_f/\eta_m$$

$$W_i = 1.75 \text{ kW}/0.80 = 2.1875 \text{ kW}$$

$$W_i = 2.2 \text{ kW}$$

**EXAMPLE 6.4** *Design forced circulation type cooling system (radiator & fan) for a 3-cylinder, 30 kW diesel engine of a tractor. The engine running at 1800 rpm consumes 5.0 kg/h diesel fuel of calorific value 43000 kJ/kg. Assume that 40% of the fuel heat is rejected by the cooling system of tractor engine. Select the size of water pump for circulation of cooling water through the engine if water temperature to be maintained is 5.5°C. Also, select the size of air fan required for the system. Assume that the temperature difference of air is to be maintained at 25°C. Assume any other data if required.*

**SOLUTION:**

3-cylinder diesel engine of tractor

Power of engine, $W_b$ = 30 kW

Engine speed, $N$ = 1800 rpm

Amount of heat removed by cooling system, $H_w$ = 40% of $H_i$

Fuel consumption of engine = 5.0 kg/hr

Calorific value of fuel = 43000 kJ/kg

Temperature difference of water circulating through engine, $\delta T_w$ = 5.5°C

Temperature difference of air passing through radiator, $\delta T_a$ =25°C

Now, we know that heat input to the engine by diesel fuel is given by

$H_i$= Fuel consumption (kg/h) × Calorific value of diesel fuel (C.V)

$$H_i = 5.0 \text{ kg/h} \times 43000 \text{ kJ/kg}$$

$$H_i = 215000 \text{ kJ/h or } 59.75 \text{ kJ/s}$$

Also,

Heat removed by the circulating water is

$$H_w = 40\% \text{ of } H_i \text{ (given)}$$

So,

$$H_w = (40/100) \times 59.75 \text{ kJ/s}$$

$$H_w = 23.90 \text{ kJ/s}$$

***i*) Frontal area of radiator ($A_f$)**

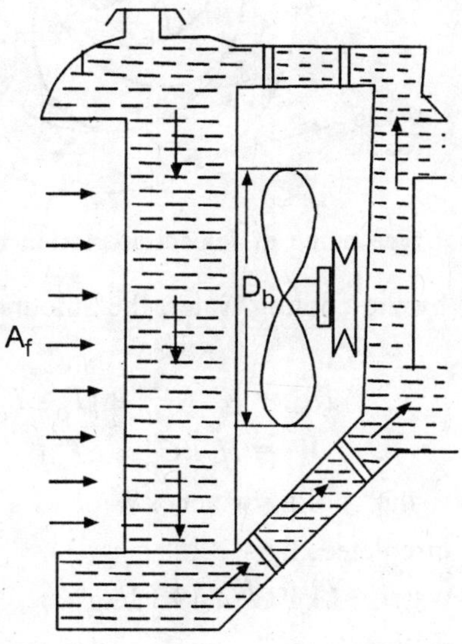


**Figure 6.4: Air circulation through radiator**

The heat removed by the cooling water must be released to the air. So, the frontal area ($A_f$) of the radiator is given by

$$A_f = H_w/(V_a \times M_a \times C_a \times \delta T_a)$$

Where $A_f$ = Frontal area of radiator, $m^2$

$H_w$ = Heat removed by the air from radiator, kW or kJ/s

$V_a$ = Velocity of air through radiator, m/s (usually 5–10 m/s)

$M_a$ = Mass of air, $kg/m^3$ (0.34 $kg/m^3$)

$C_a$ = Specific heat of air, kJ/kg°C

$\delta T_a$ = Temperature rise of air while passing through the radiator, °C

Putting values in above equation we get

$$A_f = 23.90 \text{ kJ/s}/(10 \text{ m/s} \times 0.34 \text{ kg/m}^3 \times 1.0 \text{ kJ/kg°C} \times 25\text{°C})$$

Or, $A_f = 0.28 \text{ m}^2$

***ii*) Water pump capacity ($Q_p$)**

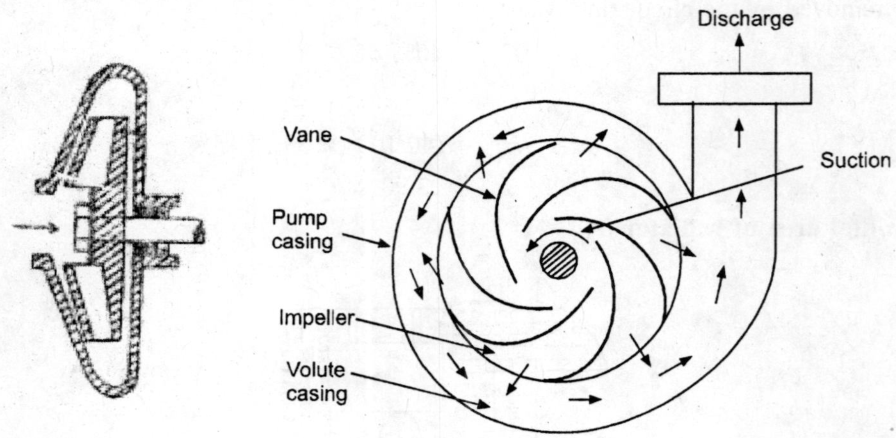


Figure 6.5: Centrifugal type pump of forced circulation type cooling system

In order to remove $H_w$ heat by the cooling water, the amount of water to be circulated by the centrifugal pump is given by

$$H_w = W \times C_p \times (T_o - T_i)$$

Or,

$$W = H_w/(C_p \times \delta T_w)$$

Where $H_w$ = Heat dissipated by the cooling water, kW or kJ/s

$W$ = Weight of water circulated, kg/s

$C_p$ = Specific heat of water, kJ/kg°C (4.19 kJ/kg°C)

$T_o - T_i = \delta T_w$ = Temperature difference between outlet and inlet of radiator, °C

Putting values in above equation, we get

$$W = 23.90 \text{ kJ/s}/(4.19 \text{ kJ/kg°C} \times 5.5\text{°C})$$

$$W = 1.037 \text{ kg/s or } 1.037\text{l/s}$$

Therefore, the pump capacity ($Q_p$) of a centrifugal type pump used in cooling system of tractor engine would be 1.037 lps or 62.25 lpm

***iii*) Design of air fan (blower) for the cooling system**

***a*) Fan output ($V_f$):**

We know that output of air fan is given by

$$V_f = A_f \times V_a$$

Where $V_f$ = Fan output, m$^3$/s

$A_f$ = Frontal area of radiator, m$^2$

$V_a$ = Velocity of air, m/s (Usually 5–12 m/s)

Putting values in above equation we get

$$V_f = 0.28 \text{ m}^2 \times 12 \text{ m/s}$$

$$V_f = 3.375 \text{ m}^3/\text{s}$$

***b*) Diameter of fan blades ($D_b$):**

We know that

$$D_b = 2(A_f/\pi)^{0.5}$$

Putting values in above equation, we get

$$D_b = 2\ (0.28\ m^2/22/7)^{0.5}$$

Or,

$$D_b = 0.5969\ m\ \text{or}\ 59.70\ cm$$

**c) Power requirement of blower fan ($W_f$):**

We know that for a blower fan

$$W_f = (V_f \times \delta P)/\eta_f$$

Where $W_f$ = Power requirement of fan,watts

$V_f$ = Fan output, $m^3/s$

$\delta P$ = Resistance to air flow through radiator, $N/m^2$ (200–300 $N/m^2$)

$\eta_f$ = Fan efficiency, %

Putting values in above equation we get

$$W_f = (0.28\ m^3/s \times 250\ N/m^2)/0.80$$

$$W_f = 87.5\ N\text{-}m/s$$

Or,

$$W_f = 87.5\ \text{watts}$$

## 6.6 THERMOSTAT VALVE

A thermostat valve regulates the temperature by causing the cooling water to bypass the radiator when engine is cold (refer Fig 6.6). This governs the water flow through the radiator and engine outlet temperature is maintained within 75–90°C at any speed or load. Normally this valve begins to open at 70–75°C and completely opens at 90°C. Based on the filling, it is of two types. *i.e.* Liquid or solid filling.

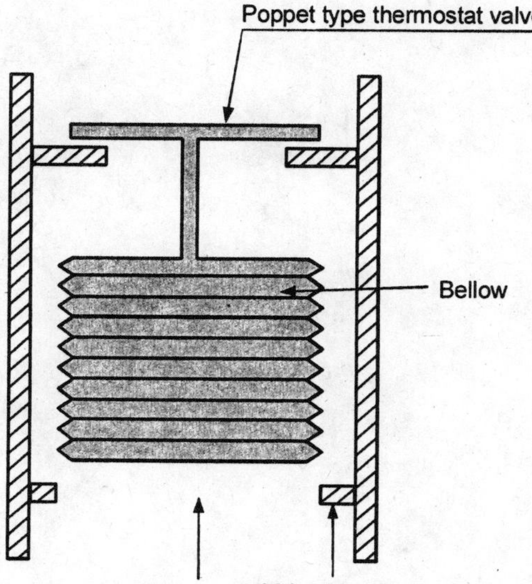


**Figure 6.6. Thermostat valve**

**Liquid filling valve:** It is a flexible corrugated cylinder partly filled with two third ethyl alcohol and one third water.

**Solid filling valve:** It is filled with wax crystals with higher coefficient of volumetric expansion.

## EXERCISES

1. A single cylinder engine 12 × 14 cm size is working on four stroke cycle engine. It operates at 1600 rpm and mean effective pressure is 7.5 kg/cm$^2$ has mechanical efficiency of 85%. It consumes 3.0 kg/hr diesel having calorific value 40000 kJ/kg. The cooling water is circulated 550 kg/hr having inlet and outlet temperatures of 30°C and 65°C. Calculate the following:

   (*i*) Brake thermal efficiency of engine

   (*ii*) Heat utilized for development of BHP

   (*iii*) Heat dissipated to cooling water

2. In a 35 kW brake power tractor engine 32% of energy goes to brake power and 16% goes to cooling water. Its radiators capacity is 12 litres of water. Calculate the depth and the face area of radiator.

CHAPTER 7

# Electrical System

## INTRODUCTION

Electrical system is important for all types of work on a tractor. The generator/dynamo generates the electric current which is stored in the battery and it is used for starting the engine of tractor and lighting purpose. In the modern tractors the electrical system is becoming more complicated as, for control of engine temperature and pressure latest controls and instrumentations are used. Now-a-days, electrical and electronic instrumentations are preferred in hydraulic system shift speeds in tractor. Electronic fuel control systems are also being employed in modern diesel engines to control fuel rates. These systems employ some type of electrically manipulated fuel injectors. Electrically drawn comfort items such as AC, radio, automatic control of hydraulic functions, electrical remote controls have increased the level of sophistication. The major electrical components used in a tractor are shown in Fig. 7.1.

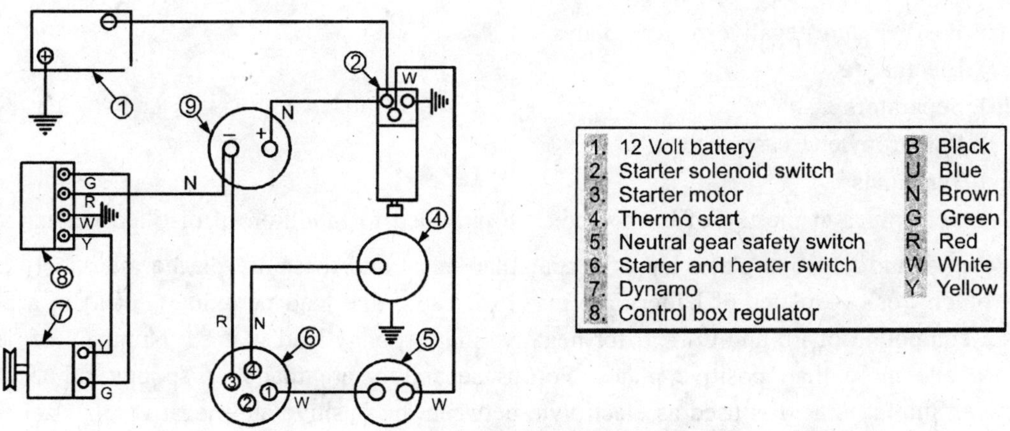


**Figure 7.1. Electrical components of tractor**

Main components of electrical system of a tractor are:

(*i*) Battery

(*ii*) Generator/dynamo

(*iii*) Cutout relay or current-voltage regulator

(*iv*) Self starter

(*v*) Electrical wiring

(*vi*) Electric units/solenoid switch

## 7.1 BATTERY

Battery is an energy storage device which provides energy for starting of tractor and also for lighting purpose when tractor engine is not running. A lead acid battery stores electrical energy in the form of chemical energy and current is produced by chemical action when circuit is completed (Fig.7.2).

**Figure 7.2: Lead acid battery of tractor**

Main components of lead acid battery are:

(*i*) Positive and negative battery plates
(*ii*) Electrolyte
(*iii*) Separators
(*iv*) Polypropylene case or box
(*v*) Terminals
(*vi*) Vent plugs at the top of battery box are provided for addition of distilled water.

Positive and negative plates are of rectangular shape and these are placed alternately parallel to each other. Positive plates of battery are made of lead. The lead peroxide ($PbO_2$) in a positive plate is a compound of Pb and $O_2$ and for negative plate spongy lead is used. Numbers of negative plates are one more than positive plates. Porous separators are made of spongy rubber or bad conductors. Sulphuric acid is used as electrolyte between the positive and negative plates. The level of electrolyte above battery plates should be 6 mm. A fully charged lead acid battery electrolyte has 36% sulphuric acid and 64% water in it and the electrolyte has a specific gravity of 1.27. Casing of battery is made of polypropylene or hard rubber. The casing is provided with a inter cell connection and battery terminals. Vents are provided on the cover of battery for addition of distilled water and testing of battery.

A single cell in a lead acid battery develops a potential difference of 2V at full charge. Fig. 7.3 shows how a voltmeter is used to check the voltage across the battery terminals. When the battery is used, it discharges and the current flows at a potential difference due to the chemical reactions that occurs in the battery. When load is applied to battery terminals, the reactions as depicted in Table. 7.1 occur where oxygen ($O_2$) at positive plate ($PbO_2$) combines with the hydrogen (H) which is ionized in the electrolyte of the battery and form lead sulphate ($PbSO_4$) and water ($H_2O$). The discharging cycle of battery is given in eq. 7.1 below.

$$PbO_2 \cdot Pb + 2H_2SO_4 \leftrightarrow 2\ PbSO_4 + 2H_2O \qquad ...(7.1)$$

The increase in water results in dilution of electrolyte and lowering of specific gravity. The specific gravity of discharged battery is about 1.10. The battery should be recharged when its specific gravity falls below 1.225 otherwise its life will reduce drastically. For maintaining proper level of electrolyte in the battery distilled water should be used as impurities shorten the life of battery.

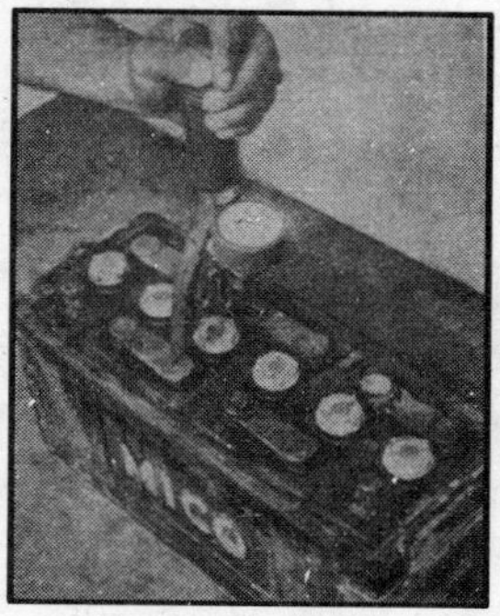

Figure 7.3. Checking voltage of battery cell

**TABLE 7.1: Chemical changes in a discharged battery**

| Battery component | Fully charged battery | Complete discharged battery |
|---|---|---|
| Positive plate | $PbO_2$ | $PbO_2$<br>$PbSO_4$ |
| Negative plate | Pb | Pb<br>$PbSO_4$ |
| Electrolyte | $H_2SO_4$ | $H_2O$<br>$H_2SO_4$ |

### 7.1.1. Recharging of Battery

It is reverse of battery discharge and is an electrochemical process due to supply of electric current in the opposite direction which is accomplished by generator/dynamo provided in the electrical system. Charging of battery reverse the reactions at both plates of battery and increases the acid concentration in the electrolyte. So, during recharging of battery the lead sulphate ($PbSO_4$) and water ($H_2O$) react with each other and sulphuric acid is formed and free oxygen will combine with lead at the positive plate to form lead peroxide ($PbO_2$) as shown by eq.7.2 below.

$$2\ PbSO_4 + 2H_2O \leftrightarrow PbO_2 \cdot Pb + 2H_2SO_4 \qquad ...(7.2)$$

Usually 5–7 ampere current and charging voltage of 2.3 to 2.45 V per cell is given for charging of battery and slow charging is advisable. Before putting battery to charger its vent plugs should be removed so that gaseous products produced during charging process should escape to atmosphere.

The lead acid battery should not be allowed to discharge completely or remain at lower electrolyte concentration levels as this result in high lead sulphate concentrations at electrodes. If the battery is not used for a longer period of time and kept in discharged state, large lead sulphide crystals will be deposited at the plates and will be difficult to recharge the battery.

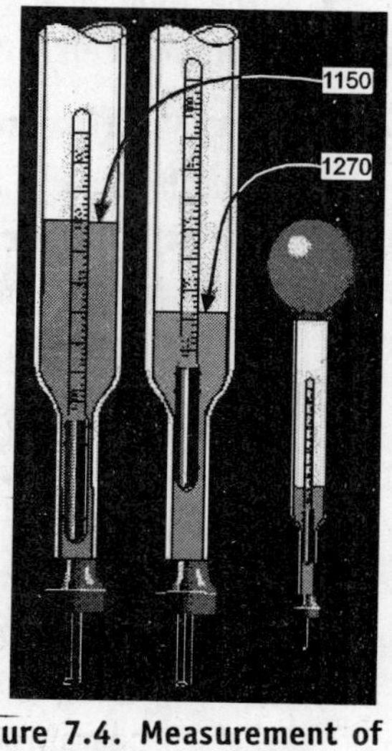


Figure 7.4. Measurement of specific gravity of battery

The voltage and charge levels of lead acid battery depends upon

- Acid concentration
- Temperature of the battery
- Load applied to battery

In a 12 V lead acid battery, the voltage of each cell is dependent on the state of charge and cell temperature. The electrolyte specific gravity is generally used as an indicator of the state of charge in the cells of battery. The measurement of specific gravity of a battery using hydrometer is shown in Fig. 7.4.

The nominal state of charge and voltage at different specific gravities of electrolyte at 27°C temperature is given in Table 7.2.

**TABLE 7.2: Electrolyte specific gravity depicting charge condition of battery**

| Specific gravity of electrolyte | Charge level (%) | Cell voltage, V |
|---|---|---|
| 1.28 | 100.00 | 2.12 |
| 1.24 | 75.00 | 2.08 |
| 1.20 | 50.00 | 2.04 |
| 1.16 | 25.00 | 2.00 |
| 1.12 | 0.00 | 1.96 |

### 7.1.2. Capacity of Battery

It is expressed in terms of ampere hours. For example a 80AH (ampere hour) capacity battery should give 5 Amp current for a period of 16 hours without dropping its voltage. Battery capacity is also rated in terms of cold cranking current and reserve capacity. Cold cranking current is the current that is supplied by the battery for a period of 30 seconds at the rating temperatures of –18°C,–29°C and provide an ending voltage of at least 1.2 V by each cell. Reserve capacity of a battery is the time that a fully charged battery can deliver 25A current at 27°C temperature and provide an ending cell voltage of at least 1.75V.

### 7.1.3. Energy Efficiency of Battery

It is defined as the ratio of discharging energy to charging energy which is about 75%. Energy efficiency of battery can be used for determination of charging requirements of the battery. Mathematically is expressed as under:

$$\eta_e = [\text{Battery discharging energy } (E_1)/\text{Charging energy of battery } (E_2)] \times 100$$

$$\eta_e = (P_1/P_2) \times (t_1/t_2) \times 100$$

where, $\eta_e$ = energy efficiency of battery, %

$E_1$ = discharging energy of battery

$E_2$ = charging energy of battery

$P_1$ = discharging power of battery

$P_2$ = charging power of battery

$t_1$ = discharging time

$t_2$ = charging time

## 7.2 GENERATOR/DYNAMO/ALTERNATOR

A generator/dynamo/alternator is a device (Fig. 7.5) which converts mechanical energy into electrical energy. It generates DC electric current which is used for continuous charging of battery while engine is running. A generator will keep the battery fully charged ensuring maximum efficiency of electrical system. The exploded view of alternator is given in Fig. 7.6.

Main components of dynamo are:

1. Armature
2. Field coils
3. Brushes and
4. End shields

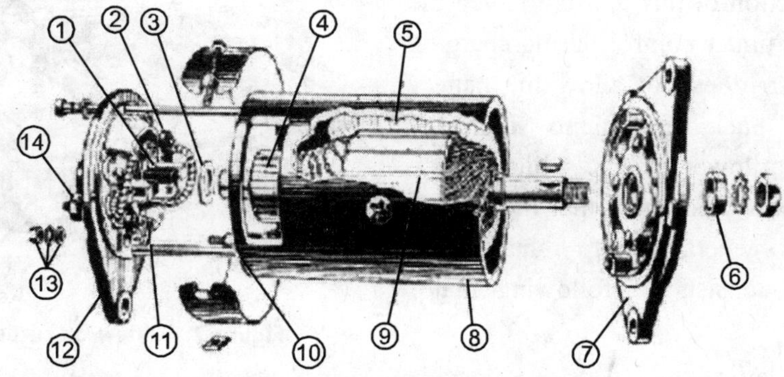


| | |
|---|---|
| 1. Brush | 8. Field frame |
| 2. Brush springs | 9. Armature |
| 3. Thrust washer | 10. Field terminal |
| 4. Commutator | 11. Brush holder |
| 5. Field coil | 12. Commutator end bracket |
| 6. Spacer | 13. Field terminal nuts and washer |
| 7. Driving end bracket | 14. Main output terminal |

**Figure 7.5. Exploded view of dynamo**

**Figure 7.6. Exploded view of alternator**

The armature or rotor consists of shaft with two sets of claw poles surrounding a coil. Voltage is applied to the rotating coil through brush and slip ring assembly, causing current to flow and rotating coil and claw poles are magnetized. The poles rotate past with in the stator coil inducing currents in the stator coils. The current induced in the stator coils of alternator is AC current which is rectified to DC current to charge the battery and supply for other electrical loads on the tractor. The dynamo gets drive through V-belt from fan belt pulley fitted on crankshaft of the engine whose speed is twice the engine speed. The drive belt of dynamo should have a proper tension so that the deflection of belt is not more than 12 mm. This will enable the dynamo/generator to keep the battery fully charged ensuring the maximum efficiency of engine.

## 7.3 CUTOUT RELAY OR CURRENT-VOLTAGE REGULATOR

A combined cutout and voltage regulator automatically controls the charging of battery (Fig. 7.7). The main function of this unit is to keep the voltage and current under control during charging of battery. This also does not allow the battery current to reverse back to dynamo when the dynamo is running at lower speeds. A high charge in the ampere meter would show that the battery has run down and generator output has arisen and *vice-versa*. It consists of following major components:

**Figure 7.7. View of cutout relay**

1. Cut out relay
2. Current regulator
3. Voltage regulator

The current and voltage regulators work on the principle of electromagnetic switch and control current and voltage respectively during charging of battery. During charging of battery when the load on alternator is low and operating speed is high, the voltage regulator will switch the excitation current on and off continuously to regulate the voltage. The voltage output from the voltage regulator should be matched with battery conditions. Lower charging voltage is required when battery temperature is high. If the battery is consistently running down, the charging circuit (dynamo and voltage regulator) requires proper testing and adjustments or replacement.

## 7.4 SELF STARTER

The self starter motor is a device which converts electrical energy into mechanical energy. The exploded view of self starter is given in Fig. 7.8. This is a high torque motor which is used for starting the engine. It is generally operated for less than 30 seconds and if engine does not start, a rest of few minutes is given to make another attempt to start the engine. It has a solenoid operated pinion which engages a replaceable gear ring on the fly wheel. The starter has a switch which is used to complete the circuit with the battery; its shaft begins to rotate along with the pinion which rotates the crank shaft of engine. After the engine is started, the starter is switched off and pinion returns to its initial position. The main components of self starter are armature, field coil, brushes and shields and drive mechanism.

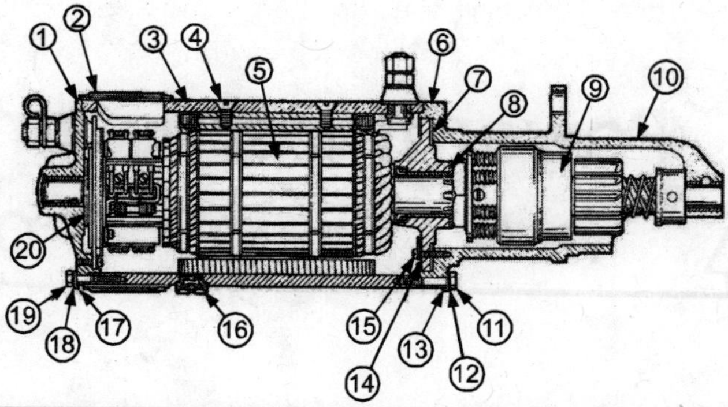


1. Commutator end bearing assembly
2. Cover and assembly
3. Frame and field assembly
4. Pole shoe screw
5. Armature assembly
6. Middle bearing assembly
8. Spacer washer
9. Bendix drive assembly
10. Drive housing assembly
11. Drive housing bolts
12. Flat washers
13. Lock washer
14. Lock washer
15. Machine screw
16. Ventilator
17. Lock washer
18. Flat washer
19. End bracket bolts
20. Brake shoe

**Figure 7.8. Exploded view of self starter**

## 7.5 ELECTRICAL WIRING

Electrical system in addition to starting of tractor provides lighting for three major functions namely safety lighting, work lighting and instrument lighting on the tractor. The electric power from the battery is distributed to a fuse box or a circuit breaker system and then individual wires to individual loads. The fuse box is provided on the instrument panel of tractor for protecting the lighting circuit. All the lights (front, back, side indicators and instrument panel lights) as well as other electrical connections of electrical system of tractor are made with suitable wiring of standard color codes.

Following important factors must be considered for selection of electrical wires (cables) for the tractor:

1. Mechanical strength of wire (cable)
2. Voltage drop
3. Connection requirements
4. Required current capacity
5. Temperature rise due to resistive heating
6. Physical exposure of the wire to the environmental temperature
7. Wire lengths

## 7.6 ELECTRIC UNITS/SOLENOID SWITCH

The solenoid switch works on the electromagnetic principle. The battery cable is connected to one terminal of solenoid switch and other is earthed to self starter. It consists of an electromagnetic coil, a plunger with fixed contact point. When switch of self starter is pressed the current flows in the coil of solenoid switch and as a result of magnetic field produced, the plunger is pushed down against spring tension. The plunger contact strip will touch the contact terminals and current will flow to the self starter. When the switch is released, the magnetic field in the coil diminishes and the plunger comes to its original position under spring tension and breaks the circuit.

CHAPTER 8

# Power Transmission System of Tractor

## INTRODUCTION

The brake power available at the fly wheel of an IC engine of a tractor is transmitted to rear drive wheels or output shaft (P. T. O. shaft or belt pulley) through clutch, gearbox, differential and final drive. This system is provided to perform following main functions:

- To transmit engine brake power from its fly wheel to tractor rear drive wheels and to multiply the torque developed by the engine.
- To engage or disengage engine power with rest of tractor power trains as per load and speed.
- To select appropriate speed ratio according to type of work and drawbar load on the tractor.
- To equalize power to the rear drive wheels of tractor for turnings.

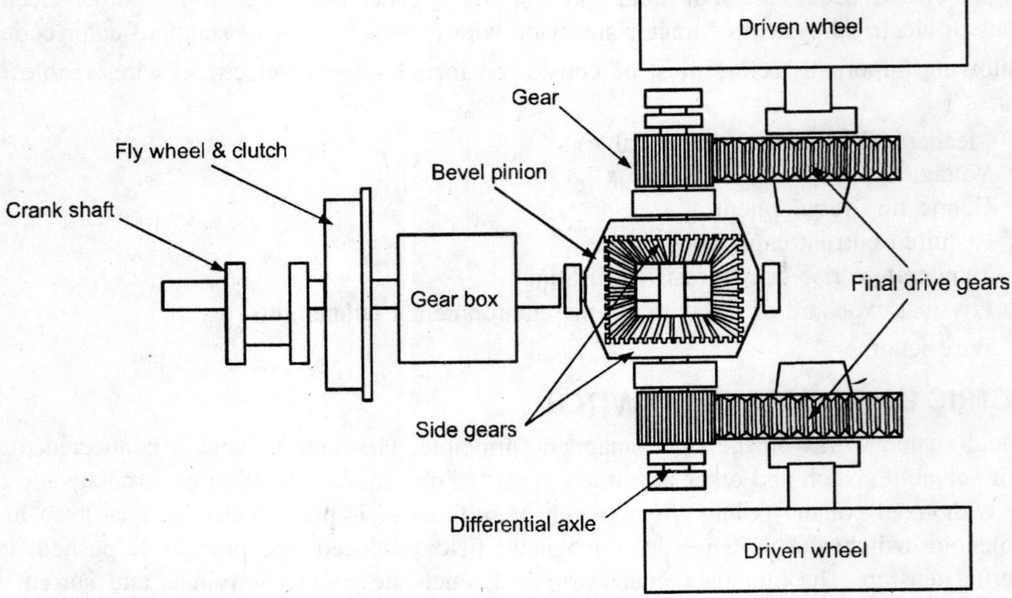


**Figure 8.1: Power transmission system of tractor**

- To provide means of reversing the tractor.
- To transmit engine power to P.T.O shaft and belt pulley for operation of implements requiring rotary power.
- To drive the pump of hydraulic system of tractor.

Various components of power transmission system of a tractor are illustrated in Fig. 8.1.

## 8.1 TRACTOR TRANSMISSION PERFORMANCE

The relationship between engine brake power and power in the drive wheels of tractor are discussed below.

### 8.1.1. Engine Brake Power

The engine brake power ($W$) is given by the following equation

$$W = \frac{2\pi N_e T_e}{6 \times 10^4} \quad \text{...(8.1)}$$

where, $W$ = engine brake power, kW

$N_e$ = engine RPM

$T_e$ = engine torque, N-m

or,

$$W = \frac{2\pi N_e T_e}{4500} \quad \text{...(8.2)}$$

where, $W$ = engine brake power, HP

$N_e$ = engine RPM

$T_e$ = engine torque, Kg-m

### 8.1.2. Power in the Drive Wheels of Tractor

The power in the drive wheels of tractor is given by

$$W_w = \frac{2\pi T_w N_w}{6 \times 10^4} \quad \text{...(8.3)}$$

where, $W_w$ = power in drive wheels of tractor, kW

$T_w$ = drive wheel torque, N-m

$N_w$ = drive wheel RPM

Based on torque speed relationship of tractor power transmission as given in eq. 8.2 and 8.3, the transmission efficiency ($\eta_t$) is given by the following equation.

$$T_e N_e \eta_t = T_w N_w = \text{Constant} \quad \text{...(8.4)}$$

where, $T_e$ = engine torque, N-m or Kg-m

$N_e$ = engine RPM

$T_w$ = drive wheel torque, N-m

$N_w$ = drive wheel RPM

$\eta_t$ = transmission efficiency, %

### 8.1.3. Drawbar Power of Tractor

It primarily depends on drawbar pull developed by the tractor and its speed of operation. The drawbar power of tractor is given by

$$W_d = \frac{P \times S}{3.6} \quad \text{...(8.5)}$$

where, $W_d$ = drawbar power, kW
$P$ = drawbar pull, kN
$S$ = speed, km/hr

or,

$$W_d = \frac{P \times S}{75} \quad \text{...(8.6)}$$

where, $W_d$ = drawbar power, HP
$P$ = drawbar pull, Kg
$S$ = speed, m/s

Pull speed curves of different kW tractors is shown in Fig. 8.2 which clearly indicates that at lower speed of operation, tractor develops maximum drawbar pull and goes on decreasing with increase in speed.

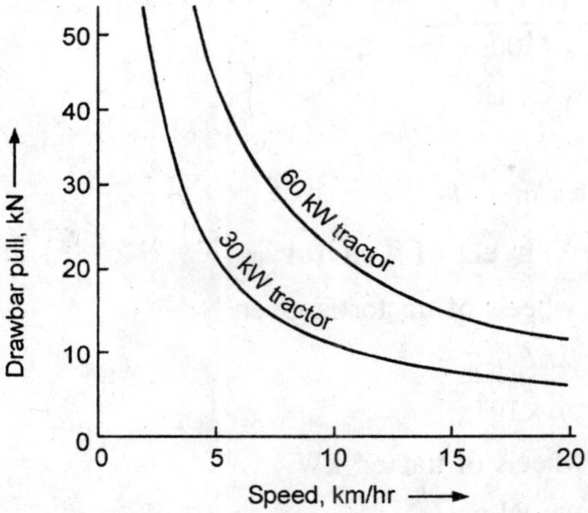


**Figure 8.2. Pull-speed curves for different tractors**

## 8.2 DESIGN OF CLUTCH FOR A TRACTOR

Clutches are used to engage or disengage power. Single plate clutch in disengaged position along with the components are shown in Figs. 8.3 and 8.4. Clutches are of various types and frictional clutches are most commonly used because of following advantages:

**Advantages of friction clutches:**

1. Slips during engagement help the drive to pick up and accelerate the load with minimum shock.
2. They need not to be unloaded before engagement.

3. These can be used at high engagement speeds.
4. Slip under momentary shock loads, provides cushioning.

**Disadvantage:** Friction clutches create problem of heat dissipation.

**Applications of friction clutches:** These are used under following conditions:

(*i*) Low torsion prime movers *i.e.* I.C Engines, motors, must start a load moving from rest.

(*ii*) When one source of power drives two or more shafts which have different cycles of stopping and starting.

**Types of friction clutches:**

**(*i*) *Axial friction clutch*:** A contact pressure is applied by shift movement along the shaft. It is of two types namely disc or cone clutch.

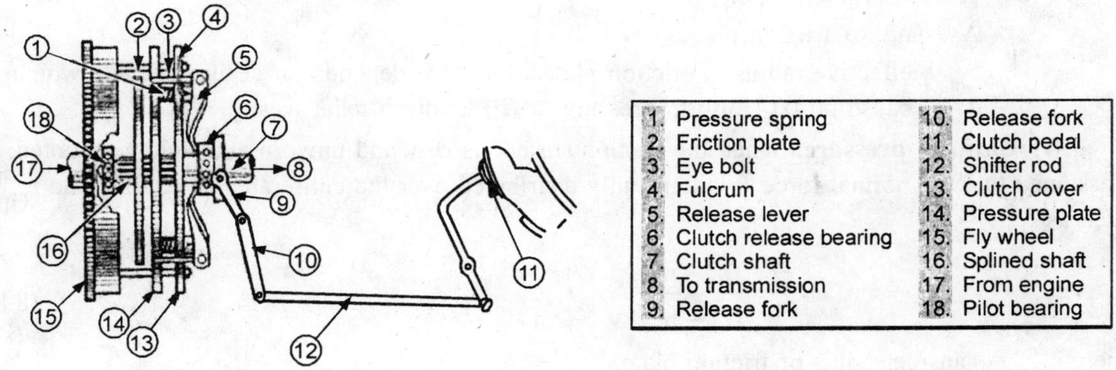


**Figure 8.3. Single plate clutch in disengaged position**

**Figure 8.4. Friction type single plate clutch**

**(*ii*) *Radial friction clutches*:** These are also known as ring or drum clutches. This can be of following three types:

(*a*) Tyre-pneumatic clutch.

(*b*) Centrifugal clutch.

(*c*) Over running or free wheeling clutch.

### 8.2.1. Design of Disc Type Clutch

There is a relationship between following parameters in a disc clutch:

- Dimensions of disc.
- Pressure applied to the friction surface.
- Coefficient of friction and
- Torsional moment developed.

Mathematically,

$$M_t = \tau = P \times \mu \times r_m \times N \quad \text{...(8.7)}$$

where, $M_t$ or $\tau$ = clutch torque, kg-cm or N-cm

$P$ = normal force, kgf or $N$ *i.e.* axial force

$\mu$ = coefficient of friction

$N$ = no. of friction planes

$r_m$ = effective radius of friction plates. Its value depends on design of plate which is based on (*i*) Uniform pressure or (*ii*) Uniform axial wear

(*i*) **Uniform pressure:** When the friction surface is new and unworn and rigidly mounted, it is assumed that the normal force $P$ is uniformly distributed over the entire area of clutch. And $r_m$ is taken as :

$$r_m = \frac{2}{3} \times \frac{(r_0^3 - r_1^3)}{(r_0^2 - r_1^2)} \quad \text{...(8.8)}$$

where, $r_0$ = outside radius of friction plate.

$r_i$ = inside radius of friction plate.

(*ii*) **Uniform axial wear :** The clutch is subjected to wear due to sliding friction and after the running in wear is ended, the wear will be uniform. The mean radius $r_m$ of the clutch is given by

$$r_m = \frac{(r_0 + r_1)}{2} \quad \text{...(8.9)}$$

When equal importance is given to durability and torsional moment, then

$$r_i / r_0 = 0.5 \text{ to } 0.7 \quad \text{...(8.10)}$$

When high torsional moment capacity is needed and wear is not a serious problem, then

$$r_i / r_0 = 0.748 \quad \text{...(8.11)}$$

Where wear is a problem, then

$$r_i / r_0 = 0.479 \quad \text{...(8.12)}$$

### 8.2.2. Design of Cone Clutch

It is comparatively powerful for a given outside diameter and axial energizing force.

**Advantages of cone clutch:**

1. Force is concentrated at a large diameter.
2. Sufficient friction surface width is provided for durability.
3. A full 360° of lining material is available.

The torsional moment developed by cone clutch is a function of

- Inner radii of functional surface
- Outer radii of frictional surface
- The cone angle, θ
- The force of engagement
- Coefficient of friction of the contact surface.

$$M_t = \frac{\mu \times F_a \times r_m}{\sin\theta} \quad ...(8.13)$$

And, $$r_m = \frac{(r_0 + r_1)}{2} \quad ...(8.14)$$

Therefore, $$M_t = \frac{\mu \times F_a \times (r_0 + r_1)/2}{\sin\theta} \quad ...(8.15)$$

And, axial force $F_a$ is given by

$$F_a = F_n\ (\sin\theta + \mu\cos\theta) \quad ...(8.16)$$

It has been found that the term $\mu\cos\theta$ is only 25% effective.

Therefore,

$$F_a = F_n\ (\sin\theta + \mu\cos\theta/4) \quad ...(8.17)$$

As $\theta \rightarrow 0$ $M_t \rightarrow$ to infinity

At $\theta = 0$ the cone becomes a drum and

At $\theta = 90°$ the cone becomes a single face disk clutch

Generally the value of θ varies from 7.5 to 30° depending on clutch facing material and type of disengagement required.

**EXAMPLE 8.1** *A tractor engine has rated output of 20 kW. Maximum torque developed by the engine is 200 N-m. The clutch used is of single plate type having both faces active. Axial pressure not to exceed 1.70 bars. Outer diameter of friction plate is 1.25 times the inside diameter. Determine the dimensions of friction plate and the axial force exerted by the springs. Assume uniform wear and coefficient of material friction as 0.3. Assume any other data required.*

**SOLUTION:**

Assume that $r_1$ = outer radius of clutch

$r_2$ = inside radius of clutch

and $$p_1 r_1 = p_2 r_2 = c = 1.70 \times 10^5 \times r_2$$

and intensity of pressure will be more at inner radius for uniform wear assumption, with the intensity of pressure not to exceed 1.70 bar

Then, $$W = 2\pi\ c\ (r_1 - r_2)$$

$$= 2\pi \times 1.70 \times 10^5 \times r_2\ (1.25\ r_2 - r_2)$$

$$= 2\pi \times 1.70 \times 10^5 \times 0.25\, r_2^2$$
$$= 2.67 \times 10^5 \times r_2^2, \text{ N}$$

We know that, Torque transmitted by the clutch plate due to both active surfaces is given by

$$T = 2 \times \frac{1}{2} \mu \times W \times (r_1 + r_2) \quad ...(8.18)$$

Putting the values in eq. 8.18, we get

$$= 0.3 \text{ W } (1.25 + 1)\, r_2$$
$$= 0.675 \text{ W } r_2$$

Therefore, $T = 0.675 \times 2.67 \times 10^5 \times r_2^2\, r_2$, N-m

But, $T = 200$ N-m (given)

Therefore, $200 = 0.675 \times 2.67 \times 10^5 \times r_2^2\, r_2$

or, $r_2 = (200/(0.675 \times 2.67 \times 105))^{1/3}$

$= 0.1035$ m or 10.35 cm

and, $r_1 = 1.25 \times 10.35$

$= 12.94$ cm

Axial force exerted by the springs on clutch plate

$$W = 2.67 \times 10^5 \times r_2^2$$
$$= 2.67 \times 10^5 \times (0.1035)^2$$
$$= 2860 \text{ N}$$

### 8.2.3. Heat Generated in Clutch (*Q*)

The heat generated (*Q*) in a clutch is given by

$$Q = \frac{T \times N_s \times t}{9.5493} \quad ...(8.19)$$

where, $Q$ = heat generated in the clutch due to slippage, J
$T$ = Average slip torque, N.m
$N_s$ = Average slip, RPM
$t$ = Total slip time for the clutch, s

### 8.2.4. Temperature of Heat Absorbing Element of Clutch (*T*)

The temperature of heat absorbing element of clutch (*T*) is given by

$$T = \frac{Q}{m \times C_p} + T_o \quad ...(8.20)$$

where, $T$ = average bulk temperature of clutch, °C
$Q$ = heat generated in clutch, J
$m$ = total mass of heat absorbing element of clutch
$C_p$ = specific heat of heat absorbing element, J/kg-°C
$T_0$ = Bulk temperature before engagement of clutch, °C

### 8.2.5. Rate of Energy Generation in Clutch (E)

The rate of energy generation in clutch is given by

$$E = \frac{T \times N_s}{9.5193\, a} \qquad ...(8.21)$$

where, $E$ = rate of energy generation in clutch, w/mm$^2$
$N_s$ = Average slip of clutch, RPM
$T$ = Average slip torque in the clutch, N.m
$a$ = Total facing area of clutch, mm$^2$

## 8.3 GEAR DRIVE DESIGN

Gear design involves

1. Adjustment of shaft center distance (CD)
2. Number of teeth on both gears
3. Gear width
4. Pressure angle
5. Helix or spiral angle
6. Optimization of gear set (Both tooth bending and surface compression stress near maximum allowable)
7. Gear ratio and
8. Noise control

### 8.3.1. Gear Terminology

The generally used terms regarding the gear is given in Fig. 8.5 and is discussed below:

$$P_c = \pi D/N \qquad ...(8.22)$$

$$P = N/D \qquad ...(8.23)$$

$$P_c \times P = \pi \qquad ...(8.24)$$

$$m = D/N \qquad ...(8.25)$$

$$m = m_n/\cos\psi \qquad ...(8.26)$$

where, $P_c$ = Circular pitch, $D$ = Pitch diameter
$N$ = Number of teeth, $P$ = Diametrical pitch
$m$ = Tooth size module, $m_n$ = Cutter module and
$\psi$ = helix angle

**Gear module (*m*)**

The gear module (*m*) is given by

$$m = D/N \qquad ...(8.27)$$

$$m = m_n/\cos\psi \qquad ...(8.28)$$

where, $m$ = tooth size module
$D$ = Nominal pitch diameter
$N$ = Number of teeth
$m_n$ = Cutter module
$\psi$ = Helix angle

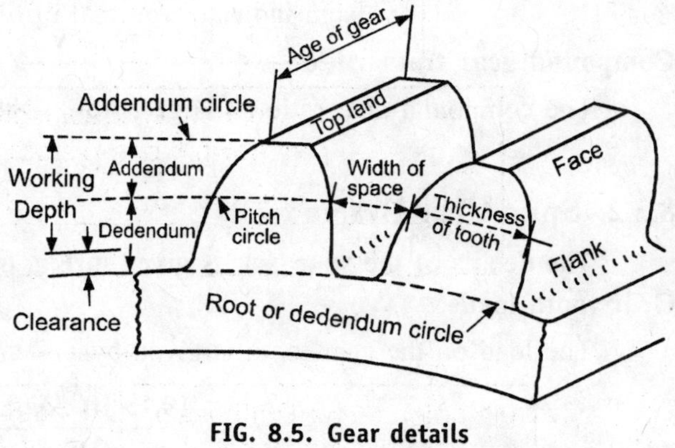


FIG. 8.5. Gear details

The tooth module (m) for various gears is given in Table 8.1.

**TABLE 8.1: Tooth module for various gears (m)**

| Sr. No. | Type of gears | Tooth module (m) |
|---|---|---|
| 1 | Transmission gears | 4 to 5 |
| 2 | Power shift planetary | 2.5 to 3.5 |
| 3 | Spiral bevel gears | 8 to 12 |
| 4 | Final drive gears | 5 to 7 |

**Pinion pitch diameter ($D_p$)**

The pitch diameter ($D_p$) of the pinion gear is given by

$$D_p = \frac{2CD}{1+R} \quad \text{...(8.29)}$$

where, $D_p$ = Pitch diameter of pinion or small gear

$CD$ = Shaft center distance

$R$ = Gear ratio larger than 1

**Pitch diameter of larger gear ($D_g$)**

The pitch diameter ($D_g$) of the larger gear is given by

$$D_g = 2CD - D_p \quad \text{...(8.30)}$$

**Gear ratios**

The gear ratio ($r_g$ or $i$) is given by

$$r_g = i = \frac{RPM_1}{RPM_2} = \frac{S_1}{S_2} = -\frac{N_2}{N_1} \quad \text{...(8.31)}$$

where, $r_g$ = Gear ratio > 1,

$S_1$ and $S_2$ = Speeds of gears, Km/hr,

$N_1$ and $N_2$ = No of teeth of gears,

– ve sign indicates reversal of direction

**Compound gear train ratio**

The compound gear ratio ($i$) is given by

$$i = i_{I} \times i_{II} \times i_{III} \times .....i_n \quad \text{...(8.32)}$$

## 8.3.2. Spur Gear Design

The details of the spur gear is given in Fig. 8.6.

**Gear tooth loads**

The load on the gear tooth is given by

$$F_t = \frac{2T}{D} = \frac{19.1\times10^6 \times kW}{DN}$$

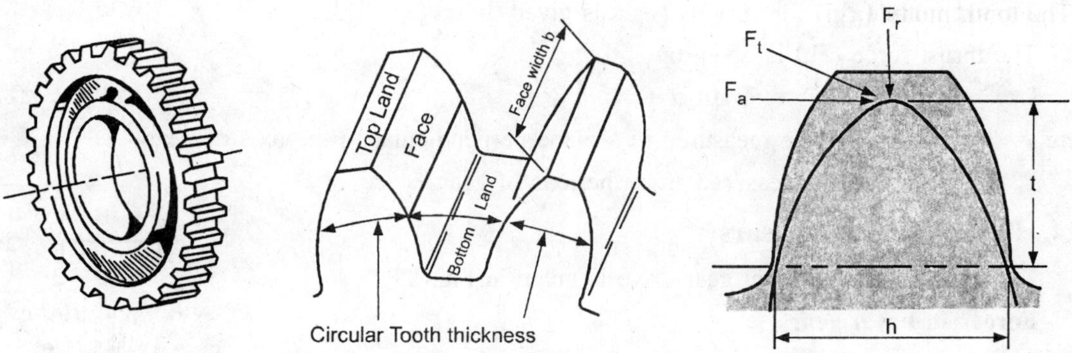


**Figure 8.6. Details of spur gear**

$$= \frac{4500 \times HP}{\pi DN} = \frac{4500 \times HP}{V_m} \qquad ...(8.33)$$

where, $T$ = torque transmitted, N-m

$D$ = pitch diameter, mm or m

$N$ = RPM of gear or shaft

$V_m$ = pitch line velocity, mpm

**Bending strength of gear tooth**

The bending strength (σ) of gear tooth is given by

$$\sigma = \frac{6M}{bh^2} = F_B/b \times 6t/h^2 = \frac{6F_B t}{bh^2} \qquad ...(8.34)$$

where, $F_B$ = Bending load in gear teeth, $N$

$b$ = Width of gear face, mm

$h$ = Thickness of tooth, mm

$t$ = Height of tooth, mm

σ = Maximum allowable bending stress, μ Pascal

### 8.3.3. Helical Gears

The forces acting on helical gear is given in Fig. 8.7 and are discussed below.

**Tangential force ($F_t$)**

The tangential force ($F_t$) is given by

$$F_t = \frac{2T}{D} = \frac{2M_t}{D} = \frac{19.1 \times 10^6 \times kw}{DN}$$

$$= \frac{4500 \times HP}{\pi DN} = \frac{4500 \times HP}{V_m} \qquad ...(8.35)$$

**Separating force ($F_r$)**

The separating force ($F_r$) is given by

$$F_r = F_t \tan \phi \qquad ...(8.36)$$

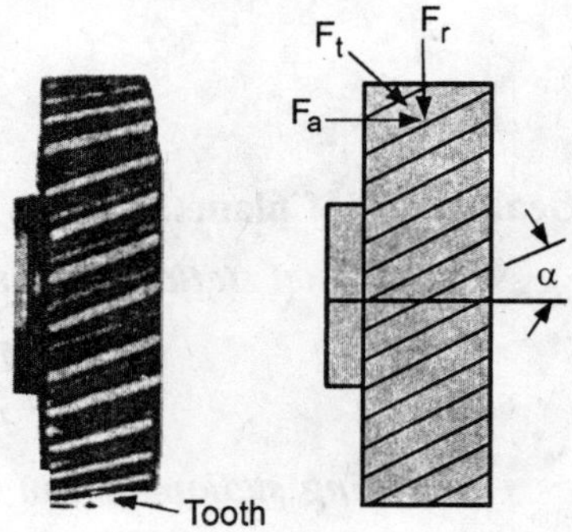


**Figure 8.7. Forces acting on helical gear**

**Thrust force ($F_a$)**

The thrust force ($F_a$) is given by

$$F_a = F_t \tan \alpha \quad ...(8.37)$$

where, $\phi$ = Pressure angle measured in a plane perpendicular to the axis of gear

$\alpha$ = Helix angle measured from the axis of gear

### 8.3.4. Design of Bevel Gears

The components of bevel gear drive is given in Fig. 8.8.

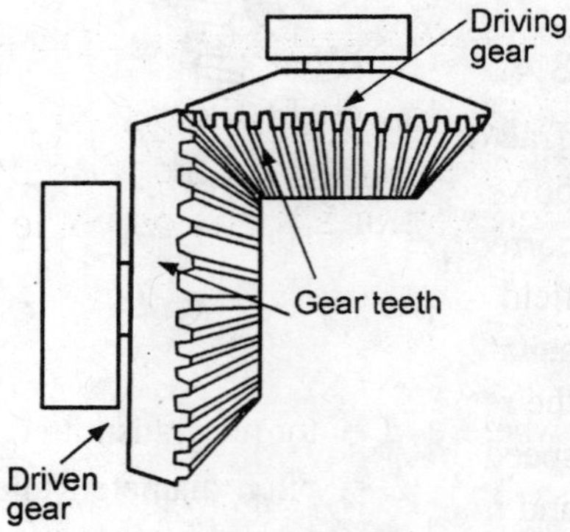


Figure 8.8. Bevel gear drive

**Forces in bevel gears**

$$F_{tm} = 2T/d_m \quad ...(8.37)$$

**Axial force ($F_n$)**

$$F_n = F_{tm} \tan\Phi \sin\delta \quad ...(8.38)$$

**Radial force ($F_R$)**

$$F_R = F_{tm} \tan\Phi \cos\delta \quad ...(8.39)$$

where, $\Phi$ = Angle between $F_{tm}$ and $F_n$, and

$\delta$ = Cone angle of bevel gears.

### 8.3.5. Planetary Gear Unit

The details of planetary gear unit is given in Fig. 8.9

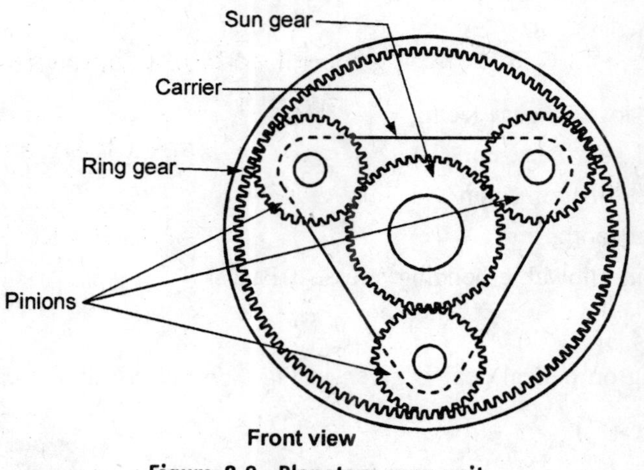


Figure 8.9. Planetary gear unit

**Gear ratios of planetary sets:**

***(i) Planet stationary sun rotating***

$$r_g = \frac{RPM_S}{RPM_R} = \frac{S_s}{S_r} = -\frac{G_r}{G_s} \quad ...(8.40)$$

***(ii) Ring stationary sun rotating***

$$r_g = \frac{RPM_s}{RPM_c} = \frac{G_r}{G_s} + 1 \quad ...(8.41)$$

***(iii) Sun stationary ring rotating***

$$r_g = \frac{RPM_r}{RPM_c} = \frac{G_r}{G_r} + 1 \quad ...(8.42)$$

where, $S_s$ & $S_r$ = Speeds of sun and ring gears

$G_r$ = Inner diameter of ring

$G_s$ = Diameter of sun gear

## 8.4. TRACTOR TRANSMISSION TYPES

Tractors are to be used for heavy field works especially tillage operations require maximum tractive power and P.T.O work where correct P.T.O speed is essential. At rated engine speed of tractor correct P.T.O speed should be available for getting maximum P.T.O power from the tractor. Most of field operations for crop cultivation need forward speeds between 3–6 km/hr. Therefore, selection of suitable speed ratios in this range for different types of field works is of vital importance. In tractor the rear drive wheels require power at lower speed and high torque whereas its engine runs at higher speed and low torque. Therefore, the purpose of gearbox transmission is to provide speed reduction and multiply the torque received from the engine. Main principle of gear train transmission is given by the following relationship.

$$\frac{N_{driver}}{N_{driven}} = \frac{T_{driven}}{T_{driver}} \quad ...(8.43)$$

where, $N_{driver}$ = speed of driving gear, rpm

$N_{driven}$ = speed of driven gear, rpm

$T_{driver}$ = number of teeth on driving gear

$T_{driven}$ = number of teeth on driven gear

Most common type of power transmissions used in tractors are as under:

- Sliding gear
- Constant mesh
- Synchronized or Synchromesh
- Power shift
- Hydro-static
- Hydro-dynamic

### 8.4.1. Sliding Gear Transmission

It is the basic and simplest type of spur gear transmission where desired speed ratios are obtained with the movement of gear lever by operator. Gear lever slides the selected gears on to their shafts. This can provide 3–4 forward speeds and one reverse speed. Sliding mesh gear box is given in Fig. 8.10.

**Advantages:**

1. It is very efficient *i.e.* it has highest transmission efficiency
2. It is simple in design and cheaper in cost.

**Disadvantages:**

1. This is limited to small tractors only.
2. Damage to teeth during gear shifting.
3. Tractor needs to be stopped before shifting the gear to prevent gear damage.

**Figure 8.10. Sliding mesh gear box**

## 8.4.2. Constant Mesh Gear Type Transmission

It is also basic and simple type of transmission where all the pairs of helical gears on main and counter shafts are always in mesh (engaged position) and do not move on their shafts (Refer Fig. 8.11). The gears are engaged or disengaged with the help of splined sleeve couplings operated by gear lever. One of the disadvantages of using constant mesh gear box is that the tractor needs to be stopped before shifting the gear to prevent teeth damage.

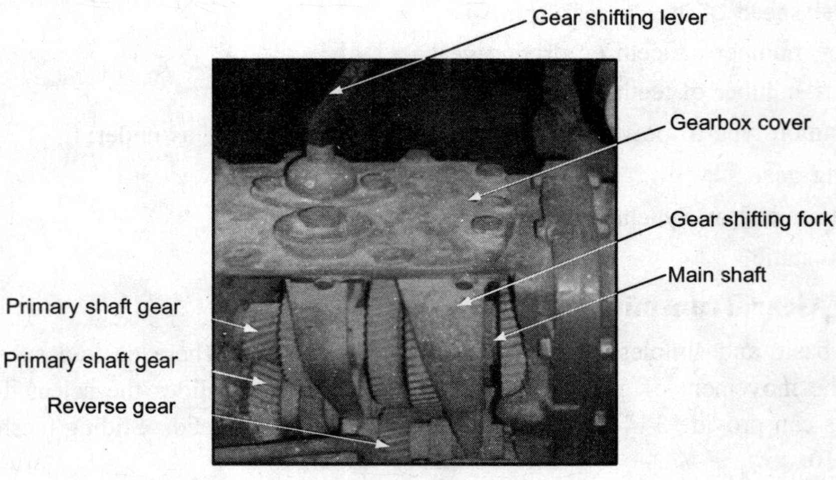


**Figure 8.11. Constant mesh type gearbox of tractor**

## 8.4.3. Synchromesh Transmission

This type of transmission is suitable for changing the speeds when tractor is moving (Refer Fig. 8.12). This also works in the same way as that of sliding gear transmission. In this synchromesh unit is provided. The synchronizing devices synchronize the speed of two gears and shafts before changing the appropriate gear. Small friction clutches usually cone type are used to synchronize the speed of collars and gears.

**Advantages:**

1. Gear shift can be made without damaging, even when tractor is moving
2. Popular in tractors when used for highway transport purpose

**Disadvantages:**

1. It has power transmission efficiency lower than sliding gear transmission.
2. This system is more costly.

**Figure 8.12. Synchromesh type gearbox**

### 8.4.4. Power Shift Transmission

In this type of transmission speed shift arrangement usually uses planetary type gear system where disc clutches are used. In the planetary type of gear box, the planet, pinion gear turns on their own axis while rotating around the sun gear. Here gears are shifted for changing gear ratios and remain in engaged position. It uses high torque friction clutches to engage gears. Planetary system is very versatile in terms of number of speeds and direction of rotation which operates with the help of brakes and clutches.

**Advantages:**

1. Gear shifting possible while moving and transmitting power
2. It decreases load on each gear tooth
3. As load is uniformly distributed in the system there will not any deflection in the shafts.
4. There is no noise during changing speed ratios and wear and tear is minimum.

**Disadvantages:**

1. It is more expensive type of transmission.
2. Less efficient as planetary gearbox can not transmit power as efficiently as spur gearbox.

### 8.4.5. Hydrostatic Transmission

This is totally hydraulically operated power transmission. It consists of a hydraulic pump driven by tractor engine coupled with hydraulic motor. The pump supplies oil at high pressure and low velocity. Both the pump and hydraulic motor are positive displacement type.

**Advantages:**

1. It provides full torque and infinite speed control.
2. Provides improved engine loading performance.

**Disadvantages:**

1. It is more complex and more expensive.
2. Engine lugging or stalling can not be stopped.
3. Its repair and maintenance cost is high.

### 8.4.6. Hydro-dynamic Transmission

It is a basic type of transmission fitted with a torque converter which can provide infinite range of speeds. Hydro-dynamic torque converter is an automatic fluid drive which operates under low pressure and high fluid velocity. The torque converter automatically adjusts the transmission torque matching to drawbar load. But, the torque converter is efficient only over a limited speed range.

**Advantages:**

1. It permits operating of tractor at higher loads in high gears.
2. It prevents engine stalling under any loads.
3. It provides wide range of gear ratios.

**Disadvantages:**

1. Its transmission efficiency is relatively low.
2. It is more complex in design and construction and hence expensive.

## 8.5 DESIGN PROCEDURE FOR GEARBOX OF A TRACTOR

### 8.5.1. Design Considerations

1. To reduce the size of gearbox, the intermediate shaft should have as high speed as possible
2. At any point of time only one set of gears should be in mesh. In other words, one set of gears must be completely disengaged before the other starts to engage.
3. The transmission ratio (*TR*) of a pair of gears in a gearbox should satisfy following condition.

$$TR \leq 2:1 \text{ and } \geq 1:4 \text{ or in other words } 0.25 \leq TR \leq 2$$

4. The speed range ratio (Maximum shaft speed divided by minimum shaft speed) should not be more than 8.
5. In case of sliding gearbox, the centre distance between two shafts should remain constant. Or in other words the sum of number of teeth of meshing gears must be constant.

$$T_1 + T_2 = T_3 + T_4 = \text{Constant}$$

6. In a gearbox same module (m) of the gear set must be used.
7. The minimum difference between the numbers of teeth of adjacent gears must be 4.
8. The minimum numbers of teeth (in a set of gears for spindle drives) should be greater than 17 to avoid interference of tooth.

**EXAMPLE 8.2** *Design a three speed gearbox for a tractor as shown in Fig. 8.13 to give speed variation between 200 and 600 rpm. The input shaft from the tractor engine runs at 1600 rpm.*

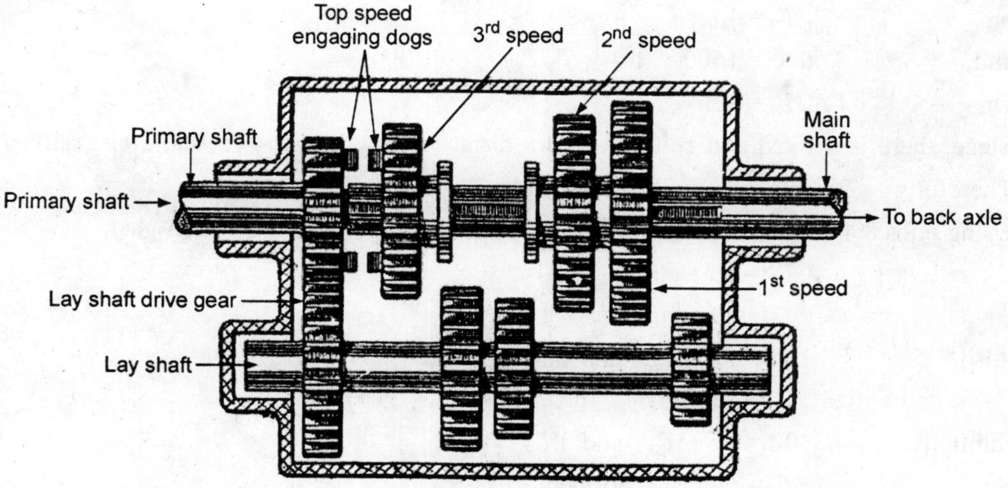


**Figure 8.13. Three speed sliding mesh gearbox**

**SOLUTION:**

Referring to Fig. 8.13, the output speed ratios from the gear box would be as under:

$$N_1 = 1600 \times \frac{T_1}{T_2} \times \frac{T_5}{T_6}$$

$$N_2 = 1600 \times \frac{T_1}{T_2} \times \frac{T_4}{T_7}$$

$$N_3 = 1600 \times \frac{T_1}{T_2} \times \frac{T_3}{T_8}$$

where, $N_1$, $N_2$ and $N_3$ are the speeds of output shaft of gearbox and $T_1$, $T_2$, $T_3$, $T_4$, $T_5$, $T_6$, $T_7$, and $T_8$ are number of teeth of gears.

And as given the output shaft speeds should vary between 200–600 rpm.

Therefore, we may take $N_1$ = 200 rpm $N_2$ = 400 rpm and $N_3$ = 600 rpm as output speeds

Assume transmission ratio between input shaft and intermediate shaft as ¼.

Therefore,

$$\frac{N_{input}}{N_{int}} = \frac{1600}{N_{int}} = 4 = \frac{T_2}{T_1}$$

or $\quad T_2/T_1 = 4$

Considering the requirement of minimum no. of teeth on the smaller gear as 17 teeth, then

$$T_2/T_1 = 4 = 80/20$$

Also, as given $200 = 600 \times 1/4 \times T_5/T_6$

or, $T_5/T_6 = 1/2$ ...(8.44)

and, $400 = 1600 \times 1/4 \times T_4/T_7$

or, $T_4/T_7 = 1$ ..(8.45)

and, $600 = 1600 \times 1/4 \times T_3/T_8$

Or, $T_3/T_8 = 1.5$ ...(8.46)

Since, there is a fixed and constant centre distance between the two shafts of gearbox

Therefore, $T_1 + T_2 = T_5 + T_6 = T_4 + T_7 = T_3 + T_8 = \text{Constant}$ ...(8.47)

Using eqns.8.44, 8.45, 8.46 and 8.47, solve for number of teeth on each gear.

$T_1 = 20$ teeth

$T_2 = 80$ teeth

Also, $100 = T_5 + T_6$ and $T_5/T_6 = 1/2$

$T_5 = 33$ and $T_6 = 67$

Similarly, $100 = T_4 + T_7$ and $T_4/T_7 = 1$

So, $T_4 = 50$, $T_7 = 50$ teeth

And $100 = T_3 + T_8$ and $T_3/T_8 = 1.5$

$T_3 = 60$ teeth and $T_8 = 40$ teeth

## 8.6 DIFFERENTIAL

Differential of a tractor consists of planetary gear system which has four bevel gears (two side gears and two pinions). It also has a pair of bevel gears consisting of a pinion and crown wheel fitted at right angle to each other to transmit power received from the gearbox to the rear axles. In other words, the input power to the planet carrier attached to the crown wheel and output power to the side gears mounted on the counter shafts gives drive to the rear wheels. It acts as a speed reduction and transmission of power at 90°. The differential divides the power into equal parts and finally to

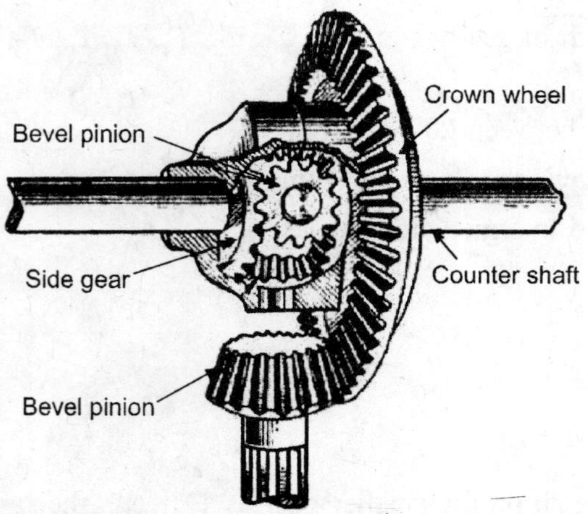


**Figure 8.14. Constructional details of differential**

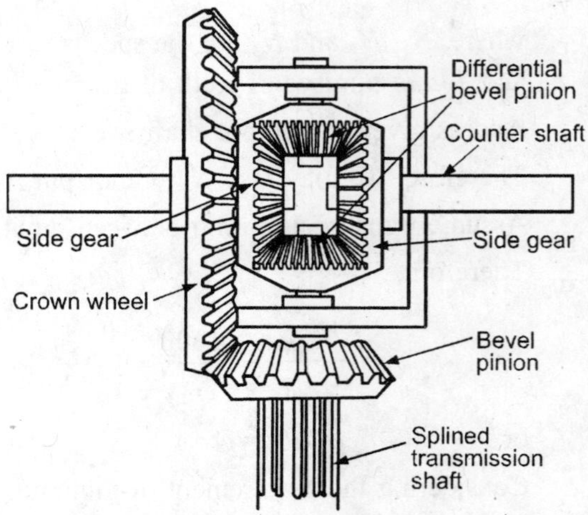


**Figure 8.15. Differential of a tractor**

the rear wheels. It allows one wheel of tractor to move faster than the other wheel while taking turns. When the tractor is moving straight ahead, the bevel pinions of differential do not rotate on their carrier shafts and both the side gears rotate at same speed. A differential lock is also provided to prevent excessive spin of one wheel than the other when a resistance to wheels is different. If one wheel of tractor gets in the mud or loose soil, the other wheel on the solid ground will not move while the other wheel spins around due to differential action. To overcome this problem differential lock is provided which allow both the wheels to move with same speed and apply equal torque. The constructional details of differential assembly are given in Figs. 8.14. and 8.15.

The torque transmitted by both the axles of tractor would be equal as the bevel pinions of differential are exerting equal torque on both the side gears.

Transmission efficiency of differential of tractor is given by

$$\eta_d = \frac{W_a}{W_{bp}} \qquad \text{...(8.48)}$$

where, $\eta_d$ = Transmission efficiency of differential

$W_a$ = power output through both the axles, kW

$W_{bp}$ = power input to differential through bevel pinion, kW

Also,

$$T_{bp} \times N_{bp} \times \eta_d = (T_{al} \times N_{al} + T_{ar} \times N_{ar}) \qquad \text{...(8.49)}$$

where, $T_{bp}$ = torque input to bevel pinion of differential, Nm

$N_{bp}$ = RPM of bevel pinion

$T_{al}$ = torque output from left axle, N.m

$T_{ar}$ = torque output from right axle, N.m

$N_{al}$ = RPM of left axle

$N_{ar}$ = Rpm of right axle

$\eta_d$ = transmission efficiency of differential, %

While moving straight, the torque in both the axles should be equal

Therefore, $$T_{al} = T_{ar} = T_a \qquad \text{...(8.50)}$$

where, $T_a$ = rear wheel axle torque.

And average speed of the axle ($N_a$) would be

$$N_a = (N_{al} + N_{ar})/2 \qquad \text{...(8.51)}$$

From eqns. 8.49, 8.50 and 8.51

We get,

$$T_{bp} \times N_{bp} \times \eta_d = T_a \times N_a \times 2$$

or

$$T_a = \frac{T_{bp} \times N_{bp} \times \eta_d}{2N_a} \qquad \text{...(8.52)}$$

$$T_a = \left[\frac{N_{bp}}{N_a}\right] \times \left[\frac{\eta_d}{2}\right] \times T_{bp} \qquad \text{...(8.53)}$$

### 8.6.1. Speed Division by the Differential

While taking turns, the role of differential comes into picture and as per the principles of differential gears, the reduction in speed of inner sun gear will be added up to the speed of outer sun gear. The speed of crown wheel during turnings would be average speed of two drive wheels of the tractor as given by following equation.

$$N_c = (N_i + N_o)/2 \quad \text{...(8.54)}$$

where, $N_c$ = crown wheel speed, rpm

$N_i$ = inner wheel speed, rpm

$N_o$ = outer wheel speed, rpm

### 8.6.2. Design of Bevel Gears of Differential

The following points should be taken into account while designing a bevel gear drive for a differential:

1. The gear should have sufficient strength so that, it does not fail at starting torques under dynamic running conditions.
2. The teeth must have very good wear characteristics so that the life of gear is long.
3. The suitable material must have very good wear characteristics so that life of gear is long.
4. The drive should be compact and properly designed.
5. The proper lubrication arrangement should be made.

**Design procedure**

**1. *Pitch diameters of bevel gears*:** Let the number of teeth be $N$ and module be $m$.

Then, $D_1 = PCD = N \times m/10$

Velocity ratio $= VR = 1.7$

Take $\sigma_2 = 1/VR = 1/1.7$ or $\sigma_2 = 30.4°$ and $\sigma_1 = 90° - 30.4° = 59.6°$

Thus, the reference angle for tooth of gear = 30.4°.

Thus, the reference angle for tooth of pinion = 59.6°

Pitch line Velocity: Pitch line velocity of pinion and gear is calculated by

$$V_m = 3.14 \times D_1 \times N_1/(60 \times 100), \text{ m/s}$$

**2. *Determination of maximum tooth load*:** Assuming that the full load acts on entire length of rotor which is driven by these gears. So, the transmitted teeth load is given by

$$F_t = HP \times 75/V_m, \text{ kgf} \quad \text{...(8.55)}$$

**3. *Materials for bevel gears and designed stresses*:** Let the material for gears be 15Ni2Cr1Mo15 (Nickel chromium molybdenum steel) having ultimate strength $s_u$ = 9000 kg/cm$^2$

Taking factor of safety 2.5 for the case hardened steel

Then, design stress

$$s_d = \sigma_u/2.5, \text{ kgf/cm}^2$$

4. ***Dynamic load on bevel gears***: Given in machine design hand books

$$F_d = C_v N_{sf} K_m F_t \quad ...(8.56)$$

where $F_d$ = dynamic load, kgf

$C_v$ = Velocity factor = $3.5 + V_m^{0.5}/3.5$

$V_m$ = mean velocity

$N_{sf}$ = service factor = 1.5

$K_m$ = load distribution factor = 1.25

$F_t$ = tooth load

Find $F_d$ = ? kgf

5. ***Calculation of $P_c$ and $P_d$***: The circular pitch = $P_c = \lambda m$

Diametric pitch $P_d = 1/m$

6. ***Calculation of face width***: Adopting a 20° in volute teeth profile (the gear Lewis form factor is given by

$$Y_v = 0.154 - 0.912/Z_v \quad ...(8.57)$$

For straight bevel gears = $Z_1/\cos\sigma_1$ or $Z_2/\cos\sigma_2 = Z_v$ ...(8.58)

$Z_v$ = virtual number of teeth

$Z_1$ and $Z_2$ = number of teeth in pinion and gear respectively

$\sigma_1$ and $\sigma_2$ = reference cone angle in degrees

$Y_v = \pi \times Y_v$

Applying Lewis eqn.

$$F_s = \frac{\sigma_u \times b \times Y_v \times (1 - b/R)}{P_d} \quad ...(8.59)$$

where $F_s$ = strength of tooth in kgf

$\sigma_u$ = design bending stress, 3200kg/cm$^2$ for used material

$R$ = cone distance

$b$ = face width

$P_d$ = diametrical pitch

If $b$ is small, then we can take another value.

**Check for dynamic load:**

Dynamic load is given by Buckingham equation.

$$F_d = F_t + \left[\frac{0.164\,Vm\,(bc + F_t)}{0.164\,V_m + 1.485\sqrt{(bc + F_t)}}\right] \quad ...(8.60)$$

where, $V_m$ = pitch line velocity m/s

$c$ = constant whose values for 20° full length steel gear is given by $c = 11860 \times e$

$E$ = permissible error in action corresponding to a pitch line velocity ($V$)

Therefore, $F_d$ must be below the maximum permissible contact compressive stress.

**Check for maximum wear:**

Formula for maximum wear is given by

$$F_w = d \times Q \times K \times b \qquad \text{...(8.61)}$$

where, $F_w$ = wear load

$d$ = Pitch circle diameter

$Q$ = ratio factor 22/(2 + 1)

$$k = \text{load factor} = (\sigma_c)^2 \times \frac{\sin\alpha\left(\dfrac{1}{\sigma_1}+\dfrac{1}{\sigma_2}\right)}{1.4} \qquad \text{...(8.62)}$$

$\alpha$ = pressure angle

$b$ = face width

$c$ = design compression strength

It can be checked that $F_w$ must be greater than $F_d$ then only gears are safe for severe services also.

## 8.7 FINAL DRIVE

It is a further reduction in wheel speed by using a set of two spur gears on each axle. It is provided near the rear drive wheels of tractor. The size of driving gear is small and that of driven gear is much larger than driving gear. The main purpose of final drive is to reduce the rear wheel speed and increase torque for development of more traction. It also helps in minimizing the number of gears and shafts in the gearbox. It is provided in the transmission system of tractor for following main reasons:

1. To provide a permanent gear reduction between engine and rear wheels
2. To transmit the power from the gearbox through 90°.

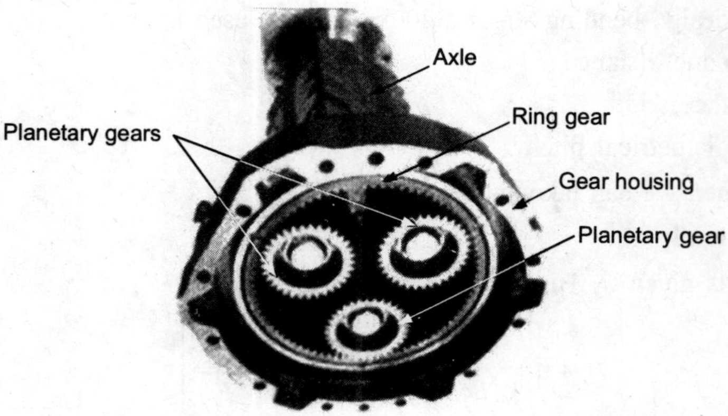


**Figure 8.16. Planetary gear with straight axle**

Planetary gear type of final drive with straight axle as shown in Fig. 8.16 is smaller and compact. This is very durable under heavy loads as the torque load is uniformly distributed over several planetary gears.

## 8.8 P.T.O. SHAFT

Power take off (PTO) shaft is an attachment in the power train of a tractor. Used to provide power of tractor with the help of telescopic shafting for operating the mechanisms of rotavator, sugarcane cutter planter, post hole digger, threshers, combines, potato digger and groundnut diggers etc. It is provided at midway of rear of tractor to drive field machines which require rotary power to operate their mechanisms during field or stationary works like threshing of crops, pumping water etc. Power take off (P.T.O) shaft is located in relation to drawbar of tractor in such a way that the drawbar and universal joints do not swing sideways. The tractor PTO shaft is shown in Figs. 8.17 and 8.18.

**Figure 8.17(a) Tractor P. T. O. shaft**

**Figure 8.17(b) Tractor P. T. O. shaft with cover**

There are three basic types of PTO namely continuous running PTO, independent PTO and transmission driven PTO. Recommended PTO speeds are 540 and 1000 rpm. In modern tractors two standard PTO speeds *i.e.* 540 ±10 rpm and 1000 ± 25 rpm with 6 and 21 teeth in splined shafts respectively are available. 1000 rpm shaft is shorter than 540 rpm shaft which provides more telescoping space and simplifies hitching of P.T.O operated implements with tractor. It also transmit nearly twice power than the existing 540 rpm PTO for a given torque. A live, constant running PTO will continue to operate with a dual clutch or second clutch even when the tractor is in stationary condition.

## 8.9 BELT PULLEY

It is also an attachment in the power train of a tractor to transmit power for operating stationary implements like irrigation pump sets, chaff cutters etc. It is provided on the right side of the operator for easy adjustments and operation.

### 8.9.1. Belt Pulley Operating Speed ($V$)

The belt pulley speed of a tractor is estimated by following relationship.

$$V = \pi DN \qquad ...(8.63)$$

where $V$ = belt speed, m/s
$D$ = diameter of pulley, m
$N$ = RPM of pulley

According to ASAE and SAE standards for belt pulley of a tractor:

1. Standard belt speed should be 940 ± 30.5 m/min
2. Minimum width of tractor belt pulley shall be such as to provide for the use of a 15 cm wide belt.

## EXERCISES

1. In a HMT-7511 Tractor engine 50 kW is transmitted at 2000 rpm by a multiple disc clutch. The clutch material has coefficient of friction of 0.35, and the axial intensity of pressure is not to exceed 1.5 bars. Outside radius of clutch is 1.5 times the internal radius. The external radius is 12.50 cm. Determine the number of plates needed to transmit the required torque. Assume uniform wear conditions.
2. A multiple disc clutch plate having four active frictional surfaces has outer and inner radi of 12.5 and 7.5 cm. Determine the maximum axial intensity of pressure needed between the discs for transmitting 25 kW at 1800 rpm . Assume uniform wear and the coefficient of friction as 0.3.
3. A tractor engine is fitted with a single plate clutch and develops a maximum torque of 30 kW at 2200 rpm. The total side load on the clutch plate is 2500 N. The outside diameter of plate is 25 cm,. Consider that both the sides of plate are active and coefficient of friction is 0.3. Determine the inner diameter of clutch plate. Assume uniform wear conditions.
4. How much maximum torque can be transmitted by a single plate clutch of 200 mm dia (inside) and 250 mm outside dia. Assume coeff. of friction as 0.4 and clamping force as 100 N.
5. A 50 HP tractor engine has a rated speed of 2000 rpm and is provided with single plate dry clutch (both sides effective). The pressure plate of the clutch has a maximum pressure intensity of 1.0 Kg/cm$^2$. The coefficient of friction of material may be assumed as 0.3. Assuming that maximum wear principle exists and its side thrust is to be taken by 4 springs of 3.0 cm diameters. Calculate the following dimensions of the clutch plate.
   (*a*) Inside and outside dimensions of the plate if 20% overload on tractor is permissible.
   (*b*) Side thrust taken by each spring
   (*c*) Quantity of heat generated by slipping clutch plate if 100% slippage is recorded for a period of 10 seconds
   (*d*) Multiple disc clutch for above tractor
6. A 40 HP tractor having rated engine rpm of 2800 is provided with a single dry clutch (both sides effective). The pressure plate of clutch has a maximum pressure intensity of 0.8 Kg/cm$^2$. The coefficient of friction of plate material may be taken as 0.25. Assuming that the uniform wear principle exists and its side thrust to be taken by 6 springs of 2.5 cm diameter. Calculate the following dimensions of clutch plate.
   (*a*) Inside and outside diameter of plate if 25% overload of tractor is exerted.
   (*b*) Side thrust taken by each spring
   (*c*) Quantity of heat generated by slipping plate if 20% of slippage is recorded for a period of 5 seconds
   (*d*) Design a multiple clutch for above tractor.
7. A single plate clutch with both sides effective is to transmit 15 kW at 2000 rpm. The axial pressure is limited to 0.1 N/mm$^2$. The outer diameter of the friction lining is 1.5 times the inner diameter. Design suitable dimensions of the friction lining, Assume uniform wear conditions. The coefficient of friction may be taken as 0.3.

8. A single disc clutch with both sides of disc effective is used to transmit 12 hp power at 900 rpm. The axial pressure is limited to 0.85 kgf/cm$^2$. If the external diameter of friction lining is 1.25 times the internal diameter, find the required dimensions of the friction lining and axial force exerted by the springs. Assume uniform wear conditions. The coeff. of friction may be taken as 0.3.
9. A friction clutch is required to transmit 35 bhp at 2000 rpm. It is to be single plate disc type with both side of plate effective; the pressure of 0.75 kg/cm$^2$ is being applied axially by means of spring. If the outer diameter of the clutch is 30 cm, find out the inner diameter of the clutch and total force exerted by the spring. Assume the coefficient of friction as 0.3 and wear of clutch to be uniform. Assume any data required.
10. In a 45 kW tractor engine running at a speed of 2000 rpm is having a single plate clutch both sides effective. If maximum intensity of pressure on surface of clutch is to be 10 N/cm$^2$ and coefficient of friction is 0.3. Determine the outer and inner diameters of the clutch plate.
11. A single plate friction clutch for a 25 kW tractor engine running at 2200 rpm has both sides effective. The axial pressure is limited to 10 N/cm$^2$ and outer diameter of clutch is 1.65 times its inner diameter. Then calculate the dimensions of friction lining of clutch plate if principle of uniform wear exists and coefficient of friction is 0.3.
12. How much maximum torque can be transmitted by a single plate clutch of 200 mm internal diameter and 2250 mm outside diameter? Assume coefficient of friction to be 0.4 and clamping force of 100 N.
13. A single plate clutch has an effective area of 800 cm$^2$ and effective torque radius of 10 cm. What torque can the clutch transmit without slipping if total spring force is 2.67 KN and coefficient of friction is 0.6.
14. A multiple disc clutch, steel or bronze is to transmit 15 HP at 1050 rpm. The inner radius of contact is 10 cm and outer radius of is 12.5 cm. The coefficient of friction is 0.3. The maximum allowable pressure is 3.5 kg/cm$^2$
    (*a*) How many total discs will be required?
    (*b*) What axial force is required?
15. A safety single plate clutch in a rotavator is to operate at 120 rpm. Inner and outer diameters of clutch are 8 and 24 cm respectively. Calculate the force required for each spring if total 5 springs are used. Clutch is to operate 20 kW and coefficient of friction is 0.6.
16. In a tractor of 15 HP, a spur gear box is provided for gear change. Assuming that starting torque is 20% higher, determine the bending stress in gear teeth if width of gear is 2.5 cm, diametrical pitch is 2 cm and pinion has 30 teeth. The gear and pinion are 20° full depth involute type.
17. A planetary gear unit is provided in final drive of the tractor. The number of teeth of planetary gears are as under:
    (*i*) Input sun : 56 teeth
    (*ii*) Planets : 32 teeth
    (*iii*) Ring : 146 teeth
    (*iv*) If sun is rotating at 500 rpm, determine the speeds of output shafts when
    (*v*) (*a*) Planet stationary (*b*) Ring stationary

**18.** 20 kW power is transmitted by a single reduction gear. The pitch circle diameter of pinion is 200 mm and its speed is 750 rpm. The teeths are of involute profile with pressure angle equal to 20°. Calculate the radial and tangential forces acting on wheel when transmitting the given power.

**19.** Maximum PTO power output of a diesel tractor was 33.44 kW at a PTO rpm of 540 and engine speed of 2440 rpm.

(*a*) What is the gear ratio between the speed of engine and PTO

(*b*) What torque was measured at PTO

(*c*) Assuming that efficiency of gear reduction between engine and PTO as 97%, what torque and power would be measured at the engine.

**20.** A spur gearbox transmits power in a 33.44 kW tractor from 2440 engine rpm to low speed shaft running at 640 rpm. The starting torque is 10% higher than average running torque. Determine the bending stress in gear teeth if width of gear is 2.5 cm, diametrical pitch is 2 cm and pinion has 30 teeth. The gear and pinion are 20° full depth involute type.

**21.** A planetary system provided in the final drive of a tractor has number of teeths are as follows:

(*i*) Input sun : 56 teeth

(*ii*) Planets : 22 teeth    Output ring : 101 teeth

The input sun is rotating at 1000 rpm, for this situation how fast the output ring will turn?

**22.** A 35 hp tractor has a four speed sliding gear box. The speed ratios of the driving shaft to the driven shaft are approximately; 4 : 1, 2.5 : 1, 1.5 : 1, and 1 : 1 in the first, second, third and top gear respectively. The pitch of the gears in the module is 3.72 mm and center to center distance between mating gears is 80 mm. Design a suitable gear box for above speed ratios. Assume the minimum number of teeth on the pinion to be 14.

**23.** Explain the construction and working of a synchromesh type gear box with help of neat sketch.

**24.** State the application of power take off drives, their standardization, loads imposed on them and recommended load limits.

**25.** The PTO Power output of a tractor was 63.44 kW at a PTO speed of 540 rpm and engine speed of 2447 rpm. What is the gear ratio between engine and PTO?

**26.** A tractor has reduction between engine and wheels. Efficiency of each reduction is 95%. If engine is producing 46 hp at 1300 rpm, what are the rpm and hp of rear axle?

**27.** A rolling machine is powered by electric motor with a v-belt drive to a gear box. The motor rated speed is 1440 rpm and roller rotates at 90 rpm. The gearbox gear ratio is 9:1, its efficiency is 95% and its output shaft is directly connected to the roller it drives. The motor pulley is 7.5 cm diameter and v-belt system is 95% efficient

(*a*) What will be size of pulley on the gear box shaft?

(*b*) When motor is delivering 5 hp, what torque and hp are being delivered to the roller.

**28.** A planetary gear drive has following details

(*i*) No. of teeth on ring gear : 70

(*ii*) No. of teeth on sun gear : 35

(*iii*) Speed of sun gear : 120 rpm

(*iv*) Direction of rotation of sun gear : anticlockwise

29. If the gear drive comes to the sun gear and ring gear is held stationary and power output is through planet carrier, then calculate the following:

(*a*) Speed of planet carrier (*b*) Direction of rotation of planet carrier.

30. In the differential of a tractor a bevel pinion of 10 teeth has input torque of 1550 N.m at a speed of 550 rpm and drives its crown wheel having 41 teeth. The side gears of differential are connected to rear axle through planetary gear sets which provide speed reduction of 5 : 1. Assume that efficiency of differential is 0.975 and tractor is moving straight ahead on level ground, then calculate the following:

(*a*) Speed of rear axle (*b*) Torque in rear axle (*c*) Power in each rear axle.

31. In the final drive of 45 kW tractor, the reduction gear of 35 cm pitch circle diameter running at a speed of 450 rpm. Calculate the load on the reduction gear of final drive of tractor.

32. The final dive of a tractor has set of spur gears with a speed reduction of 5 : 1. The driving gear has 70 teeth with circular pitch of 25 mm. The torque input from the differential to driving gear of final drive is 850 N.m. Calculate the power transmitted by the axle of tractor at a speed of 160 rpm.

33. Design a four speed sliding gearbox for a 30 kW tractor which should have following speed ratios:

| Gear | Speed ratio |
|---|---|
| $1^{st}$ | 4 : 1 |
| $2^{nd}$ | 2.75 : 1 |
| $3^{rd}$ | 1.45 : 1 |
| $4^{th}$ | 1 : 1 |

Assume any other data required.

34. The transmission efficiency of a gear box of a tractor is 96%. The input and output torques of the gearbox are 150 N.m and 650 N.m respectively. Then calculate the desired gear ratio of the gear box.

35. The power transmission units of a tractor engine running at a speed of 1600 rpm have following gear ratios:

(*a*) Gearbox–3 : 1 (*b*) Differential gears–3 : 1 (*c*) Final drive–4.5 : 1

Then calculate the speed of axle of tractor. Also determine the forward speed of tractor if its drive wheel diameter is 1.6 m.

36. A planetary gear drive has following specifications:

(*a*) No. of teeth on sun gear : 18

(*b*) No. of teeth on ring gear : 54

(*c*) No. of teeth on each planet : 12

When drive is given to the sun gear and ring gear is held stationary, then calculate the gear ratio between the planet carrier and sun gear.

37. A belt pulley fitted on P.T.O shaft of a tractor is required to operate a power thresher at a speed of 750 rpm. Select the dimensions of belt pulley and thresher pulley for carrying out threshing of wheat crop satisfactorily.

38. A planetary gear system provided in the final drive of a tractor has following specifications:

    (*a*) Number of teeth on input sun gear : 56

    (*b*) Number of teeth on planets : 22

    (*c*) Number of teeth on output ring : 101

    If the input sun gear is rotating at a speed of 1000 rpm, then how fast the output ring will turn?

39. A 40 kW tractor has reduction between engine and wheels as below:

    (*a*) Gear change : 1.40

    (*b*) Differential : 3.86

    (*c*) Final drive : 5.63

    If the efficiency of each reduction is 95% and rated engine speed is 1800 rpm, what are the rpm and torque at the rear axle? Also determine PTO power of the tractor.

40. In above tractor a spur gearbox is provided for gear change. Assuming that starting torque of the engine is 20% higher than running torque, determine the bending stress in the gear teeth if width of gear is 2.5 cm, diametrical pitch is 2 cm and pinion has 30 teeth. The gear and pinion are 20° full depth involute type.

41. A four wheel tractor develops a drawbar power (PS) of 26.5 hp while pulling a M.B plough at a forward speed of 4.5 km/hr. The pull of implement is 1600 kg. If rear wheel radius of tractor is 60 cm, determine the engine torque and HP at a rated speed of 2250 rpm. The transmission system efficiency may be taken as 95%.

42. A spur gearbox is provided in above tractor for gear change. Assuming that starting torque is 10% higher, determine the bending stress in gear tooth if width of gear is 2.5 cm, diametrical pitch is 2 cm and pinion has 30 teeth. The gear and pinion are $20^0$ full depth involute type.

43. A tractor engine is operating at 1800 rpm having 15 cm belt pulley. What would be diameter of pulley on a feed grinder to obtain 3500 rpm with 5% slip of belt?

44. In a 39 HP tractor, the engine torque and speeds are 10 kg-m and 2150 rpm respectively and output torque and speeds of rear wheels are 350 kg-m and 50 rpm respectively. What are the gear ratios and efficiency of this transmission? If the reduction between engine and wheels are as under:

    (*a*) Gear change : 1.8

    (*b*) Differential : 3.86

    (c) Final drive : 6.19

    Determine the torques and speeds of each drive.

45. A planetary system is provided in final drive of a tractor. The input sun has 39 teeth, the ring gear has 81 teeth and the carrier is the output member. Determine the input output ratio and efficiency.

46. What is drawbar pull normally available from a tractor engine having 37 kW at 2400 rpm?

47. Calculate the speed of belt pulley of 40 cm diameter rotating at 3500 rpm?

48. A tractor engine develops a brake power of 24 kW at 2000 rpm when engaged in 1st gear reduction ratio of 40:1 through main gear box and 4:1 through final differential unit. The overall efficiency in 1st gear is 90%, determine the torque, speed and power at differential wheel.

49. The 2nd gear of the tractor gearbox of 10 cm gear is rotating at 1500 rpm. It is transmitting 1.5 kg-m torque. Determine the power transmitted by the gear.

50. Pull type machines require a draft of 2 KN while operating at a speed of 5.4 km/hr. Calculate the power developed by the tractor.

51. What is the maximum possible speed at which a tractor can operate a 3 × 30 cm M.B plough going 15 cm deep? The soil resistance of 0.6 kg/cm$^2$. The tractor consumes 8 litres of diesel/hr, the calorific value of fuel is 8900 Kcal/litre. The thermal, mechanical and transmission efficiencies being 35, 75 and 82%. Neglect other losses.

52. In a gearbox clutch shaft pinion has 14 teeth and gear main shaft pinion has 32 teeths. The corresponding lay shaft pinion has 36 and 18 teeth. The rear axle ratio is 3.7:1 and effective radius of rear tire is 35.5 cm. Calculate the tractor speed in the above arrangement at an average engine speed of 2500 rpm.

53. Five spur gears A, B, C, D and E are used for power transmission. A has 50 teeth and runs at 300 rpm. B has 80 teeth, C has 60 teeth, D has 40 teeth and E has 120 teeth. What would be the speed of gear B, C, D and E?

54. A spur gear drive transmits 10 kW from high speed shaft running at 1440 rpm to low speed shaft running at 360 rpm. The starting torque is 50% higher than average running torque. Determine the bending stress in the gear teeth if width of gear is 2.5 cm, diametrical pitch is 2 cm and pinion has 30 teeth. The gear and pinion are of 20° full depth involute types.

55. A rotary of a power tiller is to be operated by 10 kW diesel engine. The speed of engine shaft is 970 rpm and that of rotary is to be 330 rpm. The minimum centre distance between engine and rotary shaft is to be 550 mm. Design a suitable chain drive.

CHAPTER 9

# HYdraulic System of a Tractor

## INTRODUCTION

Hydraulic system in a tractor is provided to enable the tractor operator:

- To raise or lower heavy implements as per requirements.
- To control implement depth during field operation with minimum efforts.

## 9.1 FUNDAMENTALS OF FLUID POWER TRANSMISSION

Fluid power is based on the principle of Pascal's law which states that pressure applied to a fluid is transmitted equally in all directions. Hydraulic Fluid is assumed as incompressible. The fluid pressure controls the force of output. ($P = F/A$ = force/area). The fluid flow controls the speed of output. The required flow in lpm is given by

Required flow in lpm = Volume of fluid displacement in litres/time

where, time is in minutes for complete stroke.

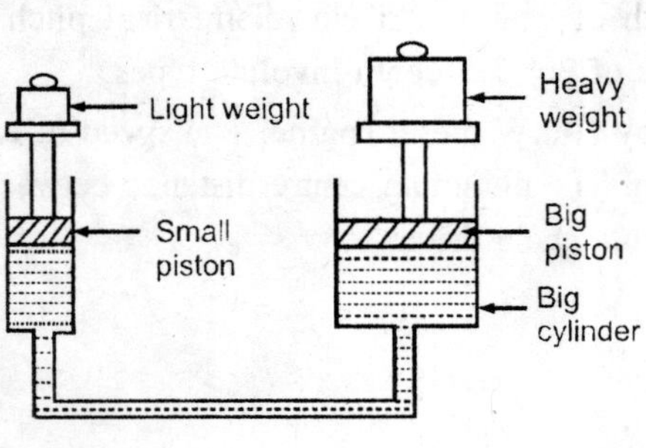


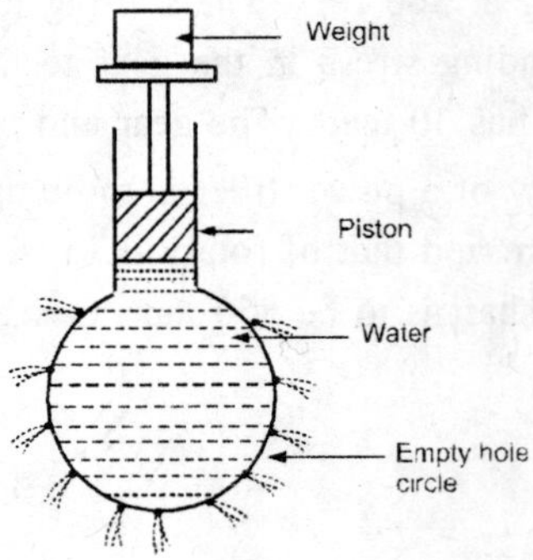


**Hydrodynamics:** Transmits power through high velocity and low pressure.

**Hydrostatics:** Transmits power through high pressure and low velocity.

### 9.1.1. Basic Components of Fluid Power Transmission

The basic components of fluid power transmission are as follows:

1. Fluid 2. Reservoir 3. Filter 4. Pump 5. Actuator-linear or rotary
6. Directional control valves 7. Pressure control valves-Relief valve for safety
8. Flow control valves 9. Lines-pressure, return, intake.

#### 1. Fluid

Fluid acts as a means of transmitting power to remote locations, lubricates and cools the components. It also picks up contaminants and carries then to filter for removal. Viscosity is most important property of hydraulic fluids. Generally, fluid viscosities are recommended between 12 to 48

MPa by the manufacturers at operating temperature of pump. Otherwise, the performance of the pump will be affected considerably. Each tractor manufacturer specifies the hydraulic fluid that will meet requirements of both transmission and hydraulic systems. The oil temperature should be kept below 60°C to reduce oxidation of oil. Additives are needed to reduce wear in gear/vane type pumps above 7 MPa operating pressures.

## 2. Reservoir

Reservoir holds the fluid for components and allows large particles to settle and entrained air to escape. It also dissipates heat. It supplies extra oil needed when hydraulic cylinder is extending. It also provides space for extra returning oil when cylinder is retracting. In the modern tractors transmission case also serves as hydraulic reservoir. The reservoir is vented to atmosphere to accommodate changing oil levels. The air vent is provided with a filter to prevent dirt/dust entry into the reservoir.

## 3. Filter

Filter removes small particles from the fluid. Filters are nominally rated according to the size of particles that are predominantly trapped. Change filters on regular basis, if bypass valves are used.

## 4. Pumps

Pumps convert mechanical power to fluid power. Hydraulic pumps which are mainly used are gear type (Fig. 9.1), roller vane type (Fig. 9.2) or axial piston variable flow type. The pressure developed by three main types of hydraulic pumps are as follows:

1. Fixed gear/vane pump : Pressure up to 10.3 MPa
2. Pressure balanced gear/vane pump : 13.8–24.1 MPa
3. Pinion type pump : 27.6–34.5 MPa

The common speed of operation of pumps ranges from 3000 to 5000 rpm

The fluid and shaft power of pumps are given by eqns. 9.1 and 9.2.

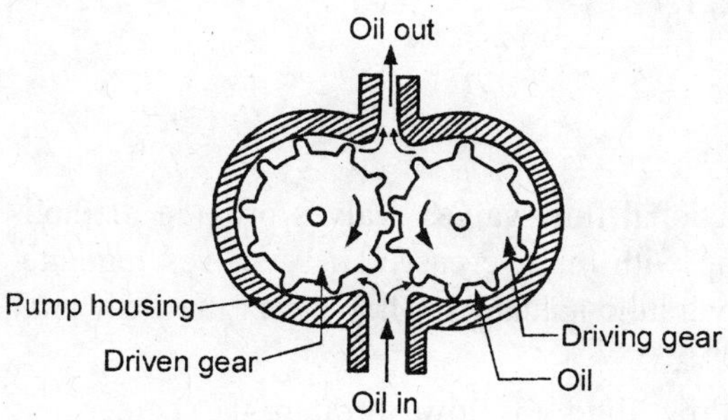


**Figure 9.1: Gear type oil pump**

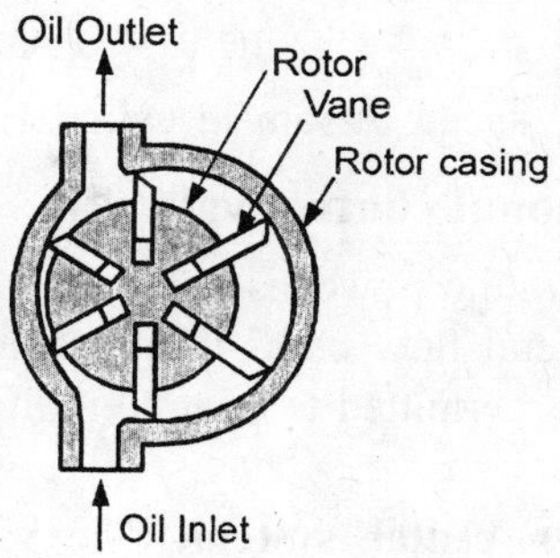


**Figure 9.2: Vane pump**

**Fluid power of pump ($W_f$)**

The fluid power of pump ($W_f$) is given by

$$W_f = \frac{Q \times P}{60} \quad ...(9.1)$$

where, $W_f$ = fluid power, kW

$Q$ = pump discharge, l/m $P$ = pressure across the pump, MPa

**Shaft power of pump ($W_s$)**

The shaft power of pump ($W_s$) is given by

$$W_s = T \times N \times 1.05 \times 10^{-4} \quad ...(9.2)$$

where, $W_s$ = shaft power of pump, kW ; $T$ = input shaft torque, N-m

$N$ = shaft speed, rpm

Also,

$$W_s = W_f / \eta_m \quad ...(9.3)$$

where, $\eta_m$ = mechanical efficiency or overall efficiency of pump.

## 5. Actuator-linear

Converts fluid power to linear mechanical power. Single acting and double acting hydraulic cylinders are given in Figs. 9.3 and 9.4.

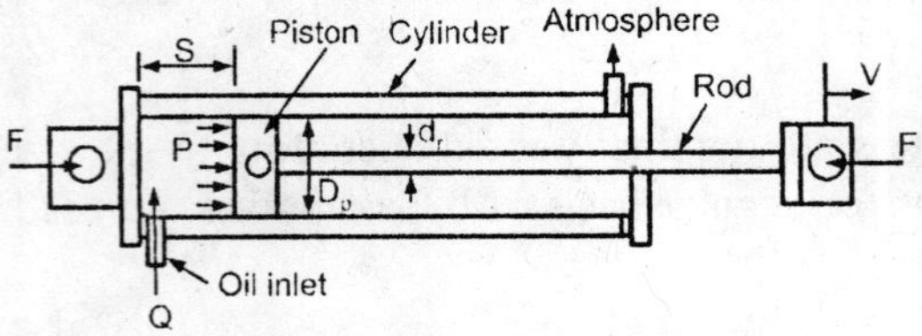


**Figure 9.3: Single acting hydraulic cylinder**

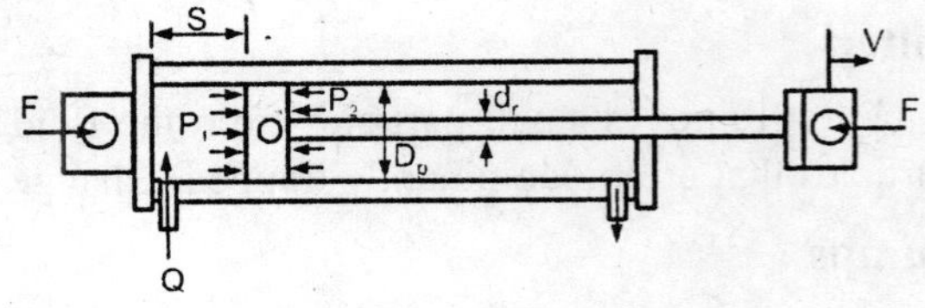


**Figure 9.4: Double acting hydraulic cylinder**

Force in the cylinder is given by

$$F_e = P \times A_c$$

$$F_{re} = P \times (A_c - A_r)$$

where, $F_e$ = extension force in the cylinder, N ; $F_{re}$ = retraction force in the cylinder, N

$P$ = fluid pressure in actuator, N/mm$^2$ ; $A_c$ = cross sectional area of ram, mm$^2$

$A_r$ = cross sectional area of rod, mm$^2$

Power developed by the actuator ($W_a$) in kW is given by

$$W_a = F_e \times V/1000$$

where, $V$ = speed of ram in cylinder, m/s.

## 6. Directional control valves

Hydraulic power is controlled by directional flow valves. Valves provide methods to control one or several flow paths from a single pump with relative ease. These valves regulate the rate of flow that is permitted to operate individual hydraulic actuators. They direct the flow path of fluid in two ways.

**Open center system:** The valves allow fluid to flow through the center and return to reservoir when the system is in neutral. At idle; maximum flow, near zero pressure. A constant flow pump is generally used.

open port-floating position control

closed port-locking position control

**Closed center system:** The valves allow no fluid to flow through the center when the system is in neutral. At idle; near zero flow, relief pressure. A variable flow pump is generally used, which stops pumping when the valve is closed.

open port-floating position control

closed port-locking position control

Directional control valves may be of following types:

**Poppet valve:** It is constructed of a poppet held tightly against a seat by a small spring force.

**Spool valves:** These are basically a shaft sliding in a bore. The shaft has grooves around circumference, which makes it look like a spool. Spool valves may be two way (Fig. 9.5), three way (Fig. 9.6) or four way type depending on to the number of hydraulic lines connected to the valve, the number of operating positions for the spool and how the hydraulic lines are inter connected when the spool is in neutral position.

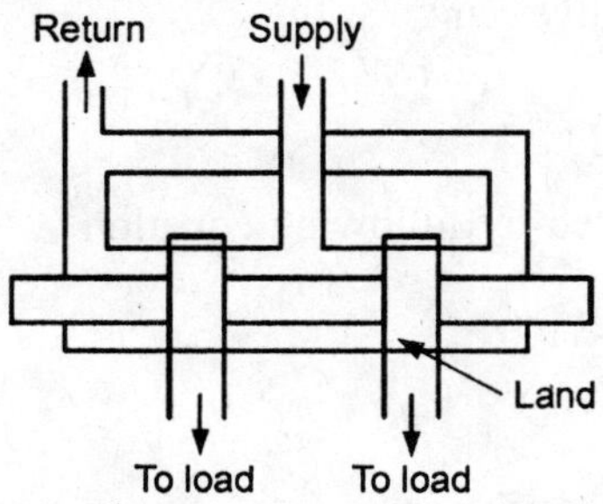


**Figure 9.5: Two way spool valve**

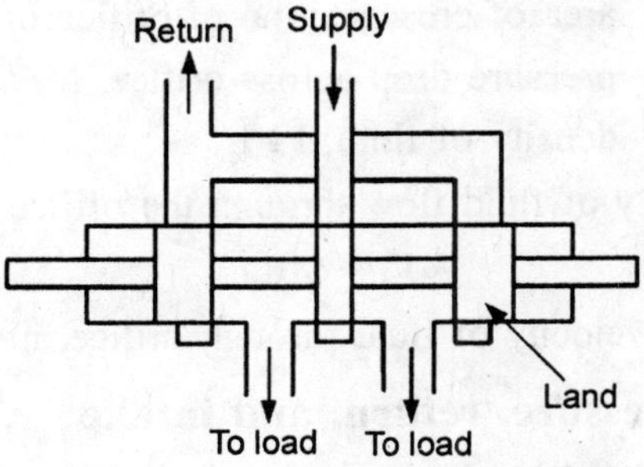


**Figure 9.6: Three way spool valve**

## 7. Pressure control valves

It is used to control pressure in the system. These are provided to protect the components within hydraulic circuit from damage from excessive pressure. Theses are also called as safety relief valves. Relief valve is essential for safety as it sets maximum pressure in the system. The most basic type is a poppet held against a cone seat by spring force. Pilot operated pressure regulator valve provides fast action to respond flow changes. Other common types of valves are: Pressure reducing, sequence, unloading valves etc.

## 8. Flow control valves

It is used to control fluid flow in the system (speed of actuators). Check valve allows fluid flow in one direction, no flow in the other direction. Needle valve-acts like variable orifice to restrict flow. Pressure compensated valves-automatically adjust the fluid flow to compensate for pressure variations in the system. Ball valves (Fig. 9.7) and Spool valves (Fig. 9.8) are used for controlling the flow of fluid.

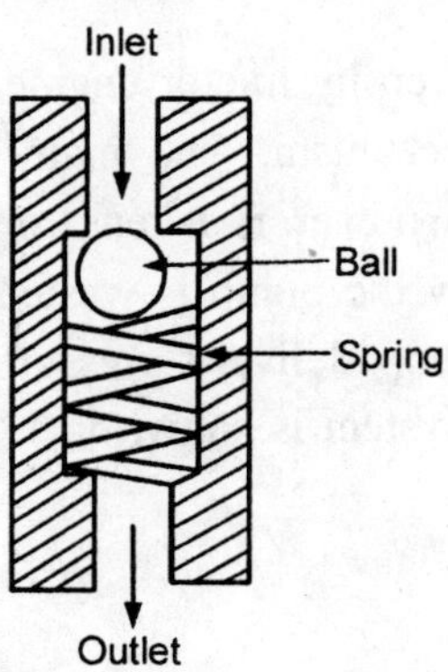


**Figure 9.7: Ball type flow control valve**

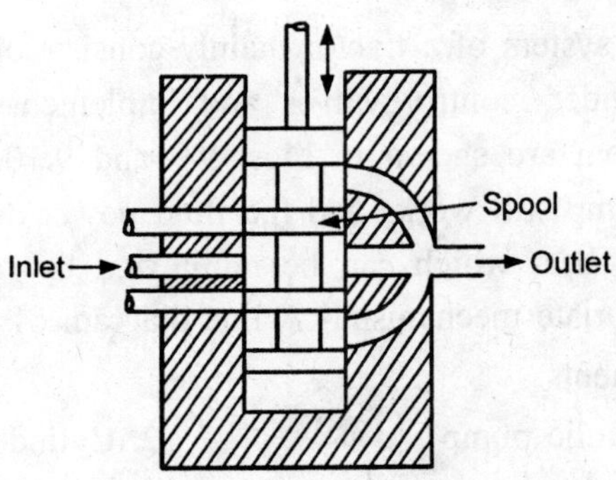


**Figure 9.8: Spool type flow control valve**

Following orifice equation can be used to calculate the flow rate ($Q$) at a given pressure drop across the orifice.

$$Q = 2.68 \times 10^{-2} \times C_d \times a \times \sqrt{\left(\frac{\delta P}{\rho}\right)}$$

where, $Q$ = fluid flow rate through control valve, l/m

$C_d$ = confinement of discharge, dimensionless

$a$ = area of cross section of orifice of control valve, $cm^2$

$\partial P$ = pressure drop across orifice, MPa

$\rho$ = density of fluid, kg/l

Velocity of fluid flow through the orifice is calculated by following equation

$$V_o = Q/6a$$

where, $V_o$ = velocity of fluid through orifice, m/s.

### 9. Lines-pressure, return, and intake

Hydraulic lines are used to convey the fluid to remote locations under pressure and dissipate heat developed in the system. The lines should be strong enough to with stand the fluid pressure developed during operation and their size should be such that the pressure drop is minimum. Rigid lines are made of steel while flexible are made from reinforced rubber. Wall thickness of conduit pipe used for fluid pressure lines is calculated based on maximum pressure and hoop stresses developed that would cause failure of conduit pipe along a line parallel to its centerline. It is given by

$$t_w = \frac{P_{max} \times (d_c/2)}{S_d}$$

where, $t_w$ = wall thickness of conduit pipe, cm

$P_{max}$ = maximum allowable pressure, MPa

$d_c$ = conduit diameter, cm

$S_d$ = Design stress for the pipe line, MPa

## 9.2 HYDRAULIC SYSTEM OF TRACTOR

The hydraulic system of a tractor mainly consists of pump driven by tractor engine or power train, hydraulic cylinder, control valves and implement lifting mechanism. The main components of hydraulic system are shown in Figs. 9.9 and 9.10. When no power is taken from the hydraulic system, the pump still works and the fluid power developed by the pump is wasted. This power is converted into heat which can be minimized by reducing pump delivery pressure and discharge through appropriate mechanism. A line diagram of hydraulic system is shown in Fig. 9.11.

Components:

1. Hydraulic pump
2. Cylinder
3. Control valve
4. Hand control lever
5. Walking beam
6. Implement lift arm

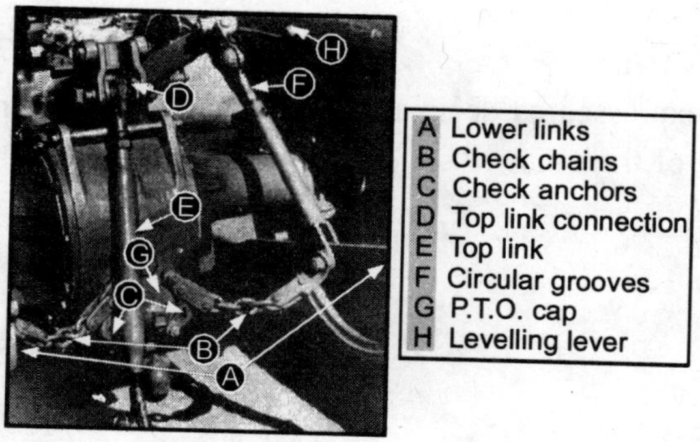


Figure 9.9: Links in tractor hydraulic system

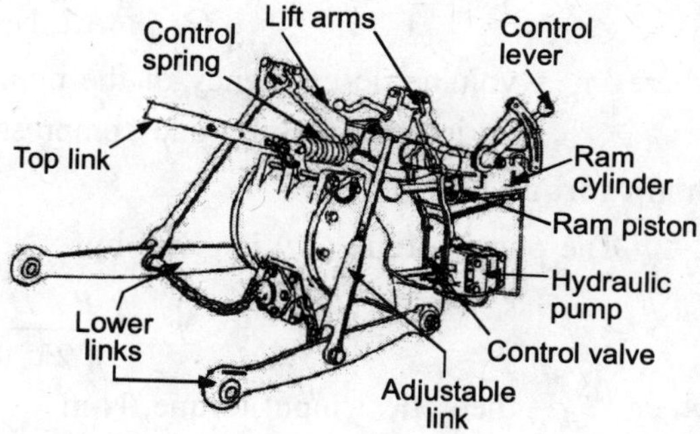


Figure 9.10: Hydraulic system of a tractor

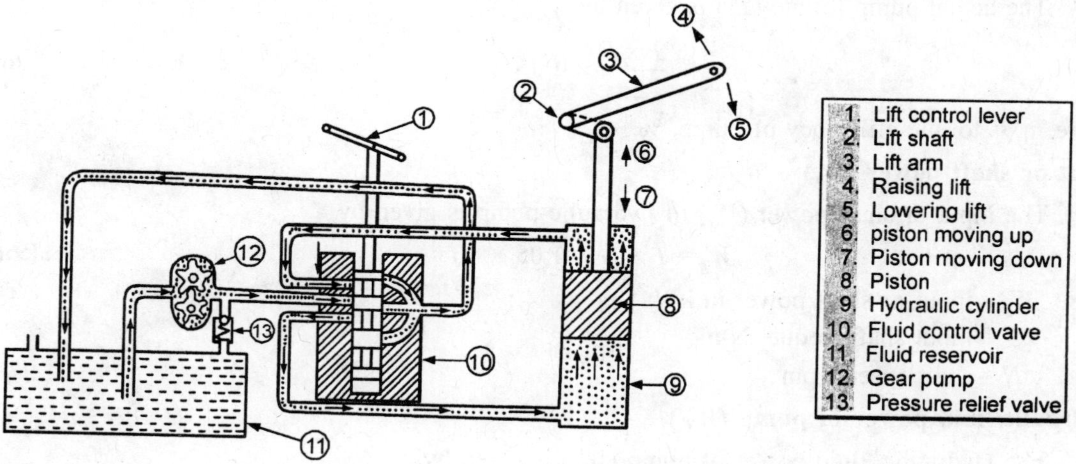


Figure 9.11: Line diagram of hydraulic system of tractor

## 9.3 HYDRAULIC PUMP PERFORMANCE

### 9.3.1. Pump Discharge

The discharge of hydraulic pump is given by

$$Q_{th} = D_p \times N \quad \text{...(9.4)}$$

where, $Q_{th}$ = theoretical flow, l/min

$D_p$ = volume of displacement of pump in one revolution, l/rev

$N$ = pump speed, rpm

For plunger barrel type pumps, the discharge is given by

$$Q_{th} = \text{A.L.N.} \times 10^{-3} \quad \text{...(9.5)}$$

where, $A$ = area of plunger, $cm^2$

$L$ = length of stroke, cm

$N$ = pump speed, rpm.

The actual discharge of hydraulic pump is given by

$$Q_{act} = D_p \times N \times \eta_v \quad \text{...(9.6)}$$

Or, for plunger barrel type pumps

$$Q_{act} = \text{A.L.N} \times 10^{-3} \times \eta_v \quad \text{...(9.7)}$$

where, $\eta_v$ = volumetric efficiency of the pump, % expressed as decimal fraction and is dependent on internal leakage and compressibility of the oil.

**Pump torque ($T_p$)**

The pump torque ($T_p$) is given by

$$T_{th} = \frac{P \times D}{2\pi} \times 100 \quad \text{...(9.8)}$$

where, $T_{th}$ = theoretical input torque, N-m

$P$ = pump outlet pressure minus pump inlet pressure (bar).

The actual pump torque ($T_p$) is given by

$$T_{ac} = \frac{P \times D}{2\pi} \times 100 \times \eta_t \quad \text{...(9.9)}$$

where, $\eta_t$ = torque efficiency of pump, %.

**Input or shaft power ($W_s$)**

The input or shaft power ($W_s$) of hydraulic pump is given by

$$W_s = T \times N \times 1.05 \times 10^{-4} \quad \text{...(9.10)}$$

where, $W_s$ = input or shaft power in kW

$T$ = input shaft torque, N-m

$N$ = shaft speed, rpm

**Hydraulic/fluid power of pump ($W_f$)**

The Hydraulic/Fluid power of pump ($W_f$) is given by

$$W_f = \frac{Q \times P}{60} \quad \text{...(9.11)}$$

where, $Q$ = actual pump discharge, l/m

$P$ = pressure across the pump, MPa

Also

$$HP_f = \frac{Q \times H}{75} \quad \text{...(9.12)}$$

where, $Q$ = actual pump discharge, l/s

$H$ = Head, m

**Overall efficiency of pump ($\eta_m$)**

Overall efficiency of pump ($\eta_m$) is given by

$$\eta_m = \frac{W_f}{W_s} \quad \text{...(9.13)}$$

where, $W_f$ = Hydraulic/fluid power of pump

$W_s$ = input or shaft power in kW

This is also equal to the product of torque and volumetric efficiencies, *i.e.*

$$\eta_m = \eta_t \times \eta_v$$

### 9.3.2. Pump Performance Characteristics

The pump performance characteristics can be established by comparison between the pump performances at no load and at load at a given condition of speed, pressure and displacement. The typical pump performance curves for a variable displacement piston pump are shown in Fig. 9.12.

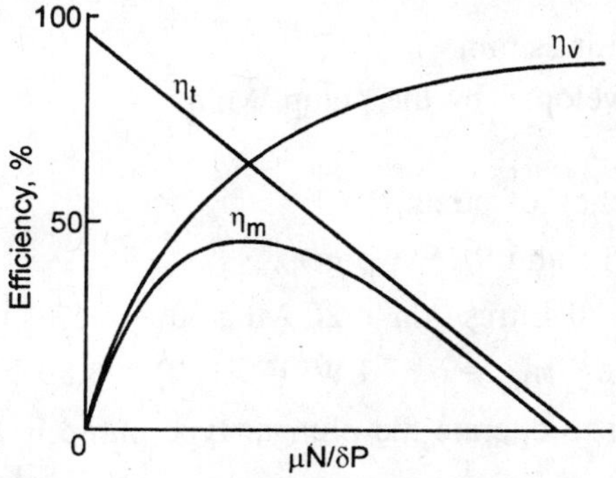


**Figure 9.12: Typical torque ($\eta_t$), volumetric ($\eta_v$) and overall ($\eta_m$) efficiencies of pump**

## 9.4 SOLVED PROBLEMS ON PUMPS FOR HYDRAULIC SYSTEM

**EXAMPLE 9.1** *Design a plunger barrel type hydraulic pump to deliver a pump discharge of 20 litres/min at a speed of 1000 rpm. The pump efficiency should be 75%. Also find out power required to operate the pump if pressure developed in the pump is 20 MPa.*

**SOLUTION:**

Pump discharge ($Q$) = 20 litres/min = $20 \times 10^3$ cm$^3$/min

Pump efficiency ($\eta$) = 75%

Pump speed ($N$) = 1000 rpm

Pressure developed by the pump = 20 MPa

Assume that the stroke bore ratio of plunger pump is 1.1

So, $L/D = 1.1$ or $L = 1.1D$ take $L = 35$ mm

Now, We know that for a plunger barrel type of pump

Theoretical volume of oil pumped/min ($V$) = A.L.N

and, Actual volume ($Q$) = $V \times \eta$ = A.L.N. $\eta_v$ ...(9.14)

where, $A$ = area of plunger, cm$^2$

$L$ = length of stroke, cm

$N$ = pump speed, rpm

$\eta_v$ = volumetric efficiency of pump, %

Putting the values in eq. 9.14, we get

$$20 \times 10^3 \text{ cm}^3/\text{min} = \pi/4 \times D^2 \times 3.5 \text{ cm} \times 1000 \times 75/100$$

or, $$D^2 = (20 \times 10^3 \times 4 \times 100)/(\pi \times 3.5 \times 1000 \times 75)$$

$$D = 3.11 \text{ cm say } 31.5 \text{ mm}$$

So, designed dimensions of pump plunger is 31.5 mm diameter and 35 m stroke length.

**Power requirement of the pump:** The power requirement for development of fluid pressure of 20 MPa is calculated as under:

Fluid Power $(W_f) = Q \times P/60$ ...(9.15)

Shaft Power $(W_s) = W_f/\eta_m$ ...(9.16)

where, $W_f$ = Fluid power, kW

$Q$ = Pump discharge, Litres/min

$P$ = Fluid pressure developed by the pump, MPa

$W_s$ = Shaft power, kW

$\eta_m$ = mechanical efficiency of pump, %

Putting values in eqns. 9.15 and 9.16, we get

$$W_f = 20 \text{ Litres/min} \times 20 \text{ MPa}/60 = 6.67 \text{ kW}$$

And, Shaft power $W_s = W_f/\eta_m = 6.67 \text{ kW}/ (75/100) = 8.89 \text{ kW}$

Therefore, power required to operate the plunger type pump is 8.89 kW.

**EXAMPLE 9.2** *A plunger barrel type hydraulic pump is required to deliver fluid at the rate of 91.6 litres/min at a speed of 1500 rpm against a fluid pressure of 15 MPa. Calculate pump efficiency if shaft power needed to operate the pump is 27.5 kW. Also determine torque requirement of the pump.*

**SOLUTION:**

Pump discharge $(Q)$ = 91.6 litres/min

Pump speed $(N)$ = 1500 rpm

Pressure developed by the pump = 15 MPa

Shaft power $(W_s)$ = 27.5 kW

We know that

Fluid Power $(W_f) = Q \times P/60$ ...(9.17)

Shaft Power $(W_s) = W_f/\eta_m$ ...(9.18)

From eqn. 9.17,

$$W_f = 91.6 \text{ litres/min} \times 15 \text{ MPa}/60$$
$$= 22.9 \text{ kW}$$

From eqn. 9.18,

$$W_s = W_f/\eta_m$$

or

$$\eta_m = W_f/W_s$$
$$\eta_m = 22.9/27.5 = 0.833 \text{ or } 83.3\%$$

**Torque requirement of pump $(T_p)$**

We know that, torque required for the pump is given by

$$T_p = \delta p \times D_p/2\pi\eta_t \quad ...(9.19)$$

where, $T_p$ = torque required to drive the pump, N-m

$\delta p$ = Pressure developed across the pump, MPa

$D_p$ = pump displacement, $cm^3$/rev

$D_p$ = $Q/N$ = (91.6 litres/min × $10^3$ $cm^3$/liter)/1500 = 61.1 $cm^3$/rev

Putting the values in eqn. 9.19, we get,

$$T_p = 15 \text{ MPa} \times 61.1\text{cm}^3/\text{rev}/(2\pi x\ 83.3/100)$$

$$= 175.04 \text{ N-m}$$

**EXAMPLE 9.3** *A hydraulic pump operating at a speed of 1800 rpm at 15 MPa pressure has a displacement of 20.5 cm³/min. Calculate the following if mechanical and torque efficiencies of the pump are 85% and 90% respectively.*

*(a) Delivery rate of pump in litres/min*

*(b) Shaft power of the pump*

*(c) Torque required for driving the pump.*

**SOLUTION:**

Pump speed ($N$) = 1800 rpm

Pump displacement ($D_p$) = 20.5 $cm^3$/rev

Pressure developed = 15 MPa

Overall efficiency of pump ($\eta_m$) = 85%

Torque efficiency of pump ($\eta_t$) = 90%

**(a) Pump delivery rate ($Q$)**

Pump Delivery Rate ($Q$) is given by

$$Q = D_p \times N$$

$$Q = 20.5 \text{ cm}^3/\text{rev} \times 10^{-3} \text{ litres/cm}^3 \times 1800 \text{ rpm}$$

$$= 36.9 \text{ litres/min}$$

**Ans.**

**(b) Shaft power ($W_s$)**

We know that

Fluid Power ($W_f$) = $Q \times P/60$

$$W_f = (36.9 \text{ litres/min} \times 15 \text{ MPa})/60$$

$$= 9.225 \text{ kW}$$

Also, Shaft Power ($W_s$) = $W_f/\eta_m$

$$W_s = W_f/\eta_m = 9.225\text{kW}/0.85$$

$$= 10.853 \text{ kW}$$

Therefore shaft power of the pump would be 10.853 kW.

**(c) Torque requirement of pump ($T_p$)**

We know that, torque required for the pump is given by

$$T_p = \delta p \times D_p/2\pi\eta_t$$

$$T_p = (15 \text{ MPa} \times 20.5 \text{ cm}^3/\text{rev})/(2\pi \times 0.90)$$
$$T_p = 57.55 \text{ N-m}$$

The torque required to operate the pump would be 57.55 N-m

**EXAMPLE 9.4** *A gear type pump operating at a speed of 2200 rpm is developing a pressure of 10 MPA requires input power of 10.7 kW. If its mechanical efficiency is taken as 70%, calculate oil flow rate in the pump in litres/min and its displacement volume per revolution. Also calculate theoretical discharge of pump if its volumetric efficiency is 80%.*

**SOLUTION:**

Shaft power ($W_s$) = 10.70 kW

Pressure developed ($P$) = 10 MPa

Mechanical efficiency of pump ($\eta_m$) = 70%

Pump speed ($N$) = 2200 rpm

We know that

$$\text{Shaft Power } (W_s) = W_f/\eta_m$$

Or
$$W_f = W_s \times \eta_m$$
$$= 10.7 \text{ kW} \times 70/100$$
$$= 7.49 \text{ kW}$$

Also,
$$\text{Fluid Power } (W_f) = Q \times P/60$$

Or
$$Q = W_f \times 60/\text{P}$$
$$= 7.49 \text{ kW} \times 60/10 \text{ MPa}$$
$$= 44.94 \text{ Litres/min}$$

Displacement volume per revolution is given by

$$D_p = Q/N = 44.94 \times 10^3/2200 = 24.42 \text{ cm}^3/\text{rev.}$$

The theoretical discharge of pump ($Q_{th}$) is given by

$$Q_{th} = Q_a/\eta_v$$
$$Q_{th} = 44.94 \text{ litres/min}/0.80$$
$$= 56.17 \text{ litres/min}$$

**EXAMPLE 9.5** *A gear pump operating at a speed of 2200 rpm developing a pressure of 10 MPa requires input power of 10.70 kW. Its torque efficiency may be taken 70%. Calculate the oil flow rate of pump in litres per minute and its displacement volume/rev. Also calculate theoretical discharge of pump if its volumetric efficiency is 80%.*

**SOLUTION:**

$$W_s = 10.70 \text{ kW}$$
$$P = 10 \text{ MPa}$$
$$N = 2200 \text{ rpm}$$
$$\eta_t = 70\%$$
$$\eta_v = 80\%$$

Now, $\eta_m = \eta_t \times \eta_v$

$$\eta_m = 0.70 \times 0.80 = 0.56$$
$$W_s = W_f / \eta_m = Q \times P/(60 \times \eta_m)$$

$\therefore$ $10.70 \text{ kW} = Q \times 10 \text{ MPa}/(60 \times 0.56)$

Or, $Q = 10.70 \times 60 \times 0.56/10 = 35.95$ litres/min

Displacement volume per revolution is given by

Also, $D_p = Q/N = (35.95 \text{ l/m} \times 10^3 \text{ cm}^3/\text{l})/2200$

$$= 16.34 \text{ cm}^3/\text{rev}$$

The theoretical discharge of pump ($Q_{th}$) is given by

$$Q_{th} = Q/\eta_v$$
$$Q_{th} = 35.95/0.8$$
$$= 44.94 \text{ litres/min}$$

## 9.5 DESIGN OF HYDRAULIC CYLINDERS

Hydraulic cylinder converts fluid power into linear mechanical force which can be used for lifting/lowering of implements attached to the tractor and control depth of operation in the field. According to fluid flow and forces acting and specific applications, the hydraulic cylinders can be classified as:

1. Single acting
2. Double acting
3. Double acting double rod
4. Telescoping and
5. Cushioned top type

Single acting hydraulic cylinders are most commonly used in hydraulic systems of tractors. Single acting type and double acting type hydraulic cylinders are given in Fig. 9.13 and 9.14.

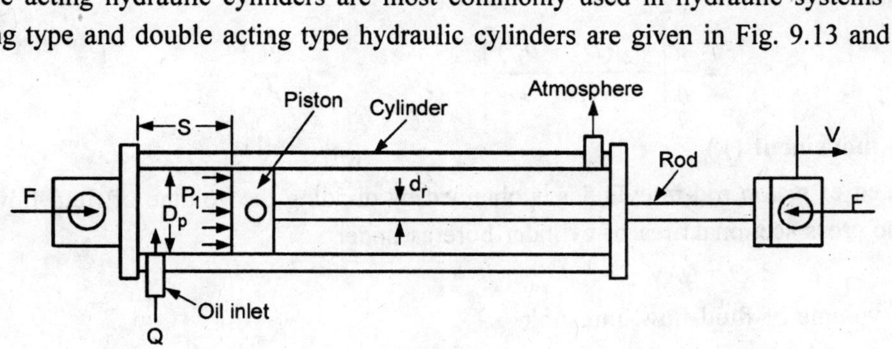


**Figrue 9.13: Single acting type hydraulic cylinder**

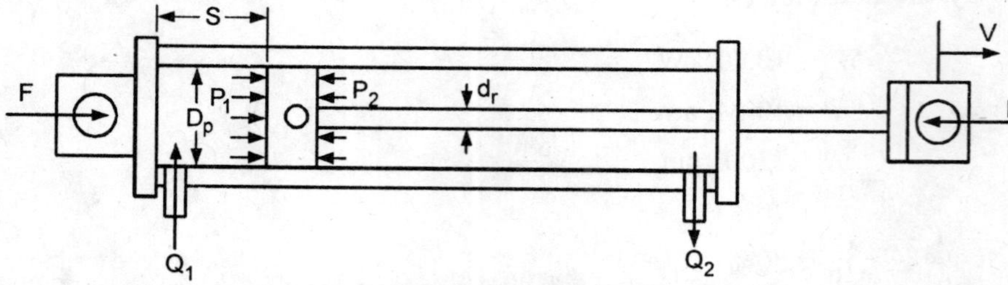


**Figure 9.14: Double acting type hydraulic cylinder**

**Fluid force acting in cylinder (*F*)**

Neglecting inertia force in the hydraulic cylinders, hydrostatic force transmission is given by

$$F = \frac{P_1 A_1 - P_2 A_2}{10} \qquad \text{...(9.20)}$$

and $\quad A_1 = (\pi/4)\, D_p^2 \quad \text{and} \quad A_2 = (\pi/4)\,(D_p^2 - d_r^2)$

Or,

$$F = \frac{\pi}{4}\left[\frac{p_1 D_p^2 - p_2 (D_p^2 - d_r^2)}{10}\right] \qquad \text{...(9.21)}$$

where, $P_1, P_2$ = hydraulic pressures, MPa
$D_p$ = piston diameter, cm
$d_r$ = rod diameter, cm
$S$ = stroke, cm
$A_1$ = piston area of the cap end, $cm^2$
$A_2$ = piston area at the rod end, $cm^2$
$F$ = Force or load moved by hydraulic cylinder, kN

In case the return oil line from the rod end is connected back to reservoir at atmospheric pressure, then the piston is extending and

$$F_e = \frac{\pi}{4}\left[\frac{p_1 D_p^2}{10}\right] \qquad \text{...(9.22)}$$

When the supply is to the rod end and the cap end is vented to atmosphere, the piston is retracting. Then,

$$F_{re} = \frac{\pi}{4}\left[\frac{p_2 (D_p^2 - d_r^2)}{10}\right] \qquad \text{...(9.23)}$$

**Speed of rod movement (*V*)**

The speed of piston rod in cylinder is obtained by dividing the volume of fluid flow into the cylinder by the cross sectional area of cylinder bore as under:

$$Q = 6AV \qquad \text{...(9.24)}$$

where, $Q$ = volume of fluid flow, litres/min
$A$ = cross sectional area, $cm^2$
$V$ = velocity of piston, m/s

**Power developed by the actuator ($W_a$)**

The power developed by hydraulic cylinder in kW is given by

$$W_a = F_e \times V/1000 \quad ...(9.25)$$

where, $F_e$ = Force developed by piston during extending, kN

$V$ = speed of ram in cylinder, m/s

**EXAMPLE 9.6** *A double acting hydraulic cylinder as shown in Fig. 9.14 has a diameter of 7.0 cm and its rod diameter is 2.5 cm. Assume that maximum pressure in the system is 18 MPa and pump discharge is 70 litres/min. Inlet end of cylinder port is connected to the pump while, the other end port is connected to oil reservoir. Calculate the following:*

*(a) Maximum load moved by the cylinder when piston is extending.*

*(b) Maximum load moved by the cylinder when piston is retracting.*

*(c) Piston speed when extending.*

**SOLUTION:**

$$D_p = 7.0 \text{ cm}$$
$$d_r = 2.5 \text{ cm}$$
$$P = 18 \text{ MPa}$$
$$Q = 70 \text{ lpm}$$

Now, $A_p = \pi/4\ D_p^2 = \pi/4\ (7.0)^2 = 38.5 \text{ cm}^2$

$A_r = \pi/4 d_r^2 = \pi/4\ (2.5)^2 = 4.8 \text{ cm}^2$

Now, $A_2 = A_p - A_r = 38.5 \text{ cm}^2 - 4.8 \text{ cm}^2 = 33.7 \text{ cm}^2$

Since, rod end of the cylinder is connected to reservoir, so, $P_2 = 0$

Therefore, maximum force/load moved while piston is extending is given by

$$F_e = P_1 \times A_p - P_2 \times (A_p - A_r)/10$$
$$F_e = 18 \text{ MPa} \times 38.5 \text{ cm}^2 - 0 \times 33.7 \text{ cm}^2/10 = 68.5 \text{ kN}$$

When the piston is retracting in the cylinder then, $P_1 = 0$.

Therefore,

$$F_{re} = 0 \times 38.5 \text{ cm}^2 - 18 \text{ MPa} \times 33.7 \text{ cm}^2$$
$$= -60.66 \text{ kN}$$

Piston speed while extending is given by

$$V = Q/6A_p$$

Or, $V = 70 \text{ litres/min}/(6 \times 38.5 \text{ cm}^2)$

$= 0.303 \text{ m/s}$

Again, piston speed when cylinder is retracting is given by

$$V = Q/6\ (A_p - A_r)$$
$$V = 70 \text{ litres/min}/(6 \times 33.7 \text{ cm}^2) = 0.346 \text{ m/s}$$

Now, Oil flow rate during retracting is given by

$$Q = 6\ V \cdot A_p$$

Or, $Q = 6 \times 0.346 \text{ m/s} \times 38.5 \text{ cm}^2$

$= 79.97$ litres/min

Therefore, Oil flow rate when piston is retracting is 79.97 litres/min to the reservoir and the pump is supplying only 70 litres/min. Therefore, the oil reservoir should have enough space to accommodate extra oil returning from the system.

**EXAMPLE 9.7** *Calculate the cylinder diameter of a double acting hydraulic cylinder if maximum safe load moved during extension is 75kN when the pump develops a pressure of 17.5 MPa at an oil discharge of 70 litres/min. Assume that rod diameter is 2.54 cm and stroke length is 20 cm. Also calculate the speed of piston during extension and safe load moved by the cylinder during retraction. What will be oil discharge when cylinder is retracting?*

**SOLUTION:**

$$F_e = 75 \text{ kN}$$

$$Q = 70 \text{ litres/min}$$

$$P = 17.5 \text{ MPa}$$

$$d_r = 2.54 \text{ cm}$$

$$D_p = ?$$

We know that $A_p = \pi/4\ D_p^2$

$$A_r = \pi/4 d_r^2 = \pi/4\ (2.54)^2 = 5.07 \text{ cm}^2$$

Now for double acting hydraulic cylinder

$$F = \frac{\pi}{4}\left[\frac{p_1 D_p^2 - p_2(D_p^2 - d_r^2)}{10}\right]$$

While cylinder is extending $P_2 = 0$

and $$F_e = \frac{\pi}{4}\left[\frac{17.5 \text{ MPa} \times D_p^2 - 0 \times (D_p^2 - d_r^2)}{10}\right]$$

$$75 \text{ kN} = \frac{\pi}{4}\left[\frac{17.5 MPa \times D_p^2}{10}\right]$$

Or, $D_p^2 = 75 \times 10/(17.5 \times \pi/4)$

and $A_p = (\pi/4) \times D_p^2 = 42.856 \text{ cm}^2$

When the cylinder is retracting $P_1 = 0$

Therefore maximum load during retracting is

$$F_{re} = -P_2 \times (A_p - A_r)/10$$

$$= -17.5 \text{ MPa } (42.856\text{-}5.07)/10$$

$$= -66.13 \text{ kN}$$

Piston speed ($V$) during extending is given by

$$V = Q/6A$$

Or, $$V = 70 \text{ litres/min}/6 \times 42.857 = 0.272 \text{ m/s}$$

Similarly, speed at which cylinder is retracting is given by

$$V = Q/6(A_p - A_r)$$

$$= 70 \text{ litres/min}/6 \times 37.787 \text{ cm}^2$$

$$= 0.309 \text{ m/s}$$

Oil flow rate during retracting is given by

$$Q = 6\, A_p \times V = 6 \times 42.857 \text{ cm}^2 \times 0.309 \text{ m/s}$$

$$= 79.39 \text{ litres/min}$$

Thus, when cylinder is retracting, it is returning oil flow at the rate of 79.39 litres/min to the reservoir and the pump is supplying only 70 litres/min. Therefore, the oil reservoir should have enough space to accommodate extra oil returning from the system.

## 9.6 HYDRAULIC CONTROL IN TRACTOR

The different controls used in tractor are shown in Fig. 9.15.

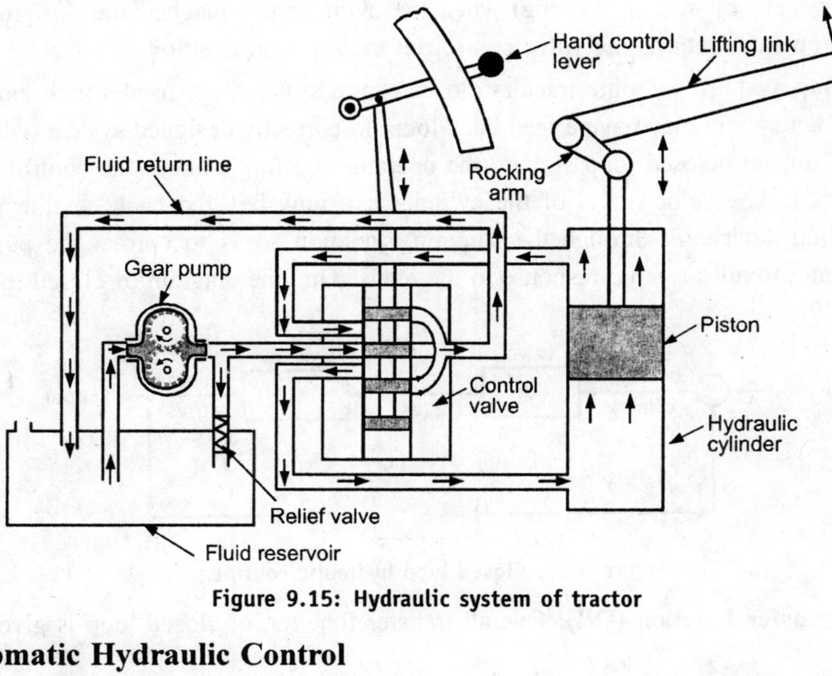


**Figure 9.15: Hydraulic system of tractor**

### 9.6.1. Automatic Hydraulic Control

This is also known as an automatic control or feed back system. This compares the output signals to the input signals and uses the difference to change the output. These can be open loop control system or closed loop control system. The main difference between the two systems is that the open centre system maintains a constant flow of oil, and the closed system maintains a constant pressure when not in use. These are discussed below.

**Open loop system:** The open-centre system was the first type used on farm tractors, and even today it is most commonly used. In this type of system a valve '*V*' is used to direct the fluid to a cylinder, '*C*'. The line diagram of open loop system is given in Fig. 9.16.

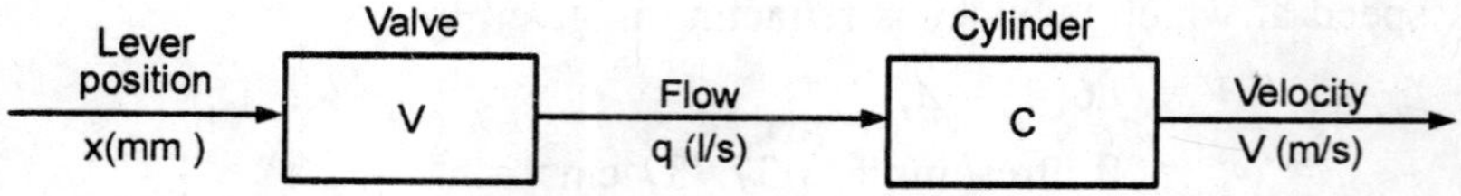


**Figure 9.16. Open loop hydraulic control**

The transfer function of valve *V* is the ratio of output '*q*' (fluid discharge, l/s) to input '*x*' (control lever displacement, mm) *i.e.* $q/x$ and the transfer function of cylinder '*C*' is ratio of output '*v*' (velocity of piston/s) to input '*q*' (pump discharge, l/s) *i.e.* $v/q$. The overall transfer function of the system can be combined simply by multiplying $V \times C$ as given below:

$$\text{Transfer Function } (O/I) = \frac{q}{x} \times \frac{v}{q} = \frac{v}{x}$$

In this type of system the hydraulic cylinder may have a stroke control device that returns the fluid to sump when cylinder reaches the end of stroke. At the end of stroke pressure builds up, causing the valve to return to neutral position. In most cases the operator is quite capable of being a part of control system by sensing (seeing) when the cylinder has reached the desired position, at which point the operator returns the valve control lever to neutral position.

**Closed loop system:** In some tractors closed-centre systems are used which employs piston type pumps. Such a system may have a feed back loop. In correctly designed system, when valve '*V*' and cylinder '*C*' are into closed loop system, the operator can forget about the control. F is now in the feed back loop. The velocity, '*v*' of the cylinder can now be "fed back" to the valve '*V*' by means of signaling device, *F*, through the summing junction so as to correct the position of the valve. This system provides a rapid response to the loads. The line diagram of closed loop system is given in Fig. 9.17.

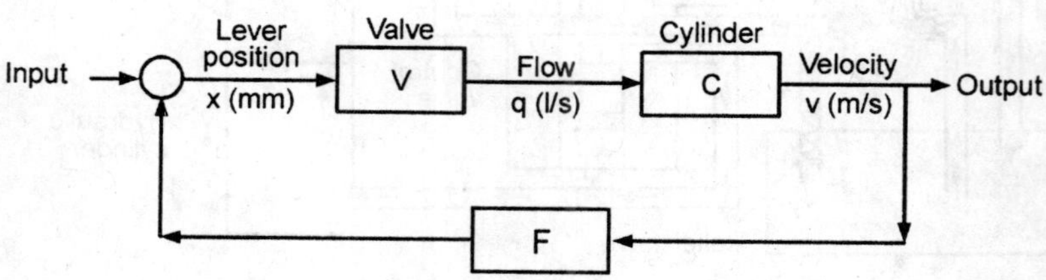


**Figure 9.17: Closed loop hydraulic control**

**Overall transfer function (O/I):** Overall transfer function of closed loop is given by

$$\frac{O}{I} = \frac{v \times c}{(1 + VCF)}$$

where, $V$ = valve in which the input is the motion of spool ($x$) and output is fluid flow rate ($q$). The output /input ratio of valve is also known as flow gain, L/s/mm.

$C$ = dynamic behavior *i.e.* Velocity of cylinder ($v$) of the system (Cylinder + hydraulic oil + masses attached to the cylinder).

$F$ = feedback loop force (draft sensing force), which might be either a mechanical linkage attached to an "error bar" or pressure line to sense the load on, or position of the output of the cylinder.

### 9.6.2. Automatic Position Control System

Automatic position control system is normally associated with a three point hitch system. It provides automatic control of an attached implement and allows the operator to pre select and to position the implement as controlled by the hand control lever. The relative position of hand lever and hydraulic cylinder are always identical. Within the limit of the relief valve controlling the maximum pressure, the hydraulic cylinder will automatically move the implement to its predetermined position and maintain it there, regardless of any leakage in the system. This system is not used with a remote cylinder. The different position of hydraulic quadrant during operation is given in Fig. 9.18.

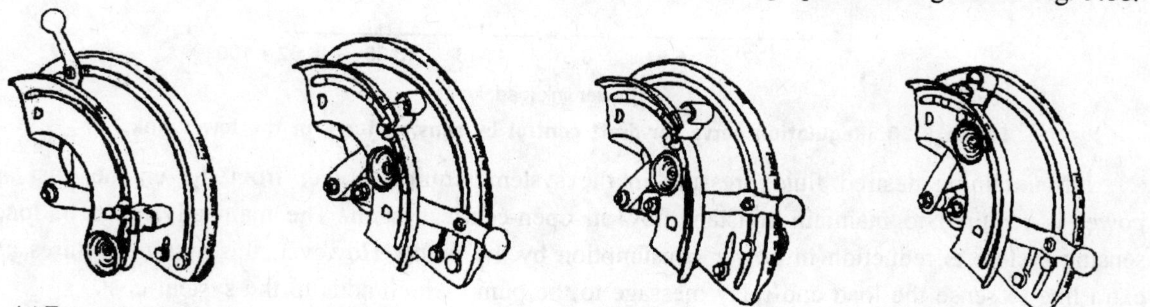

(a) Transport position (b) Normal ploughing (c) Shallow cultivation (d) Operation of external hydraulic equipment

**Figure 9.18: Different position of hydraulic quadrant during operation**

### 9.6.3. Automatic Draft Control System

Automatic draft control system will automatically raise or lower the implement as the draft of attached implement increases or decreases. The position of hand control lever, in effect, establishes the draft to be maintained

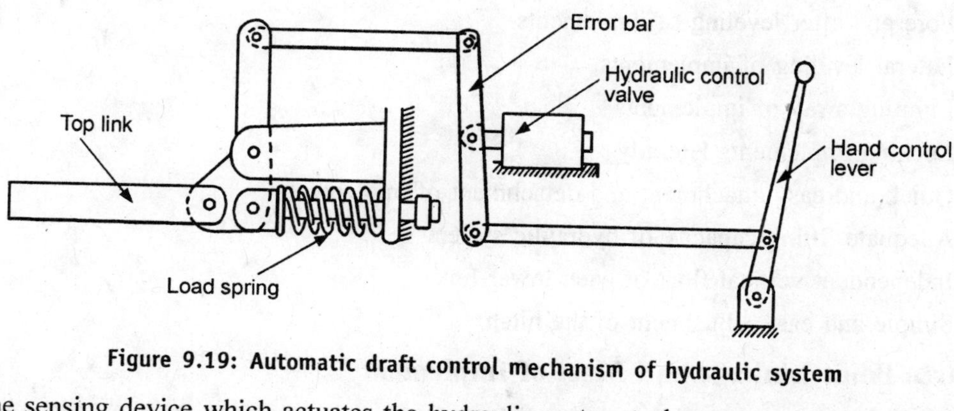


**Figure 9.19: Automatic draft control mechanism of hydraulic system**

The sensing device which actuates the hydraulic system to lower or raise the hitch system is located on either the lower links or upper link, depending upon the size of tractor (Refer Fig. 9.19). The load sensing system senses the load and sends a message to the pump causing it to provide just enough pressure to overcome the load. Under no-load conditions, it works under less pressure. Regulation of draft sensing mechanism is given in Fig. 9.20 and it is calculated as given below:

$$\text{Regulation (\%)} = 100\,(F_r - F_l)/F_r \quad ...(9.26)$$

where, $F_r$ = Average force to start hitch to raise

$F_l$ = Average force to start hitch to lower

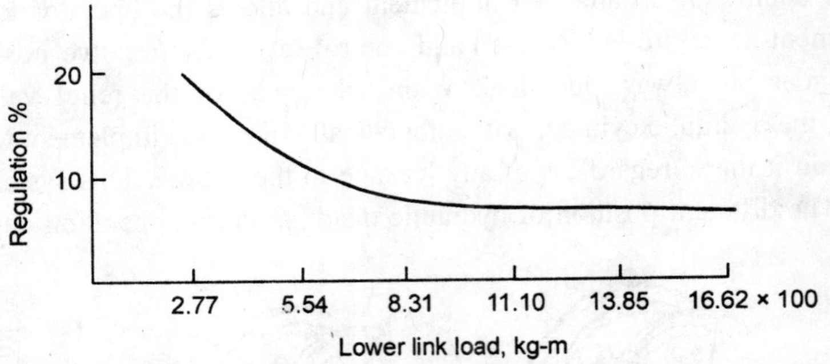


**Figure 9.20: Regulation curve for draft control by sensing force in the lower link**

Maintaining desired fluid pressure in the system requires power from the engine, just as power is required to maintain constant flow in open-centre system. The main advantage of load sensing system is reduction in power consumption by the pump. However, this system requires an extra line to sense the load and relay message to the pump which adds to the system cost.

## 9.7 HITCH SYSTEM FOR FARM MACHINERY

**Design requirements:** Tractor three point hitch system should have following important features:

- Depth control of implement
- Load transfer to drive wheels
- Lateral sway and central ability
- Interchangeability of implements and tractors
- Fore and after leveling of implements
- Lateral leveling of implements
- Limiting sway of implements
- Locking implements laterally
- Quick and easy attachment and detachment of implements
- Adequate lifting capacity of hydraulic system
- Independent vertical float of each lower link
- Simple and easy adjustment of the hitch

### 9.7.1. Three Point Linkage and Mast of Implement

The various components of three point linkage is given in Fig. 9.21. The major functions of various components of three point linkage are given in Table 9.1. The type of load which acts on different links is given in Table 9.2.

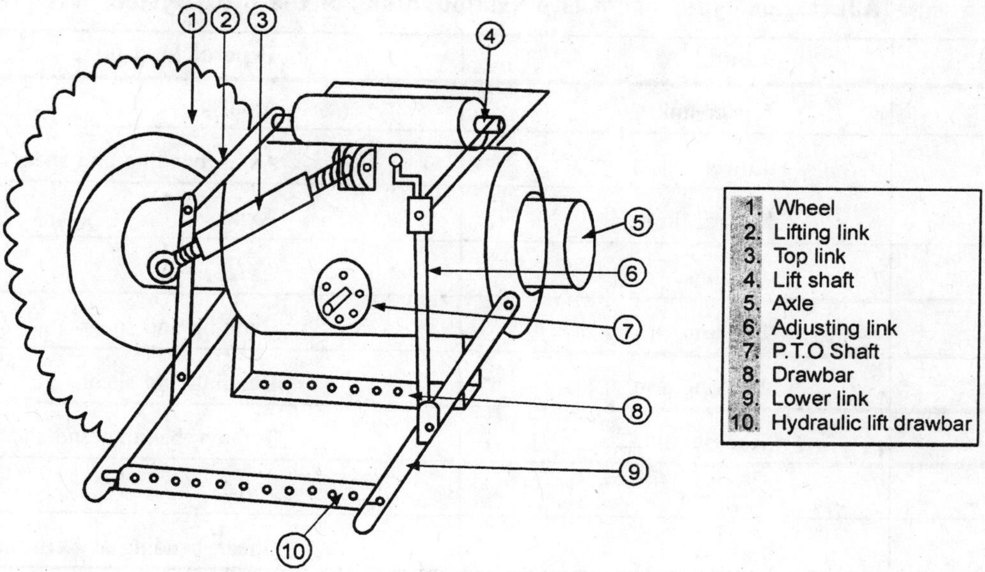


**Figure 9.21: Various components of three point linkage**

**TABLE 9.1: Major functions of various components of hitch system**

| S. No. | Component | Numbers | Functions |
|---|---|---|---|
| 1 | Upper link | 1 | Basic component of hitch system. Connects implement to tractor. Transfers hitching forces of tractor to implement and implement to tractor. |
| 2 | Lower link | 2 | -do- |
| 3 | Lateral limiters | 2 | Limits the travel of implement in horizontal plane thereby inhibits the lateral sway. |
| 4 | Lift link | 2 | Lifts the implement and supports the implement in transport position. It provides lateral stability and leveling to the implement. |
| 5 | Lift arm | 2 | It provides the lateral stability. It lifts implement by giving needed force and motion to lift link and supports implement in transport position. |
| 6 | Rocking arm | 1 | It connects cylinder and rockshaft. It converts linear motion of cylinder into rotation. |
| 7 | Rockshaft | 1 | It transmit the rotating motion of rocking arm to lift arm. |
| 8 | Cylinder | 1 | It is a source of power for lifting implement. It gives linear motion to rocking arm. |

**TABLE 9.2: Types of loads on various links of the hitch system**

| S. No. | Link | Type of load (s) |
|---|---|---|
| 1 | Upper link | Axial |
| 2 | Lower link | Axial, bending and shear |
| 3 | Lateral limiters | Axial |
| 4 | Lift link | Axial |
| 5 | Lift arm | Bending and shear |
| 6 | Rocking arm | Bending and shear |
| 7 | Rockshaft | Torsion, bending and shear |
| 8 | Cylinder | Axial |
| 9 | Pins | Shear, bending and crushing |

Different symbols used in hydraulic circuits are given below.

**HYDRAULIC CIRCUIT SYMBOLS**

| **PUMPS** | |
|---|---|
| Hydraulic pump<br>Fixed displacement |  |
| Variable displacement |  |
| **MOTOR AND CYLINDERS** | |
| Hydraulic motor<br>Fixed displacement |  |
| Variable displacement |  |
| Cylinder, Single acting | 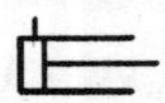 |
| Cylinder, Double acting | |
| Single end rod | 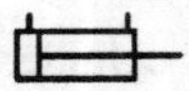 |
| Double end rod | 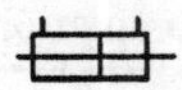 |
| Adjustable cushion advance only |  |
| Differential piston | 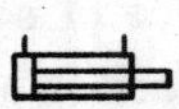 |

| **MISCELLENEOUS UNITS** | |
|---|---|
| Electric motor |  |
| Accumulator, Spring loaded |  |
| Accumulator, Gas charged |  |
| Heater |  |
| Cooler |  |
| Temperature controller |  |
| Filter, Strainer |  |
| Pressure switch |  |
| Pressure indicator |  |
| Temperature indicator |  |
| Direction of shaft rotating (Assume arrow on near side of shaft) |  |

| **LINES** | |
|---|---|
| Line working (Main) | ——— |
| Line pilot (For control) | – – – – |
| Line, liquid (Drain) | - - - - - - |
| Flow, Direction of — Hydraulic | → |
| Flow, Direction of — Pneumatic | → |
| Lines crossing |  |
| Lines joining |  |
| Line with fixed restriction |  |
| **VALVES** | |
| Check valve | 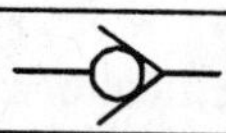 |
| On-Off valve (Manual) |  |
| Pressure relief valve, Direct acting | 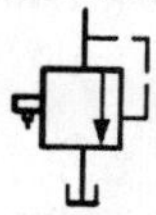 |
| Pressure reducing valve, Direct acting (infinite positioning, normally open for single part) | 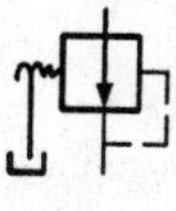 |
| Flow control valve, Adjustable (Non compensated) |  |
| Flow control valve, Adjustable (Pressure compensated with reverse by-pass) | 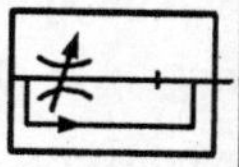 |
| Two-way (Two ports), Two positions | 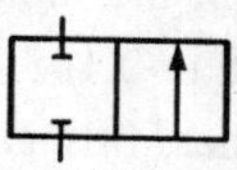 |
| Three-way (Three ports), Two positions | 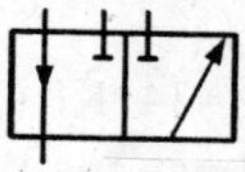 |

| | |
|---|---|
| Four-way (Four ports), Two positions |  |
| Four-way, Three position, Closed centre | 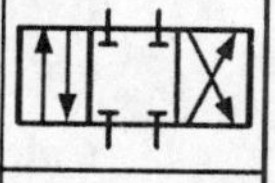 |
| Four-way, three position, Two ports, Open centre (Random) | 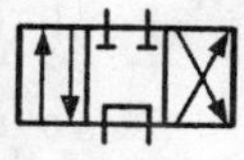 |
| Horizontal bars indicate valve capable of infinite positioning within limits | 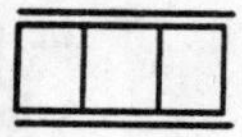 |
| Central (Add divisions and internal parts) |  |
| **ACTUATORS AND CONTROLS** | |
| Spring |  |
| Manual (General symbol; no specific type) | 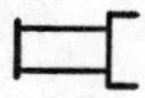 |
| Push button |  |
| Push-pull lever | 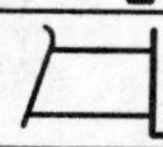 |
| Pedeal or Treadle | 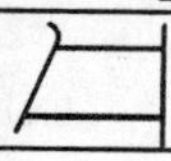 |
| Mechanical | 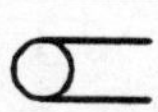 |
| Detent (Vertical line indicates which detent is in use) | 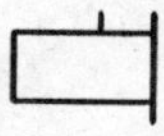 |
| Pressure compensated | 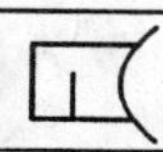 |
| Solenoid, Single winding | 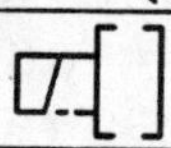 |
| Reversing Motor | 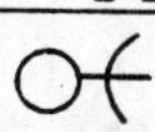 |
| Pilot pressure, Remote supply | 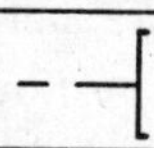 |
| Pilot pressure, Internal supply | 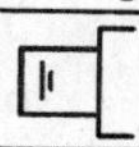 |
| Pilot Differential | 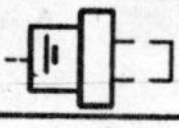 |

## EXERCISES

1. A Hydraulic circuit uses 25 litres of fluid per minute. The fluid is supplied by a pump having a fixed displacement of 12.5 $cm^3$/revolution driven at 3000 rpm. The pump has a volumetric efficiency of 0.85 and torque efficiency of 0.88. The system is set at 18 MPa by the relief valve. Calculate the power required to operate the pump.
2. A hydraulic pump having 37.5 $cm^3$ displacement per revolution develops 15 MPa at 88% volumetric efficiency. At 3000 rpm the pump supplies oil to a torque converter whose shaft rotates at 60 rpm and has overall efficiency of 85%. Determine the torque available at the shaft of the pump.
3. A gear pump is provided in hydraulic system of a tractor has following specifications:

   (*i*) Pump discharge = 70 litres/min (*ii*) Rated speed of pump = 2200 rpm

   (*iii*) Pump displacement = 30 $cm^3$/rev (*iv*) Pressure developed = 20 MPa

   (*v*) Power input to pump = 27.5 kW

   Calculate the following:

   (*a*) Volumetric and torque efficiencies of pump

   (*b*) Theoretical discharge and torque of pump

   (*c*) Power efficiency of pump

   (*d*) Power converted into heat
4. A piston plunger type pump has following specifications:

   (*i*) Pump discharge = 48.5 litres/min (*ii*) Rated speed = 2000 rpm

   (*iii*) Pump displacement = 37.5 $cm^3$/rev (*iv*) Pump pressure = 35.5 MPa

   (*v*) Power input = 32.4 kW

   Calculate the following:

   1. Theoretical discharge and torque of pump
   2. Volumetric and torque efficiencies of the pump
   3. Power efficiency of pump
   4. Power converted into heat
5. A Hydraulic circuit uses 25 litres of fluid per minute. The fluid is supplied by a pump having a fixed displacement of 12.5 $cm^3$/revolution driven at 3000 rpm. The pump has a volumetric efficiency of 0.85 and torque efficiency of 0.88. The system is set at 18 MPa by the relief valve. Calculate the power required to operate the pump.
6. In hydraulic power transmission system, motor converts fluid power to rotary mechanical power output. In such a system the output torque from the motor is 90 N-m at 225 rpm. The required flow rate is 30 l/min, the motor displacement is 0.105 litres per revolution and motor overall efficiency is 75%. The total pressure loss in lines, fittings, valves etc. is negligible. Calculate the volumetric efficiency of the motor.
7. A hydraulic pump has an inlet pressure of –34 KPa vacuum and a discharge pressure of 3440 kPa. The diameter of suction line is 32 mm and the discharge line is 19 mm. The pump

discharges oil at 1.15 L/s and density, of the oil is 0.88 Kg/L. Neglect friction and efficiency. Determine the power in kilowatts required to rotate the pump.

8. How much load can be lifted by hydraulic system having cylinder diameters of 5 mm and 50 mm. The load on small cylinder is 5 Kgf?

9. Compute the force to move a piston in a hydraulic cylinder at a velocity of 25 cm/s. Assume pressure is zero and cylinder is full of oil. Given, piston diameter is 50 mm, piston length is 50 mm, cylinder diameter is 50.01 mm, oil viscosity is 5 centistokes, and oil density is 0.88 kg/L.

10. A hydraulic system consists of a directional control valve (DCV), variable displacement pump, and double acting cylinder. The valve operates the double acting cylinder, in addition to having positions for extending and retracting the cylinder. The valve has a neutral and a float position. Sketch the system using hydraulic circuit (HC) symbols and state which type of system is this.

11. A pump delivers oil at the rate of 40 l/min to a 10 cm diameter cylinder for producing 2200N force. Calculate
    (*i*) Pressure required
    (*ii*) Hydraulic power required

12. A hydraulic pump having 37.5 $cm^3$ displacement per revolution develops 15 MPa at 88% volumetric efficiency. At 3000 rpm the pump supplies oil to a torque converter whose shaft rotates at 60 rpm and has overall efficiency of 85%. Determine the torque available at the shaft of the pump.

13. Calculate the power required to drive pump at 3000 rpm, if change in pressure across the pump is 250 bars. Assume flow of oil as 0.105 l/min.

14. Compute the force to move a piston in a hydraulic cylinder at a velocity of 25 cm/s. Assume pressure is zero and cylinder is full of oil. Given, piston diameter is 50 mm, piston length is 50 mm, cylinder diameter is 50.01 mm, oil viscosity is 5 centistokes, and oil density is 0.88 kg/L.

15. Explain automatic draft and depth control system in the hydraulic system of a tractor.

# CHAPTER 10

# Mechanical and Power Steering of Tractor

## INTRODUCTION

In order to have effective control on tractor at different speeds, loads and road conditions for steering it in left or right directions steering mechanism is provided. The concept of steering is simple-you turn the steering wheel, the front wheels turn accordingly, and the tractor changes direction However, precise steering control requires understanding of interaction between tire and operating conditions (field conditions & road). The tire and field conditions and road act as source of information seen by the operator as force that govern tractor's motion. For an active steering system, actual steer angle can be different from driver command angle to either alter driver's perception of tractor handling or to maintain control during extreme maneuvers. Steering can be either power or manual.

**Good steering system of a tractor should have:**

*i)* Steering geometry *i.e.* front end alignment of the tractor on undulating fields and during overload should remain unaltered

*ii)* Minimum force requirement for steering the tractor in left or right direction

*iii)* Self adjustment and self alignment during operation of tractor

## 10.1 MECHANICAL STEERING SYSTEM OF TRACTOR

The basic category of steering system most commonly used has pitman arms with a steering 'box'. The components of a mechanical steering system of a tractor usually include the steering linkages, steering gear box, the steering column and wheel. Pitman arm mechanism has a steering 'box' where the shaft from the steering wheel comes in and a lever arm known as the pitman arm comes out. The tie rods connect to the pitman arm. The traditional advantage of this system is that it gives bigger mechanical advantage and thus works well on heavier vehicles and tractors. Figure 10.1 depicts details of a conventional mechanical steering mechanism of a tractor.

**Figure. 10.1: External components of tractor steering mechanism**

### 10.1.1. Components of Mechanical Type Steering System

As shown in 10.1 above main components of a conventional manual steering mechanism of a tractor are:

*i)* **Steering wheel:** It is made up of steel rod with a hub welded in its centre. The hub has got a key groove or splines for firm fitting on upper end of steering shaft. The steering wheel is manually operated by the tractor driver for easy steering of tractor as per requirements under actual field as well as road conditions.

*ii)* **Outer tube or column:** It is made up of hollow steel tube in which steering shaft is fitted with a bearing and the shaft moves/rotates in it. One end of the column is fixed on steering box.

*iii)* **Bearings:** The steering shaft is fitted in the outer tube or column with the help of roller bearing so that it rotates freely in the outer tube.

*iv)* **Steering shaft:** The shaft is made of high quality steel. To the upper end of shaft steering wheel is fixed while the lower end of shaft is firmly attached to the worm in the steering box.

*v)* **Steering box:** Steering box is provided to convert the rotary motion of steering shaft fitted with worm into to and fro motion of drop arm attached to sector or gear. In this type of steering box, the end of the shaft from the steering wheel has a worm gear attached to it. It meshes directly with a sector gear or full gear. When the steering wheel is turned, the shaft turns the worm gear, and the sector gear pivots around its axis as its teeth are moved along the worm gear. The sector gear mounted on the cross shaft to which pitman or drop arm is attached. When the sector gear turns, it turns the cross shaft, which rotates the pitman or drop arm. The drag link connected to drop arm is pushed or pulled by rotation of steering wheel resulting in movement of stub axle towards right or left. The steering boxes are of many types but basic categories of boxes are worm gear type or worm & sector type. The following figure shows the active components that are present inside the worm and sector steering box. The steering box is sealed and filled with grease.

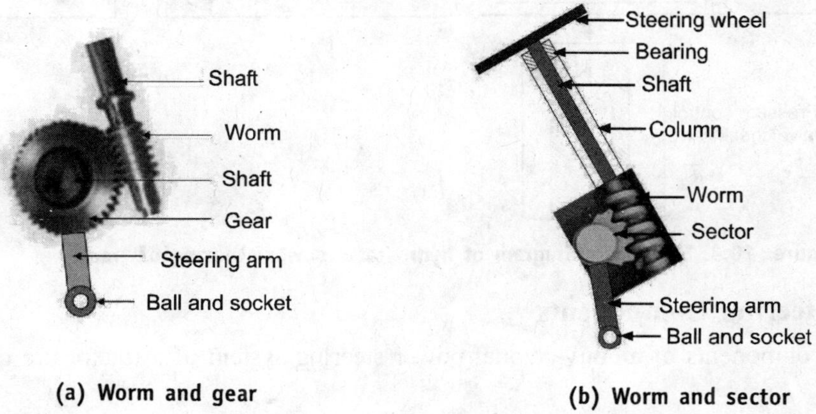


(a) Worm and gear

(b) Worm and sector

Figure 10.2: Steering gear box

*vi)* **Drop arm/steering arm:** It is a forged link having splines on one end which fitted to the shaft of sector or gear and other end with tapered hole to which tie rod is attached with the help of ball and socket.

*vii)* **Steering linkage:** Ball & socket, tie rod, tie rod pin & hub are important components of steering linkage which results in movement of stub axle towards right or left. Front wheel of tractor is mounted on the stub axle.

## 10.2 POWER STEERING OF TRACTOR

Power steering does the job of making the tractor turn via the steering wheel with a minimum amount of effort by using a fluid pump for ease of operation. The pump drives the power steering fluid through high pressure lines into a steering gearbox that has valves, seals and gears. Oil is pressurized by the steering/charge pump and routed through the steering valve. The Steering system is protected by a relief valve located in the steering valve. Excess oil comes across the relief valve and returns to reservoir via filter. The steering system goes over relief in full right hand or left hand turns.

When the steering wheel is turned, pressurized oil is routed through the steering valve to the balanced steering cylinder through the pressure hoses. The steering cylinder converts the hydraulic flow to mechanical movement to turn the wheel as desired. The force on the steering wheel is sensed by a device known as **rotary valve.** A power-steering system should assist the driver only when he is exerting force on the steering wheel *i.e.* when starting a turn. When the driver is driving in a straight line, the system shouldn't provide any assistance.

The power steering design means selection of appropriate sizes of system elements according to their functions. These functions are generation, transmission, control and application of fluid power for proper operation of steering system of a tractor.

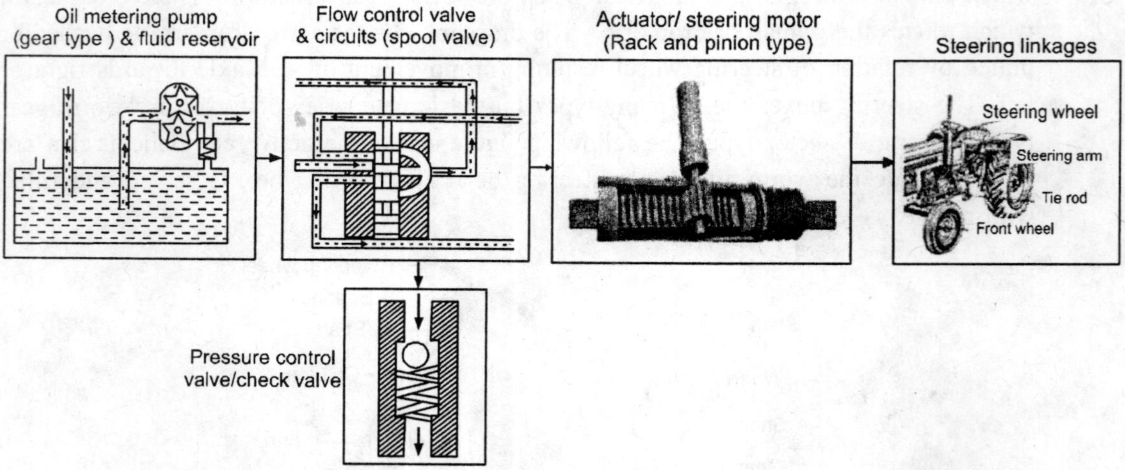


**Figure. 10.3: Schematic diagram of hydrostatic power steering of tractor**

### 10.2.1. Power Steering Components

The major components of a conventional power steering system of a tractor are discussed as under:

*i)* **Fluid & Fluid reservoir:** Fluid acts as a means of transmitting power to remote locations, lubricates and cools the components. It also picks up contaminants and carries to filter for removal. Viscosity is most important property of hydraulic fluid. Generally recommended fluid viscosities range between 12 and 48 MPa by the manufacturers at operating temperature of pump. Otherwise, the performance of the pump will be affected considerably. Each tractor manufacturer specifies the hydraulic fluid that will meet requirements of both transmission and hydraulic systems. The oil temperature should be kept below 60°C to reduce oxidation of oil. Additives are needed to reduce wear in gear/vane type pumps above 7 MPa operating pressures reservoir holds the fluid for components, Allows large particles to settle and entrained air to escape. It also dissipates heat. It supplies extra oil needed when hydraulic cylinder is extending. It also provides space for extra returning oil when cylinder is retracting. In the modern tractors transmission case also serves as hydraulic reservoir. The reservoir is vented to atmosphere to accommodate changing oil levels. Filter is provided to block away all foreign particles. The air vent is provided with a filter to prevent dirt/dust energy into the reservoir.

*ii)* **Pump:** Pump converts mechanical power to fluid power. Such device increases the mechanical energy of the fluid when the fluid is moved through flow system. Hydraulic pumps which are mainly used are gear type, roller vane type or axial piston variable flow type. These are positive displacement pumps which admit a fixed volume of liquid through inlet and discharge under pressure through outlet. Positive displacement pumps are used where higher head increases without velocity changes are required. The hydraulic power for the steering is provided by any of following types of pumps:

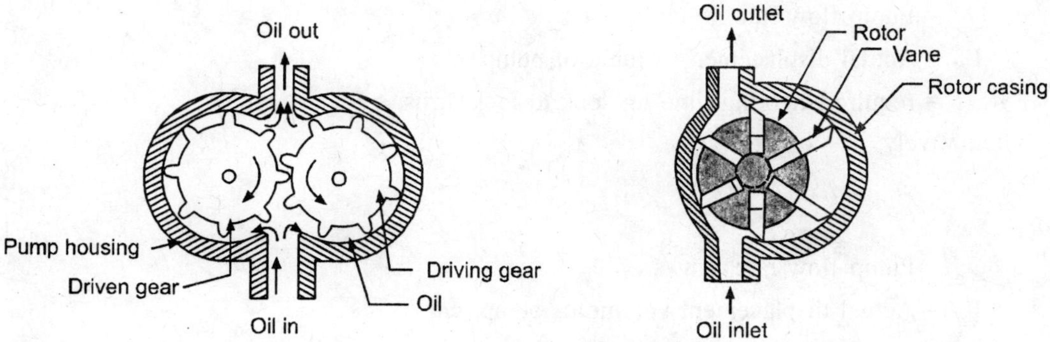


**(a) Gear type oil pump** **(b) Vane pump**

**Fig. 10.4: Types of pumps for power steering**

**Functions of pump of power steering:** Main functions of a pump of power steering are:

*i)* Hydrostatic steering in the tractor

*ii)* To maintain oil flow through oil filter and cooler

*iii)* To provide back pressure on the pump

*iv)* To provides makeup oil for internal leakage in the system

**Table 10.1: Details of pumps used in power steering**

| Type of steering system | Type of pump | Operating pressure (MPa) |
|---|---|---|
| Open center steering | I. Fixed clearance high quality | |
| | *a*) Gear | 10.30 |
| | *b*) Vane | -do- |
| | II. Pressure balanced & clearance compensated | |
| | *a*) Gear | 13.8 to 20.7 |
| | *b*) Vane | -do- |
| | c) Latest design gear type | 24.1 |
| Closed center self contained steering | Piston type pump | 27.6–34.5 |
| Operating speed of pumps | Ranges between 3000–5000 pm | |
| Pump drive | Most power steering pumps are either belt driven or gear driven | |

**Characteristics of pumps:**

**Pump discharge ($Q_p$):** The pump flow rate or discharge ($Q_p$) is given by

$$Q_p = 0.06\ V_d \times \mathrm{t} \quad \text{...(10.1)}$$

where;

$Q_p$ = Pump flow rate, l/min

$V_d$ = Actual displacement volume of pump, $cm^3$

$t$ = required steering time for lock to lock turns, s

Alternatively,

$$Q_p = V_d \times t \quad \text{...(10.2)}$$

where;

$Q_p$ = Pump flow rate, $cm^3/s$

$V_d$ = Actual displacement volume of pump, $cm^3$

t = required steering time for lock to lock turns, s

**Pump displacement ($V_d$):**

$$V_d = Q_p \times t/0.06,\ cm^3 \quad \text{...(10.3)}$$

where;

$Q_p$ = Pump flow rate, l/min

$V_d$ = Actual displacement volume of pump, $cm^3$

$t$ = required steering time for lock to lock turns, s

or,

$$V_d = Q_p \times t \quad \text{...(10.4)}$$

Where; $Q_p$ = Pump flow rate, $cm^3/s$
$V_d$ = Actual displacement volume of pump, $cm^3$
$t$ = required steering time for lock to lock turns, s

**EXAMPLE 10.1** *If a hydraulic pump is rotating at a speed of 2000 rpm with a displacement of 25 cc/rev. Calculate the theoretical discharge of pump. If the pump has a volumetric efficiency of 90% how much flow is created by the pump?*

**SOLUTION:**

Pump speed, $N_p$ = 2000 rpm
Pump displacement, $D_p$ = 25 cm3/rev
Volumetric efficiency of pump, $h_v$ = 90%
Now, we know that,

$$Q_t = D_p \times N_p$$

or,

$$Q_t = 2000 \text{ rpm} \times 25 \text{ cm}^3\text{/rev}$$
$$= 50000 \text{ cm}^3\text{/min or 50l pm}$$ **Ans.**

Also we know that;

$$Q_a = Q_t \times \text{Volumetric efficiency of pump } (h_v)$$
$$= 50 \text{ lpm} \times 0.90$$
$$= 45 \text{ lpm}$$ **Ans.**

**Fluid power of pump ($W_f$):**

Pump power output can be determined based on its output flow rate and outlet pressure as under:

The fluid power of pump ($W_f$) is given by

$$W_f = \frac{Q \times P}{60}$$

where,

$W_f$ = fluid power, kW
$Q$ = pump discharge, l/m
$P$ = pressure across the pump, MPa

**Shaft power of pump ($W_s$):**

The shaft power of pump ($W_s$) is given by

$$W_s = T \times N \times 1.05 \times 10^{-4}$$

where

$W_s$ = shaft power of pump, kW
$T$ = input shaft torque, N-m
$N$ = shaft speed, rpm

**Pump input power requirement ($W_p$):** In order to drive hydraulic pump to produce an output flow and to overcome the load (outlet pressure) input power is required. Although modern hydraulic pumps are well designed and quite efficient, yet, these are not 100% efficient in converting the mechanical input power into output hydraulic power as some of the power is lost in the pump. We can use pump efficiency to measure the power loss. So, the input power requirement for the hydraulic pump of power steering is given by

$$W_p = V_d \times \delta p \times n / (10^6 \times \eta_m) \quad ...(10.5)$$

Where; $W_p$ = Power required for the pump, kW

$V_d$ = Actual displacement volume of pump, $cm^3$

$dp$ = Pressure rise in the pump, Pa

$n$ = Pump speed, rev/s

$\eta_m$ = Pump overall efficiency, % = $\eta_v \times \eta_t$

$\eta_v$ = Volumetric efficiency of pump, %

$\eta_t$ = Torque efficiency of pump, %

**Overall efficiency of pump ($h_m$):**

Overall efficiency of pump ($\eta_m$) is given by

$$\eta_m = \frac{W_f}{W_s}$$

Where $W_f$ = Hydraulic/fluid power of pump, kW

$W_s$ = input or shaft power in kW

This is also equal to the product of torque and volumetric efficiencies, *i.e.*

$$h_m = \eta_t \times \eta_v$$

**EXAMPLE 10.2** *If a pump delivers 30lpm at 40 MPa, how much fluid power the pump develops?*

**SOLUTION:**

Actual pump discharge, $Q_a$ = 30lpm

Pump pressure, $P$ = 40 MPa

The power requirement for development of fluid pressure of 40 MPa is calculated as under:

Fluid Power ($W_f$) = Q.P/60

$W_f$ = 30 Litres/min × 40 MPa/60 = 20.0 kW **Ans.**

**EXAMPLE 10.3** *what maximum flow could you expect from a 10 kW power unit if the hydraulic system pressure was 30MPa?*

**SOLUTION:**

Fluid Power ($W_f$) = 10 kW

Pump pressure, $P$ = 30 MPa

We know that;

Fluid Power ($W_f$) = Q.P/60

Or, $Q = W_f \times 60/P$

$Q$ = 10 kW × 60/30 MPa = 20 lpm **Ans.**

**EXAMPLE 10.4** *A hydraulic pump of a power steering requires 9 kW input power to deliver 20 lpm of hydraulic oil at 20 MPa. The pump capacity is 25 lpm. Determine the pump efficiencies..*

**SOLUTION:**

Input power of pump ($W_i$) = 9 kW

Actual pump discharge, $Q_a$ = 20lpm

Pump pressure, $P$ = 20 MPa

Theoretical Pump capacity, $Q_t$ = 25 lpm

Now, we know that;

The power requirement for development of fluid pressure of 20 MPa is calculated as under:

Fluid Power ($W_f$) = Q.P/60

$W_f$ = 20 Litres/min × 20 MPa/60 = 6.67 kW

Now, we know that overall efficiency of pump is given by

Overall efficiency of pump ($\eta_m$ )

= (Power output of pump ($W_f$)/Pump input power ($W_i$)) × 100

$h_{tm}$ = ($W_f/W_i$) × 100

= (6.67 kW/9 kW) × 100

= 74.11% **Ans.**

**Volumetric efficiency ($\eta_v$):**

**Volumetric efficiency of pump ($\eta_v$) = ($Q_a/Q_t$) × 100**

Or,

Putting values we get;

$\eta_v$ = (20 lpm/25 lpm) × 100

= 80.0% **Ans.**

Also we know that;

Overall efficiency of pump is also equal to the product of torque and volumetric efficiencies, *i.e.*

$$h_m = \eta_t \times \eta_v$$

Putting values in above equation, we get;

$$0.7411 = \eta_t \times 0.80$$

Or, $\eta_t = (0.7411/0.80) \times 100$

$\eta_t = 92.63\%$ Ans.

**EXAMPLE 10.5** *Determine the theoretical and actual fluid discharge and mechanical (input) power for a pump delivering 50 lpm with a pressure rise of 20MPa if volumetric and mechanical (torque) efficiencies of the pump are 95% and 90%, respectively.*

**SOLUTION:**

Pump discharge, $Q_p$ =50 lpm

Pump pressure, $P$ = 20 MPa

The power requirement for development of fluid pressure of 20 MPa is calculated as under:

Fluid Power $(W_f) = Q_p.P/60$

$W_f$ = 50 Litres/min × 20 MPa/60 = 16.67 kW

Now, we know that overall efficiency of pump is given by

Overall efficiency of pump $(\eta_m) = \eta_t \times \eta_v$

Or, $\eta_m = 0.90 \times 0.95 = 0.855$

Also,

Input power to pump $W_i$ = Fluid power $(W_f)/(\eta_m)$

Or, $W_i$ = 16.67 kW/0.855

= 19.497 kW **Ans.**

Also,

We know that for a hydraulic pump

$$\eta_v = Q_p/Q_t$$

Where;

$\eta_v$ = Volumetric efficiency of pump, %

$Q_p$ = Actual discharge of pump. lpm

$Q_t$ = Theoretical discharge of pump. lpm

Or, $Q_t = Q_p/\eta_v$ = 50 lpm/0.95

$Q_t$ = 52.63 lpm

**EXAMPLE 10.6** *A hydraulic pump with 140 cm³/rev displacement develops a pressure of 30 MPa; how much torque will it theoretically take to turn this pump? If the same pump is 90% mechanically efficient (10% friction & drag), how much torque the prime mover is required to deliver?*

**SOLUTION:**

$$D_p = 140\ \text{cm}^3/\text{rev}$$
$$\delta P = 30\ \text{MPa}$$
$$\eta_t = 90\%$$

We know that, theoretical torque required for the pump is given by

$$T = \delta p.D_p/2\pi \qquad ...(10.6)$$

Where $T$ = Theoretical torque required to drive the pump, N-m

$\delta p$ = Pressure developed across the pump, MPa

$D_p$ = Pump displacement, $\text{cm}^3$/rev

Now, putting the values in above eqn. we get,

$$T = 30\ \text{MPa} \times 140\text{cm}^3/\text{rev}/2\pi$$
$$= 668.18\ \text{N-m}$$

Now,

Actual torque required to drive the pump, $T_p = T/\eta_t$

$$T_p = 668.18\ \text{N-m}/0.90$$
$$= 742.42\ \text{N-m}$$

**Ans.**

**EXAMPLE 10.7** *Determine the theoretical and actual torque requirement to turn a 40 cm³/rev hydraulic pump if the pressure rise is 20MPa and mechanical (torque) efficiency is 90%.*

**SOLUTION:**

$$D_p = 40\ \text{cm}^3/\text{rev}$$
$$\delta P = 20\ \text{MPa}$$
$$\eta_t = 90\%$$

We know that, theoretical torque required for the pump is given by

$$T_p = \delta p.\ D_p/(2\pi \times \eta_t) \qquad ...(10.7)$$

Where,

$T_p$ = Actual torque required to drive the pump, N-m

$\delta p$ = Pressure developed across the pump, MPa

$D_p$ = Pump displacement, $\text{cm}^3$/rev

$\eta_t$ = Torque efficiency of pump, %

Now, putting the values in above eqn, we get,

$$T_p = 20\ \text{MPa} \times 40\text{cm}^3/\text{rev}/(2\pi \times 0.90)$$
$$= 141.41\ \text{N-m}$$

**Ans.**

*iii)* **Actuators:** Convert fluid power to linear mechanical power. The fluid pressure energy of pump is directed to the actuator (stroke or angular rotation type) which transmits the fluid energy into the form of mechanical energy to the linkage of steering system. Stroke or rotary type actuators *i.e.* cylinder or rack and pinion are mostly used in the power steering. Their effectiveness usually ranges between 80–95%, however, cylinder type actuator has higher efficiency than the rotary rack and pinion type. Single acting and double acting hydraulic cylinders are given in Figs.10.5 and 10.6.

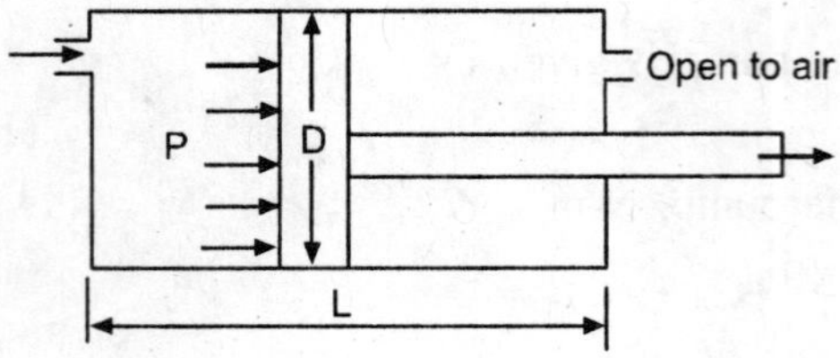


Figure. 10.5: Single acting hydraulic cylinder

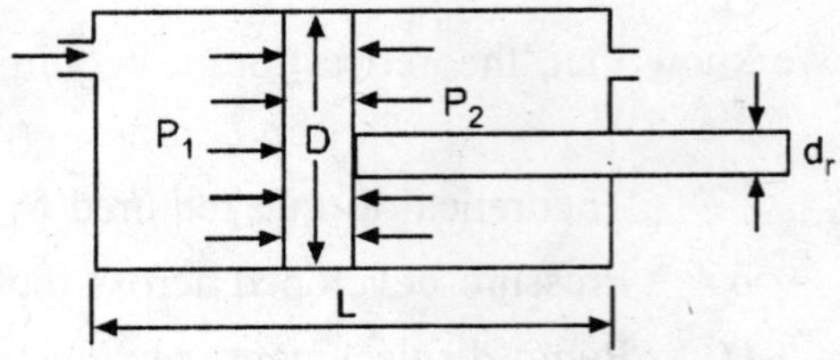


Figure. 10.6: Double acting hydraulic cylinder

Force in the cylinder is given by

$$F_e = P \times A_c \quad \text{...(10.7)}$$

$$F_{re} = P \times (A_c - A_r) \quad \text{...(10.8)}$$

Where $F_e$ = extension force in the cylinder, N

$F_{re}$ = retraction force in the cylinder, N

$P$ = fluid pressure in actuator, N/mm$^2$

$A_c$ = cross sectional area of ram, mm$^2$

$A_r$ = cross sectional area of rod, mm$^2$

**EXAMPLE 10.8** *If a 250-N force is applied to the top of a piston of hydraulic actuator and the force produces 750 Pa of pressure. Determine the area as well as diameter of the piston?*

**SOLUTION:**

Applied force, $F$ = 250 N

Pressure on piston head,

$$P = 750 \text{ Pa}$$

$$P = \frac{F}{A}$$

Now, we know that

Putting values in above equation we get

$$750Pa = \frac{250N}{A}$$

Or, $$A = \frac{250N}{750Pa}$$

Also, $$A = 0.334\text{m}^2$$

$$A = \pi/4 \times d^2$$

Or, $$d^2 = A \times 4/\pi = 0.334 \text{ m}^2 \times 4/\pi$$

Or, $$d = 0.652 \text{ m}$$ **Ans.**

**Power developed by the actuator ($W_a$):**

Power developed by the actuator in kW is given by

$$W_a = F_e \times V/1000 \quad ...(10.9)$$

Where,

$V$ = speed of ram in cylinder, m/s.

However, this will depend on the type of actuator, its output as stroke or angular rotation and location of actuator in the linkage. The actuator of power steering is designed based on following equation:

$$d = ((4\alpha T_k/\pi \times L_a \times P_e \times \eta_a \times \eta_l) + d_r)^{0.5} \quad ...(10.10)$$

Where,

$d$ = piston diameter, mm

$\alpha$ = Lock-to-lock steering angle at kingpin or hinge, rad

$T_k$ = Torque required at kingpin or hinge, N-mm

$L_a$ = Actuator piston stroke, mm

$P_e$ = Effective pressure at piston face, MPa

$\eta_a$ = Overall efficiency of actuator, %

$\eta_l$ = Linkage efficiency, %

$d_r$ = piston rod diameter, mm (wherever applicable)

Also,

$$D_a = (\alpha\, T_k/(L_a \times P_e \times \eta_a \times \eta_l)) \quad ...(10.11)$$

Where,

$D_a$ = Actuator displacement, mm$^2$

**Kingpin torque ($T_k$):**

The kingpin torque in a steering system depends on vertical load on front wheel ($W_{fw}$), coefficient of friction ($\mu_e$) and kingpin offset (e) and can be calculated by following equation:

$$T_k = \mu_e \times W_{fw}\, (w_t^2/8 + e)^{0.5} \quad (10.12)$$

Where;

$T_k$ = Torque required at kingpin or hinge, N-mm

$\mu_e$ = Effective coefficient of friction between tyre and surface

$W_{fw}$ = Vertical load on front wheel of tractor, N

$w_t$ = Nominal front tyre width, mm

$e$ = kingpin offset, mm

There is a minimum kingpin torque for an optimum value of kingpin offset. The kingpin offset usually varies with different surface conditions; however, in loose soil conditions where rolling resistance is high, lower kingpin offset is better suited for heavily loaded tyres. Thus, highest turning torque of steering should be according to axle load and different surface and soil conditions as it will display excellent performance under average to maximum load conditions. However maximum power steering forces should be limited to 110% of maximum design condition. Based on values of kingpin torque the work output of actuator is determined for the purpose of its design.

**Flow control valves:** These are used to control fluid flow in the system (speed of actuators). Flow control valve assembly is installed in the outlet line of power steering pump. It diverts fluid flow to the pump reservoir. It also pulses on and off to control amount of fluid diverted. Check valve allows fluid flow in one direction, no flow in the other direction. Needle valve-acts like variable orifice to restrict flow. Pressure compensated valves-automatically adjust the fluid flow to compensate for pressure variations in the system. Ball valves (Fig. 10.7) and Spool valves (Fig.10.8) are used for controlling the flow of fluid. Since spool valves are simple in construction and operation, these are commonly used in power steering system of a tractor. As the pressure drop across the control valve remains constant for any duration of fluid supply and load pressure, the steering rate is only a function of valve opening. Generally, two types of 4-way spool valves namely open center & closed center are commonly used in steering system.

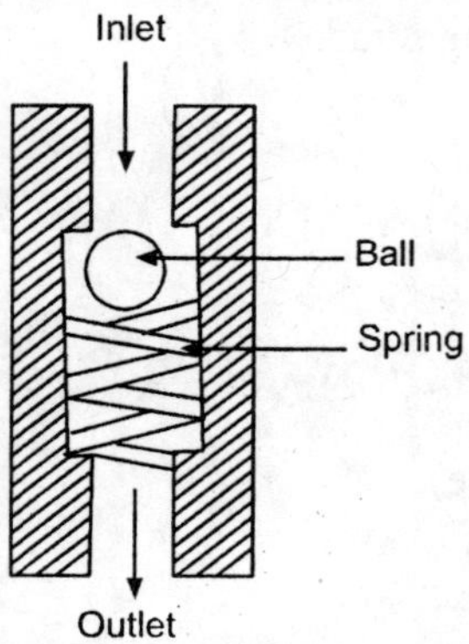


**Figure. 10.7: Ball type flow control valve**

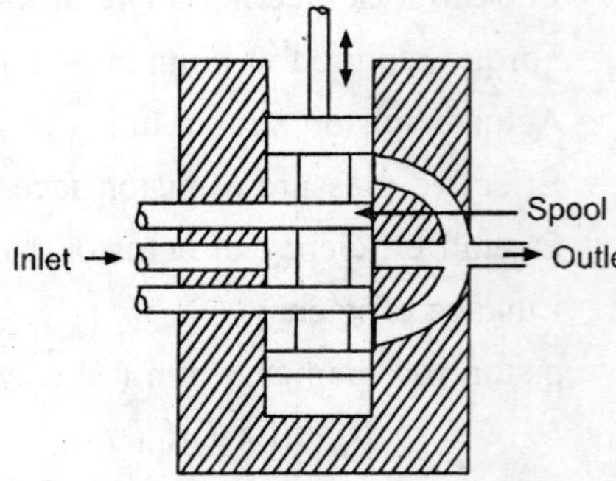


**Figure. 10.8: Spool type flow control valve**

In design of oil passages/orifices of hydraulic system, accurate assessment of pressure drops/ losses at different flow rates is very essential. Primary pressure losses in the hydraulic circuits largely depend on the fluid flow velocity ($V$), surface roughness of the passage and temperature and viscosity of the fluid. For better performance, oil operating temperatures of should range between 65–93°C and oil viscosities of 70–100 SUS at 65°C and 45–60 SUS at 93°C respectively. The recommended oil flow velocities in different passages are given in table below:

**Table: 10.2: Fluid flow velocities in hydraulic circuits**

| Particular of fluid passage | Flow velocity ($V$), m/s |
|---|---|
| Suction lines | 1.50 |
| High pressure lines | 9.10 |
| Delivery & return lines | 5.30 |
| Valve apertures and orifices | >9.50 |

In addition to above, pressure losses in hydraulic circuits occur due to entry & exist of oil, expansion and contraction of passages, pipe bends, fittings, valves and orifices. The pressure drop across a smooth orifice with a passage length equal to its diameter is given by:

$$\delta P = 0.90\ \rho\ (Q_p/A_0)^2 \qquad \text{...(10.13)}$$

Where; $\delta P$ = Pressure drop across the orifice, dynes/cm$^2$

$\rho$ = Mass density of fluid, dyne-s$^2$/cm$^4$

$Q_p$ = Fluid flow rate from the pump, cm$^3$/s

$A_0$ = Minimum cross section flow area of orifice, cm$^2$

So, based on total pressure drop in the orifice for a given flow rate, the size of orifice ($d_o$) can be determined for the hydraulic circuit.

**Inlet hose check valve:** Inlet hose check valve controls pressure to steering gear valve. This valve keeps fluid from backing up through the inlet hose if the vehicle strikes a pothole or a bump when the flow rate is low. It increases or decreases steering effort.

Following orifice equation can be used to calculate the flow rate ($Q$) at a given pressure drop across the orifice.

$$Q = 2.68 \times 10^{-2} \times C_d \times a \times \sqrt{\left(\frac{\delta P}{\rho}\right)} \qquad \text{...(10.14)}$$

Where; $Q$ = fluid flow rate through control valve, l/m

$C_d$ = confinement of discharge, dimensionless

$a$ = area of cross section of orifice of control valve, cm$^2$

$\partial P$ = pressure drop across orifice, MPa

$\rho$ = density of fluid, kg/l

Velocity of fluid flow through the orifice is calculated by following equation

$$V_o = Q/6a$$

Where,

$V_o$= velocity of fluid through orifice, m/s

*v)* **Pressure relief valve:** It is used to control pressure in the system. These are provided to protect the components within hydraulic circuit from damage from excessive pressure. It reduces pressure by returning oil to the tank. Theses are also called as safety relief valves. Relief valve is essential for safety as it sets maximum pressure in the system. In normal position the valve is closed. If the opening pressure is reached at the input, the output opens. When the pressure drops below the preset level, the valve closes again. The most basic type is a poppet held against a cone seat by spring force. Pilot operated pressure regulator vale provides fast action to respond flow changes. Other common types of valves are: Pressure reducing, sequence, unloading valves etc.

*vi)* **Hoses:** Hoses or Hydraulic lines are used to convey the fluid to remote locations under pressure and dissipate heat developed in the system. These are used for connection of power pack with the circuit. Return lines are provided for recycling oil to the tank. The lines should be strong enough to with stand the fluid pressure developed during operation and their size should be such that the pressure drop is minimum. Rigid lines are made of steel while flexible are made from reinforced rubber. Wall thickness of conduit pipe used for fluid pressure lines is calculated based on maximum pressure and hoop stresses developed that would cause failure of conduit pipe along a line parallel to its centerline. It is given by

$$t_w = \frac{P_{max} \times (d_c/2)}{S_d} \qquad ...(10.15)$$

Where, $t_w$ = wall thickness of conduit pipe, cm

$P_{max}$ = maximum allowable pressure, MPa

$d_c$ = conduit pipe diameter, cm

$S_d$ = Design stress for the pipe line, MPa

*vii)* **Gearbox:** The gearbox of power steering of a tractor, interprets the steering wheel command by sensing the pressure. The main gearbox housing, made of cast iron, usually contains four power steering line inlets in its casing (from fluid reservoir, one from the pump and two fluid lines to actuator). The fluid pump that drives power steering fluid through high pressure lines into the steering gearbox having valves, seats and gears. The **rotary valve** is a device which senses the force on the steering wheel and actuates only with detected pressure. Steering wheel rotation sensor determines which direction and how quickly the steering wheel is being turned. A torsion bar works in conjunction with the rotary valve which consists of a thin rod of metal. Its upper end is connected to the steering wheel and lower end to the worm or pinion gear that turns the wheels when turning torque (pressure) is applied by the operator. It activates when turning left or right from the commands of the steering wheel. It provides full power assistance needed to make quick steering maneuver at high speeds. The splined input shaft with a universal coupler or a rag-joint flange is fitted at the top of the gearbox and connected directly to the steering column.

The rack and pinion type steering gears are commonly used in modern power steering systems. It is relatively simple in construction and low cost gearbox. The part of the sector shaft fitted inside the gearbox with needle bearings contains several gear teeth. These teeth mesh with the power piston inside the gearbox. Steering gear valve contains small hydraulic pistons. The power piston moves back and forth inside the gearbox. When the worm gear and input shaft turn, it moves the piston back and forth. The outside of the piston has teeth that mate with the sector shaft. The power piston's movement causes the sector shaft to rotate, which turns the pitman arm, which turns the steering linkage. Pistons also use power steering pump pressure to oppose movement of the steering gear. When the steering wheel is not being turned, both the hydraulic lines of the valve provide the same amount of fluid pressure to the steering gear. On the other hand, if the spool valve is turned one way or the other by the operator, ports open up to provide high-pressure fluid to the appropriate line for easy steering to the right or left.

*viii)* **Steering linkage:** The splined sector shaft, fitted at the bottom of the gearbox is attached to a tie rod on the pitman arm. The pitman arm controls the steering linkage of the wheels. Ball & socket, tie rod, tie rod pin & hub are important components of steering linkage which results in movement of stub axle towards right or left. Front wheel of tractor is mounted on the stub axle.

## 10.3 STEERING GEOMETRY

It is the front end alignment of tractor for easy and safe steering performance. Various adjustments are discussed as under:

*i)* **Ackerman steering:** When front wheel axles of tractor instead of swinging of complete axle, the wheels swing individually on stub axle and the king pin then it is known as Ackerman steering. In this, the chassis is narrowed at front to accommodate tyres during taking turns as the steering arms are fixed to stub axle slanted towards the centre of tractor in such a way that centre line drawn from kingpin and tie-rod ball pin joins at focal point. This type of arrangement makes the tractor to move in true circle and there will not be any side slippage/undue wear of front tyres during taking turns.

*ii)* **Camber angle:** For easy steering of front wheels of tractor, the kingpin load needs to be reduced. This is accomplished by tilting the front wheels outward at the top when viewed from the front. The kingpin is also tilted vertically in such a way that centre line of kingpin and tyre where tyre touches the ground. So, the angle between the plane of front wheel and vertical axis is known as camber angle. In tractors it usually ranges between 0.5°–2.5° (positive). When the front wheels of tractor are tilted in at the top, the camber angle is negative.

*iii)* **Kingpin inclination:** It is defined as the angle by which kingpin in the tractor front wheel is inclined in such a way that the centre line of kingpin and centre line of cambered wheel meet at a point where front wheel touches the ground. It ranges between 6.30°–9° depending on the tractor make and model.

*iv)* **Caster angle:** In order to maintain the load of tractor ahead of centre of front tyre, caster angle is provided. This is the angle by which the kingpin is set at the back of vertical line drawn the centre of spindle body.

*v)* **Toe-in:** Toe-in is known as the distance between two front wheels in the front at hub height (At the front of wheels it is less than the distance at the back). Toe-in is provided to counter the slippage effect in tyres of front wheels due to cambering of wheels. With proper camber angle and toe-in, the tractor will move forward without any side slippage. Toe-in varies from tractor to tractor; however, it ranges between 0–10 mm depending upon make of tractor. It is always measured at hub height and adjusted with the help of toe-in gauge through tie-rod and ball joint socket as per requirements.

*vi)* **Toe-out:** When the distance of front wheels at front is more than the distance at the back of front wheels, it is called as toe-out. This is provided to avoid slippage of tyres when the tractor is taking turns. This can be adjusted by bending the steering arms towards the centre of tractor as well as downwards.

**Table: 10.3: Specifications of steering of various tractors**

| Particulars | Eicher | Escorts | Ford | International | Massey Ferguson |
|---|---|---|---|---|---|
| Type of steering box | Worm & peg | Bevel pinion with sector | Ball & nut | Worm & peg | Re-circulating ball type |
| Camber angle | 2.5° | — | 2° | 3.5° | 2° |
| Caster angle | 0° | 3.30° | 5° | 3° | 5° |
| Kingpin inclination | 9.30° | 6.30° | 9° | 6.5° | 9° |
| Steering play | — | — | — | 3.0° | 0.5° |
| Toe in (mm) | 5–9 | 6–8 | 0.0–12.7 | 8 | 3 |

## EXERCISES

1. A gear type hydraulic motor of a power steering having displacement of 70 $cm^3$/rev has input pressure of 20 Mpa produces a torque of 150 N-m at a speed of 15 revolution per second. If the viscosity of oil is 20 mPa-s. Calculate theoretical torque and torque efficiency of hydraulic motor.
2. A double acting actuator of a power steering has following details:
   *i)* Cylinder bore = 5.0 cm
   *ii)* Stroke length = 10 cm
   *iii)* Rod diameter = 1.0 cm
   *iv)* Piston velocity = 0.50 m/s
   Calculate the following:
   *a)* Oil inflow rate
   *b)* Oil pressure required to move a load of 10 kN
3. In a power steering, the oil of 0.88 kg/l density and 25 mPa-s viscosity is flowing at the rate of 50 lpm through an orifice of 4 mm diameter. Calculate the following:
   *i)* Velocity of fluid flow through orifice
   *ii)* Pressure drop across the orifice
4. In a hydraulic circuit of a power steering, the fluid flow rate is 80 lpm with an allowable pressure drop of 0.20 Mpa, then, calculate the diameter of hose pipe. Take density of hydraulic fluid as 0.88 kg/L and its viscosity 25 mPa-s.

# CHAPTER 11

# Traction

## INTRODUCTION

Tractor engine power for accomplishing useful work is generally transmitted by following three modes:

(*i*) **P.T.O shaft:** This is primarily used for positive rotary drives to the mechanisms of the machines such as rotavator, sugarcane cutter planter, pumping set, vertical conveyer reapers, threshers etc. It is most efficient method of tractor power use.

(*ii*) **Hydraulic power:** This is generally used in hydraulic system of tractor for controlling the mounted implements. Remote hydraulic cylinders are also used in certain applications such as power harrow, tipping trailers.

(*iii*) **Drawbar power:** This is the most widely used mode of tractor power usage on the farm. This is least efficient as its utilization for pulling the loads depends on traction developed by the rear drive wheels of tractor.

## 11.1 TRACTION

Traction is the driving force developed by the interaction between the mechanical driving members such as wheels, tracks or other traction devices and the soil surface. The extent of traction force developed will depend upon the engine power available at the drawbar of the tractor.

### 11.1.1. Factors Affecting Traction

Main factors affecting the traction of drive wheel or track which can be controlled by the operator for improving traction are discussed as under :

1. **Soil type and surface condition:** The performance of traction devices largely depends on the type of soil and its surface condition. Similarly, soil moisture content also has considerable bearing on the traction of drive wheel.
2. **Travel reduction or slippage(S):** Whenever a traction wheel moves over soil surface pulling a load, travel reduction or slippage takes place. At increased loads the slippage increases considerably and becomes a limiting factor in development of maximum drawbar pulls in tractors. It results in excessive tyre wear, soil compaction and field efficiency. The slippage is defined as

$$S = \frac{(D_n - D_l)}{D_n} \times 100 \qquad ...(11.1)$$

where, $S$ = slippage or travel reduction, %

$D_n$ = distance traveled at no load, m

$D_l$ = distance traveled with load, m

Alternatively,

$$S = (V_t - V_a)/V_t$$

Or, $$S = (1 - V_a/V_t) \qquad ...(11.2)$$

where, $V_t$ = theoretical wheel speed = $r\omega$, m/s

$V_a$ = actual wheel speed, m/s

$r$ = rolling radius of wheel on hard surface, m

$\omega$ = angular velocity of wheel, rad/s.

The normal expectable wheel slippage is given in Table 11.1.

**TABLE 11.1: Normal acceptable wheel slippage**

| Sr. No. | Types of tractor wheels | Slippage (S), % |
|---|---|---|
| 1 | Rubber tyre wheel–2 wheel drive | 16.00 |
| 2. | Rubber tyre wheel–4 wheel drive | 12.00 |
| 3 | Track type tractors | 7.00 |

**3. Rolling resistance or towed force ($R_r$):** Rolling resistance is defined as the force required in the direction of travel to overcome the resistance of motion over the soil surface. It depends on following factors:

- Speed
- Soil firmness
- Wheel dimensions (diameter and width)
- Tyre lug type
- Tyre lug height
- Tyre inflation pressure

Now, from figure of a towed wheel (Fig. 11.1) where no axle torque is acting

$$R_r \,.\, r - R_v \,.\, x = 0 \qquad ...(11.3)$$

Or $$x = (R_r/R_v) \times r \quad \text{(Because } R_v = W\text{)}$$

$\therefore$ $$x = (R_r/W) \times r \qquad ...(11.4)$$

where, $x$ = distance of point of action of rolling resistance ahead of wheel centre line, cm

$R_r$ = rolling resistance of wheel, N or kg

$r$ = rolling radius of wheel, cm

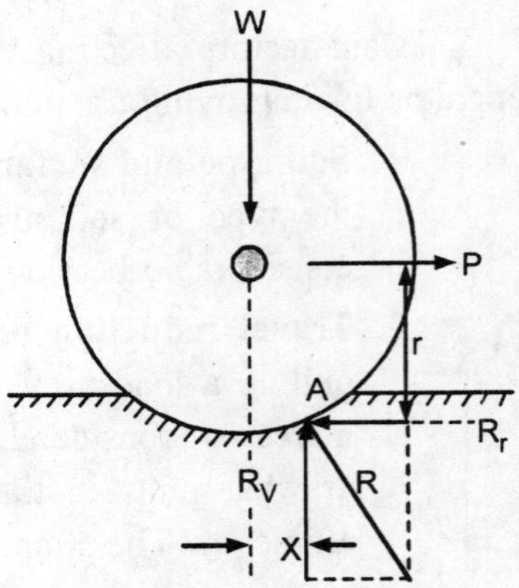


**Figure 11.1: Forces acting on a towed wheel**

**Motion resistance ratio (ρ) :** It is defined as the ratio of rolling resistance force and normal load on the traction wheel

$$r = R_r/W \qquad ...(11.5)$$

Therefore putting this value in eq. 11.4, we get,

$$x = r\,.r \qquad ...(11.6)$$

**4. Weight on rear wheels:** Weight on rear wheels of tractor has considerable effect on the drawbar pull developed by it during its use. The tractive-ability of tractor is affected by vertical soil reaction against the traction wheels. It is static weight on the rear wheels plus weight transferred from the implement and front end of tractor during use. In tractors using three points mounted implements, weight transfer phenomena exists which increase the weight of rear drive wheels. Transfer of weight from front end of tractor to rear takes place when tractor is operated under drawbar load as the pulled load tends to rotate front end of tractor up around rear axle. The effect of drawbar pull on weight transfer of tractor is given in Fig. 11.2.

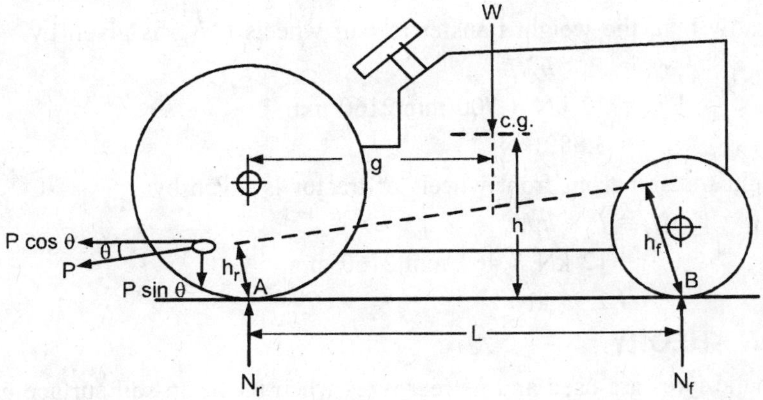


**Figure 11.2: Effect of drawbar pull on weight transfer of tractor**

The amount of weight transfer depends on drawbar load and hitch height. Higher the amount of pulled load and higher the hitch point, the more weight is transferred from front to rear. The weight transfer by drawbar load decreases the soil reaction from the front wheels by an amount $\Delta N_f$ and increases by an amount $\Delta N_r$ which result in increased drawbar pull in 2-wheel drive tractor as given below.

$$\Delta N_f = P \times h_r / L \quad ...(11.7)$$

$$\Delta N_r = P \times h_f / L \quad ...(11.8)$$

where, $P$ = drawbar pull, $N$ or kg

$h_r$ = distance of drawbar pull from point '$A$', cm

$h_f$ = distance of drawbar pull from point '$B$', cm

$L$ = wheel base, cm

**EXAMPLE 11.1** *A tractor with a total weight of 28 kN having wheel base of 2160 mm has front and rear wheel reactions of 9.0 kN and 19.0 kN respectively. It pulls a drawbar load of 12 kN at drawbar in such a way that $h_f$ is 700 mm and $h_r$ is 460 mm respectively. Calculate the weight transfer in rear wheel and front wheels occurring due to above pull developed by the tractor.*

**SOLUTION:**

Weight of tractor = 28 kN

$N_f = 9.0$ kN

$N_r = 19.0$ kN

$L = 2160$ mm

$h_f = 700$ mm

$h_r = 460$ mm

$P = 12$ kN

Now, we know that, the weight transfer to rear wheels ($\Delta N_r$) is given by

$$\Delta N_r = P \times h_f / L$$

$$= 12 \text{ kN} \times 700 \text{ mm}/2160 \text{ mm}$$

$$= 3.889 \text{ kN}$$ **Ans.**

Again, weight transfer from front wheels of tractor is given by

$$\Delta N_f = P \times h_r / L$$

$$= 12 \text{ kN} \times 460 \text{ mm}/2160 \text{ mm}$$

$$= 2.55 \text{ kN}$$

## 11.2 TRACTION THEORY

In tractor's pneumatic tyres are used and its rear tyres when move on soil surface have to overcome the rolling resistance or towing force as shown in Fig. 11.3.

Now summing up the forces in horizontal direction, we get:

$$P = F - R_r \qquad ...(11.9)$$

where, $P$ = drawbar pull, $N$ or kg

$F$ = tractive force in direction of motion, N or kg

$R_r$ = rolling resistance opposing motion of wheel, N or kg

Bekker suggested following equation for estimation of tractive force '$F$' in the drive wheel

$$F = A.C + W \tan \phi \qquad ...(10.10)$$

Or,

$$F = A\,(C + p \tan \phi) \qquad ...(10.11)$$

where, $A$ = contact area, $cm^2$

$C$ = cohesion of soil, $N/cm^2$ or $kg/cm^2$

$\phi$ = angle of internal friction of soil, degrees

$p$ = average normal soil pressure, $N/cm^2$ or $kg/cm^2$

$p = W/bl$ for track type devices

$p = W/0.78\,bl$ for pneumatic tyres.

$W$ = weight on drive wheel, N or kg

$b$ = tyre width, cm

$l$ = length of contact of tyre on soil surface, cm

So, tractive force on drive wheel is directly related with tyre contact area and vertical load on the wheel.

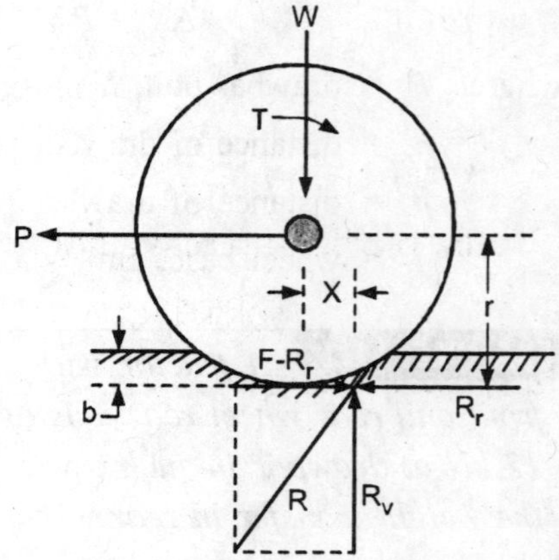


**Figure 11.3: Forces acting on rear drive wheels of tractor**

**EXAMPLE 11.2** *Determine traction force developed by a track type wheel 30 cm wide and 150 cm contact length weighing 15 kN moving on a soil having following parameters:*

$$C = 1.3 \text{ N/cm}^2 \quad ; \quad K_c = 3 \quad ; \quad \phi = 28° \quad ; \quad n = 0.2$$

*Assume that lugs on the track are such that the soil is sheared off in a plane area at ends of lugs.*

**SOLUTION :**

$W = 15$ kN ; $C = 1.3$ N/cm$^2$

$b = 30$ cm ; $l = 150$ cm

$K_c = 3$ ; $\phi = 28°$

$n = 0.2$

Now, we know that shearing force or tractive force is

$$F = AC + W \times \tan\phi \qquad ...(11.12)$$

or

$$F = b.l.C + W \times \tan\phi \qquad ...(11.13)$$

Putting values in eqns.11.12 and 11.13, we get,

$$F = 30 \text{ cm} \times 150 \text{ cm} \times 1.3 \times 10^{-3} \text{ kN/cm}^2 + 15 \text{ kN} \times \tan 28°$$

$$F = 5.85 \text{ kN} + 15 \times 0.531 = 5.85 \text{ kN} + 7.9756 \text{ kN}$$

$$F = 13.825 \text{ kN}$$ **Ans.**

## 11.2.1. Gross Tractive Resistance ($\mu_g$)

Gross tractive resistance ($\mu_g$) of wheel is given by

$$\mu_g = \frac{F}{R_v} = \frac{T}{rW} = 0.75\,(1 - e^{-0.3C_nS}) \qquad ...(11.14)$$

Gross tractive force '$F$' would be

$$F = 0.75 \text{ W } (1 - e^{-0.3\,C_nS}) \qquad ...(11.15)$$

For concrete surface $C_n = \infty$

Therefore, gross tractive force for concrete surface would be

$$F = 0.75 \text{ W} \qquad ...(11.16)$$

and, net tractive coefficient ($\mu$) as

$$\mu = \frac{P}{R_v} = \frac{P}{W} = 0.75\,(1 - e^{-0.3C_nS}) - \left[\frac{1.2}{C_n} + 0.04\right] \qquad ...(11.17)$$

Now, dividing eqn. 10.9 by $W$ we get

$$P/W = F/W - R_r/W \qquad ...(11.18)$$

or,

$$\mu = \mu_g - \rho \qquad ...(11.19)$$

## 11.2.2. Dynamic Tractive Coefficient ($\mu_d$)

It is also known as dynamic traction ratio and defined as ratio of dynamic pull and dynamic weight on driving wheels.

**For 2-wheel drive tractor:** For a rear wheel drive tractor dynamic traction ratio is given by

$$\mu_d = P/(R_v + \Delta N_r) \quad ...(11.20)$$

where, $P$ = drawbar pull, kN or kg

$R_v$ = static weight on rear wheels, kN or kg

$\Delta N_r$ = weight transfer to rear wheel, kN or kg

**For 4-wheel drive tractor:** For a four wheel drive tractor dynamic traction ratio is given by

$$\mu_d = P/W \quad ...(11.21)$$

where, $W$ = weight of tractor, kN, or kg.

Higher value of $\mu_d$ is required for obtaining higher drawbar pulls. It can be improved by proper lug design and use of radial ply tyres.

Again, taking summation of moment about wheel (Refer Fig. 10.2), we get

$$T - (F\text{-}R_r)\, r - R_v \times x = 0 \quad ...(11.22)$$

Or, $T - F \times r + R_r \times r - R_v \times x = 0$ ...(11.23)

But, $R_r \times r - R_v \times x = 0$ ...(11.24)

So, $T - F \times r = 0$ ...(11.25)

Or, $T = F \times r$ ...(11.26)

Therefore, torque developed in the drive wheel is product of gross tractive force '$F$' and rolling radius '$r$' of the drive wheel. The rolling resistance of drive wheel due to soil compaction can be estimated assuming that the energy required to overcome rolling resistance is equal to work done in soil deformation. $R_r$ is calculated by following equation.

$$R_r = \frac{2}{\left[(n+1)(K_c + bK_\phi)^{1/n}\right]} \times \left[\frac{W}{2l}\right]^{(n+1)/n} \quad ...(11.27)$$

where, $R_r$ = rolling resistance or towed force, N or kg

$n$ = coefficient of wheel sinkage

$K_c$ = cohesion modulus of soil deformation

$K_\phi$ = friction modulus of soil deformation

$b$ = width of track, cm

$l$ = length of track in contact, cm

### 11.2.3. Coefficient of Rolling Resistance (ρ)

It is defined as the ratio of rolling resistance force to normal load on the traction device.

$$\rho = R_r/W = 1.2/C_n + 0.04$$

where, $C_n = CI \times b \times d/W$

where, $C_n$ = wheel numeric, for compact dry soils = ∞

$CI$ = cone index

$d$ = overall tyre diameter

$W$ = normal dynamic load, N or kg

Now for dry hard soils

$$R_r/W = 1.2/\infty + 0.04$$

or, $$R_r = 0.04W \quad ...(11.28)$$

Thus, by finding tractive force '$F$' and rolling resistance '$R_r$' of drive wheel of tractor, net or useful pull can be computed by following equation

$$P = F - R_r \quad ...(11.29)$$

**EXAMPLE 11.3** *A rear wheel drive tractor weighing 28 kN is pulling a load on a soil surface in such a way that reactions on front and rear wheels are 10 kN and 18 kN respectively, which has following parameters:*

*(i) Soil cohesion = 1.2 N/cm²* *(ii) Angle of soil friction = 21°*
*(iii) Cohesion modulus of deformation = 3* *(iv) Friction modulus of deformation = 0.5*
*(v) Coefficient of sinkage of soil = 0.2* *(vi) Tractor tyre width = 286 mm*
*(vii) Length of contact of tyre = 550 mm*

*Assume that lugs on tyre are such that the soil is sheared off in a plane area at the ends of lugs. Determine maximum drawbar pull developed by the drive wheels of tractor (Refer Fig. 11.4).*

**SOLUTION:**

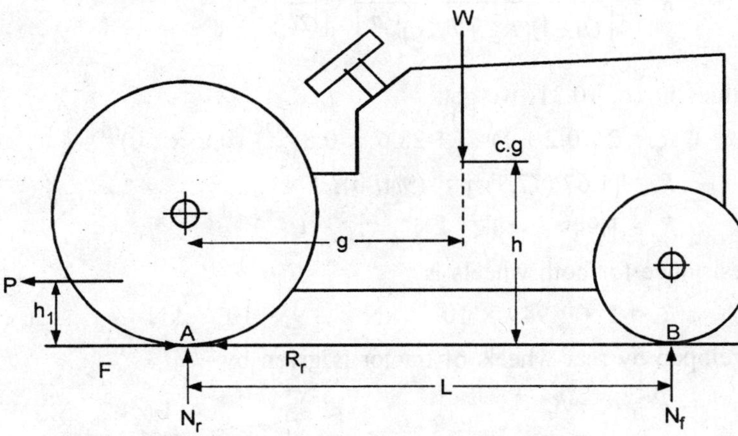


**Figure 11.4: Tractor pulling load on horizontal surface**

Weight of tractor = 28 kN

$N_f$ = 10 kN

$N_r$ = 18 kN

Soil cohesion = 1.2 N/cm²

Angle of soil friction = 21°

Cohesion modulus of deformation = 3

Friction modulus of deformation = 0.5

Coefficient of sinkage of soil = 0.2

Tractor tyre width, $b = 286$ mm

Length of contact of tyre, $l = 500$ mm

Now area of contact of pneumatic tyre,

$$A = 0.78 \text{ bl}$$

$$A = 0.78 \times 28.6 \times 50 = 1115.4 \text{ cm}^2$$

Now, tractive effort developed by the drive wheel is

$$F = AC + N_r/2. \tan \phi \qquad \text{...(11.30)}$$

where, $N_r / 2 = 18$ kN/2 = 9 kN.

Putting the values in eqn. 10.30, we get,

$$F = 1115.4 \text{ cm}^2 \times 1.2 \times 10^{-3} \text{ kN/cm}^2 + 9 \text{ kN} \times \tan 21°$$

$$F = 1.34 \text{ kN} + 3.456 \text{ kN}$$

$$F = 4.796 \text{ kN}$$

Now, tractive force developed by both the rear wheels

$$2F = 2 \times 4.796 \text{ kN} = 9.592 \text{ kN}$$

Again, we know that

$$R_r = \frac{2}{\left[(n+1)(K_c + bK_\phi)^{1/n}\right]} \times \left[\frac{W}{2l}\right]^{(n+1)/n} \qquad \text{...(11.31)}$$

Putting the values in eq. 10.31, we get,

$$R_r = 2/[(0.2 + 1)\ (3 + 28.6 \times 0.5)^{1/2}]\ (9/2 \times 50)^{(0.2 + 1)\ /\ 0.2}$$

Or, $R_r = [1.67/(17.3)^5] \times (9/100)^6$ kN

Or, $R_r = 1.949 \times 10^{-11}$ kN

And rolling resistance for both wheels is

$$R_r = 2 \times 1.949 \times 10^{-11} \text{ kN} = 3.9 \times 10^{-11} \text{ kN}$$

Now, pull developed by rear wheels of tractor is given by

$$P = F - R_r \qquad \text{...(11.32)}$$

Putting the values in eqn. 10.32, we get

$$P = 9.592 \text{ kN} - 3.9 \times 10^{-11} \text{ kN}$$

$$P = 9.591 \text{ kN}$$

**Ans.**

**EXAMPLE 11.4** *A tractor weighing 28 kN is climbing a slope of 20% and it has a wheel base of 2250 cm, drawbar height is 400 mm, centre of gravity is acting at 900 mm ahead of rear axle and 800 mm above the ground as given in Fig. 11.5. The area of contact of each wheel with soil is 1850 cm². Cohesion of soil is 0.5 N/cm² and angle of internal friction of soil is 28°. Ignoring rolling resistance and assuming that the pull is parallel to the soil surface, find the maximum draw bar pull exerted by the tractor.*

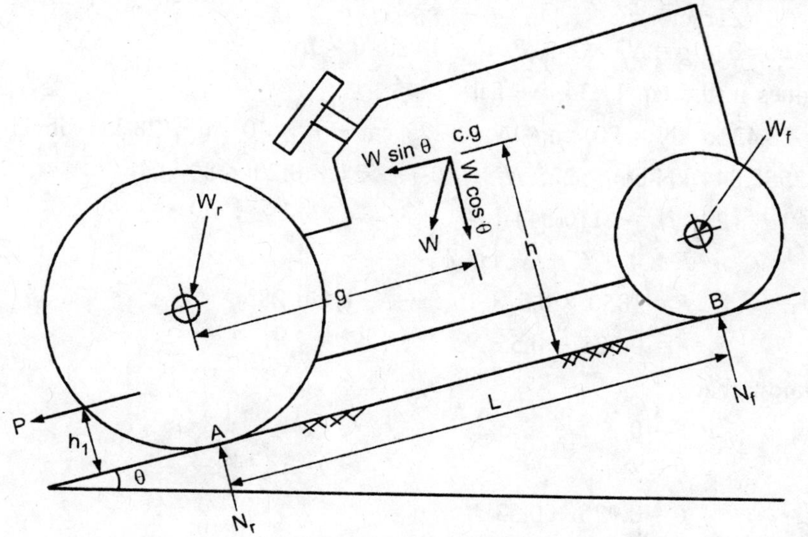


**Figure 11.5: Tractor pulling load while climbing a slope**

**SOLUTION:**

Weight of tractor, $W = 28$ kN

Wheel base, $L = 2250$ cm

Distance of c.g. of tractor, $g = 900$ mm ahead of rear wheel axle

Height of c.g. of tractor from ground surface, $h = 800$ mm

Area of contact of each wheel with soil, $A = 1850\ \text{cm}^2$

Cohesion of soil, $C = 0.5\ \text{N/cm}^2$

Angle of internal friction of soil, $\phi = 28°$

Slope of soil surface, $S = 20\%$

Since slope is 20%

Therefore, from Fig. 11.5,

$$\text{Slope} = \sin\theta = 20/100 = 0.2$$

Or, $\sin\theta = 0.20$

Or, $\theta = 11.54°$

Now, assume that, $N_f$ and $N_r$ are the reactions at the front and rear wheels

$$\sum F_v = 0,$$

$$N_r + N_f - W\cos\theta = 0$$

Or, $$N_r + N_f = W\cos\theta \qquad ...(11.33)$$

Putting the values in eqn. 10.33, we get,

$$N_r + N_f = 28\text{ kN} \times 0.9797 = 27.4316\text{ kN}$$

Now, taking moments about '$A$' we get

$$\sum M = 0$$

$$W \cos \theta \times g = N_f \times L + Pxh_1 + W \sin \theta \times h \qquad ...(11.34)$$

Putting values in the eq. 11.34, we get

$$28.4316 \text{ kN} \times 90 \text{ cm} = N_f \times 225 \text{ cm} + P \times 40 \text{ cm} + 28 \text{ kN} \sin 11.54° \times 80 \text{ cm}$$

or, $2558.844 \text{ kN-cm} = 225\ N_f + 40\ P + 28 \times 0.20 \times 80$

or, $40\ P + 225\ N_f = 2110.844 \qquad ...(11.35)$

Again, $F = A \times C + N_r \tan \phi$

or, $F = 1850 \times 0.5 \times 10^{-3} + N_r \times \tan 28°$

$F = 0.925 + 0.53\ N_r \qquad ...(11.36)$

Also we know that

$$\text{P-F} = 0$$

or, $P = F$

Therefore, $P = 0.925 + 0.53\ N_r$

Now putting values of $P$ in equation 11.35 we get

$$40\ (0.925 + 0.53\ N_r) + 225\ N_f = 2110.844$$

or, $21.2\ N_r + 225\ N_f = 2073.844 \qquad ...(11.37)$

Solving eqns. 11.33 and 11.37, we get

$$N_f = 7.322 \text{ kN}$$

And $N_r = 27.4316 - N_f = 27.4316 - 7.332 = 20.1096 \text{ kN}$

Maximum drawbar pull developed by tractor ($P$):

Now, $P = 0.925 + 0.53\ N_r \qquad ...(11.38)$

Putting value of $N_r$ in eqn. 10.38, we get

$$P = 0.925 \text{ kN} + 0.53 \times 20.1096 \text{ kN}$$

$$P = 0.925 \text{ kN} + 10.658 \text{ kN} = 11.583 \text{ kN}$$

Therefore,

Maximum permissible drawbar pull developed by the tractor would be **11.583 kN.** **Ans.**

### 11.2.4. Tractive Efficiency (TE)

Tractive efficiency of a drive device is a measure of efficiency with which it transforms torque acting on axle of traction device in to drawbar pulls. It is defined as the ratio of output power to input power of traction device. It is also referred to as fraction of axle power converted to drawbar power by the drive wheels. Following important parameters generally reduce the tractive efficiency of traction device:

- rolling resistance
- slip
- friction
- deflection in tractive device
- steering

The tractive efficiency is given by

$$TE = \text{Output power/Input power} = \text{Drawbar power/Axle power}$$

$$TE = \frac{P \times V_a}{T\omega} = \frac{P \times V}{T\,(V_t/r)}$$

or $$TE = \frac{\frac{P}{W} \times (1 - S)}{\frac{F}{W}} \quad ...(11.39)$$

where, $P$ = drawbar pull, kN or kg
$V_t$ = theoretical wheel speed, m/s
$r$ = radius of drive wheel, m
$W$ = weight of tractor, kN
$F$ = tractive force, kN
$V_a$ = actual wheel speed, m/s
$T$ = axle torque, kN.m
$\omega$ = angular velocity of drive wheel, rad/s
$S$ = wheel slip, %

From equation. 11.39, it is clear that traction efficiency is maximum at relatively lower slip and decreases with increasing slip.

Also, $$TE = P \times S/(3.6 \times W_a) \quad ...(11.40)$$

where, $P$ = drawbar pull, kN
$S$ = actual forward speed of tractor, km/hr
$W_a$ = axle power, *kW*.

**EXAMPLE 11.5** *A rear wheel drive tractor having total weight of 25 kN with a wheel base 2200 mm and centre of gravity is 900 mm ahead of rear wheel axle centre line. The tractor is pulling a load of 16 kN on concrete road at a forward speed of 7.2 km/hr and drawbar height is 400 mm as given in Fig. 10.6. The axle power of tractor is 35 kW. Determine:*

*(i) Weight transfer to the rear wheels*
*(ii) Coefficient of traction*
*(iii) Tractive efficiency*

**SOLUTION:**

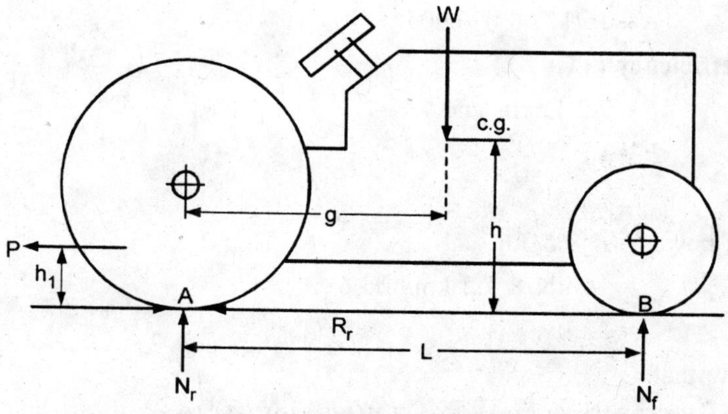


**Figure 11.6: Tractor pulling load on horizontal surface**

$W$ = 25 kN

$L$ = 2200 mm = 2.20 m

$G$ = 900 mm = 0.9 m

Pull, $P = 16$ kN

Speed, $S = 7.2$ km/hr

Axle power, $W_a = 35$ kW

Drawbar height, $h = 400$ mm $= 0.4$ m

**(*i*) Weight transfer to rear wheels ($\Delta N_r$)**

We know that; $\Delta N_r = P \times$ hitch height/L ...(11.41)

$\Delta N_r = 16$ kN $\times$ 0.4 m/ 2.2 m

$\Delta N_r = 2.909$ kN **Ans.**

**(*ii*) Coefficient of traction (μ)**

From Fig. 11.6

$$N_r + N_f = W \quad ...(11.42)$$

Or, $N_r = W - N_f$

Now, taking moment about '*A*' we get

$$P \times h_l + N_f \times L - W \times g = 0$$

Or, $P \times h_1 + N_f \times L = W \times g$

Or, $N_f = (W \times g - P \times h)/L$ ...(10.43)

Putting the values in eqn. 11.43, we get

$N_f = (25$ kN $\times$ 0.9 m $-$ 16 kN $\times$ 0.4m)/2.2 m

$N_f = 7.32$ kN

Again based on eqn. 11.42, we get

$N_r = 25$ kN $-$ 7.32 kN $=$ 17.68 kN

Now, we know that

$\mu = F/N_r = P/N_r$

$\mu = 16/17.68 = 0.905$ **Ans.**

**(*iii*) Tractive efficiency (TE)**

Now, Speed, $S = 7.2$ km/hr and

Drawbar pull, $P = 16$ kN

Therefore,

Drawbar power $= P \times S/3.6$

$= 16$ kN $\times$ 7.2 km/hr/3.6

$= 32$ kW

Now, we know that

$TE =$ (Drawbar power, kW/$W_a$, kW) $\times$ 10 ...(11.44)

Putting the values in eqn. 11.44, we get,

$TE =$ (32 kW/35 kW) $\times$ 100

$TE = 91.43$ **Ans.**

## 11.3 TRACTOR TYRES

Tyre design, soil conditions and method of their use has considerable effect on tractive performance of pneumatic tyres. They carry full load of the tractor and bear the continuous friction of soil surface. Rear tyres of tractor are lugged types which are suitable for development of traction. Rubber manufacturers association has determined load and torque limits for each tyre. Front tyres of tractor are non-lugged or ribbed tyres which are used for steering purpose. They also act as a buffer between the surface and the tractor.

Main functions of tyres are:

(*i*) To carry load of tractor

(*ii*) To provide grip on soil surface for development of better traction

(*iii*) To transmit engine power from transmission system to the ground and move tractor forward

(*iv*) To absorb small shocks from the ground and dampen vibrations to some extent

(*v*) To absorb retarding force during application of brakes on the tractor

### Composition of pneumatic tyres

Tyres consist of beads, body plies, casing, side walls, lugs, breakers etc. which is discussed below.

**Beads:** These are rubber enclosed bundles of wires that anchor tyre to the wheel rim. All the plies are tied to these bundles of wires and prevent change of shape of tyre and fit on the rim.

**Body plies:** These are layers of rubber–cushioned fabrics or cords tied to the beads and extend across the face of tyre. Each ply is insulated from the other. Ply rating is an index of tyre strength factor of load carrying capacity. Generally front and rear tyres of tractor are available from 4 to 6 ply ratings. The designation of ply rating has been accepted by the association of tyre manufacturers to identify a given type of tyre with its maximum recommended load. These plies are separated from each other by resilient rubber compound. Earlier tyres had biased ply construction where one ply runs from one bead to another at an angle. Radial ply tyres have gained popularity in the recent years. Their construction is similar to previous tyres except that the plies are perpendicular to tyre beads. These tyres can operate even at lower inflation pressure and have greater area of contact with ground surface.

**Casing:** Casing of tyre is made up of layers of rubber and cushioned cord or fabrics. It contains strength of inflation pressure which supports the tractor load and also dampens the surface shocks.

**Side walls:** These are the protective rubber coverings on both sides of casing. Side walls of tyres are subjected to small continuous deflection and sudden shocks during operation of tractor.

**Lugs:** The outer edge of rear tyre has rubber lugs, treads which penetrates into soil and improve traction. The tyres should be mounted on the rim in such a way that 'V' pattern points downwards at the front of tyre. Lug type and height have considerable effect on traction developed by the wheels. Small lugs are more efficient on firm soils to develop good traction. But, in under soft wet soil conditions larger lug size with sharp corners will give better performance. Similarly lug spacing and lug angle effect the tyre performance under actual field conditions. Wider lug spacing increases power efficiency due to decreased soil distribution but difficulty in driving on hard soil surface is observed. Significantly lower tyre wears are found in tyres with smaller lug angles. This is quite significant for use of tractors in transportation works. Front tyres of tractor have ribs which penetrate into soil surface and helps in turning of tractor.

**Breakers:** These are extra plies provided under the treads/lugs. It helps the treads to absorb sudden shocks and gives enough strength to tyre against blows due to rough surface or obstacles.

**Tyre size:** Traction produced by a tyre is directly proportional to the weight it carries. Selection of tyre size is based on weight required to obtain desired drawbar horsepower from the tractor. Use of higher size tyres increases weight carrying capacity of tyre. However, proper amount of weight on tyre should produce lower rolling resistance and slippage losses. For rear wheel drive tractors the slippage should be between 12% on hard ground and 22% on soft soil surfaces. The tractor tyres are designated by the tyre width and rim diameter where tyre is mounted in a recommended rim *e.g.* 11.2/10-28, where 11.2/10 inch is nominal tyre width and 28 inches is rim diameter.

**Ballast:** Usually, to take advantage of the increased pulling ability, more ballast (weight) must be added to maintain effective traction. Extra weight is used to properly ballast a tractor for field operations. Heavy draft loads require more ballast than lighter loads. Ballast is the use of additional weights to obtain optimum weight to tractor in order to improve its traction. Ballasting can be done with the following methods.

(*i*) Mounting cast iron weights
(*ii*) Liquid ballast and
(*iii*) Dry ballast.

There are certain safe limits on the total weight of the rear tyres of tractor as excessive loading of rear tyres would result in:

- Increased soil compaction
- Increased fuel consumption
- Design life of final drives is reduced
- Reduced tyre life

If it is convenient for light loads, remove extra ballast to reduce rolling resistance and improve fuel economy as well as reduce the potential for soil compaction. The optimum rear wheel weight of tractor under different soil conditions can be estimated as given in Table 11.2.

**TABLE 11.2: Optimum weight on rear wheels**

| Cohesive soil | Non-cohesive soil |
|---|---|
| $\text{Weight (kg)} = \dfrac{110 \times PTO}{\text{actual speed (km/hr)}}$ | $\text{Weight (kg)} = \dfrac{123 \times PTO}{\text{actual speed (km/hr)}}$ |

**Tyre inflation:** The tyre inflation pressure should be maintained at recommended levels. Both under-inflation and over inflation are harmful. It should not be lower than the recommended value as this will reduce the tyre life due to damaged cord and diagonal breaks in cord fabric in the side walls and buckling of side walls. The size of tractor and the recommended inflation pressure is given in Table 11.3.

**TABLE 11.3: Tractor tyre size and recommended inflation pressure**

| Sr. No. | Tyre size | Ply rating | Recommended inflation pressure, Kg/cm$^2$ |
|---|---|---|---|
| **I. Rear tyres** | | | |
| 1. | 11.2/10 × 28 | 4 | 1.10 |
| 2. | 11.2/10 × 28 | 6 | 1.85 |
| 3. | 12.4/11 × 28 | 4 | 1.00 |
| 4. | 12.4/11 × 28 | 6 | 1.50 |
| .5. | 13.6/12 × 28 | 6 | 1.40 |
| 6. | 14 × 28 | 6 | 1.25 |
| **II. Front tyres** | | | |
| 1. | 5.00 × 16 | 6 | 3.60 |
| 2. | 5.50 × 16 | 4 | 2.25 |
| 3. | 6.00 × 16 | 4 | 2.25 |
| 4. | 6.00 × 16 | 6 | 3.40 |
| 5. | 6.00 × 19 | 6 | 3.40 |
| 6. | 6.50 × 20 | 6 | 3.10 |

## EXERCISES

1. A tractor has front and rear wheel reactions of 10 and 15 kN respectively. Its wheel base is 2000 mm. How far is the C.G of tractor from the rear axle of tractor?
2. A tractor weighing 25 kN is operating on level ground and has front and rear wheel reaction 10 and 15 kN respectively. While operating on level ground, it is exerting a pull of 16 kN as shown in Fig. 11.7. The line of pull is such that $h_r$ and $h_f$ are 300 mm and 930 mm respectively. Determine the rear and front wheel normal reaction of tractor.

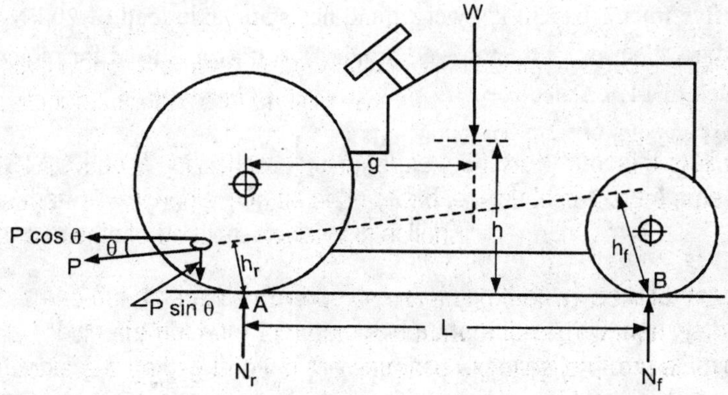


**Figure 11.7: Effect of drawbar pull on weight transfer of tractor**

3. A rear wheel drive tractor has a wheel base of 2250 mm. The front and rear wheel reactions are 12 and 20 kN respectively. Coefficient of traction is 0.6 and rear axle torque is adequate. How much load this tractor would pull horizontally when height of drawbar is 400 mm above the ground. Is pull limited by the stability of front wheels?
4. In a rear wheel drive tractor under no load, rear and front wheel reactions are 12 kN and 18 kN respectively. The drawbar height is 450 mm and the wheel base is 2000 mm. If the coefficient of traction is 0.6, what horizontal pull on the level ground the tractor will exert. Neglect rolling resistance of tractor.
5. A Massey Ferguson Tractor moves 20 m distance in 5 revolutions of rear wheels at no load on firm ground and 14.6 m in 5 revolutions when ploughing the field with a mounted disc plough. Calculate the slippage in tractor wheels.
6. A rear wheel drive tractor weighing 36 kN has wheel base 2250 mm. Horizontal distance from the C. G.. of tractor to rear axle is 800 mm . Calculate:
   (*a*) Static weight on the front wheel
   (*b*) Static weight on rear wheel axle
7. A rear wheel drive tractor weighing 36 kN has wheel base 2250 mm. Horizontal distance from the C. G. of tractor to rear axle is 800 mm. It is pulling a loaded tractor trailer with a level drawbar pull of 15 kN and the drawbar height is 450 mm. Calculate the weight transfer and dynamic weights on
   (*a*) Front axle (*b*) Rear axle
8. A rear wheel drive tractor has total weight of 32 kN and wheel base of 2200 mm. The centre of gravity is 750 mm ahead of rear wheel axle centerline. The tractor is pulling a level drawbar pull of 16 kN on concrete road. The height of drawbar is 425 mm. The axle power of tractor is 35 kW. The actual travel speed and no load tractor speed are 5.5 km/hr and 5.8 km/hr respectively. Calculate the following:
   (*a*) Slippage or travel reduction (*b*) Dynamic load on rear axle
   (*c*) Tractive efficiency (*d*) Dynamic traction ratio
9. A Farmtrac tractor has total weight of 32.5 kN and a wheel base of 2500 mm. The static weight of front axle is 14.5 kN. The tractor pull is level at a drawbar height of 420 mm. Calculate the critical pull at which the front wheel of tractor would lift off the ground.
10. A rear wheel drive tractor has 30 kN weight and has static axle load of 20 kN and axle power is 35 kW. No load travel speed of tractor is 5.7 km/hr. The tractor is used for ploughing a field where slippage is limited to 14%. Calculate:
    (*a*) Actual travel speed and (*b*) Drawbar pull

CHAPTER 12

# Mechanics of Tractor Chassis and Stability

## INTRODUCTION

Performance of rear wheel drive tractors especially tractiveability, stability, riding and handling can be well understood by the statics and dynamics of tractor. This can be evaluated with the help of static equilibrium analysis.

## 12.1 STATIC EQUILIBRIUM OF TRACTOR

Tractiveability and stability of tractor depends upon interaction of all external forces. The analysis of external forces acting on tractor can be done by considering it as a free body as shown in Fig. 11.1.

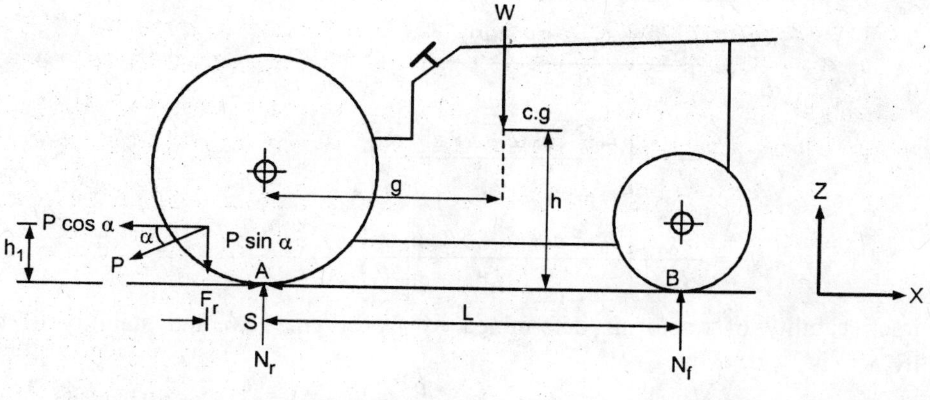


**Figure 12.1: Free body diagram of tractor chassis with external forces**

Now, referring to free body diagram of tractor (Fig. 12.1) under static condition, various forces acting on the tractor are

$W$ = Weight of tractor, kg or kN

$P$ = Drawbar pull of implement, kg or kN

$N_f$ = Ground reaction at front wheels, kg or kN

$N_r$ = Ground reaction at rear wheel, kg or kN

$F_r$ = Tractive force at rear wheel, kg or kN

$L$ = Wheel base of tractor, mm

$g$ = Distance from rear axle centre to c.g of tractor

$h$ = Height of c.g from the ground, mm

$S$ = Distance from the rear axle centre to the point of hitch, mm

$h_1$ = Height of drawbar hitch point from ground, mm

$\alpha$ = Angle of line of pull with the horizontal, degrees

Now, according to Newton's law of motion for a free body under steady state condition:

$$\sum F_x = 0$$

and $$\sum F_z = 0$$

and taking moment about point '*A*'

$$\sum M = 0$$

Now, $$\sum F_x = 0$$

$$F_r - P \sin \alpha = 0 \quad ...(12.1)$$

$$\sum F_z = 0$$

$$N_r + N_f - W - P \cos a = 0 \quad ...(12.2)$$

And taking moment about point '*A*' $\sum M = 0$

$$W_g - h_1 P \cos \alpha - SP \sin \alpha - N_f L = 0 \quad ...(12.3)$$

Or, $$\frac{Wg}{L} = \frac{h_1 P \cos \alpha - SP \sin \alpha}{L} + N_f \quad ...(12.4)$$

Or, $$N_f = \frac{Wg}{L} - \left[\frac{h_1 P \cos \alpha - SP \sin \alpha}{L}\right] \quad ...(12.5)$$

And, $$N_r = \frac{Wg}{L} + \left[\frac{h_1 P \cos \alpha - SP \sin \alpha}{L}\right] \quad ...(12.6)$$

The tractiveability of tractor is determined by $N_r$ or eq. 12.6 and stability of tractor is determined by $N_f$.

## 12.2 WEIGHT TRANSFER PHENOMENON

In eqn. 12.4, term $(h_1 \times P \cos \alpha$ - S P sin $\alpha)/L$ is known as weight transfer from the front axle to the rear wheels of tractor due to drawbar pull of mounted implement. So, whenever a tractor pulls a load through hitch point above ground level weight is transferred from the front wheels to the rear wheels. Although there is no actual shift of weight, the changes in soil reactions of rear ($N_r$) and front ($N_f$) are commonly known as weight transfer. When the pull exerted by the tractor is parallel to the ground surface, the weight transferred to rear axle is equal to the weight lost by the front wheels. Weight transfer is a function of height of hitch point and wheel base *i.e.* when height of hitch point ($h_1$) is increased, weight transfer increases and it also increases with decrease in wheel base ($L$). In order to avoid overturning of tractor this term $(h_1 \times P \cos \alpha - S P \sin \alpha)/L$ must be less than $Wg/L$.

Or, $Wg/L \geq (h_1\ P \cos\alpha - S\ P \sin\alpha)/L$

In case, $Wg/L \leq (h_1 \times P \cos\alpha - S\ P \sin\alpha)/L$,

then, through the weight transfer effect the drawbar pull may cause the $N_f$ to become zero and this effect stability of tractor as the tractor will leave the ground and overturn rearwards. There must be enough weight on the front wheels of tractor for steering. Proper amount of pull, its direction and height above ground surface can transfer adequate quantity of weight to the rear wheels of tractor without affecting its steerability. In rear wheel drive tractors the total static weight on rear wheels is generally kept 60–70% for development of adequate traction and proper stability.

## 12.3 MAXIMUM PERMISSIBLE DRAWBAR PULL (*P*)

The maximum drawbar pull at which the tractor will become unstable is given by

$$P = \frac{Wg}{h_1\ P \cos\alpha - S \sin\alpha} \quad ...(12.7)$$

The drawbar pull of tractor can be increased by

- Increasing weight of tractor ($W$)
- Increasing wheel base ($L$)
- Decreasing hitch point ($h_1$ and $S$)
- Maximum achievable drawbar pull is also limited by tractive condition of surface on which tractor is operating.

**EXAMPLE 12.1** *A tractor with a total weight of 30 kN having wheel base of 2200 mm has c.g. located 800 mm ahead of centre of rear axle. It pulls a drawbar load of 16 kN at drawbar at an angle of 15° with the horizontal. The hitch point is located 400 mm above ground surface 300 mm behind the centre of rear axle. Calculate the reactions on rear and front wheels of tractor. Also calculate the weight transfer to rear wheel occurring due to above pull developed by the tractor. (Refer Fig.* 12.1).

**SOLUTION:**

Weight of tractor, $W = 30$ kN

Wheel base, $L = 2200$ mm

Drawbar pull, $P = 16$ kN

Angle of pull, $\alpha = 15°$

Height of drawbar, $h_1 = 400$ mm

Distance point of hitch from rear wheel axle, $s = 300$ mm

Distance of c.g from rear wheel axle centre, $g = 800$ mm

We know that,

$$N_f = \frac{Wg}{L} - \left[\frac{h_1\ P \cos\alpha - SP \sin\alpha}{L}\right] \quad ...(12.8)$$

Putting the values in eq. 12.8, we get

$$N_f = 30 \times 800 /2200 - (400 \times 16 \times \cos 15° - 300 \times 16 \times \sin 15°)/2200$$

Or, $N_f = 10.90 - (2.809 - 0.565) = 10.90 \text{ kN} - 2.24 \text{ kN} = 8.66 \text{ kN}$ **Ans.**

Again, $$N_r = \frac{Wg}{L} + \left[\frac{h_1 P\cos\alpha - SP\sin\alpha}{L}\right] \quad ...(12.9)$$

Putting the values in eq. 12.9, we get,

$$N_r = 30 \times 800/2200 + (400 \times 16 \times \cos 15° - 300 \times 16 \times \sin 15°)/2200$$

Or, $N_r = 10.90 \text{ kN} + 2.24 \text{ kM} = 13.14 \text{ kN}$ **Ans.**

Now, weight transfer from front wheels to rear wheels is given by

$$\Delta N_r = \left[\frac{h_1 P\cos\alpha - SP\sin\alpha}{L}\right] \quad ...(12.10)$$

Putting the values in eq. 12.10, we get,

$$\Delta N_r = (400 \times 16 \times \cos 15° - 300 \times 16 \times \sin 15°)/2200$$

Or, $\Delta N_r = 2.809 \text{ kN} - 0.565 \text{ kN} = 2.24 \text{ kN}$ **Ans.**

**EXAMPLE 12.2** *A tractor weighing 28 kN is climbing a slope of 20% and it has a wheel base of 2250 mm, drawbar height of 400 mm, centre of gravity is acting at 900 mm ahead of rear axle and 800 mm above the ground. The area of contact of each wheel with soil is 1850 cm². Cohesion of soil is 0.5 N/cm² and angle of internal friction of soil is 28°. Ignoring rolling resistance and assuming that the pull is parallel to the soil surface, find the maximum draw bar pull exerted by the tractor. (Refer Fig. 12.2)*

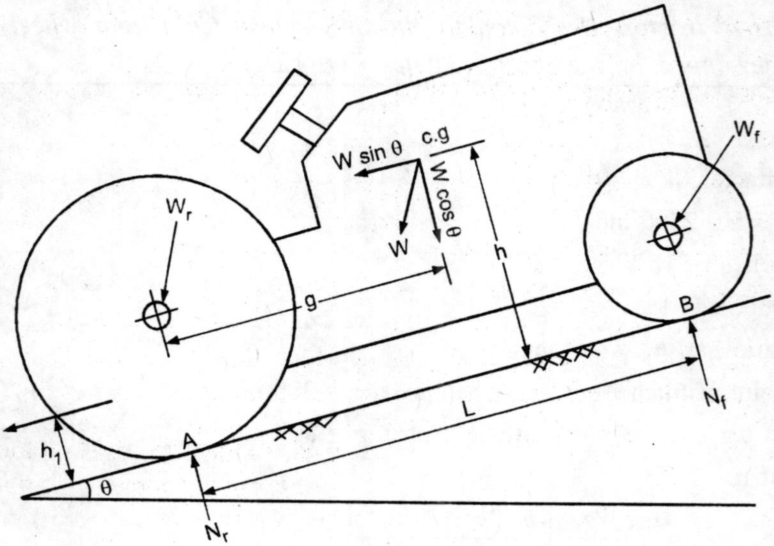


**Figure 12.2: Tractor pulling load while climbing a slope**

**SOLUTION:**

Weight of tractor, $W = 28$ kN

Wheel base, $L = 2250$ mm

Distance of c.g of tractor, $g = 900$ mm ahead of rear wheel axle

Height of c.g of tractor from ground surface, $h = 800$ mm

Area of contact of each wheel with soil, $A = 1850\ \text{cm}^2$

Cohesion of soil, $C = 0.5\ \text{N/cm}^2$

Angle of internal friction of soil, $\phi = 28°$

Slope of soil surface, $S = 20\%$

Since slope is 20%

Therefore, from Fig. 12.2,

$$\text{Slope} = \sin\theta = 20/100 = 0.2$$

Or, $\sin\theta = 0.20$

Or, $\theta = 11.54°$

Now, assume that, $N_f$ and $N_r$ are the reactions at the front and rear wheels

$$\sum F_v = 0,$$

$$N_r + N_f - W\cos\theta = 0$$

Or, $N_r + N_f = W\,\text{Cos}\,\theta$ ...(12.11)

Putting values in eqn. 12.1, we get,

$$N_r + N_f = 28\ \text{kN} \times 0.9797 = 27.4316\ \text{kN} \qquad ...(12.12)$$

Now, taking moments about '$A$' we get

$$\sum M = 0$$

$$Wg\cos\theta = N_f L + Ph_1 + W h \sin\theta \qquad ...(12.13)$$

Putting the values in eq. 12.13, we get

$$28.4316\ \text{kN} \times 90\ \text{cm} = N_f \times 225\ \text{cm} + P \times 40\ \text{cm} + 28\ \text{kN}\sin 11.54° \times 80\ \text{cm}$$

Or, $2558.844\ \text{kN} - \text{cm} = 225\,N_f + 40\,P + 28 \times 0.20 \times 80$

Or, $40\,P + 225\,N_f = 2110.844$ ...(12.14)

Again, $F = A.\,C + N_r \tan\phi$

Or, $F = 1850 \times 0.5 \times 10^{-3} + N_r \times \tan 28°$

$F = 0.925 + 0.53\,N_r$ ...(12.15)

Also we know that

$$P - F = 0$$

Or, $P = F$

Therefore, $P = 0.925 + 0.53\,N_r$

Now putting the values of $P$ in eq. 12.5, we get

$$40\ (0.925 + 0.53\ N_r) + 225\ N_f = 2110.844$$

Or, $$21.2\ N_r + 225\ N_f = 2073.844 \quad ...(12.16)$$

Solving eqns. 12.2 and 12.16, we get,

$$N_f = 7.322 \text{ kN}$$

And

$$N_r = 27.4316 - N_f = 27.4316 - 7.332$$
$$= 20.1096 \text{ kN}$$

Maximum drawbar pull developed by tractor ($P$):

Now, $$P = 0.925 + 0.53\ N_r \quad ...(12.17)$$

Putting value of $N_f$ in eq. 12.17, we get

$$P = 0.925 \text{ kN} + 0.53 \times 20.1096 \text{ kN}$$
$$P = 0.925 \text{ kN} + 10.658 \text{ kN} = 11.583 \text{ kN}$$

Therefore,

Maximum permissible drawbar pull developed by the tractor would be 11.583 kN **Ans.**

## 12.4 LONGITUDINAL STABILITY OF TRACTOR AT NO LOAD

### 12.4.1. Tractor moving uphill

The maximum upgrade slope ($\theta_{lim}$) for the tractor moving up hill is given by

$$\tan \theta_{lim} = g/h \quad ...(12.18)$$

where, $\theta_{lim}$ = maximum upgrade angle upto which tractor is stable, degrees

$g$ = perpendicular distance from rear axle to $c.g.$ of tractor, mm

$h$ = height of $c.g.$ from ground, mm

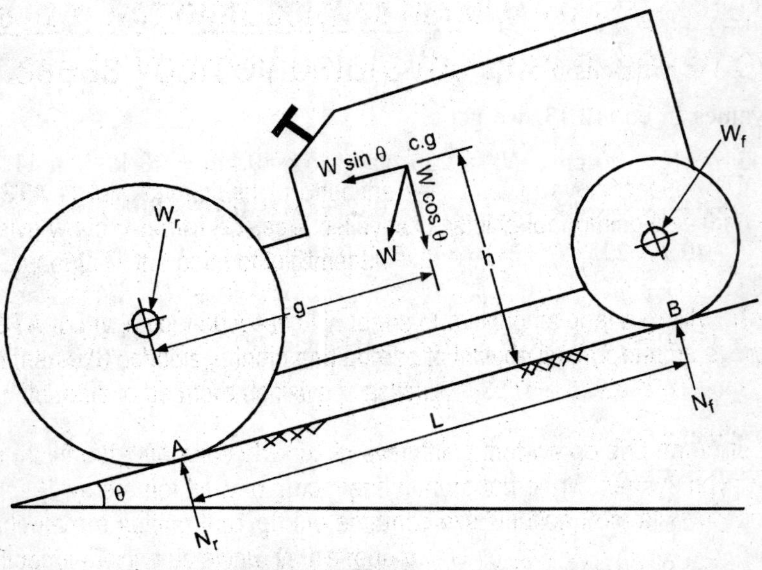


**Figure 12.3. Tractor climbing a slope at no-load**

### 12.4.2. Tractor Moving Down Hill

The maximum downgrade slope ($\theta_{lim}$) is given by

$$\tan \theta_{lim} = x/h \quad ...(12.19)$$

where, $\theta_{lim}$ = maximum down grade angle up to which tractor is stable, degrees

$x$ = perpendicular distance from front axle to *c.g.* of tractor, mm

$h$ = height of *c.g.* from ground, mm

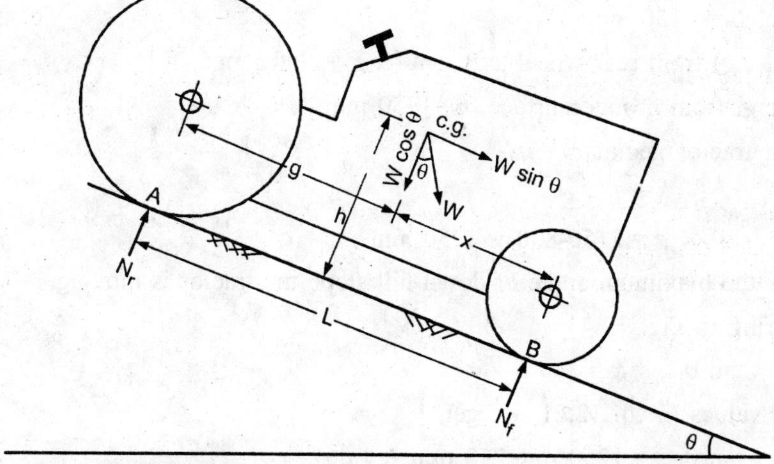


**Figure 12.4: Tractor moving downhill at no-load**

**EXAMPLE 12.3** *A tractor weighing 28 kN has wheel base of 2150 mm and moving uphill at no load. Its c.g. is located 900 mm ahead of centre of rear wheel axle and 750 mm above the ground surface. Determine the maximum up hill slope the tractor can climb without overturning backwards. (Refer Fig. 12.3)*

**SOLUTION:**

Weight of tractor, $W$ = 30 kN

Wheel base, $L$ = 2150 mm

Distance of *c.g.* from rear wheel axle centre, $g$ = 900 mm

Height of *c.g.* from ground surface, $h$ = 750 mm

Let, $\theta_{lim,}$ is the maximum angle of uphill slope the tractor is climbing.

Now, referring to Fig. 12.3

$$\tan \theta_{lim} = g/h \quad ...(12.20)$$

Putting the values in eq. 11.20, we get

$$\tan \theta_{lim} = 900 \text{ mm}/750 \text{ mm} = 1.2$$

Or, $\theta_{lim} = \tan^{-1} 1.2$

$\theta_{lim}$ = 50.19 degrees **Ans.**

**EXAMPLE 12.4** *A tractor weighing 28 kN has wheel base of 2150 mm and moving downhill at no load. Its c.g. is located 900 mm ahead of centre of rear wheel axle and 750 mm above the ground surface. Determine the maximum down hill slope the tractor can move safely without overturning foreword. (Refer Fig. 12.4)*

**SOLUTION:**

Weight of tractor, $W$ = 30 kN

Wheel base, $L$ = 2150 mm

Distance of *c.g.* from rear wheel axle centre, $g$ = 900 mm

Height of *c.g.* from ground surface, $h$ = 750 mm

Now, From tractor geometry

$$x = L - g$$

$$x = 2150\text{-}800 = 1250 \text{ mm}$$

Let, $\theta_{lim,}$ is the maximum angle of down hill slope the tractor is moving.

Now, referring to Fig. 12.4

$$\tan \theta_{lim} = x/h \tag{12.21}$$

Putting the values in eq. 12.21, we get,

$$\tan \theta_{lim} = 1250 \text{ mm}/750 \text{ mm} \doteq 1.667$$

Or, $$\theta_{lim} = \tan^{-1} 1.667$$

$$\theta_{lim} = 59.04 \text{ degrees}$$ **Ans.**

## 12.5 LATERAL STABILITY OF TRACTOR

When tractor is operating in field or road straight ahead with no wheel slippage both the wheels of tractor move at equal speed and equal power is transmitted to both the wheels and its differential only works when the tractor is taking turns. During turns, the side towards which is turned, that wheel turns at slower speed than the outer wheel of tractor. When one wheel of tractor is braked during turning, the speed of other wheel will be doubled. Similarly, torque transmitted during turning of tractor is doubled in the outer wheel when one wheel is completely stopped. The torque would be equal to

$$T_t = \frac{HP \times 60 \times 75}{2\pi N} \text{ (in kg-m)} \qquad ...(12.22)$$

This torque would be twice the torque developed by the tractor during straight movement. The top plan, side elevation and back view of the tractor taking turn are given in Fig. 12.5, 12.6 and 12.7 respectively.

While taking short turns with the tractor at relatively high speeds, a centrifugal force will act at centre of gravity of tractor which is given by following equation.

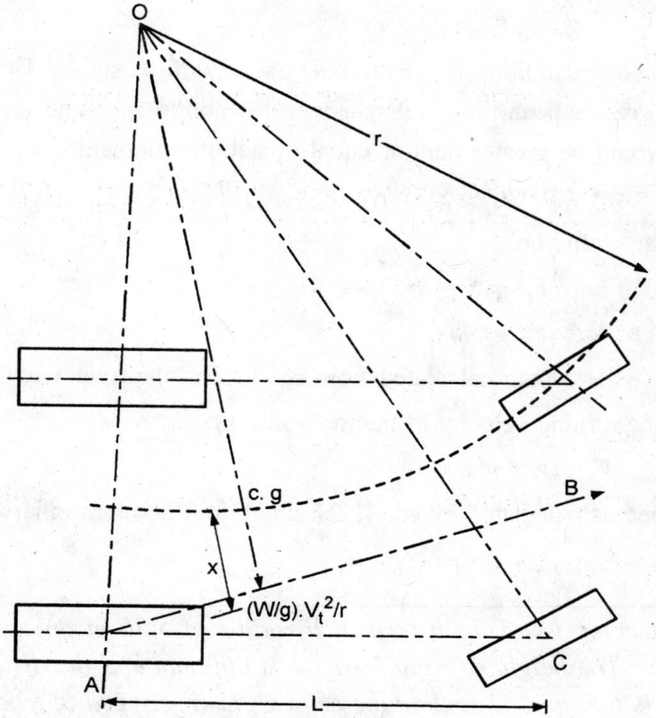


Figure 12.5. Top plan of tractor taking turn

$$F_c = (W/g)\ V_t^2/r \qquad \text{...(12.23)}$$

where $F_c$ = Centrifugal force acting at *c.g.* of tractor, kg or kN

$W$ = Weight of tractor, kg, or kN

$V_t$ = Critical turning speed of tractor, m/s

$r$ = Turning radius of tractor measured from *c.g.* of tractor to turning centre, *m*

$g$ = gravitational constant

This force will cause instability of tractor in lateral direction.

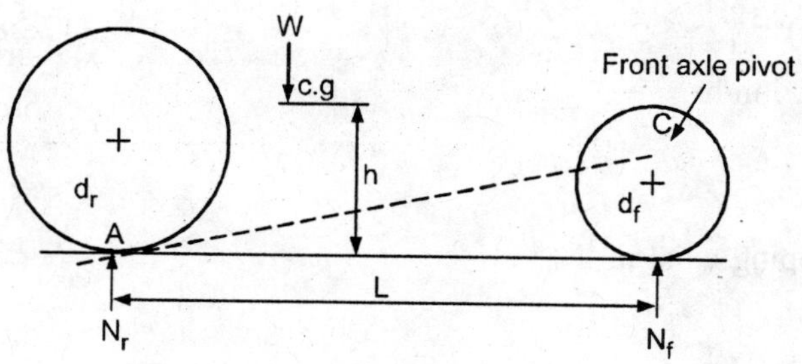


Figure 12.6: Side elevation of tractor taking turn

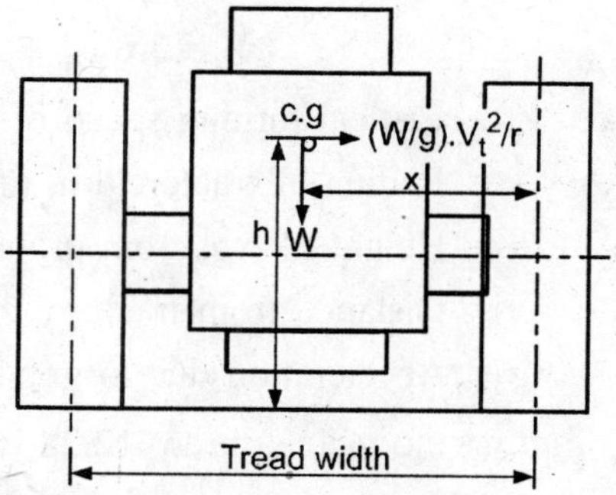


Figure 12.7: Back view of tractor

In order to bring the tractor to stability the stability moment *i.e.* '*Wx*' must be greater than the moment due to centrifugal force.

Or, $$Wx \geq W\,(V_t^2/g \times r)\,h \qquad ...(12.24)$$

As long as the above condition is satisfied the tractor will be stable. The tractor will overturn laterally when the soil reaction on the outer rear wheel becomes zero and under this condition the overturning moment would be greater than or equal to stability moment. *i.e.*

$$Wx \leq W\,(V_t^2/g \times r)\,h \qquad ...(12.25)$$

And limiting case would be

$$x = (V_t^2/g \times r)\,h$$

Or, $$r = (V_t^2/g)\;h/x \qquad ...(12.26)$$

If turning radius is less than calculated from eq. 12.26, the tractor will overturn.

Similarly, limiting turning velocity of tractor would be

$$V_t = (g \times r \times x/h)^{0.5} \qquad ...(12.27)$$

The turning speed as calculated by eq. 12.27 should not be more otherwise the tractor would be unstable.

**EXAMPLE 12.5** *A tractor is taking a turn at a radius of 5.56 m on concrete road without application of brakes. The height of c.g. of tractor is 900 mm and the distance of c.g from the tractor tipping axis is 600 mm. Calculate the critical turning speed of tractor at which lateral tipping of tractor would begin.*

**SOLUTION:**

Radius of tractor turn, $r$ = 5.56 m

Height of c.g. from ground, $h$ = 900 mm

Distance from tractor c.g. to tipping axis, $x$ = 600 mm

Acceleration due to gravity, $g$ = 9.8 m/s$^2$

Let $V_t$ be the tractor turning speed, m/s

Now, we know that;

$$V_t = 3.6\,(g \times r \times x/h)^{0.5} \qquad ...(12.28)$$

where, $V_t$ = Critical turning speed of tractor, km/hr

$r$ = Radius of tractor turn, m

$h$ = Height of *c.g.* from ground, m

$x$ = Distance from tractor *c.g.* to tipping axis, m

$g$ = Acceleration due to gravity, m/s$^2$

Putting the values in eq. 12.28, we get,

$$V_t = 3.6\;[(9.8)\;(5.56)\;(0.600)/0.900]^{0.5}$$

Or, $$V_t = 3.6 \times 6.027 = 21.70 \text{ km/hr}$$ **Ans.**

## 12.6 WEIGHT TRANSFERENCE IN WALKING TYPE 2-WHEEL TRACTOR (POWER TILLER)

The mechanics of power tiller (2-wheel tractor) chassis is the same in principle as in case of conventional four wheel tractor, but the power tiller chassis requires support when pulling a draw bar load in the field. This support can be provided by any one or more of the following:

*i*) Tool, implement or trailer at the rear

*ii*) By a rear wheel

*iii*) A counter balance weight at the front of power tiller

*iv*) By the operator through handles

Let us consider a 2-wheel tractor pulling a load at its draw bar on an uphill slope (Figure: 12.8) as shown below:

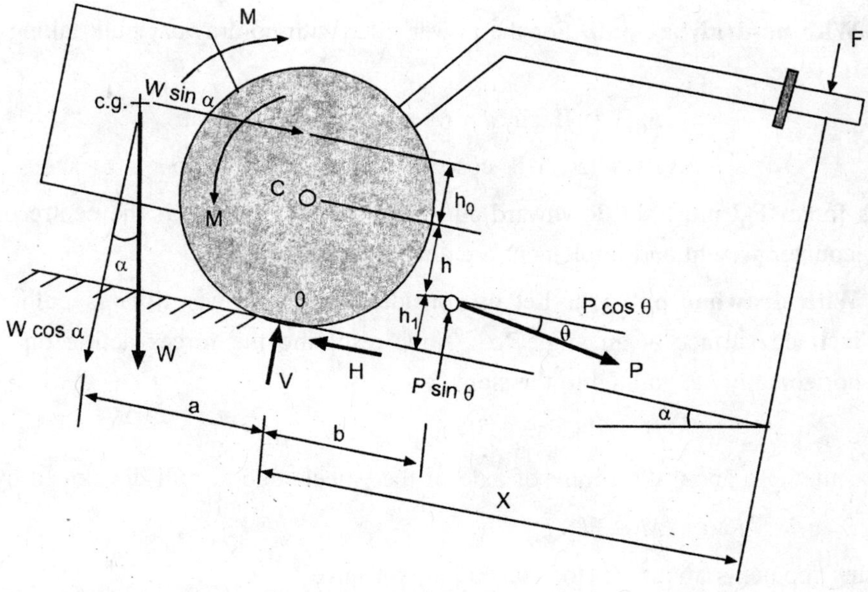


**Figure 12.8. Weight transfer analysis in two wheel tractor on slope**

Normally the location of centre of gravity (*c.g.*) of power tiller would be such that at no-drawbar pull the tractor would tip forward and a counter acting force '*F*' acting downward on its handles would be required to balance it during operation. When the tractor is pulling a load *i.e.* draw bar pull acts, and net moment on the chassis of power tiller will be acting clockwise as shown in figure above and the tractor tends to balance itself during operation.

Now, referring to free body diagram of power tiller (figure above) under static condition, various forces acting on the tractor are

$W$ = Weight of tractor, kg or kN

$F$ = Counter acting force on the handles of power tiller, kg or kN

$M$ = Moment on the chassis of power tiller due to weight, kg-mm or kN-mm

$P$ = Drawbar pull of implement, kg or kN

$V$ = Vertical component or ground reaction at the wheel, kg or kN

$H$ = Draft or tractive force at the wheel, kg or N

$a$ = Distance from axle centre to *c.g.* of tractor, mm

$b$ = Distance from the axle centre to point of hitch, mm

$h_1$ = Height of hitch point from ground, mm

$h_g$ = Height of c.g. from axle centre of wheel, mm

$a$ = Upgrade slope, degrees

$q$ = Angle of line of pull with the horizontal, degrees

***i)* With no-drawbar pull:** For the power tiller with no-drawbar pull, taking moments about '*O*', we get

$$F_0.X = W \sin\alpha \times (r + h_g) = W \cos\alpha \times a$$

**Or,** $$F_0 = (a/X)\, W \cos\alpha - ((r + h_g)/X)\, W \sin\alpha \quad ...(12.29)$$

This force '$F_0$' must act downward as shown in figure above if the centre of gravity of the power till, counter weight and implement are ahead of the axle.

***ii)* With drawbar pull (*P*):** Let us consider that the power tiller is pulling a load on an inclined surface at an angle 'α'. Now, resolving the forces acting on the power tiller horizontally *i.e.* parallel to the slope.

$$H = P \cos\theta + W \sin\alpha \quad ... (12.30)$$

Now, moment about the centre of axle of the wheels due to pull developed by the tractor

$$M = H \times r \quad ... (12.31)$$

Taking moments about '*C*' for the tractor, we have

$$M + W \sin\alpha \times h_g + P\sin\theta \times b + F.X. = W \cos\alpha \times a + P\cos\theta \times (r - h_1) \quad ...(12.32)$$

Putting values of H and M from equations (12.30) & (12.31) we get

$$(P \cos\theta + W \sin\alpha)r + W \sin\alpha \times h_g + P \sin\theta \times b + F.X = W \cos\alpha \times a + P \cos\theta \times (r - h_1)$$

Or, $$F = (a/X)W \cos\alpha - ((r + h_g)/X)\, W \sin\alpha - (h_1/X)\, P \cos\theta - (b/X)\, P \sin\theta \quad ...(12.33)$$

But,

$$(a/X)W \cos\alpha - ((r + h_g)/X)\, W \sin\alpha = F_o$$

So,

$$F = F_0 - (h_1/X) \times P \cos\theta - (b/X) \times P \sin\theta \quad .... (12.34)$$

## 12.7 CENTRE GRAVITY OF TRACTOR

Centre gravity of tractor refers to a point on the body of tractor at which its weight is acting. In rear wheel drive tractors it is usually located at about $2/3^{rd}$ of wheel base ahead of rear wheel axle. Exact location of *c.g.* of a tractor can be determined by using any of the following three methods:

(*i*) Suspension method

(*ii*) Balancing method

(*iii*) Weighing method

### 12.7.1. Determination of Centre of Gravity by Weighing Method

This is the most commonly used method for determination of *c.g.* of four wheel tractor. However, this method also does not consider the effect of movement of oil in crank case, transmission oil and fuel in the partly filled tanks as well as weight and position of operator. So, following assumptions are made in this method.

(*i*) The tractor tyres are rigid and there is no deflection during weighing

(*ii*) The shift of fluid, coolant, and lubricating oil when tractor is tilted are ignored.

Consider that a tractor has weight '*W*' and wheel base '*L*'. The longitudinal and vertical location of its centre of gravity is found out by weighing the front axle of tractor to determine $N_f$.

First the weight on the front wheels of tractor is taken on the level ground as shown Fig. 12.9.

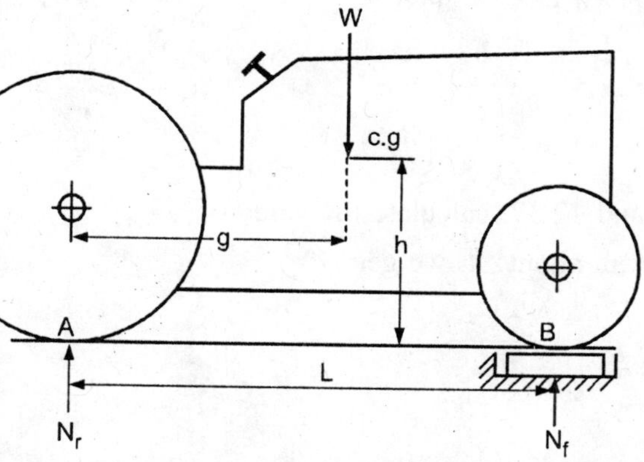


**Figure 12.9: Forces on tractor at level ground**

Referring to free body diagram of forces on level ground, $N_r$ and $N_f$ are the soil reactions against the rear and front wheels respectively.

Now, taking moment about '*A*' we get

$$g = N_f \times L/W \quad ...(12.35)$$

Thus, location of *c.g.* from rear wheel axle of tractor would be at a distance '*g*' and can be calculated by using eq. 12.35.

Determination of height of *c.g.* is quite difficult. This is determined by elevating the front axle of tractor and geometry of tractor in raised position is used for calculation of *c.g.* of tractor. Again, the tractor front wheels are lifted by a known height '$h_1$'which should be adequate to obtain significant difference between reactions $N_f$ and $N_f$ which are measured with the help of weighing scale. The forces acting on a tractor when the front wheels are lifted is shown in Fig. 12.9.

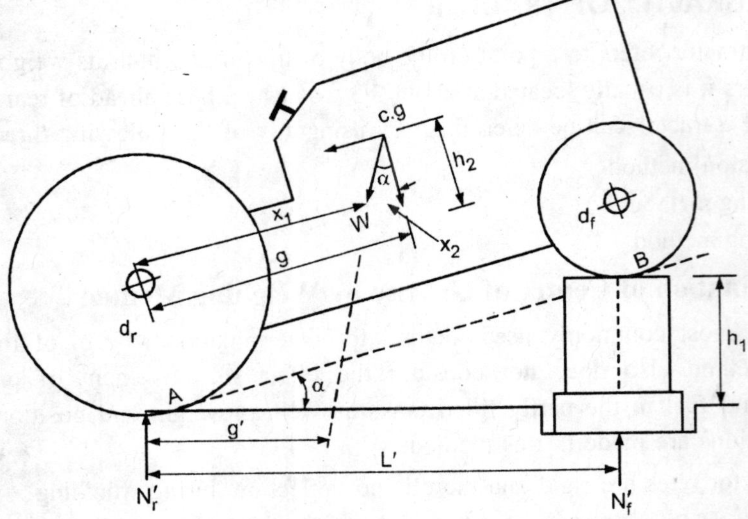


**Figure 12.10: Forces on tractor during front wheels lifted**

Now, the location of *c.g.* is calculated by using the geometry of tractor as given below:

$$L' = \left[ L + \frac{(d_r - d_f)}{\tan \alpha} \right] \cos \alpha \qquad \text{...(12.36)}$$

Also,

$$\sin \alpha = \frac{h_1}{L - \left( \frac{d_f}{2} \right) \sin \alpha} \qquad \text{...(12.37)}$$

Using eqs. 12.36 and 12.37, calculate the value of '*L*'

Again taking moment about '*A*' we get,

$$g' = \frac{N'_f \times L'}{W} \qquad \text{...(12.38)}$$

Also from geometry

$$\tan a = \frac{x_2}{h_2} = \frac{(g - x_1)}{h_2} \qquad \text{...(12.39)}$$

or,

$$h_2 = (g - x_1) \tan \alpha \qquad \text{...(12.40)}$$

Also,

$$\cos \alpha = g'/x_1$$

or,

$$x_1 = g'/\cos \alpha$$

Putting the value of $x_1$ in eq. 12.40, we get

$$h_2 = (g - g'/\cos \alpha)/\tan\alpha$$

Now, height of c.g from ground surface '*h*' is given by

$$h = d_r/2 + h_2$$

where, $h$ = distance of *c.g.* from ground surface, mm

$d_r$ = diameter of rear wheel of tractor, mm

$h_2$ = distance of *c.g.* from center line of rear wheel axle, mm

**EXAMPLE 12.6** *A tractor has following specifications:*

*Total weight of tractor, W = 25 kN*

*Wheel base L = 2170 mm*

*Diameter of rear wheels* $d_r$ *=1450 mm*

*Diameter of front wheels,* $d_f$ *= 740 mm*

*Weight of front wheels on level ground,* $N_f$ *=8.5 kN*

*Weight on front wheels when lifted 420 mm above ground,* $N_f'$ *= 7.5 kN*

*Determine the location of c.g. of tractor.*

**SOLUTION:**

Refer to Fig. 12.9 of tractor on level ground. $N_r$ and $N_f$ are the reactions on rear and front wheels.

Then, $$g = N_f x\ L/W \quad ...(12.41)$$

Putting the values in eqn. 12.35, we get

$$g = 8.5 \times 2170/25 = 737.8 \text{ mm}$$

Now, again refer to Fig. 12.10, when front wheel is raised by 420 mm.

Now, from geometry of tractor

$$L' = \left[ L + \frac{(d_r - d_f)}{\tan \alpha} \right] \cos \alpha \quad (12.42)$$

Putting the values in eq. 12.42, we get

$$L' = [2170 + (1450 - 740) \tan \alpha) \cos \alpha$$

or, $$L' = (2170 + 710 \tan \alpha) \cos \alpha \quad ...(12.43)$$

Again, $$\sin \alpha = h_1/\ (L - (d_f/2) \sin \alpha) \quad ...(12.44)$$

or, $$\sin \alpha = 420/\ (2170 - (740/2) \sin \alpha)$$

or, $$2170 \sin \alpha - 370 \sin^2\alpha = 420$$

or, $$\sin \alpha = 0.195$$

or, $$\alpha = 11.25 \text{ degrees}$$

And, $$\cos \alpha = 0.980$$

Putting the values in eq. 12.43, we get,

$$L' = (2170 + 710 \tan 11.25) \cos 11.25$$

$$L' = 2265.00 \text{ mm}$$

Now, taking moment about '*A*' we get;

$$g' = N'_f \times L'/W$$

or, $$g' = 7.5 \times 2265/25 = 679.5 \text{ mm}$$

Again from geometry of tractor

$$h_2 = (g - g'/\cos \alpha)/\tan \alpha \quad ...(12.45)$$

Putting the values in eq. 12.45, we get,

$$h_2 = (737.8 - 679.5/\cos 11.25)/\tan 11.25$$

or, $$h_2 = (737.8 - 693.4)/0.1989 = 223.22 \text{ mm}$$

Now, $$h = d_r/2 + h_2$$

or, $$h = 1450/2 + 223.22 = 948.22 \text{ mm}$$

Therefore, the location of c.g of tractor would be 737.8 mm ahead of rear axle and 948.22 mm above the ground surface.

## EXERCISES

1. A tractor has front and rear wheel reactions of 10 and 15 kN respectively. Its wheel base is 2000 mm. How far is the C.G of tractor from the rear axle of tractor?
2. A tractor weighing 25 kN is operating on level ground and has front and rear wheel reaction 10 and 15 kN respectively. While operating on level ground, it is exerting a pull of 16 kN. The line of pull is such that $h_r$ and $h_f$ are 300 mm and 930 mm respectively (Refer Fig. 12.11). Determine the rear and front wheel normal reaction of tractor.

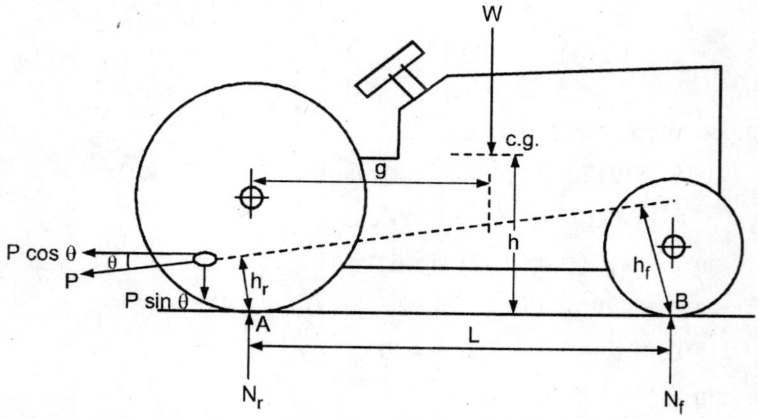


**Figure 12.11: Tractor on operating on level ground**

3. A tractor has front and rear wheel reactions of 10 and 15 kN respectively. Its wheel base is 2000 mm. How far is the C.G. of tractor from the rear axle of tractor?
4. A tractor weighing 25 kN is operating on level ground and has front and rear wheel reaction 10 and 15 kN respectively. While operating on level ground, it is exerting a pull of 16 kN. The line of pull is such that $h_r$ and $h_f$ are 300 mm and 930 mm respectively (Refer Fig. 11.10). Determine the rear and front wheel normal reaction of tractor.
3. A rear wheel drive tractor weighing 36 kN has wheel base 2250 mm. Horizontal distance from the C.G of tractor to rear axle is 800 mm. It is pulling a loaded tractor trailer with a level drawbar pull of 15 kN and the drawbar height is 450 mm. Calculate the weight transfer and dynamic weights on (*a*) Front axle (*b*) Rear axle.

4. A Farmtrac tractor has total weight of 32.5 kN and wheel base of 2500 mm. The static weight of front axle is 14.5 kN. The tractor pull is level at a drawbar height of 420 mm. Calculate the critical pull at which the front wheel of tractor would lift off the ground.

5. A tractor weighing 25 kN has a wheel base of 2150 mm. Its front and rear wheel reactions are 9.5 kN and 15.5 kN respectively on level ground. The respective wheel diameters are 750 mm and 1470 mm. When the front end of tractor is raised by 0.50 m, the reaction at front wheel observed was 8.0 kN. Calculate the position of centre of gravity of tractor.

6. A rear wheel drive tractor weighing 28 kN has a wheel base of 2200 mm and its centre of gravity is located 980 mm ahead of rear axle centre line. The tractor is pulling a load of 14 kN at an angle of 15°. The height of hitch point is 420 mm and 350 mm behind the centre of rear axle. Determine the weight transfer on the rear axle of tractor.

7. Calculate the centre of gravity of tractor which has following specifications:

   Weight of tractor = 32 kN

   Weight on front wheel at level ground = 12kN

   Diameter of rear wheels =1450 mm

   Diameter of front wheels = 700 mm

   Weight on the front wheel raised by 480 mm from the ground = 10.5 kN

Fig. 12.12 shows the forces on tractor at level ground and Fig. 12.13 shows the forces on tractor during front wheels lifted.

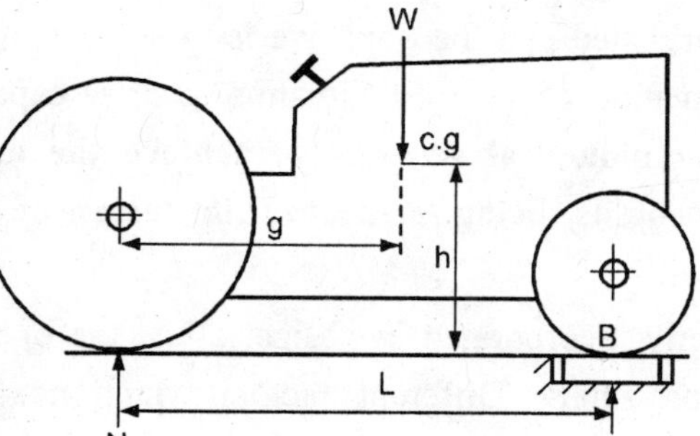


Figure 12.12: Forces on tractor at level ground

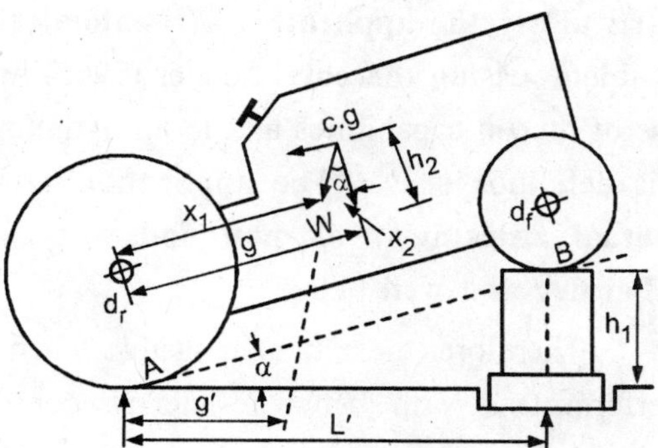


Figure 12.13: Forces on tractor during front wheels lifted

8. A four wheel tractor weighing 28 kN has its c.g. at a height of 950 mm and 1050 mm ahead from the centre line of rear axle and tread width of 1500 mm. Determine the stable turning radius for the tractor when operating at a speed of 12.5 km/hr.

9. A tractor is taking a turn at a radius of 6.0 m on concrete road without application of brakes. The height of c.g. of tractor is 900 mm and the distance of c.g. from the tractor tipping axis is 650 mm. Calculate the critical turning speed of tractor at which lateral tipping of tractor would begin.

CHAPTER 13

# Human Engineering in Tractor Design

## INTRODUCTION

Man as a source of power has very limited power, but as a controller has got unlimited capabilities. Human engineering or ergonomics deals with this aspect of man-machine system which means engineering the product or machine to fit the operator. Modern ergonomics (ergo = work; nomos = laws in greek) virtually became a field of specialization during the second world war, because at that time the objectives was to have maximum operational efficiency, which lead to multi disciplinary approach. There is a slight variation between the approaches of USA and European Scientist, the first category deals mainly with integration of man-machine system, whereas the later deal with welfare of the individual concerned. According to British Research Society (1949), **"Ergonomics deals with the relationship between man and his occupation, equipment and environment, particularly the application of anatomical, physiological and psychological knowledge to the problem arising thereof."** Zander (1965) however stated that the objective is to achieve a rational use of human capabilities and to an optimum adaptation of the work situation to these capabilities. His definition state, **"The application of human biological sciences to achieve the optimum mutual adjustment of man and work, the benefits being measured in terms of human efficiency and well being.**

Therefore, these human factors when properly incorporated in design, allow the operator to perform task with better efficiency, comfort and safety. Different factors which need to be consideredin tractor/farm machinery design from human factor point of view are:

- Operator-Machine interface
- Operator exposure to environmental factors
- Location, arrangement and easy operation of controls
- Operator seating
- Noise and its controls
- Vibration and its control in tractor

This chapter provides detailed information and principles of human factors that are essential in the design of a tractor operator's workplace.

## 13.1 THE OPERATOR-MACHINE INTERFACE

In any activity, the tractor operator receives and processes information and then acts upon it. There are many interfaces between the tractor operator and the tractor; they include various actions such as:

- Riding in and out daily many times
- Maintenance such as cleaning, servicing and refueling
- Riding on and operating the controls for performing desired tasks

Therefore, when a tractor operator operates the tractor, the sensing and decision making and muscular powers of the operator are attached to an engineering system (tractor). The tractor operator uses sensory system; hearing, sight, sense of smell, touch, heat/cold or feels through nervous system to the brain. The brain feels senses and interprets the inputs from the machine; the operator will then take action as a result of the decision and to interface the control instruments through manipulation to achieve the desired output of the tractor as shown in Fig. 13.1.

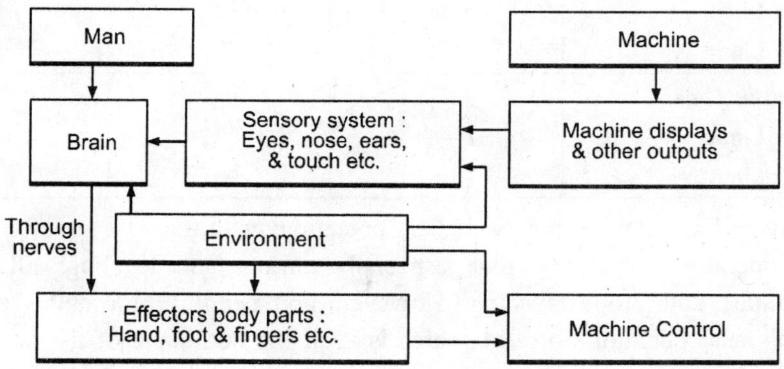


**Fig. 13.1: Man-machine interface**

For design of workplace for a tractor operator, Hansson *et. al.* (1970) reported that following important factors/parameters should be kept in view:

1. Safety, comfort and convenience of the operator.
2. Location and construction of the operator's work place.
3. The work place should be located on the machine so that visibility in the driving position is good without requiring the operator to work in an awkward, tiring position.
4. The operator should be able to change his working position easily.
5. Levers, pedals and instruments should be conveniently and logically located.
6. The work place should fit both tall and short operators.
7. The work area should be free of sharp edges and obstructions such as transmission cases.

## 13.2 THE OPERATOR EXPOSURE TO ENVIRONMENTAL FACTORS

Agricultural tractors are generally used under varying agro-climatic conditions. The tractor operators are exposed directly to thermal stresses due to excessive environmental temperatures, humidity, wind, dust and even chemicals during spraying and dusting operations. These environmental parameters especially temperature, humidity, air flow and dust concentrations have considerable bearings on performance and safety of tractor operator. Most of the parameters are interrelated and the tractor operator needs to be provided with a comfortable environment in order to enhance his work efficiency and safety. These parameters must be considered for design of operators enclosures of tractor to minimize their effect and provide thermal comfort and quality air in the enclosures. The comfort and bearable zones of temperature, humidity and air ventilation rates are reported in Table 13.1. However, the effect of ultraviolet radiations on humans is not known so far.

**TABLE 13.1: Comfort and bearable zones of different environmental parameters**

| Sr. No. | Environmental Zone | Environmental Parameters | | |
|---|---|---|---|---|
| | | Temperature (°C) | Humidity (%) | Ventilation rate ($m^3$/min) |
| I | **Comfort Zone** | | | |
| | Lower Limit | 18 | 30 | 0.37 |
| | Upper Limit | 24 | 70 | 0.57 |
| II | **Bearable Zone** | | | |
| | Lower Limit | – 1 | 10 | 0.14 |
| | Upper Limit | 38 | 90 | 1.4 |

**Dust exposure:** During performance of field operations with tractor a lot of dust is generated near the tractor operator's breathing zone especially during land leveling, tillage, harvesting (combining operation) and crop threshing. However, no specific information about the dust concentration levels near operator's breathing area is available but, some of the dust concentration reported in field operations are:

- In tillage operations peak dust concentrations of 577 mg/$m^3$ with mean value of 146 mg/$m^3$ have been reported
- Permissible guideline limit for dust concentration on combines in Netherlands is 15 mg/$m^3$.
- In tractor's pressurized cab at 50 Pa fitted with air filters of fine quality, dust concentration of 24.7 mg/$m^3$ in operator's breathing zone has been found.

**Exposure to chemicals :** Greater use of pesticides in the field crops exposes the tractor operator to hazardous chemicals during plant protection operations. Therefore, in pesticide application operations the tractor operator should either use personal protective equipments or tractor cab/ enclosure as a protective device.

## 13.3 THERMAL COMFORT FOR TRACTOR OPERATOR

**Thermal comfort:** It is defined as state of mind that expresses satisfaction with the thermal environment. Thermo-dynamic heat exchange process between tractor operator and his environment was given by Gagge *et. al* (1941) as given below:

$$S = M - E \pm R \pm C - W \qquad ...(13.1)$$

where, $S$ = amount of heat gained or lost, if body is in thermal balance, $S = 0$.

If $S$ has positive value, it will cause the mean body temperature to rise and negative value will cause it to fall.

$M$ = metabolism, 70–140 watts/m$^2$
$E$ = evapotranspiration
$R$ = Radiation
$C$ = Convection
$W$ = work accomplished

The above heat exchange is related with the operator's body surface area. The metabolic rate for a tractor operator will be in the range of 70–140 watts/m$^2$. Average body surface area of a man will be 2m$^2$ resulting in 140–348 watts. In order to maintain thermal equilibrium tractor enclosure environment must be maintained to balance the metabolism of tractor operator.

## 13.3.1. Metabolic Heat of Operator

Amount of heat produced in the body by metabolism depending on activity being performed by the operator is expressed by the following **metabolic energy equation**:

$$I = W + M + S \qquad ...(13.2)$$

where, $I$ = energy input via nutrition
$W$ = external work done by the operator
$M$ = metabolic heat generated in the body of operator
$S$ = energy stored in the body

Or

$$I - W = \text{Constant} = M + S \qquad ...(13.3)$$

The system is in balance if all the metabolic energy $M$ is dissipated to environment without change in quantity $S$. The metabolic energy required to perform different physical activities is given in Table 13.2.

**TABLE 13.2: Metabolic energy required to perform different physical activities**

| Activity | Heat produced | |
|---|---|---|
| | (Kcal/min) | (KJ/min) |
| Basal condition | 1 | 4.3 |
| Light physical work | <3.50 | <13.0 |
| Moderately heavy physical work | 3.50–5.25 | 13.0–22.0 |
| Heavy physical work | >5.25 | 22.0 |

## 13.3.2. Heat Exchange Between Operator Body and Environment

Heat from the tractor operator body is exchanged with the environment through Radiation ($R$), Convection ($C$) and Evaporation ($E$) as given below:

$$M \pm R - E = \pm S \qquad ...(13.4)$$

where, $M$ = heat metabolism (according to level of physical activity)
$C$ = convection heat gain or loss
$R$ = radiation heat gain or loss
$E$ = evaporative heat loss
$S$ = amount of heat gain or loss by tissues of body. In case of thermal equilibrium $S = 0$

***Heat exchange through radiation***

Radiant heat gain or loss by the tractor operator is given by

$$R = 5.7\ (t_s - t_r) \quad \text{...(13.5)}$$

where, $R$ = radiant loss or gain, kcal/m$^2$/hr

$t_s$ = skin temperature, °C

$t_r$ = radiant temperature of surface, °C

***Heat exchange through convection***

The heat gain or loss by the operator through convection is given by

$$C = 0.5\sqrt{V}\ (t_s - t_a) \quad \text{...(13.6)}$$

where, $C$ = amount of heat loss/gain in kcal/m$^2$/hr

$V$ = air speed, m/min

$t_s$ = skin temperature, °C

$t_a$ = air temperature, °C

## 12.3.3. Thermal Comfort in Operator Enclosures

**Tractor enclosure design:** The tractor operator's enclosure must provide clear air and proper air velocity, temperature and humidity for his thermal comfort to enhance his work efficiency and safety. Therefore, the enclosure design must include cab pressurization, filtration, air filtration, air movement, heating, cooling and window defrosting etc.

**Comfort equation:** To predict comfortable environment in terms of combination of air temperature, mean radiant temperature, air humidity and relative velocity, Fanger (1972) developed following comfort equation:

$$F\ (H/A_{Du}, I_{cl}, t_a, t_{mrt}, P_a, V) = 0 \quad \text{...(13.7)}$$

where,

$H/A_{Du}$ = internal heat production per unit body surface area ($A_{Du}$ = DuBois area)

A tractor operator will expend 150 kcal/h.m$^2$

Secondary person will average 50 kcal/h.m$^2$

$I_{cl}$ = thermal resistance of clothing

Heavy clothing values of 0.5, 1.0, 1.5 clo respectively.

$t_a$ = air temperature. °C

$t_{mrt}$ = mean radiant temperature, °C

On bright sunny day $t_{mrt}$ can be 5°C to 10°C above cab air temperature

$P_a$ = pressure of water vapour in ambient air

$V$ = relative air velocity, m/s. Cab air velocity should be in the range of 1 to 3 m/s.

Above comfort equation developed by Fanger can be effectively used to predict the effect of any combination of environmental factors on the comfortable environment for a clothed tractor operator performing field operations especially during summer season.

**Effective Temperature Scale (*ET*):** Effective temperature is based on simple model of human physiological response and is defined as an empirical index for human thermal comfort. Most individual will be comfortable if *ET* (Effective Temperature) is between 24°C and 27°C. The operator can make appropriate adjustments to meet his comfort by changing following environmental factors:

- Air speed and its direction
- Air temperature
- Clothing worn

## 13.4 SPATIAL, VISUAL AND CONTROL REQUIREMENT OF THE OPERATOR

**Work place layout:** The layout of workplace should be compatible with not only system performance requirement but also with the user. It should also ensure safety and comfort of operator and controls must be within the reach to minimize error. Proper workplace layout requires consideration of workplace dimensions, controls and operations being controlled with due regard to:

(*i*) The operator's size
(*ii*) His position and the directions in which he can most easily work
(*iii*) The optimum spaces in which he can manipulate the controls
(*iv*) Arrangement of controls and displays
(*v*) Visual requirement for maximum operator efficiency
(*vi*) *Working posture of the operator viz. sitting, standing or squatting*
(*vii*) Special influence such as protective clothing.

To decide about proper workplace layout following important factors must be considered:

1. Anthropometric parameters of operators
2. Placement of operator on tractor for optimum work task vision or vision of displays
3. Placement of controls in optimum areas for the operators.

### 13.4.1. Anthropometric Data

Human being must not only fit spatially in a man task system, but must also be able to move in the work space. With the aid of anthropometric data we can provide an optimum work space layout, including good posture, contributing to considerable decrease in work load and an improvement in the performance. In design of work space and other facilities various considerations need to be taken. In particular, the type of people and their dody dimensions as given in Table 13.3. Normally, during collection of human engineering data skip the first and last five percentile. Thus while designing a seat, it should be designed to accommodate a reasonable range of individuals, usually from $5^{th}$ to $95^{th}$ percentiles. The seat must be adjustable in a fast, easy and safe way- in horizontal and vertical direction to realize an adoption to the measurements of various population groups. Seat should be designed to take maximum weight expected. In order to realize a good performance, it is necessary that the movements of the body members are in synchrony, simple and logical motions are made, which can be performed almost automatically by the central nervous system. Lower percentile values of seat height and seat depth should be taken. Layout studies can be carried out to find maximum and optimum work space area.

**TABLE 13.3 : Body dimensions of tractor operators**

| Sr. No | Dimensions | Percentile | | |
|---|---|---|---|---|
| | | 5th | 50th | 95th |
| 1. | Height, cm | 162 | 173 | 185 |
| 2. | Seating height erect, cm | 84 | 91 | 97 |
| 3. | Seating height normal, cm | 80 | 87 | 93 |
| 4. | Knee height, cm | 49 | 54 | 59 |
| 5. | Popliteal height, cm | 39 | 44 | 49 |
| 6. | Elbow rest height, cm | 19 | 24 | 30 |
| 7. | Thigh clearance height, cm | 11 | 15 | 18 |
| 8. | Buttock knee height, cm | 54 | 59 | 64 |
| 9. | Buttock Popliteal length, cm | 44 | 50 | 55 |
| 10. | Elbow to elbow breadth, cm | 35 | 42 | 51 |
| 11. | Seat breadth, cm | 31 | 36 | 40 |
| 12. | Weight, Kg | 58 | 75 | 98 |

## 13.4.2. Placement of Operator for Optimum Vision

The seat of tractor must give the operator an optimum field of vision and be in a position on the tractor which helps give him comfortable and safe operating conditions. Tractor operator may require vision to front and rear, or front and sides. A wide field of vision is required for both short and long ranges. Moreover close range vision is required during handling of mounted implements. These visibility requirements are satisfied by upright seating posture in order to permit easy movements of head and upper torso from the front, to side, or rear as required gathering necessary visual information. Good visibility for the operator is more important than excessive number of displays, especially when the machine is operating satisfactorily. The display area has to be close to the operator's line of vision which require only minimum eye movements away from his task. The guidelines given in Figs. 13.2 and 13.3 and Table 13.4 would be quite helpful in designing the location of displays of tractor in relation to the operator.

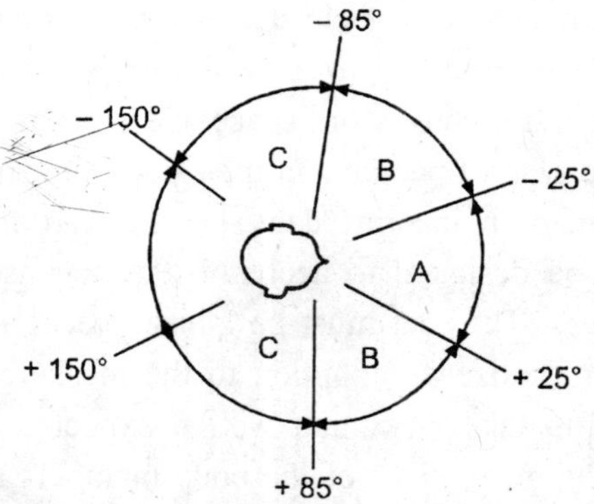


A- Stationary field B- Eye field C- Head field

**Figure 13.2: Visual field of tractor operator in horizontal place**

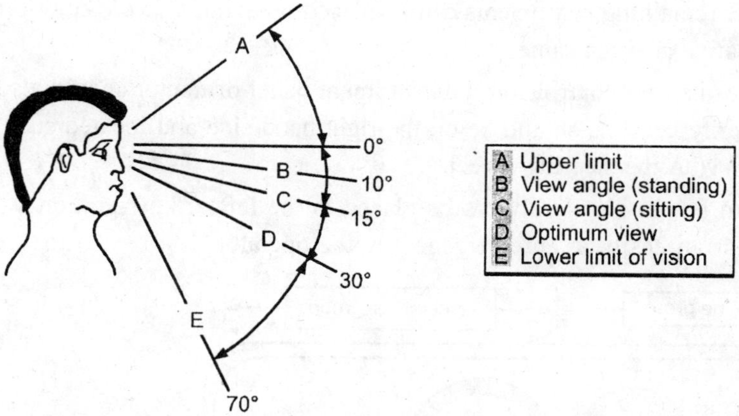


**Figure. 13.3: Visual field of tractor operator (vertical plane)**

**TABLE 13.4: Optimum vision of operators**

| Type of movement | Direction | Lateral | | Direction | Vertical | |
|---|---|---|---|---|---|---|
| | | Opt. | Max. | | Opt. | Max. |
| Head rotation only | Left and right | 0 | 60 | Up and down | 0 | 50 |
| Eye rotation only | -do- | 15 | 35 | -do- | 0<br>30 | 25<br>35 |
| Head and eye rotation | -do- | 15 | 95 | -do- | 0<br>30 | 75<br>85 |

## 13.4.3. Design of Instrument Panel of Tractor

Good visibility for the tractor operator is more important than abundant displayed information about the tractor. In order to have proper visibility over the various displays, the instrument panel of tractor should be close to the operator's line of vision with minimum eye movement away from the tasks. This would require prime instrument panel that would enhance operator's performance and minimize error. The instruments and panel controls should be logically positioned on the tractor so that all operators become familiar with the system and be able to drive the tractor with confidence. The instrument panel grouping in a tractor is given in Fig. 13.4.

For instrument panel design main guidelines to be followed are:

1. The instrument panel designed should be symmetrical as far as possible.
2. A central zone of high priority instruments panel should be in 30° cone for easy eye movements which is 380 mm wide at 700 mm from the operator's eye.
3. Similar functions instruments or controls should be grouped on the panel.
4. The size of related group of instruments should be same.
5. The gauges should be grouped in the priority zone horizontally and according to their functions *e.g.* engine gauges to the left, steering column, or tachometer or group of indicator lights at the panel center and other functional gauges to the right side.

6. All other remaining instruments can be placed on either side of the priority group and keep their relative position same.
7. The placement of controls on the instrument panel of tractor should also follow standards. The priority controls should be on the right hand side and located such that they may not interfere with the steering wheel.
8. The horn button should always be placed to the left of key ignition switch so that it can be found out easily in an emergency by the operator.

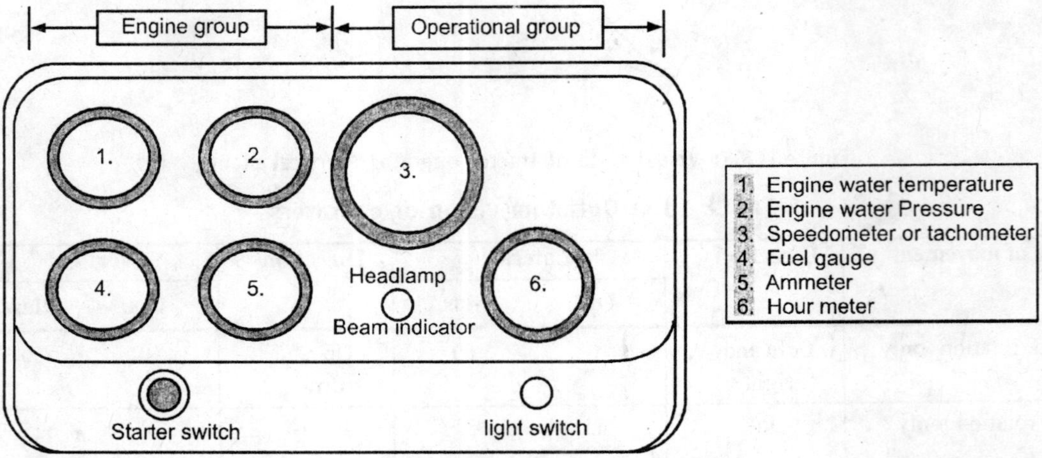


**Figure 13.4: Instrument panel grouping in a tractor**

## 13.4.4. Control Requirements of Operator

A control is a device or hardware that can be considered as a link between the tractor and operator which converts the output of operator into input and change of state of tractor. Concept of optimum dimensions and limiting dimensions is used in placement of controls in space and dimensions usually chosen to define boundaries of the space is estimated to cater for $5^{th}$ to $95^{th}$ percentiles of operators. The optimum dimension defines the most desirable space or ideal area for the location of most important and frequently used controls both in neutral position as well as in working position in any direction. The limiting dimensions define the acceptable but not the most desirable space for location of controls as the controls are neither too close nor too far from the operator. Generally following two types of controls are used in tractors.

(*i*) Hand controls

(*ii*) Foot controls.

**13.4.4.1. Hand controls:** Variety of hand controls is commensurate with the versatility of the hands. Hand controls can be operated either in sitting position or standing position but, seated position is preferred to the standing position especially when the controls are used for any length of time. Use of controls in standing position is less efficient and results in fatigue. Moreover, the accuracy of movement will be lesser in standing position. Hand controls are precise and have high speed. Certain hand controls can be used effectively without vision or without looking at the control *e.g.* gear levers. Hand controls are much more accurate and are preferred to foot control where, (*i*) Accuracy of control positioning is important.

(*ii*) Continuous or prolonged application of moderate or large forces (89N or more) is necessary.

**Location of Hand controls :** The comfort zones are easy to reach and the controls which do not require movement of upper body should be located based on anthropometric dimensions of tractor operators. The comfort angles of hands should be maintained for easy reach of controls. The forearm should not be raised much above the horizontal to avoid fatigue. The controls must look efficient, attractive and easy to use. When all controls in a tractor are put together, it is desirable that these are logically arranged in orderly manner and well balanced and well placed that enables the operator to perceive the interrelationship. Preferred hand should be used where speed, accuracy or strength of controls movement is important. The optimum area of hand controls for adult operators in seated position is given in Fig. 13.5.

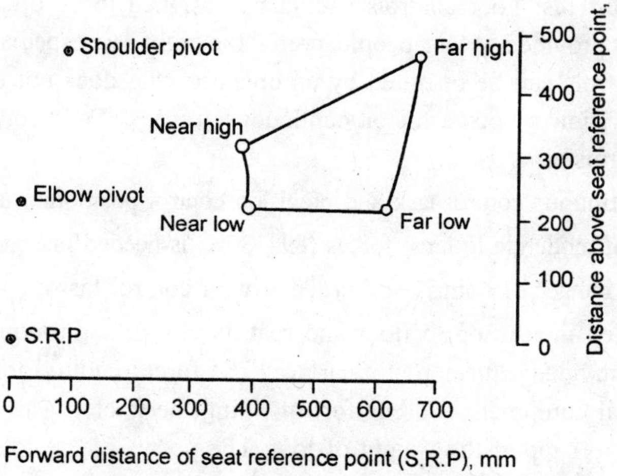


**Fig. 13.5: Optimum area of hand controls for adult operators in seated position**

For proper location of hand control following points must be kept in mind.

1. Normally the dimensions of control placement are with respect to seat reference point.
2. The reference point should be adjustable at least 75 mm horizontally and 125 mm vertically.
3. Recommended dimensions for optimum manual control area is about 600 mm wide and 300 mm to either side of midline.
4. When all controls cannot be placed with in the optimum area, locations immediately adjacent to optimum control areas are more desirable than those farther away.
5. The upper arm should make 50° angles with the upper body line and the fore arm should be 165° to the upper arm.
6. The controls must be kept approximately in a line ahead of shoulder joint so that the elbow is not required to move sideways from the body at angle more than 20°.

7. Grouping of the controls is important. Primary controls which are used continuously for a longer period of time should be placed as near to or within the horizontal planes 0–300 mm.
8. The controls such as engine and transmission (throttle, gear shift), hydraulic function controls which require accurate manipulation should be grouped and placed on the right hand side of operator.
9. The controls which generally do not require accurate adjustment *i.e.* P.T.O clutch, differential lock, parking brake can be provided towards left hand side of operator. However, these must be visible and reached easily by the operator. Steering wheel can be operated by left hand during use of other controls.
10. A difference in shape in knobs of different controls will help avoid errors in their use separately. Moreover clearance between the adjacent knobs should be 25–50 mm. If these controls are used blindly their spacing should be 125–175 mm with shape coded knobs.

**13.4.4.2. Foot controls:** Foot controls should be designed to be operated in seated position and backrest should be provided. Most people prefer the right leg especially for critical tasks. A maximum of 4 foot controls can be operated by an operator who does not require skill or practice. These are best for provision of powerful or continuous force. Foot controls are to be used in preference to hand controls where,

(*a*) There is continuous control task and precision control positioning is not important.

(*b*) Application of moderate to large forces (89–130N) is needed intermittently or continuously.

(*c*) Hands are in danger of being overburdened with control tasks.

Pedals are provided in relation to floor and seat, based on anthropometric data of operators. The pedals should be provided with non slip surface. The force required to operate each control is dependent on mechanical equipment and comfort of riding the tractor. The restoring force of pedal should be large enough to support the weight of foot. The pedals are divided into two groups:

(*i*) **Group-I:** When the force used by the leg is above 44–89N, *e.g.* brake pedals

(*ii*) **Group-II:** Where small force (about 44N) is largely obtained from the ankle for continuous operation *e.g.* accelerator pedal.

**Location of foot controls :** After determination of optimum seat position on the tractor, location of most frequently used controls in relation to seat should be provided for comfort and safety of operator. The size, shape and location of foot controls and the space in which the operator has to work must be decided based on anthropometric dimensions of operators from $5^{th}$ percentile to $95^{th}$ percentile. Both small and large operators sit with their heels on the same heel point. The optimum foot pedal area may be selected by locating the comfort zones which are easy to reach. The optimum pedal area for location of foot controls both in neutral position and when displaced in any direction is shown in Fig. 13.6. The angle of comfort of leg 20° either side of centre may be taken for location of foot controls and accordingly brake pedal and clutch pedals may be positioned.

(*a*) For light pedal pressures (44–89N), the foot should be applied to the pedal so that long axis of the tibia (lower leg) is immediately over and in line with the axis of pivot of pedal.

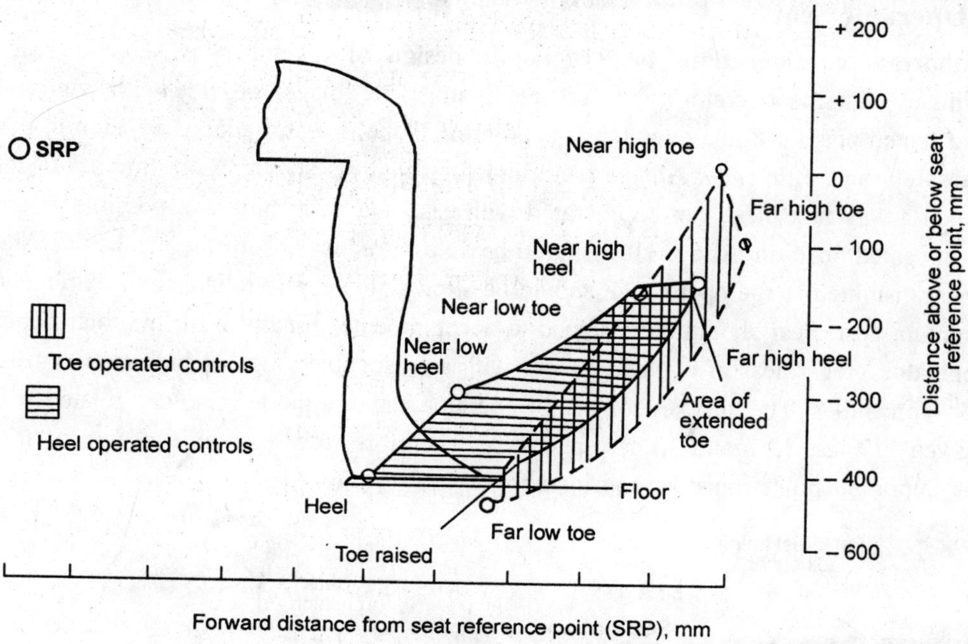


**Fig. 13.6: Optimum foot pedal area for seated tractor operator**

(*b*) The long axis of foot and lower leg should form 90° angle, thus requiring least muscular effort to hold the foot in position.

For location of foot controls in seated position in optimum areas, there are following three main considerations:

**(*i*) The fore and aft location:** The distance from seat reference point (S.R.P) to pedal is an important determinant of amount of pressure exertible on the foot control, as smaller the distance more the exertible force.

**(*ii*) Vertical location:** Where comfort matters more than the exertible force, the foot pedals can be placed below S.R.P. by vertical distances varying from type of task performed.

**(*iii*) Lateral fore and aft location:** As pedals are moved laterally from midline of leg, the exertible force decreases and discomfort of operator increases. The reduction in exertible force is related with the lateral distance and is given in Table 13.5.

**TABLE 13.5: Relation between lateral distance of leg and exertible force**

| Sr. No. | Lateral distance on either side of leg, mm | Reduction in exertible force (%) |
|---|---|---|
| 1. | 75 | 10.0 |
| 2. | 175 | 27.0 |
| 3. | 250 | 37.0 |

Therefore, when placement of pedal at leg mid line is not possible, it should be displaced only 75–125 mm from mid line.

## 13.4.5. Operator Seat

**Important considerations for ergonomic design of tractor seat:** Tractor seat is most closely linked with the operator's comfort and it must be able to provide with comfortable and controlled seated posture to the operator. It must provide the operator adequate vision to perform all the tasks safely and efficiently. All the hand and foot controls should be positioned in relation to seat in such a way that these can be operated with ease and with minimum possible efforts by the operator in seated position. Above all it should be able to reduce/absorb the mechanical shocks and vibrations transmitted to the operator. It should be strong, stable, and reliable and extremely durable with minimum cost. Seat should be designed to accommodate, equally well, the total population of tractor operators, regardless of age and gender with a reasonable range of individuals, usually from $5^{th}$ to $95^{th}$ percentiles. The top view of tractor operator seat and the terminology related with tractor seat is given in Figs. 13.7 and 13.8 respectively. Therefore, for ergonomic design of tractor seat following important points must be considered:

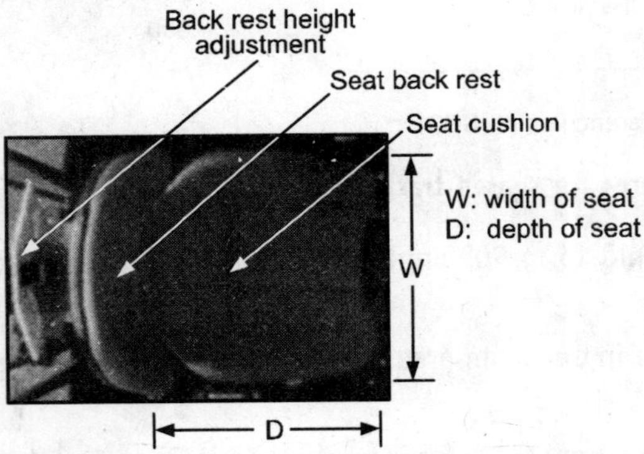


**Figure 13.7: Top view of tractor operator seat**

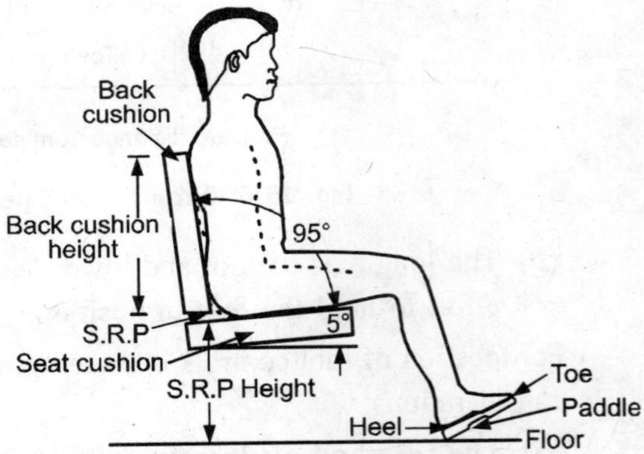


**Figure 13.8: Tractor operator seat**

1. **Seat height range:**

(*i*) The seat height should accommodate 5 to 95% population. So, based on anthropometric data, the seat height for small people with a 10 cm seat adjustment to accommodate larger people should be selected.

(*ii*) Seat adjustments should provide at least 150 mm of fore and aft movement for accommodating larger size operators.

(*iii*) Seat adjustments should provide at least 100 mm of vertical movement to accommodate larger size operators.

2. **Seat width:** The seat width should be selected for 95% population.

3. **Seat depth:** Again, it should accommodate 95% population.

4. **Seat cushion:**

(*i*) Weight of buttocks and thighs should be properly supported by a seat cushion. Human buttocks have bony structure known as **ischial tuberosities** are capable of transmitting body weight directly and uniformly from spinal column to the seat cushion. If seat cushion is not properly designed according to physiology of buttock region, after a prolonged time (2 to 4 hours) it may result in high degree of discomfort or pain to the operators.

(*ii*) Most of body weight of operator should be supported by ischial tuberosities. Peak pressure under the ischial tuberosities should be limited to 90 g/cm$^2$ by providing flat and firm cushion in the central region of seat.

(*iii*) The pressure in the thighs of operator should be limited to 30 g/cm$^2$ to avoid pinching of nerves of thighs which can be accomplished by cushion contour, cushion tilt, cushion firmness at the front and seat height above the foot support.

(*iv*) The seat cushion should be elevated by 5 degree seat angle from horizontal from the front side of seat.

**5. Back cushion:**

1. In order to minimize backache and fatigue the upper body of operator should be properly supported by cushion known as lumbar support according to natural geometrical shape of spinal column for the required operating posture.
2. The included angle between the thigh and spine or angle between back rest and seat should be at least 95°.
3. Backrest must support the lumbar back properly for longer period of sitting. The lumbar support should be adjustable to fit particular operating conditions.
4. The back cushion/support up to sacral level (75 to 150 mm above seat cushion in compressed position) should provide firm support to the operator's back during normal operation *i.e.* reaction forces due to foot pedal operations.
5. For free swing of shoulders and arms the back cushion width of tractor seat should be limited to 330 mm.
6. For free swing of shoulders and arms the back cushion height of tractor seat should be limited to 300 mm.

**6. Arm rests:**

(*i*) Armrests should be provided for support and comfort to shoulders.

(*ii*) Armrests should be adjustable vertically for varying sizes of persons.

**7. Location of controls in relation to seat:**

(*i*) All the hand and foot controls should be positioned in relation to seat in such a way that these can be operated with ease and with minimum possible efforts by the operator in seated position.

(*ii*) Leg to thigh angle should 110–120° for pedal operation with a minimum foot- to-leg angle of 90°.

Based on anthropometric data of tractor operators the optimum design of seat incorporating all the desirable features are reported in Fig. 13.9 and Table 13.6 given below:

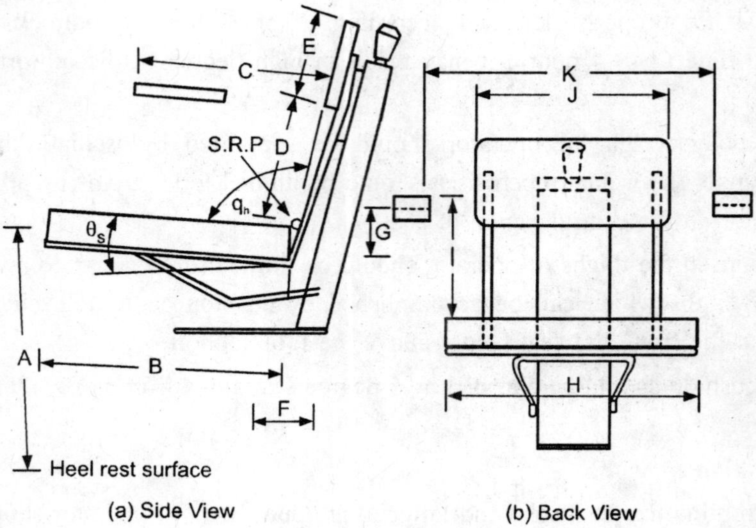


**Figure 13.9: Optimum design of tractor seat**

**TABLE 13.6 : Optimum tractor seat design dimensions, mm**

| Sr. No. | Description | Item | Maximum | Minimum | Nominal |
|---|---|---|---|---|---|
| 1. | S.R.P height | *A* | — | 375 | 400 |
| 2. | Seat depth | *B* | 400 | 375 | — |
| 3. | Distance of arm length from seat back | *C* | 150 | 125 | — |
| 4. | Distance of S.R.P from lower end back | *D* | 200 | 175 | — |
| 5. | Back cushion length | *E* | 150 | 125 | — |
| 6. | Fore and aft. Adjustment | *F* | 150 | 100 | — |
| 7. | Vertical adjustment | *G* | | | |
| 8. | Seat cushion width | *H* | — | — | 475 |
| 9. | Back cushion width | *I* | 325 | — | — |
| 10. | Arm rest height | *J* | 250 | 200 | — |
| 11. | Arm rest lateral spacing | *K* | — | — | 475 |
| 12. | Seat cushion angle | $\theta_s$ | 7° | 5° | — |
| 13. | Back cushion angle | $\theta_b$ | 115° | 110° | — |

**EXAMPLE 13.1** *Using anthropometric data provided in Table 13.3, determine the operator work place dimensions for the following:*

*(i) Seat height range*
*(ii) Seat depth (front range)*
*(iii) Seat width*
*(iv) Arm rest width and height*
*(v) Height inside the tractor cab*

**SOLUTION :**

(*i*) **Seat height range:** The seat height should accommodate 5–95% population. So, based on anthropometric data, we select the seat height for small people with a 10 cm adjustment to accommodate larger people with seat adjustments.

So, seat height = Popliteal height (39 cm) + 10 cm adjustment = 49 cm

(*ii*) **Seat width:** The seat width should be selected for 95% population. So, from data the seat width should be 40 cm.

(*iii*) **Seat depth:** Again, it should accommodate 95% population. It is equal to buttock popliteal length. It should be less than 55 cm

(*iv*) **Arm rest width and height:** From data, seat elbow height for 5% population = 19 cm

And, elbow breadth for 95% population = 51 cm

(*v*) **Height inside the cab:** The height inside the cab should be 5–10 cm more than normal seating height.

So, Height = 93.0 cm + 7 cm = 100 cm Ans.

## 13.5 OPERATOR EXPOSURE TO NOISE

Zander (1965) stated that the application of human biological sciences to achieve the optimum mutual adjustment of man and work, the benefits being measured in terms of human efficiency and well being. Human factors when properly incorporated in design, allow the operator to perform task with better efficiency, comfort and safety. In tractor design, noise is one of the important factors which need to be considered, as the design of tractor operator work place has direct impact on noise levels at operators' ear level. Noise is unwanted sound and its effect depends on frequency, sound pressure level and duration of exposure. Noise in tractor is generated due to rotating and reciprocating parts, vibrations in engine components, exhaust gases and flow of hydraulic fluids. It is transmitted by the moving (rotating, reciprocating and vibrating) structural components of tractor or air borne or combination of the two. The tractors generate sound in the range of 125–500 Hz while the hearing range of human ear is 16 to 22,000 Hz depending upon age and ear sensitivity. Hence, continued exposure of tractor noise to its operator will have harmful effects on their comforts and efficiency. Noise has annoying and damaging effect. Therefore, the design of mechanical components of tractor and its engine to limit the sound energy levels to acceptable levels for operator's comfort and efficiency is a challenge for the design engineers.

**Noise:** It is defined as acoustic sound or unwanted sound and is wasted energy damaging to human ear which is physically speaking, mechanical vibrations in gaseous, fluid or solid medium. It is characterized by frequency, amplitude and phase. The simplest vibration is a pure tone that consists of sinusoid with frequency (Fig. 13.10).

The frequency is given by

$$f = 1/T \qquad \text{...(13.8)}$$

where, $T$ = period in seconds.

The magnitude of noise is usually expressed in terms of RMS (root mean square) value, which is given by

$$A_{RMS} = (1/\sqrt{2})\ A_{PEAK} \qquad \text{...(13.9)}$$

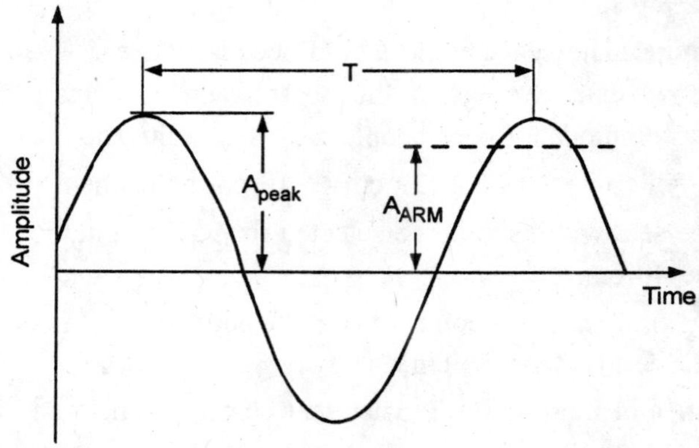


**Figure 13.10: Sinusoidal sound wave with peak and RMS amplitudes**

It is measured with the help of noise level or decibel meter which has got three frequency weighing scales A, B and C. It is expressed in terms of dB (A). The sound level meter incorporates electrical circuits known as weighing networks. A, B, C scale operating conditions can be selected on the sound level meter. Least sensitivity is provided in A-scale and highest in C-scale. A-scale is used for measuring frequencies that human ear can detect.

**Sound pressure level (SPL):** It is expressed as sound pressure level (SPL) relative to reference sound pressure.

$$SPL = 20 \log P/P_0,\ dB \qquad ...(13.10)$$

And
$$SPL = 20 \log P/0.00002 \qquad ...(13.11)$$

where, $P$ = measured RMS sound pressure, $N/m^2$

$P_0$ = reference sound pressure, $N/m^2$

log = logarithm to the base 10

**EXAMPLE 13.2** *In a tractor near its exhaust pipe at a sound pressure of 1 N/m² the noise level recorded is 94 dB. Calculate the increase in sound level if the sound pressure is doubled.*

**SOLUTION:**

Sound pressure = 1 $N/m^2$

Noise level at 1 $N/m^2$ sound pressure = 94 dB

Now, we know that

$$SPL = 20 \log P/P_0,\ \text{dB}$$

Or,
$$SPL = 20 \log P/0.0002,\ \text{dB}$$

Now,
$$SPL_1 = 94 \text{ dB (given)}$$

When
$$P_2 = 2\ P_1 = 2 \times 1\ N/m^2$$

Then, $SPL_2 = 20 \log 2.0/0.0002$, dB

$SPL_2 = 20 \log 10^5$

$SPL_2 = 20 \times 5 = 100$ dB

Therefore, increase in sound level due to doubling in sound pressure in tractor exhaust pipe is

$SPL_2 - SPL_1 = 100 - 94 = 6$ dB **Ans.**

**Sources and effect of noise on tractor operator:** According to Nebraska's Organization for Economic Cooperation and Development (OECD). Tractor Tests the tractor noise levels at the operator's site will be in the range of 89–98 dB (A). Almost all the models of tractors manufactured in India also produce noise level in the range of 88–100 dB (A). Noise levels of farm machinery ranged from 90 to 97 dB (A) for the operations normally carried out by the operators.

**Noise sources in tractor:** One of the major problems associated with the tractors is the high level of noise emission. Main sources of noise in tractors given under different categories are as :

1. Tractor engine:High noise generating components in tractor engine are:

   (*a*) Engine exhausts (*b*) Intake
   (*c*) Combustion (*d*) Piston slap
   (*e*) Fuel injection pump (*f*) Valve train
   (*g*) Gears (*h*) Bearings
   (*i*) Crank shaft (*j*) Engine fan

2. Hydraulic system
3. Differential (power transmission system)
4. Brakes etc.

Out of the above noise sources in a tractor, the noise produced by combustion and piston slap are the biggest sources of noise. It is mainly caused due to pressure pulsation and turbulent flow created by sudden opening and closing of inlet and exhaust valves. The tractor operators in India are exposed to noise levels above the safe permissible limit drawn by Occupational Safety and Health Agency (OSHA), ILO and BIS in 90% of models of all category of tractors.

**Levels of noise of different sources:** The generation and transmission of noise by various sources depend on the frequency and level of noise. It has been reported that highest sound levels on tractors were in the frequency range of 75 to 300Hz (Weston, 1963). Noise levels of different sources are given in Table 13.7.

Reference air borne sound pressure level (SPL) = 0.00002 N/m$^2$ = 0 dB.

The noise conservation measures are mandatory at 65 dB (A) and noise controls are required when noise levels reach 90 dB (A) for 8 hours a day (Annony and Laird, 1994).

**Principal effects of noise:** Communication between man and his tasks (or men) takes place through hearing. Human ear converts the sound wave into neural signals which can be transmitted to brain. Exposure to noise may adversely affect overall efficiency, safety and hearing ability of the workers. The entire spectrum of audible noise range from 20 Hz to 20 kHz and deterioration in threshold of hearing (DITH) was observed in all the audible frequencies if dose of noise is continuous for longer period of time. The noise generated is beyond tolerable limits. OSHA in USA

**TABLE 13.7: Different sources and levels of noise**

| Sr. No. | Source | Level |
|---|---|---|
| 1. | Air borne sound (Ref.) | 0 dB |
| 2. | Quite room | 40 dB |
| 3. | Conversation (1 m) | 60 dB |
| 4. | Vacuum cleaner | 72 dB |
| 5. | Modern Tractor with cab | 80 dB (at operator's ear) |
| 6. | Tractors without cab | 89–98 dB (at operator's ear) |
| 7. | Threshers and Combine harvesters | 90–98 dB |
| 8. | Power operated spray pumps | 90–98 dB |
| 9. | Power Tiller operator zone | 105–110 dB |
| 10. | Milling machine (1.2 m) | 86 dB |
| 11. | Cotton ginning Machines | 96 dB |
| 12. | News paper press | 97 dB |
| 13. | Power lawn mover | 98 dB |
| 14. | Textile room | 107 dB |
| 15. | Pneumatic chipper (2m) | 113 dB |
| 16. | Teenage Rock 'n' roll band | 114 dB |

has set permissible noise exposure level of 90 dB (A) to 8 hours per day. The average working hours per day of farm machinery operators vary from 12–14 in sowing and harvesting season and 5–6 hrs in lean season. The exposure to noise in sowing/ harvesting season is sufficient to cause noise induced hearing loss (NIHL). The noise environment and its severity associated with the tractors may have following main effects on the operators:

1. Undesired physiological reactions as noise is annoying (objectionable to unbearable).
2. Lowering of concentration, fatigue due to longer exposure and interference which decreases the speed, quality and precision of work. Longer exposure to noise may affect the performance in terms of rhythm disturbance and interference with worker to worker communication in a team.
3. Hearing loss due to continuous and prolonged exposure to high noise levels.
4. Damage to hearing caused by noise (temporary and permanent) due to hearing thresh hold shift. Excessive noise would cause more strain on operator and may result in permanent hearing loss. They experience stress related disorders and suffer temporary or permanent shifts to hearing ability. This is due to deterioration in threshold of hearing (DITH).
5. Heart rate of tractor operator increase with increased exposure of noise.
6. Greater incidence of physical illness and increased strain among those exposed to high intensity noise. Evidence of pathological effect of continuous exposure of 95 dB (A) or more was reported by Janesar (1969).

## Overall effect of several noise levels

There are situations in which several noise sources, their levels must be combined to predict the overall effect on the operators who are exposed to such type noise sources. A convenient method of combining decibels is by use of following methods:

***(i)* By using Table 13.8 for combining decibels of multiple noise sources**

**TABLE 13.8: Determining combined decibels of multiple noise sources**

| **Difference between two noise levels (dB)** | 0 | 1 | 2 | 3 | 4 | 5 | 6 | 7 | 8 | 9 | 10 | 11 | 12 |
|---|---|---|---|---|---|---|---|---|---|---|---|---|---|
| **Quantity of noise to be added to higher noise level** | 3.0 | 2.6 | 2.1 | 1.8 | 1.4 | 1.2 | 1.0 | 0.8 | 0.6 | 0.5 | 0.4 | 0.3 | 0.2 |

***(ii)* By combining all the sources together:**

The sound power of two or more than two sources can be combined by using following equation

$$SPL_c = 10 \log [10^{L1/10} + 10^{L2/10} + 10^{L3/10} + \cdots\cdots + 10^{Ln/10}] \quad ...(13.12)$$

where, $SPL_c$ = Combined sound power level, *dB*

$L_1$, $L_2$, $L_3$, $L_n$ = sound power levels of individual machines, *dB*

**By using following chart :** The sound pressures levels of different sources can be combined together as per Fig. 13.11.

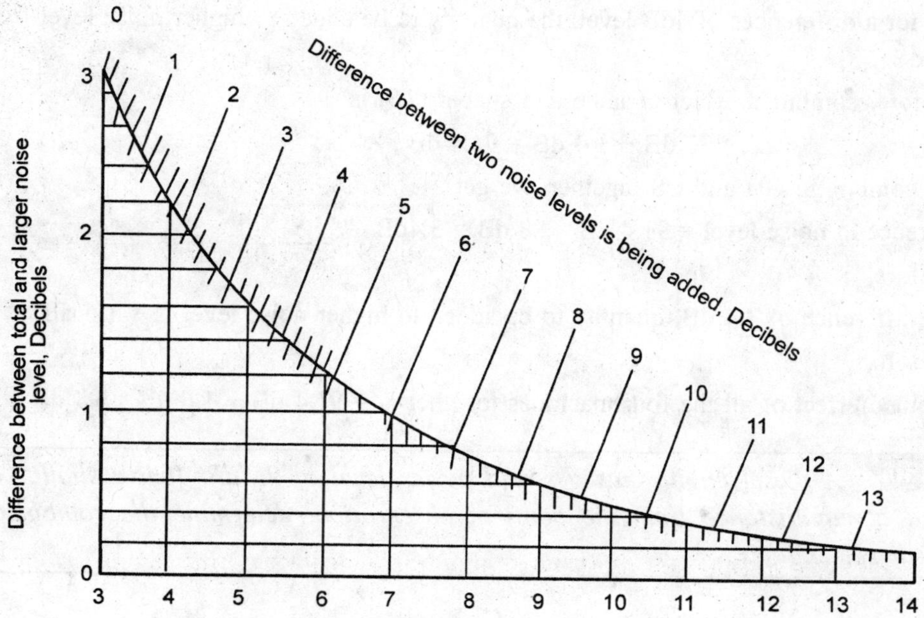


**Figure 13.11: Determining combined decibles of multiple noise sources**

**EXAMPLE 13.3** *In a tractor repair workshop following machines with their noise levels are working together:*

*(i) Generator: 85 dB* *(ii) Drilling machine: 85 dB*

*(iii) Lathe machine: 90 dB* *(iv) Shaping machine: 86 dB.*

*Calculate the combined noise level of all the machines in the workshop.*

**SOLUTION:**

Noise levels of various machines are

Generator = 85 dB

Drilling machine = 85 dB

Lathe machine = 90 dB

Shaping machine = 86 dB

Now, considering generator drilling machine, we can find that

Difference in noise level = 85 dB – 85 dB = 0 dB

Now, from the decibel scale (Table 13.8) for a difference of 0 dB, 3dB is to be added to the higher noise level

Therefore, combined noise level of generator and drilling machine (GD) is

$$GD = 85 \text{ dB} + 3 \text{ dB} = 88 \text{ dB}$$

Again, taking Lathe and shaping machines together we get

Difference = 90 dB – 86 dB = 4 dB

Now, for a differences of 4dB level, the quantity to be added to higher noise level from Table 13.8, is 1.4 dB

Therefore, combined effect of lathe and shaper (*LS*) is

$$LS = 90 \text{ dB} + 1.4 \text{ dB} = 91.4 \text{ dB}$$

Now, combining GD and LS together, we get

Difference in noise level = 91.4 dB – 88 dB = 3.4dB

Therefore,

For a difference of 3.4 dB, quantity to be added to higher noise level is = 1.6 dB

Therefore,

Combined effect of all the four machines together is = 91.4 dB + 1.6 dB = 93 dB **Ans.**

**EXAMPLE 13.4** *A diesel engine has a sound power level of 95 dB. If five similar engines are located at equidistance from the point of observation, determine the combined effect of all the diesel engines.*

**SOLUTION:**

$$L_1, L_2, L_3, L_4, L_5 = 95 \text{ dB}$$

Now, we know that for two or more than two sources of power, the combined effect is given by

$$SPL_c = 10 \log [10^{L1/10} + 10^{L2/10} + 10^{L3/10} + \cdots + 10^{Ln/10}] \quad ...(13.13)$$

But, $L_1 = L_2 = L_3 = L_4 = L_5 = L = 95$ dB

So, eq. 13.13 becomes

$$SPL_c = 10 \log [n \times 10^{L/10}] \quad ...(13.14)$$

where, $N$ = number of noise sources.

Putting values in eqn. 12.14, we get,

$$SPL_c = 10 \log [5 \times 10^{95/10}]$$

Or,
$$SPL_c = 10 \log [5 \times 10^{9.5}]$$

$$SPL_c = 10 \times 10.199 \text{ dB}$$

$$SPL_c = 101.99 \text{ dB}$$ **Ans.**

**EXAMPLE 13.5** *If tractor noise from two components i.e. transmission is 80 dB and from engine is 80 dB, then calculate the overall noise level in the tractor by using Fig. 12.11.*

**SOLUTION:**

Sound levels in transmission = 80 dB

Sound levels in tractor engine = 80 dB

Now,

Difference between the two noise levels is = 80 dB – 80 dB = 0 dB

Referring to the Fig. 12.11, we find that for 0 dB difference, the quantity of noise to be added to higher level would be 3 dB.

Therefore, resultant noise level in the tractor = 80 dB + 3 dB = 83 dB **Ans.**

**OSHA Act for operators' exposure to noise levels :** The operator's exposure to noise levels is based on Occupational Safety and Health Agency (OSHA) which has given acceptable levels of operator's exposure to tractor noise. For eight hours per day, the sound level should not exceed 90 dB (A). Even higher sound levels can be tolerated for a shorter period of time. According to OSHA's standard, at a noise level of 90 dB scales, the exposure level is calculated by

$$D_{ei} = \frac{\text{Actual time of exposure noise level}}{\text{Calculated permissible exposure level time}}$$

$$D_{ei} = T_{ai} / T_{ci} \quad ...(13.15)$$

The permissible dose of noise exposure to the operators as per OSHA's Act is given in Table 13.9.

OSHA's sound regulations indicate that for each increase of 5 decibels (A scale), the operator's exposure time is reduced by ½. According to this regulation, the exposure time for an operator would be: 85 dB (A) = 16 hrs; 90 dB (A) = 8 hrs; 95 dB (A) = 4 hrs; 100 dB (A) = 2 hrs and so on.

**TABLE 13.9: OSHA's (Occupational Safety and Health Act) noise criteria**

| Sr. No. | Duration per day, (hours) | Sound level dB(A) |
|---|---|---|
| 1. | 32 | 80 |
| 2. | 16 | 85 |
| 3. | 8 | 90 |
| 4. | 6 | 92 |
| 5. | 4 | 95 |
| 6. | 3 | 97 |
| 7. | 2 | 100 |
| 8. | 1.5 | 102 |
| 9. | 1 | 105 |
| 10. | 0.5 | 110 |
| 11. | 0.25 | 115 |
| 12. | 0.125 | 120 |
| 13. | 0.063 | 125 |
| 14. | 0.032 | 130 |

**TABLE 13.10: ISO proposed sound pressure levels at specific frequencies**

| Sr. No. | Exposure time)/ Frequency(Hz) | Sound pressure level (dB) 63 | 125 | 250 | 500 | 1000 |
|---|---|---|---|---|---|---|
| 1. | 8 h | 97 | 91 | 87 | 84 | 82 |
| 2. | 4 h | 100 | 94 | 90 | 87 | 85 |
| 3. | 2 h | 103 | 97 | 93 | 90 | 88 |
| 4. | 1 h | 106 | 100 | 96 | 93 | 91 |
| 5. | 15 min | 110 | 104 | 100 | 97 | 95 |
| 6. | 7 min | 122 | 116 | 112 | 109 | 107 |

**EXAMPLE 13.6** *A tractor operator while performing field operations is exposed to following levels of noise during the work:*

| *Sr. No.* | *Time of day* | *Noise Level, dB* |
|---|---|---|
| *1* | *7.00–9.00 AM* | *90* |
| *2.* | *9.00–11.30 AM* | *95* |
| *3.* | *11.30–13.00 PM* | *70* |
| *4.* | *13.00–14.00 PM* | *94* |
| *5.* | *14.00–17.00 PM* | *85* |

*Calculate the dose of equivalent noise level to which the operator is exposed over the whole day and what protection measures you would suggest for the operator? Assume that permissible noise level is 90 dB.*

**SOLUTION:**

According to OSHA's Standard, at a noise scale of 90 dB, the exposure level is calculated as

$D_{ei}$ = Actual time of exposure noise level/Calculated permissible exposure level time

Or $D_{ei} = T_{ai} / T_{ci}$

Necessary calculations in this regard are tabulated in Table 13.11.

**TABLE 13.11: Calculated time for different noise levels**

| Sr. No | Time of day | Noise Level, *dB* | Actual duration ($T_{ai}$), hrs | Calculated time ($T_{ci}$) hrs |
|---|---|---|---|---|
| 1 | 7.00–9.00 AM | 90 | 2.0 | 8.0 |
| 2. | 9.00–11.30 AM | 95 | 1.5 | 4.0 |
| 3. | 11.30–13.00 PM | 70 | 1.0 | 128.0 |
| 4. | 13.00–14.00 PM | 94 | 1.0 | 4.6 |
| 5. | 14.00–17.00 PM | 85 | 3.0 | 16.0 |

Now, based on Table 13.11

$$D = 100 \sum_{i=1}^{n} T_{ai} / T_{ci} \qquad \text{...[13.16 (a)]}$$

$$D = 100\ [2/8 + 1.5/4 + 1/128 + 1/4.6 + 3/16]$$

$$D = 100\ [0.25 + 0.375 + 0.0078 + 0.217 + 0.1875]$$

$$D = 103.73\ \%$$

Since, the noise dose is more than 100%, therefore, the operator is advised to use protective ear plugs. **Ans.**

**Protection from noise:** It is accepted fact that a permanent exposure to sound pressure level of 85 dB (A) or more should be protected to avoid damage of ears. For favorable conditions the workers must be protected from high noise either by technical means or by personal means. The noise levels can be controlled by following methods:

(*i*) Control at source of sound: By reducing the noise generated at the source itself *i.e.* modification of source to make it less noisy or by proper maintenance

(*a*) Lubricating the machine

(*b*) Rubber mounting.

(*ii*) To replace the machine with quieter machines or replacement of machines components with less noisy components.

(*iii*) By enclosing the source or by reducing noise transmission from source

(*iv*) By modifying the acoustic properties of surroundings *i.e.* use of dampening and visco-elastic material for muffing the noise such as fiber glass, and high efficiency foams.

(*v*) Modifying noise path by using acoustic barriers, acoustic enclosures or operating booths. These can reduce noise by 5–8 dB (A) while complete enclosures *i.e.* cabs can reduce noise levels by 20 dB (A).

(*vi*) Regular maintenance and replacement of worn out parts at appropriate time.

(*vii*) Sound absorption by baffles and mufflers

(*viii*) By using personal protective devices/equipments such as ear muffs, and ear plugs to guard the ears from excessive noise. At least 10 dB (A) should be reduced by these devices/aids

(*ix*) By proper layout of machines.

(*x*) Reduction in exposure time of workers.

## EXERCISES

1. Show by calculations that by doubling the sound pressure level, 6 dB increase in sound level is achieved.
2. A tractor is producing 80 dB noises while a generator is generating 90dB noise. What is the resultant noise level?
3. A tractor has a sound pressure of 93 dB. Determine the sound power of four similar identical tractors operating at the same distance from the point of observation.
4. A tractor operator is exposed to following levels of noise during work:

| Time | Noise Level (dB) |
|---|---|
| 7.00–9.00 | 95 |
| 9.00–11.30 | 90 |
| 11.30–12.30 | 94 |
| 12.30–13.0 | 70 |
| 13.00–16.0 | 85 |

Calculate the dose of equivalent noise level to which the operator is exposed over the whole day. Assume the permissible noise level is 90 dB.

5. Following machines with noise levels are working together in a shop

| | |
|---|---|
| Machine 1 | 80 dB |
| Machine 2 | 80 dB |
| Machine 3 | 87 dB |
| Machine 4 | 82 dB |

Calculate the combined noise level.

6. In a tractor, the noise level measured at the operator's ear level and the bystander's position are found to be 84 dBA and 76 dBA respectively. What would be the corresponding RMS values in N/$m^2$ at these positions?
7. A test engineer has isolated a pure-tone noise in a tractor and determined its frequency to be 8000Hz and peak to peak amplitude to be 0.01 Pa. Determine the period, RMS sound pressure

and resulting sound pressure level. Should the engineer be concerned about eliminating or reducing the source of noise?

8. Sound was measured at 80 dB in the operator's station on a tractor. What is the RMS sound pressure in Newton per square meter ($N/m^2$)? If the sound pressure increased eight times, determine the resulting sound pressure in decibels. Why the decibel scale is used in sound measurement rather then a sound pressure scale?
9. Two components of sound have been identified in a tractor and measured at 74 dB and 81 dB. What is the resulting noise level?
10. What is the maximum theoretical sound pressure in decibels that can exist?

## 13.6 VIBRATIONS IN TRACTOR

**Human exposure to vibrations:** Any engineering system possessing mass and elasticity are capable of relative motion. When this motion repeats after a given interval of time, then this motion is known as vibration. In many cases it is undesirable and is a form of wasted energy. This is particularly true in tractors and farm machinery as they generate noise, break down parts and transmit unwanted forces and movements to different components. Vibrations and noise in tractor are generated due to rotating and reciprocating parts, vibrations in engine components, exhaust gases and flow of hydraulic fluids. These are transmitted by the moving (rotating, reciprocating and vibrating) structural components of tractor or air borne or combination of the two. The physical objects have their individual resonant frequencies which are a function of their mass. Tractors with pneumatic tyres have resonant frequencies primarily in the range of 1 to 4 Hz and for track type tractors more than 4Hz. It is important to note that in the frequency range of 4 to 8-Hz, human tolerance to vibration is minimum. Exposure of human body to vibrations can result in

- Biological effects
- Mechanical effects
- Physiological effects and
- Psychological effects

**Vibration:** It can be defined as an oscillatory motion of mechanical system and can generate sound in a gas, fluid, or solid medium. Vibration is characterized by frequency, amplitude and phase. In the simplest case mechanical vibration can be derived from simple harmonic wave form shown in Fig. 13.12.

In vibration analysis, the frequency of periodic motion is number of cycles per unit time and it is a function of time period as given below.

$$f = 1/T \qquad ...(13.16)$$

where $T$ = period in time required for a periodic motion to repeat itself in seconds

The frequency of vibration can be sinusoidal, complex or random. It is important to note that in the frequency range of 4 to 8Hz, human tolerance to vibration is a minimum.

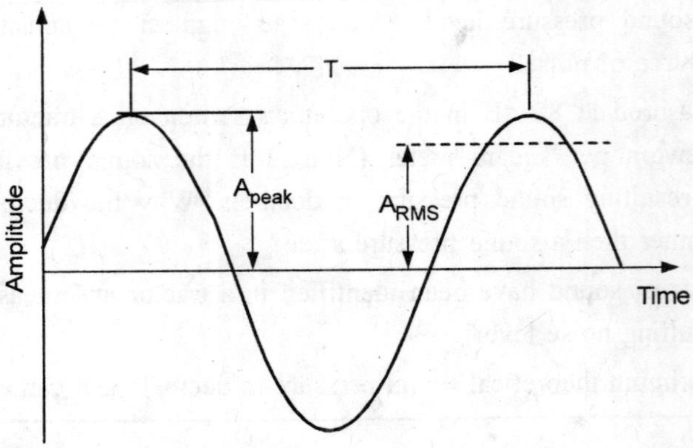


Figure 12.12: Simple harmonic vibration wave

**Natural frequency ($\omega_n$):** It is the frequency of system having free vibration without friction.

**Damped frequency ($\omega_d$):** Damped frequency is the frequency of a system having free vibration and with friction.

Vibration can be mathematically be described by displacement function.

**Displacement function (X):** The amplitude can be cm or m of displacement which may be either a half–wave single-amplitude or full-wave double amplitude displacement.

$$X = A \sin \omega t \qquad ...(13.17)$$

where, $X$ = Displacement, m

$A$ = peak amplitude, m

$\omega$ = frequency of vibration, rad/s

$t$ = time, s

**Velocity function (V):** It is first derivative of displacement, usually in cm or m/s but it is not often used.

$$V = \delta X/\delta t = \omega A \cos \omega t \qquad ...(13.18)$$

where, $V$ = Velocity, m/s.

**Acceleration function ($a$):** It is second derivative of displacement function usually in cm or m/s$^2$ and some times expressed as peak or maximum $g$.

$$a = \delta^2 X/\delta t^2 = -\omega^2 A \sin \omega t \qquad ...(13.19)$$

where, $a$ = acceleration, m/s$^2$.

Acceleration is directly proportional to the displacement and square of the frequency.

**Acceleration function ($a$):** Vibration is measured by accelerometer and readout is expressed as acceleration, RMS

$$a_{RMS} = (1/\sqrt{2})\ (\omega^2 A) \qquad ...(13.20)$$

It is convenient to express acceleration in term of g's. *i.e.*

$a/g$ or $a_{RMS}/g$

Or, $a/9.81$ and $a_{RMS}/9.81$

Vibration levels are expressed in dB. A convenient reference level for vibration is $1 m/s^2$ RMS. Also, vibration levels are expressed in decibels as given below:

$$Val = 20 \log V/V_0, \text{ dB} \quad ...(13.21)$$

where, $V_0$ = reference level = $1\ m/s^2$ RMS

$Val$ = vibration acceleration level, dB

$V$ = measured RMS acceleration, $m/s^2$

Displacement and maximum acceleration (in g units) are used most commonly in characterizing intensity of sinusoidal vibration.

## Types of Vibrations

The vibrations in a system can be of following two types:

**1. Forced vibration :** It is defined as the periodic motion observed, as the system is displaced from its static equilibrium position. The forces acting are spring force, the friction force, the weight of the vibrating mass and external forces acting on the system during its vibratory motion. The system will tend to vibrate at its natural frequency at forced vibration. This will follow the frequency of the excitation force. In the presence of friction, the portion of motion not sustained by sinusoidal excitation force will gradually die out. As a result of this the system will vibrate at the frequency of excitation force regardless of initial conditions or natural frequency of the system. The part of sustained vibration is called as steady state vibration or response of the system. This can be described for general single degree of freedom system by differential equation of following form:

$$m \frac{\delta^2 x}{\delta t^2} + c \frac{\delta x}{\delta t} + kx = F(t) \quad ...(13.22)$$

where, $m$ = mass

$k$ = spring constant (force per unit deflection)

$c$ = damping constant (force per unit velocity) viscous damping where resisting force is proportional to velocity.

$x$ = displacement of mass from static equilibrium position, which can be linear or angular

$\delta^2 x/\delta t^2$ = acceleration function

$\delta x/\delta t$ = velocity function

$F(t)$ = external force acting, a function of time

Also, $$F(t) = F_0 \sin \omega t \quad ...(13.23)$$

where, $F_0$ = amplitude of external force applied

$\omega$ = frequency

**2. Free vibration:** It is defined as the periodic motion observed as the system is displaced from its static equilibrium position. The forces acting are spring force, the friction force and the weight of the vibrating mass. This may occur when after an initial disturbance, no external force is present *i.e.* $F(t) = 0$. The vibration will diminish with time due to presence of friction. This is sometimes called as transient vibration. The differential equation for free vibration would be as under:

$$m \frac{\delta^2 x}{\delta t^2} + c\frac{\delta x}{\delta t} + kx = 0 \qquad ...(13.24)$$

where, $m$ = mass

$k$ = spring constant (force per unit deflection)

$c$ = damping constant (force per unit velocity) viscous damping where resisting force is proportional to velocity.

$x$ = displacement of mass from static equilibrium position, which can be linear or angular

$\delta^2x/\delta t^2$ = acceleration function

$\delta x/\delta t$ = velocity function

## Vibrations in tractor chassis

The tractor driving may have considerable ill-effects on the health of operator. This is largely due to effect of vibrations and shock continuously acting on human body and setting up harmful stamina and partly to the need to keep the body in cramped condition and unhealthy posture for long periods. Tractor ride vibration intensities are normally related with the ground speed. The vibrations become intolerable as the speed is increased. Tractors with pneumatic tyres have resonant frequencies primarily in the range of 1 to 4 Hz and for track type tractors more than 4Hz. It is important to note that human tolerance to vibration is minimum in the frequency range of 4 to 8-Hz, According to survey majority of large tractors are found to be operating at less than two-third of maximum power because of following reasons.

- Operator's inability or unwillingness to withstand the ride at full speed.
- Ride induced vibrations do have ill-effects on the operators.

Therefore, proper care must be taken in designing tractors particularly their seat

- To reduce vibrations and shocks to a minimum by appropriate suspension and shock absorption
- To arrange the tractor controls in a manner to a comfortable posture and minimum effort.

Vibration input to tractor seat due to vertical motion of tractor body as tractor ride vibration intensities are positively related with ground surface and ground speed during field operations is given by following equation.

$$Z_i = Z_t + \theta\ g \qquad ...(13.25)$$

where, $Z_i$ = Vertical motion input to tractor seat, m

$Z_t$ = Vertical motion of tractor c.g , m

$\theta$ = Rotation or pitch about tractor c.g, radians

$g$ = Longitudinal distance from tractor seat to c.g, m

## Tractor Seat Design

***(a)* From vibration point of view:** Fig. 13.13 shows a tractor seat suspension for vertical vibrations transmitted by the tractor chassis to the seat and experienced by the tractor operator.

During the process of whole body vibration of tractor operator, the vibration transmitted to the body can be amplified or attenuated due to body posture, type of seat and frequency of vibration. The dynamic performance of seat suspension can be analyzed based on output vibration in response to a given input vibration, which can be expressed as a function of

- frequency of input vibration
- seat spring rate and
- mass damping properties

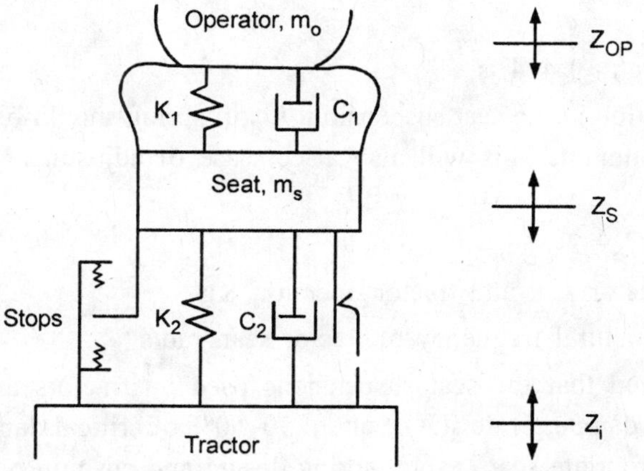


**Fig. 13.13: Tractor operator seat suspension**

Now, for steady state vibration input ($Z_i$) to above tractor seat suspension system, the transmissibility is expressed as :

$$\text{Transmissibility } (T) = \frac{\text{Magnitude of output vibration } (Z_o)}{\text{Magnitude of input vibration } (Z_i)}$$

Therefore, for a linear seat suspension system, the transmissibility function for a steady state input vibration can be expressed as:

$$T = \frac{\left|(1 + 4\zeta^2 \, (\omega_t/\omega_n)^2\right|}{\sqrt{\left[((1 - (\omega_t/\omega_n)^2 + 4\zeta^2 \, (\omega_t/\omega_n)^2\right]}} \quad ...(13.27)$$

where, $T$ = transmissibility of vibrations

$\zeta$ = damping ratio = $C/C_c$

$C$ = actual seat suspension damping rate or coefficient, N/m.s

$C_c$ = critical damping rate, N/m.s

(When $\zeta = 1.0$, the suspended mass will return to equilibrium position in the least time without oscillation. On the other hand if $\zeta = 0$, the damping will be zero, transmissibility would be infinite and the operator would experience mechanical shocks during operation of tractor or any agricultural machine. In case of a seated operator there is an amplification effect at various body locations especially in the range of 3.5 to 4.0 Hz. On the other hand at frequencies 5 to 6 Hz the transmissibility is reduced to about the amplitude of tractor chassis vibration).

$\omega_t$ = frequency of tractor chassis, rad/s

$\omega_n$ = undamped natural frequency of tractor seat suspension, rad/s = $(K/M)^{1/2}$, rad/s

$K$ = seat spring rate, N/cm or N/mm

$M$ = mass of tractor seat and operator, Kg

From eq. 13.27, it is clear that $\omega_n$ (undamped natural frequency) of the seat is a vital parameter for matching with vibration input from the tractor. The value of $\omega_n$ (undamped natural frequency) of the seat should be less than the frequency input from the tractor chassis.

Therefore,

$$\omega_t > 1.414\ \omega_n$$

to avoid vibration attenuation in the seat suspension. A soft spring should be used to keep the natural frequency value to a minimum. This will also affect ease of adjustment and convenience of the operator.

Also, $$C_c = 2\ M\omega_n \quad ...(13.28)$$

where, $M$ = mass of tractor seat and tractor operator, Kg

$\omega_n$ = undamped natural frequency of tractor seat, rad/s

It has been observed that the seat suspensions used on tractors and agricultural machines would normally require a damping rate ($C$) of about 30–50% of critical damping rate ($C_c$). Damping can be controlled by appropriate seat design, spring design and cushion of seat. Thus, the physical effects of vibration on whole body of operator are greatly influenced by body posture, and materials provided between the body and source of vibration i.e. seat, cushion and springs etc.

A properly designed seat can effectively reduce the vibration intensity which would otherwise be transmitted to operator, especially in low frequency range (2 to 5 Hz) and may have considerable ill-effects on the health of operator. The tractor seat suspensions are comprised of cushions mounted to resilient spring/damper to reduce the level of input tractor chassis vibrations.

**EXAMPLE 13.7** *Design a seat suspension (Refer Fig. 13.13) for*

(1) *Seat and operator mass of 90 kg*

(2) *Transmissibility of 0.315*

(3) *Tractor chassis frequency of 4 Hz and*

(4) *Static spring deflection of seat and operator of 10 cm.*

*Determine:*

1. *The undamped natural frequency of the seat.*
2. *Spring and shock absorber design values.*
3. *The decibel reduction in RMS acceleration that the seat suspension* provides.

**SOLUTION:**

$M = M_o + M_s = 90$ kg

Transmissibility ($T$) = 0.315

Tractor chassis frequency ($\omega_t$) = 4 Hz

**(a) Natural undamped frequency of seat ($\omega_s$):**

Now, we know that

$$K = M/k = 90 \text{ kg} \times 10\text{N/kg} / (10 \text{ cm}/100 \text{ cm/m})$$
$$= 9000 \text{ N/m}$$

Also, $\omega_s = (K/M)^{1/2} = (9000 \text{ N/m} / 900 \text{ N})^{1/2}$

$$\omega_s = 3.16 \text{ rad/s}$$

And, $C_c = 2\ M.\ \omega_s = 2 \times 90 \times 3.16 = 568.8$ rad/s

Now, $\omega_t/\omega_s = 4 \text{ Hz}/3.16 \text{ Hz} = 1.12$

But, it is given that the frequency ratio should not be less than 1.0. So, we can take the value as 1.45.

**(b) Spring (K) and shock absorber (c) values:**

$$K = M/k = 90 \text{ kg} \times 10 \text{ N/kg}/(10 \text{ cm}/100\text{cm/m}) = 9000 \text{ N/m}$$

And, $C_c = 2\ M.\ \omega_s = 2 \times 90 \times 3.16 = 568.8$ rad/s

Now,
$$T = \frac{\left|(1 + 4\zeta^2 (\omega_t/\omega_n)^2\right|}{\sqrt{\left[\left((1-(\omega_t/\omega_n)^2\right)^2 + 4\zeta^2 (\omega_t/\omega_n)^2\right]}} \qquad ...(13.29)$$

Putting values in eqn. 13.29, we get

$$0.315 = [(1 + 4\ \zeta^2\ (1.45)^2)/[\{1 - (1.45)^2)\}^2 + 4\ \zeta^2\ (1.45)^2]]^{0.5}$$

Or, $(0.315)^2 = [(1 + 4\ \zeta^2\ (1.45)^2)/[\{1 - (1.45)^2)\}^2 + 4\ \zeta^2\ (1.45)^2]]$

Or, $-7.576\ \zeta^2 = 0.8795$

Or, $\zeta = 0.340$

Also we know that

$$\zeta = C/C_c$$

Putting values we get

$$0.340 = C/568.8$$

Or, $C = 0.340 \times 568.8 = 193.39$ N/m **Ans.**

**(c) Decibel reduction in RMS acceleration by the seat suspension:**

We know that $a_Z = \text{Transmissibility} \times RMS\ Z_{in}$ ...(13.30)

When no damping is provided to the seat, according to eq. 12.30

$$a_{Z1} = 1 \times \text{RMS } Z_{in}$$

Again, when seat suspension is provided with damping

$$a_{Z2} = \text{Transmissibility} \times \text{RMS } Z_{in}$$
$$a_{Z2} = 0.315 \times \text{RMS } Z_{in}$$

Therefore, percent reduction in vibrations by the seat suspension is

$$(a_{Z1} - a_{Z2}/a_{Z1}) \times 100 = (Z_{in} - 0.315\ Z_{in}/Z_{in}) \times 100$$

Percent reduction in vibrations by the seat suspension = 68.85% **Ans.**

### Effects of whole body vibration on operators

Whole body vibration is transmitted through the seat or feet and hand arm of the worker operator who drive the vehicle/machine over rough and uneven surface as a main part of their job. Large shocks and jolts may cause the health risks including back pain.

*Exposure of human body to vibrations can result in Biological, Mechanical, Physiological and Psychological effects as given below:*

1. There may be direct mechanical interference with the activity due to whole body vibrations.
2. The whole body vibrations may result in increased working stress level, tension and deformation as a source of localized pain and fatigue.
3. General discomfort and anxiety with certain subjective sensations which may be annoying to the operators.
4. Abdominal, chest and testicular pains which may be contributing to operator's long term health.
5. There may be indirect physiological induced alterations/effects on metabolism.
6. The combined mechanical, physiological and psychological responses to sinusoidal vibrations can effect the operator's ability to perform control functions in different types of tasks as under: (*i*) Visual tasks: dial reading, visual scanning, (*ii*) Simple motor task that require precision and coordination, (*iii*) Psychomotor tasks including tracking tasks
7. Fatigue in the body.

### Reducing vibrations risks

- Mount vibrating equipment on spring or compression pads.
- Use materials that generate less vibrations.
- Considering the choice of seat (including suspension seats) and the choice of tyres, and
- Regular maintenance of vehicles (including their seats and suspension) and maintenance of unmade roads and ground conditions throughout sites to suit the machines that use them will greatly reduce shocks and jolts.
- Designing the layout of workplace sites to reduce the need to transport materials, and so reduce the WBV exposure of drivers/operators;
- Providing suitable and sufficient information and training for employees:
- Limiting the duration and magnitude of exposure - when all reasonably practicable steps have been taken to reduce the vibration magnitude, and taking account of the fact that there is no personal protective equipment available for WBV, the final resort for compliance with the exposure limit value is to limit the duration of exposure;
- Ensuring the work schedules have adequate rest periods - a recommended precautionary measure is to take a short break between operating mobile machinery and manual handling of materials, to give tired muscles time to recover before handling heavy loads,
- Protecting employees from cold and damp - cold exposure may accelerate the onset or worsen the severity of back pain. It is good practice to ensure that those working in the cold are provided with warm, and (if necessary) waterproof clothing.
- Reducing exposure below the exposure limit value - you must not permit an employee to be exposed above the exposure limit value.

Extra care will be needed to ensure that the exposure of those who are particularly sensitive to WBV is kept to a minimum, that they are given and take account of adequate information, instruction and training, and that symptoms of back pain or other diseases are monitored.

## Sound Level Meter

Sound level meter is an important engineering equipment meant for recording the level of noise in decibels (dB). To measure noise produced by a source at a particular location, SLM (sound level meter) is positioned in desired location with no obstruction from the sound source. ***The basic parts of SLM includes microphone, amplifiers, weighting networks and display meter.***

***Working of SLM :*** Any sound pressure coming from the source (mechanised vehicles, fire engines, police cars, ambulance, trains and social gatherings) reaches to the microphone. ***Microphone*** then acts as a pressure transducer (device converter) and mimics (imitate) the pressure pattern of source and converts it into electrical signal. This electrical signal thereafter is boosted in preamplifier and then modified by the weighting network. The modified signal is again boosted in magnitude through amplifier. A ***rectifier*** is fixed in SLM which converts the amplified signal from A.C. (Alternate current) to D.C. (direct current). This process cause the needle of the display meter to record and register the SPL (sound pressure level) in decibels (dB) or Hz (Hertz).

***Readings of SLM :*** Following steps should be taken before registering the readings of SLM.

(*i*) SLM should be mounted (placed) on a ***eripod*** (*i.e.*, stool or table). (*ii*) Operator of SLM should stand at least 1/2 metre away from nearest edge of meter. (*iii*) Outdoor sound measurement are to be taken one metre to 1½ metre above the ground level. (*iv*) The SLM should be kept or positioned 3½ m away from the reflecting surfaces such as buildings and vehicles so that sound pressure coming from the source is not interfered.

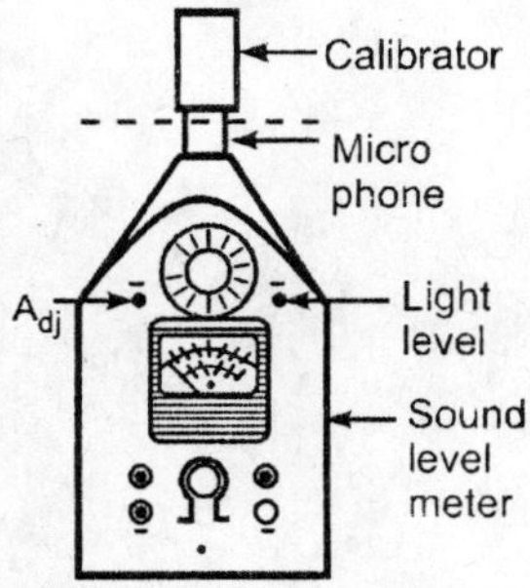


**Fig. 13.14 Sound Level Meter**

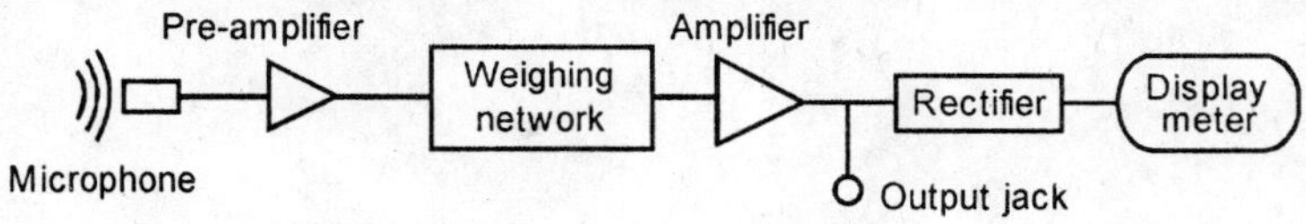


## EXERCISES

1. An accelerometer mounted on the waist of a seated tractor operator records a vertical RMS acceleration of 1.5 m/s$^2$ at 8 Hz. What is the most likely source of this vibration? Would it be desirable for the operator to experience this level of vibration? Why? What is the amplitude of this vibration in mm?
2. If the RMS acceleration in above problem were decreased by 10 dB because of improved seat design, what would be the resulting RMS acceleration? How many hours could the operator tolerate this level of vibration?
3. Using the anthropometric data from following table, determine the operator work place dimensions for
   (*a*) Seat height range (*b*) seat width (*c*) seat depth (front-rear)
   (*d*) arms rest width and height (*e*) height inside a cab.
4. Design a seat suspension for
   (1) Seat and operator mass of 100 kg
   (2) Transmissibility of 0.400
   (3) Tractor chassis frequency of 5 Hz and
   (4) Static spring deflection of seat and operator of 10 cm.
   (*a*) Determine the undamped natural frequency of the seat.
   (*b*) Determine spring and shock absorber design values.
   (*c*) Determine the decibel reduction in RMS acceleration that the seat suspension provides.
   (*d*) Using ISO 2631 criteria, how long should a tractor driver be exposed to a tractor chassis input of 1 RMS m/s$^2$ for the suspension you designed?
   (*e*) If the tractor chassis frequency decreases, will the seat suspension be more or less effective? Why?

# APPENDIX

# Annexure-I

**TABLE No. 1: Tractor manufacturers in India**

| Sr. No. | Addresses |
|---|---|
| 1. | Bajaj Tempo Limited, (Tractor Division) Akurdi, **PUNE-411035** Ph. 020-776381 |
| 2. | Eicher Tractors, Marketing Division, 59, NIT, **FARIDABAD-121001** Ph. 8233751 Fax: 8233233 |
| 3. | Escorts Limited, Agricultural Machinery Division, 18/4, Mathura Road, **FARIDABAD-121007**, Ph. 284911, Fax: 284839 |
| 4. | Gujrat Tractors Limited, Vishwamatri Railway Station, Over bridge VADODRA- 390001 |
| 5. | HMT Limited (Tractor Business Group), 54, Madhya Marg, Sector 7C, **Chandigarh-160010** Ph. 548501, 771495 Fax: 0172-548525, 549842 |
| 6. | Indofarm Equipment Ltd; S.C.O. 859, N.A.C. Manimajra, Kalka Road, **Chandigarh** |
| 7. | International Tractors Limited, Sonalika House, 283, AGCR Enclave, KARKARDOOMA, **Delhi-110092** Ph. 22373785/89/91 |
| 8. | John Deere Pvt. Ltd; Pune Nagar Road, Sanaswadi, Taluka-Shirur, Distt. **PUNE-412208** |
| 9. | Mahindra and Mahindra Ltd; Tractor Division, Mahindra Tower, Road No. 13, WORLI, **MUMBAI-400018** |
| 10. | New Holland Tractors (India) Pvt. Ltd; 210, Okhla Industrial Area-III, **New-Delhi-110020** |
| 11. | Partap Steels Limited, (Automotive Division), 21/3, Mathura Road, **Ballabgarh121004** Ph.42071 |
| 12. | Punjab Tractors Limited, **Sahibjada Ajit Singh Nagar-160055** Near Chandigarh |
| 13. | Standard Combines (P) Ltd; (Tractor Division), Handiaya Chowk**BARNALA-148101** Ph. 0167-3937981, 3938033, Fax: 3930833 e-mail: scombine@sifty.com |
| 14. | SAME Greaves Tractors Ltd, 72, Spicot, Industrial Complex, RANIPET-3 |
| 15. | Tractors and Farm Equipment Limited, 35, Nungambakkam High Road, CHENNAI-600034 |
| 16. | VST Tillers and Tractors, **Bangalore** |

**TABLE No. 2: Different makes of tractors manufactured in India and their HP range and year of commencement**

| Sr. No. | Manufacturer | Technical Collaborator | Year of commen-cement | Horse Power Range |
|---|---|---|---|---|
| 1. | Eicher Tractors Limited, Faridabad | Gebr, Eicher Tractorenfabrik, West Germany | 1961 | 26–60 |
| 2. | TAFE, Chennai | Massey Ferguson, UK | 1961 | 30–75 |
| 3. | Gujrat Tractors, Vadodra | Motkov-Parha, Czechoslovakia | 1963 | 35–60 |
| 4. | Escorts Limited, Faridabad | Ursus, Poland | 1964 | 30–70 |
| 5. | Mahindra and Mahindra Limited, Mumbai | International Harvesters, UK | 1965 | 30–60 |
| 6. | HMT Limited, Pinjore | Motkov-Parha, Czechoslovakia | 1971 | 25–75 |
| 7. | Punjab Tractors Limited, Mohali, Punjab | CMERI, India | 1974 | 25–55 |
| 8. | VST Tillers and Tractors, Bangalore | Mistsubishi, Japan | 1983 | <25 |
| 9. | Bajaj Tempo Limited, Pune | Indegenous | 1997 | 30–50 |
| 10. | International Tractors (Sonalika), Hosiarpur | Renault, France | 1998 | 30–60 |
| 11. | New Holland Tractors, Noida | New Holland, Italy | 1999 | 35–70 |
| 12. | John Deere, Pune | John Deere, USA | 1999 | 40–55 |
| 13. | Same Deutz-Fahar, Tamil Nadu | Same Deutz-Fahar, Italy | 1999 | 35–60 |
| 14. | Standard Tractors, Sangrur | Indigenous | 2000 | 30–50 |
| 15. | Indofarm Tractors, Punjab | Ursus, Poland | 2000 | 30–50 |
| 16. | Preet Tractors, Nabha, Punjab | Indigenous | 2002 | 35 |

# Annexure-II

## TYPES OF TRACTORS

- **Crawler:** The track-type tractors have limited use in agriculture. Used for special earth moving jobs on farms and for land cleaning
- **Standard row-crop:** Primarily for traction through rear wheels. These are especially adapted for use on row crops, allowing quick attachment of various tillage and cultivation tools and implements
- **High Clearance tractor:** These are modified row crop tractors designed especially for crops that require extra clearance such as cane, cotton Arhar etc.
- **Utility tractor:** Generally has less clearance than standard or row crop tractors. Used for many jobs on the farm and equipped with front loader
- **Orchard Tractor:** Small or medium size general purpose machine (Track or wheel type) which can be better operated around the trees. Their heights are lower with few projecting parts.
- **Multipurpose Tractor:** It can be operated in either direction. It not only carries the implement but, also furnishes power
- **Lawn and garden tractor:** This has power output of less than 15 kW and primarily used for care of lawns. These tractors have very low clearance and are for light duty use.
- **Power tiller:** It is a two wheel tractor guided by hand and used commonly in rice growing regions of Japan and Southeast Asia. It is equipped with a rotary tiller and powered by single cylinder engine of 5–12 kW.
- **Tree Skidder:** Four wheel drive tractor for moving tree trunks out of forests. It is combination of Agricultural and industrial tractor.
- **Skid-steer loader:** Used when turning room is restricted, such as in dairy or fruit storage building.
- **Four wheel drive with smaller front steering wheels:** These are developed so as to produce more drawbar power. It is simply a standard or a row crop tractor with front wheels also being driven.

**Four wheel drive with equal sized wheels and articulated frame steering:** This tractor has become particularly popular in Japan because of its excellent steering and traction characteristics in soft, wet rice fields. Their size varies in United States and Canada from 100 kW to more than 300 kW. In Europe 4WD drive tractors may be as small as 15 kW and are specially used in vineyards. These can be steered by pivoting the tractor in the centre (frame steer) or steering the wheels.

# Annexure-III

**TABLE No. 1: Model and power range of tractors**

| Sr. No. | Model | Number of Cylinders | Capacity ($Cm^3$) | Max. pto power (kW) | SFC at max. power (g/kWh) | weight/pto power (Kg/kWh) | Power kW | Engine Power (HP) |
|---|---|---|---|---|---|---|---|---|
| 1. | Eicher 241 NC | 1 | 1557 | 15.1 | 262 | 109.93 | 17.6 | 24 |
| 2. | Eicher 242 NC | 1 | 1558 | 14.1 | 267 | 114.54 | 19.2 | 24 |
| 3. | Eicher 312 Super | 2 | 1790 | 20.3 | 259 | 85.47 | 27.6 | 30 |
| 4. | Eicher 364 NC | 2 | 1963 | 22.9 | 272 | 76.2 | 31.1 | 40 |
| 5. | Eicher 485 DI | 3 | 2945 | 30.6 | 276 | 66.85 | | 44 |
| 6. | Eicher 380S | 3 | | 27.23 | | | | 38 |
| 1. | Escorts 325 M | 2 | 1795 | 16.6 | 288 | 100 | 24.4 | 25 |
| 2. | 325 M (10+2) | 2 | 1795 | 17.9 | 288 | | 24.4 | 27 |
| 3. | 335 M (10+2) | 2 | 1960 | 22.2 | 268 | | 30.2 | 35 |
| 4. | Escorts 335 M | 2 | 1960 | 20.9 | 250 | 83.97 | 30.3 | 35 |
| 5. | Escorts 340 M | 3 | 3120 | 33.2 | 339 | 54.97 | 40.3 | 54 |
| 6. | 355 (6+2) | 3 | | 28 | 256 | | 38.2 | |
| 7. | Escorts 355 M | 3 | 2727 | 29.6 | 245 | 62.67 | 45.1 | 55 |
| 8. | Escort 435 | 3 | 2450 | | | | | 35 |
| 1. | Farmtrac 50 | 3 | 2868 | 31 | 297 | 59.35 | 40.1 | 47 |
| 2. | Farmtrac 60 | 3 | 3147 | 33.3 | 253 | 59.31 | 45.3 | 50 |
| 3. | Farmtrac 55 | 3 | 2868 | 32.9 | 248 | 40.14 | 44.7 | 47 |
| 4. | Farmtrac 50 XL | 3 | | 29.8 | 258 | | 44,7 | 47 |
| 5. | Farmtrac 35 | 3 | 2150 | 24.3 | 242 | 76.75 | 24.3 | 39 |
| 1. | HMT 1811 | 2 | 1560 | 12.3 | 274 | 128.46 | 16.7 | 20 |
| 2. | HMT 2522 Edi | 2 | 1560 | 16.1 | 266 | 102.48 | 22.5 | 25 |
| 3. | HMT 2522 | 2 | 1560 | 16.6 | 256 | 87.95 | 22.5 | 25 |

| | | | | | | | | |
|---|---|---|---|---|---|---|---|---|
| 4. | HMT 3022 | 2 | 1798 | 22.1 | 265 | 75.57 | 30 | 30 |
| 5. | HMT 3511 | 3 | 2340 | 22.5 | 254 | 84.44 | 31.3 | 35 |
| 6. | HMT 3522 DX | 3 | 2340 | 22.5 | 254 | 83.55 | 30.7 | 39 |
| 7. | HMT 4022 | 3 | 2340 | | | | | 40 |
| 8. | HMT 4511 | 3 | 2698 | 30.5 | 274 | 69.67 | 41.4 | 45 |
| 9. | HMT 5911 | 4 | 3456 | 37.2 | 264 | 63.71 | 52.9 | 58 |
| 10. | HMT 7511 | 4 | 4160 | | | | | 75 |
| 1. | Hindustan G 312 | 2 | 1798 | 18.7 | 271 | 91.18 | 28.3 | |
| 2. | Hindustan G 453 DI | 3 | 2697 | 32.3 | 290 | 61.61 | 43.3 | |
| 3. | Hindustan Super G 614 | 4 | 4160 | 39.2 | 285 | 68.88 | 53.5 | |
| 4. | Hindustan G 614 | 4 | 4667 | 48.9 | 277 | 55.52 | | |
| 1. | Indofarm 2040 DI | 3 | 2503 | 24.5 | 257 | 81.22 | | 40 |
| 2. | Indofarm 2050 DI | 3 | 2503 | 31.6 | 274 | 61.71 | | 50 |
| 1. | John Deere 5103 | 3 | 2900 | 35.00(26.1) | 266 | 73.77 | | 40 |
| 2. | John Deere 5203 | 3 | 2900 | 44.20(33.0) | 238 | 55.34 | | 47 |
| 3. | John Deere 5310 | 3 | 2930 | 50.50(37.7) | 182 | 56.01 | | 55 |
| 1. | Mahindra 225 DI | 2 | 1261 | 12 | 264 | 142.92 | 17.3 | 30 |
| 2. | Mahindra 265 DI | 3 | 1788 | 22.8 | 249 | 76.10 | 31.0 | 36 |
| 3. | Mahindra B-275 DI | 3 | 1892 | 23.3 | 256 | 74.68 | 30.5 | 36 |
| 4. | Mahindra 365 DI | 3 | 1810 | 21.9 | 255 | 78.54 | | 33 |
| 5. | Mahindra 475 DI | 4 | 2384 | 29 | 238 | 61.38 | | 40 |
| 6. | Mahindra 585 DI | 4 | 2523 | 31.2 | 233 | 59.94 | 42.4 | 50 |
| 7. | Mahindra 595 DI | 4 | | 32.59 | 255 | | 44.2 | |
| 8. | Mahindra 605 DI | 4 | 3193 | 40.0 | 255 | | | 60 |

Continued...

(*Continued....* TABLE No. 1)

| Sr. No. | Model | Number of Cylinders | Capacity ($Cm^3$) | Max. pto power (kW) | SFC at max. power (g/kWh) | weight/pto power (Kg/kWh) | Power kW | Engine Power (HP) |
|---|---|---|---|---|---|---|---|---|
| 1. | Sonalika Int DI 730 | 2 | 1570 | | | 58.00 | | 30 |
| 2. | Sonalika Int DI 740 | 3 | 2400 | 24.5 | 255 | 77.96 | 33.3 | 40 |
| 3. | Sonalika Int. DI 750 | 3 | 2500 | | | 68.05 | | 50 |
| 4. | Sonaqlika 760 | 4 | 3457 | | | | | 60 |
| 5. | Sonalika 745 | 3 | 2592 | 28.87 | 259 | 75.86 | | 45 |
| 1. | Swaraj 722 FE | 1 | 1425 | 9 | 268 | | 12.2 | 24.5 |
| 2. | Swaraj 720 | 1 | 1425 | 9 | 268 | 138.89 | 12.2 | |
| 3. | Swaraj 724 | 2 | 1728 | 16.3 | 294 | 110.43 | 22.1 | 25 |
| 4. | Swaraj 724 FE | 2 | 1728 | 16 | 259 | 107.81 | 21.7 | 25 |
| 5. | Swaraj 735 | 3 | 2592 | 23.7 | 298 | 80.17 | 32.1 | 39 |
| 6. | Swaraj 735 FE | 3 | 2592 | 25.1 | 250 | 73.11 | 32.2 | 39 |
| 7. | Swaraj 744 FE | 3 | 3136 | 30.88 | | 62.50 | | 48 |
| 8. | Swaraj 855 | 3 | 3308 | 33.9 | 257 | 57.27 | 46.1 | 55 |
| 1. | Standard 335 | 3 | 2340 | | | | | 35 |
| 2. | Standard 345 | 3 | 2696 | 30.6 | 291 | | | 45 |
| 3. | Standard 460 | 4 | 3456 | | | | | 60 |
| 4. | Standard 475 | 4 | 4156 | as | | | | 75 |
| 1. | Same Greaves 503 | 3 | 3000 | 36.4 | 249 | 50.14 | 49.3 | 50 |
| 2. | Same Greaves 603 | 3 | 3000 | 39.7 | 255 | 51.13 | | 60 |
| 3. | Same Greaves 453 | 3 | 3000 | 29.35 | | 60.65 | | 42 |
| 1. | TAFE 18 DI | 2 | | 12.3 | 257 | | 16.8 | |
| 2. | TAFE 25 DI | 2 | 1670 | 17.7 | 269 | 90.41 | 24.2 | 28.4 |
| 3. | TAFE 30 DI | 3 | 1788 | 25.1 | 258 | 65.74 | 29.3 | 31.4 |
| 4. | TAFE MF 1035 | 3 | 2365 | 23.7 | 311 | 62.03 | 32.2 | 36.5 |

| | | | | | | | | |
|---|---|---|---|---|---|---|---|---|
| 5. | TAFE 1035 DI | 3 | 2365 | 24.9 | 243 | 65.66 | 31.1 | 36.5 |
| 6. | MF 245 J | 3 | 2500 | 30.5 | 256 | 58.2 | 41.5 | 47.6 |
| 7. | TAFE 5900 DI | 4 | 3330 | 38.0 | 266 | 58.68 | 51.7 | 60 |
| 1. | TEMPO OX 25 | 4 | 1797 | 18.2 | 258 | 76.92 | | 27 |
| 2. | TEMPO OX 35 | 3 | 1947 | 20.1 | 277 | | | 35 |
| 3. | TEMPO OX 45 | 4 | 2596 | 29 | 254 | 62.76 | 39.4 | 45 |
| 4. | TEMPO Balwan | 4 | 2594 | | | | | 50 |
| 1. | Veer Partap 1027 | 1 | 1559 | 14.1 | 276 | 115.25 | 19.1 | 24 |
| 2. | Veer Partap | 3 | 2365 | 25.1 | 245 | 64.74 | 34.1 | 35 |
| 3. | Veer Partap Belarus | 4 | 4940 | 44.8 | 267 | 74.77 | 23 | 62 |
| 1. | Ford 3030 | | | | | | 33.7hp | 35 |
| 2. | Ford 3230 | 3 | 2500 | 28.6 | 250 | 58.74 | 38.8hp | 42 |
| 3. | Ford 3630 | 3 | 2710 | 33.8 | 256 | 46.00 | 46.0 | 50 |
| 4. | Ford 5630 | 4 | 3613 | 43.4 | 252 | 59.00 | | 70 |

**Source :** TMA data

**TABLE No. 2: Technical details of Eicher tractors manufactured in India**

| Sr. No. | Particulars | Make and models of tractors | | | | |
|---|---|---|---|---|---|---|
| | | **Eicher-241** | **Eicher-242 NC** | **Eicher-310 NC** | **Eicher-312 NC** | **Eicher364 NC** |
| **1.** | Engine Model | Eicher-241 | Eicher-242 NC | Eicher-310 | Eicher-312 | Eicher 364-NC |
| **2.** | HP | 24 (15.1) | 24 | 24.4 (17.9) | 30 | 35 |
| **3.** | No. of Cylinders | 1 | 1 | 2 | 2 | 2 |
| **4.** | Bore (mm) | 115 | 115 | 100 | 100 | 100 |
| **5.** | Stroke (mm) | 150 | 150 | 114 | 114 | 125 |
| **6.** | Compression Ratio | | | 17:1 | | 16.3:1 |
| **7.** | Displacement Volume (cc) | 1557 | 1558 | 1790 | 1790 | 1963 |
| **8.** | Rated Speed (RPM) | 1650 | 1650 | 2150 | 2150 | 2150 |
| **9.** | Maximum Torque (N-m) | 93.90 (NM) | 10.9 Kg-m | 8.2 Kg-m (80.0 N-m) | 10.75 | 12.7 Kg-m |
| **10.** | PTO Power, HP (kW) | 15.1 kW | 14.1 kW | 24.4 (17.9) | 20.3 kW | 22.9 kW |
| **11.** | SFC , g/kW/hr (g/hp/hr) | 262 | 267 (175) | 276 (203) | 259 | 272 (180) |
| **12.** | Tyre Size | | | | | |
| | Front | 5.50 × 16 | 5.50 × 16 | 6.00×16 | 60 × 16 | 6.00 × 16 |
| | Rear | 12.4 × 28 | 12.4 × 28 | 12.4×28 | 12.4 × 28 | 12.7 × 28 |
| **13.** | Lift Capacity (Kgf) | 1000 | 6.47 (kN) | 1025 | 4.91 (kN) | 1200 |
| **14.** | No. of Gears | | | | | |
| | Forward | 6 | 8 | 8 | 8 | 8 |
| | Reverse | 2 | 2 | 2 | 2 | 2 |
| **15.** | PTO | | | | | |
| | No. of Splines | 6 | 21 | 21 | 21 | 21 |
| | PTO RPM | 540 | 1021 | 1000 | 1331 | 540 |
| **16.** | Type of Clutch | Single | Single (dry) | Single (dry) 250 mm | Single (dry) | Single (dry) 251 mm |
| **17.** | Electric Battery | 12.V, | 12 V, | 12 V, | 12 V, | 12 V, |
| **18.** | Overall Dimensions | | | | | |
| | Length mm | 3072 | 3135 | 3105 | 3025 | 3003 |
| | Width mm | 1635 | 1650 | 1631 | 1620 | 1615 |
| | Height mm | 2010 | 2000 | 2169 | 2165 | 2330 |
| **19.** | Ground Clearance (mm) | 380 | 390 | 331 | 340 | 340 |
| **20.** | Weight of Tractor (Kg) | | 1765 | 2050 | | 1790 |
| **21.** | Address of Manufacturers | Eicher Tractors, Marketing Division, 59, NIT,FARIDABAD-121001 Ph. 8233751 Fax: 8233233 | | | | |

*Continued....*

(*Contdinued...* TABLE No. 2)

| Sr. No. | Particulars | Make and models of tractors | | | |
|---|---|---|---|---|---|
| | | Eicher-368 | Eicher-480 DI | Eicher-485 DI | Eicher-6100 |
| 1. | Engine Model | Simpson | Eicher-480 | Eicher-485 DI | Eicher-6100 Euro |
| 2. | HP (kW) | | 44 | 44 | 61 |
| 3. | No. of Cylinders | 3 | 3 | 3 | 3 |
| 4. | Bore (mm) | 100 | 91.4 | 100 | 108 |
| 5. | Stroke (mm) | 125 | 127 | 125 | 120 |
| 6. | Compression Ratio | 17:1 | 18.5:1 | | 16.5:1 |
| 7. | Displacement Volume | 2945 | 2500 | 2945 | 3300 |
| 8. | Rated Speed (RPM) | 2150 | 2150 | 2150 | 2250 |
| 9. | Maximum Torque (N-m) | 11.30 kg N | 16.4 kg-m | | 163 NM |
| 10. | PTO Power, HP(kW) | 34.0(25.0) | 39.7 HP | 41.0 HP | 40.2 |
| 11. | Specific Fuel Consumption (g/kW/hr) | 249(183) | 245 | | 255 |
| 12. | Tyre Size | | | | |
| | Front | 6.00 × 16 | 6.00 × 16 | 6.00 × 16 | 7.5 × 16 |
| | Rear | 12.4 × 28 | 13.6 × 28 | 13.6 × 28 | 16.9 × 30 |
| 13. | Lift Capacity (Kgf) | 1200 | 1200 | 1200 | 2000 |
| 14. | No. of Gears | | | | |
| | Forward | 8 | 8 | 8 | 12 |
| | Reverse | 2 | 2 | 2 | 8 |
| 15. | PTO | | | | |
| | No. of Splines | 21 | 6 | | 6 |
| | PTO RPM | 1616 | 540 | 540 | 540 |
| 16. | Type of Clutch | Single dry 280 mm | Single (dry) 280 mm | Single (dry) 280 mm | Dual Disc (294.9) |
| 17. | Electric Battery | 12V, 70 Ah | 12V, 70 Ah | 12V, 88 Ah | 12 V, 125 Ah |
| 18. | Overall Dimensions | | | | |
| | Length | 3435 | 3525 | | 4025 |
| | Width | 1650 | 1700 | | 1940 |
| | Height | 2087 | 2170 | | 2595 |
| 19. | Ground Clearance (mm) | 345 | 320 | | 440 mm |
| 20. | Weight of Tractor (Kg) | 1820 | 2030 | 2045 | 2865 |
| 21. | Address of Manufacturers | Eicher Tractors, Marketing Division, 59, NIT, FARIDABAD121001 Ph. 8233751 Fax: 8233233 | | | |

**Table No. 3: Technical details of Escorts tractors manufactured in India**

| Sr. No. | Particulars | Make and models of tractors | | | | |
|---|---|---|---|---|---|---|
| | | Escort-325 | Escort-335 | Escort-340 | Escort-430 Powertrac | Escort-435 Powertrac |
| 1. | Engine Model | Escort | Escort | Escort 3.273 | Escort3.179 | Escort3.215 |
| 2. | HP (kW) | 27 | 35 | 40 | 30 | 35 |
| 3. | No. of Cylinders | 2 | 2 | 3 | 3 | 3 |
| 4. | Bore (mm) | 97.6 | 102 | 105 | 91 | 91 |
| 5. | Stroke (mm) | 120 | 120 | 105 | 92 | 110 |
| 6. | Compression Ratio | | | | | |
| 7. | Displacement Volume | 1795 | 1960 | 2728 | 1790 | 2450 |
| 8. | Rated Speed (RPM) | 2200 | 2200 | 2200 | 2200 | |
| 9. | Maximum Torque (N-m) | 96.6 | | 15 kg-m | 11.2 kg-m | 13.2 kg-m |
| 10. | PTO Power, HP(kW) | 16.6 kW | 20.9 kW | 37 (33.2) | | |
| 11. | Specific Fuel Consumption (g/kW/hr) | 288 | 268 | 250 | | |
| 12. | Tyre Size | | | | | |
| | Front | 5.5 × 16 | 6 × 16 | 6.00 × 16 | 6.00 × 16 | 6.00 × 16 |
| | Rear | 12.4 × 28 | 12.4 × 2.8 | 12.4 × 28 | 12.4 × 28 | 12.4 × 28 |
| 13. | Lift Capacity (Kgf) | 8.70 (kN) | 8.11 (kN) | 1000 | 1000 | 1000 |
| 14. | No. of Gears | | | | | |
| | Forward | 10 | | 6 | 6 | 8 |
| | Reverse | 2 | | 2 | 2 | 2 |
| 15. | PTO | | | | | |
| | No. of Splines | 21 | 21 | 8 21 | 6 | 21 |
| | PTO RPM | 1000 | 1000 | 540 1000 | 540 | 1000 |
| 16. | Type of Clutch | Single | Single | Single(dry) 280 mm | Single(dry) 250 mm | Single(dry) 250 mm |
| 17. | Electric Battery | 12.V | 12.V | 12V, 100Ah | 12V,70Ah | 12V,70Ah |
| 18. | Overall Dimensions | | | | | |
| | Length mm | 3140 | 3150 | 3380 | 3275 | 3275 |
| | Width mm | 1710 | 1708 | 1690 | 1860 | 1860 |
| | Height mm | 2045 | 2055 | 2070 | 2070 | 2070 |
| 19. | Ground Clearance (mm) | 375 | 380 | 360 | 360 | 360 |
| 20. | Weight of Tractor (Kg) | | | 1865 | 1740 | 1740 |
| 21. | Address of Manufacturers | Escorts Limited, Agricultural Machinery Division, 18/4, Mathura Road, FARIDABAD-121007, Ph. 284911, Fax: 284839 | | | | |

*Continued....*

(*Contdinued...* Table No. 3)

| Sr. No. | Particulars | Make and models of tractors | | | |
|---|---|---|---|---|---|
| | | Escort-440 Powertrac | Escort-455 Powertrac | Farmtrac-30 Hero | Farmtrac-35 Champion |
| 1. | Engine Model | Escort | Escort | Escort | Escort ADI |
| 2. | HP (kW) | 40 | 55 | 30 | 39 |
| 3. | No. of Cylinders | 3 | 3 | 3 | 3 |
| 4. | Bore (mm) | 105 | 105 | 91 | 91 |
| 5. | Stroke (mm) | 105 | 120 | 92 | 110 |
| 6. | Compression Ratio | 175:1 | 175:1 | 18:1 | 18:1 |
| 7. | Displacement Volume | 2727 | 3117 | 1795 | 2150 |
| 8. | Rated Speed (RPM) | 2200 | 2200 | 2200 | 2200 |
| 9. | Maximum Torque (N-m) | | 188.7 Nm | 10.18 kg.m | 12.4 kg.m |
| 10. | PTO Power, HP (kW) | 29.2 (387) | 35.5 | 28.2 (20.7) | 33.0 (24.3) |
| 11. | Specific Fuel Consumption (g/hp/hr) | 253 kg (186)g | 270 | 252 (185) | 242 (178) |
| 12. | Tyre Size<br>Front<br>Rear | <br>6.00 × 16<br>14.9 × 28 | <br>7.50 × 16<br>16.9 × 28 | <br>6..00 × 16<br>12.4 × 28 | <br>6.00 × 16<br>12.4 × 28 |
| 13. | Lift Capacity (Kgf) | 1300 | 1300 | 1050 | 1050 |
| 14. | No. of Gears<br>Forward<br>Reverse | <br>8<br>2 | <br>8<br>2 | <br>8<br>2 | <br>8<br>2 |
| 15. | PTO<br>No. of Splines<br>PTO RPM | <br>6<br>1000 | <br>6<br>540 | <br><br>540 | <br><br>540 |
| 16. | Type of Clutch | Single(dry) | Single(dry) | Single(dry) | Single (dry) |
| 17. | Electric Battery | 12 V, 70 Ah | 12V, 100Ah | 12V, 70 Ah | 12V, 70Ah |
| 18. | Overall Dimensions<br>Length<br>Width<br>Height | | <br>3550<br>1865<br>2210 | <br>3260<br>1715<br>2070 | <br>3265<br>1705<br>2060 |
| 19. | Ground Clearance (mm) | | 430 | 375 | 370 |
| 20. | Weight of Tractor (Kg) | | 2135 | 1860 | 1865 |
| 21. | Address of Manufacturers | Escorts Limited, Agricultural Machinery Division, 18/4, Mathura Road, FARIDABAD-121007, Ph. 284911, Fax: 284839 | | | |

*Continued....*

(*Contdinued...* Table No. 3)

| Sr. No. | Particulars | Make and models of tractors | | | |
|---|---|---|---|---|---|
| | | **Farmtrac-50** | **Farmtrac-55** | **Farmtrac-60** | **Farmtrac-70** |
| 1. | Engine Model | Escort | Escort | Escort | Escort |
| 2. | HP | 45 | 47 SAE | 50 | 60 |
| 3. | No. of Cylinders | 3 | 3 | 3 | 3 |
| 4. | Bore (mm) | 106.68 | 106.68 | 111.7 | 111.76 |
| 5. | Stroke (mm) | 106.68 | 106.68 | 106.68 | 111.76 |
| 6. | Compression Ratio | | | | 16.6:1 |
| 7. | Displacement Volume (cc) | 2868 | 2868 | 3147 | 3292 |
| 8. | Rated Speed (RPM) | 2000 | 2000 | 2000 | 2200 |
| 9. | Maximum Torque(N-m) | 158.6 | 17.2 kg-m | 20.6 kg-m | 19.3 kg.m |
| 10. | PTO Power HP(kW) | 31 kW | 40 HP | 44.7(33.3) | 52.2(38.4) |
| 11. | Specific Fuel Consumption (g/kW/hr) | 297 | 297 | 253(186) | 273(201) |
| 12. | Tyre Size<br>Front<br>Rear | <br>6.00 × 16<br>13.6 × 28 | <br>6.00 × 16<br>13.6 × 28 | <br>6.00 × 16<br>13.6 × 28 | <br>7.50 × 16<br>16.9/14 × 30 |
| 13. | Lift Capacity (Kgf) | 1050 | 1050 | 1050 | 1050 |
| 14. | No. of Gears<br>Forward<br>Reverse | <br>8<br>2 | <br>8<br>2 | <br>8<br>2 | <br>8<br>2 |
| 15. | PTO<br>No. of Splines<br>PTO RPM | <br>6<br>540 | | <br>6<br>540 | |
| 16. | Type of Clutch | Single(dry) | Single(dry)<br>280 mm | Single (dry)<br>280 mm | Single dry<br>280 mm |
| 17. | Electric Battery | 12V, 88Ah | 12V, 88 Ah | 12V, 88Ah | 12V, 88Ah |
| 18. | Overall Dimensions<br>Length mm<br>Width mm<br>Height mm | <br>3235<br>1700<br>2160 | | <br>3310<br>1710<br>2180 | <br>3540<br>1233<br>2350 |
| 19. | Ground Clearance (mm) | 355 | | 360 | 470 |
| 20. | Weight of Tractor (Kg) | | 1955 | 1985 | 2370 |
| 21. | Address of Manufacturers | Escorts Limited, Agricultural Machinery Division, 18/4, Mathura Road, FARIDABAD-121007, Ph. 284911, Fax: 28483 | | | |

TABLE No. 4: Technical details of Ford tractors manufactured in India

| Sr. No. | Particulars | Make and models of tractors | | |
|---|---|---|---|---|
| | | Ford-3230 | Ford-3630 | Ford-5630 |
| 1. | Engine Model | Ford | Ford | Ford |
| 2. | HP | 40 | 50 | 70 SAE |
| 3. | No. of Cylinders | 3 | 3 | 4 |
| 4. | Bore (mm) | 91.4 | 100 | 100 |
| 5. | Stroke (mm) | 127 | 110 | 115 |
| 6. | Compression Ratio | 18.5:1 | 17 : 1 | 17 : 1 |
| 7. | Displacement Volume | 2500 | 2710 | 3613 |
| 8. | Rated Speed (RPM) | 2000 | 2500 | 2500 |
| 9. | Maximum Torque (N-m) | 15.45 kg.m | 141.7(14.45) | 195.2(19.90) |
| 10. | PTO Power, HP (kW) | 38.8(28.6) | 33.8(46°) | 43.4(59.0) |
| 11. | Specific Fuel Consumption, g/kW/hr (g/hp/hr) | 250 (184) | 256 (188) | 252 (185) |
| 12. | Tyre Size | | | |
| | Front | 6.00 × 16 | 6.00 × 16 | 7.50 × 16 |
| | Rear | 12.4 × 28 | 13.6/16.9 × 28 | 18.4 × 3 |
| 13. | Lift Capacity (Kgf) | 103.2 | 1750 | 1950 |
| 14. | No. of Gears | | | |
| | Forward | 8 | 8 | 8 |
| | Reverse | 2 | 2 | 2 |
| 15. | PTO | | | |
| | No. of Splines | 6 | 6 | 6 |
| | PTO RPM | 540 | 540 | 540 |
| 16. | Type of Clutch | Dual (dry) 279.4 mm | Dual (dry) 279.4 mm | Dual (dry) 279.4mm |
| 17. | Electric Battery | 12V, 88Ah | 12V, 88Ah | 12V,100Ah |
| 18. | Overall Dimensions | | | |
| | Length | 3270 | 2900 | 3890 |
| | Width | 1682 | 1410 | 1995 |
| | Height | 2260 | 2380 | 2585 |
| 19. | Ground Clearance (mm) | 385 | 425 | 532 |
| 20. | Weight of Tractor (Kg) | 1680 | 2090 | 2475 |
| 21. | Address of Manufacturers | New Holland Tractors (India) Pvt. Ltd; 210, Okhla Industrial Area-III, New-Delhi-110020. | | |

**TABLE No. 5: Technical details of HMT tractors manufactured in India**

| Sr. No. | Particulars | Make and models of tractors | | | | |
|---|---|---|---|---|---|---|
| | | **HMT-1811** | **HMT-2522 EDI** | **HMT-2522** | **HMT-3022 Edi** | **HMT-3511** |
| 1. | Engine Model | HMT-1811 | HMT | HMT (IDI) AVL design | HMT(DI) | HMT |
| 2. | HP (kW) | 20 | 25 | 25 | 30 | 35 |
| 3. | No. of Cylinders | 2 | 2 | 2 | 2 | 3 |
| 4. | Bore (mm) | 95 | 95 | 95 | 102 | 95 |
| 5. | Stroke (mm) | 110 | 110 | 110 | 110 | 110 |
| 6. | Compression Ratio | 17.4:1 | 17.4:1 | 17.4:1 | 17:1 | 17.9:1 |
| 7. | Displacement Volume | 1560 | 1560 | 1560 | 1798 | 2340 |
| 8. | Rated Speed (RPM) | 2000 | 2100 | 2100 | 2100 | 2000 |
| 9. | Maximum Torque(N-m) | | 87.8 | 8.23 kg.m | | 108.5 |
| 10. | PTO Power | 17 (12.3 ) | 16.1 kW | 21.2(15.6 ) | 22.1 kW | 22.5 kW |
| 11. | Specific Fuel Consumption (g/kW/hr) | 274 | 266 | 279 (205) | 265 | 254 |
| 12. | Tyre Size | | | | | |
| | Front | 5.50 × 16 | 6.00 × 16 | 5.00 × 15 | 6.00 × 16 | 6.00 × 16 |
| | Rear | 11.2 × 28 | 12.4 × 28 | 8.00 × 18 | 12.4 × 28 | 12.4 × 28 |
| 13. | Lift Capacity (Kgf) | 800 | 800 | 549 | 1000 | 1200 |
| 14. | No. of Gears | | | | | |
| | Forward | 10 | 10 | 10 | 10 | 8 |
| | Reverse | 2 | 2 | 2 | 2 | 2 |
| 15. | PTO | | | | | |
| | No. of Splines | 6 | 6 | 6 | 545 | 519 |
| | PTO RPM | 545 | 545 | 540 | 210-1074 | 258-1095 |
| 16. | Type of Clutch | Dual (dry) | Dual (dry) | Dual (dry) | Dual (dry) | Dual (dry) |
| 17. | Electric Battery | 12V, 75Ah | 12V, 88Ah | 12V, 88Ah | 12V, 88Ah | 12V, 88Ah |
| 18. | Overall Dimensions (mm) | | | | | |
| | Length | 3096 | 3230 | 2830 | 3230 | 3310 |
| | Width | 1680 | 1710 | 1385 | 1710 | 1710 |
| | Height | 1505 (Steer.) | 2011 | 1435 | 1532 (Steer.) | 2075 |
| 19. | Ground Clearance (mm) | 390 | 360 | 165 | 385 | 390 |
| 20. | Weight of Tractor (Kg) | 1580 | 1670 | 1460 | 1670 | |
| 21. | Address of Manufacturers | HMT Limited (Tractor Business Group), 54, Madhya Marg, Sector 7C, Chandigarh-160010 Ph. 548501, 771495 Fax: 0172-548525, 549842 | | | | |

*Continued....*

(*Contdinued...* TABLE No. 5)

| Sr. No. | Particulars | Make and models of tractors | | | |
|---|---|---|---|---|---|
| | | **HMT-3022** | **HMT-3522 DX** | **HMT-4022** | **HMT 4511** |
| 1. | Engine Model | HMT (DI) | HMT (AVL) | HMT (AVL) DI | HMT 4511 |
| 2. | HP | 30 | 39 | 40 | 45 |
| 3. | No. of Cylinders | 2 | 3 | 3 | 3 |
| 4. | Bore (mm) | 102 | 95 | 95 | 102 |
| 5. | Stroke (mm) | 110 | 110 | 110 | 110 |
| 6. | Compression Ratio | | 17.4:1 | 17.4:1 | 17:1 |
| 7. | Displacement Volume | 1798 | 2340 | 2340 | 2698 |
| 8. | Rated Speed (RPM) | 2100 | 2100 | 2100 | 2200 |
| 9. | Maximum Torque(N-m) | | | | 149.7 |
| 10. | PTO Power, HP (kW) | | | | 30.5 kW |
| 11. | Specific Fuel Consumption (g/bhp/hr) | 265 | | | 274 |
| 12. | Tyre Size<br>Front<br>Rear | | <br>6.00 × 16<br>12.4 × 28 | <br>6.00 × 16 8PR<br>13.6 × 28 10PR | <br>6.00 × 16<br>13.6 × 28 |
| 13. | Lift Capacity (Kgf) | | 1200 | 1200 | 1200 |
| 14. | No. of Gears<br>Forward<br>Reverse | <br>10<br>2 | <br>8<br>2 | <br>8<br>2 | <br>8<br>2 |
| 15. | PTO<br>No. of Splines<br>PTO RPM | | <br>545<br>271–1150 | <br>545<br>271–1150 | <br>545<br>284–1205 |
| 16. | Type of Clutch | Dual (dry) | Dual (dry) 280 mm | Multiple 295 mm | Dual (dry) |
| 17. | Electric Battery | | 12V, 88Ah | 12V, 88Ah | 12V, 88Ah |
| 18. | Overall Dimensions<br>Length<br>Width<br>Height | | <br>3310<br>1710<br>2008 | | <br>3520<br>1940<br>2135 |
| 19. | Ground Clearance (mm) | | 325 | | 390 |
| 20. | Weight of Tractor (Kg) | | 1880 | 2050 | 2035 |
| 21. | Address of Manufacturers | HMT Limited (Tractor Business Group), 54, Madhya Marg, Sector 7C, Chandigarh-160010 Ph. 548501, 771495 Fax: 0172-548525, 549842 | | | |

*Continued....*

(*Contdinued...* **TABLE No. 5**)

| Sr. No. | Particulars | Make and models of tractors | | |
|---|---|---|---|---|
| | | HMT-4922 | HMT-5911 | HMT-7511 |
| 1. | Engine Model | HMT AVL | HMT | 4R1040 |
| 2. | HP (kW) | 50 | 58 | 75 |
| 3. | No. of Cylinders | 3 | 4 | 4 |
| 4. | Bore (mm) | 102 | 100 | 105 |
| 5. | Stroke (mm) | 110 | 110 | 120 |
| 6. | Compression Ratio | 17.4:1 | 17:1 | 17:1 |
| 7. | Displacement Volume | 2698 | 3456 | 4160 |
| 8. | Rated Speed (RPM) | 2200 | 2200 | 2200 |
| 9. | Maximum Torque(N-m) | | | |
| 10. | PTO Power | | 37.2 kW | |
| 11. | Specific Fuel Consumption (g/kW/hr) | | 264 | |
| 12. | Tyre Size | | | |
| | Front | 6.00 × 16 | 6.50 × 20 | 6.50 × 20 |
| | Rear | 13.6 × 28 | 16.9 × 28 | 18.4/15 × 30 |
| 13. | Lift Capacity (Kgf) | 1200 | 1700 | 2000 |
| 14. | No. of Gears | | | |
| | Forward | 8 | 10 | 8 |
| | Reverse | 2 | 2 | 2 |
| 15. | PTO | | | |
| | No. of Splines | 545 | 540 | 540 |
| | PTO RPM | 284–1205 | 273–1331.6 | 306–1331.6 |
| 16. | Type of Clutch | Dual (dry) | Dual (dry) | Dual(dry) |
| 17. | Electric Battery | 12V, 88Ah | 2, 12V | 2, 12V |
| 18. | Overall Dimensions (mm) | | | |
| | Length | | 3655 | 3870 |
| | Width | | 1850 | 1860 |
| | Height | | 2220 | 2512 |
| 19. | Ground Clearance (mm) | | 470 | 550 |
| 20. | Weight of Tractor (Kg) | 2340 | 2375 | 3300 |
| 21. | Address of Manufacturers | HMT Limited (Tractor Business Group), 54, Madhya Marg, Sector 7C, Chandigarh-160010 Ph. 548501, 771495 Fax: 0172-548525, 549842 | | |

**TABLE No. 6: Technical details of Hindustan tractors manufactured in India**

| Sr. No. | Particulars | Make and models of tractors | | | |
|---|---|---|---|---|---|
| | | Hindustan G 312 | Hindustan G 453 DI | Hindustan Super G 61 | Hindustan G 614 |
| 1. | Engine Model | | | | |
| 2. | HP (kW) | | | | |
| 3. | No. of Cylinders | 2 | 3 | 4 | 4 |
| 4. | Bore (mm) | 102 | 102 | 105 | 105 |
| 5. | Stroke (mm) | 110 | 110 | 120 | 120 |
| 6. | Compression Ratio | | | | |
| 7. | Displacement Volume | 1798 | 2697 | 4160 | 4667 |
| 8. | Rated Speed (RPM) | 2000 | 2200 | 1650 | 2000 |
| 9. | Maximum Torque (N-m) | 90.2 | 153.5 | 19.94 kg.m | 196 |
| 10. | PTO Power. HP (kW) | 28.3 (20.8) | 32.3 kW | 53.5 (39.2) | 48.9 kW |
| 11. | Specific Fuel Consumption (g/kW/hr) | 271 | 290 | 285 (210) | 277 |
| 12. | Tyre Size<br>Front<br>Rear | <br>5.50 × 16<br>12.4 × 28 | <br>6.00 × 16<br>13.6 × 28 | <br>6.50 × 16<br>16.9/14 × 28 | <br>6.5 × 16<br>16.9 × 28 |
| 13. | Lift Capacity (Kgf) | 6.85 | 8.08 kN | | 9.68 kN |
| 14. | No. of Gears<br>Forward<br>Reverse | <br>8<br>2 | <br>10<br>2 | <br>8<br>2 | <br>8<br>2 |
| 15. | PTO<br>No. of Splines<br>PTO RPM | <br>6<br>540 | <br>6<br>540 | <br>6<br>540 | <br>6<br>540 |
| 16. | Type of Clutch | Single | Dual | Single dry | Dual |
| 17. | Electric Battery | 12 V | 12 V | 12V, 88Ah | 12 V |
| 18. | Overall Dimensions<br>Length mm<br>Width mm<br>Height mm | <br>3065<br>1645<br>2240 | <br>3255<br>1800<br>2275 | <br>3645<br>1910<br>2017 | <br>3770<br>1910<br>2200 |
| 19. | Ground Clearance (mm) | 360 | 455 | 410 | 410 |
| 20. | Weight of Tractor (Kg) | | | 2615 | |
| 21. | Address of Manufacturers | Gujrat Tractors Limited, Vishwamatri Railway Station, Overbridge VADODRA-390001 | | | |

**TABLE No. 7: Technical details of Indofarm and John Deere tractors manufactured in India**

| Sr. No. | Particulars | Make and models of tractors | | | | |
|---|---|---|---|---|---|---|
| | | Indofarm 2040 DI | Indofarm 2050 DI | John Deere 5103 | John Deere 5203 | John Deere 5310 |
| 1. | Engine Model | 2040 DI | 2050 DI | 3029DPY03 | 3029DPY02 | 3029DPY01 |
| 2. | HP (kW) | 40 | 50 | 40 | 47 | 55 |
| 3. | No. of Cylinders | 3 | 3 | 3 | 3 | 3 |
| 4. | Bore (mm) | 91.44 | 91.44 | 106.5 | 106.5 | 106.5 |
| 5. | Stroke (mm) | 127 | 127 | 110 | 110 | 110 |
| 6. | Compression Ratio | 16.5:1 | !6.5:1 | 17.4:1 | 17.4 : 1 | 17.8 : 1 |
| 7. | Displacement Volume (cc) | 2503 | 2503 | 2900 | 2900 | 2930 |
| 8. | Rated Speed (RPM) | 2000 | 2250 | 2300 | 2300 | 2400 |
| 9. | Maximum Torque (N-m) | | 160–165 | 170–175 | 13.39 kg.m | 178 Nm |
| 10. | PTO Power, HP(kW) | 33.3(24.5) | 42.9(31.6) | 33.2(24.4) | 44.20 | 50.50 |
| 11. | SFC,g/kW/hr (g/hp/hr) | 257(189) | 274(202) | 266(196) | 238 (175) | 243 (179) |
| 12. | Tyre Size | | | | | |
| | Front | 6.00 × 16 | 6.00 × 16 | 6.00×16 8 ply | 6.00×16 8pr | 6.50×20 8 pr |
| | Rear | 12.4 × 28/ 13.6 × 28 | 13.6 × 28/ 14.6 × 28 | 12.4×28 12pl | 13.6×28 12pl | 16.9×28 12pr |
| 13. | Lift Capacity (Kgf) | 1000 | 1200 | 1220 | 1550 | 2000 |
| 14. | No.of Gears | | | | | |
| | Forward | 8 | 8 | 8 | 8 | 8 |
| | Reverse | 2 | 2 | 2 | 2 | 2 |
| 15. | PTO | | | | | |
| | No. of Splines | 21 | 21 | 6 | 6 | 6 |
| | PTO RPM | 976 | 1098 | 540 | 540 | 540 |
| 16. | Type of Clutch | Single/dual | Single/dual | Single | Single/dual | Dual |
| 17. | Electric Battery | 12V, 100Ah | 12V, 100Ah | 12V,80Ah | !2V, 88Ah | 12V, 88Ah |
| 18. | Overall Dimensions | | | | | |
| | Length | 360 | 3670 | 3335 | 3360 | 3500 |
| | Width | 1675 | 1745 | 1650 | 179 | 1865 |
| | Height | 2220 | 2280 | 2205 | 2215 | 2320 |
| 19. | Ground Clearance(mm) | 380 | 395 | 365 | 420 | 450 |
| 20. | Weight of Tractor (Kg) | 1990 | 1950 | 1795 | 1835 | 2110 |
| 21. | Address | Indofarm Equipment Ltd., S.C..O, 859, N.A.C Manimajra, Kalka Road, Chandigarh | | John Deere Pvt. Ltd., Pune Nagar Road, Sanaswadi, Taluka- Shirur, Distt. PUNE - 412208 | | |

**TABLE No. 8: Technical details of Mahindra tractors manufactured in India**

| Sr. No. | Particulars | Make and models of tractors | | | | |
|---|---|---|---|---|---|---|
| | | Mahindra Yuvraj | Mahindra 225 DI | Mahindra 265 DI | Mahindra B-275 DI | Mahindra 365 DI |
| 1. | Engine Model | MDI-1365 | | MDI-1765 | MDI-1815 | MDI-1815 |
| 2. | HP 25 | 25 | 30 | 36 | 33 | |
| 3. | No. of Cylinders | 2 | 2 | 3 | 3 | 3 |
| 4. | Bore (mm) | 88.9 | 88.9 | 88.9 | 88.9 | 88.9 |
| 5. | Stroke (mm) | 110 | 101.6 | 96.0 | 101.6 | 97.2 |
| 6. | Compression Ratio | | | | | |
| 7. | Displacement Volume | 1365 | 1261 | 1788 | 1892 | 1810 |
| 8. | Rated Speed (RPM) | 2400 | 2300 | 2300 | 2300 | 2300 |
| 9. | Maximum Torque (N-m) | | 53.6 | 103.8 | 110.5 | 98.8 |
| 10. | PTO Power,HP(kW) | | 12.0 | 22.8 | 23.3 | 21.9 |
| 11. | Specific Fuel Consumption (g/kW/hr) | | 264 | 249 | 256 | 255 |
| 12. | Tyre Size | | | | | |
| | Front | 6.00 × 16 | 6.0 × 16 | 6.00 × 16 | 6.00 × 16 | 6.00 × 16 |
| | Rear | 12.4 × 28 | 12.4 × 28 | 12.4 × 28 | 12.4 × 28 | 12.4 × 28 |
| 13. | Lift Capacity (Kgf) | | 8.88 (kN) | 7.03 (kN) | 8.10 (kN) | 7.22 (kN) |
| 14. | No. of Gears | | | | | |
| | Forward | 8 | 8 | 8 | 8 | 8 |
| | Reverse | 2 | 2 | 2 | 2 | 2 |
| 15. | PTO | | | | | |
| | No. of Splines | 6 | 8 | 6 | 6 | 6 |
| | PTO RPM | 627 | 2 | 627 | 627 | 627 |
| 16. | Type of Clutch | Single (dry) | Single | Single (dry) | Single (dry) | Single (dry) |
| 17. | Electric Battery | 12V, 80Ah | 12 Vs | 12V, 88Ah | 12V, 88Ah | 12V, 88Ah |
| 18. | Overall Dimensions | | | | | |
| | Length mm | | 3067 | 3050 | 3065 | 3070 |
| | Width mm | | 1645 | 1630 | 1630 | 1630 |
| | Height mm | | 2035 | 2020 | 2035 | 2030 |
| 19. | Ground Clearance (mm) | | 312 | 325 | 338 | 355 |
| 20. | Weight of Tractor (Kg) | 1770 | | 1735 | | 1745 |
| 21. | Address of Manufacturers | Mahindra and Mahindra Ltd; Tractor Division, Mahindra Tower, Road No. 13, WORLI, MUMBAI-400018 | | | | |

**(*Contdinued*... TABLE No. 8)**

| Sr. No. | Particulars | Make and models of tractors | | | | |
|---|---|---|---|---|---|---|
| | | **Mahindra 445 Arjun** | **Mahindra 475 DI** | **Mahindra 565 Arjun** | **Mahindra 575 DI** | **Mahindra 585 DI** |
| 1. | Engine Model | NE 342 | MDI-2385 | NE 452 | | MDI30013 |
| 2. | HP (kW) | 42 | 40(33) | 52 | 40(29.4) | 50(40) |
| 3. | No. of Cylinders | 3 | 4 | 4 | 4 | 4 |
| 4. | Bore (mm) | | 88.9 | | 88.9 | 88.9 |
| 5. | Stroke (mm) | | 96.0 | | 101.6 | 101.6 |
| 6. | Compression Ratio | 19.4:1 | | | | 18 : 1 |
| 7. | Displacement Volume | 2394 | 2384 | 3054 | 2523 | 2523 |
| 8. | Rated Speed (RPM) | 2100 | 2300 | 2100 | 2300 | 2600 |
| 9. | Maximum Torque (N-m) or kg-m | 15.5 kg-m | | 19.9 kg-m | 147.0 Nm | 132.3 Nm |
| 10. | PTO Power, HP(kW) | 36.5 HP | 29.0 kW | 47.5 HP | 29 KW | 31.2 kW |
| 11. | Specific Fuel Consumption, g/kW/hr (g/hp/hr) | 188g/bhp | 238 | 175g/bhp | 233 (171) | 333 |
| 12. | Tyre Size<br>Front<br>Rear | <br>6.00 × 16<br>13.6 × 28 | <br>6.00 × 16 P<br>12.4 × 28 12P | <br>6.00 × 16<br>14.9 × 28 | <br>6.00 × 16<br>13.6 × 28 | <br>6.00 ×16.8PR<br>13.6 × 12PR |
| 13. | Lift Capacity (Kgf) | 1200 | | 1800 | 1000 | 11.97 KN |
| 14. | No. of Gears<br>Forward<br>Reverse | <br>8<br>2 | <br>8<br>2 | <br>8<br>2 | <br>8<br>2 | <br>8<br>2 |
| 15. | PTO<br>No. of Splines<br>PTO RPM | <br>6<br>540 | <br>6<br>540 | <br>6<br>540 | <br>6<br>540 | <br>6<br>540 |
| 16. | Type of Clutch | Diagphargm 279.4 mm | single (dry) 279.4 mm | Diaphragm 279.4 mm | Single (dry) 280 mm | Singe/Dual 279.4 mm |
| 17. | Electric Battery | 12V, 88Ah | 12V, 75 Ah | | 12,V | 12V, 88Ah |
| 18. | Overall Dimensions<br>Length<br>Width<br>Height | <br>3530<br>1845<br>2010 | | <br>3480<br>1940<br>2120 | <br>3117<br>1770<br>2020 | <br>3135<br>1755<br>2040 |
| 19. | Ground Clearance (mm) | 385 | | | 350 | 372 |
| 20. | Weight of Tractor (Kg) | 2350 | 1780 | | 1870 | 1900 |
| 21. | Address of Manufacturers | Mahindra and Mahindra Ltd; Tractor Division, Mahindra Tower, Road No. 13, WORLI, MUMBAI-400018. | | | | |

*Continued....*

**(*Continued...* TABLE No. 8:)**

| Sr. No. | Particulars | Make and models of tractors Mahindra 605DI Arjun |
|---|---|---|
| 1. | Engine Model | NE 457 |
| 2. | HP (kW) | 60 |
| 3. | No. of Cylinders | 4 |
| 4. | Bore (mm) | 94 |
| 5. | Stroke (mm) | 115 |
| 6. | Compression Ratio | 19.4:1 |
| 7. | Displacement Volume | 3192 |
| 8. | Rated Speed (RPM) | 2100 |
| 9. | Maximum Torque (N-m) or kg-m | 20.7 kg-m |
| 10. | PTO Power, HP(kW) | 51.4 (37.8 ) |
| 11. | Specific Fuel Consumption, g/kW/hr (g/hp/hr) | 240(177) |
| 12. | Tyre Size | |
| | Front | 7.50 × 16 |
| | Rear | 16.9 × 28 |
| 13. | Lift Capacity (Kgf) | 1800 |
| 14. | No. of Gears | |
| | Forward | 8 |
| | Reverse | 2 |
| 15. | PTO | |
| | No. of Splines | 6 |
| | PTO RPM | 683 |
| 16. | Type of Clutch | Single/Dual 279.4 mm |
| 17. | Electric Battery | 12V, 88Ah |
| 18. | Overall Dimensions | |
| | Length | 3480 |
| | Width | 1965 |
| | Height | 2255 |
| 19. | Ground Clearance (mm) | 445 |
| 20. | Weight of Tractor (Kg) | 2320 |
| 21. | Address of Manufacturers | Mahindra and Mahindra Ltd; Tractor Division, Mahindra Tower, Road No. 13, WORLI, MUMBAI-400018. |

**TABLE No. 9: Technical details of Same Greaves tractors manufactured in India**

| Sr. No. | Particulars | Make and models of tractors | | | |
|---|---|---|---|---|---|
| | | Same Greaves 393 | Same Greaves 453 | Same Greaves 503 | Same Greaves 603 |
| 1. | Engine Model | S 1000.3W | S 1000.3W | S1000.3W | S 1000.3 W |
| 2. | HP (kW) | 35(22) | 42(32) | 50 (37) | 60 (44) |
| 3. | No. of Cylinders | 3 | 3 | 3 | 3 |
| 4. | Bore (mm) | 105 | 105 | 105 | 105 |
| 5. | Stroke (mm) | 115.5 | 115.5 | 115.5 | 115.5 |
| 6. | Compression Ratio | 17:1 | 17:1 | 17:1 | 17:1 |
| 7. | Displacement Volume | 3000 | 3000 | 3000 | 3000 |
| 8. | Rated Speed (RPM) | 2200 | 2200 | 2350 | 2350 |
| 9. | Maximum Torque(N-m) | 145 N-m | 145 N-m | 234 N-m | 234 N-m |
| 10. | PTO Power (kW) | 29.35 kW | 29.35kW | 49.5(36.4) | 39.7 kW |
| 11. | Specific Fuel Consumption, g/kW/hr (g/hp/hr) | | | 249 (183) | 255 |
| 12. | Tyre Size<br>Front<br>Rear | <br>6.00 × 16 8p<br>12.4 × 28 12 P | <br>6.00 × 16 8p<br>12.4 × 28 12 P | <br>6.00 × 20 12 PR<br>14.9 × 28 12 P | <br>6.00 × 16 8p<br>16.9 × 28 12 P |
| 13. | Lift Capacity (Kgf) | 2000 | 2000 | 2000 | 2000 |
| 14. | No. of Gears<br>Forward<br>Reverse | <br>8<br>2 | <br>8<br>2 | <br>8<br>2 | <br>8<br>2 |
| 15. | PTO<br>No. of Splines<br>PTO RPM | <br>6<br>540 | <br>6<br>540 | <br>6<br>540 | <br>6<br>540 |
| 16. | Type of Clutch | Single | Single/dual | Single/dual | Single/dual |
| 17. | Electric Battery | 12 V, 80 Ah | 12 V, 80 Ah | 12 V, 80 Ah | 12V, 80 Ah |
| 18. | Overall Dimensions<br>Length<br>Width<br>Height | <br>3365<br>1645<br> | <br>3365<br>1645<br> | <br>3365<br>1645<br>2415 | <br>3365<br>1645<br> |
| 19. | Ground Clearance (mm) | | | 270 | 390 |
| 20. | Weight of Tractor (Kg) | 1780 | 1780 | 1940 | 2030 |
| 21. | Address of Manufacturers | SAME Greaves Tractors Ltd, 72, Spicot, Industrial Complex, RANIPET-632403 | | | |

TABLE No. 10: Technical details of Standard tractors manufactured in India

| Sr. No. | Particulars | Make and models of tractors | | | | |
|---|---|---|---|---|---|---|
| | | Standard 335 | Standard 345 | Standard 450 | Standard 460 | Standard 475 |
| 1. | Engine Model | SE-335/std | SE345/std | SE450/std | SE460/std | SE475/std |
| 2. | HP 35 | 45 | 50 | 60 | 75 | |
| 3. | No. of Cylinders | 3 | 3 | 4 | 4 | 4 |
| 4. | Bore (mm) | 95 | 102 | 95 | 100 | 105 |
| 5. | Stroke (mm) | 110 | 110 | 110 | 110 | 120 |
| 6. | Compression Ratio | 17.4 : 1 | 17 : 1 | | | |
| 7. | Displacement Volume (cc) | 2340 | 2696 | 3120 | 3456 | 4156 |
| 8. | Rated Speed (RPM) | 2200 | 2200 | 2250 | 2200 | 2200 |
| 9. | Maximum Torque (N-m) | 132 | 160.9 | | | |
| 10. | PTO Power, HP(kW) | 21.8 | 30.6 | | | |
| 11. | SFC (g/kW/hr) | 310 | 291 | | | |
| 12. | Tyre Size<br>Front<br><br>Rear | <br>6.00×16 8 PR<br><br>12.4×28 12 PR | <br>6.00×16 8 PR<br><br>13.6×28 12 PR | <br>6.00×16 8 PR<br><br>13.6×28 12 PR | <br>6.50×20 8 PR<br><br>16.9×28 12 PR | <br>6.50×20 8 PR<br><br>16.9×28 12 PR |
| 13. | Lift Capacity (Kgf) | 1200 | 1200 | 1200 | 1500 | 1500 |
| 14. | No. of Gears<br>Forward<br>Reverse | <br>10<br>2 | <br>10<br>2 | <br>10<br>2 | <br>10<br>2 | <br>10<br>2 |
| 15. | PTO<br>No. of Splines<br>PTO RPM | <br>21<br>467/480 | <br>21<br>467/480 | <br>21<br>540/972 | <br>21<br>540/972 | <br>21<br>540/972 |
| 16. | Type of Clutch | Single(dry) | Single(dry) | Dual | Dual | Dual |
| 17. | Electric Battery | 12V, 70Ah | 12V, 70Ah | | | |
| 18. | Overall Dimensions<br>Length<br>Width<br>Height | <br>2980<br>1350<br>2025 | <br>2980<br>1840<br>2035 | <br>3492<br>1840<br>2052 | <br>3730<br>1940<br>20+0 | <br>3730<br>1940<br>2185 |
| 19. | Ground Clearance (mm) | 396 | 496 | 436 | 475 | 475 |
| 20. | Weight of Tractor (Kg) | 2096 | 2120 | 2158 | 2325 | 2450 |
| 21. | Address of Manufacturers | Standard Combines (P) Ltd; (Tractor Division), Handiaya Chowk BARNALA-148101 Ph. 0167-3937981, 3938033, Fax: 3930833 e-mail: Scombine@sifty.com. | | | | |

**TABLE No. 11: Technical details of Sonalika tractors manufactured in India**

| Sr. No. | Particulars | Make and models of tractors | | | | |
|---|---|---|---|---|---|---|
| | | Sonalika 725 DI | Sonalika 730 DI | Sonalika DI 730 III | Sonalika DI 732 III | Sonalika DI 735 |
| 1. | Engine Model | S-217 | S-217 | IT-3092 | IT-3095 | IT-3097 |
| 2. | HP | 25 SAE | 30 SAE | 30 SAE | 32 SAE | 35 SAE |
| 3. | No. of Cylinders | 2 | 2 | 3 | 3 | 3 |
| 4. | Bore (mm) | 91.4 | 91.4 | 92 | 95 | 97 |
| 5. | Stroke (mm) | 127 | 127 | 110 | 110 | 110 |
| 6. | Compression Ratio | | 18.5:1 | | | |
| 7. | Displacement Volume (cc) | 1670 | 1670 | 2194 | 2338 | 2438 |
| 8. | Rated Speed (RPM) | 2000 | 2000 | 2100 | 2100 | 2100 |
| 9. | Maximum Torque (N-m) | | | | | |
| 10. | PTO Power, HP (kW) | | | | | |
| 11. | SFC (g/kW/hr) | | | | | |
| 12. | Tyre Size<br>Front<br>Rear | <br>6.00 × 16<br>12.4 × 8 | <br>6.00 × 16<br>12.4 × 8 | <br>6.00 × 16<br>12.4 × 8 | <br>6.00 × 16<br>12.4 × 8 | <br>6.00 × 16<br>12.4 × 8 |
| 13. | Lift Capacity (Kgf) | 1200 | 1200 | 1200 | 1200 | 1200 |
| 14. | No. of Gears<br>Forward<br>Reverse | <br>6<br>2 | <br>6<br>2 | <br>6<br>2 | <br>8<br>2 | <br>8<br>2 |
| 15. | PTO<br>No. of Splines<br>PTO RPM | <br>1000 ± 25 | <br>844 | <br>540 ± 10 | <br>540 ± 10 | <br>540 ± 10 |
| 16. | Type and Size of Clutch | Single(dry) 280 mm | Single(dry) 280 mm | Single(dry) 280 mm | Single(dry) 280 mm | Single(dry) 280 mm |
| 17. | Electric Battery | 12V, 70Ah | 12V, 70Ah | 12V, 70Ah | 12V, 70Ah | 12V, 70Ah |
| 18. | Overall Dimensions (mm)<br>Length<br>Width<br>Height | | <br>3400<br>1600<br>2400 | | | |
| 19. | Ground Clearance (mm) | | 380 | | | |
| 20. | Weight of Tractor (Kg) | | | | | |
| 21. | Address of Manufacturers | International Tractors Limited, Sonalika House, 283, AGCR Enclave, KARKARDOOMA, Delhi-110092 Ph. 22373785/89/91 | | | | |

*Continued....*

(*Continued*.... TABLE No. 11)

| Sr. No. | Particulars | Make and models of tractors | | | | |
|---|---|---|---|---|---|---|
| | | Sonalika DI 740 | Sonalika DI745 III | Sonalika DI 750 II | Sonalika DI 750 III | Sonalika DI-55 |
| 1. | Engine Model | Simpson-324 | IT-3100 | IT-3102 | IT-4095 F | IT-4100N |
| 2. | HP (kW) | 40 SAE | 45 SAE | 50 SAE | 50 SAE | 55 SAE |
| 3. | No. of Cylinders | 3 | 3 | 3 | 4 | 4 |
| 4. | Bore (mm) | 88.9 | 100 | 102 | 95 | 100 |
| 5. | Stroke (mm) | 127 | 110 | 110 | 110 | 110 |
| 6. | Compression Ratio | 17.5:1 | 17.5:1 | | 17.4:1 | 17 : 1 |
| 7. | Displacement Volume )cc) | 2400 | 2592 | 2695 | 3120 | 3456 |
| 8. | Rated Speed (RPM) | 2000 | 2100 | 2100 | 2100 | 2200 |
| 9. | Maximum Torque (N-m) or (Kg-m) | 13.00 kg.m | | | 13.99 kg.m | 185.5 Nm<br>18.92 kg m |
| 10. | PTO Power, HP(kW) | 33.0(24.3) | | | 42.6(31.3) | 36.6(49.8) |
| 11. | SFC (g/kW/hr) | 262(193) | | | 259(190) | 270(198) |
| 12. | Tyre Size<br>Front<br>Rear | <br>6.00 × 16<br>12.4 × 28 | <br>6.00 × 16<br>12.4 × 28 | <br>6.00 × 16<br>13.6 × 28 | <br>6.00 × 16<br>13.6 × 28 | <br>6.00 × 16<br>13.6 × 28/<br>14.9 × 28 |
| 13. | Lift Capacity (Kgf) | 1200 | 1600 | 1600 | 1200 | 1800 |
| 14. | No. of Gears<br>Forward<br>Reverse | <br>8<br>2 | <br>8<br>2 | <br>8<br>2 | <br>8<br>2 | <br>8<br>2 |
| 15. | PTO<br>No. of Splines<br>PTO RPM | <br>21<br>844 | <br>1000 ± 25<br>540 ± 10 | <br>1000 ± 25<br>540 ± 10 | <br>21<br>1074 | <br>21<br>1074 |
| 16. | Type and Size of Clutch | Single/Dual 280 mm | Single/Dual 280 mm | Single/Dual 280/295 mm | Dual (dry) 305 mm | Dual(dry) 280/295 mm |
| 17. | Electric Battery | 12V, 70 Ah | 12V, 70 Ah | 12V, 70 Ah | 12V,70 Ah | 12V,99 Ah |
| 18. | Overall Dimensions<br>Length<br>Width<br>Height | <br>3450<br>1690<br>2140 | | | <br>3745<br>1720<br>2120 | <br>3750<br>1700<br>2145 |
| 19. | Ground Clearance (mm) | 370 | | | 385 | 410 |
| 20. | Weight of Tractor (Kg) | 1910 | | | 2130 | 2135 |
| 21. | Address of Manufacturers | International Tractors Limited, Sonalika House, 283, AGCR Enclave, KARKARDOOMA,Delhi-110092 Ph. 22373785/89/91 | | | | |

*Continued....*

(*Continued....* **TABLE No. 11**)

| Sr. No. | Particulars | Make and models of tractors<br>Sonalika DI 60 |
|---|---|---|
| 1. | Engine Model | IT-4100N |
| 2. | HP (kW) | 60 SAE |
| 3. | No. of Cylinders | 4 |
| 4. | Bore (mm) | 100 |
| 5. | Stroke (mm) | 110 |
| 6. | Compression Ratio | 17:1 |
| 7. | Displacement Volume (cc) | 3456 |
| 8. | Rated Speed (RPM) | 2200 |
| 9. | Maximum Torque (N-m) or (Kg-m) | 178.6 (18.2) |
| 10. | PTO Power, HP(kW) | 37.9 (51.6) |
| 11. | SFC (g/kW/hr) | 254 g/kwh |
| 12. | Tyre Size | |
| | Front | 6.50 × 20 |
| | Rear | 16.9 × 28 |
| 13. | Lift Capacity (Kgf) | 1800 |
| 14. | No. of Gears | |
| | Forward | 8 |
| | Reverse | 2 |
| 15. | PTO | |
| | No. of Splines | 21 |
| | PTO RPM | 1074 |
| 16. | Type and Size of Clutch | Dual (dry) 280/295 mm |
| 17. | Electric Battery | 12V, 99Ah |
| 18. | Overall Dimensions | |
| | Length | 3763 |
| | Width | 1840 |
| | Height | 2140 |
| 19. | Ground Clearance (mm) | 460 |
| 20. | Weight of Tractor (Kg) | 2190 |
| 21. | Address of Manufacturers | International Tractors Limtied, Sonalika House, 283, AGCR Enclave, KARKARDOOMA, Delhi – 110092 Ph. 22373785/89/91 |

TABLE No. 12: Technical details of Swaraj tractors manufactured in India

| Sr. No. | Particulars | Make and models of tractors | | | | |
|---|---|---|---|---|---|---|
| | | Swaraj 720 | Swaraj 722 FE | Swaraj 724 FE | Swaraj 724 | Swaraj 733 FE |
| 1. | Engine Model | S 720 | S-15 | Swaraj | Swaraj | RB-3TR Kirloskar |
| 2. | HP (kW) | 19.5 SAE | 24.5 SAE | 25 | 25 | 34 SAE |
| 3. | No. of Cylinders | 1 | 1 | 2 | 2 | 2 |
| 4. | Bore (mm) | 110 | 120 | 100 | 100 | 110 |
| 5. | Stroke (mm) | 116 | 126 | 110 | 110 | 116 |
| 6. | Compression Ratio | | 17:1 | 17:1 | 17:1 | 17:1 |
| 7. | Displacement Volume | | 1425 | 1728 | 1728 | 2204 |
| 8. | Rated Speed (RPM) | 1800 | 1900 | 2000 | 2000 | 2000 |
| 9. | Maximum Torque(N-m) | 54.4 | 7.79 kg.m | 9.66 kg.m | | 11.00 kg.m |
| 10. | PTO Power (kW) | 9.0 | 18.57(13.6) | 22.1(16.2) | 16.3kW | 29.2(21.5) |
| 11. | Specific Fuel Consumption (g/kW/hr) | 268 | 269 (198) | 256 (189) | 294 | 263 (193) |
| 12. | Tyre Size<br>Front<br>Rear | <br>5.50 × 16<br>11.2 × 28 | <br>5.50 × 16<br>12.4 × 28 | <br>5.50 × 6<br>12.4 × 28 | <br>5.50 × 16<br>12.4 × 28 | <br>6.00 × 16<br>12.4 × 28 |
| 13. | Lift Capacity (Kgf) | 800 | 1000 | 800 | 800 | 1000 |
| 14. | No. of Gears<br>Forward<br>Reverse | <br>4<br>2 | <br>6<br>2 | <br>6<br>2 | <br>6<br>2 | <br>6<br>2 |
| 15. | PTO<br>No. of Splines<br>PTO RPM | <br>21<br>1000 | <br>21<br>1000 | <br>21<br>1000 | <br>21<br>1000 | <br>6<br>1000 |
| 16. | Type of Clutch | Single (dry) 215 mm | Single(dry) 233 mm | Single(dry) 225 mm | Single (dry) 225 mm | Single (dry) |
| 17. | Electric Battery | 12V, | 12V,70Ah | 12V, 70Ah | 12V, 70Ah | 12V, 88Ah |
| 18. | Overall Dimensions<br>Length mm<br>Width mm<br>Height mm | <br>2940<br>1500<br>2010 | <br>2985<br>1610<br>2037 | <br>3285<br>1675<br>2120 | | <br>3290<br>1680<br>2120G |
| 19. | Ground Clearance (mm) | 290 | 332 | 385 | | 385 |
| 20. | Weight of Tractor (Kg) | 1250 | 1710 | 1730 | 1800 | 1750 |
| 21. | Address of Manufacturers | Punjab Tractors Limited, S.A.S Nagar-160055, Near Chandigarh | | | | |

*Continued....*

(*Continued...* **TABLE No. 12)**

| Sr. No. | Particulars | Make and models of tractors | | | |
|---|---|---|---|---|---|
| | | **Swaraj 735** | **Swaraj 735FE** | **Swaraj 744 FE** | **Swaraj 855** |
| 1. | Engine Model | RB-3TR Kirloskar | RB-3TR Kirloskar | RB30TR Kirloskar | RB33TR Kirloskar |
| 2. | HP | 39 SAE | 39 SAE | 48 SAE | 55 SAE |
| 3. | No. of Cylinders | 3 | 3 | 3 | 3 |
| 4. | Bore (mm) | 100 | 100 | 110 | 110 |
| 5. | Stroke (mm) | 110 | 110 | 110 | 116 |
| 6. | Compression Ratio | 17:1 | 17:1 | 17:1 | 17:1 |
| 7. | Displacement Volume (cc) | 2592 | 2592 | 3136 | 3308 |
| 8. | Rated Speed (RPM) | 2000 | 2000 | 2000 | 2000 |
| 9. | Maximum Torque (N-m) | | 11.6 kg.m | 165.6 | 172.6 Nm |
| 10. | PTO Power kW | | 33.7(24.8) | 30.4 | 33.9kW |
| 11. | SFC (g/kW/hr) (g/hghr) | 298 | 251 (185) | 255 (18.8) | 257 |
| 12. | Tyre Size | | | | |
| | Front | 6.00 × 16 | 6.00 × 16 | 6.00 × 16 | 6.00 × 16/ 6.50 × 20 |
| | Rear | 12.4 × 28 | 12.4 × 28 | 13.6 × 28 | 13.6/16.9 × 28 |
| 13. | Lift Capacity (Kgf) | 1000 | 1000 | 1000-1500 | 1000-1500 |
| 14. | No. of Gears | | | | |
| | Forward | 6 | 8 | 8 | 8 |
| | Reverse | 2 | 2 | 2 | 2 |
| 15. | PTO | | | | |
| | No. of Splines | 21 | 21 6 | 21 6 | 21 |
| | PTO RPM | 1000 | 1000 540 | 1000 540 | 1000 |
| 16. | Type of Clutch | Single (dry) 254 mm | Single (dry) | Single/dual | Dual (dry) 305 mm |
| 17. | Electric Battery | 12V, 88Ah | 12V,88Ah | 12 V,88Ah | 12V, 100Ah |
| 18. | Overall Dimensions | | | | |
| | Length | | 3435 | 3430 | 3430 |
| | Width | | 1675 | 1730 | 1730 |
| | Height | | 2120 | 2170 | 2170 |
| 19. | Ground Clearance (mm) | | 390 | 405 | 405 |
| 20. | Weight of Tractor (Kg) | 1900 | 1820 | 1930 | 1930 |
| 21. | Address of Manufacturers | Punjab Tractors Limited, Sahibjada Ajit Singh Nagar-160055 Near Chandigarh | | | |

**TABLE No. 13: Technical details of TAFE tractors manufactured in India**

| Sr. No. | Particulars | Make and models of tractors | | | | |
|---|---|---|---|---|---|---|
| | | **TAFE 25 DI** | **TAFE 30 DI** | **TAFE MF 1035** | **TAFE 1035 DI** | **MF 245 J** |
| 1. | Engine Model | | TAFE-30 | Simpson P3 TA | S-324 DI | S-325 |
| 2. | HP (kW) | 28.4 | 31.4 | 36.5(26.85) | 36.5(26.85) | 47.65(35.07) |
| 3. | No. of Cylinders | 2 | 3 | 3 | 3 | 3 |
| 4. | Bore (mm) | 88.9 | 88.9 | 88.9 | 88.9 | 91.4 |
| 5. | Stroke (mm) | 96.0 | 96.0 | 127 | 127 | 127 |
| 6. | Compression Ratio | 17:1 | 17:1 | 16.5:1 | 17.5:1 | 18.5:1 |
| 7. | Displacement Volume (cc) | 1670 | 1788 | 2365 | 2400 | 2500 |
| 8. | Rated Speed (RPM) | 2250 | 2250 | 2000 | 2000 | 2250 |
| 9. | Maximum Torque (N-m) | 10.6 kg-m | 10.0 kg-m | 13.3 kg-m | 14.0 kg-m | 17.7 kg-m |
| 10. | PTO Power HP(kW) | 17.7 kW | 28.3(20.8) | 28.4(20.9) | 32(24.9) | 41.5(30.5) |
| 11. | Specific Fuel Consumption (g/kW/hr) | 269 | 258 | 311 | 243 | 256 |
| 12. | Tyre Size<br>Front<br>Rear | <br>6.0 × 16<br>12.4 × 28 | <br>6.00 × 16<br>12.4 × 28 | <br>6.00 × 16<br>12.4 × 28 | <br>6.00 × 16<br>12.4 × 28 | <br>6.00 × 16<br>12.4 × 28 |
| 13. | Lift Capacity (Kgf) | 8.43 (kN) | 9.41 (kN) | 9.00 (kN) | 8.47 (kN) | 12.14 (kN) |
| 14. | No. of Gears<br>Forward<br>Reverse | <br>6<br>2 | <br>6<br>2 | <br>6<br>2 | <br>6<br>2 | <br>6<br>2 |
| 15. | PTO<br>No. of Splines<br>PTO RPM | <br>6<br>540 | <br>6<br>540 | <br>6<br>540 | <br>6<br>540 | <br>6<br>540 |
| 16. | Type of Clutch | Single (dry) 254 mm | Single/dual 254 mm | Single (dry) 280 mm | Single/dual 305 mm | Single |
| 17. | Electric Battery | 12V, 80 Ah | 12V, 75Ah | 12V,85Ah | 12V, 90Ah | 12 V, |
| 18. | Overall Dimensions<br>Length mm<br>Width mm<br>Height mm | <br>3095<br>1630<br>2015 | <br>3120<br>1650<br>2170 | <br>3145<br>1645<br>2165 | <br>3030<br>1650<br>2175 | <br>3080<br>1680<br>2200 |
| 19. | Ground Clearance (mm) | 325 | 325 | 325 | 320 | 355 |
| 20. | Weight of Tractor (Kg) | | 1600 | 1470 | 1580 | 1700 |
| 21. | Address of Manufacturers | Tractors and Farm Equipment Limited, 35, Nungambakkam High Road, CHENNAI - 600034. | | | | |

*Continued....*

(*Continued...* TABLE No. 13)

| Sr. No. | Particulars | Make and models of tractors | |
|---|---|---|---|
| | | **TAFE 4410 Samrat** | **TAFE 5900 DI** |
| 1. | Engine Model | SJ 325 | S-423 |
| 2. | HP (kW) | 44 | 60 |
| 3. | No. of Cylinders | 3 | 4 |
| 4. | Bore (mm) | | 91.4 |
| 5. | Stroke (mm) | | 127 |
| 6. | Compression Ratio | | 18.5:1 |
| 7. | Displacement Volume (cc) | | 3330 |
| 8. | Rated Speed (RPM) | | 2300 |
| 9. | Maximum Torque (N-m) | | 17.87 kg.m |
| 10. | PTO Power HP(kW) | | 51.7(38.0) |
| 11. | Specific Fuel Consumption (g/kW/hr) | | |
| 12. | Tyre Size | | |
| | Front | 6.66 × 16 | 7.50 × 16 |
| | Rear | 12.4 × 28 | 16.9 × 28 |
| 13. | Lift Capacity (Kgf) | | |
| 14. | No. of Gears | | |
| | Forward | 8 | 8 |
| | Reverse | 2 | 2 |
| 15. | PTO | | |
| | No. of Splines | 6 | 6 |
| | PTO RPM | 540 | 540 |
| 16. | Type of Clutch | Dual (dry) | Dual (dry) |
| 17. | Electric Battery | 12V, 70Ah | 254/305 |
| 18. | Overall Dimensions | | |
| | Length | 3210 | 3600 |
| | Width | 1700 | 2000 |
| | Height | 2230 | 2400 |
| 19. | Ground Clearance (mm) | 375 | 420 |
| 20. | Weight of Tractor (Kg) | 1850 | 2230 |
| 21. | Address of Manufacturers | Tractors and Farm Equipment Limited, 35, Nungambakkam High Road, CHENNAI-600034. | |

**TABLE No. 14: Technical details of Tempo tractors manufactured in India**

| Sr. No. | Particulars | Make and models of tractors | | | |
|---|---|---|---|---|---|
| | | TEMPO OX 25 | TEMPO OX 35 | TEMPO OX 45 | TEMPO Balwan |
| 1. | Engine Model | D301 DI | TD 1950F | TD 2600F | TD 2600F |
| 2. | HP (kW) | 27 | 35 | 45 | 50 |
| 3. | No. of Cylinders | 4 | 3 | 4 | 4 |
| 4. | Bore (mm) | 78.0 | 90.9 | 90.9 | 90.9 |
| 5. | Stroke (mm) | 94.0 | 100 | 100 | 100 |
| 6. | Compression Ratio | 18.55:1 | 18.3:1 | 18.5:1 | 18.5:1 |
| 7. | Displacement Volume (cc) | 1797 | 1947 | 2596 | 2594 |
| 8. | Rated Speed (RPM) | 2200 | 2200 | 2200 | 2200 |
| 9. | Maximum Torque (N-m) | 93.8 | 103.3 | 14.3 kg.m | 1530 Nm |
| 10. | PTO Power, HP(kW) | 24.7 (18.2) | 26.9 | 42.8 (31.5) | 31.8 (kN) |
| 11. | Specific Fuel Consumption (g/kW/hr) | 258 (190) | 277 | 247 (182) | 248 |
| 12. | Tyre Size | | | | |
| | Front | 5.50 × 16 | 6.00 × 16 | 6.00 × 16 | 6.00 × 16 |
| | Rear | 11.2 × 28 | 12.4 × 28 | 13.6 × 28 | 1.3.4 × 28 |
| 13. | Lift Capacity (Kgf) | 1155 | 1400 | 1475 | 1475 |
| 14. | No. of Gears | | | | |
| | Forward | 8 | 8 | 8 | 8 |
| | Reverse | 4 | 4 | 4 | 4 |
| 15. | PTO | | | | |
| | No. of Splines | 6 | 6 | 6 | 6 |
| | PTO RPM | 540, 1000 | 540, 1000 | 540, 1000 | 540, 1000 |
| 16. | Type of Clutch | Single (dry) 254 mm | Single/dual 300 mm | Dual (dry) 300 mm | Dual (dry) 305 |
| 17. | Electric Battery | 12V, 55Ah | 12V, 70Ah | 12V, 70Ah | 12V, 70Ah |
| 18. | Overall Dimensions | | | | |
| | Length | 3170 | 3350 | 3360 | 3340 |
| | Width | 1480 | 1690 | 1680 | 1690 |
| | Height | 1960 | 2100 | 2085 | 2117 |
| 19. | Ground Clearance (mm) | 320 | 370 | 402 | 402 |
| 20. | Weight of Tractor (Kg) | 1450 | 1750 | 1850 | 1900 |
| 21. | Address of Manufacturers | Bajaj Tempo Limited, (Tractor Division) Akurdi, PUNE-411035 Ph. 020-776381 | | | |

**TABLE No. 15: Technical details of Veer Pratap tractors manufactured in India**

| Sr. No. | Particulars | Make and models of tractors | | |
|---|---|---|---|---|
| | | Veer Partap 1027 | Veer Partap | Veer Partap Belarus |
| 1. | Engine Model | PS1027 | PS 3035 | D 65M |
| 2. | HP (kW) | 24 | 35 | 62 |
| 3. | No. of Cylinders | 1 | 3 | 4 |
| 4. | Bore (mm) | 115 | 88.9 | 110 |
| 5. | Stroke (mm) | 150 | 127 | 180 |
| 6. | Compression Ratio | 17.7:1 | 16.5:1 | |
| 7. | Displacement Volume (cc) | 1559 | 2365 | 4940 |
| 8. | Rated Speed (RPM) | 1650 | 2000 | 1750 |
| 9. | Maximum Torque (N-m) | 10.3 kg-m | 13.3 kg-m | 277 Nm |
| 10. | PTO Power, HP(kW) | 14.1 kW | 25.1 kW | 44.8 kW |
| 11. | Specific Fuel Consumption (g/kW/hr) | 276 | 254 (187) | 267 |
| 12. | Tyre Size | | | |
| | Front | 6.00 × 16 | 6.00 × 16 | 7.50 × 20 |
| | Rear | 12.4 × 28 | 12.4 × 28 | 15.5 × 39 |
| 13. | Lift Capacity (Kgf) | 7.17 (kN) | 882 | 14.4 kN |
| 14. | No. of Gears | | | |
| | Forward | 8 | 8 | 8 |
| | Reverse | 2 | 2 | 2 |
| 15. | PTO | | | |
| | No. of Splines | 21 | 21 | 21 |
| | PTO RPM | 1021 | 1238 | 540 |
| 16. | Type of Clutch | Single | Single (dry) 250 mm | Dual (dry) |
| 17. | Electric Battery | 12 V | 12 V | 12 V |
| 18. | Overall Dimensions | | | |
| | Length | 3065 | 3145 | 4165 |
| | Width | 1665 | 1655 | 1994 |
| | Height | 1460 (st.) | 2170 | 2860 |
| 19. | Ground Clearance (mm) | 400 | 360 | 450 |
| 20. | Weight of Tractor (Kg) | 1625 | 1600 | 3350 (W.E) |
| 21. | Address of Manufacturers | Partap Steels Limited, (Automotive Division), 21/3, Mathura Road, Ballabgarh121004 Ph.42071 | | |

### TABLE No. 16: Heat of combustion of different fuels

| Sr. No. | Fuel | Formula | Heat Value (kJ/kg) |
|---|---|---|---|
| 1. | Natural Gas | $CH_4$ | 55006 |
| 2. | Gasoline (Octane) | $C_8H_{18}$ | 47889 |
| 3. | Diesel (Cetane) | $C_{16}H_{34}$ | 47261 |

**COMBUSTION :**

**Fuel + Air = > Carbon Dioxide + Water + Nitrogen + Heat**

### TABLE No. 17: Composition of air

| Sr. No. | Gas/Air | Percent/molecules |
|---|---|---|
| **Composition of air by mass** | | |
| 1. | Oxygen ($O_2$) | 23.19 |
| 2. | Nitrogen ($N_2$) | 76.81 |
| 3. | Air | 1kgm $O_2$ + 3.31 kgm $N_2$ = 4.31 kgm air |
| **Composition air by volume** | | |
| 1. | Oxygen ($O_2$) | 20.99 |
| 2. | Nitrogen ($N_2$) | 79.01 |
| 3. | Air | 1 mol $O_2$ + 3.764 mol $N_2$ = 4.764 mol air |

### TABLE No. 18: Approximate Coefficient of traction for different surfaces

| Sr. No. | Surface type | Traction Factors | |
|---|---|---|---|
| | | Rubber tyres | Track tyres |
| 1. | Rough concrete | 0.88–1.0 | 0.45 |
| 2. | Clay loam dry | 0.50–0.58 | |
| 3. | Clay loam, wet | 0.40–0.49 | |
| 4. | Rutted clay loam | 0.40–0.44 | |
| 5. | Loose sand | 0.20–0.35 | 0.30 |
| 6. | Quarry pit | 0.60–0.70 | |
| 7. | Gravel road (loose not hard) | 0.36 | |
| 8. | Packed snow | 0.20 | |
| 9. | Ice | 0.12 | 0.12* |
| 10. | Firm earth | 0.70–0.90 | 0.90 |
| 11. | Loose earth | 0.40–0.50 | 0.60 |

*Semi-skeleton shoes 0.27

**TABLE No. 19: Tractive and Transmission Coefficients**

| Sr. No. | Surface condition | Light load pull =10% wt. | Medium drawbar load | Heavyload, without excessive wheel slip |
|---|---|---|---|---|
| 1. | Concrete | 0.75 | 0.85 | 0.9 |
| 2. | Firm untilled field | 0.60 | 0.75 | 0.80 |
| 3. | Tilled reasonably firm | 0.40 | 0.55 | 0.65 |
| 4. | Freshly ploughed soil | 0.25 | 0.40 | 0.45 |

**TABLE No. 20: Approximate drawbar pull (Kg) per gross ton weight of tractor**

| Sr. No. | Type of surface | Steel tyres plain bearings | High pressure rubber tyres anti-friction bearings | Low pressure Rubber tyres anti-friction bearings | Track type wheels |
|---|---|---|---|---|---|
| 1. | Smooth concrete | 18.144 | 15.876 | 15.876 | 24.948 |
| 2. | Mecadam, Good | 31.752 | 27.216 | 27.216 | 31.752 |
| 3. | Earth Roads, dry, dusty | 54.432 | 45.36 | 36.288 | 36.288 |
| 4. | Unploughed Earth Terrain | 77.112 | 68.04 | 54.432 | 45.36 |
| 5. | Ploughed earth, dry (stubble field) | 99.792 | 86.184 | 68.04 | 54.432 |
| 6. | Earth road, rutted, uneven or muddy surface | 117.936 | 99.792 | 81.648 | 63.504 |
| 7. | Loose sand and gravel | 140.616 | 122.472 | 108.864 | 77.112 |
| 8. | Very muddy rads, wet sticky soil construction hauls | 181.440 | 158.76 | 145.152 | 102.06 |

The above figures are approximate but are considered sufficiently accurate for estimating purpose

**TABLE No. 21: Soil Conditions and Usable Power (kW)**

| Condition of soil | Usable drawbar power as %age of Max. PTO HP | Ratio of max. PTO HP to usable dbhp |
|---|---|---|
| Firm | 66.0% | 1.52 |
| Tilled | 57% | 1.75 |
| Soft/Sandy | 50% | 2.00 |

**TABLE No. 22: Soil Conditions and wheel slip**

| Wheel slip | Type of soil condition |
|---|---|
| 4–8% | Concrete |
| 8–10 | Firm soil |
| 11–13% | Tilled soil |
| 14–16% | Soft soils and sand |

**TABLE No. 23: Speed of tractor (Km/hr) for a given tyre size and wheel RPM**

| RPM | Tyre Size | | | | | | | | | |
|---|---|---|---|---|---|---|---|---|---|---|
| | 12 × 38 | 11 × 38 | 10 × 38 | 9 × 38 | 9 × 36 | 9 × 32 | 11 × 28 | 10 × 28 | 10 × 24 | 9 × 24 |
| 12 | 3.36 | 3.20 | 3.04 | 3.04 | 2.88 | 2.56 | 2.56 | 2.56 | 2.24 | 2.24 |
| 13 | 3.52 | 3.36 | 3.36 | 3.20 | 3.20 | 2.88 | 2.88 | 2.72 | 2.40 | 2.40 |
| 14 | 3.84 | 3.68 | 3.52 | 3.52 | 3.36 | 3.04 | 3.04 | 2.88 | 2.72 | 2.56 |
| 15 | 4.16 | 4.00 | 3.84 | 3.68 | 3.52 | 3.36 | 3.20 | 3.20 | 2.88 | 2.72 |
| 16 | 4.32 | 4.16 | 4.16 | 4.00 | 3.84 | 3.52 | 3.52 | 3.36 | 3.04 | 2.88 |
| 17 | 4.64 | 4.48 | 4.32 | 4.16 | 4.00 | 3.68 | 3.68 | 3.52 | 3.20 | 3.20 |
| 18 | 4.96 | 4.80 | 4.64 | 4.48 | 4.32 | 4.00 | 3.84 | 3.84 | 3.36 | 3.36 |
| 19 | 5.12 | 4.96 | 4.80 | 4.64 | 4.48 | 4.16 | 4.16 | 4.00 | 3.52 | 3.52 |
| 20 | 5.44 | 5.28 | 5.28 | 4.96 | 4.80 | 4.32 | 4.32 | 4.16 | 3.84 | 3.68 |
| 21 | 5.76 | 5.60 | 5.44 | 5.28 | 4.96 | 4.64 | 4.48 | 4.48 | 4.00 | 3.84 |
| 22 | 6.08 | 5.76 | 5.60 | 5.44 | 5.28 | 4.80 | 4.80 | 4.64 | 4.16 | 4.00 |
| 23 | 6.24 | 6.08 | 5.92 | 5.6 | 5.44 | 4.96 | 4.96 | 4.8 | 4.32 | 4.16 |
| 24 | 6.56 | 6.40 | 6.08 | 5.76 | 5.76 | 5.28 | 5.28 | 4.96 | 4.48 | 4.48 |
| 25 | 6.88 | 6.56 | 6.40 | 6.08 | 5.92 | 5.44 | 5.44 | 5.28 | 4.80 | 4.64 |
| 26 | 7.04 | 6.88 | 6.72 | 6.24 | 6.24 | 5.76 | 5.60 | 5.44 | 4.96 | 4.80 |
| 27 | 7.36 | 7.20 | 6.88 | 6.56 | 6.40 | 5.92 | 5.92 | 5.60 | 5.12 | 4.96 |
| 28 | 7.68 | 7.36 | 7.20 | 6.72 | 6.72 | 6.08 | 6.08 | 5.92 | 5.28 | 5.12 |
| 29 | 7.84 | 7.68 | 7.36 | 7.20 | 6.88 | 6.40 | 6.24 | 6.08 | 5.44 | 5.28 |
| 30 | 8.16 | 8.00 | 7.68 | 7.36 | 7.20 | 6.56 | 6.56 | 6.24 | 5.60 | 5.44 |
| 31 | 8.48 | 8.16 | 8.00 | 7.68 | 7.36 | 6.72 | 6.72 | 6.56 | 5.92 | 5.76 |
| 32 | 8.60 | 8.48 | 8.16 | 8.00 | 7.68 | 7.04 | 6.88 | 6.72 | 6.08 | 5.92 |
| 33 | 8.76 | 8,64 | 8.48 | 8.16 | 7.84 | 7.20 | 7.20 | 6.88 | 6.24 | 6.08 |
| 34 | 9.08 | 8.76 | 8.64 | 8.48 | 8.16 | 7.36 | 7.36 | 7.04 | 6.40 | 6.24 |
| 35 | 9.70 | 9.08 | 8.76 | 8.64 | 8.32 | 7.68 | 7.52 | 7.36 | 6.56 | 6.40 |
| 36 | 9.86 | 9.54 | 9.08 | 8.76 | 8.64 | 7.84 | 7.84 | 7.52 | 6.88 | 6.56 |

**TABLE No. 24: Area commanded by different power sources for timely operations**

| Sr. No | Power Source | Population/1000 ha | Area commanded by the source (ha) |
|---|---|---|---|
| 1 | Tractors | 66 | 15 |
| 2 | Power Tiller | 200 | 5 |
| 3 | Draught Animal | 1000 | 2 per pair of animal |

**TABLE No. 25 : Capacity, draft and power requirements of various agricultural machines**

**(A) Tractor operated machinery**

| Sr. No. | Implement | Size, mm | Capacity ha/hr | Draft and powerrequired Draft, kg | Power, HP |
|---|---|---|---|---|---|
| 1. | MB Plough | 2–3 bottom, 300 mm each | 0.25 | 630–845 g/cm$^2$ of f.s | 25–35 HP |
| 2. | Disc plough | 2–3 discs 990–1110 mm | 0.25 | 350–630 g/cm$^2$ of f.s | 23–25 |
| 3. | Disc harrow | 10–16 discs 1150–1900 | 0.50 | 120–150 kg/m | 20–45 |
| 4. | Paddy harrow | 10–12 discs | 0.5 | 60–190 kg/m | 20–45 |
| 5. | Cultivator | 7–15 tynes 1370–3050 | 0.8–1.0 | 110–270 kg/m | 20–45 |
| 6. | Rotavator | 1500–2500 | 0.20–0.30 | | 35–55 |
| 7. | Ridger | 2–3 bottoms | | 600–1000 kg for straight ridging | 35-45 |
| 8. | Seed-cum-fertilizer drill | 7–13 tynes | 0.4-0. | 45–120 kg/m | 20–45 |
| 9. | Potato planter | 2–4 rows | 0.15–0.25 | 120–180 kg/m | 35–45 |
| 10. | Sugarcane planter | 2 row 600–900 mm | 0.6 | 120–180 kg/m | 35–45 |
| 11. | Reaper harvester (VCR) | 4220 mm | 0.4 | 90–150 kg/m | 25–35 |
| 12. | Groundnut digger | 1340 mm | 0,25 | -do- | 35–45 |
| 13. | Potato digger | 460–530 mm | 0.15 | -do- | 35–45 |
| **(B) Power operated machinery** | | | | | |
| 14. | Power thresher | - | 2–15 q/h | | 5–20 |
| 15. | Combine harvester (TD) | 2.1–4.7 m | | 6.8–12.7 hp/m cutter bar | |
| 16. | Combine self propelled | 2.1–4.7 m | | 6.8–10.2 hp/ m cutter bar | |
| 17. | Grain binder | | | 100–220 kg/m | |
| 18. | Sugarcane crusher | 3 roller | 550–227 kg/hr | | 8–25 |
| 19. | Chaff cutter | - | 1 ton/h | 0.79–1.67 hp/ton | 15 |
| 20. | Irrigation pumps | 100–150 | 8–25 l/s | - | 3–10 |
| 21. | Submersible pumps | 150–300 | 2–80 l/s | - | 5–60 |

**Unit draft of different soils:**

| | | |
|---|---|---|
| Light soil | : | 2.1–4.1 N/cm$^2$ |
| Medium soil | : | 3.4–6.2 N/cm$^2$ |
| Heavy soils | : | 5.88–14.71 N/cm$^2$ |
| Very heavy soils | : | 8.82–14.71 N/cm$^2$ |

**Table No. 26: Ploughing resistance**

| Sr. No. | Type of soil | Resistance (kN/$m^2$) |
|---|---|---|
| 1. | Very light blowing sand | 34.5 |
| 2. | Medium loam | 68.95 |
| 3. | Heavy clay | 103.4 |

**Table No. 27 : Operation/Implement wise draft and power requirement**

| Sr. No. | Implement | Draft and Power requirement |
|---|---|---|
| I | **Tillage** | |
| 1. | Disc Harrow | 60–190 kg/m |
| 2. | Disc Tiller | 220–520 kg/m |
| 3. | Duch Foot Cultivator | 130–240 kg/m |
| 4. | Extreme up to Plough | 1260.4 |
| 5. | Heavy Duty Tandem Harrow | 120–150 kg/m |
| 6. | Heavy Plough | 630–845 |
| 7. | Light Plough | 140–350 |
| 8. | Medium Plough | 350–630 |
| 9. | Roller | 45–90 kg/m |
| 10. | Spike Tooth Harrow | 45–90 kg/m |
| 11. | Spring Tooth Harrow | 110–270 kg/m |
| 12. | Tandem Harrow | 250–340 kg/m |
| 13. | TD Ridger | 600–1000 kg |
| II | **Planting** | |
| 1. | Grain Drill | 45–120 kg/m |
| 2. | Row Crop Planter | 120–180 kg/m |
| III | **Cultivation** | |
| 1. | 3TyneCultivator / Trifali | 40–50 kg/m |
| 2. | Bakhar Blades | 90–150 kg/m |
| 3. | Cultivator | 30–140 kg/m |
| 4. | Rotary Hoes | 45–120 kg/m |
| IV | **Harvesting** | |
| 1. | Crop Picker | 2–5 (PTO h.p)/row |
| 2. | Grain Binder | 100–220 kg/m |
| 3. | PTO Operated Combine | 6.8–13.7 h.p/m of cutter bar |
| 4. | Reaper | 90–150 kg/m |
| 5. | Self Propelled Combine | 6.8–10.2 h.p/m of cutter bar |
| 6. | Silage Cutter | 0.79–1.67 h.p/hr/ton |

**Table No. 28: Distribution of tractor power loading**

| Sr. No. | % of Maximum Power | % of Total Time |
|---|---|---|
| 1. | >80 | 16.8 |
| 2. | 80–60 | 23.9 |
| 3. | 60–40 | 22.6 |
| 4. | 40–20 | 17.5 |
| 5. | <20 | 19.2 |

**Table No. 29: Matching size of mould board ploughs for different horsepower range of tractors**

| | Type of soil | | | | | |
|---|---|---|---|---|---|---|
| | Clay loam | | Silty clay loam and silty loam | | Sandy loam | |
| PTO hp | Size (cm × No.) | Speed (Kmph) | Size (cm × No.) | Speed (Kmph) | Size (cm × No.) | Speed (Kmp h) |
| 46-55 | 30 × 3 | 4–4.5 | 30 × 3 | 4.5–5.0 | Ploughing not | |
| 41-45 | 30 × 3 | 3–3.5 | 30 × 3 | 4.5–5.0 | recommended | |
| 31-40 | 25 × 3 | 3–3.5 | 25 × 3 | 4.5–5.0 | | |
| 26-30 | 30 × 2 | 3–3.5 | 30 × 2 | 4.5–5.0 | | |
| 25 and below | 25 × 2 | 2–3.5 | 25 × 2 | 3.5–5.0 | | |

**Table No. 30 : Matching harrows (two gangs with 60 cm disc dia and spacing of 23 cm) for different horsepower range of tractors**

| | Type of soil | | | | | |
|---|---|---|---|---|---|---|
| | Clay loam | | Silty clay loam and silty loam | | Sandy loam | |
| PTO hp | Size (cm × No.) | Speed (Kmph) | Size (cm × No.) | Speed (Kmph) | Size (cm × No.) | Speed (Kmp h) |
| 46–55 | 11 × 11 | 5–6.0 | 11 × 11 | 6–7.0 | 11 × 11 | 7–8.5 |
| 41–45 | 9 × 9 | 5–6.0 | 9 × 9 | 6–7.0 | 9 × 9 | 7–8.5 |
| 31–40 | 8 × 8 | 6–7.0 | 8 × 8 | 7–8.0 | 8 × 8 | 8–8.5 |
| | 7 × 7 | 6–8.0 | 7 × 7 | 7–8.0 | 7 × 7 | 8–8.5 |
| 26–30 | 7 × 7 | 6–7.0 | 7 × 7 | 7–8.0 | 7 × 7 | 8–8.5 |
| | 6 × 6 | 8–8.5 | | | | |
| 25 and below | 6 × 6 | 5–6.0 | 6 × 6 | 6–7.0 | 6 × 6 | 6–7.5 |
| | 5 × 5 | 5–6.0 | 5 × 5 | 5–70 | 5 × 5 | 7–8.0 |

**Table No. 31: Matching cultivators (with 22.5 spacing) for different horsepower range of tractors**

| PTO hp | Type of soil | | | | | |
|---|---|---|---|---|---|---|
| | Clay loam | | Silty clay loam and silty loam | | Sandy loam | |
| | Size (cm × No.) | Speed (Kmph) | Size (cm × No.) | Speed (Kmph) | Size (cm × No.) | Speed (Kmph) |
| 46–55 | 17 | 5–6.0 | 21 | 5–6.0 | 21 | 6–8.0 |
| 41–45 | 15 | 5–6.0 | 17 | 5–6.0 | 21 | 5–6.0 |
| 31–40 | 13 | 5–6.0 | 15 | 5–6.0 | 17 | 5–6.0 |
| 26–30 | 11 | 5–6.0 | 13 | 5–6.0 | 15 | 5–6.0 |
| 25 and below | 9 | 5–6.0 | 11 | 5–6.0 | 13 | 5–6.0 |

**Table No. 32: Turning Times and Field Conditions**

| Sr. No. | Type of turns | Time lost |
|---|---|---|
| I. | Correct turns | 12–15% time lost |
| II. | Undesirable turns | 50% increase in turning time |
| III | Wrong turns | Double turning time |

**Table No. 33 : Rate of planting by different sizes of machines**

| Planter size | Width (m) | Operating speed | Field (%) | Area, ha/hr Efficiency | Ha per day 12-hour |
|---|---|---|---|---|---|
| 4 row, 100 cm | 4.0 | 5 km/hr | 71 | 1.42 | 17.04 |
| 4 row, 75 cm | 3.0 | 5 km/hr | 69 | 1.035 | 12.42 |
| 5 row, 60 cm | 3.0 | 5 km/hr | 67 | 1.005 | 12.06 |

**Table No. 34 : Power requirements for different harvesting machines**

| Sr. No. | Components of power required in the machine | Harvesting/Digging machine | | |
|---|---|---|---|---|
| | | Grain combines | Potato Digger | Forage harvester |
| 1. | Force for rolling the machine ,$F_r(N)$ | $1.2\text{-}2 \times 10^3$ | $3.6\text{-}6 \times 10^3$ | $2.5\text{-}5 \times 10^3$ |
| 2. | No load power, $W_n$ (kW) | 8–9.5 | 8–10 | 5.5–7.0 |
| 3. | Specific power for normal operation, $W_w$ (kW-sec/kg of material) | 5.1–5.8 | 2.8–4.5 | 2.5–3.5 |

(*Source*: Klenin *et. al.*)

**Table No. 35 : Power required for threshing of different crops**

| Sr. No. | Crop | Power requirement | |
|---|---|---|---|
| | | kWh/t of crop | kWh/t of grain |
| 1. | Wheat | 4–7.5 | 9–15 |
| 2. | Gram | 3.5–4.5 | 7–8.5 |
| 3. | Sorghum | 2.5–3.5 | 3.5–5.5 |
| 4. | Paddy | 2–3 | 3.5–5 |
| 5. | Maize | 2–3 | 3–4 |
| 6. | Soybean | 3–5.5 | 10–14 |

## Table No. 36: Mechanical properties of different materials (MKS Units)

| Sr. No. | Materials and Composition | Ultimate tensile ($kg/cm^2$) | Yield point strength | Ultimate shear ($kg/cm^2$) ($kg/cm^2$) | Young's modulus strength ($kg/cm^2$) | Modulus of rigidity© of elasticity(E) | Brinell Hardness ($kg/cm^2$) |
|---|---|---|---|---|---|---|---|
| 1. | **Cast iron** | 700–2000 | – | 1100 | $1–1.5 \times 10^6$ | $0.6–0.8 \times 10^6$ | 150–225 |
| 2. | **Wrought iron** | 2200–4500 | – | 2700 | $1.8–2 \times 10^6$ | $0.75–0.95 \times 10^6$ | 75–100 |
| 3. | **Steel** | | | | | | |
| | (*i*) Mild steel (0.28% C) | 4000–6000 | | 3500 | $2.1 \times 10^6$ | $0.8 \times 10^6$ | 150 |
| | (*ii*) Medium carbon steel (0.55%C) | 7500 | | 3700* | $2.15 \times 10^6$ | $0.8 \times 10^6$ | 200 |
| | | | | 0.1% PS | | | |
| | (*iii*) High carbon steel | 19970 | 10890 | | $2.18 \times 10^6$ | $0.8 \times 10^6$ | 550 |
| 4. | **Alloy steels** | | | | | | |
| | (*i*) Manganese steel (1.5% M, 0.29% C) | 6500 | 3800 | 3300* | $2160 \times 10^3$ | | 187 |
| | (*ii*) Nickel steel (3.5% Ni, 0.43% C) | 10350 | 9175 | 8600* | $2120 \times 10^3$ | | 293 |
| | (*iii*) Nickel-Chromium steel (3.5% Ni, 0.31% C, 0.7% Cr) | 9780 | 8850 | 8100* | $2130 \times 10^3$ | | 277 |
| | (*iv*) Nickel-Chromium-Molyb-denum-V steel | 12000 | 11180 | 10590* | $2150 \times 10^3$ | | 340 |
| | (*v*) Carbon-Chrome Ball Bearing Steel | 14150 | 13400 | 11700* | $2110 \times 10^3$ | | 402 |
| | (*vi*) Silicon-Manganese steel (hardened) | 14680 | 12770 | 10900* | $2030 \times 10^3$ | | 418 |
| | (*vii*) Stainless steel | 8150 | 6250 | 5500* | $2190 \times 10^3$ | | 241 |
| | (*viii*) Very high speed steel | 8400 | 4600 | 3380* | $2360 \times 10^3$ | | 241 |

| 5. | **Non-ferrous Alloys** | | | | | | |
|---|---|---|---|---|---|---|---|
| | **I. Tin-base alloys** | | | | | | |
| | (*i*) 91.0 Sn, 5.5 Sb, 4.5 Cu | 925 | 315 | | | | 17 |
| | (*ii*) 83.3Sn, 8.3 Sb, 2.0 Cu | 1260 | 475 | | | | 27 |
| | (*iii*) 65.0 Sn, 15.0Sb, 2.0 Cu | 1080 | 360 | | | | 22.5 |
| | **II. Lead-based Alloys** | | | | | | |
| | (*i*) 85 Pb, 15 Sb | 920 | 220 | | | | 15 |
| | (*ii*) 85 Pb, 10 Sb, 5 Sn | 1125 | 245 | | | | 19 |
| | (*iii*) 75 Pb, 15 Sb, 10 Sn | 1136 | 250 | | | | 22.5 |
| | **III. Copper-based Alloys** | | | | | | |
| | (*i*) Manganese-Brass (60Cu,1Mn,39 Zn) | 5645 | | | | | 140 |
| | (*ii*) Bronze (85 Cu, 15 Sn) | 2160 | | | | | 100 |
| | (*iii*) Phosphor-Bronze (89 Cu, 10 Sn) | 2900 | | | | | 100 |
| | (*iv*) Gun-metal (88 Cu, 10 Sn, 2 Pb) | 2740 | | | | | 65 |
| | (*v*) Lead-Bronze (80 Cu, 10 Sn, 10Pb) | 2420 | | | | | 65 |

**Represents 0.1% Proof Stress**

## Table No. 37: Mechanical properties of differents materials (SI Units)

| Sr. No. | Materials and Composition | Ultimate tensile strength ($MN/m^2$) or MPa | Yield point ($MN/m^2$) or MPa | Ultimate shear strength ($MN/m^2$) or MPa | Young modulus of elasticity(E) ($MN/m^2$) | Modulus of rigidity© ($MN/m^2$) | Brinell Hardness |
|---|---|---|---|---|---|---|---|
| | 1. Cast iron | 68.5–196.2 | – | 108 | $9.8–14.7 \times 10^4$ | $5.89–7.85 \times 10^4$ | 150–225 |
| | 2. Wrought iron | 4415.8–441.5 | – | 265 | $17.7–19 \times 10^4$ | $7.36–9.32 \times 10^4$ | 75–100 |
| 3. | **Steel** | | | | | | |
| | (*i*) Mild steel (0.28% C) | 392.4–588.6 | | 343.4 | $20.6 \times 10^4$ | $7.85 \times 10^4$ | 150 |
| | (*ii*) Medium carbon steel (0.55%C) | | | 363 | $21.1 \times 10^4$ | $7.85 \times 10^4$ | 200 |
| | (*iii*) High carbon steel | 883 | 0.1% PS 1068.3 | | $21.4 \times 10^4$ | $7.85 \times 10^4$ | 550 |
| 4. | **Alloy steels** | | | | | | |
| | (*i*) Manganese steel (1.5% M, 0.29% C) | 637.7 | 372.8 | 324* | $21.19 \times 10^4$ | | 187 |
| | (*ii*) Nickel steel (3.5% Ni, 0.43% C) | 1015.3 | 900 | 843.7* | $20.8 \times 10^4$ | | 293 |
| | (*iii*) Nickel-Chromium steel (3.5% Ni, 0.31% C, 0.7% Cr) | 959.5 | 868.2 | 794.6* | $20.89 \times 10^4$ | | 277 |
| | (*iv*) Nickel-Chromium-Molyb-denum-V steel | 1177.2 | 1096.8 | 1038.9* | $21.09 \times 10^4$ | | 340 |
| | (*v*) Carbon-Chrome Ball Bearing Steel | 1388.1 | 1314.5 | 1147.8* | $20.7 \times 10^4$ | | 402 |
| | (*vi*) Silicon-Manganese steel (hardened) | 1440 | 1252.8 | 1069.3* | $19.91 \times 10^4$ | | 418 |
| | (*vii*) Stainless steel | 799.5 | 613.1 | 539.6* | $21.48 \times 10^4$ | | 241 |
| | (*viii*) Very high speed steel | 824 | 451.3 | 331.6* | $23.15 \times 10^4$ | | 241 |

| 5. | **Non-ferrous Alloys** | | | | | | |
|---|---|---|---|---|---|---|---|
| | **I. Tin-base alloys** | | | | | | |
| | (*i*) 91.0 Sn, 5.5 Sb, 4.5 Cu | 90.7 | 30.9 | | | | 17 |
| | (*ii*) 83.3Sn, 8.3 Sb, 2.0 Cu | 123.6 | 46.6 | | | | 27 |
| | (*iii*) 65.0 Sn, 15.0Sb, 2.0 Cu | 105.9 | 35.3 | | | | 22.5 |
| | **II. Lead-based Alloys** | | | | | | |
| | (*i*) 85 Pb, 15 Sb | 90.3 | 21.6 | | | | 15 |
| | (*ii*) 85 Pb, 10 Sb, 5 Sn | 110.4 | 24.0 | | | | 19 |
| | (*iii*) 75 Pb, 15 Sb, 10 Sn | 111.4 | 24.5 | | | | 22.5 |
| | **III. Copper-based Alloys** | | | | | | |
| | (*i*) Manganese-Brass (60Cu,1Mn,39 Zn) | 55.38 | | | | | 140 |
| | (*ii*) Bronze (85 Cu, 15 Sn) | 211.9 | | | | | 100 |
| | (*iii*) Phosphor-Bronze (89 Cu, 10 Sn) | 284.5 | | | | | 100 |
| | (*iv*) Gun-metal (88 Cu, 10 Sn, 2 Pb) | 268.8 | | | | | 65 |
| | (*v*) Lead-Bronze (80 Cu, 10 Sn, 10Pb) | 237.4 | | | | | 65 |

Represents 0.1% Proof Stress

### Table No. 38: Tensile and Compressive Strengths of different materials

| Sr. No. | Material | Tensile strength | | Compressive Strength | |
|---|---|---|---|---|---|
| | | MKS Units ($Kg/mm^2$) | SI Units ($N/mm^2$) | MKS Units ($Kg/mm^2$) | SI Units ($N/mm^2$) |
| 1. | Cast iron | 7–20 | 68.7–196.2 | 40–95 | 392.4–932.0 |
| 2. | Grey cast iron | 10–30 | 98.1–294.3 | 40–180 | 392.4–1765.8 |
| 3. | High grade cast iron | 30–90 | 294.3–882.9 | | |
| 4. | Wrought iron | 22–45 | 215.8–441.5 | 27 | 265.0 |
| 5. | Mild steel | 30–80 | 294.3–784.8 | 43 | 422.0 |
| 6. | Medium carbon steel | 75 | 735.75 | | |
| 7. | High carbon steel | 90 | 882.9 | | |
| 8. | Aluminum | 5–20 | 49.0–192.2 | | |
| 9. | Aluminum alloy | 10–60 | 98.1–588.6 | | |
| 10. | Copper | 15–30 | 147.2–294.3 | | |
| 11. | Zinc | 5.5–9.5 | 49.0–93.2 | | |
| 12. | Brass | 30–60 | 294.3–588.6 | | |
| 13. | Bronze | 30–70 | 294.3–686.7 | | |
| 14. | Nylon | 6–20 | 58.9–199.2 | | |
| 15. | Soft PVC | 1–2 | 9.81–19.6 | | |
| 16. | Phenol resin | 4–5 | 39.2–49.0 | | |
| 17. | Glass fibre | 70–1000 | 686.7–9810 | | |
| 18. | Wood | 5–20 | 49.0–199.2 | 2.5–8 | 24.5–78.5 |
| 19. | Laminated wood | 9–26 | 88.3–255.0 | 7–19 | 68.7–186.4 |
| 20. | Steel wire | 40–120 | 392.4–1177.2 | | |
| 21. | Flat belts | 2–5 | 19.6–49.0 | | |

### Toble No. 39: Allowable stresses in gear teeth

| Sr. No. | Gear Velocity (m/s) | Allowable stress (S) in gear teeth | Endurance strength ($S_e$) | |
|---|---|---|---|---|
| 1. | <10 m/s | $S_e$ {3/(3 + V)} | **Material** | $S_c$ ($MN/m^2$) |
| 2. | 10–20 m/s | $S_e$ {6/(6 + V)} | Cast iron | 55 |
| 3. | >20 m/s | $S_e$ {4.6/(5.6 + vV)} | Bronze | 83 |
| | | | Mild steel | 103 |
| | | | Carbon steel | 70–350 |
| | | | Forged steel | 160 |
| | | | Cast steel | 100 |
| | | | Steel (general) | 1/3rd ultimate strength of material |

**Table No. 40: Space requirements for storage of farm machines**

| Sr. No. | Machinery | Space requirement(m) | | |
|---|---|---|---|---|
| | | Width | Height | Length |
| 1. | Tractor | | | |
| | 15–25 hp range | 1.50 | 1.5 | 2.75 |
| | 25–35 hp range | 2.25 | 1.5 | 3.6 |
| | 40–50 hp range | 2.25 | 1.5 | 3.6 |
| 2. | Combines Tractpr drawm) | | | |
| | 1.5–1.8 m | 2.75–3.6 | 2.55 | 5–6 |
| | 3.6 m | 4.0 | 3.6 | 6.7 |
| | 5.0 m | 6.0 | 4.25 | 7.5 |
| 3. | Cultivator | 4.5 | — | 2.4 |
| 4. | Grain drill | 3.3 | 1.75 | 1.9 |
| 5. | Spike tooth harrow | 1.2 | — | 1.9 |
| 6. | Spring tooth harrow | 1.0 | — | 1.9 |
| 7. | T.D Harrow | 3.0 | — | 2.6 |
| 8. | Potato Digger | 1.5 | — | 2.4 |

# Objective Type Questions with Answers

## CHAPTER-1 ENGINE WORKING PRINCPLE AND DESIGN

1 Top of piston is called as:

*a*) Head *b*) Crown
*c*) Skirt *d*) Lands

2 Compression rings are provided in the piston at

*a*) Skirt *b*) piston grooves near piston head
*c*) Top of piston *d*) Sleeve

3 Crank shaft of engine are made of

*a*) Cast iron *b*) Cast steel
*c*) Drop forged steel *d*) Both *b*) and *c*)

4 Pistons are attached with crank shaft with the help of

*a*) Cam shaft *b*) Timing gear
*c*) Connecting rod *d*) None of the above

5 Usually the types of cylinder liners used in engines are

*a*) Dry *b*) Wet
*c*) Both *a*) and *b*) *d*) None of the above

6 Valves are made of high grade

*a*) Carbon steel *b*) Alloy steel
*c*) Cast iron *d*) None of the above

7 Piston ring is made of

*a*) Copper *b*) Cast iron
*c*) Pressed steel alloy *d*) Both *b*) and *c*)

8 The firing order of four cylinder engine is

*a*) 1234 *b*) 2134
*c*) 1342 *d*) 4321

9 Worn out rings in an IC engine results in

*a*) Less development of power *b*) Failure to start the engine
*c*) Poor thermal efficiency *d*) Both *a*) & *b*)

10 The cam shaft of an engine gets drive from

*a*) Flywheel *b*) Piston
*c*) Crankshaft *d*) None of the above

11 The ignition timing of 4-stroke cycle engine is controlled by

*a*) Cam *b*) Crank

*c*) Connecting rod *d*) Timing gear

12 Exhaust valve of a tractor engine remains open for about

*a*) 1250 *b*) 1550

*c*) 1950 *d*) 2250

13 In diesel engine fresh air enters the cylinder through

*a*) Exhaust valve *b*) Carburetor

*c*) Inlet valve *d*) None of the above

14 Function of cam shaft in tractor engine is

*a*) To drive crank shaft *b*) To drive water pump

*c*) To drive valve assembly *d*) To drive crank pulley

15 Usually compression ring end gap of water cooled diesel engine is kept at

*a*) 0.07-0.08 mm per inch bore dia *b*) 2.5-0.3 mm per mm of bore dia

*c*) 2.5-0.3 mm per inch bore dia *d*) 0.06-0.08 mm per mm bore dia

16 Usually gasket used in exhaust manifold of tractor engine is

*a*) Fiber *b*) Copper and rubber

*c*) Copper and asbestos *d*) Fiber and copper

17 Normally tappet clearance is adjusted when

*a*) Inlet valve is closed *b*) Exhaust valve is closed

*c*) Rocking position *d*) Both valves closed

18 Diesel engine works on the principle of

*a*) Otto cycle *b*) Diesel cycle

*c*) Both *a*) and *b*) *d*) None of the above

19 The material of construction of connecting rod is

*a*) Cast iron *b*) Mild steel

*c*) Nickel *d*) Drop forged steel

20 Wall thickness of a dry liner is

*a*) 0.01-0.03D *b*) 0.03-0.035D

*c*) 0.035-0.05D *d*) more than 0.05D

21 In a 4-stroke cycle engine for best results stroke bore ratio (*L*/*D*) should be equal to

*a*) 1.0 *b*) 1.25

*c*) 1.5 *d*) 1.75

22 Piston head is designed on the basis of

*a*) Strength *b*) Heat dissipation

*c*) Both *a*) and *b*) *d*) None of the above

23 Mostly the type of piston pin used is

*a*) Semi floating *b*) Floating

*c*) Fixed *d*) None of the above three

24 In a crankshaft, left hand crank web as compared to right hand crank web is ________ stressed.

*a*) Less *b*) More
*c*) Equal *d*) None of the above

25 The gas load in the connecting rod of an engine is maximum at

*a*) TDC b ) BDC
*c*) Both *a*) and *b*) *d*) None of the above

26 Piston skirt takes the side thrust of

*a*) Rings *b*) Connecting rod
*c*) Piston pin *d*) None of the above

27 The crankshaft is designed for

*a*) Bending moments *b*) Twisting moments
*c*) Both *a*) and *b*) *d*) None of the above

28 Number of power strokes in 2-stroke cycle engine as compared to 4-strokes cycle engine are

*a*) Twice *b*) Half
*c*) Equal *d*) None of the above

29 Large size flywheel is used in the following engine

*a*) 4-stroke cycle engine *b*) 2-stroke cycle engine
*c*) Petrol engine *d*) All above three

30 The gap between the rocker arm and valve stem of an engine is known as

*a*) Clearance volume *b*) Tappet clearance
*c*) Ring gap *d*) None of the above

**Answers:**

| 1. | 2. | 3. | 4. | 5. | 6. | 7. | 8. | 9. | 10. |
|---|---|---|---|---|---|---|---|---|---|
| *a*) | *b*) | *d*) | *c*) | *c*) | *b*) | *d*) | *c*) | *d*) | *c*) |
| 11. | 12. | 13. | 14. | 15. | 16. | 17. | 18. | 19. | 20. |
| *d*) | *d*) | *c*) | *c*) | *a*) | *c*) | *c*) | *b*) | *d*) | *b*) |
| 21. | 22. | 23. | 24. | 25. | 26. | 27. | 28. | 29. | 30. |
| *c*) | *c*) | *b*) | *a*) | *a*) | *b*) | *c*) | *a*) | *a*) | *b*) |

## CHAPTER-3 AIR FUEL SUPPLY SYSTEM OF TRACTOR

1. Fuel injection pump is a part of

*a*) Diesel engine *b*) Petrol engine
*c*) Electric motor *d*) None of the above

2. In tractor engines most common type of air cleaner used is

*a*) Dry paper type *b*) Oil bath type
*c*) Fin type *d*) None of the above

3. Air lock in diesel engine results in
   *a*) Engine develop less power  *b*) Engine fails to start
   *c*) Insufficient torque  *d*) None of the above
4. Excessive smoke coming out from an IC engine is due to
   *a*) Improper fuel  *b*) Excessive load
   *c*) Rich mixture  *d*) All above three
5. In 4-stroke cycle engine the valve timing is controlled by
   *a*) Cam shaft  *b*) Idler gear
   *c*) Timing gear  *d*) Piston
6. A CI engine of a tractor is provided with a
   *a*) Carburetor  *b*) FI pump
   *c*) Both *a*) & *b*)  *d*) None of the above
7. Extent of fuel wasted due to selection of wrong gear with tractor is
   *a*) 10-15 %  *b*) 16-20 %
   *c*) 25-30 %  *d*) More than 30 %
8. Which grade of oil is used in air cleaner during summer?
   *a*) SAE-20  *b*) SAE-30
   *c*) SAE-40  *d*) None of the above
9. Compression ratio of a diesel engine is about
   *a*) 7:1  *b*) 10:1
   *c*) 14:1  *d*) 16:1
10. Type of fuel injectors mainly used are
   *a*) One type  *b*) Two types
   *c*) Three types  *d*) Four types
11. A 30 kW tractor is consuming diesel @ 5.1 liters per hr. Its specific fuel consumption is equal to
   *a*) 170 ml/kW-hr  *b*) 170 gm/kW-hr
   *c*) 150 ml/kW-hr  *d*) 200 ml/kW-hr
12. Optimum sp. break mean effective fuel consumption of tractor engine is
   *a*) 100-125 g/kWh  *b*) 150-200 g/kWh
   *c*) 180-210 g/kWh  *d*) more than 250 g/kWh
13. DI is direct injection in the open combustion chamber on the top of piston, over conventional engine this saves about
   *a*) 5-7 % diesel  *b*) 8-10 % diesel
   *c*) 10-15 % diesel  *d*) 15-20 % diesel
14. Cetane number is an indicator of ignition quality of
   *a*) Petrol fuel  *b*) Diesel fuel
   *c*) Both *a*) and *b*)  *d*) None of the above

8. Cause of blue smoke from exhaust of engine
   *a*) Worn out oil rings *b*) Oil viscosity is low
   *c*) Oil level in the sump is too high *d*) All above three
9. While changing the engine oil, the oil should be drained
   *a*) When the engine become cold *b*) After warming up the engine
   *c*) First change the air cleaner oil *d*) None of the above
10. Reasons for low lubricating oil pressure are
   *a*) Shortage of oil in crank case *b*) Blockage of oil in pipes
   *c*) Defective oil pressure gauge *d*) All above three
11. The oil pump of force feed lubrication system is driven by
   *a*) Crank shaft *b*) Electric motor
   *c*) Cam shaft *d*) All above three
12. The quality of lubricating oil is tested by
   *a*) Flash fire test *b*) Pour point test
   *c*) Carbon residue test *d*) Both *a*) and *b*)
13. Types of lubrication system used in IC engines are
   *a*) Splash and forced feed system *b*) Splash only
   *c*) Forced feed type only *d*) None of the above
14. In high speed tractor engines the type of lubrication system used is
   *a*) Forced feed system *b*) Splash type
   *c*) Both *a*) and *b*) *d*) None of the above
15. The material of full flow type oil filter is
   *a*) Paper *b*) Thin metal plate
   *c*) Felt & cloth *d*) All above three
16. According to API number of classes of oils for diesel engines is
   *a*) 3 *b*) 4
   *c*) 5 *d*) 6
17. The SAE number is used to grade lubricating oil for
   *a*) Viscosity *b*) Density
   *c*) Flash point *d*) Pour point

**Answers:**

| 1. | 2. | 3. | 4. | 5. | 6. | 7. | 8. | 9. | 10. |
|---|---|---|---|---|---|---|---|---|---|
| *b*) | *b*) | *b*) | *d*) | *d*) | *b*) | *a*) | *d*) | *d*) | *d*) |
| 11. | 12. | 13. | 14. | 15. | 16. | 17. | | | |
| *a*) | *d*) | *a*) | *a*) | *d*) | *a*) | *a*) | | | |

## CHAPTER-6 COOLING SYSTEM OF TRACTOR

1. In tractors, the required flow rate of water per kW is
   *a*) 0.1 *l*/s *b*) 0.16 *l*/s
   *c*) 0.2 *l*/s *d*) 0.25 *l*/s

2. Blower fan efficiency is ratio of
   *a*) Air power to input power *b*) Input power to air power
   *c*) Fan speed to crank speed *d*) None of above
3. In IC engine the circulating water is cooled by
   *a*) Radiator *b*) Water pump
   *c*) Thermostat *d*) Fins
4. Water jackets in water cooled IC engine are provided around
   *a*) The piston *b*) The cylinder
   *c*) Carburetor *d*) All above three
5. The fan of cooling system is driven by
   *a*) Crank shaft *b*) Cam shaft
   *c*) Electric motor *d*) None of the above
6. For dropping the operating temperature from 5.5 to 8.5 °C of water in the radiator, the flow rate of water per kW should be
   *a*) 0.10 *l*/s *b*) 0.14 *l*/s
   *c*) 0.16 *l*/s *d*) 0.20 *l*/s
7. Air power of a fan is a function of
   *a*) Total pressure *b*) Air flow rate
   *c*) Front area of radiator *d*) Both *b*) and *c*)
8. A 40 kW diesel tractor with a coolest temperature difference of 5.5 °C will require circulation of water at the rate of
   *a*) 1.2 *l*/s *b*) 1.75 *l*/s
   *c*) 2.5 *l*/s *d*) 3.72 *l*/s
9. A water temperature gauge in a tractor is provided to indicate
   *a*) Engine temperature *b*) Operating temperature of thermostat valve
   *c*) Water temperature in cooling system *d*) All above three
10. In air cooled engine fins are provided to
    *a*) Increase contact area for air *b*) Cool the engine
    *c*) Increase air flow rate *d*) Both *a*) and *b*)
11. A loose fan belt in a tractor will result in
    *a*) Overheating of engine *b*) Lower engine speed
    *c*) Blue smoke in engine *d*) All above three
12. Air cooled engine does not have
    *a*) Blower *b*) Fins
    *c*) Cowling *d*) Radiator
13. Which are the components of water cooled engines
    *a*) Radiator *b*) Water pump
    *c*) Thermostat valve *d*) All above three
14. In IC engine the operating temperature thermostat valve ranges between
    *a*) 35-40 °C *b*) 45-55 °C
    *c*) 60-65 °C *d*) 70-75 °C

15. The optimum operating temperature of a tractor engine is
   a) 60 °C  b) 75 °C
   c) 82 °C  d) 95 °C
16. In a tractor optimum fan belt tension of 5 kg force results in a deflection of
   a) 0.5-1.0 cm  b) 1-2 cm
   c) 2-3 cm  d) 3-4 cm
17. Air cooling system is commonly used in
   a) Tractors  b) Auto engines
   c) Small stationary engines  d) Both b) and c)
18. Normally operating temperature of air cooled engine as compared to water cooled engine is
   a) More  b) Less
   c) Equal  d) None of the above
19. A bellow type thermostat valve contains
   a) Alcohol  b) Ether
   c) Alcohol and Ether  d) None of the above
20. The quantity of air required in air cooling is dependent on
   a) Front area of radiator
   b) Velocity of air through radiator
   c) Rise in temperature of air after passing through the radiator
   d) All of the above

**Answers:**

| 1. | 2. | 3. | 4. | 5. | 6. | 7. | 8. | 9. | 10. |
|---|---|---|---|---|---|---|---|---|---|
| b) | a) | a) | b) | a) | c) | d) | d) | c) | a) |
| 11. | 12. | 13. | 14. | 15. | 16. | 17. | 18. | 19. | 20. |
| a) | d) | d) | d) | c) | b) | d) | a) | a) | d) |

## CHAPTER-7 ELECTRICAL SYSTEM

1. The electrolyte level above the plates in a tractor battery should be
   a) 1 cm  b) 2 cm
   c) 3 cm  d) 4 cm
2. Most common type of battery used in tractor engine is
   a) Dry battery  b) Hot plate battery
   c) Lead acid battery  d) All above three
3. Number of cells in a storage battery of tractor is
   a) 2  b) 4
   c) 6  d) 9
4. Electrolyte in battery of tractor is
   a) (65 % $H_2SO_4$ + 35 % distilled water)  b) (65 % distilled water + 35 % $H_2SO_4$)
   c) (65 % HCL + 35 % distilled water)  d) (65 % $H_2SO_4$ + 35 % HCL)

5. What is used for charging the battery in a tractor
   *a*) Dynamo  *b*) Starter motor
   *c*) Alternator  *d*) Both *a*) or *c*)
6. Positive plate of battery is made of
   *a*) $PbO_2$  *b*) $PbSO_4$
   *c*) Both *a*) and *b*)  *d*) None of the above
7. While charging battery with a dynamo
   *a*) Acid becomes thick  *b*) Battery voltage increases
   *c*) Increase in density  *d*) None of the above
8. Generally looseness in dynamo belt should be
   *a*) 4-5 mm  *b*) 6-12 mm
   *c*)12-15 mm  *d*) 20 mm
9. Electrical system of a tractor has following main components
   *a*) Battery  *b*) Alternator
   *c*) Cut out  *d*) None of the above
10. The self starter switch should not be pressed for more than
   *a*) 20-25 seconds  *b*) 25-30 seconds
   *c*) 15-20 seconds  *d*) 35-50 seconds

**Answers:**

| 1. | 2. | 3. | 4. | 5. | 6. | 7. | 8. | 9. | 10. |
|---|---|---|---|---|---|---|---|---|---|
| *a*) | *c*) | *c*) | *a*) | *c*) | *a*) | *d*) | *b*) | *d*) | *c*) |

## CHAPTER-8 POWER TRANSMISSION SYSTEM OF TRACTOR

1. Generally gears used in the transmission are
   *a*) Spur gears only  *b*) Helical gears only
   *c*) Helical and spur gears  *d*) Bevel gears
2. The standard PTO speed of tractor is
   *a*) 540 rpm  *b*) 1000 rpm
   *c*) Both *a*) & *b*)  *d*) None of the above
3. When one wheel of tractor is brakes the speed of other wheel is increased by
   *a*) 2 times  *b*) 3 times
   *c*) 4 times  *d*) None of the above
4. The grade of oil in tractor gearbox is
   *a*) SAE-30  *b*) SAE-40
   *c*) SAE-60  *d*) SAE-90
5. The differential is provided in the tractor as a compensating device during
   *a*) Straight drive  *b*) Turnings
   *c*) Slopes  *d*) None of the above
6. Type of gear box used in a tractor is
   *a*) Constant mesh  *b*) Sliding mesh
   *c*) Synchromesh  *d*) All above three

7. Main components of power transmission system are
 a) Clutch & flywheel b) Reverse axle and differential
 c) Cam shaft d) Both a) and b)
8. The clutch transmits power from tractor engine to
 a) Gearbox b) Differential
 c) Final drive d) Cam shaft
9. Tractor PTO gets its drive from
 a) Engine directly b) PTO shaft
 c) Gearbox d) Cam shaft
10. The ratio of inside to outside radius of clutch plate should be
 a) 1.0 b) 1.2
 c) 0.67 d) 0.9
11. Transmission efficiency is highest in
 a) Power shift gear box b) Sliding gear box
 c) Constant mesh gear box d) Synchromesh gear box
12. Tractor will exert more pull but result in higher fuel consumption, if tractor is operated at
 a) High gears b) Lower gears
 c) Both a) and b) d) None of the above
13. The extent of total mechanical power loss in a tractor is
 a) 10-20 % of IHP b) 10-20 % of BHP
 c) 10-20 % of FHP d) FHP
14. Most used power outlet of a tractor is
 a) Drawbar in the rear b) PTO shaft
 c) Belt pulley d) None of the above
15. Tractor engine power at right angle is transmitted by
 a) Differential b) Clutch assembly
 c) PTO shaft d) Belt pulley
16. Torque or power is transmitted by clutch is due to
 a) Meshing of gears b) Friction
 c) Coupling of shafts d) Inertia
17. Multiple disc type clutches can be
 a) Wet type b) Dry type
 c) Both a) and b) d) None of the above
18. Gears used in tractor usually are made of
 a) Alloy steel b) Cast iron
 c) Cast steel d) Chrome
19. In tractor engine type of timing gear used is
 a) Spur gear b) Helical gear

c) Bevel gear d) All above three

20. A safety clutch is used to prevent

a) Slippage b) Overload

c) Both a) & b) d) None of the above

**Answers:**

| 1. | 2. | 3. | 4. | 5. | 6. | 7. | 8. | 9. | 10. |
|---|---|---|---|---|---|---|---|---|---|
| c) | c) | a) | d) | b) | b) | d) | a) | d) | c) |
| 11. | 12. | 13. | 14. | 15. | 16. | 17. | 18. | 19. | 20. |
| b) | b) | b) | a) | a) | b) | c) | a) | a) | b) |

## CHAPTER-9 HYDRAULIC SYSTEM OF TRACTOR

1. Most commonly used pump in hydraulic system is

a) Plunger type b) Gear type

c) Multiple cylinder reciprocating type d) Both b) and c)

2. When hydraulic system of a tractor lifts the implement very slowly, it is due to

a) Defective pump b) Defective control valve

c) Clogged safety valve d) All above three

3. The function of three point linkage in a tractor is to

a) Hitch the implement b) Lift the implement

c) Carry the implement d) All above three

4. Hydraulic system of a tractor works on the principle of

a) Newton's law b) Pascal's law

c) Gravity d) None of the above

5. Main components of hydraulic system are

a) Oil pump b) Power cylinder & piston

c) PTO shaft d) Both a) and b)

6. Oil pump in hydraulic system of tractor develops oil pressure

a) 50-75 kg/cm$^2$ b) 75-100 kg/cm$^2$

c) 110-125 kg/cm$^2$ d) 135-150 kg/cm$^2$

7. The spool type oil control valves of a tractor hydraulic system are of

a) One type b) Two type

c) Three type d) None of the above

8. The oil control valve of hydraulic system mainly does following function

a) Control direction of oil flow b) Control quantity of oil flow

c) Both a) and b) d) None of the above

9. The function of power cylinder and piston assembly of hydraulic system is

a) To convert hydraulic power into mechanical power

b) To convert mechanical power into hydraulic power

c) Both a) and b) d) None of the above

10. The reasons for hydraulic pump not developing required pressure are
   a) Low oil level in tank b) Poor quality of oil
   c) Improper pump speed d) None of the above

**Answers:**

| 1. | 2. | 3. | 4. | 5. | 6. | 7. | 8. | 9. | 10. |
|---|---|---|---|---|---|---|---|---|---|
| d) | d) | d) | b) | d) | d) | b) | c) | a) | d) |

## CHAPTER-10 MECHANICAL AND POWER STEERING OF TRACTOR

1. Steering system of a tractor consists of
   a) Drop arm b) Tie rod
   c) Both a) and b) d) Rim
2. Drop arm is a component of
   a) Hydraulic system b) Steering
   c) Transmission d) None of the above
3. Caster angle is
   a) Angle between caster line of tyre and vertical
   b) Angle between centre line of tyre and centre line of king pin
   c) Angle between centre line of king pin and vertical
   d) Angle between centre line of king pin and centre line of stub axle
4. In steering mechanism of tractor the front wheel alignment is made by
   a) Toe-in b) Radius rod
   c) Both a) and b) d) None of the above
5. The radius rod of steering mechanism of a tractor is pivoted on the
   a) Gearbox b) Clutch housing
   c) Toe-in d) None of the above
6. The tie-rod of steering mechanism of tractor is actuated by
   a) Tie-rod b) Wheel spindle
   c) Drag link d) Toe-in
7. The worm of steering shaft of a tractor is meshed with
   a) Worm gear b) Radius rod
   c) Sector on vertical shaft d) Tie-rod
8. Excessive vibrations in steering wheel of a tractor indicates
   a) High speed of tractor b) Less toe-in
   c) High Toe-in d) Both b) and c)
9. Toe-in provided in a tractor should be
   a) 5-7 mm b) 7-10 mm
   c) 10-12 mm d) 12-15 mm
10. The camber is a component of

*a*) Clutch  *b*) Differential
*c*) Steering mechanism  *d*) Hydraulic system

**Answers:**

| 1. | 2. | 3. | 4. | 5. | 6. | 7. | 8. | 9. | 10. |
|---|---|---|---|---|---|---|---|---|---|
| *c*) | *b*) | *d*) | *c*) | *b*) | *c*) | *c*) | *d*) | *b*) | *c*) |

**CHAPTER-11 TRACTION**

1. An Agricultural tractor gets its driving force from its
   *a*) Engine  *b*) Drive wheels
   *c*) Dynamo  *d*) Both *a*) and *b*)
2. The front wheels of tractor helps in
   *a*) Steering the tractor  *b*) Development of drawbar pull
   *c*) Applying brakes  *d*) None of the above
3. Weight transfer in a tractor is affected by
   *a*) Wheel diameter  *b*) Wheel base
   *c*) Height of hitch point  *d*) Both *b*) and *c*)
4. A tractor tyre is specified by
   *a*) Rim diameter  *b*) Width of rim
   *c*) Both *a*) and *b*)  *d*) None of the above
5. Higher tractive efficiency is obtained in
   *a*) Loose soils  *b*) Firm dry soils
   *c*) Wet soils  *d*) None
6. Tractive coefficient in a dry field as compared to others is
   *a*) Minimum  *b*) Maximum
   *c*) Equal  *d*) None of the above
7. We increase the pulling power of tractor by
   *a*) High hitch point  *b*) Ballasting rear wheels
   *c*) Both *a*) and *b*)  *d*) None of above
8. Optimal wheel slip for ballasting purpose is
   *a*) 8 %  *b*) 10 %
   *c*) 15 %  *d*) 18 %
9. We increase weight transfer in a tractor through application of
   *a*) Front wheel ballasting  *b*) Pull
   *c*) Both *a*) and *b*)  *d*) None of the above
10. Traction is developed by interaction between soil and mechanical devices such as
   *a*) Wheels  *b*) Tracks
   *c*) Frog  *d*) Both *a*) and *b*)

**Answers**

| 1. | 2. | 3. | 4. | 5. | 6. | 7. | 8. | 9. | 10. |
|---|---|---|---|---|---|---|---|---|---|
| *b*) | *a*) | *d*) | *c*) | *b*) | *b*) | *c*) | *a*) | *c*) | *d*) |

## CHAPTER-13 HUMAN ENGINEERING IN TRACTOR DESIGN

1. Tractor engine speed is indicated by

*a*) Tachometer *b*) Hour meter
*c*) Flow meter *d*) Dynamometer

2. On tractor instrument panel engine gauges are located to the

*a*) Right *b*) Left
*c*) Randomly *d*) All above three

3. White light other than head light or plough light on tractor is

*a*) Parking light *b*) Direction indicator light
*c*) Hazard light *d*) Both *b*) and *c*)

4. Oil pressure gauge in tractor is meant for indicating

*a*) Compression pressure *b*) Hydraulic oil pressure
*c*) Oil pressure in lubricating system *d*) Fuel injection pressure

5. The maximum permissible noise level from tractor near operator's ear is

*a*) 60 dB *b*) 75 dB
*c*) 90 dB *d*) 105 dB

6. For accurate design of tractor seat, the value of transmissibility should be considered as

*a*) Less than 0.3 *b*) 0.4-0.5
*c*) less than 1.0 *d*) 1.0

7. The study of man-machine system is known as

*a*) Man-machine interface *b*) Environment
*c*) Machine control *d*) All above three

8. The force needed to operate brake pedals ranges between

*a*) 20-30 N *b*) 30-40 N
*c*) 44-89 N *d*) More than 89 N

9. Tractor controls are designed for

*a*) $5^{th}$ percentile *b*) 50 percentiles
*c*) $5^{th}$ to $95^{th}$ percentiles *d*) 95 percentile

10. Normally the dimensions of control placement are w.r.t

*a*) Midline *b*) Seat reference point
*c*) Tractor C.G *d*) None of the above

11. A control transmits the information from

*a*) The man to the machine *b*) The machine to man
*c*) Both *a*) and *b*) *d*) None of the above

12. Range of knee comfort angle (in degrees) for tractor operator should be:

*a*) 95-135 *b*) 80-95
*c*) 170-196 *d*) None of the above

13. The Sound pressure level (SPL), measured in decibels, can be written as:
   *a*) SPL = 20 log Pr/Po  *b*) SPL = 30 log Po/Pr
   *c*) SPL = 20 log Po/Pr  *d*) None of the above

14. The environmental temperature for comfort zone should be between
   *a*) 10-12 °C  *b*) 12-15 °C
   *c*) 18-24 °C  *d*) 24-26 °C

15. Visual displays are the most common in use and involve user's
   *a*) visual capabilities  *b*) skills
   *c*) Both *a*) and *b*)  *d*) None of the above

16. Heat produced per minute by human being for doing moderately heavy work is
   *a*) Less than 13 kJ  *b*) 13-22 kJ
   *c*) 22.9 kJ  *d*) more than 30kJ

17. Some of the environmental factors affecting task performance of an operator are:
   *a*) Noise and vibrations  *b*) dust and smoke
   *c*) Both *a*) and *b*)  *d*) None of the above

18. Maximum actuating force (N) to operate clutch pedal is:
   *a*) 150 N  *b*) 250 N
   *c*) 350 N  *d*) 450 N

19. For Moderate work the oxygen consumption and pulse rate ranges between
   *a*) 0.5 - 1.0 l/min and 90-110 beats per minute respectively
   *b*) 0,5-1.5 l/min and 110-120 beats/minute respectively
   *c*) 1.0-1.5 l/min and 70-90 beats/min respectively
   *d*) None of the above

20. According to occupational safety and health act, the tractor operator should not be exposed to 90dB noise for more than
   *a*) 30 minutes  *b*) 1 hour
   *c*) 4 hrs  *d*) 8 hrs

21. Uncomfortable body posture of operator in different activities reduces
   *a*) work efficiency  *b*) capacity
   *c*) safety  *d*) All of the above

22. Transmissibility of tractor seat suspension vibrations depends on
   *a*) Seat spring rate  *b*) Mass damping
   *c*) Frequency of input vibration  *d*) All above three

**Answers:**

| 1. | 2. | 3. | 4. | 5. | 6. | 7. | 8. | 9. | 10. |
|---|---|---|---|---|---|---|---|---|---|
| *a*) | *b*) | *b*) | *c*) | *c*) | *c*) | *a*) | *c*) | *c*) | *c*) |
| 11. | 12. | 13. | 14. | 15. | 16. | 17. | 18. | 19. | 20. |
| *a*) | *a*) | *c*) | *c*) | *c*) | *b*) | *c*) | *c*) | *a*) | *d*) |
| 21. | 22. | | | | | | | | |
| *d*) | *d*) | | | | | | | | |

# Index


A

Absolute viscosity, 152,153,154
Acceleration function, 306
Accelerometer, 306
Acceptable wheel slippage, 248
Ackerman steering, 245
Actuator-linear, 208
Adiabatic compression, 5
Adiabatic expansion, 5
Adjusting screw, 87
Air
–cleaners, 104
–cooling system, 156
–flow through radiator, 163
–fuel ratio, 107,109
–fuel supply system, 104
–fuel mixture, 3
Allowable stresses, 357
Alloy steels, 353
Angle of internal friction, 250
Anthropometric data, 285
Area commanded, 348
Arm rests, 293
Armature, field coils, brushes and, end shields, 175
Atomization of fuel, 126
Automatic
–draft control system, 223
–hydraulic control, 221
–position control system, 223
Axial, 226
–friction clutch, 181
–thickness of rings, 49
–housing, 97

B

Back cushion, 293
Balancing method, 225
Ball type flow control valve, 209
Ballast, 260
Battery, 172
Beads, 259
Bearable zones, 282
Bekker's equation, 250
Belt horse power, 24
Belt pulley, 199
Bending and shear, 226
Big end, 60
Body dimensions, 256
Body plies, 259
Bore, 21
Bottom dead centre, 21
Brake power, 23
Breakers, 260
Bronze, 354
Buckingham equation, 197
Buckling load, 59

C

Cam, 87
Camber angle, 245
Capacity of battery, 174
Capacity, draft and power requirements of, 349
Carbon-chrome ball bearing steel, 353
Carburetor type, 3
Casing, 259
Cast iron weights, 260
Cast iron, 353
Caster angle, 245
Castings and housings, 96
Centre of gravity, 275
Chaff cutter, 349
Checking voltage, 173
Chemical combustion equation, 107
Closed
–center system, 208
–loop system, 222
–type, 122

Coefficient of
- –rolling resistance, 252
- –traction (ρ), 258
- –traction, 346

Cohesion, 251
- –modulus, 251

Combine harvester ($t_d$), 349

Combined
- –self propelled, 349
- –mechanical and pneumatic type governor, 137
- –pneumatic and mechanical type governor, 137

Compound gear train ratio, 186

Combustion
- –chambers, 129, 186
- –of diesel fuel, 107

Comfort equation, 284

Comfort zone, 282

Composition of air, 346

Compressed natural gas (cng), 1

Compression
- –ignition, 3
- –process, 5
- –ratio (r), 7, 22

Cone clutch, 182

Connecting rod section, 58

Constant
- –mesh gear type, 190
- –pressure cycle, 7
- –speed governor, 135
- –volume cycle, 5

Constructional details, 194

Control requirement, 288

Convection (c), 283

Cooling fan efficiency ($\eta_f$), 157,164

Copper-based alloys, 354

Crank case breather, 148

Crank pin, 72

Crawler, 316

Critical damping rate, 309

Cubic capacity, 22

Cultivator, 349

Current regulator, 176

Current-voltage regulator, 176

Cushioned top type hydraulic cylinder, 217

Cut-off ratio, 7

Cutout relay, 176

Cylinder, 39, 225

Cylinder head, 33

## D

Damped frequency, 306

Damping constant, 307

Damping rate or coefficient, 309

Damping ratio, 309

Delivery valve, 114

Design of
- –35hp tractor, 37
- –bevel gears, 188
- –clutch, 180
- –connecting rod, 53
- –crankshaft, 70
- –cylinder, 39
- –cylinder head, 43
- –flange and studs, 41
- –fly wheel, 64
- –fuel injection pump for diesel engine, 114
- –hydraulic cylinder, 217
- –instrument panel, 287
- –piston, 45
- –procedure for gearbox, 192
- –radiator, 160
- –valve, 81
- –valve gear mechanism, 79

Design requirements, 224

Diameter of fan blades ($d_b$), 164

Diesel cycle, 3

Different makes of tractors manufactures, 315

Differential, 194
- –equation, 307

Dimension chart of piston & cylinder, 54

Dimensions of ring, 50

Directional control valves, 208

Disc
- –harrow, 341
- –plough, 349
- –type clutch, 182

Displacement
- –function, 306
- –volume of engine, 22

Distributor type fuel injection system, 114

Drawbar
- –power of tractor, 180
- –power, 24, 247
- –pull (p), 265, 347

Drop arm, 232

Dry
- –ballast, 260
- –liner, 31
- –type air cleaner, 156

Dubois area, 284

Dust
- –concentrations, 282
- –exposure, 282

Dynamic
- –load, 197
- –tractive coefficient, 251

E_______

Effect of environment on horse power, 24

Effective temperature scale, 285

Effects of noise, 297

Efficiency of fi pump, 119

Effort of governor, 143

Electrical components, 171

Electrical wiring, 177

Electrolyte, 172, 174

Energy
- –efficiency of battery, 174
- –fluctuation in flywheel, 64
- –of diesel fuel atomization, 127
- –supplied by fuel, 27

Engine
- –and their classifications, 1
- –brake power, 179
- –components, 95
- –terminology, 21

Environmental factors, 281

Ergonomics, 280

Evaporation (e), 283

Exhaust
- –process, 5
- –valve., 17

External
- –combustion engines, 1
- –components, 11

F_______

Factors affecting traction, 247

Field conditions, 352

Filter, 207

Final drive, 198

Firing interval, 18

Firing order, 17

Fixed piston pin, 52

Flange, 43

Flow control valves, 209

Fluid, 206
- –flow velocities, 242
- –force acting in cylinder, 218
- –power of pump, 207

Flywheel section, 68

Foot controls, 288

Forced
- –analysis, 82
- –circulation type cooling system, 159
- –feed lubricating system, 147
- –vibration, 307

Fore and aft location, 291

Four stroke, 4

Four wheel drive, 316

Free body diagram, 263

Free vibration, 307

Frequency, 307

Friction
- –clutches, 181
- –modulus, 251

Frictional power, 23

Fuel
- –feed rate, 108
- –injection system, 110
- –injection time, 127

Fulcrum pin, 84

Full floating piston pin, 52

G_______

Gagge, 282

Gasoline engine, 3

Gear, 97
- –drive design, 185
- –module (m), 185
- –ratios of planetary sets, 188

–ratios, 186
–terminology, 185
–tooth loads, 186
–type oil pump, 149
Generator/dynamo/alternator, 175
Governors, 135
–hunting, 144
–performance characteristics, 142
–regulation, 139
Grain binder, 349
Gross tractive resistance, 251
Groundnut digger, 349
Gudgeon pin, 52
Gun-metal, 354

**H**

Hand controls, 288
Hansson, 281
Hartnell governor, 143
Head or crown, 46
Heat
–balance equation, 27
–engine, 1
–exchange, 283
–converted to useful work, 29
–lost due to incomplete combustion, 29
–lost in cooling system, 29
–lost in exhaust gases, 29
–of combustion, 346
Height of cylinder, 41
High
–carbon steel, 353
–clearance tractor, 316
–speed, 3
Hitch system for farm machinery, 224
Hoses, 243
Horse power (h.p), 22
Human
–engineering, 280
–factors, 280
Hydraulic
–circuit symbols, 226
–fluid power of pump (wf ), 151, 212
–governor, 137
–power, 247
–pump performance, 211
–system, 206
–type governor, 135
Hydrodynamics, 206
–transmission, 192
Hydrostatic-transmission, 191
Hydrostatics, 206

**I**

I.C. engine energy flow, 1
Indicated power ($w_i$), 22
Individual or in-line injection pump, 112
Injection delay, 127
Inlet hose check valve, 243
Inlet valve, 16, 88
Input or shaft power ($w_s$), 151, 212
Instrument panel, 288
Intake valve, 88
Internal combustion engines, 2
Internal components, 11
Irrigation pumps, 349

**J**

Journals, 78

**K**

Kilowatt (kw), 22
Kinematic viscosity, 154
Kingpin inclination, 245
Kingpin torque ($t_k$), 241

**L**

Lateral limiters, 225
Lateral stability, 270
Lawn and garden tractor, 316
Lead
–acid battery, 172
–based alloys, 354
–bronze, 354
–peroxide, 172
Least radius of gyration, 59
Left hand crank web, 73
Levels of noise, 297
Lewis eqn, 197
Lift arm, 225
Lift link, 225
Liquefied petroleum gas (lpg), biogas, producer gas, 1

Liquid
–ballast, 260
–filling valve, 170
–or water cooling system, 156
Longitudinal stability, 268
Lower
–groove, 54
–link, 225
Lubrication, 146
Lugs, 259

**M**

Main bearings, 73
Manganese steel, 353
Manganese-brass, 354
Mast of implement, 224
Matching
–cultivators, 352
–harrows, 351
–size, 95
Materials of construction, 95
Mean effective pressure, 24
Mechanical
–efficiency, 27
–or centrifugal governors, 135
–properties, 353
–steering system, 230
Medium
–carbon steel, 353
–speed, 3
Metabolic
–energy equation, 283
–heat, 283
Mild steel, 353
Miscellaneous parts, 99
Mobile, 3
Mobility, 2
Motion resistance ratio, 248
Multi-hole nozzle, 125
Multiple cylinders, 3
Multipurpose tractor, 316

**N**

Natural frequency, 306
Newton's law of motion, 264
Newtonian fluids, 152
Nickel steel, 353
Nickel-chromium steel, 353
Nickel-chromium-molyb-denum-v steel, 353
Noise sources, 297
Noise, 295
Non-ferrous alloys, 353

**O**

Oil
–bath air cleaner, 105
–filters, 148
–pump, 149
Open
–center system, 208
–chamber, 129
–combustion chambers, 129
–loop system, 222
–type injector, 122
Operator seat, 292
Operator-machine, 281
Optimum vision, 286
Orchard tractor, 316
Orifice equation, 210
OSHA act, 301
Otto cycle, 3
Outer tube or column, 231
Overall
–effect, 299
–efficiency of pump ($\eta_m$), 151, 212
–transfer function (o/i), 222

**P**

P.T.O. shaft, 199, 247
Paddy harrow, 349
Parts of fuel injection system, 112
Pascal's law, 206
Performance of fan of cooling system, 163
Peripheral velocity of fan blades ($u_t$), 164
Phosphor-bronze, 354
Pinion pitch diameter, 186
Piston
–barrel, 51
–movement, 2
–pin or gudgeon pin or wrist pin, 52
–fixed, 52
–full floating, 52
–semi floting, 52

–rings, 46, 48
–speed ($n_s$), 22
Planetary gear unit, 188
Plastic parts, 99
Ploughing resistance, 350
Plunger diameter, 120
Pneumatic
–type governor, 137
–tyres, 259
Poiseville's law of viscosity, 153
Polypropylene, 172
Poppet or mushroom valve, 80
Poppet valve, 209
Porter governor, 143
Position of engine, 3
Positive and negative battery plates, 172
Potato
–digger, 349
–planter, 349
Power, 22
–chart, 19
–developed by the actuator ($w_a$), 219, 242
–of governor, 143
–process, 5
–required for threshing, 352
–requirement of fan ($w_f$), 164
–requirement of the pump, 214
–requirements, 151
–shift transmission, 191
–steering, 232
–take off horse power, 23
–thresher, 349
–tiller, 316
–transmission system, 178
Pre-combustion chamber, 130
Pressure
–control valves, 209
–relief valve, 243
Principle requirements of fuel supply, 110
Properties of lubricating oil, 152
Protection from noise, 303
Pull-speed curves, 180
Pumps, 207
–discharge, 211
–performance characteristics, 213
–torque, 151, 212
Push rod, 86

Q

Quantity
–of air intake, 106
–of oil pumped by gear pump, 150

R

Radial friction clutches, 181
Radial ribs, 48
Radiation (r), 283
Radiator, 160
Range of governor equilibrium speed, 139
Rankine formula, 49
Reaper harvester (vcr), 349
Reboring factor, 40
Recharging of battery, 173
Reciprocating engine, 2
Reference level, 307
Regulation, 224
–curve, 224
Relationship between different horse powers, 25
Replaceable type, 149
Reservoir, 207
Ridger, 349
Right hand crank web, 74
Rms (root mean square) value, 295
Rocker arm assembly, 82
Rocker arm, 85
Rocking arm, 225
Rockshaft, 225
Rolling resistance, 248
Rotavator, 349
Rules for finding firing order, 17

S

Society of automative engine power, 24
Seat
–cushion, 292
–depth, 292
–height, 292
–width, 292
Seed-cum-fertilizer drill, 349
Second moment of intertia, 60
Self starter, 176

Semi-divided combustion chamber, 130
Sensitiveness of governor, 142
Separators, 172
Shaft power of pump, 208
Sheet metal, 99
Side clearance, 54
Side walls, 259
Silicon-manganese steel, 353
Simple watt governor, 143
Single acting double acting hydraulic cylinder, 217
Single cylinder, 3
Single degree of freedom, 307
Single hole pintel type nozzle, 126
Sir Issac Newton, 152
Skid-steer loader, 316
Skirt, 51
–length, 51
Sleeve lift, 139
Sliding gear transmission, 189
Slippage, 247
Slow speed, 3
Small end, 61
Soil conditions, 347
Soil type, 247
Solenoid switch, 177
Solid filling valve, 170
Sound pressure level, 296
Spark ignition, 3
Spatial, visual req. for operator, 285
Specific fuel consumption, 26, 123
Specific gravity of battery, 173
Speed
–division by the differential, 196
–of rod movement (v), 218
–of tractor, 348
Splash type, 147
Spongy lead, 172
Spool type flow control valve, 209
Spool valves, 209
Spring constant, 311
Spur gear design, 186
Stability of governor, 144
Stainless steel, 353
Standard row-crop, 316
Static equilibrium of tractor, 263
Stationary, 2
Steady state vibration, 307
Steel, 353
Steering
–box, 231
–geometry, 245
–linkages, 232
–shaft, 231
–system, 230
–wheel, 231
Stroke, 21, 120
–bore ratio, 21
Structural parts of tractor, 98
Submersible pumps, 349
Suction process, 5
Sugarcane
–crusher, 349
–planter, 349
Surface condition, 247
Suspension method, 275
Swept volume, 22
Swirl chamber, 130
Synchromesh transmission, 190
Tensile and compressive strengths, 357

T

Thermal
–comfort, 282
–efficiency, 5, 26
Thermo siphon type, 158
Thermodynamic cycle, 3
Thermostat valve, 169
Thickness of
–cylinder, 40
–jacket wall, 41
–piston head, 46
–water space, 41
Three point linkage, 224
Tin-base alloys, 353
Toe-in, 245
Toe-out, 245
Tooth module, 186
Top dead centre, 21

Top land, 50
Torque (t), 25, 151
Torsion, bending and shear, 226
Total fuel delivery rate, 120
Towed force, 248
Traction theory, 250
Traction, 247
Tractive and transmission coefficients, 347
Tractive efficiency, 24, 256, 258
Tractor
–components, 95
–design, 280
–manufacturers, 314
–moving down hill , 269
–moving uphill, 268
–seat design, 308
–transmission performance, 179
–transmission types, 189
–tyres, 259
Transfer function, 222
Transmissibility (t), 309
Travel reduction, 247
Tree skidder, 316
Turning times, 352
Two stroke, 4
Types of
–fuel injection pumps, 111
–injectors, 121
–nozzles, 125
–tractors, 316
Tyre inflation, 260
Tyre size, 260

U

Ultimate Crushing Stress, 59
Unaccounted Losses, 29
Uniform Axial Wear, 182
Uniform Pressure, 182
Unit Draft, 349
Upper Groove, 44
Upper Link, 225
Usable Power, 347
Utility Tractor, 316

V

Valve
–seat angle, 82
–stem diameter, 82
–timing diagram, 16
Variable speed governor, 135
Velocity function, 306
Very high speed steel, 353
Vibration acceleration level, 307
Vibrations, 305
Viscosity, 152
–index (vi), 154
Voltage regulator, 176
Volume of air required, 157
Volumetric efficiency, 25

W

Wankel rotary, 2
Washable type filters, 149
Water cooling system, 157
Water pump, 165
Weighing method, 275
Weight transfer phenomenon, 264
Weight transference in power tiller, 273
Wet liner, 39
Wheel slip, 347
Whole body vibration, 312
Work place layout, 285
Worm and gear, 231
Worm and sector, 231
Working principle, 10
Wrought iron, 353

Z

Zander, 295
Zone comfort, 282
–bearable, 282